The
Contemporary African American
Novel

BERNARD W. BELL

The Contemporary African American Novel

Its Folk Roots and Modern Literary Branches

UNIVERSITY OF MASSACHUSETTS PRESS
AMHERST AND BOSTON

Printed in the United States of America
LC 2004013508
ISBN 1-55849-472-3 (library cloth ed.); 473-1 (paper)

Set in Palatino by Binghamton Valley Composition
Printed and bound by The Maple-Vail Book Manufacturing Group

Library of Congress Cataloging-in-Publication Data

Bell, Bernard W.
The contemporary African American novel : its folk roots and modern literary branches / Bernard W. Bell.
p. cm.
Sequel to: The Afro-American novel and its tradition.
Includes bibliographical references and index.
ISBN 1-55849-473-1 (pbk. : alk. paper)—ISBN 1-55849-472-3 (library cloth : alk. paper)
1. American fiction—African American authors—History and criticism. 2. American fiction—20th century—History and criticism. 3. Literature and folklore—United States. 4. African Americans—Intellectual life. 5. African Americans in literature. 6. African Americans—Folklore. 7. Folklore in literature. I. Title.
PS374.N4B45 2004
813'.509896073—dc22

2004013508

British Library Cataloguing in Publication data are available.

Every black scholar should try (1) to make some contribution to general theoretical work in his discipline. . . . So, while rooting oneself in fighting for one's people, one also tried to make a contribution at the highest theoretical level of scholarship; (2) to decide upon some aspect of the social structure in which to become an expert at the empirical level . . . ; and (3) to select a problem that contributed to racial advancement, as we used to call it. Today we call it Black liberation.

St. Clair Drake
Quoted in Manning Marable,
Dispatches from the Ebony Tower

When we read a novel of Dostoevski, or see a play by Tchehov, for the first time, I think we are fascinated by the odd way in which Russians behave; later we come to recognize that theirs is merely an odd way of expressing thoughts and feelings which we all share. And though it is only too easy for a writer to be local without being universal, I doubt whether a poet or novelist can be universal without being local too. Who could be more Greek than Odysseus? Or more German than Faust? Or more Spanish than Don Quixote? Or more American than Huck Finn? [Or more African American than the nameless protagonist in Invisible Man*?] Yet each one of them is a kind of archetype in the mythology of all men everywhere.*

T. S. Eliot
"American Literature and Language," in
To Criticize the Critic

Contents

Contents

Memoir
On Becoming an African American Scholar Activist

"EVERYTHING now, we must assume, is in our hands," African American gay novelist, playwright, and essayist James Baldwin reminded us in the biblical and black spiritual jeremiad at the end of *The Fire Next Time* (1963); "we have no right to assume otherwise. If we—and now I mean the relatively conscious whites and the relatively conscious blacks, who must, like lovers, insist on, or create, the consciousness of the others—do not falter in our duty now, we may be able, handful that we are, to end the racial nightmare and achieve our country, and change the history of the world."[1] Like many black American men of the pre–World War II generation who are what some readers of Marxist Antonio Gramsci's *Prison Notebooks* (1971) might call organic intellectuals[2] and agents of social change, my soul looks back in wonder how we collectively and individually got over the life crises of our sociohistorical separation from primary communities, our sociopsychological transitional experience with hybrid identities, and our ultimate sociocultural reincorporation.[3]

In our rites of passage many of us have come this far mainly by faith, resourcefulness, and resilience in challenging the legacy of slavery and social hierarchy that subjected and continues in many ways to subject Negroes with one drop of black blood, especially those whose skin was darker than a brown paper bag, to racial prejudice, discrimination, and exclusion. For example, in *The Future of the Race* (1996), Henry Louis Gates Jr., the distinguished brown-skinned critic and chair of the African American Studies Department at Harvard University, tells this story about the brown paper bag ritual that he encountered as a student at Yale in the 1960s:

> Some of the brothers who came from private schools in New Orleans held a "bag party." As a classmate explained it to me, a bag party was a New Orleans custom wherein a brown paper bag was stuck on the door. Anyone darker than the bag was denied entrance. That was one cultural legacy that would be put to rest in a hurry—we all made sure of that. But in a manner of speaking, it was replaced by an opposite test whereby those

> who were deemed "not black enough" ideologically were to be shunned. I was not so sure this was an improvement.[4]

Thus, African Americans, especially native-born male intellectuals and agents of progressive social change, owe an immense debt to our primary racial, ethnic, and national communities. We are especially obligated to the ancestors and elders on whose shoulders we stand, for our modern and contemporary survival strategies for reconciling our double consciousness (dual racial and cultural identities) and for our distinctive vernacular theories of an African American cultural and literary tradition.

"The whole history of the progress of human liberty shows that all concessions, yet made to her august claims, have been born of earnest struggle. . . . This struggle," Frederick Douglass wrote in a letter to white abolitionist Gerrit Smith in 1849, "may be a moral one; or it may be a physical one; or it may be both moral and physical; but it must be a struggle."[5] When I was a latchkey kid in grammar school during World War II, I would occasionally upset my brown-skinned, working-class, single mother by visiting my equally brown-skinned but estranged father and my short, wiry, witty paternal grandfather, who lived at 1915 North Capitol Street, only two blocks from my school in Northwest Washington, D.C. Although I rarely saw my father during these after school visits and never developed a relationship with him, Grandpa Weaver loved to tell me stories, and I loved to listen. Often, these stories would be about his strategies for resisting antiblack racism in the army during World War I and in his everyday experiences with the tragicomic ironies of "separate but equal" racial segregation in the army and the nation's capital. Wryly critical of the ways of black and white folks, he sometimes began the stories with the same popular black folk saying: "If you're white, you're alright. If you're brown, stick around. But if you're black, oh brother, get back, get back!" Underscoring the fact that most folks in our primary speech community knew from their everyday experiences that racial prejudice and segregation actually meant an unequal and unjust division of power, privilege, preference, and resources, he would usually close the storytelling sessions in his living-room or on the front porch of his two-story red brick home with the trenchant vernacular moral lesson of courage, resilience, and resourcefulness: " 'Member, son, it takes shit, grit, and motherwit to survive in dis man's world."

Also, before migrating to Harlem and the South Bronx at the end of World War II, my mother and I used to make frequent visits to kinfolks outside the District of Columbia in Norbeck, Maryland, especially in the summer. Usually during these visits, my mother's oldest and most maternal sister, Aunt Gretna, would affectionately call me "Benniewix" and welcome me with a big hug before strengthening our family bond with my favorite communal and spiritual ritual. While she was baking bread in the oven of a huge wood-burning stove in her equally huge kitchen, she would tell me and her daughter, Little Gretna, who was a year younger than I, stories about having Jesus in our lives, and she would hum spirituals. After taking two or three pans out of the oven and piling butter on the big, fluffy, golden brown chunks of hot white bread for us, she would say: "Don't y'all forget yo blessing. And 'member, de Lord helps dem dat helps demselves." Her tall, dark-skinned husband, Uncle Jim, a construction worker and the protector and provider of the family who, unlike my Uncles Angel and David, brought his paycheck home every Friday and with whom she shared authority, would sometimes walk through the kitchen on these occasions. When he overheard her, he would say in his usual soft-spoken manner with a smile on his face, "Ya think long, ya think wrong," reminding us that she didn't mean for us to help ourselves to another chunk of bread without her permission. These anecdotes are examples of the bidialectalism and residually oral forms of the African American vernacular roots of my authenticity, authority, and agency, key terms indicating a significantly, predominantly, or exclusively black American identity formation and primary reference group orientation that will be defined more fully in chapter 1. These are the sociolinguistic, cognitive, and affective roots of my double consciousness, ambivalence, and code-switching as a modern African American organic intellectual as well as an African American vernacular critic, literary scholar, and social activist in the tradition of W. E. B. Du Bois and Sterling A. Brown, two of my elders, ancestors, and primary intellectual role models.

Grounded in the specific experiences of enslaved black people of primarily West and Central African ancestry and culture with antiblack racism in the United States[6] and in the hybrid cultural heritage of our African American folk and vernacular tradition, *The Contemporary African American Novel: Its Folk Roots and Modern Literary Branches* is a sequel to *The Afro-American Novel and Its Tradition* (1987). The hybridity of African American folk and our vernacular tradition has deep historical roots in South Carolina, the Georgia Sea Islands, and Louisiana that have been transplanted and that have developed contemporary branches nationally, especially in Northern and Midwestern industrialized cities. In *The Souls of Black Folk* (1903), Great Barrington–born W. E. B. Du Bois, who bore witness as a visibly mixed black New England Brahmin to the lives of black peasants, sharecroppers, and farmers as a teacher in Tennessee and who wrote a thesis on it as a doctoral student in Berlin, identifies the folk struggling up from slavery at the end of the nineteenth century as "the black artisan."[7] In *The New Negro* (1925), Philadelphia-born Alain Locke, a similarly light-skinned black intellectual educated at Harvard and the University of Berlin, calls the modern transplanted and transformed folk of Harlem in the 1920s "the New Negro," "the migrant masses," and "the Negro . . . peasant matrix of that section of America that has most undervalued him." In *The Big Sea* (1940), the light-skinned black poet Langston Hughes, born in Joplin, Missouri, and educated at Lincoln ("black Princeton") University, simply refers to the folk of the Harlem Renaissance as "ordinary Negroes."[8] The *Oxford English Dictionary* reminds us that the term "vernacular" has shifted from its Latin root *verna,* meaning "a home-born slave," to include "a language or dialect: That is naturally spoken by the people of a particular country or district" and "arts, or features of these: Native or peculiar to a particular country or locality."[9] As a literary history that deploys the biologically and culturally mixed heritage of black folk in the United States, both Southern rural and Northern urban, as a dominant trope, and as a critical study that reaffirms the strategic essentialism of African American literature and hybrid identity formations, this book is more dialectic and cyclical than linear despite the designated time frames in the chapter headings.

The Contemporary African American Novel: Its Folk Roots and Modern Literary Branches is not only a diachronic but also a synchronic critical study that charts frequently concurrent and overlapping residual and emergent as well as dominant cultural, narrative, and aesthetic movements. For example, as one aspect of the African American aesthetic that moves cyclically from residual to emergent, the Blues Aesthetic "arises as a late nineteenth-century/early twentieth-century secular thrust of the African-American musical culture, whose oldest musical and lyrical heritage was Africa but whose changing contemporary expression summed up their [African American] lives and history in the West."[10] This book, therefore, begins with a critique of contemporary cultural and literary theories and ideologies for representing and reading the authenticity, authority, and agency of African American culture and character. This critique illuminates why and how the dominant African American aesthetic focuses on the nature and function of the shifting grounds for discovering and constructing truth, ethics, and politics as well as beauty in art and literature primarily by, for, and about black Americans. Chapters 2–8 will identify and examine closely the relationship of class and cultural formations to the pattern of residual, emergent, and dominant African American narrative and aesthetic movements. These chapters revise, expand, and enrich the coverage of women and contemporary male writers by including homosexual romances and novels as well as science fiction and detective novels that, like other subgenres in the narrative tradition, are written by and about biracial, bicultural African Americans speaking for themselves. More than literary history, *The Contemporary African American Novel: Its Folk Roots and Modern Literary Branches* is also a theoretical and methodological study of the rhetoric, dialectics, and dialogics of the African American novel and romance, especially their constructions of cultural and political identities.

More specifically, this book is a call for a reinvigorated discourse on the liberating impact of vernacular and literary cultural production by African American novelists and on continuity and change in the tradition of the African American novel. I began it in the 1990s as a response to the impact of Eurocentric postmodernism and postcolonialism on my vernacular theory of contemporary African American novelists and novels, especially critiques of vernacular criticism and cultural nationalism that unqualifiedly repudiate all master narratives and boundaries, heuristic as well as historical, as inherently fixed and essentialist. "Too often," as poststructuralist feminist critic Diana Fuss clearly and persuasively demonstrates, "constructionists presume that the category of the social automatically escapes essentialism, in contradistinction to the way the category of the natural is presupposed to be inevitably entrapped within it. But there is no compelling reason to assume that the natural is, in essence, essentialist and that the social is, in essence, constructionist."[11] Finally, this book is a response to the overwhelmingly positive critical reception of *The Afro-American Novel and Its Tradition*. The questions raised in that book concerning the politics of identity remain inextricably linked to the poetics and rhetoric of the African American novel, as well as to the lessons learned from my elders and ancestors about the Southern down-home Jim Crow survival rituals and Northern school of hard knocks: store-front churches, barbershops, schoolyards, basement parties, rooftop gang rituals, and the ebony tower. My modern street-wise urban elders and peers, who used to call me "Schoolboy" and went out of their way to keep me out of harm's way, included pimps, prostitutes, pushers, junkies, number runners, pickpockets, shoplifters, gamblers, and everyday hustlers, who made a living any way that they could, as well as occasionally preachers, teachers, and cultural and social welfare workers.

In situating the authenticity, authority, and agency of my identity as an African American cultural and literary critic, I assume, like most black Americans in the United States of my pre–World War II and Swing Age generation, that the world is interpreted from the vantage point of different, often still separated, and unequal racial and ethnic spaces and communities. My generation bore witness to the sounds of the big bands of Cab Calloway, Count Basie, and Duke Ellington as well as to the mass demonstrations by African Americans protesting Italy's invasion of Ethiopia in 1935. Many postmodern and some postcolonial theorists, as illustrated in chapter 1, advocate seeing the world from multiple transnational and transcultural subject positions while paradoxically and often unconsciously grounding the subjectivities of themselves and others, as Afro-British Paul Gilroy does in his critical study of black modernity and double consciousness, in the ethnocentric norms of their own Anglocentric or Eurocentric background, primary speech community, and predominantly white middle-class living space. Gilroy, for example, constructs his diasporic theory of the Black Atlantic and cultural hybridity by focusing on "the special relationships between 'race,' culture, nationality, and ethnicity which have a bearing on the histories and political cultures of Britain's black citizens."[12] In contrast, the dynamics of my identity formation and cultural productions are explicitly grounded in the African Americentric[13] core of my sociohistorical, sociocultural, and sociopsychological double consciousness and code-switching or blending of Standard American English (SAE) and African American Vernacular English (AAVE) vocabulary, pronunciation, grammar, and tropes as a revisionist African American male vernacular cultural and literary critic. In the field of cultural production, according to sociologist Pierre Bourdieu, symbolic and cultural capital are particularly important. Whereas symbolic capital refers to the "degree of accumulated prestige, celebrity, consecration or honour and is founded on a dialectic of knowledge . . . and recognition . . . cultural capital . . . [is] a form of knowledge, an internalized code or a cognitive acquisition which equips the social agent with empathy towards, appreciation for or competence in deciphering cultural relations and cultural artifacts."[14] African and African American vernacular revisionist cultural and literary critics use our cultural capital and double consciousness to contest and complicate the master narratives and myths of the natural, universal superiority of Western culture and the innate purity, unity, and dominance of white people, especially men. We also use our double consciousness to express either an Afrocentric or African Americentric type of modernism and postmodernism that acknowledges the limitations and possibilities of cultural relativism and provisional truths in the quest for personal and collective freedom, literacy, and wholeness.

Because they will be explained more fully in chapter 1, let me here just briefly define the terms "Eurocentric," "Afrocentric," and "African Americentric" as unstable, shifting geopolitical and philosophical concepts that basically indicate whether Europe or Africa or the United States is at the center of one's vision of the world and method of interpreting it and literary texts. The history of imperialism and the Atlantic slave trade as well as of foreign-born immigration and native-born migration clearly indicates that the relation of the lighter peoples of the world to the darker is marked by racial and cultural mixture. Rather than indicating a direct, mechanistic correlation between a writer's social position and the type of literary text that he or she produces, the dominant aesthetic tradition of the African American novel reveals that the text is not only an indirect, imaginative representation of the racial, class, and gender identity formation or position of the author and of the group to which he or she implies a primary commitment. The text is also a product of the complex conditions of the production, circulation, and consumption of socially significant symbolic acts and goods for a marketplace of different types of resisting readers.

I deploy rhetorical, dialectical, and dialogical critical strategies to reexamine and reconstruct the relationship between conventionally classified—but far from pure, static, and mutually exclusive—black and white cultures, especially their vernacular and literary traditions, mainly in the United States. As elaborated more fully in chapter 2, my critical theory and analyses of the culture of Americans of sub-Saharan black African descent are grounded primarily in the sociohistorical and sociocultural specificity of the dynamic pattern of our everyday and mythic experiences in antagonistic cooperation with the dominant white social formation in the United States. I am therefore committed to an aesthetic that imaginatively seeks to challenge and change insidious contemporary language and other institutional manifestations of the system of antiblack racism in the United States. Contemporary antiblack racism includes racial profiling, racial brutality by police officers, racial discrimination in the justice system and media, and racial economic redlining, which are fostered by negative stereotypes and representations of nonwhite people, sometimes expressed by ourselves, that serve to maintain and perpetuate the power, preferential treatment, and privileges of the white ruling class and its nonwhite supporters.

In other words, like Bourdieu's theory and rigorous analysis of the cultural field, my analysis adapts a radical contextualization of literary texts:

> It takes into consideration not only works themselves, seen relationally within the space of available possibilities and within the historical development of such possibilities, but also producers of works in terms of their strategies and trajectories, based on their individual and class habitus, as well as their objective position within the field. It also entails an analysis of the structure of the field itself, which includes the positions occupied by producers (e.g. writers, artists) as well as those occupied by all the instances of consecration and legitimation which make cultural products what they are (the public, publishers, critics, galleries, academies and so forth). Finally, it involves an analysis of the position of the [literary] field within the broader field of power.[15]

More specifically for this study, although my analytic method includes the social conditions of the production, circulation, and consumption of novels as symbolic texts and acts, I am primarily committed to the validation and valorization of the authentic everyday voices and previously excluded experiences of ordinary black Americans in the revisionist tradition of black and white social scientists, humanists, and artists. This tradition includes Carter G. Woodson, John B. Cade, Charles S. Johnson, Lawrence D. Reddick, Melville J. Herskovits, Benjamin A. Botkin, Kenneth M. Stampp, Norman R. Yetman, George P. Rawick, and John W. Blassingame, as well as Du Bois and Brown.

Highlighting the problems of the authenticity, authority, and agency of African American voices, the self-liberated slave John Little told an interviewer in 1855 after escaping to Canada: "Tisn't he who has stood and looked on, that can tell you what slavery is—'tis he who has endured."[16] How do auditors and readers assess the authenticity and authority of the pronunciation, vocabulary, and grammar of this and similar voices that were and are usually recorded, interpreted, and published by white interviewers and editors? How do readers and critics move beyond the popular cultural legacy of the cacography, malapropisms, anachronisms, anomalies, and ridicule of African American language, culture, and character spawned by the plantation and blackface minstrel traditions? White authorities and masters, too often with the complicity and collusion of members of the oppressed group, not only controlled the past, they also controlled and control the written histories. "Seldom before or since has racism been so pervasive and so academically respectable in America as during the early years of the twentieth century," writes sociologist Norman Yetman. "The assumption of the innate and inherited inferiority of non–Anglo Saxon racial and ethnic groups permeated and dominated intellectual as well as popular thought. Social, scientific, and historical thought both mirrored and reinforced this racism."[17]

For example, in twentieth-century historiography and popular culture in the United States, Ulrich B. Phillips's *American Negro Slavery* (1918) and *Life and Labor in the Old South* (1929) and Stanley Elkins's *Slavery* (1959) provoked early revisionist scholarship by providing academic respectability for the negative stereotypes of black Americans as biologically and culturally inferior. These stereotypes were first popularized on stage in the 1830s in the minstrel tradition of blackfaced white men mocking black culture, language, and character. They were also popular in antebellum and postbellum writings by such authors as John Pendleton Kennedy, Joel Chandler Harris, and Thomas Nelson Page, who either sympathetically supported or nostalgically glorified the plantation tradition of the Old South. In their representations of the Old South from the perspective of the white planter class, slavery was a paternalistic agricultural economic system. Influenced by his Southern heritage to devalue and dismiss the testimonies, the oral history, of ex-slaves as unintelligent, unintelligible, and unreliable, Phillips valorized the popular representations of African Americans as descendants of culturally, morally, and intellectually deficient contented slaves in his comprehensive study of American slavery. Because "the typical Negroes" were naturally "impulsive and inconstant, sociable and amorous, voluble, dilatory, and negligent, but robust, amiable, obedient and contented," Phillips writes, "they have been the world's premium slaves."[18]

According to Elkins, slavery in the United States was a closed social system, more like Nazi concentration camps than like slavery in Latin America and the Caribbean, in which enslaved Africans and their descendants were infantile laborers and Sambos who were "docile but irresponsible, loyal but lazy, humble but chronically given to lying and stealing."[19] This thesis was a counterdiscourse not only to the revisionist scholarship of John Hope Franklin's classic comprehensive black history *From Slavery to Freedom* (1947) and Kenneth Stampp's history of American slavery *The Peculiar Institution* (1959), but also to earlier revisionist scholarship inspired by the Harvard-educated black historians W. E. B. Du Bois and Carter G. Woodson. In 1896, Du Bois published *The Suppression of the African Slave Trade to the United States of America, 1638–1870*, and in 1915 Woodson founded the Association for the Study of Negro Life and History and in 1916 the *Journal of Negro History*. In the 1920s and 1930s black and white revisionist scholars and cultural workers in the United States began to recover, reclaim, and reassess missing or misrepresented texts and absent black voices for the reconstruction of a more diverse and democratic usable American past. It is also very important to note here that 1896 was the year that the *Plessy v. Ferguson* U. S. Supreme Court decision, which will be examined more closely later in this book as the disingenuous modern law that transformed the Southern ritual and trope of Jim Crow into a national reality, established that racial segregation was reasonable and legal where separate but equal public facilities were provided. Racially segregated and unequal public facilities, as were generally the rule rather than the exception, were thus a violation of federal law that was rarely if ever prosecuted. Segregation and antiblack racism also challenged black Americans to create and maintain alternative, often parallel, social and cultural systems for survival as a people.

In the tradition of African American cultural resistance and resiliency, as quiet as it is kept, the first major projects to collect and preserve the life stories of ex-slaves were at black institutions, Fisk University in Tennessee in 1928 and Southern University in Louisiana in 1929, under the direction of such sociologists as Charles S. Johnson at Fisk and such historians as John B. Cade at Southern. Although the interviews collected by black staff members of Johnson's Social Science Institute were a major source for his analysis in *Shadow of the Plantation* (1934), the first major study to reveal the plantation system from the slaves' point of view, the interviews were not published until the 1970s. Also in 1934, Lawrence Reddick, a graduate student participant in the Fisk project and a faculty member at Kentucky State College, led a Federal Emergency Relief Administration (FERA) pilot project of twelve "Black white-collar workers" who collected approximately 250 interviews in Indiana and Kentucky, though what was said to be their inadequate interviewing experience resulted in the disapproval of the proposal for a more ambitious project until the Federal Writers' Project (FWP) established a similar study. Reddick's ambitious but unrealized proposal to employ 500 black college-educated workers to interview the surviving ex-slave population systematically was supported by Johnson and cosponsored by Woodson and the Association for the Study of Negro Life and History.[20] The interviews directed at Southern by Cade were summarized in 1935 in the article "Out of the Mouths of Ex-Slaves,"[21] but the more than 400 interviews with ex-slaves in thirteen states that he directed while at Prairie View State College during 1935–38 remain unpublished.

Although we hear the stories of ex-slaves filtered through the voices and inscribed by the pens of African American historians, including Du Bois's revisionist classic study *Black Reconstruction in America* (1935), the voices of enslaved Africans and African Americans were not generally valued in white American historiography until the Black Studies movement inspired revisionist scholarship in the 1960s. This was the case even though more than 2,000 interviews with those who endured slavery, as well as commentaries and autobiographies by them, were compiled in seventeen states by the FWP in 1936–39. During this period, Henry G. Alsberg was the national director of the FWP; George Cronyn, the associate director; Sterling A. Brown (1936–38) the national editor for Negro affairs; and John Lomax (1936–37) and Benjamin Botkin (1937–39) the national folklore editors for this project. Because of his prestige, Lomax, probably the most distinguished Southern white folklorist and popularizer of American folksongs, was primarily responsible in 1937 for systematically extending the Slave Narrative Collection program through the different states. "The interview method of collecting folklore and a corollary emphasis upon the collection of life-history materials, both of which he introduced, became a hall mark of Writers' Project research," Yetman notes.[22]

As a nationally respected Howard University associate professor, published poet and essayist, and scholar of black and white American poetry, fiction, and drama, Brown, the "light, bright, damned-near white" son and grandson of ex-slaves,[23] who wryly called himself the black sheep of his family, was exceptionally well qualified for his responsibilities of coordinating "all the Writers' Project's studies by and about Blacks . . . and monitoring the number of Blacks employed in the Project."[24] At the beginning of their careers, such now distinguished black writers as Roi Ottley, Willard Motley, Frank Yerby, Zora Neale Hurston, Margaret Walker, Arna Bontemps, Claude McKay, Richard Wright, and Ralph Ellison were employed on state projects during Brown's tenure as national editor. But we should not forget that most of the interviewers were unemployed white artists and writers with obvious class, racial, and regional biases that distorted the collection of the ex-slave narratives and the writing of guidebooks in states like Texas, Mississippi, and South Carolina. Alsberg, Brown, and Botkin therefore provided specific, detailed guidelines to the state field collectors and directors and revised the interviewers' questionnaires designed by Lomax in order to improve "the level of authenticity and honesty in their presentation of this material."[25] But Texas and Mississippi state directors either extensively revised or failed to send interviews to the national office that questioned the popular legend of slavery as a paternalistic Southern social system of benevolent white masters and contented black slaves.

Because of the popularity of blackface minstrel stereotypes created by white performers to ridicule black character and culture while reifying the myth of white supremacy, these guidelines and questionnaires were especially needed for the recording and interpretation of the ex-slaves' unique Gullah dialect and culture in the coastal areas of South Carolina and Georgia. Based on his experience with and respect for authentic black folk speech, developed primarily while he was a teacher in Virginia, and demonstrated in his published poetry and criticism, especially a seminal article in 1933 on black stereotypes in American literature, Brown also recommended that "truth to idiom be paramount, and exact truth to pronunciation secondary."[26] Even so, the racial, regional, class, and gender biases of many of the interviewers and state editors resulted in either violations of or uneven adherence to Brown's standard of authenticity.

As my venerable teacher, mentor, and friend, Brown, who was a social realist and modernist in critical theory and poetic practice, is most important in my rites of passage in becoming an African Americentric scholar and activist. Unlike the focus on the African past and African diaspora of many Afrocentrics, my primary scholarly comparative methodology focuses on the double consciousness and hybrid identity formations resulting from the acculturative process in the United States that transformed Africans into African Americans. This is not a philosophical issue of whether identity is the product of either nature or nurture. Rather, it is the anthropological proposition that identity is a complex dialectic process that takes place between nature and nurture. Other important revisionists who influenced me in my journey as an African Americentric scholar include the anthropologist Melville J. Herskovits, who, along with Brown, was prominent among the consultants on African American culture to Gunnar Myrdal's landmark study, *An American Dilemma* (1944). Herskovits's *Myth of the Negro Past* (1941) is a provocative, valuable, revisionist seminal study of African cultural survivals in the United States and Caribbean that reconstructs Du Bois's concept of double consciousness and introduces the African acculturative process of retention, reinterpretation, and syncretism. Continuing the revisionist tradition in 1945, Botkin edited *Lay My Burden Down,* the first modest folk history of excerpts and selections from narratives in the Slave Narrative Collection of the FWP. Even more impressive are Kenneth Stampp's *Peculiar Institution* (1956) and Charles Nichols's *Many Thousand Gone* (1963), classic histories by a white and a black scholar that challenged traditional historiography by including black voices across the nation telling their stories from the social margins about the legacy of slavery.

Elkins's comparative study of slavery in Latin America, the Caribbean, and Nazi concentration camps was primarily a response to Stampp's displacement of the moral and scholarly authority of Phillips and the Sambo identity with evidence from the testimonies of former plantation slaves themselves. Challenging the assumptions and extending the evidence of Phillips, this testimony from the traditionally devalued and unacknowledged voices of the peculiar institution supported Stampp's thesis that enslaved black Americans "were merely ordinary human beings, that innately Negroes *are*, after all, only white men with black skins, nothing more, nothing less."[27] But my rites of passage into manhood as an African American revisionist scholar, vernacular theorist, modernist critic, and social activist challenged the authority of this well-intentioned declaration of the norms of Negro identity.

In the 1970s several books recovered and reassessed the voices in the Slave Narrative Collection of the FWP for the pedagogical, cultural, and research projects fostered by the Black Studies movement. These include Yetman's valuable *Life under the "Peculiar Institution"* (1970), Rawick's impressive nineteen-volume *From Sundown to Sunup* (1972), and Blassingame's provocative *Slave Community* (1972) and *Slave Testimony* (1977). These revisionist studies challenged the standard representation of African American character and culture as deviant and deficient by the historiography of Phillips and Elkins. Elkins's *Slavery* was an important influence on the controversial representation of Nat Turner and his slave revolt in 1831 as deviant in William Styron's 1968 Pulitzer Prize–winning *Confessions of Nat Turner*. In response to the misrepresentation of African American culture and character by Elkins and Styron, I wrote the first articles in my rites of passage as a revisionist scholar and activist in 1968.

According to family legend, however, my rites of passage into manhood began during the economic depression of the 1930s below the Mason-Dixon line, the eighteenth-century geographical boundary between Maryland and Pennsylvania that marked the political and cultural line between the North and South. Born and raised in early childhood in the racially segregated black speech communities and public schools of Washington, D.C., and Norbeck, Maryland, where neither the outdated books and inadequate supplies nor the curriculum and physical plant were the equal of facilities and resources in white schools, I am the only son of a single black mother. A high school graduate and avid reader, she insisted that I read such authors as Paul Laurence Dunbar, Langston Hughes, Louisa May Alcott, Robert Louis Stevenson, Mark Twain, and Edgar Allan Poe, as well as the comic books that I usually preferred to read. With my migration to New York during World War II, I learned the urban strategies of survival as a manchild in the mean streets and racially nonsegregated public schools of the Promised Land in the increasingly black and Puerto Rican speech communities of the South Bronx. I was nevertheless required in grade school to participate in speech therapy classes to correct my African American Vernacular English. Although my after-school hustles (delivering groceries; shining shoes; washing cars and windows; cleaning fish in a Jewish market and hallways in my housing project; playing blackjack; pitching nickels and dimes; shooting dice; shoplifting; snatching handbags; and watching out for cops at gambling dens) and my mother's monthly welfare checks helped us to survive the hard times, I was fortunate to escape the fate of many of my peers in such gangs as the Happy Gents, Coppians, Slicksters, Puerto Rican Tigers, and Irish Dukes. Graduating from De Witt Clinton High School at seventeen, I entered the liminal stage of my rites of passage into manhood by joining the military and learning the strategies of killing and survival as a U.S. Marine in Europe and the Far East during the Korean War. In the late 1950s I returned to revitalize the core black culture of my identity by reintegrating into the predominantly African American community of the nation's capital, especially the Northeast Housing Projects on Benning Road. I became a husband, a father of three sons, and a graduate of the predominantly black Howard University, as well as a D.C. high school teacher, scholar activist, doctoral student, and ultimately a faculty member in the Black Studies movement of 1968–69 at the University of Massachusetts in Amherst.

Actually, my authority and agency as an African American scholar and activist began to transform my consciousness and commitment during the Mississippi freedom rides and schools in 1962 with the inspiration of my mentor, Sterling A. Brown, whom I affectionately and respectfully called "Prof." As a Korean veteran who had to take remedial English in order to attend Howard University under the GI Bill and as the first college student in my family, I realized that I was not the turn-the-other-cheek type of person required to participate in nonviolent civil rights demonstrations. But while working as a graduate research assistant with Prof at Howard on the critical debate of whether Herman Melville's "Benito Cereno" was most meaningfully read as a realistic or allegorical short story of a black slave revolt at sea, I became deeply involved in revisionist scholarship on slavery and in theories of social realism and modernism. It was also in his office during this time that I first met Student Nonviolent Coordinating Committee (SNCC) activists Michael Thelwell, Stokely Carmichael, Charlie Cobb, Courtland Cox, and Cleve Sellers, who were undergraduate college students recruiting volunteers for the Civil Rights movement and freedom schools in Alabama and Mississippi.

Inspired by my research and Prof's profound spiritual, political, and scholarly identification with Southern rural and urban working-class blacks, as well as with young undergraduate student activists and future SNCC leaders in the Black Power movement of the mid-1960s, I became more politically active as a cultural worker and critic. Because I was an ex-Marine who did not believe in nonviolence, and because I was a father who drove a cab and worked as an airline chef to support my wife and three sons, I was neither willing nor able to participate in street demonstrations. But I did participate with Prof and other student activists in supporting lectures, forums, and meetings on the Howard campus and in the city concerning everything from sit-ins, freedom schools, and voting registration drives to poetry readings, agitprop theater, and other cultural performances. This phase of my agency as a scholar of African American social neorealism and modernism culminated with Prof and me participating in the extraordinary 1963 March on Washington and paying tribute to the legendary and venerable pioneer African American scholar and activist W. E. B. Du Bois at the news of his death during the march.

The next stage of my rites of passage as a revisionist African Americentric literary and cultural critic committed to validating and valorizing black American voices from the bottom and margins of society was the completion of a master's thesis, *Anger in the Novels of Ralph Ellison, John O. Killens and James Baldwin*, at Howard University in 1966. After accepting a fellowship in 1967 to study with Professor Sidney Kaplan, a 1949 Bancroft Prize–winning specialist in American and African American Studies, at the University of Massachusetts, I began achieving national recognition in 1968 and 1969 with my publication of scholarly book reviews in the *Michigan Review* and *American Dialog*. These essays challenged the pseudo-Freudian Stanley Elkins–influenced representation by William Styron of the Virginia slave revolt of 1831 and of its legendary messianic leader, Nat Turner, as an aberrant act by a sexually repressed violent predator of white women.

During the same period, two major academic and political developments resonated deeply in my life. The first was the completion of my doctoral dissertation, *The Afro-American Novel and Its Tradition*, under the direction of Professor Kaplan. The second was the impact on me of Ralph Ellison's *Shadow and Act* (1964), Frantz Fanon's *Wretched of the Earth* (1968) and Harold Cruse's *Crisis of the Negro Intellectual* (1968) and of my participation as a Phi Kappa Phi honors graduate student in the historically neglected Black Studies movement at the University of Massachusetts in transforming me into a postcolonial African Americentric vernacular theorist, literary critic, and social activist. Even more remarkable than San Francisco State University, the University of Massachusetts movement established departments, rather than programs, of African American studies at the elite private institutions of Amherst, Smith, Mount Holyoke, and Hampshire Colleges, as well as a department named in honor of W. E. B. Du Bois at the Amherst campus of the University of Massachusetts. As a graduate student and faculty member, I not only co-founded the W. E. B. Du Bois Department of African American Studies at the University of Massachusetts, but also served as interim chairman of the department and as the first chairman of the Five-College Executive Committee of African American Studies.

Although generally neglected in major reports by the Ford Foundation and books by specialists such as Thomas Sowell, Nick Aaron Ford, and Perry A. Hall on the Black Studies movement,[28] the Du Bois Department of African American Studies was probably the most politically and intellectually diverse and dynamic revisionist development in a white institution of higher education at that time on the East Coast if not in the nation. Under the charismatic leadership of Michael Thelwell, a prize-winning Jamaican writer, SNCC political activist, and compelling orator, and under my academic and administrative leadership, our faculty included the following: Algerian Ambassador Cherif Guellal, Herbert Aptheker, Chinua Achebe, Johnnetta Cole, Ivanhoe Donaldson, Max Roach, Archie Shepp, Playthell Benjamin, William Strickland, John Bracey, Paul Carter Harrison, Nelson Stevens, Olufemi Richards, Julius Lester, Acklyn Lynch, Ernest Mkalimoto, Chester Davis, Esther and Eugene Terry, Ray Miles, and Sidney Kaplan. As a faculty member in the Department of English at the University of Massachusetts for twenty-four years as well as in the W. E. B. Du Bois Department of African American Studies during its most turbulent early years, I also founded the Black Faculty Association and the Minority Faculty Association in order to increase the recruitment, retention, and power of black and nonwhite minority faculty.

My participation in the African American Studies movement to challenge and change the literary canon, academic curriculum, and critical pedagogy continued in the 1970s. In 1971 I published a pioneering essay on Jean Toomer, "A Key to the Poems in *Cane*," in the *College Language Association Journal*, and in 1972 I edited the anthology *Modern and Contemporary Afro-American Poetry* as a pedagogical collection of poems that reveals in some depth the vitality and versatility of some of the best modern and contemporary African American poets. As one of the Broadside Press Critics, I also published a pioneering monograph on Johann Gottfried von Herder and African American vernacular poetic theory and practice in 1974, *The Folk Roots of Contemporary Afro-American Poetry*. I joined the Department of English at the Pennsylvania State University (PSU) in 1991 and coordinated the development of an undergraduate and graduate program in African American literature that ranks among the nation's top programs of its type. I was also active at PSU in developing the African and African American Studies Department, in negotiating mutually agreeable terms in 2001 between black student demonstrators and the university president for implementing a more vigorous diversity plan at the university, and in organizing the Africana Research Center.

In addition to lecturing and teaching in America, Europe, and Africa at such universities as Harvard, Chicago, Morgan State, Heidelberg, Lisbon, Coimbra, Salamanca, and the Sorbonne and to authoring, editing, or coediting seven books and publishing more than fifty articles, I have received several awards as a scholar and activist. They include the College Language Association Creative Scholarship Award in 1989, the Du Bois/Garvey Pan African Unity Award in 1999, and an induction into the International Literary Hall of Fame for Writers of African Descent in 2000. Internationally, I have been honored to serve as a Visiting Professor at the University of Freiburg in Germany in 1974–75, as a member of the colloquium at the Second World Black and African Festival of Arts and Culture in Lagos, Nigeria, in 1977, and as a Senior Fulbright-Hays Scholar at the University of Coimbra in Portugal in 1982–83, at the University of Salamanca in Spain in 1996, and at Beijing Foreign Studies University in the People's Republic of China in 2004.

But I still draw strength as an African Americentric scholar and critic from memories of the sociocultural rituals and stories of my primary speech community. Particularly indelible are memories of those about the souls and ways of black folk recounted by my single mother, paternal grandfather, and kinfolk in Washington and by my aunts, uncles, cousins, and up-South extended family in Maryland. Equally strong are memories of the survival strategies of my black peers and elders in the turbulent streets of the South Bronx, where I and thousands of black Southerners and Puerto Ricans migrated after World War II. Even though my wife, sons, and I have lived for many years in predominantly white communities, these memories were enriched and extended further by vital links with my wife's family in North and South Carolina, especially my sage, septuagenarian Cousin Tea Baby, who is more appropriately and respectfully known as Mother McClellan to other Church of God in Christ members. These links with and memories of traditional and contemporary Southern black American speech communities and culture are also invigorated by my wife's tragicomic stories about her family's strategies for surviving intraracial and interracial color lines in getting an education and religion, as well as picking cotton and doing domestic work for white folks during her childhood in Monroe, North Carolina, before moving to Philadelphia and Washington, D.C.

As a boy, I was nurtured primarily in exclusively black storytelling sessions while participating in the vibrant culture of an up-South rural community. This culture included church revivals and camp meetings, picnics, apple orchard and corn-field raids, skinny dipping in water holes, fruit and vegetable picking, wood-sawing and water hauling chores, chicken and fish fry parties, hog-slopping and hog-killing rituals, squirrel and rabbit hunting, horse-shoe games, and caddying with black men from 7th and T Streets at the nearby whites-only golf club across the road from my Aunt Gretna's house in Norbeck. Later, from 169th Street and Brook Avenue to 174th and Claremont Parkway in the South Bronx, the black Baptist church, schoolyards, front stoops, rooftops, street corners, pool halls, gambling dens, barber shops, community centers, and house parties became the primary sites for sustained and substantive immersion with my predominantly black peers and elders in the African American vernacular tradition. In the predominantly white USMC, I traveled to many countries and reconstructed my identity within and against the different cultures and languages of the peoples of Puerto Rico, Spain, France, Italy, Sicily, Turkey, Greece, Algeria, and Japan. And as a student at Howard University, working at night as a cab driver and airline chef, I drank deeply from the reservoir of knowledge and the inspirational example of such distinguished and varied black educators and scholars as Sterling Brown, E. Franklin Frazier, Rayford Logan, Kelly Miller, Frank Snowden, William Banner, Arthur P. Davis, Chancellor Williams, Owen Dodson, John Lovell, Jose Ferrer Canales, Margaret Butcher, and Dorothy Porter.

This autobiographical sketch does not mean that I intend to flip the script in this book in order either to demonize whiteness and matriarchy or to deify blackness and patriarchy. Nor is it intended as an immodest advertisement for myself and an intemperate sweeping indictment of the black bourgeoisie, Whitey, Oreos, neoconservative blacks, radical Afrocentrics, angry black feminists, transnational Anglocentrics, multicultural buppies, or platinum album–selling rappers and their associates for the victimization of ostensibly powerless black folks. It certainly doesn't mean that only black folks can understand black culture or teach black literature. Rather, this autobiographical sketch seeks to offer a useful personal model of rites of passage—the three major phases of separation, transition or liminality, and incorporation that mark an individual's life crises—for assessing the authenticity, authority, and agency of a revisionist African Americentric critic and text. The language, knowledge, and power of my voice emanate from the storytelling lessons and scholarly legacy of my ancestors and elders as well as from a post-1980s sensibility of many people, especially men, in the United States of sub-Saharan black African descent and bicultural heritage. This model is an interdependent configuration of chromosomes, color, ethnicity, class, gender, geography, age, culture, sexuality, consciousness, commitment, conscience, and choice. But it assumes that an Afrocentric or African Americentric critic and text will be significantly grounded in and will manifest a viable link to, or politically activist knowledge of, the sociohistorical and sociopsychological dynamics of traditional and contemporary black American culture, language, and character. It also assumes that the critic will be as formally educated in and committed to the interdisciplinary field of African American Studies, including having membership in and providing professional support for its major historical institutions, as he or she is or would be in any traditional discipline. In such cases, however, a black Afrocentric or African Americentric native-speaker and code-switching critic would probably manifest more authenticity, authority, and agency in interpreting ethnic commonplaces and nuances in the language of literature by, about, and primarily for African American readers than would a white critic.

My rites of passage as an African Americentric critic and cultural worker therefore map the roots and branches of the authenticity, authority, and agency of my identity and of the struggle of African Americans through vernacular and literary cultural production to affirm their humanity, to resist domination, and to attain their full civil rights as citizens with dignity in the United States. "Power concedes nothing without a demand," Frederick Douglass wrote. "It never did, and it never will. Find out just what people will submit to, and you have found out the exact amount of injustice and wrong which will be imposed upon them; and these will continue till they are resisted with either words or blows, or with both."[29] In their everyday struggle for identity, status, and power to fit into or to change an unjust and unequal social system, the authors and texts under examination in this work illuminate the complexity and paradoxes of our hybrid identity formations. The authors and novels that I examine here reveal that a change in the tradition of the African American novel is underway. They also reveal how our identities are both a product of and a process in a specific time and place of a core of ethnic beliefs and values derived from the complex, dynamic relationship of our chromosomes, color, ethnicity, class, gender, geography, age, culture, sexuality, consciousness, commitment, conscience, and choice. When I was inducted into the International Literary Hall of Fame for Writers of African Descent at the Gwendolyn Brooks Center in Chicago in

2000, my soul clapped hands and sang, to borrow a phrase from William Butler Yeats and Paule Marshall, as I heard the voices of my elders and ancestors rising above the praise songs of my contemporary community of writers and cultural workers: "Boy, you've done good. You're sure enough a credit to the race. But don't ya git weary 'cause the Lord ain't through with you yet!"

I am indebted for assistance in completing this book to more folks that I could reasonably remember or list in this acknowledgment. But let me begin with praise for the graduate students, colleagues, and readers who encouraged me with the candor and cooperation of their constructive and often cogent commentaries on sections and chapters of this work in progress. I am particularly appreciative of the contributions of Gigi Marino, Melanie Levinson, Musa al Halool, Mule Katwiwa, Susan Searls, Carol Davenport, Janet Cooper, Vorris Nunley, Dyon Stefanon, Howard Rambsy II, Mursalata Muhammad, Jeffrey Pruchnic, Steele Nowlin, Christopher White, and Pia Deas. These students were in my graduate courses on the relationship of Eurocentric modernist and postmodernist literary theories and texts to the cultural production and narratives of African Americans from the New Negro movement of the 1920s to the New Black Aesthetic movement of the 1990s. Levinson, Searls, Davenport, Muhammad, Cooper, Nunley, Rambsy, Stefanon, Pruchnic, Nowlin, White, and Deas also provided valuable service as research assistants and, in the case of Cooper and Stefanon, as highly perceptive assistant editors at different stages of the more than ten years that this project was in progress. The assistance of Breyan Strickler in the final stage of production of this book is also gratefully acknowledged.

Colleagues who have either read chapters in progress or at various times discussed with me the issues I raise have also provided valuable contributions to the final shape of the book even when I have not always heeded their cautionary advice about the risks of engaging so many provocative cultural and literary theories, theorists, and practices. I am particularly indebted to Professors Alan Sica, James Stewart, Keith Gilyard, Jerry Ward, Trudier Harris, Chester Fontenot, Houston Baker Jr., and Hortense Spillers. I am also deeply appreciative of the patience, cooperation, and editorial assistance of the director, Bruce Wilcox, and staff of the University of Massachusetts Press, and especially of copyeditor Kay Scheuer, in producing this sequel to *The Afro-American Novel and Its Tradition*.

Introduction

THE *Contemporary African American Novel: Its Folk Roots and Modern Literary Branches* is a sociohistorical, sociocultural, and sociopsychological critical history of the contemporary African American novel as a socially symbolic act of cultural politics and narrative discourse. The strategic essentialism and oppositional discourse for interpreting African American narratives that I proposed in the introduction and first chapter of *The Afro-American Novel and Its Tradition* in 1987 has its origins in two interrelated theories. The first is a sociohistorical, sociocultural, and sociopsychological theory of Du Boisian double consciousness and double vision. And the second is a vernacular theory of residual oral forms: oratory (including everyday speech acts), myth (including its ritual reenactment), legend, tale, and song or music. In the earlier book I analyzed the relationship of double consciousness and the five vernacular oral forms to the distinctive thematic, stylistic, and structural characteristics of the African American novel from its beginnings in 1853 to major achievements in the genre in 1983. For example, in 1983 Alice Walker's National Book Award and Pulitzer Prize–winning *The Color Purple* marked the culmination of the achievement of black female novelists, and John Edgar Wideman's Homewood trilogy revitalized the power of an Afrocentric aesthetic for black male novelists.

Because this book begins in 1962 but focuses primarily on novels and romances published between 1983 and 2001, chapter 1 maps the terrain and definition of the terms for understanding the book's rhetoric, politics, and poetics of representation. Chapters 2–5 are revisions and summaries of chapters 1–8 in *The Afro-American Novel and Its Tradition*. More specifically, chapters 2 and 3 survey the sociohistorical, sociocultural, and sociopsychological landscape and roots, as well as the peaks and valleys of the African American novel and its tradition from 1853 to 1962. Chapters 4 and 5 update and clarify the theoretical and critical issues initially outlined in chapters 7 and 8 of the earlier work about neorealism, modernism, and postmodernism in the contemporary African American novel. Responding to recent debates in literary and cultural theory, chapters 4 and 5 also closely examine more than 40 novels published between 1962 and 1983 by more than 20 novelists that illustrate the importance of authenticity, authority, and agency in assessing the literary use of African American residually oral forms, especially black American speech, music, and religion. The novelists include John Oliver Killens, John A. Williams, Alice Walker, Gayl Jones, Toni Cade Bambara, Toni Morrison, Margaret Walker, Ernest Gaines, William Melvin Kelley, Ronald Fair, John Edgar Wideman, Clarence Major, Charles Stevenson Wright, Hal Bennett, and Ishmael Reed.

The memoir "On Becoming an African American Scholar Activist," introduction, chapters 1, 6–8, and the conclusion of this book are completely new. They examine continuity and change between 1983 and 2001 in the Afrocentric and African Americentric tropes of identity in African American novels and romances. In general, whereas Afrocentric tropes focus on the African diaspora, African Americentric tropes emanate from the United States. Chapter 6 examines primarily the texts published since 1983 by Paule Marshall, Albert Murray, Gloria Naylor, Al Young, David Bradley, and Leon Forrest. Chapter 7 covers Charles Johnson and the neo-Black Aesthetic novelists who have emerged since 1983 such as Nathaniel Mackey, Trey Ellis, Percival L. Everett and Colson Whitehead. Expanding on Samuel Delany's concept of paraliterature, chapter 8 focuses primarily on the science fiction of Delany and Octavia Butler, the gay novels of E. Lynn Harris, Larry Duplechan, and Randall Kenan, and the detective narratives of Barbara Neely and Walter Mosley.

Between 1983 and 2001, the outstanding achievements of black women novelists culminated in four prestigious international and national nominations and awards. In addition to Walker's Pulitzer Prize in 1983 for *The Color Purple,* Toni Morrison received the Nobel Prize for Literature in 1993, Gayl Jones's *Healing* was a finalist for the National Book Award in 1998, and Gloria Naylor's *Women of Brewster Place* received an American Book Award in 1999. Trey Ellis's *Right Here, Right Now* also received an American Book Award in 1999. The *Esquire* and *USA Today* Best First Novel of the Year Awards went to Colson Whitehead's *Intuitionist* in 2000, and his *John Henry Days* was a finalist for the Pulitzer Prize in 2001. These novels by contemporary black males mark the challenge of a black neomasculinist satirical interrogation and exploration of an African American vernacular tradition and the emergence of what some artists and critics perceive as a postmodern neo–Black Aesthetic.

The Afro-American Novel and Its Tradition developed a vernacular theory of the African American novel as "a hybrid narrative whose distinctive tradition and vitality are derived basically from the sedimented indigenous roots of black American folklore and literary genres of the Western world."[1] Two of the basic assumptions of my narrative theory in the first book have been indirectly and implicitly challenged by the categorical antiessentialism of many white and nonwhite postmodern and postcolonial cultural critics. The first basic assumption is that by custom and law "there has always been a cultural and social boundary in America beyond which the black American could not go." The second is that "the Afro-American novel is not merely a branch of the Euro-American novel but also a development of the Afro-American oral tradition," including religious and political master narratives.[2] My response to antiessentialist indirect challenges is this updated reassessment and reaffirmation of the validity of my vernacular theory and critical practice of analyzing the African American novel holistically as a socially symbolic act and imaginative reconstruction of the quest of African Americans for personal and social freedom, literacy, and wholeness.[3]

In the 1980s and 1990s cultural debates in the media and academies about the formation of literary canons and sociocultural identities began to shift from black nationalism and feminism to questions concerning the significance of masculinity, sexuality, multiculturalism, and postmodernism. Because definitions of masculinity will be discussed fully in chapter 8, it will suffice here to remind readers that identity formations are fluid processes, not static products, that some critics conflate the biological category of race with the cultural classification of ethnicity, and that there are many different types of masculine identities. According to sociologist Clyde W. Franklin II, the complex socialization of many African American males involves a "lethal socialization triangle." This triangle includes "(1) a type of primary group socialization providing mixed messages regarding the meaning of Black masculinity; (2) a peer group socialization source that teaches innovative Black masculine traits, and (3) a mainstream . . . socialization source that sends Black men mixed messages regarding competitiveness, aggressiveness, passivity, inferiority, and invisibility."[4] Although Franklin's value judgment of the socialization process of many African American males as lethal is disturbing, the socialization triangle is nevertheless useful in examining the identity formations of black males in African American novels published since 1983.

According to the Gay/Lesbian Almanac, the term "sexuality" is a Victorian invention "referring to the quality of being sexual or having a sex, possessing sexual powers or feelings, or being conscious of our preoccupation with sex."[5] Assuming, however, that the history of sexuality must be understood as "the chronicle of an increasing repression" since the seventeenth century, theorist Michel Foucault argues provocatively in *The History of Sexuality* that "the idea that there have been repeated attempts, by various means, to reduce all of sex to its reproductive function, its heterosexual and adult form, and its matrimonial legitimacy fails to take into account the manifold objectives aimed for, the manifold means employed in the different sexual politics concerned with the two sexes, the different age groups and social classes."[6] Although I am similarly interested in the relationship between power, knowledge, and sexual identity, my primary focus in this book, especially in chapter 8, is on the relationship among male sexuality, race, and ethnicity. Of particular interest will be the impact on narrative discourses of social marginality and sexual choice or condition on the health, unity, and diversity of black communities.

Multiculturalism may be defined as the social theory and practice that shifts the dynamics of power from the distinctive history of nonwhite slavery, Negrophobic segregation, and antiblack racism in the United States to an ostensibly progressive rejection of reductive racial binarisms of white oppressors and black victims. At its best, multiculturalism shifts the discourse and struggle for social justice from the unscientific and often stereotypic racial categories of white and black to diverse groups committed to the construction of a new social order that privileges mixed ethnic and other cultural identities. In *Multi-America* (1998), satirist and cultural critic Ishmael Reed's seminal anthology of diverse dissenting ethnic voices, Afrocentric scholar Maulana Karenga defines multiculturalism as "thought and practice informed by a profound appreciation for diversity, which expresses itself in four fundamental ways." These include mutual respect, mutual rights and responsibilities, mutual commitment to a relentless quest for common ground, and mutual commitment to "*a social ethics of sharing*."[7] Political scientist Manning Marable has called for a "'radical multiculturalism,' which means people of different backgrounds cohering around left-wing political causes."[8] As an African Americanist, I advocate a commitment to a radical democracy. This commitment involves the validation of the economics of slavery and politics of racial segregation as the major determinants of African American biracial and bicultural identity[9] as well as the cooperation of progressive members of all ethnic groups with mutual respect for the rights and responsibilities of each in the social reconstruction of the United States.

Unfortunately, however, multiculturalism too frequently represents a confusing reductive social construction and amalgamation of the different histories, cultures, and identities of all nonwhite ethnic and other immigrant, migrant, and minority groups in the United States, especially Native Americans, African Americans, Latino Americans, and Asian Americans.[10] But a closer examination of American identity formations beneath the surface of their popular names reveals a generally unacknowledged complexity. Among other things, all members of racial and ethnic groups did not arrive voluntarily in the New World and United States, especially in the cities, at the same time, in the same manner, or for the same reasons. Historically, although African Americans have been socially classified in census records as the largest racial minority group in the United States in part because of our mixed sub-Saharan African ancestry and because of the "one-drop rule," we have never been a homogeneous national and ethnic group. Geographically, generationally, socially, and culturally, there are distinctive, frequently disruptive intraracial differences and inequities among African Americans as well as interracial conflicts with Anglo-Americans and Euro-Americans. These differences and inequities began most unjustly with the racialization of slavery in Maryland in the seventeenth century and its sanctioning in the U.S. Constitution in the eighteenth century, culminated in the nationalization of racial segregation as the law of the land in the *Plessy v. Ferguson* Supreme Court decision of 1896, and were most meaningfully reconciled in the Civil Rights movement of the 1960s, especially in the Civil Rights Acts of 1964 and 1965. Until the violent response of African Americans to justice denied in the brutal beating of Rodney King by Los Angeles police in 1992, the post-1965, post–Civil Rights generation of African Americans and nonwhite ethnic immigrants had little or no shared direct experience with or shared indirect memories of blatant Negrophobic laws and menacing public signs, of systematic social inequality, of flagrant public hatred and physical violence expressed by antiblack white racists and their assimilated allies. Consequently, racial and ethnic solidarity and pride did not shape the consciousness and commitment of most post-1965, post–Civil Rights generation African Americans in a manner and to a degree similar to that of the pre-1965 generation. The members of each generation, to paraphrase social theorist Frantz Fanon, are challenged therefore not only to discover their mission and cultural identity, but also to fulfill or betray their personal and collective agency in the reconstruction of a more just social order.

Anthropologist Joe Chung Fong advances a similar perspective on generational and ethnic difference in his article "Ethnic Conflict and Harmony between African and Asian Americans in the United States." Because the amendments in 1965 to the Immigration and Nationality Act "allowed twenty thousand persons per country to emigrate from the eastern hemisphere and did away with the quota system for Asian countries. Korean and other 'new' Asian immigrants were allowed to come to the United States in significant numbers after 1965. The critical point here is that there remains a distinctive difference socially and culturally between the post-1965 Koreans and pre-1965 Asian immigrants."[11] Even though pluralism or multicultural unity with diversity in the United States was embodied in a national motto, "E Pluribus Unum," on currency until the Cold War with Russia heated up in 1956, when it was replaced by "In God We Trust," it is actually a modern socioeconomic ideal for many people rather than a socioeconomic reality. Racial, political, and cultural identities, rather than class, are the central differences. In contrast to the French-speaking black Haitians, the Spanish-speaking immigrants from both Cuba and Puerto Rico identify themselves predominantly as white Caribbeans. Also, whereas Haiti has been an independent black nation since 1804, Puerto Rico is a protectorate of the United States, and Cuba is an independent neo-Marxist nation. As nonwhite Haitian American immigrants are probably most acutely aware, there is "a universe of difference . . . between the experience of the Cuban man who arrived in the United States as a child with his parents after fleeing Castro's revolution and the Puerto Rican woman who is a third-generation single mother on the Lower East Side."[12]

It is common knowledge, moreover, that the popular terms and misnomers for racially mixed ethnic groups of people of Spanish-speaking ancestry who either immigrate to or are born in the United States are Hispanic and Latino.[13] But it is not common knowledge that between 1940 and 1960 the U.S. Census Bureau classified all Latin Americans as white ethnics, a population that census estimates predicted would surpass by 2002 the approximately 35 million racial population of African Americans. When the Census Bureau in 2000 gave citizens the choice of multiple racial identifications, Jamaican American sociologist Orlando Patterson notes, 48 percent of the Latino ethnic population identified themselves as purely white rather than racially mixed.[14] On one level, this racial choice expresses the degree to which many Latinos have also internalized and accepted the antiblack racism of the United States as the price of assimilation as American citizens. According to prize-winning author and Chicana activist Ana Castillo, a 1989 University of Chicago study reveals "that deep divisions based on race exist between black Hispanics and white Hispanics in the United States."[15] Even so, for political and economic reasons the leaders of many Latino organizations have increasingly reconciled intragroup color, class, and generational differences in order to form coalitions with African Americans and to benefit from affirmative action programs. At their best, then, multiculturalism and multiculturalists not only conflate but also homogenize racial and ethnic differences in the reconstruction of the imbalances and inequities of social power. At their worse, however, they disingenuously appropriate and deracinate the historically specific racial segregation, exploitation and sociopsychological trauma of African Americans that was nationally sanctioned by law in 1896. Although the *Brown v. Board of Education of Topeka* Court declared in 1954 that "Separate educational facilities are inherently unequal," it was not until the *Gayle v. Browder* Court concluded in 1956 that state statutes requiring racial segregation on the buses of Montgomery, Alabama, were unconstitutional that the separate-but-equal law was finally overturned.[16]

As for postmodernism, which will be defined more fully in subsequent chapters, it basically means the movement in critical theory and practice beyond the conventional assumptions about the essential nature of truth, reality, and art. Unquestionably, because African Americans have historically contested myths about the natural biological and cultural superiority of white people, multiculturalism and postmodernism are relevant to the construction and interpretation of the emancipation and empowerment of multiple identities in some of the motifs and leitmotifs of contemporary African American novels in this book. But my primary focus is on the specific post-1962 biracial, bicultural identities and aesthetics of African American novelists, critics, and readers. I hope to achieve this by situating my African Americentric approach to the novel as a spatially and temporally specific postcolonial socially symbolic act. Unlike postcolonialists, whose critical theory and practice emanate from their particular experiences with European and British colonialism in Africa, Asia, India, Latin America, and the Caribbean, I derive my postcolonial African Americentric approach from my core linguistic, belief, and value systems as a black American of African descent and bicultural heritage in the United States. Therefore, the dialectic tension between nonwhite racial and ethnic groups and the structures of white power and dominance in the United States between 1962 and 2001 is at the center of this book.

Throughout the rites of passage examined here, we not only become aware of continuity and change in the tradition of the novel, we also discover that the more things change, the more they remain the same. Irony and parody, tragicomedy and wry humor, ambiguity and ambivalence, segregation and integration, and accommodation and resistance are still salient characteristics of the double consciousness, of repetition with a black difference, and of African American culture and character in the journey from slavery to freedom. "Many of the people I see who are thought of as black could just as well be white in their appearance. Many of the white people I see are black as far as I can tell by the way they look. Now, that's it for looks," says one of the Southern-born, nearly ninety-year-old wise narrators in *Drylongso*. "Looks don't mean much. The thing that makes us different is how we think. What we believe is important, the ways we look at life." Although "white people have the power . . . the mojo and the sayso, . . . it is not hard to tell that they don't really know everything. . . . Pretending to know everything or just pretending to be better than you know you are must be a terrible strain on anybody."[17] The voice of this black elder thus reminds us of a common theme in the contemporary African American novel: there are racially and ethnically different ways of knowing and being in the world with others that ought to be mutually respected as we strive to assert and acknowledge our mutual rights and responsibilities in the construction of a more just, compassionate, and democratic social system.

In examining the identity formations that are imaginatively represented by more than 100 novelists in more than 200 novels published between 1962 and 2001, I will be guided by the ancestral voices of the elders of black communities such as those in *Drylongso* and those in my past. I will also be responding to the most significant contemporary voices of postcolonialists and postmodernists. The primary focus of my close analysis is on approximately 40 novels and romances published or reprinted between 1983 and 2001. The analysis will subordinate attention to the narrative deployment of residual oral African American forms in these texts to an examination of the relationship of language to knowledge and power in the construction of the authenticity, authority, and agency, key terms that are defined in chapter 1, of the implied authors and characters in the texts.

Whether read for verisimilitude as closed texts with definite meanings or as open-ended texts with indeterminate meanings, contemporary African American novels challenge readers by the imaginative deployment of language and speech to examine and even question the social construction of their identities and world, especially their systems of language, belief, and values. It is therefore not my purpose here to rehearse either the history of race as an idea, especially the nature versus nurture debate between Herder and Kant and other Enlightenment scientists and philosophers, or the history of antiblack racism in the United States.[18] Because race has always mattered regardless of how unscientifically we construct or interpret it, my purpose in general is to examine the relationship between race and culture in identity formations in the United States and in particular to examine the relationship between language, knowledge, and power in the contemporary African American novel.

In explaining the formal relations of parts of the text to the whole and the manner in which the language of the text mediates between the author's vision of reality and the reader's, I remain indebted to Wayne C. Booth's *Rhetoric of Fiction.*[19] More important than whether the story is told from a first-person or third-person point of view are whether the narrator is dramatized in his or her own right and whether his or her values are shared by the author. Dramatized narrators, both male and female, are generally as fully drawn characters as those they tell about, and their characteristics and beliefs are often very different from those of the "implied author" who creates them. The implied author, who should not be confused with the actual author, is the implicit picture the reader discerns of an author who stands behind the scenes imaginatively constructing and manipulating narrative elements when the narrator is undramatized. Unless this author is explicitly identified, there will be no difference between his characteristics and those of the undramatized narrator. In such cases the term author-narrator is generally used.

In discussing the various kinds of involvement or detachment among author, narrator, characters, and reader, most of our attention will be directed to the moral, political, and ideological qualities of the narrator, for the reliability or unreliability of the narrator is of vital importance to the integrity of the text. A reliable narrator is trustworthy and speaks for or acts in accord with the implied author's norms; an unreliable narrator is untrustworthy and does not. By proceeding, then, from significant historical events that produced the hybrid culture and double consciousness of black Americans to the manner in which they symbolically reenact and illumine the paradoxes and ambivalences of their experiences in romances and novels, I am attempting to provide a literary history and critical study that affirms a respect for the complex, reciprocal relationship between the principles of narrative form and social reality.

The Contemporary African American Novel: Its Folk Roots and Modern Literary Branches is therefore more than an academic exercise in canon reformation. I hope that it will contribute to an invigorating discourse on the manner and degree to which the identities of black American citizens of African descent and bicultural heritage are both a product and a process of the complex relationship of our chromosomes, color, ethnicity, class, gender, geography, age, culture, sexuality, consciousness, commitment, conscience, and choice. This book demonstrates that the struggle of black Americans for power, status, and community in an emerging, radically new social order of mutually respected, enacted, and enforced human and civil rights and responsibilities begins even though it does not end in the United States.

1 / *Mapping the Rhetoric, Politics, and Poetics of Representation in the Contemporary African American Novel*

> Fiction is of great value to any people as a preserver of manners and customs—religious, political and social. It is a record of growth and development from generation to generation. *No one will do this for us; we must ourselves, develop the men and women who will faithfully portray the inmost thoughts and feelings of the Negro with all the fire and romance which lie dormant in our history,* and, as yet, unrecognized by writers of the Anglo-Saxon race.
>
> PAULINE E. HOPKINS
> *Contending Forces*

IF it walks like a duck, quacks like a duck, and swims like a duck, then it must be a duck. This well-known folksaying, with its focus on knowledge acquired by perceptions of the bodies and behavior of others, is true on one level for many people. But as demonstrated by RuPaul, the successful black drag queen talk-show host; by Chester Himes, the social and sexual boundaries-crossing, prize-winning black masculinist detective novelist; and by Samuel Delany, the celebrated prize-winning black gay science fiction novelist and critic—the truth of performative racial and gender identities complicates rather than cancels the truth of core identities. As Ralph Ellison brilliantly demonstrates in the Liberty Paint Company episode in *Invisible Man,* in which the purest white paint in the nation is made by the nameless black protagonist mixing ten drops of black graduate with white paint, even in the modern African American novel the relationship between neither the racial and cultural identities of people in the United States nor their language, knowledge, and power is ever pure and simple.

Beginning in the 1960s and culminating in the 1980s and 1990s, poststructural, postmodern, and postcolonial critical theories and practice had a significant impact on the authenticity, authority, and agency of African American culture and several contemporary black American novelists. In appropriately interpreting the latter three concepts in the various contexts of this book, readers should keep in mind that authenticity means more than believing something is based on fact, that authority implies more than influencing thought or behavior, and that agency involves more than changing events by speech acts. These terms and other increasingly rarefied literary jargon will be defined more fully later in this chapter. The paradigmatic shift in the representation and interpretation of culture in the 1980s and 1990s vigorously promoted the transgression of racial, class, gender, and genre boundaries, as well as the antiessentialist social construction of identities. Influenced by Roland Barthes's poststructuralist declaration of the death of the author and celebration of the reader's pleasure in the endless play of language in "writerly texts,"[1] this shift in models of literary theory and critical practice also encouraged the discursive, indeterminate, open-ended reconstruction and representation of identity formations in several African American novels and romances. But what you see and what you hear are neither always true nor always what you get. As the critical examination in this book of the roots and modern branches of the contemporary African American novel demonstrates, the relationship between race, culture, and identity is as complex as the relationship between language, knowledge, and power.

"From Phyllis [*sic*] Wheatley to Charles Chesnutt, to the present generation of American Negro writers," LeRoi Jones wrote in 1962 with disdain for the apparent imitation by black writers of the literary standards of white middle-class models and with a call for the emulation of the emotional truth and beauty of spirituals, blues, and jazz, "the only recognizable accretion of tradition readily attributable to the black producer of a formal literature in this country, with a few notable exceptions, has been of an almost agonizing mediocrity."[2] But, like Jones's ideological indictment of black literature, contemporary reports of the death of the authenticity, authority, and agency of the author in the African American novel are not only premature but also grossly exaggerated. From the early petitions of enslaved Africans in 1773 for permission to purchase their freedom and return to Africa to the neoslave narratives of Margaret Walker, Ernest Gaines, Ishmael Reed, Toni Morrison, Sherley Anne Williams, and Charles Johnson, the literary tradition of African Americans has been fundamentally characterized by an emancipatory, life-enhancing social and cultural movement and by striving in the rhetoric, politics, and poetics of representation to reconcile the double consciousness of Americans of African descent. From William Wells Brown's *Clotel* (1853), Harriet E. Wilson's *Our Nig* (1859), and James Weldon Johnson's *Autobiography of an Ex-Colored Man* (1912) to Alice Walker's *The Color Purple* (1982), Samuel Delany's *Flight from Neveryon* (1985), Walter Mosley's *Devil in a Blue Dress* (1990), E. Lynn Harris's *Invisible Life* (1992), Trey Ellis's *Platitudes* (1988), and Colson Whitehead's *John Henry Days* (2001), we bear witness to the complex rhetoric, politics, and poetics, especially intertextuality, of the representation of African American character and culture in the tradition of the African American novel.

With the continuing production, marketing, and reception of new voices and texts, the process of reassessing and reconstructing the canon of African American literature and the tradition of the African American novel necessarily continues. But the more things change, the more they remain the same in the process of interpreting and interrogating the authenticity, authority, and agency of texts, authors, and critics. In other words, like Ishmael Reed, Clarence Major, and Toni Morrison in their experiments with postmodernism, I am as respectful of moral and cultural continuities as I am of discontinuities in forms of language, knowledge, and power in reconstructing the world that we have inherited from our ancestors into a more just and democratic social order. As a reassessment and reconstruction of the canon of the African American novel and its tradition in light of literary and cultural debates of the 1980s and 1990s, *The Contemporary African American Novel: Its Folk Roots and Modern Literary Branches* is therefore overdue.

The interdisciplinary examination in this book of the double consciousness and double vision in contemporary African American novels reveals continuity and change in the major thematic, structural, and stylistic dualisms in the narratives. Like the multiple conflicts, ironies, and paradoxes in what Mikhail Bakhtin in *The Dialogic Imagination* calls double-voiced and dialogic texts, which stress the social nature of language and speech events, these dualisms are neither mutually exclusive nor absolute. They are dynamic rather than static, and they vary in the domination of different configurations in different texts. The major dualisms under examination are racial or biological (black vs. white), ethnic or cultural (Afrocentric vs. Eurocentric or oral vs. literary), generic (romance vs. novel), gender (male vs. female), class (folk or working class vs. middle class), regional (Southern vs. Northern and rural vs. urban), and sexual (heterosexual vs. homosexual). In addition, the adequacy of the thick description and of the close critical examination of romances and novels in this book is enhanced by the rhetorical, dialectical, or dialogical analysis that the structure and style of each text suggest is most appropriate.

The questions raised more than fifteen years ago in *The Afro-American Novel and Its Tradition* concerning the politics of identity remain inextricably linked to the poetics and rhetoric of the African American novel. I have therefore attempted in this new book to improve the accessibility of relevant literary theories and interdisciplinary analyses to researchers, students, and general readers by minimizing rather than completely eliminating critical jargon. The confusing variety of contemporary critical terms, concepts, and questions debated in academic and public forums compels me to address some of these questions and clarify the appropriate formal language for these terms and concepts. With the indulgence of specialists who are already familiar with the technical language of sociocultural theory and practice, it is necessary, to paraphrase the celebrated novelist and anthropologist Zora Neale Hurston, to go there with general readers to know there. Among other things, this means that we need to interpret both oral and written texts in their appropriate contexts instead of displacing them with intertextual analyses. It is also imperative to use any means necessary, including, with appropriate linguistic improvisation and code-switching, the master's tools or Eurocentric language and conventions to critique our own complex identities and world. We must therefore examine the concept and process of discursive personal and group identity formations, especially such contemporary terms as "essentialism," "authenticity," "authority," and "agency," as well as "postmodern," "poststructural," "postcolonial," and "Afrocentric."

In addition, the politics of identity formation compels me to address the following questions about the politics of representation: Who represents what to whom, for what reasons, through what institutions, to what effect, to whose benefit, and at what costs?[3] These questions will be addressed from a postcolonial African Americentric neomasculinist position that illuminates the distinctive ironies and paradoxes of the legacy of colonialism and antiblack racism in the United States and critiques the nature of violence in the identity formation of contemporary black males without injudiciously demonizing or glorifying it or them for a political or religious agenda. The sources of black male socialization and neomasculinist identities are, as noted by social scientists Richard G. Majors and Jacob U. Gordon, "conflicting expectations held by people in three related, though distinct, social worlds comprising Black males' society: (1) the Black males' peer group; (2) the Black males' primary group; and (3) 'mainstream society.'"[4] While rejecting the calls for the feminization of America by some critics and for the return to patriarchy of others, my African Americentric neomasculinist position respects the validity and complexity of the politics of gender, class, and sexual differences in the quest for the empowerment of black men and women, as well as the viability of a revised vernacular theory of the African American novel.

My revised indigenous African American vernacular and rhetorical approach judiciously and improvisationally responds to the challenges of multicultural, abstruse postcolonial, and postmodern theories. It privileges a cyclical rather than an ascending dialectic for understanding history and developing consciousness that moves from thesis to antithesis to synthesis to a new thesis.[5] As the rhetorical style and structure of the texts warrant, I also alternatively employ a dialogics of racial difference in critical interpretations of the novel that affirm the significance of authenticity, authority, and agency in the emergence of a new social order of radical democracy.

More specifically, this chapter maps and examines fundamental issues in African American cultural and literary theory and practice in five stages. The first stage outlines and critiques some of the problems that many readers, especially African Americans, have with postmodernism, poststructuralism, postcolonialism, and Afrocentricity in the construction and interpretation of African American texts and identity formations. The second stage develops a postcolonial African Americentric, neomasculinist sociohistorical theory of antiblack racism and internal colonialism in the United States. By neomasculinism I mean neither the celebration nor the advocacy of a resurgency of black male chauvinism and exploitation of black women. Rather, I mean the representation and interrogation in contemporary African American novels and romances of the economic, moral, and political tensions between heterosexuals and homosexuals as well as between violent and nonviolent impulses as central to the identity formation of black males. By internal colonialism I mean the domination by white European and British colonists and their descendants over indigenous native peoples, Mexicans, enslaved Africans and their descendants as a domestic or internal colony. African Americentrism challenges the categorical propositions about identity formation by the most conservative assimilationist and most radical Afrocentric, postcolonial, feminist, and multicultural theorists.

Rather than a systematic exposition of a colonial and neo-Marxist model of capitalism, the third stage in examining the complexity and paradoxes of the issues in the representation of African American identities in novels primarily of the 1980s and 1990s sets forth an African Americentric vernacular theory of culture and literature. It focuses specifically and systematically on an explanation of the following issues and relationships: language, culture, and values in studies by Benjamin Whorf and Geneva Smitherman; language, knowledge, and power in studies by Foucault, Bakhtin, and Terry Eagleton; and language, power, and identity formation as manifested in Standard American English (SAE), Language of Wider Communication (LWC), African American Vernacular English (AAVE), and strategic essentialism; and authority, authenticity, and agency as addressed by Wideman, Charles Taylor, Lionel Trilling, and Marvin E. Olsen.

The fourth stage outlines the core values of African American communities and neomasculine identity formations that are a product and process of shared experiences, beliefs, languages, memories, and stories that are celebrated, challenged, or rejected in selected African American novels and romances primarily of the 1980s and 1990s, as well as in much criticism of the period. And the fifth and final stage of this chapter outlines some continuities and changes between the deployment of the vernacular tradition in *The Afro-American Novel and Its Tradition* and the deployment of rhetoric, dialectics, and dialogics as analytical strategies in this present volume.

A Critique of Eurocentric, Afrocentric, and Americentric Cultural Theories, Critics, and Criticism

Is the issue of race, class, or gender the dominant problem for many contemporary critics with Eurocentric, Afrocentric, and Americentric cultural theories? Even though in theory, as many black feminists contend, race, class, and gender are an inseparable matrix, in practice the social, cultural, and literary criticism of popular black feminists like bell hooks, who identify patriarchy as the arch-enemy of social systems, invariably privileges the empowerment of women over the other two categories. In contrast, even though I also assume that race, ethnicity, class, and gender are intimately linked, the theory, history, and analysis in this book stress race and ethnicity over class and gender for three reasons. First, I question the authority of some postcolonial discourse on immigrant groups crossing boundaries and assimilating into a nation that misleadingly stresses surface similarities over historical, geographical, and cultural differences. Second, I challenge the authority and agency of implied authors, narrators, and characters, like Walker's Shug Avery in *The Color Purple*, who believe that "Man corrupt everything" and that the feminization of men is the panacea for patriarchy as a system of male domination.[6] Third and finally, I feel compelled to respond to narratives and discourses by black feminists, critics, and pundits that reinforce and perpetuate negative images of black males as sex-crazed dogs, domestic abusers, dead-beat dads, drug addicts, and moral degenerates. Because I am neither an Africanist nor an Egyptologist, I am also less concerned with Afrocentric discourse on the ancient civilizations of our precolonial African past even though such dialectic (i.e., either/or) and dialogic (i.e., both/and) challenges to the hegemony of Eurocentric cartography, historiography, and epistemology are salutary though occasionally strident. Despite their waning appeal in the academy, postmodern models of ahistorical, fragmented multicultural identities are also not my central concern. Instead, I am primarily concerned with renewing and reinvigorating discourse on the liberating impact of cultural and literary production by Americans of African descent and bicultural African American heritage in the United States in resistance to domination as an internal black colony and in reconciling the conflicts of our dual identities as African Americans.

It would be unreasonable, however, to throw out the baby that is the relentless struggle of African Americans for freedom, justice, equality, and unity as subjects and agents of change with the dirty water of binarisms that reinscribe negative racial, class, and gender stereotypes. But it would be disingenuous to argue that "radical black subjectivity" can be constructed without the transformative knowledge and power of master narratives that critique as they construct new radical democratic communities. "The questioning of the universal and totalizing in the name of the local and particular does not automatically entail the end of all consensus," writes postmodern critic Linda Hutcheon with a supporting quote from critic Victor Burgin. "'Of course moralities and histories are "relative," but this does not mean they do not exist.'"[7]

In expanding the theory of an African American literary tradition in which the dialectic tension between an essential racial and ethnic identity and a socially constructed one is central, *The Contemporary African American Novel: Its Folk Roots and Modern Literary Branches* is more rigorous than *The Afro-American Novel and Its Tradition*. It is more rigorous in its interrogation of the deployment of an indigenous oppositional vernacular and counterdiscourse strategy. It closely examines the different types and degrees of emancipatory individual and collective resistance to and transformations of racial, ethnic, class, and gender oppression. It also examines the problem of the ahistoricism and obscurantism of postmodern theories and criticism by such critics as Gayatri Spivak and Homi Bhabha. For this interrogation and examination, I have found Linda Hutcheon's *Poetics of Postmodernism* (1988) and *Politics of Postmodernism* (1989) helpful, despite their disturbing limitations.

Because postmodernism is more fully examined in chapter 5, it is sufficient for clarity here to state that the confusion over the definition and evaluation of postmodernism is best resolved by recognizing the existence of two opposed camps:

> the radically antagonistic and the provisionally supportive. The tone of the former group ranges from sly irony to rabid rage. Curiously, this camp encompasses the opposition of the neoconservative right, the liberal center, and the Marxist left. However positioned politically, the objections seem to be consistently to what are perceived as, on the one hand, the ahistoricism and pastiched depthlessness of the postmodern and, on the other, its crossing of boundaries of genres and discourse once considered discrete and firm. . . . The work of those provisionally or tentatively supportive of postmodernism ranges from descriptive accounts of the postmodern in terms of its incredulity toward grand totalizing narratives to more tendentiously rueful acknowledgments that we are all part of the postmodern, whether we like it or not.[8]

This explanation by Hutcheon is helpful in characterizing the resistance that most black American critics have to postmodernism.

As the reader has already probably realized, my own resistance to postmodernism derives mainly from two sources. The first is its ahistoricism—especially its appropriation of the experience of "Otherness" while separating the politics of difference from the politics of race in the construction of identity and the assertion of agency. And the second is its categorical rejection of totalizing narratives. Hutcheon contends that "there is no dialectic in the postmodern: the self-reflexive remains distinct from its traditionally accepted contrary. . . . The result of this deliberate refusal to resolve contradictions is a contesting of . . . the totalizing master narratives of our culture, those systems by which we usually unify and order (and smooth over) any contradictions in order to make them fit." As a problematizing force, however, postmodernism not only "raises questions about (or renders problematic) the common-sensical and the 'natural,'" it also devalues and often disparages them. Moreover, contrary to Hutcheon's claim, insofar as postmodernism "never offers answers that are anything but provisional and contextually determined (and limited)," it is also dialectic.[9]

Chapters 5–7 therefore examine the relationship in the contemporary African American novel of the doubleness of Hutcheon's "paradoxical postmodernism of complicity [with] and critique [of]" power and domination to Du Bois's double consciousness, double vision, and socialized ambivalence.

However, this work does not reinscribe the perception of a sociocultural, sociopolitical, marginal, and provincial identity of black Americans under the sign "Afro-Americans," whose hybridity is marked by its prefix and hyphen. Instead, the dual racial and cultural identity of Americans of sub-Saharan black African descent is holistically reconfigured and reinscribed in the title and most of the text of this book as "African American." This shift in naming correlates with the transforming dialectics and dialogics of the social and rhetorical power relations inspired by the Black Power and Black Arts movements of the 1960s and 1970s, as well as by the Black Feminist movement of the 1970s and 1980s in the United States.

Neither the Hegelian nor the Marxist quest for knowledge of the ultimate reality through exclusively rational or material dialectics resolves its dynamic tensions in a permanent closure or stasis. Nevertheless, there is some merit to Hutcheon's argument about the nondialectic style and structure of postmodernism as it applies to her central concern with disruption and discontinuity in white Eurocentric postmodernism. In contrast, as I have already stated and will demonstrate in subsequent chapters, African American experiments with postmodernism are generally more ambivalent and subversive or transgressive in their interrogation and reinscription of master narratives. But some of the parodic, ironic, and metafictional narratives of writers such as Ishmael Reed, Clarence Major, William Melvin Kelley, Toni Morrison, Charles S. Wright, Hal Bennett, and Alice Walker are ostensibly similar to the white postmodernist narratives that Hutcheon cites, but with a black difference. Because the narratives of these writers are generally nonrepresentational and experimental rather than antirepresentational and experimental, they are actually modernist rather than postmodernist in structure and style. The relatively few African American postmodernist texts, by novelists like Reed and Major, "challenge the process of meaning-making in the production and reception of art, but also in broader discursive terms: . . . [they foreground] how we make historical 'facts' out of brute 'events' of the past, or, more generally, how our various sign systems grant meaning to our experience."[10]

Although useful for specialists in charting shifts in representational and interpretative strategies, the meaning of the above terms and theories as used by many nonblack, non-American major theorists and critics is alienating for many readers, especially African Americans. Many readers are alienated by the arrogance of the critics and the obscurantism of their styles and language, which more often impede than enhance the understanding and appreciation of literary texts. Some of the philosophers and critics, and their frequently used terms include the following: Ludwig Wittgenstein ("language games"), Ferdinand de Saussure ("langue" and "parole"), Antonio Gramsci ("hegemony" and "subaltern"), Wolfgang Iser ("implied reader"), Roland Barthes ("writable text"), Jacques Derrida ("deconstruction" and "transcendental signifier"), Jean-François Lyotard ("*postmodern* as incredulity toward metanarratives" and "the grand narrative"), Roman Ingarden ("indeterminacies"), Frantz Fanon ("The colonial world is a Manichean world"; "culture is the expression of national consciousness"; "liberation implies the use of all means, and that of force first and foremost"), Gayatri Spivak ("subaltern silence" and "identitarianism"), Linda Hutcheon ("ironic discontinuity"), Michel Foucault ("archeology of knowledge," "discourse," and "genealogy"), Mikhail Bakhtin ("dialogism" and "heteroglossia"), Jacques Lacan ("imaginary"), Gilles Deleuze and Félix Guattari ("territorialization" and "deterritorialization"), Edward Said ("nativism"), and Homi Bhabha ("Third Space" and "stereotype as an ambivalent mode of knowledge and power").[11] The degree of usefulness or alienation these terms present to readers of these theorists varies. As I hope my use of some of these theorists and terms demonstrates, the degree varies based on the specific historical, geographical, institutional, and ideological sites from and contexts in which the theorists engage relationships, on the one hand, of language to knowledge and power, and, on the other, of authenticity to authority and agency. Readers should therefore be mindful that most of these critics ground their theorizing in the historical and geopolitical specificity of the sites of their national origin and their elite class and institutional positions. They also share a passion for writing obscure prose for only other academics.

Because they categorically reject fundamental principles of biological and metaphysical essence, stability, unity, and meaning in their notion of human identities and subjects, most Eurocentric postmodern, poststructural, and postcolonial critics dogmatically advocate an exclusively discursive, fluid social or cultural construction of identity. Jean-François Lyotard's theory of the postmodern condition, for example, is grounded in his disillusionment in France and Quebec in the 1970s with Marxist orthodoxy and the totalizing dialectic philosophy of Hegel and Jürgen Habermas. In *The Postmodern Condition,* Lyotard argues that the status of knowledge as a kind of discourse has radically changed since societies entered the postindustrial age of computers and since cultures entered the postmodern age of the crisis in legitimating a law or truth as a norm by such authorities as legislators and scientists at the end of the 1950s. These transformations, he claims, "have altered the game rules for science, literature, and the arts," especially in "the context of the crisis of narratives." According to Lyotard, the "grand narrative has lost its credibility, regardless of what mode of unification it uses, regardless of whether it is a speculative narrative or a narrative of emancipation."[12] This postmodern incredulity of master narratives, such as racial, ethnic, and national myths and epics of origin and unity, ostensibly devalues my quest to develop a coherent theory of the distinctive generic history of the African American novel by undermining the validity of both a linear and a dialectical evolution of history and language.

Similarly, the Algerian-born, Western-educated, emigrant philosopher Jacques Derrida's poststructural theory of a transcendental signifier indirectly challenges my theoretical position on African American religion and spirituality by deconstructing the conventional belief in a single sign or essence, such as God, the Spirit, or the Self, "as the foundation or origin of all thought, language, and experience."[13] As literary critic Jonathan Culler reveals, Derrida's method of deconstructing "a discourse is to show how it undermines the philosophy it asserts, or the hierarchical oppositions on which it relies, by identifying in the text the rhetorical operations that produce the supposed ground of argument, the key concept or premise."[14] However, as I will demonstrate below, this shift by many academic critics to fashionable postmodern and postcolonial theories of identity formation reduces emancipatory narratives and the liberation struggle of colonized subjects in the United States and their descendants against domination and for political and cultural authority, authenticity, and agency to mere rhetoric, counterdiscourse, and language games.

Edward Said, the Palestinian-born, Western-educated, Arab-American postcolonialist literary critic, indirectly contests my theory of a vernacular tradition as the originary site of an indigenous hybrid African American culture by implicitly associating it with nativism, that is, "demagogic assertions about a native past, narrative or actuality that stands free from worldly time itself."[15] According to Said's apparent indictment of all theories of vernacular or indigenous native cultures, "the exhilarating heyday of decolonization and early Third World nationalism" has degenerated into "nationalist appeals to pure or authentic Islam, or to Afrocentrism, *negritude,* or Arabism."[16] Without closely examining the texts of such leading proponents of Afrocentrism as Maulana Karenga and Molefi Asante, Said fallaciously implies that all Afrocentrism in the United States is as demagogic and purist as his single example of Marcus Garvey's Back-to-Africa movement of the 1920s. As an epistemology and methodology, Afrocentrism, as demonstrated since the 1980s in the annual conferences of the National Council of Black Studies and in African Americanist critic Perry A. Hall's *In the Vineyard,* is actually a broad, diverse, and useful alternative racial and cultural system of cognitive, ethical, and sociolinguistic practices to the global domination of Eurocentrism.

In addition to their obscure styles, Gayatri Spivak and Homi Bhabha have been criticized as elite expatriate literary postcolonials whose analyses frequently reduce the political and historical to pessimism and semiotics, as in the systematic study of signs. In "Can the Subaltern Speak?" for example, Spivak filters her theory of the improbability of the subaltern or oppressed subjects speaking for themselves through the lens of her East Indian birth, education, and experiences as a postcolonial emigrant and intellectual. She uses Hindu law and the colonial debates on the burning of Indian widows on their husbands' pyres to make her case for the intersection of colonialism and patriarchy.[17] Spivak writes, "as a literary critic, I tactically confronted the immense problem of the consciousness of the woman as subaltern. I reinvented the problem in a sentence and transformed it into the object of simple semiosis."[18] While useful as a literary tool for deconstructing Eurocentric policies and practices from an East Indian perspective, Spivak's methodology is inadequate for analyzing the nuances of the authenticity, authority, and agency of the themes, narrators, characters, styles, and structures of the struggle with African American double consciousness and against various forms of domination in novels and romances by black Americans.

Homi Bhabha was also born in India and educated in India and England before becoming a postcolonial intellectual, literary critic, and emigrant to academies in the United States. As E. San Juan Jr. reminds us in *Beyond Postcolonial Theory* (1998), Bhabha focuses abstractly and rhetorically on the poststructuralist "*differance* of writing" found in the cultural performances of privileged positions and experiences. These performances and positions include "the history of postcolonial migration, the narratives of cultural and political diaspora, the major social displacements of peasants and aboriginal communities, the poetics of exile, [and] the grim prose of political and economic refugees."[19] Bhabha's antiessentializing postcolonial theory in *The Location of Culture* (1994) relies heavily on notions of hybridity, liminality, and ambivalence in the discursive construction of identity.

On the surface I also may be considered a literary postcolonialist critic in my use of hybridity, liminality, and ambivalence in my earlier study of the African American novel. But this book should reveal that among other differences, it strives to be less obscure, more historically specific about the duality and double consciousness of African American identity, and more influenced by the radical theories of identity transformation of Du Bois, Melville Herskovits, Frantz Fanon, Ralph Ellison, Harold Cruse, Stuart Hall, and Victor Turner. In this sense, my African Americentric revisionist approach, which is more black cultural nationalist than integrationist, is informed by a transformative vision that is based on the enduring validity of Du Bois's theory and trope of double consciousness as the distinctive sign of African American culture and character.[20] In other words, a personal and professional grounding in the culture and revisionist scholarship of Afrocentrics and African Americentrics is most appropriate for the study of the authenticity, authority, and agency of African American literature in general and the tradition of the African American novel in particular.

Although "postcolonial" designates a general division in geopolitics between the colonizers and the colonized, the concept has various temporal and spatial origins that are often confusing. Defined as "the conquest and control of other people's land and goods," colonialism "is not merely the expansion of various European powers into Asia, Africa or the Americas from the sixteenth century onwards; it has been a recurrent and widespread feature of human history." But "modern European colonialism was distinctive and by far the most extensive of the different kinds of colonial contact."[21] For Filipino postcolonial critic San Juan, postcoloniality has its contemporary birth in "the emergence of immigrant and refugee intellectuals from the Empire's hinterlands in Western institutions of higher learning" and in the provocative debate initiated by Aijaz Ahmad's *In Theory, Classes, Nations, Literatures.* This 1992 neo-Marxist critique of the romantic idealization of the Third World, the technologically underdeveloped nonwhite postcolonial nations, by Western intellectuals like Fredric Jameson was followed in 1995 by a critique of the "eclectic, sometimes dilettantish" politics of literary postcoloniality of Spivak and Bhabha. "It is not clear how the celebration of a postcolonial transnational, electronically produced cultural hybridity is to be squared with this systematic decay of countries and continents," San Juan writes perceptively, "and with decreasing chances for substantial proportions of the global population to obtain conditions of bare survival, let alone electronic literacy and gadgetry."[22]

In contrast to Eurocentric and Anglocentric literary postcolonialism, the political concept of postcolonialism and the Third World in the United States as a liberation movement was inspired in the 1960s by the psychological and political theory of revolutionary nationalism in Fanon's *Wretched of the Earth*. The indigenous origins of postcolonialism in the United States include the trenchant cultural, economic, and political critique of Harold Cruse's *Crisis of the Negro Intellectual* and, most dramatically, the resurgent Black Power liberation movement against antiblack racism by the Student Nonviolent Coordinating Committee and other activist political organizations. For African American academics and activists, postcolonialism also has its origins in the anticolonial liberation struggles in Africa, Latin America, and the Caribbean, beginning with the independence of the Sudan in 1956, of Ghana in 1957, and of Cuba in 1959. But the oppressed and dispossessed peoples of the world are still struggling with the tragic fact that a "country may be both postcolonial (in the sense of being formally independent) and neo-colonial (in the sense of remaining economically and/or culturally dependent) at the same time."[23]

Finally, African American postcolonial literature and narratives have their roots in the emancipatory petitions and narratives of peoples of African descent and heritage, such as *The Interesting Narrative of the Life of Olaudah Equiano, or Gustavus Vassa, The African* (1789), that contest enslavement and reject domination by British and European subjects doing the colonial period. It is therefore, as literary and cultural critic Ania Loomba notes in *Colonialism/Postcolonialism*, "more helpful to think of postcolonialism not just as coming literally after colonialism and signifying its demise, but more flexibly as the contestation of colonial domination and the legacies of colonialism." This position allows us "to include people geographically displaced by colonialism such as African-Americans or people of Asian or Caribbean origin in Britain as 'postcolonial' subjects although they live within metropolitan cultures."[24] Despite the historical importance of class struggle, antiblack racism and intraracial ethnic conflict are for most African American scholar-activists and cultural workers, unlike for most East Indian postcolonialists, as central to geopolitical change at the dawn of the twenty-first century as W.E.B. Du Bois predicted the problem of the color line would be at the dawn of the twentieth.

Ranging from reformist to revolutionary, the concept of Black Power is therefore fundamentally a call for group unity and spatial or territorial solidarity based on cultural and revolutionary nationalism. But the Black Power movement of the 1960s generally stressed African cultural heritage or confrontational Marxist class politics over personal consent in the struggle to achieve collective and individual self-determination in the process of deconstructing de jure and de facto dual social systems of antiblack racism. In this context, postcolonialism signifies the contemporary struggle of a class of racialized subjects for liberation from political violence and disfranchisement, economic exploitation, and cultural misrepresentation and dispossession. Postcolonialism is also a political, economic, and cultural movement for the construction of a new social order of freedom, justice, and radical democracy.

How, then, does postcolonial discourse relate to the more recent controversial theory and practice of Afrocentricity? Although Maulana Karenga's *Introduction to Black Studies* (1982) and Molefi Kete Asante's *Afrocentricity: The Theory of Social Change* (1980) are major texts in promoting a systematic Afrocentric epistemology and methodology, Asante has become the most popular spokesman in the 1980s and 1990s for the Afrocentric movement. He has not only developed his ideas on the topic in a series of books, but also institutionalized the theory and practice by establishing the first Afrocentric doctoral program in the nation at Temple University.[25] As a sign of the theoretical shift in black nationalist ideology, "Afrocentricity is the belief in the centrality of Africans in post modern history."[26] Although he has more reasonably expanded his theory to include Central Africa in subsequent editions of his book, Asante still argues that an "Afrocentric analysis reestablishes the centrality of the ancient Kemetic (Egyptian) civilization and the Nile Valley cultural complex as points of reference for an African perspective in much the same way as Greece and Rome serve as reference points for the European world."[27] In contrast to most Eurocentrics, however, leading Afrocentrics like Asante and Karenga do not seek to validate and valorize a distinctive African legacy of knowing and being in the world with others by either suppressing or merely tolerating alternative cultural systems. But as historian Wilson Moses reminds us, Asante did not actually coin the term "Afrocentric." In a 1962 typed draft titled "Proposed plans for an Encyclopedia Africana," Du Bois indicated that the study would be "unashamedly Afro-Centric, but not indifferent to the impact of the outside world upon Africa or to the impact of Africa upon the outside world." In this geopolitical and epistemological sense of the term, Du Bois was an Afrocentric even though, unlike Asante, he did not make Egypt central to either his theory or his methodology.[28]

Asante was apparently more strongly influenced by *The African Origin of Civilization* and other pioneering texts in French by Cheikh Anta Diop in focusing on Egypt as a classical African civilization. According to African Americanist Perry A. Hall, "As a body of thought, Asante's work reads, at some points, like ideology, sometimes like mysticism or theology, and sometimes like an intellectual paradigm."[29] Karenga, the founder of the Afrocentric theory of Kawaida with seven cardinal principles for African American unity that are celebrated during the annual holiday of Kwanzaa, which he also established, expands on Asante's idea of ancient Egypt in the 1993 revision of *Introduction to Black Studies*. In contrast, Joseph E. Holloway, a pan-African historian, argues in "The Origins of African-American Culture" that "the Bantu of Central Africa had the largest homogeneous culture among the imported Africans and the strongest impact on the development of African American culture."[30] Afrocentrics thus not only risk conflict with nonblack groups by encouraging racial chauvinism, but also risk romantically celebrating a mythic and legendary past at the expense of pragmatically addressing social problems in the present and future. Similar to proponents of Eurocentrism, in other words, Asante, Karenga, Holloway, and other Afrocentrists argue with various degrees of scholarly rigor and romantic passion from different ideological positions for different primary audiences. Compared with Eurocentrists, however, Afrocentrists in the tradition of the African American novel seem more passionately and politically committed to respect for cultural diversity and to efforts for social change.

Why, then, are so many people in colleges and universities condemning Afrocentricity, while celebrating postcoloniality? "Whereas Afrocentricity is often dismissed as methodologically sloppy, anti-intellectual identity politics, postcoloniality is affirmed as theoretically sophisticated oppositional discourse," writes African Americanist Ann duCille. Identifying herself as neither a proponent of Afrocentricity nor an opponent of postcoloniality, duCille argues that "the most critical factor in the current reception of these two resistance narratives may have more to do with market than with methodology—that is, with the academic merchandising of *different* difference. If postcoloniality is discourse—an exotic, foreign field whose time has come within the U.S. academy—Afrocentricity is 'dat course'—local color (homeboys and girls) whose foreignness has become all too familiar."[31]

While the term "postcolonial" may be new for many readers, duCille reminds us, the thematizing of relations of power between colonizer and colonized is not: "In the U.S. black intellectuals such as W. E. B. Du Bois, Alexander Crummell, Pauline Hopkins, and Anna Julia Cooper engaged in such thematizing in the late nineteenth and early twentieth centuries. More recently, but still years—even decades—before the rise of postcoloniality as an academic discipline, black activists, scholars, writers, and theorists such as Marcus Garvey, C. L. R. James, Frantz Fanon, and Aimé Césaire explored and exploded colonial and postcolonial power relations." Among the many African, African American, African Caribbean and other scholars of African descent that she names "who continue to problematize and critique the relationship between Prospero and Caliban, metropole and province" are Cheikh Anta Diop, Stuart Hall, Sylvia Wynter, Selwyn Cudjoe, Paget Henry, Paul Gilroy, and Hazel Carby.[32] Although my African Americentric approach to the tradition of the African American novel incorporates Afrocentric insights about our African cultural legacy, this study focuses more sharply on literary representations of the duality and double consciousness of contemporary African American male identity formations in the United States than readers usually find in works by East Indian and African Caribbean postcolonialists.

On one level, moreover, East Indian postcolonialty seems to be an opportunistic appropriation of the history, culture, and politics of resistance of African, African Caribbean, and African American postcolonial and black cultural nationalist critics and writers. On another level, however, the oppositional discourse of some East Indian and Middle Eastern postcolonial critics that categorically rejects, while paradoxically reconstructing, binary interpretive models suggest the complexities of cultural identities. As Edward Said explains in *Culture and Imperialism* (1993), the oppositional discourse of these critics probably comes mainly from their own political, cultural, and literary history of struggle, including complicity with colonialism and neocolonialism, especially British.

In their Olympian disdain of the ostensible ahistoricism of some Afrocentric reconstructions of an African past, such as the first edition of Asante's *Afrocentricity* in 1980, too many academic critics and political pundits engage in equally ahistorical, essentializing, fallacious reasoning. They ignore, for example, the fact that the knowledge and power which inform the construction of all personal and group identities—including their own—are products of shifting classical and contemporary social myths and rituals, as well as of empirical facts and reasoned thinking. This is most dramatically and frequently demonstrated by the thematic, stylistic, and structural importance of such myths as white supremacy and the American Dream, as well as of such rituals as the actual and symbolic lynching of black males in the African American novel.

With a fascinating and often empowering combination of fact and fiction, many contemporary African Americanists are therefore assigning more importance in their studies to the many West and Central African regions and peoples whose cultures were creatively blended by captive Africans and their descendants with elements of British and indigenous American cultures in the United States into a mixed or creolized African American culture. In the sense that African Americanists like Manning Marable, James Stewart, Michael Dyson, and others ground their theories and methodologies in the legacy of cultural syncretism while stressing the contemporary social thought and cultural practice of African Americans in the United States and respecting the contributions of Afrocentrics, they may be classified as African Americentrics.[33] In 1966 even Karenga was more of an African Americentric than Afrocentric when he created the Kawaida philosophy and Kwanzaa in order to ritualize a connection with Africa and to reinforce cultural and political unity and pride in the African American community.[34] An extraordinarily popular African American cultural holiday, Kwanzaa is reportedly celebrated by millions of black folk in the United States from December 26 to January 1.

Contemporary black nationalism—which ranges from racial and ethnic pride to various types of radical pan-Africanism and Afrocentrism—has frequently been treated with scorn or ridicule for several reasons by its opponents, both black and white. Two of the most popular reasons, especially for feminists, are the essentialist and male chauvinist assumptions and practices of many black nationalists of the 1960s. Another reason is the call of some black nationalists for pan-Africanism, a totalizing unity of Africans on the continent of Africa and dispersed Africans in the New World. And a fourth is the religiously or politically derived millenarian, teleological, or providential, occasionally apocalyptic, vision of a new world order of redemption for the just and retribution for the unjust constructed by many black cultural nationalists, revolutionaries, and novelists. In his trenchant examination of the roots of African American history, black historian Wilson J. Moses argues that Afrocentrism is both an ideology and a secular religion. "Afrocentrism, like most ideologies, contains both a utopian history and a millenarian future," he writes. "It fixates on an idealized past before the white man's 'Destruction of Black Civilization,' and predicts an Ethiopian revival, a messianic era of peace and goodwill, 'when the black man comes into his own.' "[35] Even though the language of Afrocentrism is no more romantic, mythic, or reprehensible than other ideologies, including Eurocentrism and Americentrism, the tone of Moses' criticism suggests that it is.

Actually, attacks on the ideology and methodology of African Americanists and Afrocentrists come from all directions. In addition to the reasonable criticism of many black feminists about male chauvinism and to the unreasonable bigotry about the superiority and universality of Western culture of white neoconservatives like Allan Bloom and Lynne Cheney, and of white old guard liberals like Arthur M. Schlesinger Jr. and Mary Lefkowitz,[36] these attacks also come from others, black and white. Some of these critics unjustifiably claim to have more knowledge about and respect for the diversity and interdisciplinarity of African American Studies and Ethnic Studies than those they critique. Neoconservative critics should at least be as knowledgeable about the research of major black academic specialists in the discipline under examination as most major African Americanists are about the scholarship and publications of white liberals and conservatives. They should also acknowledge the freedom of others to construct alternative, including radical and romantic, counternarratives and interpretive models that are accessible to their primary readers.

Many black scholars, critics, artists, and other cultural workers are suspicious of the unrelenting and frequently hypocritical attacks on their calls and quests for racial and ethnic unity as essentialism and romanticism. Ironically, Henry Louis Gates Jr., the author of *The Signifying Monkey* (1988), one of the most outstanding Afrocentric and essentialist critical studies of African American literature, which grounds its theory in the Yoruba myth-legend of Esu-Elegbara, the trickster figure, is also one of the most frequently cited severe critics of black essentialists and radical Afrocentrics. More frequently, the antiessentialist, anti-Afrocentric attacks come from white intellectuals (e.g., Werner Sollors, Barbara Johnson, Mary Lefkowitz, and George Hutchinson).[37] These intellectuals have in different degrees appropriated or repudiated African diasporic cultures (i.e., the cultures of the dispersed nonwhite peoples of African descent in the Americas—North, South, and Central—and the Caribbean) and literatures with different motives and objectives. For example, Sollors, a professor of English and the former head of the Department of African American Studies at Harvard University, challenges the "assumption that experience is first and foremost ethnic." In his self-authenticating argument as an ethnic and racial outsider in African American Studies, he contends that "the relativist position of ethnic insiderism uses ethnicity . . . to aggrandize and to wrap a cloak of legitimacy and authenticity around the speaker who invokes it."[38]

Although ostensibly sincere, well intentioned, and objective, many African Americanist scholars who are ethnic outsiders by personal and professional choice have managed in the 1980s and 1990s to revitalize their own Eurocentric or Anglocentric visions, academic careers, political agendas, integrationist poetics, and ethnic voices while devaluing or increasingly displacing the radical democratic voices for social change of black cultural nationalist and African American postcolonial critics. This does not mean "that only biological insiders can understand and explicate the literature of race and ethnicity."[39] Rather, it means that Afrocentric and African Americentric revisionist scholars and critics in the academy who are biological and cultural insiders are probably better able to understand and explicate the nuances of the culture and literature of their race and ethnicity. However, even racial and ethnic insiders, especially those who no longer live in predominantly African American communities, vary in the degree to which they are in touch with and attuned to the truths and realities of the daily lives of ordinary black people.

"Various characteristics common to Black Arts writing make it unappealing to many literary scholars," a black literary critic argues: "it often confuses social theory with aesthetics, failing to articulate the complex relationship between the two; much of it is predicated upon crude, strident forms of nationalism that do not lend themselves to careful analysis; and too often the work is marred by the swaggering rhetoric of ethnic and gender chauvinism."[40] The four scapegoats most frequently invoked, explicitly or implicitly, during the 1980s and 1990s in general attacks on major black cultural critics and vernacular theorists in African American Studies as being provincial, romantic, radical, racist, or anti-Semitic are East Coast orators and academics. The two most popularly known orators are the militant, often politically controversial Professor Leonard Jefferies, the former head of the Department of African American Studies at City College of New York, and zealous Minister Louis Farrakhan of the Nation of Islam. The more substantive and academic, yet equally controversial, are Professor Addison Gayle Jr., the editor of *The Black Aesthetic* (1971) and author of *The Way of the New World* (1976), a critical study of the black American novel, and Professor Molefi Asante, the founder and former head of the Department of African and African American Studies at Temple University, whose Afrocentric scholarship is probably the most often quoted and distorted.

More subtle and surprising is the response by Barbara Johnson, the white deconstructionist critic and former acting chair of the Department of African American Studies at Harvard University, to a conference paper in 1987 by her colleague Henry Louis Gates, that validated the vernacular roots of the African American literary tradition. Although intriguing and informative, her critique fallaciously assumes that despite his familial roots in West Virginia, extraordinary academic background, scholarly achievements, and advocacy of signifying as an African American vernacular theory of reading Gates is unaware that "the terms 'black' and 'white' often imply a relation of mutual exclusion." Johnson also intimates that Gates' use of these racial categories, as well as his ambiguous use of "we" in his outline of an Afro-American tradition, is a reductive, oversimplistic racial binarism of "pure, unified, and separate traditions."[41] In contrast, Professor George Hutchinson's indictment of major black specialists on the Harlem Renaissance for their allegedly simplistic racial and cultural dualisms is more egregious and sweeping. In *The Harlem Renaissance in Black and White* (1995) Hutchinson disarmingly grounds his claim for personal authority and knowledge of the African diaspora on working as a well-digger and living with a Mossi family in Upper Volta from 1975 to 1977. Fallaciously assuming that the binary racial language of black critics established and perpetuates the myth of "the purity of blood," he then treats them with transparent pity and contempt. Unfortunately, the illuminating focus of his book on the network of left-wing white intellectuals and of interracial and intraracial personal and institutional relationships concerning cultural nationalism during the Harlem Renaissance is frequently overshadowed by the arrogance of his patronizing critique of the studies of the Harlem Renaissance by virtually all major black African Americanists. From historians Harold Cruse, Nathan Huggins, David Levering Lewis, and Wilson Moses, on the one hand, to literary critics George Kent, Henry Louis Gates, Houston Baker, Karla Holloway, and Hazel Carby on the other—all are judged guilty of deliberate and deceptive "misleading dualisms," "oversimplifications," and "reductive readings of interracial dynamics in the 1920s."[42]

A transnational example of undocumented or inadequately supported sweeping indictments of black scholars for ideological differences concerning African cultural continuities in the New World and for their use of oppositional models of racial and cultural discourse is *The Black Columbiad* (1994). Werner Sollors and Maria Diedrich, a professor of English at the University of Hannover, are the German editors of this informative collection of essays on the theme of defining moments in African American literature and culture. In attempting to establish the authority of the nonblack transnational and transcultural contributors to their anthology and their own readings of African American texts, Sollors and Diedrich combine the specious with the self-evident in this vague, undocumented attack on oppositional readings: "The genius and imaginative courage of New World black cultures are lost and the scarring quality of the African diaspora is denied in romantic or sentimental readings of these cultures that insist on African survivalism, on an uninterrupted continuity of the African and African American experience. In reality the relationship is much more complex, and involves appropriations, retrievals, inventions, and discontinuous, fragmented memories."[43]

In my more than thirty years of experience in this field, I have discovered no major, nationally respected African Americanist scholar who seriously argues for "an uninterrupted continuity of the African and African American experience." Rather, as Sollors probably knows, most specialists in the field rely in part on the cultural relativism of anthropologist Franz Boas. But they rely even more on anthropologist Melville Herskovits's theory of retention, reinterpretation, and syncretism, especially the last, in their interpretations of continuities and discontinuities in African culture in the diaspora of the Caribbean and the Americas. On the one hand, increasingly more children and grandchildren of the former colonial empires write back from the luxury of distinguished administrative posts and academic chairs in white institutions in an effort to resurrect and reassert their ancestral hegemony. On the other hand, many nationally respected African Americanists are increasingly responding to their challenge. These African Americanists also acknowledge in lectures and print the historically complex complicity and contestation of power relationships among, as well as between, the colonizers and the colonized.

The authenticity, authority, and agency of these African Americanists derive from many sources. But the primary sources are their own everyday experiences and the formal studies of such scholars as Boas, Du Bois, Herskovits, Ana Julia Cooper, Basil Davidson, E. Franklin Frazier, Carter G. Woodson, Lorenzo Dow Turner, Cheikh Anta Diop, Albert Memmi, Frantz Fanon, Gilbert Freyre, Herbert Aptheker, Sterling Brown, David Dalby, Robert Farris Thompson, and V. F. Mudimbe. The history of some major black leaders, like Martin Delany, working with white leaders in the American Colonization Movement in the nineteenth century, is one of the most dramatic cases of the complex, frequently ironic and paradoxical relationship between authenticity, authority, and agency. More contemporary cases include Richard Wright, Zora Neale Hurston, Ishmael Reed, and Toni Morrison. As bell hooks observes in *Yearning* (1990), "When white critics write about black culture 'cause it's the 'in' subject without interrogating their work to see whether or not it helps perpetuate and maintain racist domination, they participate in the commodification of 'blackness' that is so peculiar to postmodern strategies of colonization."[44] This commodification of blackness is even apparent in the well-intentioned forewords, introductions, and afterwords to studies of black culture by such white artists and scholars as Adrienne Rich, John Callahan, and Missy Dehn Kubitschek. Rich in *Of Woman Born*, Callahan in *In the African American Grain*, and Kubitschek in *Claiming the Heritage* privilege their positions as white ethnic outsiders whose personal experience with a black servant or stranger was transformative in empowering them to become authoritative voices on black literature and history. The more things change, the more they remain the same. Ann duCille wittily signifies on these appropriations of the black "Other" by white intellectuals as the Driving Miss Daisy Syndrome: "an intellectual sleight of hand that transforms power and race relations to make best friends out of driver and driven, master and slave, boss and servant, white boy and black man."[45]

As the important revisionist scholarship of the 1960s and 1970s by Herbert Aptheker, August Meir, Herbert Gutman, Eugene Genovese, Kenneth Stampp, Sidney Kaplan, and Lawrence Levine suggests, however, not all white academics and critics are exploiters of blackness. Yet, although these "white," mainly Jewish, American voices as well as "black" voices from Europe and Third World countries provide important revisionist and, occasionally, invaluable perspectives, all of these voices differ from those of African Americans and should complement rather than displace absent or silenced African American voices.[46] It is reassuring, then, to have the authenticity, authority, and agency of one's voice acknowledged by family, friends, and folks who live in black communities, as well as by African Americanists in the academy. Regardless of skin color and a desire for border-crossing, aspiring specialists in African American culture have to do more than go there to know there if they have not actually lived the life of the black folks that they preach, sing, write, or teach about. On some level, as my peers used to rap back in the day in the South Bronx, "you've got to pay some dues and live the blues in order to walk that walk and talk that talk; in order to get down with the grits and greens and the rice and beans; and in order to get hooked up with the latest happenings." Personal experience with the double consciousness of African Americans provides the social and cultural ambivalence encoded in profiling and performing the latest African American styles of hair, clothing, jewelry, music, dance, and rap. In short, the authority, authenticity, and agency of African Americanists in the academy are a product and process of the courage, compassion, and commitment manifested on at least two levels. The first level is their critique of the impact of postmodernism, postcolonialism, and Afrocentricity on cultural texts, and the second level is their participation in working together seriously and sincerely with black working-class folks and their children in the academies as well as black middle-class academics and professionals for a more just and equal social system.

A Postcolonial African Americentric, Neomasculinist Theory of Antiblack Racism and Internal Colonialism

Moving to the second stage of this chapter, let me propose a postcolonial African Americentric neomasculinist theory of antiblack racism and internal colonialism for the construction and interpretation of contemporary identity formations and African American novels. Although the experiences of the conquest and control of peoples of black African descent in the diaspora and of red, black, brown, and yellow peoples in the United States during the seventeenth, eighteenth, and nineteenth centuries were similar, colonization was hardly the same for each group. The forms of colonization and each group's responses to it varied with time, place, and colonizer. As sociologist Robert Blauner explains in his valuable collection of essays *Racial Oppression in America* (1972), in a way similar to the manner that "developing capitalism in Europe produced social classes out of a medley of rural and urban strata and status groups, the colonial system brought into being races from an array of distinct tribes and ethnic peoples. It was European conquest and colonial wardship that created 'the Indian' . . . And as a result of slavery the 'Negro race' emerged from the heterogeneity of African ethnicity."[47] In contrast to the assimilationist theory of immigrant groups that enter a society or nation voluntarily to become citizens by replacing their old culture with the new dominant culture, colonized groups are introduced to or segregated in the dominant society and culture by force or violence; "they are conquered, enslaved, or pressured into movement"[48] and consent to become deracinated subjects. In a seminal 1962 article, "Revolutionary Nationalism and the Afro-American," Harold Cruse called this condition "domestic colonialism," but Blauner analyzes it as "internal colonialism" in order to emphasize the differences in setting and consequences between it and classical colonialism.[49] But are human subjects merely the products of economic and social determinism?

Challenging prevailing contemporary notions of social determinism and the exclusive social construction of human identity, recent developments in DNA research, especially the Human Genome Project, vindicate the mother wit of many ordinary black folks as well as the belief of many scientists that human gender and cultural identity formations are a dynamic product and complex process of biology and culture, nature and nurture. "Race is a social concept, not a scientific one," declares Dr. J. Craig Venter, head of the Celera Genomics Corporation. "We all evolved in the last 100,000 years from the same small number of tribes that migrated out of Africa and colonized the world."[50] Before the recent survey of the human genome by geneticists and other scientists, and long before babies were technologically produced in bottles, tubes, and dishes, Simone de Beauvoir wrote in *The Second Sex* (1952) that one is not born a woman, and Ralph Ellison wrote in *Shadow and Act* (1953) that one must will oneself to be a Negro. But even before Beauvoir and Ellison developed theories of the sociocultural and sociopsychological construction of identities, the vernacular and literary tradition of our enslaved African and colonized African American slave and Jim Crowed ancestors taught many of us, as modern black feminist critic Hortense Spillers wryly remarks, that mama's baby was papa's maybe. Even during slavery, as revealed in Linda Brent's slave narrative, *Incidents in the Life of a Slave Girl* (1861), women could and did assert power in various ways over reproduction.

Yesteryear, before some of the most radical, sexually liberated white women, like Andrea Dworkin, considered men not only expendable but also extraneous, ordinary black folks of my generation learned in our folklore that even during slavery women controlled in different ways and to different degrees two keys to power: the key to the kitchen and the key to the bedroom and reproductivity. "'Cause wimmens got dem two little keys, de mens thinks dey is de boss an de wimmen knows dey is boss." Long before I read Zora Neale Hurston's recording of this power in *Mules and Men*, I heard older women in my community pass this saying on to younger women. Even when black women were raped by force, the power to name the biological father as well as the child depended not only on the political economy of slavery, urbanization, and industrialization, but also on the language, knowledge, and will of the mother. Black women, as black historian Deborah Gray White reveals in *Aren't I a Woman* (1985), were not merely the victims of white male dominance and aggression. Nor were they innately passive subjects dominated or controlled by black men. Whether by the interracial unions of rape, seduction, concubinage, or marriage as illustrated in novels from Brown's *Clotel* to Butler's *Kindred*, black women as subjects and agents made choices about the manner and degree to which they would reject, resist, or accommodate white male desire and dominance as they adopted or rejected the traditional ways of their racial, ethnic, class, and gender communities in doing things and constructing their identities.[51] "The salient theme emerging from domestic life in the slave quarters," as black social critic Angela Y. Davis notes, "is one of sexual equality. The labor that slaves performed for their own sake and not for the aggrandizement of their masters was carried out on terms of equality."[52]

Some African American writers, according to Afro-British cultural critic Paul Gilroy, collapse the synonyms "Afrocentricity" and "Africentricity" into "Americocentricity" by sometimes sanctioning "a crucial and regrettable slippage from the vernacular and the popular to the provincial and the parochial."[53] However, because Gilroy acknowledges that elements of "political sensibility and cultural expression transmitted from black America" are "central, though no longer dominant" in black vernacular culture in Britain, his argument "that Britain's black settler communities have forged a compound culture from disparate sources" that challenge the "absolutist conceptions of cultural difference" of some African American intellectuals is at best Anglocentric and problematic to a native-born African Americentric scholar activist.[54] By using the term "African Americentric," I mean to resurrect neither mid-nineteenth-century cultural provincialism and economic protectionism nor the turn-of-the-twentieth-century jingoism and imperialism of American exceptionalism. While implicitly acknowledging the complex interrelationship of chromosomes, color, ethnicity, class, gender, geography, age, culture, sexuality, consciousness, commitment, conscience, and choice in identity formations, African Americentrism names the specific historical and national grounding in the United States of my dual mode of epistemological, ontological, and cultural inquiry in a particular language and worldview.

My African Americentric theory and practice derive most directly from the paradoxical and ironic tensions between the everyday experiences of black Americans encoded in the vernacular tradition and the four principal American national grand narratives: the Bible, especially Genesis, Exodus, and Revelation; the Declaration of Independence, especially the Preamble; the Constitution of the United States, especially Article I, Sections 2 and 9, Article IV, Section 2, and the Thirteenth, Fourteenth, and Fifteenth Amendments; and the myth of the American Dream. As forms of rhetoric, the Declaration of Independence and the Constitution of the United States are performative speech acts and texts whose illocutionary force dramatically calls into being and establishes an independent new nation of people. Too often, readers forget the stories of the congressional meetings behind the texts that reveal the political, economic, and racial motives of the slave owners and aristocrats who wrote both documents in order to justify to other white men more than to God their construction of an independent nation primarily for white people and their descendants. In the debates and deliberations of the convention, the Founding Fathers removed Thomas Jefferson's criticism of slavery and the king from later drafts of the Declaration of Independence in 1776 at the insistence of Southern representatives. As James Madison's "Notes" from the Constitutional Convention of 1787 reveal, the delegates struck a major compromise with North Carolina, South Carolina, and Georgia concerning their right to import Negro slaves, including the disingenuous use of the term "persons" to avoid the use of slavery in the Constitution.[55] Because of the national legacy of racialized slavery and segregation, an African Americentric literary critic examines issues of race, ethnicity, class, gender, and culture in the historical experiences and oppositional discourse of peoples of sub-Saharan black African descent, primarily in the United States and secondarily in the African diaspora of the Caribbean and the Americas. As outlined in the African American residual oral forms of oratory, myth, legend, tale, and song in chapter 2, African Americentrism also challenges the myths of white supremacy, especially interpretations of the biblical curses on Cain and Ham as the legacy of peoples of African descent, and of a color-blind Constitution of the United States.

Despite their varying backgrounds and worldviews, few high school graduates and contemporary readers are unaware of the colonial conquest, enslavement, and denigration of black Africans and nonwhite indigenous peoples in the New World by white European and English colonists and colonialists. History and literature reveal that it was mainly the ancestors and elders of contemporary white readers who established the mythological racial hierarchies, ethnic boundaries, and pseudoscientific typologies of human beings that rationalized their military, cultural, political, and economic domination of nonwhite peoples. For example, many readers are familiar with the mythification of Europe's colonizing of America in *The Tempest* (1611), William Shakespeare's last play. This myth of the colonization of the "brave new world" and the lives of its native peoples is symbolized by the magical powers of Prospero, the Duke of Milan, whose land was usurped by his brother, and by Caliban, the naïve aborigine whose land is usurped by Prospero and whose life is reduced to that of a "savage and deformed slave." Rebuking Prospero for stealing his island and enslaving him, Caliban declares: "You taught me language, and my profit on't / Is, I know how to curse. The red plague rid you / For learning me your language!"[56] American high school graduates and readers are probably more familiar with the fugitive slave Jim's rebuke of Huck Finn's bigotry in Mark Twain's *Adventures of Huckleberry Finn* (1884). Some readers are even familiar with the more aggressive rebuke of Zack Edmonds by Lucas Beauchamp, the proud, racially mixed sexagenarian grandson of the slave owner Carothers McCaslin, in William Faulkner's *Go Down, Moses* (1942). Zack was rebuked for ostensibly sexually abusing Molly Beauchamp, Lucas's wife. This literature by Twain and Faulkner challenges readers to acknowledge our personal and collective responsibility for the American national sin of slavery and the moral cowardice of perpetuating racial violence, divisions, inequities, and injustice by legal segregation and antiblack racism.

Where and when, however, do we locate the origin of antiblack racism? And if the past is prologue to the present, how is this narrative of the colonial past related to the postcolonial formation of African American identities and texts? As black philosopher Lewis R. Gordon cogently explains in *Bad Faith and Antiblack Racism* (1995), antiblack racism is the belief and practice that institutionally and structurally construct black people as biologically or culturally inferior and subhuman by nature. From our ancestors and elders, black folks of my generation learned that the struggle to survive antiblack racism requires resilience, resourcefulness, resistance, reform, and, if necessary, revolutionary action. The cultural origins of antiblack racism are most comprehensively and clearly revealed in Winthrop D. Jordan's *White over Black: American Attitudes toward the Negro, 1550–1812* (1968). They can be traced back to the European religious wars against the Islamic Moors in Africa and the 1493 Bulls of Pope Alexander VI. These edicts divided the non-Christian world between Spain and Portugal, granting them the absolute power to claim the lands and to transform nonwhites and non-Christians into Christians, servants, and slaves.

In Britain the origins of antiblack racism can be traced back to the seventeenth-century idea and eighteenth-century hierarchic classification system of all inanimate things and forms of life in the Great Chain of Being. But antiblack racism in the United States has its mythic origins in the Book of Genesis, especially, on the one hand, in the covenant between God and a "chosen people," and, on the other, in the curse of Cain and Noah on an unfavored group of people. The biological and legislative origins of antiblack racism have two major sources. They are, first, the Virginia and Maryland laws of 1662 and 1663 that declared captive black Africans slaves for life and, second, the state miscegenation laws, beginning with Maryland in 1661, prohibiting interracial marriage, cohabitation, or fornication between white colonists and people of varying percentages of Negro ancestry, descent, or blood. These miscegenation statutes also have their origins in Negrophobia, the historical and irrational fear by most white people that was spawned and spread by stereotypes of peoples of African descent as beasts, savages, and criminals. After the Civil War, especially between 1882 and 1927, this fear culminated in ritualized horrific lynchings by white mobs primarily of black males, who were frequently accused of sexual indiscretions with white women.[57] State miscegenation laws were not declared unconstitutional until the U.S. Supreme Court decision of 1967 in the case of *Loving v. Virginia.* And despite the efforts of black leaders like Ida B.

Wells and Walter White, and their white allies, including the belated activism in the 1930s of The Association of Southern Women for the Prevention of Lynching, a federal anti-lynching law was never passed.

The most ironic early expression of antiblack racism and advocacy of the myth of white supremacy in the United States, however, was inscribed by Thomas Jefferson in his 1787 *Notes on the State of Virginia*. Because blacks "are inferior to whites in the endowments both of body and of mind," Jefferson argued disingenuously, they should, when and if freed, "be removed beyond the reach of mixture" and "staining the blood" of the superior race.[58] But DNA tests on the Y chromosome of a male descendant of Jefferson in 1999 and a romantic TV serial on the Jefferson and Hemings relationship in 2000 provide dramatic scientific and cultural support for the truth of the black folk legend and the novel *Clotel; or, The President's Daughter* (1853) by William Wells Brown. Jefferson, one of the Founding Fathers and the third president of the United States, was also the father of one or more children by his slave mistress, Sally Hemings.

In the 1960s and 1970s black and white intellectuals and activists reconstructed the nineteenth-century concept advanced by black nationalists and novelists Martin Delany, Alexander Crummell, and W. E. B. Du Bois of the segregated black American community in the United States as an internal colony.[59] Because most peoples of black sub-Saharan African descent in the New World are products of the dual processes of colonization and colonialization initiated by the expansion of white Europeans over five centuries ago, Africans in the New World shared on one level a common historical frame of reference. But, as social scientists Benjamin B. Ringer and Elinor R. Lawless persuasively argue in *Race-Ethnicity and Society* (1989), the pattern of white European conquest and settlement in the New World varied with time, place, colonizer, and colonized. Specifically, as a result of the tri-racial system of transplanted refugees from the slave revolutions in Barbados in 1670 and Saint Dominique in 1791, the colonial heritage of eighteenth-century blacks in the United States, especially in South Carolina, as revealed in historian Peter H. Wood's prize-winning *Black Majority* (1974), and Louisiana, as noted in historian Gwendolyn Midlo Hall's prize-winning *Africans in Colonial Louisiana* (1995), was and is similar to, yet vitally different from, that of blacks in other nations in the New World.

This vitally important difference in heritage was expressed in the duality of what I broadly interpret as the principal secular master narratives of the United States. The texts and stories of the origins of the Declaration of Independence and the Constitution of the United States, including the Bill of Rights, constructed a society whose institutions primarily represented the racial, religious, economic, and cultural image and interests of white people as subjects, especially the power of upper-class males. At the same time, paradoxically, the colonialist heritage of the United States continued its racial subjugation, extermination, and segregation of nonwhites by force and fraud, establishing and perpetuating a web of arbitrary legal and political white domination and control.[60] Commenting in a contemporary interview on the relationship of his use of ideologies and strategies of space to power, Foucault states: "Once knowledge can be analysed in terms of region, domain, implantation, displacement, transposition, one is able to capture the process by which knowledge functions as a form of power and disseminates the effects of power. There is an administration of knowledge, a politics of knowledge, relations of power which pass via knowledge and which, if one tries to transcribe them, lead one to consider forms of domination designated by such notions as field, region and territory."[61]

For example, in his dissenting opinion to *Plessy v. Ferguson*, the 1896 Supreme Court decision that established "separate but equal" as the legal basis for racial segregation in the nation, Justice John Marshall Harlan nevertheless expressed the traditional white majority belief in a distinction between social and political equality:

> The white race deems itself to be the dominant race in this country. And so it is in prestige, in achievements, in education, in wealth, and in power. So, I doubt not that it will continue to be for all time, if it remains true to its great heritage and holds fast to the principles of constitutional liberty. But in view of the Constitution, in the eye of the law, there is in this country no superior, dominant, ruling class of citizens. There is no caste here. Our Constitution is color-blind, and neither knows, nor tolerates classes among citizens. In respect of civil rights, all citizens are equal before the law.

With unintended irony and obvious bigotry, Justice Harlan affirms that the dominance of the white race is self-evident and eternal, while simultaneously declaring that the Constitution is the color-blind, classless guarantor of equality before the law.[62]

Once again, the more things change, the more they remain the same. It was white Europeans and white ethnic British Americans, in other words, not black artists, intellectuals, and cultural nationalists, who first constructed the political, pseudoscientific, and juridical institutions and classification systems that universally and hierarchically assigned individual and group identities to people by race or blood. As Ringer and Lawless remind us in *Race-Ethnicity and Society*, the Constitution of the United States, the principal political master narrative of the nation, disingenuously inscribes the classic binarism between "we," the white colonizers and colonists, in its Preamble, and "they," the Native Americans and enslaved Africans. In each case, after the human and political identity of "Indians" is erased in Article I, Section 2, enslaved and imported Africans are rhetorically, legally, and politically deracialized and transformed into property in Article I, Section 9, and Article IV, Section 2, while paradoxically designated as "other Persons."[63]

More specifically, both before and after the landmark 1896 Supreme Court decision that reaffirmed the power of white Americans to separate themselves from the cradle to the grave from Negro Americans, white Americans were determined to maintain their political, economic, and cultural domination by defining and devaluing the identity of Negroes. In the twenty states that chose to include definitions in their prohibition of interracial marriage, called mongrelization and miscegenation during the nineteenth century, "the state legislatures used one of two criteria: ancestry or descent, and percentage of Negro blood."[64] It is important to remember that long before the racialism of Marcus Garvey and the Nation of Islam these state miscegenation laws reinforced the social construction of the purity and supremacy of the white race by codifying the belief that anyone with any black ancestry or blood was a Negro: the one-drop rule. Among other things, the one-drop rule, which is unique to the United States and which has been internalized by many white and black Americans, contravenes the biblical injunction "He hath made of one blood all the nations of the earth" (Acts 17:26), which was popular in nineteenth-century black sermons. On one level, the paradox and irony of this biblical injunction, metaphysical signifier, and biological symbol were first invoked in African American literature by Olaudah Equiano/Gustavus Vassa at the end of the first chapter in his classic slave narrative, *The Interesting Narrative of the Life of Olaudah Equiano*. This biblical reference also inspired Pauline Hopkins's magazine novel *Of One Blood*, published in 1902–3.[65] On another level, the absurdity of the one-drop of black blood rule is satirized in the Liberty Paint Company episode in Ellison's *Invisible Man*. As stated earlier, in this book I define racial and ethnic identity as a complex, dynamic configuration in which the following constituent elements are assigned different weights and dominance in the subject's construction and representation of himself or herself: chromosomes, color, ethnicity, class, gender, geography, age, culture, sexuality, consciousness, commitment, conscience, and choice.

As indicated above, antiblack state laws prohibiting interracial marriage were not nullified by the Supreme Court until 1967, thirteen years after the Supreme Court's public school desegregation decision that reversed the "separate-but-equal" decision of 1896. Moreover, racial profiling—from shopping while black (SWB) in nonblack stores, driving while black (DWB) anywhere, and paying more for goods and services because we are black (the Black Tax)—is still the price that most people of my race and ethnicity pay regardless of class for being black Americans. Dualistic models and oppositional discourse, from Manichean allegory to the Du Boisian trope of double consciousness, are therefore valid, though not morally equivalent, critical models to deploy strategically in specific contexts. For these rhetorical strategies, as illustrated in the tradition of the African American novel, illuminate on different levels the paradoxes and ironies of the historical experiences and cultural expressions, both oral and written, of Americans of African descent.

As the everyday experiences of most black folks and the innovative writings of such law professors and critical race theorists as Derrick Bell, Kimberle Crenshaw, Richard Delgado, Neil Gotanda, Gary Peller, and Kendall Thomas demonstrate, antiblack racism, including the criminalizing of blackness and blackening of crime, is arguably still the norm in the United States.[66] In response to black intellectual entrepreneur Henry Louis Gates's claim in a different context that race is "the ultimate trope of difference," a feminist critic argues that gender is equally a trope of difference that shares with race "a similar structure of identity categories whose enactment and boundaries are culturally policed."[67] But one of the motivations for this sequel to *The Afro-American Novel and Its Tradition* is the antiblack-male spirit of the times and the survival of strong, socially responsible black men. These are the times that try the souls of men, especially if we are black, heterosexual, over thirty-five, neomasculinist brothers in spirit who still love, but do not all abuse, wine, whiskey, women, and song. From many in the media, academies, conservative think tanks, and several best-selling black feminist novels, the most frequent stories that we hear in the United States about black men are bad news. The news is that we are all dogs, robbers, homophobes, drug addicts, dope dealers, abusers of women and children, repressed rapists, dead-beat dads, racial purists, or ethnic extremists who are destined for death—physical, moral, or spiritual—at an early age. These are the contemporary negative stereotypes perpetuated in the dominant discourse, in the media, and in many African American novels. Many black male rappers and entertainers who boastfully and brotherly call each other "dawg," from rappers Snoop Doggy Dog and Bow Wow to comedians Cedric the Entertainer and Harvey, also uncritically perpetuate and reinforce the negative sociolinguistic construction of black male sexuality and identity.

The more things change, the more they remain the same. Both traditional and contemporary definitions of masculine identity stress sexual aggression and dominance. "The sex/gender system consists of marking the categories of biological sex with socially constructed gender meanings of masculinity and femininity," states black feminist and social theorist Patricia Hill Collins. "Just as sex/gender systems vary from relatively egalitarian systems to sex/gender hierarchies, ideologies of sexuality attached to particular sex/gender systems exhibit similar diversity. Sexuality is socially constructed through the sex/gender system on both the personal level of individual consciousness and interpersonal relationships and the social structural level of social institutions."[68] One of the most valuable and provocative debates on the inevitability or myth of male dominance is between sociologist Steven Goldberg in *The Inevitability of Patriarchy* (1974) and anthropologist Eleanor Burke Leacock in *Myths of Male Dominance* (1981). As their book titles indicate, Goldberg argues that biological differences in the levels of testosterone in males and females determine their physical and social dominance. Leacock invokes her personal experience and professional cross-cultural studies to argue that the subordination of women is neither biological nor universal, especially with the impact of modern technology. Goldberg rather boldly defines male dominance as "the *feeling* acknowledged by the emotions of both men and women that the woman's will is somehow subordinate to the male's and that general authority in dyadic and familial relationships, in whatever terms a particular society defines authority, ultimately resides in the male."[69]

The major weakness in Goldberg's argument is that biological differences between the sexes do not always produce male domination. Because of the legacy of resistance to the oppression of slavery and of resourcefulness in surviving racial segregation, male domination was and is not an absolute in black dyadic and familial relationships. Collins and Angela Davis reveal how pornography, prostitution, and rape are forms of sexual dominance and violence that have been historically used as weapons of social control against both black men and women.[70] In addition, most black males must live with the history, memory, and reality of the different levels of lynching and emasculation—from physical, verbal, and psychological to social, economic, and political—that influence the construction, representation, and perception of their manhood. Black men were misrepresented and lynched as sexually driven beasts with an insatiable desire for raping white women. Black women were misrepresented and raped as sexually driven animals, prostitutes, and pornographic objects. In contrast to male dominance, what I mean by black neomasculinity as a standard for assessing the quality of contemporary life and literature is mutual respect, sympathy, authority, responsibility, and reciprocity between men and women, as well as the complementarity of their generative powers, particularly in sexual desire and reproduction. The head of the household, as common sense and social change dictate, should therefore be the primary individual or individuals with the emotional, economic, and ethical resources and resolve to care for and safeguard the welfare of the family. Thus, readers of African American novels, especially black gay, lesbian, detective, and science fiction narratives, should be mindful of the fact that neither black women nor black men have a monopoly on either virtue or vice, estrogen or testosterone, passivity or aggression.

Historically, black American males have never had universal, uniform power over black women, and black women and families have never been the eternal victims of black male domination and violence. What, however, are the current facts that are masked or misrepresented by the stereotypes about black men in the media and contemporary African American novels? According to the 1990 census, black men represent 6 percent of the United States population. Health statistics for 1991 indicate that black men have a life expectancy of 64.6 years, compared to white males' 72.9; have death rates of 52.9 for HIV, compared to 16.7 for white men; and have homicide rates of 72.5 per 100,000, nearly eight times higher than for white men.[71] In the most thorough report of its kind, "And Justice for Some," published in 2000 and sponsored by the Justice Department and six of the nation's leading foundations, the severity and pervasiveness of racial disparities in the juvenile justice system are revealed. Black and Latino "youths are more likely than their white counterparts to be arrested, held in jail, sent to juvenile or adult court for trial, convicted and given longer prison terms, leading to a situation in which the impact is magnified with each additional step into the juvenile justice system."[72] Thirty-three percent of black men between the ages of 20 and 29 are under the control of the criminal justice system, that is, in prison, in jail, on probation, or on parole. The number of black men in prison and jail exceeds the number enrolled in higher education. Forty-four percent of all prisoners in the United States are black, and 40 percent of the condemned on death row are black men.[73]

The Contemporary African American Novel: Its Folk Roots and Modern Literary Branches thus challenges recent literary and cultural theorists who dismiss or devalue physiological differences between men and women, including radical feminists who argue dogmatically and categorically that women can do, as well or better, *anything* that men can do. Recent scientific studies, according to journalist Dorian Sagan in a 1998 special section on women's health in the *New York Times*, reinforce the common sense of ordinary folk by demonstrating "that women can do some things better, [and] that they have many biological and cognitive advantages over men. Then again, there are some things that women don't do as well." Sagan reminds us of the importance of these biological differences. Because the connector in women between the two hemispheres of the brain is larger,

> a stroke that damages the left side of the brain leaves men barely capable of speech, while the same damage to a woman's brain is far less debilitating since she can use both sides for language. Indeed, it is not only our brain functions that apparently diverge, but just about every aspect of our physiology. The way we metabolize alcohol and drugs, the way our circulatory system works and how resistant we are to infection are all affected by our sex. Why? Hormones. . . . But the hormones we once thought were important only for pregnancy, lactation and sexual drive have profound effects on just about every organ in the body.[74]

Thus, the more things change between men and women, the more they remain the same.

To some readers this may sound very traditional or even reactionary. But it is actually intended to position this study ideologically in opposition to two fallacious assumptions. The first is that human identity is exclusively a social construction. The second is that the contemporary terms "gender" as a social construction of identity and "sex" as a biological construction of identity are mutually exclusive. Rather than mutually exclusive concepts, gender and sex, like race and ethnicity, as folk wisdom buttressed by microbiology convincingly demonstrates, are actually overlapping and intersecting physiological and social processes in the identity formation of human beings.

Again, let me be clear about why and how this book challenges the perpetuation of popular negative stereotypes in some contemporary black novels and interrogates facts and issues that, as Marvin Gaye sings in "Inner City Blues" and journalist Nathan McCall reminds us in his bestselling memoir, make many of us black men wanna holler. Its major focus is neither phallocentric nor gynocentric. It does not seek to glorify black patriarchy and machismo or to celebrate male domination and irresponsible sexual freedom. Nor is my purpose to promote black matriarchy and feminism or to trivialize the domination and victimization of women. Rather, by focusing on the impact of race, ethnicity, class, gender, and sexuality on the identity formation of African Americans in novels published by black Americans primarily between 1983 and 2001, I seek to provide a valuable updated postcolonial African Americentric theoretical and interpretive study of the African American novel and its tradition that is more democratically inclusive and respectful of difference and diversity than my earlier book on the novel.

Nowadays, as in the scientific evidence of Thomas Jefferson's fathering at least one child with his slave Sally Hemings and the genetic relationship of Israeli Jews to Palestinian Arabs and of black South African Lemba Jewish priests to white Israeli priests, we are increasingly depending on the DNA correlation of the "Y" chromosome of males to confirm human identity and family relationships.[75] Although it has been fashionable in recent years in the academy for many intellectuals to declare that race is exclusively a social construction, few people other than misguided media pundits outside of the academy believe it. Even fewer black people believe that either white Americans or the Constitution of the United States is color-blind. In fact, most nonwhite people who are confronted by discrimination and occasionally violence because of the color of their skin and eyes, the size of parts of their body, and the texture of their hair know better. Long ago, African Americans learned that even though most biological differences between the races were ostensibly superficial, the differences had a very significant impact on the quality of our lives as human beings and on the guarantee of our rights as American citizens. We also learned in the past that in all cultures there are those who can and those who cannot, those who will and those who will not, get it all together, get along, and keep it real. Getting it all together and keeping it real for readers of the African American novel and its tradition means understanding and acknowledging the complex relationship, on the one hand, between language, knowledge, and power, and, on the other, between authenticity, authority, and agency in constructing our identities and reconstructing our world.

Contemporary African American novels challenge readers by the imaginative deployment of language and speech to examine and even question the social construction of their identities and world, especially their systems of language, belief, and values. According to contemporary black novelist John Edgar Wideman, "Once a convention for dramatizing black speech appears in fiction, the literary critic should be concerned not with matters of phonetic accuracy, but with tracing the evolution of a written code and determining how that code refers to the spoken language in suggestive, artful, creative ways."[76] How, then, should readers, especially native speakers of AAVE and literary critics who are bidialectal, respond to the position of contemporary novelists and critics like Wideman in assessing black American voices and discursive strategies? Bidialectalism or diglossia is the sociolinguistic theory and practice of code-switching appropriately, based on the site, situation, and subject, between two distinct, legitimate varieties of language, in this case nonstandard AAVE and SAE. Nonstandard American English is generally acquired and used in the primary speech community of the home, and SAE is acquired and used primarily as the language of prestige and status in print and school.[77] Assuming that language is a dual system of signs for communicating ideas and feelings about reality and for establishing, maintaining, or changing power relationships with others in different spaces or sites, the most reasonable and appropriate response of readers to the language of contemporary African American novels is to focus on the problems of authenticity, authority, and agency in texts. The code-switching language and African American residually oral forms of these texts seek to illuminate what Du Bois called the double consciousness, Melville Herskovits called the socialized ambivalence, Langston Hughes called the laughing-to-keep-from-crying attitude, and Albert Murray called the antagonistic cooperation of African American everyday realities.

Rather than relying exclusively on the vernacular forms of either signifying or the blues for the distinctiveness of African American literature, keeping it real and telling it like it is for African Americentric critics and texts involve the authenticity, authority, and agency of their deployment of code-switching and five African American residually oral forms. It will suffice for now to identify oratory, myth, legend, tale, and song as the five fundamental forms, because they are fully explained in chapter 2. But I must here stipulate the layered, complex meanings of authenticity, authority, and agency in this book.

The tenth edition of *Merriam-Webster's Collegiate Dictionary* defines "authentic" as something that is "worthy of acceptance or belief as conforming to or based on fact." In *Sincerity and Authenticity* literary critic Lionel Trilling more narrowly explains authenticity "as a criterion of art and as a quality of the personal life which may be either enhanced or diminished by art."[78] In *Authentic Blackness*, a study of the representation of blackness in the New Negro movement and Harlem Renaissance, critic J. Martin Favor writes that "authenticity derives from uniqueness, but it also fixes that uniqueness to a limited range of possibilities."[79] In contrast, philosopher Charles Taylor more directly addresses the complex ethical dimensions of authenticity in *The Ethics of Authenticity*:

> Authenticity (A) involves (i) creation and construction as well as discovery, (ii) originality, and frequently (iii) opposition to the rules of society and even potentially to what we recognize as morality. But it is also true . . . that it (B) requires (i) openness to horizons of significance (for otherwise the creation loses the background that can save it from insignificance) and (ii) a self-definition in dialogue. That these demands may be in tension has to be allowed. But what must be wrong is a simple privileging of one over the other[,] of (A), say, at the expense of (B), or vice versa.[80]

Authenticity is thus conferred from without as well as from within the dialectic process of the rites of passage of one's life. Authenticity also implies both transcending or overcoming restrictive material conditions and transgressing or violating social and moral boundaries. Whether the ultimate reality and liberation are to be achieved through the power of love (*agape* or *eros*, heterosexuality or homosexuality) or the power of revolution (peaceful or violent) grounded in the actual or imagined experiences of the authors is a frequent matter of critical concern for readers of the contemporary African American novel and romance.

Although they usually overlap, authority differs from authenticity because it requires the power to influence or command thought, opinion, or behavior. According to social theorist Max Weber, power is "the probability that one actor within a social relationship will be in a position to carry out his own will despite resistance, regardless of the basis on which this probability rests."[81] In "Power as a Social Process," social scientist Marvin E. Olsen reminds us about the three grounds on which legitimate authority often rests. They "are (a) traditional values, beliefs, norms, and customs, (b) legal prerogatives established through more-or-less rational agreements, and (c) special expertise or knowledge relevant to the situation. To the extent that an actor draws legitimacy from three sources . . . his authority is especially strong."[82] Although phenotypically and sociohistorically black writers could claim the authority of their racial and cultural experience with slavery and segregation, the actual authority of the identities of peoples of African descent and their descendants in the United States, as revealed in texts that range from slave petitions and autobiographies to novels by Reed, Morrison, Trey Ellis, and Colson Whitehead, is more complex. The authority of the identities of African Americans emanates not only from the particularity of our historical struggle against slavery, colonization, and antiblack racism in the United States. It also emanates from the language of our individual and collective political agency in the present and future to maintain or change power relationships. The ways that African American novelists and novels use rhetoric, dialectics, and dialogics, especially their deployment of residually oral forms, illuminate the authority of these strategies in reconciling African American double consciousness. They also illuminate the authority of these strategies in representing the dynamic interdependence of our chromosomes, color, ethnicity, class, gender, geography, age, culture, sexuality, consciousness, commitment, conscience, and choice in the construction of the core ethnic identities and unity necessary to effect a more just community.

In narratology an agent is the representation of a human being whose speech acts influence events. But as it is used here, agency, to paraphrase Charles Taylor, is the sociocultural and sociopsychological process by which the individual assumes a responsible political position in maintaining or changing the systems of language and power by which he or she constructs and represents a personal and group identity or subjectivity of authenticity and authority.[83] In other words, agency is personal initiative and principled action in effecting social change. The history of the pan-African movement has taught African Americans that the construction of an African diasporic identity is more of a cultural and romantic ideal than, as the unrelenting fratricidal ethnic wars in sub-Saharan Africa indicate, an economic and political reality. For African Americentrics, the construction of a unifying core of shared history and feelings of racial subordination, of resistance, and of triumphant vernacular expressivity has its demographic origins in the Deep South of the United States, especially in the residually oral forms of Gullah culture (e.g., speech, myth, legend, tale, and song) in the coastal regions of Georgia and South Carolina. Varieties of its contemporary perennial life cycle and creative reconstructions occur in urban American centers of native speakers of AAVE and predominantly black inner city communities of the United States.

As Taylor explains in *Human Agency and Language*, "an individual is constituted by the language and culture which can only be maintained and renewed in the communities he is part of. . . . The community is not simply an aggregation of individuals. . . . The community is also constitutive of the individual, in the sense that the self-interpretations which define him are drawn from the interchange which the community carries on."[84] The sociocultural and sociolinguistic construction of the identities of African Americans begins with the hierarchical power relationship between the nonstandard regional dialects of enslaved Africans and the English dialect standardized for social and cultural reasons by white Americans. Addressing the question of agency in *The Afrocentric Idea*, Molefi Asante, a specialist in speech communications, argues persuasively that "the protest speaker's sensitivity to powerlessness in the society frees him or her to utilize the improvisational mechanisms of African American culture in responding to unpleasant situations."[85] The manner and degree of code-switching of novelists between the pronunciation, vocabulary, and grammar of AAVE, especially its distinctive idioms, sayings, and cultural commonplaces, and SAE in the imaginative construction of the identities of African Americans is therefore one important area of analysis for assessing the agency, as well as the authenticity and authority, of black American novelists, their characters, and their texts.

An African Americentric Vernacular Theory of Culture and Identity

In this third stage, we will reconstruct an African Americentric vernacular theory for reading contemporary African American novels. The belief that the structure of a language determines the way that speakers of that language view the world can be traced back to the nineteenth-century linguist Wilhelm von Humboldt. But in the modern era it was mainly the proponents of the Whorfian hypothesis of linguist Edward Sapir and his student Benjamin Lee Whorf, who insisted that language determines culture. In contrast, the African co-authors of *Toward the Decolonization of African Literature* (1983) argue that language embodies and expresses culture values, but "it is not the crucial generator of those values and cannot *alone* be relied upon to supply literary criteria."[86] Even though "Humboldtian (and most Whorfians, for that matter) overstate the case for language as THE determiner of thought, consciousness and behavior, nonetheless," African American sociolinguist Geneva Smitherman cogently and convincingly reminds us, "language DOES play a dominant role in the formation of ideology, consciousness, and class relations." Consciousness and ideology are therefore "largely the products of . . . the SOCIOLINGUISTIC CONSTRUCTION OF REALITY."[87]

Even though grounded in neither the history nor the culture of African Americans, the explanations of the relationship between language, knowledge, and power by French historian Michel Foucault, Russian literary theorist M. M. Bakhtin, and British literary critic Terry Eagleton are equally cogent. In *The Order of Things* (1970), Foucault states that social identity and power function through "a system of cultural unconsciouses the totality of formal structures which render mythical discourse significant, give their coherence and necessity to the rules that regulate needs, and provide the norms of life with a foundation other than that to be found in nature, or in pure biological functions."[88] In the essay "Discourse in the Novel," Bakhtin describes language in the novel as dynamic, stratified particular points of view on the world:

> As a living, socio-ideological concrete thing, as heteroglot opinion, language, for the individual consciousness, lies on the borderline between oneself and the other. The word in language is half someone else's. It becomes "one's own" only when the speaker populates it with his own intention, his own accent, when he appropriates the word, adapting it to his own semantic and expressive intention. . . . Language is not a neutral medium that passes freely and easily into the private property of the

> speaker's intentions; it is populated—overpopulated—with the intentions of others. Expropriating it, forcing it to submit to one's own intentions and accents is a difficult and complicated process.[89]

Foucault and Bakhtin thus provide provocative, nontraditional theories of the discursive and sociolinguistic process of identity or subject formation in life and literature that may be adapted by readers for the interpretation of some contemporary African American novels.

Speaking more generally about the nature of all kinds of sign systems, Eagleton writes: "Discourses, sign systems, and signifying practices of all kinds from film and television to fiction and the languages of natural science, produce effects, shape forms of consciousness and unconsciousness, which are closely related to the maintenance or transformation of our existing systems of power. They are thus closely related to what it means to be a person. Indeed 'ideology' can be taken to indicate no more than this connection—the link or nexus between discourses and power."[90] The sound and fury of national debates in the 1990s about educating students and teachers in public schools about the relationship of SAE or the LWC to AAVE or Ebonics are a dramatic illustration of the link between discourses and power in the construction of identities. Whereas SAE is the dialect sanctioned for commerce and general use by the ruling class and dominant social institutions, AAVE is the everyday dialect in the primary speech community of most inner-city, working poor black families. This raises the important question of what historical and social forces fostered the foregrounding of language in general and SAE or LWC in particular as the norm in the United States for interpreting texts and the world.

Because chapter 2 outlines the roots of AAVE, it will suffice here to remind general readers, including such celebrities as Maya Angelou, Bill Cosby, Jesse Jackson, and Oprah Winfrey, that AAVE or Ebonics is not "broken English," "bad grammar," or "merely slang." Nor is AAVE the product of archaic British words, African "thick lips and thick minds," or substandard white American dialects. According to most contemporary dialectologists, linguists, and sociolinguists, especially creolists, as well as to such professional organizations as the Linguistic Society of America and the National Council of Teachers of English, the perceptions and descriptions just noted are misrepresentations of AAVE. This contemporary misrepresentation of AAVE has its historical roots in deficit theories of the body, culture, and character of black Americans of African descent.[91] These deficit or pathological theories of AAVE were spawned by antiblack racism and class prejudice that many blacks have internalized, as well as by political and commercial national imperatives that inform the representation of African American character and culture in many contemporary African American novels.

The consensus of some linguists and most sociolinguists is that British cultural dominance in the thirteen colonies fostered the creolization process of African languages with English dialects, beginning with the pidgin languages of the seventeenth century. Characterized by the retention and reinterpretation of some African grammatical principles and forms combined with some simplified English words and sentence patterns, pidgin was a variety of English used only for trade and commerce between Africans and English-speaking peoples. When pidgin developed a more complex grammar and became the primary everyday language of a people during the eighteenth and nineteenth centuries, it became a creole language like the Gullah spoken in the South Carolina and Georgia Sea Islands. The decreolization of AAVE began primarily because of the impact of SAE on speakers of AAVE in the school system and because of major northern and western migrations of blacks in the twentieth century to segregated inner cities. But some linguists, like Professor William Labov of the University of Pennsylvania, contend that important linguistic features of AAVE are diverging farther from SAE.[92]

For African American academics and students in white colleges and universities during the Black Power and Black Arts movements, three shifts in the relationship of language, knowledge, and power are important for clarification of how the more things change, the more they remain the same in the contemporary African American novel. The first shift is the clarion call for and correlation of Black Power and Black Art in LeRoi Jones and Larry Neal's *Black Fire* (1969), a landmark anthology. The movement of black student activism from the urban centers to white academies in the struggle for Black Studies programs to validate and valorize vernacular forces and forms of knowledge and power in black America energized this shift. Among other things, *Black Fire* popularized two radical black nationalist ideas that were reclaimed and reconstructed by cultural critics Harold Cruse and Larry Neal. The first is Cruse's recovery in 1962 of Martin Delany's nineteenth-century concept of the "American Negro" as "a subject of domestic colonialism."[93] The second is Larry Neal's regeneration of W. E. B. Du Bois's concept of double consciousness and of David Walker's appeal for the redemptive power of black rebellion. What "we are asking for," Neal writes, "is a new synthesis; a new sense of literature as a living reality. But first, we must liberate ourselves, destroy the double-consciousness. We must integrate with ourselves, understand that we have within us a great vision, revolutionary and spiritual in nature, understand that the West is dying, and offers little promise of rebirth."[94]

The second shift was inspired in the late 1960s by such French intellectuals as Jacques Derrida, Roland Barthes, and Michel Foucault even though they had neither knowledge of nor research interest in African American history, culture, and character. It was the movement of critical inquiry in Ivy League institutions away from the social subversion of power by students and other political activists in the United States, ranging from the Black Studies, Black Power, and Black

Arts movements to the feminist, Ethnic Studies, gay/lesbian, and anti–Vietnam War movements, toward the linguistic subversion of power. Ostensibly ahistorical and apolitical, the linguistic movement was basically from the structuralist view of literary texts as a closed network of binary oppositions and a system of rules with a definite meaning to the poststructuralist theory that all texts are reworkings of other texts and sign systems which can not be pinned down to a single meaning. Both literary theories, especially the latter, were promoted at Yale University primarily by critics Paul de Man, J. Hillis Miller, and Geoffrey Hartman, and subsequently, in reaction to the radical political consciousness of the Black Power and Black Arts movements, by such black Yale graduate students and critics as Robert Stepto and Henry Louis Gates Jr.

The impact of structuralism on Stepto was first demonstrated in his organization of the 1977 summer seminar "African American Literature: From Critical Approach to Course Design" at Yale. According to Gates's reactionary view of the ideological struggle by Black Arts writers and cultural workers for critical authority, "the conference . . . represented an attempt to take the 'mau-mauing' out of the black literary criticism that defined the 'Black Aesthetic Movement' of the sixties and transform it into a valid field of intellectual inquiry once again."[95] Co-sponsored by the Modern Language Association and the National Endowment for the Humanities, this seminar culminated in the publication of a selection of lectures and course designs by staff members and participants in *Afro-American Literature: The Reconstruction of Instruction* (1978). Edited by Dexter Fisher and Robert Stepto, this collection promotes moving beyond the usual chronological literary survey "by examining the 'historical consciousness' of art forms and pursuing the dialectic between the various black literatures of the New World as well as that between the literature and its criticism (including, especially, the commentary that is so often appended to texts)."[96]

Even more representative of the impact of structuralism on Stepto and Gates, who was on the seminar staff, are their frequently quoted respective major studies of African American narratives: *From Behind the Veil* (1979) and *The Signifying Monkey* (1988). Although challenged by the black cultural nationalism and vernacular theory of Houston Baker, who was a Yale faculty member in 1969–70 and who influenced Gates's shift to an Afrocentric vernacular theory, their structuralist theory and practice were basically an adaptation of the linguistic theory of Ferdinand de Saussure. Saussure stressed that each sign in a language system has meaning only by its sound, image, or graphic difference from other signs in the system.[97]

" 'Language' is speech or writing viewed 'objectively,' as a chain of signs without a subject," Eagleton explains. " 'Discourse' means language grasped as *utterance*, as involving speaking and writing subjects and therefore also, at least potentially, readers or listeners."[98] Foucault and Bakhtin are mainly responsible for this shift from interpreting language as objective signs to interpreting it as discourse and dialogism, the specific utterances of individuals in particular social contexts and conflicts. This shift supported research in sociolinguistics in the 1970s that validated and valorized AAVE and other varieties of American English as legitimate rule-governed language systems. "Language, in short, was a field of ideological contention, not a monolithic system," Eagleton concludes; "indeed, signs were the very material medium of ideology, since without them no values or ideas could exist."[99]

The third important shift in the relationship of language and knowledge to power was in the rules for the formation of statements which are accepted as scientifically, linguistically, economically, and politically true. Addressing the politics of the scientific statement, Foucault states that "it's not so much a matter of knowing what external power imposes itself on science, as of what effects of power circulate among scientific statements, what constitutes, as it were, their internal regime of power, and how and why at certain moments that regime undergoes a global modification."[100] The problem of distinguishing among anthropological structures and historical events and of reconstituting how they are related should not, for Foucault, involve "analyses couched in terms of the symbolic field or the domain of signifying structures." He prefers genealogical analyses "of relations of force, strategic developments, and tactics" as in a war or battle.[101]

The reduction of personal agency in transforming self and society to mere rhetoric is clearly a risk in literature as in life. However, I believe that dialogic, as the social conflict and contentious dialogue of discourse, dialectics, as the logic of contradictions, and semiotics, as the sign systems of communication (three terms that will be more fully defined below) can account for the intrinsic intelligibility of conflict resolution and of struggles, especially of strategies and tactics, in some contemporary African American novels. While for theorist Michel deCerteau, those in power who control the spaces of articulation deploy strategies and those without power deploy tactics to contest their dispossession of space, for Foucault and some contemporary African American novelists, strategies are acts of confrontation designed to succeed in attaining objectives in specific contexts of opposition and resistance.[102]

Before Foucault became the postmodern oracle for examining the nature of power in constructing identities and various types of texts, the psychological, economic, and political systems of antiblack racism and slavery had taught black Americans that there was neither emancipation nor progress without struggle. "The limits of tyrants," Frederick Douglass wrote trenchantly in 1849, "are prescribed by the endurance of those whom they oppress."[103] Because absolute power corrupts absolutely, freedom, ancestral wisdom teaches us, is not free.

Probably the most important fundamental assumption this book makes is that language is a dual system of signs. On the one hand, language is for communicating authoritatively and authentically the beliefs and values of the author, narrators, and characters about the nature and function of reality. On the other hand, it is a system of signs for the agency of establishing, maintaining, or changing power relationships with others in order to promote more just and equitable social formations.

As outlined in chapter 2, the blues is one of the five residual oral forms essential to the authenticity and authority of a shared African American culture and character. "I can squeeze water out of a rock; I can make water come from dry sand," sings bluesman Buddy Guy. "And if you listen to my story, I'll prove I'm a natural man." Unlike most rural and urban black working-class and poor folks, many contemporary academics, black and white, are ambivalent about this masculinist vernacular boastfulness because they reject all types of essentialized and naturalized identities derived from what black anthropologist John Langston Gwaltney calls "core black culture."[104]

Core Black American Culture

The fourth stage of this chapter provides us the opportunity to examine the relevance of core black culture to the representation and interpretation of authentic African American culture and character in contemporary African American novels. *Drylongso,* Gwaltney's classic portrait of black America based on interviews with ordinary Northeastern black Americans, reveals that the "minority of black Americans who significantly depart from core black customs and values may pass, may become bourgeois in spirit as well as income, or swell the ranks of marginal drug and welfare cultures. But far more often than not, the primary status of a black person is that accorded by the people he or she lives among. It is based upon assessments of that person's fidelity to core black standards."[105] These values, as I indicate in chapter 2, are mainly a product of the European colonization of Africa and the Atlantic slave trade, as well as a product of the dynamic process of the retention, reinvention, and syncretism of vestiges of African culture and the struggles to overcome class, color, and gender domination in the New World. In the United States, although complicated by a syncretistic blend of African and non-African religious beliefs, secular myths, and rituals, these core values primarily emanate from a cyclical Judeo-Christian vision of history and of African Americans as a disinherited, colonized people, a vision that sanctions our individual and collective resilience of spirit and pursuit of social justice.

Basic black American values include a tragicomic, wry vision of life, and an extraordinary faith in the redemptive power of suffering, patience, perseverance, and compassion. These values are manifested and sanctioned in our striving to become the proud masters of our fate as individuals and as the principal providers and protectors of our families and primary communities. This core of black traditional cultural standards is neither pure nor fixed. Rather, as revealed in the Black Aesthetic movement of the late 1960s and satirized in the neo–Black Aesthetic movement of the late 1980s and 1990s, it is a dynamic biracial and bicultural identity formation with many intraracial dialectical differences, especially gender and sexuality, that the group members individually and collectively struggle to reconcile. In responding to the presence or absence of the complexity of this core of African American standards, fundamental understandings, and symbolic accord in contemporary African American novels, readers should be as open-minded in assessing the authenticity, authority, and agency of the texts as some of the texts are open-ended. However, it is equally important for readers to remember, as feminist critic Diana Fuss astutely notes in *Essentially Speaking*, that "essence is a sign, and as such historically contingent and constantly subject to change and to redefinition."[106]

Most commonly, Fuss writes, essentialism is "understood as a belief in the real, true essence of things, the invariable and fixed properties which define the 'whatness' of a given entity. . . . To some, essentialism is nothing more than the philosophical enforcer of a liberal humanist idealism which seeks to locate and to contain the subject within a fixed set of differences. . . . To others, essentialism may not be without a certain tactical or interventionary value, especially in our political struggles and debates."[107] Like Fuss's, my position is that "certain tactical or interventionary" essentialism can be deployed effectively in the service of a wide range of oppositional discourses, including progressive and reactionary, mythologizing and postmodern.

In addition to Fuss, other cultural studies and postcolonial critics who subscribe to some form of strategic essentialism range from Paul Smith and Steven Epstein to Katya Gibel Azoulay, Gayatri Chakravorty Spivak, Kadiatu Kanneh, and Stuart Hall. "Black politics—in terms of organising against racism, gaining positive, collective empowerment, recognising certain aspects of experience or identification—do need to employ certain essentialist categories in order to have any kind of strategy or existence," Kanneh persuasively argues. "Political identity often requires the need to make conscious commitments," the outstanding black Jamaican postcolonial and cultural studies theorist Hall argues even more plainly and convincingly. "Thus it may be necessary to momentarily abandon the multiplicity of cultural identities for more simple ones around which political lines have been drawn. You need all the folks together, under one hat, carrying one banner, saying we are for this, for the purpose of this fight, we are all the same, just black and just here."[108] Rather than summarily dismissed or devalued, the language of essentialism, in short, should be critiqued in the context of its use in particular configurations of power relations and knowledge production that it resists and seeks to transform.

Furthermore, in an era when it is fashionable in the academy and the media to dismiss and disavow all theories of essentialized identities, we should not "underestimate or neglect the importance of the act of imaginative rediscovery which this conception of a rediscovered, essential identity entails," as Stuart Hall wisely cautions. " 'Hidden histories' have played a critical role in the emergence of many of the most important social movements of our time—feminist, anti-colonial and anti-racist."[109] It is highly significant that this concept of cultural identity played a crucial role in all the postcolonial struggles which have so profoundly reshaped our world. Léopold Senghor, Aimé Césaire, and Frantz Fanon, as Hall reminds us, believed that our common historical experiences in the diaspora and shared cultural codes provided us "with stable, unchanging and continuous frames of reference and meaning, beneath the shifting divisions and vicissitudes of our actual history. This oneness, underlying all the other more superficial differences, is the truth, the essence . . . of the black experience. It is this identity which a . . . black diaspora must discover, excavate, bring to light and express through . . . representation."[110] Even though most postcolonial critics have shifted their theories away from cultural identities "eternally fixed in some essentialised past," Hall also reminds us that the quest for the oneness, the truth, and the essence of a people's cultural identity not only "played a critical role in all the post-colonial struggles which have so profoundly reshaped our world" but also "continues to be a very powerful and creative force in emergent forms of representation amongst hitherto marginalized peoples."[111]

It is necessary, therefore, to acknowledge our moral and political responsibility as critical readers to question both antiessentialism and essentialism as absolute truths and categorical imperatives about racial identity. This interrogation should include the new orthodoxy on the relationship of racial narratives to knowledge and power. According to African American historian Kevin K. Gaines, "it is important to realize the extent to which forms of knowing besides 'right reason'—feelings, fears, desires, and other nonrational processes—have invaded intellectual and cultural expressions regarding race, and ultimately, how these cultural narratives about race reflect power relations."[112] Epistemologically, in other words, the passions of the heart, the powers of the imagination, and our spiritual strivings, as ancestral wisdom teaches us, also have their ways of dealing with the past, present, and future paradoxes of our daily lives.

"We are a nation primarily because we think we are a nation," a sixty-one-year-old black informant told Gwaltney a decade before Benedict Anderson's theorizing on the origins of nationalism.[113] Anthropologically, "all communities larger than primordial villages of face-to-face contact (and perhaps even these) are imagined," Anderson writes. "Communities are to be distinguished, not by their falsity/genuineness, but by the style in which they are imagined."[114] Too frequently, pundits, pedants, and politicians from the left and right who inveigh against essentialism as the archetypal enemy of valid intellectual inquiries begin with two fallacious assumptions. They assume first that all oppositional models of interpretation are reductive binarisms, and second that all differential power relationships may be peacefully and permanently transcended or resolved through dialogics. However, the dialectics of our specific histories, cultures, and consciousness as black people of African and slave descent in the New World tell a different story, one that is marked by paradoxes, ironies, tragicomedy, and hope.

More specifically, as Hall cogently states: "We all write and speak from a particular place and time, from a history and a culture which is specific. What we say is always 'in context', positioned. . . . Far from being eternally fixed in some essentialised past, they [cultural identities] are subject to the continuous 'play' of history, culture and power. Far from being grounded in a mere 'recovery' of the past . . . identities are the names we give to the different ways we are positioned by, and position ourselves within, the narratives of the past."[115] In other words, scholars, students, and general readers should develop the specific historical and cultural contexts for interrogating the dialectic or dialogic construction and interpretation of our identities, texts, and strategies for social change. Enslaved Africans and black immigrants to the United States did not all arrive at the same time, in the same manner, from the same places, as contemporary novels by Morrison, Charles Johnson, Paule Marshall, and Gayl Jones reveal, even though we may now all be in the same boat of domination by the white ruling class. The process of historicizing, contextualizing, and problematizing our identities, texts, and strategies for social change will therefore improve our understanding of the complex relationship among language, knowledge, and power.

Black novelists and readers of African American novels are challenged by postmodernism to address the fundamental question of whether we human beings are the product of nature or nurture. What light does folk wisdom and the recent DNA link between Israelis and Arabs in Palestine and between many of the Lemba men of South Africa and Jewish priests in Israel shed on this question and the unrelenting fratricidal struggles for national and cultural identities by distant yet related peoples? How does the new vogue of multinational corporations cashing in on the racial and cultural hybridity of African Americans, especially the multiethnic globalization of hip-hop culture and rap music, impact on this question? More specifically, what impact does the commercial success and increased popularity of black science fiction, gay and lesbian, and detective novels and romances in the 1980s and 1990s, which are examined as paraliterature in chapter 8, have on the quest for a more just social and moral order in the tradition of the African American novel? Aren't the representation and reception of African American culture and character in novels of the 1980s and 1990s products in various ways and to different degrees of both nature and nurture: of the dynamic, distinctive configuration of our chromosomes, color, ethnicity, class, gender, geography, age, culture, sexuality, consciousness, commitment, conscience, and choice?

In their everyday struggle for identity, status, and power to fit into or to change an unjust and unequal social system, the authors and texts under examination in this study illuminate the complexity of our sexual as well as our racial and ethnic identity formations. But in interrogating the challenge of gay and lesbian narratives to the normative authority of heterosexuality, I contest the new orthodoxy of heterosexuality as homophobic. In contrast to the old orthodoxy that judged homosexuality a sin or diagnosed it as a psychiatric disease, the new orthodoxy in public discourse and some contemporary African American novels reverses the normative grouping by labeling heterosexuals who disapprove of homosexuality pathological. Whether the themes are women exploring their sexuality with other women in Ann Shockley's *Loving Her* and Alice Walker's *The Color Purple* or men engaging in sex with other men in Samuel Delany's *Mad Man* and E. Lynn Harris's *Invisible Life,* readers are challenged not only to understand the complex relationship of the authenticity, authority, and agency of the texts but also to reconstruct our belief and value systems. The fundamental question raised for readers by the authors of and narrators and characters in gay and lesbian novels and romances, as illustrated in chapter 8, is not only whether homosexuality is a matter of birth or choice, but also whether homosexuals are guaranteed the same equal rights as citizens as heterosexuals.

In the metaphysical, social, and existential construction of our complex identities as African American subjects and citizens, the fundamental questions raised in gay and lesbian novels are related to whether the truths received in our oral tradition and inscribed in our sacred texts as transcendent signifiers have more or less authority than the words inscribed in our secular master narratives and legal texts. These texts range from the Bible, the Declaration of Independence, and the Constitution of the United States to the *Brown v. Board of Education of Topeka* school desegregation decision of 1954, the *Gayle v. Browder* bus desegregation decision of 1956, and the Civil Rights Acts of 1964 and 1965, guaranteeing equal access for blacks to public accommodations, fair employment, and voting. How do average white and black American readers, in contrast to white and black intellectuals and media pundits, construct a reasonable and ethical balance in their everyday experiences between their natural and civil rights in communities of mutually respectful and responsible human beings, including black gays and lesbians?

For example, in the wake of the liberation movements in the United States of blacks and women, and especially the Stonewall rebellion of gays against police harassment in New York City in 1969, the American Psychiatric Association in 1973 declassified homosexuality as a mental illness. Subsequently, advocates of gay rights have boldly and effectively used this psychiatric declassification as a political tactic to ascribe a Freudian irrational fear of sexual intimacy with someone of the same sex to everybody who subscribes to heterosexuality as the norm and who morally objects to homosexuality. Although discrimination against homosexuals in such public areas as employment, education, and housing is illegal, it nevertheless happens. But in our private lives, many people who believe in mutual respect as a cardinal rule also believe that different strokes for different folks includes tolerance of sexual difference. However, neither in most black novels and romances nor in most black communities, do this rule and folksaying translate into sanctioning homosexuality as the social and moral equivalent of heterosexuality.

In the conservative tradition of the black Baptist and Methodist churches, God and salvation, the postmodern transcendental signifier and master plan, still reign supreme in the souls of the masses of low-income and working-class black folk, especially those of my generation. Rooted in this tradition, sexual taboos are among the many controversial aspects of black American belief and value systems. These core beliefs and values are most dramatically illustrated and contested in the narrative themes, styles, structures of James Baldwin, Hal Bennett, Alice Walker, Gloria Naylor, Ann Shockley, Samuel Delany, Larry Duplechan, E. Lynn Harris, and Randall Kenan. While sensitive to the interrelated issues of sexuality, gender, and class, this book does not seek to replace heterosexuality as a normative value in African American communities with homosexuality. Nor does it seek to replace the historical centrality of black and white racial hybridity in the United States with a multiethnic hybridity that masks or evades the power of the white ruling class and the dominance of antiblack racism in the identity formation of African Americans. Instead, I develop a postcolonial African Americentric vernacular approach to the African American novel in which antiblack racism and Du Boisian double consciousness are central to the construction and interpretation of racial and ethnic identities and texts. This African American ontological and epistemological mode of critical inquiry will illuminate the range of strategies of different authors and texts for transforming the politics of difference in power relations in the United States into a more just, peaceful, and productive democratic coexistence for all peoples.

In the preface to *Feminist Theory* (1984), bell hooks provides one of the clearest and most compelling anecdotal explanations of oppositional modes of knowing and discourse that I have encountered. Deploying the railroad tracks in her Kentucky town as the dominant historical metaphor of racial and class division, she writes:

> Living as we did—on the edge—we developed a particular way of seeing reality. We looked both from the outside in and from the inside out. We focused our attention on the center as well as on the margin. We understood both. . . . Our survival depended on an ongoing public awareness of the separation between margin and center and an ongoing private

> acknowledgment that we were a necessary, vital part of that whole. This sense of wholeness, impressed upon our consciousness by the structure of our daily lives, provided us an oppositional world view—a mode of seeing unknown to most of our oppressors, that sustained us, aided us in our struggle to transcend poverty and despair, strengthened our sense of self and our solidarity.[116]

The social boundary and symbolic legacy of railroad tracks and trains are modern signs of sociohistorically institutionalized antiblack racism, sociopsychologically internalized African American double consciousness, and socioculturally expressed transcendence, especially for black folks in the rural South. The socially symbolic legacy of these signs is voiced in African American folklore and inscribed in formal art, from the blues of the railroad tracks and train whistles in Albert Murray's *Train Whistle Guitar* (1974) to the train symbolism in John Edgar Wideman's *Sent for You Yesterday* (1983) and Colson Whitehead's *John Henry Days* (2001).

These socially symbolic sites and signs represent the paradoxical and ironic ontology and epistemology of most modern black Americans with Southern ancestry and heritage: the practical and spiritual way of coming to consciousness of being in the world with others in a racially, economically, and culturally hierarchical social system with whites on top and blacks on the bottom. For example, Ellison's Lucius Brockway and the nameless protagonist-narrator (who is significantly both an orator and a writer) are represented in the Liberty Paint factory episode of *Invisible Man* as being paradoxically both on the margins and at the center of the economic and cultural power of American society. The use of black pigment to make the company's purest white paint wryly symbolizes this paradox while simultaneously dramatizing the absurdity of the one-drop rule. Of comparable cultural and political tragicomic resonance is Morrison's ironic framing of the setting of *Sula* with "a nigger joke." The joke tells how a white master betrayed his promise of freedom and a piece of rich, fertile bottom land to his loyal slave by giving him infertile land high up in the hills. The land is high up from us, Morrison writes wryly and the master states disingenuously, "'but when God looks down, it's the bottom. That's why we call it so. It's the bottom of heaven—best land there is.'"[117]

"We need to recognize," as black British cultural studies critic Hazel V. Carby persuasively argues in "The Multicultural Wars,"

> that we live in a society in which systems of domination and subordination are structured through processes of racialization that continuously interact with all other forces of socialization. Theoretically, we should be arguing that everyone in this social order has been constructed in our political imagination as a racialized subject. In this sense, it is important to think about the invention of the category of whiteness as well as of

> blackness and, consequently, to make visible what is rendered invisible when viewed as the normative state of existence: specifically the white point in space from which we tend to identify difference. If, instead, we situated *all* North American peoples as racialized subjects of our political imagination, we would see that processes of racialization influenced all our work.[118]

The influence of these processes is most compellingly illustrated in the centrality of the social and literary construction of racial and ethnic identities, both black and white, in the work of Nobel Prize–winner Toni Morrison, including her literary criticism in *Playing in the Dark* (1992).

On another level, in "Representing Whiteness in the Black Imagination" bell hooks, who wrote her doctoral dissertation on Toni Morrison and who focuses primarily in her cultural criticism on the advocacy of feminism as a radical political movement to end sexist oppression, argues for the interrelatedness of racial, class, and sexual domination. Her analysis begins with an anecdote about the heated debates of white students in her class concerning the ways the black students expressed their knowledge about survival in a white supremacist social order. The white students' contestation of the knowledge that the black students acquired from other black folks who, as domestic servants from slavery through the present, had closely scrutinized the ways of white folks, was instructive for hooks. After illuminating the willful innocence of her white students in maintaining their power, prestige, and privilege, hooks writes perceptively: "They have a deep emotional investment in the myth of 'sameness' even as their actions reflect the primacy of whiteness as a sign informing who they are and how they think."[119] Because such systems of domination as imperialism, colonialism, and racism have resulted in many black folks internalizing negative perceptions of blackness, hooks argues, "blacks who imitate whites (adopting their values, speech, habits of being, etc.) continue to regard whiteness with suspicion, fear, and even hatred."[120] Similarly, as I did in *The Afro-American Novel and Its Tradition*, I continue to make the case in this book that ambivalence is the most common response of black people to the antiblack racism of most whites and many blacks. *The Contemporary African American Novel: Its Folk Roots and Modern Literary Branches* also continues to challenge arguments that all oppositional African American cultural nationalist models are methodologically reductionist and inadequate for illuminating critical analyses of the complexities of racial difference and cultural expressivity in life and literature.

The Vernacular Tradition and the Rhetoric, Dialectics, and Dialogics of the Contemporary African American Novel

While I am skeptical at best about the relevance to African American life and literature of the apparently infinite varieties of postmodern theory and poststructural practice, the answer to critic Tzvetan Todorov's rhetorical question in "Race, Writing, and Culture"—"Is there really no middle ground between worshipping dogmas as immutable truth and abandoning the idea of truth itself?"—is obvious.[121] Of course, there is a middle ground, but it shifts in different sociohistorical and sociocultural contexts. It shifts as people, individually and collectively, struggle to construct, maintain, or reject in life and literature different varieties and degrees of power, status, and identity. Like Fredric Jameson, I "posit, not the disappearance of the great master-narratives, but their passage underground as it were, their continuing but now unconscious effectivity as a way of 'thinking about' and acting in our current situation."[122] Authors, narrators, and characters in narratives express this struggle for authenticity, authority, and agency in relations to these buried master narratives, which Jameson calls our political unconscious, in different empowering configurations and narrative strategies of rhetoric, dialectics, and dialogics.

Although the distinctions among these empowering narrative strategies and patterns inform the analysis in *The Afro-American Novel and Its Tradition*, they are more fully developed in this volume. Since Aristotle's *Rhetoric*, Plato's *Phaedrus* and *Gorgias*, and, more recently, Wayne C. Booth's *Rhetoric of Fiction* and Mikhail Bakhtin's *Dialogic Imagination*, the distinction among rhetorical, dialectical, and dialogical discourse has been a topic of contention among their different advocates. In a 1977 interview, Foucault argues that "neither the dialectic, as logic of contradictions, nor semiotics, as the structure of communication, can account for the intrinsic intelligibility of conflicts." As a philosopher and social theorist, he therefore advocates "analyses in terms of the genealogy of relations of force, strategic developments, and tactics."[123] Although Foucault, like most postmodernists, did not focus on the identity formations and survival strategies of peoples of African descent, his definition of strategies as "winning solutions" to the oppositional strategies of others in different contexts is nevertheless useful for analyzing the various deployments of rhetoric, dialectics, and dialogics in different narratives.

In "Dialogics as an Art of Discourse in Literary Criticism," rhetorician Don Bialostosky provides an alternative, yet useful explanation of these distinctions. According to Bialostosky, dialectics seek to discover the truth of ideas or theses through the impersonal relation of such terms as confirmation and contradiction and antithesis and synthesis. Because rhetoric seeks to persuade, it is primarily concerned with the relations of agreement and disagreement among persons of divergent interests and parties. In contrast, striving "for comprehensive responsiveness and responsibility to the consequential person-ideas of a time, culture, community, or discipline," dialogic "concerns the relations among persons articulating their ideas in response to one another, discovering their mutual affinities and oppositions, their provocations to reply, their desires to hear more, or their wishes to change the subject."[124] Because of their struggle in contesting borders and crossing boundaries in their quest for self-definition and self-determination as black Americans of African descent and as individual artists, African American novelists deploy all three of these strategies and modes of discourse in deconstructing and reconstructing sacred and secular master narratives. In the tradition of the African American novel these include such core master narratives as the myths of origin and apocalypse in the Books of Genesis and Revelation respectively, the Declaration of Independence, the Constitution of the United States, and the American Dream.

The structure of my critical analysis of the tradition of the contemporary African American novel is therefore both diachronic and synchronic. The arrangement of authors and texts will illuminate thematic, stylistic, and structural change over a period of time and coexistence or coincidence of conventions in the same period of time. This dual movement of continuity and change reveals the dominance of rhetoric and dialectics in the early romances and novels, but an increasing experiment with dialogics as well as rhetoric and dialectics in contemporary narratives. Philosophical abstractions and ethical platitudes, however, are mere academic dialectics and hollow rhetoric without social dialogue, specific cultural productions, and organized political action. The most common discursive conventions that are used in distinctive patterns in the narratives examined in subsequent chapters—distinctive literary patterns which I frequently include under the tropes of double vision and repetition with a black difference—are call-and-response, irony, parody, pastiche, and paradox.

2 / *The Roots of the Contemporary African American Novel*

The history of the American Negro is the history of this strife—this longing to attain self-conscious manhood, to merge his double self into a better and truer self. In this merging he wishes neither of the older selves to be lost. He would not Africanize America, for America has too much to teach the world and Africa. He would not bleach his Negro soul in a flood of white Americanism, for he knows that Negro blood has a message for the world. He simply wishes to make it possible for a man to be both a Negro and an American, without being cursed and spit upon by his fellows, without having the doors of Opportunity closed roughly in his face.

W. E. B. DU BOIS
The Souls of Black Folk

THE quest of early African American novelists to define, chronicle, and celebrate imaginatively the experiences of black people in the United States was influenced by the impact of societal and ideological anti-black racism on the development of their distinctive hybrid culture and double consciousness. This chapter will therefore survey the sociohistorical, sociocultural, and sociopsychological landscape of the double consciousness of the majority of African Americans and of the African American novel. It will also identify and examine the African and African American folk roots, residually oral vernacular forms, literary sources, and branches of the African American novel. From the tragicomic mixed racial heritage of early female protagonists and the gift of gab and shrewdness of puttin' on massa of John, the trickster slave, to the dramatic oratorical eloquence of the old preacher John Brown and the innovative improvisational sounds of "Singing" Johnson, the creator of spirituals in Johnson's *Autobiography of an Ex-Colored Man*, the representation of the quest for black male identity in the tradition of the African American novel begins to shift its narrative blend of romance and realism. Based on the imaginative power of the authority, authenticity, and agency of the authors, characters, structures, and styles of the texts, this shift continues even more compellingly and radically in the modern and contemporary eras from the spiritual and sexual ambivalence of gay John Grimes in Baldwin's *Go Tell It on the Mountain* to the legacy of the legendary heroic physical and spiritual courage of John Henry in resisting the domination of modern technology in Whitehead's *John Henry Days*.

Sociohistorical, Sociocultural, and Sociopsychological Landscape

Is "the Negro only an American and nothing else" with "no values and culture to guard and protect"?[1] If he is not, what are the sources of the authenticity, authority, and agency of black American culture and character? To what degree are they a product of Africa? Of American racism? Of language? Of poverty or economic marginality? Of the will to be black? The notion that black Americans have no culture or that black culture is merely a colorful variety of the culture of poverty is refuted by revisionist scholarship of the 1970s in African American studies.[2] The answers to these questions concerning the identity formation of African Americans are embedded in the interdisciplinary sociohistorical, sociocultural, and sociopsychological landscape and roots of African American double consciousness and of the African American novel.

The network of understandings that defines black American culture and informs black American double consciousness has evolved from the unique pattern of experiences of black people in North America, experiences, as sociologist Robert Blauner acutely observes, "that no other national or racial minority or lower class group shared."[3] These experiences—of Africa, the transatlantic or Middle Passage, slavery, Southern plantation tradition, emancipation, Reconstruction, post-Reconstruction, Northern migration, urbanization, industrialization, and racism—have produced a residue of shared memories and frames of reference for black Americans. The most insidious and iniquitous of these experiences is racism.

Although the anthropologist Ruth Benedict has been credited as first using the term "racism" in English in the 1940s, it is common knowledge that as a condition and custom it clearly predates her modern use of the word.[4] The provocative research of social scientists Michael Omi and Howard Winant supports anecdotal and empirical evidence in the literary tradition of African Americans "that concepts of race were always politically contested" and that master narratives of the innate superiority of white people are only culturally relative and provisional as in postmodernism. According to Omi and Winant, racism is a "fundamental characteristic of social projects which create or reproduce structures of domination based on essentialist categories of race."[5] Because the racially subordinate lack the political, economic, and cultural power to institutionalize and implement structurally their prejudices and will, their oppositional strategies to the racially dominant cannot be validly called racism in reverse. When faced with such racist practices as de facto or de jure discrimination or exclusion based on fallacious assumptions and categorical propositions of biological determinism that empowers one group over another, members of subordinated or subjugated racial groups are frequently forced to unite in order to defend their interests and even their lives. "Such 'strategic essentialism' should not . . . be simply equated with the essentialism practiced by dominant groups," Omi and Winant remind us, "nor should it prevent the interrogation of internal group differences."[6]

We are also reminded that "for most of U.S. history, the state's [California's] main objective in its racial policy was repression and exclusion."[7] The first attempt to define American citizenship in the Naturalization Law of 1790 declared that only free white immigrants could qualify. Because enslaved peoples of African descent were disingenuously identified as "Persons" and thereby erased or marginalized as racialized subjects in the U.S. Constitution, the federal rights of citizenship were not conferred on black Americans until the Fourteenth Amendment in 1868. We should also be mindful of other policies and acts of racial repression and exclusion by whites. Indigenous American peoples, for example, were explicitly excluded from citizenship in the U.S. Constitution in 1787, and citizenship was not conferred upon all of them until 1924 in the Snyder Act.[8] Also, Asian immigrants did not qualify to become naturalized citizens until after the passage of the McCarran-Walter Act of 1952.[9]

Although there is no valid scientific evidence of a biological relationship between culture and race, the perception of invidious physical differences and the acquisitive urge of economic opportunism by the white majority served as the principal basis for the social exclusion, subjugation, and exploitation, the colonization and ultimate enslavement for life, of African captives and African Americans. Because African Americans are neither biologically homogeneous nor necessarily identifiable by racial features in individual cases as having African ancestry, they are not completely deprived of social mobility and do not suffer total isolation in racially segregated ghettoes, colonies, or communities. Yet the systematic barriers of exclusion and discrimination based on perceivable and socially defined racial differences, such as the position that one drop of black blood makes a person a Negro and the disingenuous "separate but equal" *Plessy v. Ferguson* Supreme Court decision of 1896 with its blatant clause stating that blacks had no rights that whites were obliged to recognize, are more important in the distinctive history of the experiences and the double consciousness of black Americans than slavery, emancipation, and the long march to the urban North.

Few black Americans would therefore seriously take issue with Ralph Ellison's rewriting of double consciousness as double vision to express his view that

> being a Negro American has to do with the memory of slavery and the hope of emancipation and the betrayal by allies and the revenge and contempt inflicted by our former masters after the Reconstruction, and the myths, both Northern and Southern, which are propagated in justification of that betrayal. It involves, too, a special attitude toward the waves of immigrants who have come later and passed us by. It has to do with a

> special perspective on the national ideals and national conduct, and with a tragicomic attitude toward the universe. . . . It involves a rugged initiation into the mysteries and rites of color. . . . It imposes the uneasy burden and occasional joy of a complex double vision, a fluid, ambivalent response to men and events which represents, at its finest, a profoundly civilized adjustment to the cost of being human in this modern world.[10]

Thus, the historical pattern of contradictions between the ideals of white America and the reality of black America as group formations based on the dynamics of culture and descent has resulted in what I prefer to examine as both ethnically and racially different cultural heritages. Like Ralph Ellison, I also prefer to interrogate the resulting process of a complex double consciousness, socialized ambivalence, and double vision as a healthful rather than pathological adjustment by blacks to the rigors of the New World.

This healthful adjustment of Africans, their acculturation, according to anthropologist and Africanist Melville Herskovits's theory of African survivals in the New World, especially in the United States, occurred through the processes of retention, reinterpretation, and syncretism.[11] Retention is the continuity of some African interpretations of phenomena, reinterpretation is the explanation of white cultural patterns according to African principles, and syncretism is the amalgamation of African and American cultural patterns and sign systems. Despite such weaknesses in Herskovits's theory as the "notion of West African cultural homogeneity that is not supported by more recent scholarship,"[12] it is conventional wisdom among African Americanists that the processes of retention, reinterpretation, and syncretism began in 1619 in the English colonies of North America when twenty captives were brought to Jamestown, Virginia, in a Dutch man-of-war and sold as servants. Although they were called "neegars" by the white colonists, they actually came from heterogeneous West African tribes or, in the more modern language of social science, ethnic groups, and their acculturation actually began before they reached North America.

Anthropologists Sidney Mintz and Richard Price reveal that new social ties and cultural patterns began to develop with the earliest interactions of captive Africans in the slave coffles and factories in Africa, as well as during the Middle Passage. They argue persuasively that "most West African religions seem to have shared certain fundamental assumptions about the nature of causality and the ability of divination to reveal specific causes." The people who practiced these African religions also shared beliefs in the need to celebrate and maintain close harmony and balance between such realms as the physical and spiritual—especially humans and deities, the living and the dead, and the community and the individual. Once an African " 'exchanged' ritual assistance" during a moment of crisis with another African from a different cultural group, "there would already exist a microcommunity with a nascent religion that was in a real sense, its own."[13]

A hybrid religion was not the only cultural form and social institution that Africans constructed during the complex acculturative process that transformed them into African Americans with mixed cultural identities. As John Hope Franklin, the doyen of African American historians, states, at least two acculturative processes involving language as well as religion were occurring at the same time in the New World. The first was interaction among Africans of various different cultures: "This produced a somewhat different set of customs and practices, but these were still manifestly rooted deep in the African experience. This was especially true where large numbers of Africans resided in the same place, as in the Sea Islands, where they could preserve certain religious practices and even language patterns. At the same time, there was the interaction of African and Western cultures, which doubtless changed the culture patterns of both groups."[14] Unlike the first white immigrants and indentured servants, the Africans were systematically deprived of their Old World cultural links and social support systems in order to transform them into slaves for life. This development, which began as early as 1640, was the result of the interplay of the economics of slavery and the psychology of racism, for the increasing demand for cheap labor led to political acts in the late seventeenth century and a social ideology by the late nineteenth century that imposed severe restrictions on the civil rights of blacks and denied their human rights.[15]

By 1638 slaves were introduced into Massachusetts, and in 1641 slavery was given legal sanction in that colony by the "Body of Liberties," statutes prohibiting human bondage "unless it be lawfull Captives taken in just warres, and such strangers as willingly sell themselves or are sold to us."[16] Virginia reinforced the system of slavery by legal statute in 1661, imposed a fine for interracial fornication in 1662, banned interracial marriages in 1691, defined slaves explicitly as real estate in 1705, and deprived freed blacks of the right to vote in 1723. According to a Maryland law of 1663, "All negroes or other slaves within the province, and all negroes and other slaves to be hereafter imported into the province, shall serve *durante vita*; and all children born of any negro or other slave, shall be slaves as their fathers were for the term of their lives."[17] Because many slaves were fathered by whites, the law was soon changed so that the mother's status determined the children's. Subsequent eighteenth- and nineteenth-century antiblack statutes and jurisprudence concerning everything from literacy to politics institutionalized the racist ideology and treatment of blacks, bondsmen and freedmen alike, as biologically and culturally inferior by nature, possessing no rights from the cradle to the grave that whites were obliged to recognize.

Despite the struggle of blacks for freedom during the War for Independence and the Industrial Revolution, the economic, political, and psychological compulsion of colonial whites to transform them into docile Christians and subhumans is a matter of record. Cotton Mather's *Rules for the Societies of Negroes* (1693) is typical of the general attitude of the Puritan and Anglican divines, whose interest in Christianizing blacks was primarily to make them obedient, honest, useful servants. That all references to slavery and the slave trade were deleted from the final draft of the Declaration of Independence because of the strong objections of some Southern and a few Northern delegates is one of several examples of the class and color interests of members of the Second Continental Congress.[18] Although manumission and antislavery societies increased after the war, the provisions of the Constitutional Convention of 1787 that sanctioned the importation of slaves until 1808 and mandated the return by the states of fugitive slaves to their owners are additional illustrations.[19] If it is true, therefore, that the framers of the Constitution were dedicated to the principle of freedom, it is no less true, as John Hope Franklin points out, that they were equally, if not even more, dedicated to the ethnocentric, socioeconomic proposition that "government should rest upon the domination of property."[20]

Nonetheless, even though the antislavery movement was apparently disrupted by the moral and political repudiation of the inalienable rights of blacks at the Constitutional Convention, many African Americans still felt that the authority of the Declaration of Independence confirmed their own convictions of equality before God and held out the promise of "Life, Liberty, and the Pursuit of Happiness" for them as well as for whites. Aware of the painful paradox of their status and struggle, many slaves futilely petitioned legislative bodies for their freedom. Others fought with greater success for theirs in the War for Independence, which for blacks was more a matter of freedom from physical bondage than freedom to participate fully in the political and economic structure of the emerging nation. After the war, the invention of the cotton gin in1793 revitalized the slave trade, and the missionary view that Africans were heathens in need of the Christianizing influence of Western civilization became the popular rationalization for zealously exploiting them. In short, the economic exploitation of early black Americans by white colonists and colonialists, together with the political and religious justification for it by the white founding fathers and Puritan divines, provides a vivid illustration of the different frames of reference within which the two races constructed their identities. For example, black abolitionist novelists like William Wells Brown and Martin Delany, on the one hand, and white novelists like the proslavery John Pendleton Kennedy and the antislavery Harriet Beecher Stowe on the other, saw the world from different vantage points. They perceived and reconstructed the reality of their identities and lives from radically different positions of power, privilege, and prestige in the racially and socially mixed but stratified antebellum and postbellum South.

Reconstruction and the rampant growth of industrial capitalism in the New South and the nation came. But on the heels of the Civil War and abolition of slavery the legendary promise of forty acres and a mule—the economic reparation and opportunity that was imperative in order for former slaves to compete equally with whites and to realize the American Dream of the times as socially equal independent farmers—was never fulfilled.[21] And the power of the black ballot was short-lived. The post-Reconstruction caste system with its Jim Crowism, disfranchisement, white terrorism, and Black Codes, which were very similar to antebellum Slave Codes, soon relegated the majority of the more than four million landless, illiterate freedmen to such a debased social status that they were little more than slaves. Thousands were lured to the cities or fled North for security. At the same time, an emerging urban black middle class, based on fair complexion, formal education, and puritan values (patriarchy, thrift, temperance, piety, and industry), began to reconstruct and to define more sharply the character and culture of the African American nation within a nation. This new class of blacks continued developing separate economic, social, and cultural institutions while simultaneously accelerating its fight for equality with the national white majority. It is not surprising, then, that early African American novelists attempted to understand and reconcile the tensions in their consciousness that resulted from these color, class, and gender conflicts and mixture of differences. On the one hand, these tensions and conflicts were between white American society and black American culture, and on the other, they were between the descendants of the free blacks and mulattoes, the relatively privileged class of phenotypically biracial house slaves who were usually fathered but unacknowledged by white males, and the unprivileged darker, less obviously racially mixed field slaves who were stereotyped as having neither history nor culture as a people other than slavery.

The popular contemporary notion of black Americans as people with no past is, for the most part, derived from the sociological theories of Gunnar Myrdal, a distinguished Swedish economist, and E. Franklin Frazier, an eminent black American sociologist. Based on the fallacious assumptions of a direct correspondence between culture and society, of culture passing in one direction from Euro-American masters to African slaves, and of white middle-class values as the norm for black Americans, Myrdal's *American Dilemma* and Frazier's *Negro in the United States* conclude that the African American was "an exaggerated American" whose values were pathological elaborations of general American values.[22] As stated earlier, research in anthropology, sociology, history, folklore, musicology, and linguistics by revisionist scholars not only challenges these conclusions. This research also convincingly supports the beliefs long held by many African Americans that the conflicts between black culture and white society have resulted in creative as well as destructive tensions in black people and their communities.

Although culture and society are closely related, the fallacious assumption of a direct correlation between them is the source of much confusion about the relationship of black American culture to white American society and of Euro-American culture to African American character. Much of this confusion, it seems to me, is a result of the historical development of the idea of culture, first, as a process of natural growth or human training; next, as a general state or habit of mind; then, as the general state of intellectual development in a society; later, as the general body of arts; and, finally, in this century, as a whole way of life.[23] Some of this confusion can be cleared up if we follow the interpretations of culture by anthropologists Clifford Geertz and Sidney Mintz. In *The Interpretation of Cultures*, Geertz defines culture as "an historically transmitted pattern of meanings embodied in symbols, a system of inherited conceptions expressed in symbolic forms by means of which men communicate, perpetuate, and develop their knowledge about and attitudes toward life." More concisely, Mintz interprets culture "as a kind of resource, and society as a kind of arena—the distinction between sets of historically available alternatives or forms on the one hand, and the societal circumstances or settings within which these forms may be employed, on the other." The emphasis is on culture as a dynamic, complex process in which organized groups in particular contexts use symbolic and material forms to "confirm, reinforce, maintain, change, or deny particular arrangements of status, power, and identity."[24]

"The cultural patterns that shape the behavior of people in groups," as sociologist Charles A. Valentine reminds us, "should not be confused with the structure of institutions or social systems, even though each is obviously dependent on the other."[25] Cultural codes such as interaction rituals and language behavior, for example, have their genesis in society but are neither lost nor acquired overnight, whether their ostensible loss is the result of the oppressive conditions imposed by the slave system or in the urban ghettos. For these codes are an integral part of a symbolic system of shared associations that has an inner coherence and logic quite different, though not completely divorced, from social or economic realities. As historian Herbert G. Gutman notes, "even in periods of radical economic and social change powerful cultural continuities and adaptations continue to shape the historical behavior of diverse working class populations."[26] Whether the means of expression is African Americans "puttin' on massa," singing sorrow songs, wailing the blues, shouting the gospel, spinning Brer Rabbit tales, rapping about the Signifying Monkey, or writing an apocalyptic novel, the meaning of these cultural forms or socially symbolic acts will be more or less apparent to those who belong to the social or ethnic group that habitually practices, acquires, or invents them. For, as Mintz writes, "appropriate practice confirms a network of understanding, or symbolic accord, corresponding to the networks of social relations within which persons define themselves, act and interact."[27] One of the major socially symbolic acts and cultural forms that contributes to the distinctive authenticity, authority, and agency of the African American novel is the slave narrative.

Slave narratives and black autobiographies provide dramatic personal testimonies of the discovery of antiblack racism in the process of secondary acculturation into the larger white society. At some point the process of surviving antiblack racism frustrates individuals in their efforts to reconcile the tension of their evolving double consciousness and to realize their potential wholeness, unity, or balance as both black people and American citizens. Most African Americans are then compelled to turn primarily to their ethnic group for protection and direction. Within the ethnic group blacks are disciplined to internalize these tensions or to transform the aborted social energy into cultural energy and expression. Over a long period, this process of acculturation has settled in the deep consciousness of the individuals who went through it as both self-protective and compensatory cultural behavior, the double consciousness that African American novelists, sometimes self-consciously but often unconsciously, illumine for readers. According to social scientists Peter Berger and Thomas Luckman, "as this experience is designated and transmitted linguistically . . . it becomes accessible and, perhaps, strongly relevant to individuals who have never gone through it."[28] Thus, as Robert Blauner notes, "the black cultural experience more resembles an alternating current than it does a direct current. The movement toward ethnicity and distinctive consciousness has been paralleled by one inducing more 'Americanization' in action and identity."[29] At the same time, of course, white American culture was becoming first Africanized and then African Americanized, especially by music.

A brief examination of the historical debate between Melville J. Herskovits and E. Franklin Frazier sheds further light on the relationship of black culture to white society and of European American culture to African American consciousness. Until the black cultural movement of the 1960s, many social scientists, taking their cue from Frazier, had strong objections to Herskovits's interdisciplinary approach and radical theories about African cultural survivals and social continuities. In their apparent eagerness to join ideological ranks against a study that stressed cultural differences between white and black Americans at a time when the nation was on the threshold of World War II, they blinded themselves to the biases of Frazier as a sociologist to blur cultural and social concepts in overstating his case concerning African survivals in the United States. As a student of Robert E. Park, an eminent social scientist at the University of Chicago, Frazier was influenced by theoretical models of the impact of modern industrialism and urbanization on American ethnic groups, especially Park's theories of social disorganization and the marginal man, that is, a racial, social, and cultural hybrid who lives on the borders or margins of two groups.[30]

Whereas social structure was an aspect of culture for white anthropologist Herskovits, culture was a product of social organization for black sociologist Frazier.

In 1937, in a sociopsychological context similar to that in which Du Bois had earlier coined the metaphor of double consciousness, which I will discuss shortly, Herskovits described the adjustment of Haitians to the sociopsychological conflict resulting from the contradictory imperatives of European and African cultural traditions as "socialized ambivalence." This process creates the many shifts in allegiance that continually take place and the changes in attitude in everyday association. It involves selection, revamping, and recombining the elements of the contributing cultures, "with the result that the ensuing combinations, though of recognizable derivation, differ from their aboriginal forms." By proposing socialized ambivalence as "a more realistic understanding of the individuals in other cultures who have likewise fallen heir to conflicting traditions," Herskovits indirectly and anthropologically reinterprets and extends the sociopsychological process that Du Bois in 1897 developed as a metaphor to describe the bicultural identity of black Americans.[31] Relying on this psychological model, analogical reasoning, comparative historical analysis, and vague, new anthropological concepts, Herskovits, in *The Myth of the Negro Past*, boldly challenged the prevailing ideology of his day concerning black Americans as a socially disorganized people without a past. As indicated earlier in this chapter, he advanced the theory that through the processes of retention, reinterpretation, and syncretism the African heritage was a continuing force in black American life. This heritage was primarily the culture of West and Central African peoples of the Sudanic and Bantu language groups south of the Sahara, especially the Yoruba and Dahomeans. "The weakest part of Herskovits' argument," according to historian Albert J. Raboteau, "is his contention that he has found African retentions in the institutional form and theology of certain types of black churches. He is more convincing when he speaks of 'patterns of motor behavior' and 'folk belief" that involve the acculturative processes of reinterpretation and syncretism."[32]

Frazier also disagreed with Herskovits's theory of African retentions, arguing in *The Negro in the United States* that over the years African social institutions like the extended family system, the primary institution of cultural transmission, were destroyed by slavery. Although on its surface this seems plausible, on a deeper symbolic level many slave narratives and nineteenth-century novels, like *Clotel*, *Blake*, and *Iola Leroy*, reveal a unique blend of extended and nuclear family systems whose ruptured yet still vital filial ties prompted countless postbellum freedmen to undertake long, arduous searches to reunite their dispersed families. The treatment of surrogate black families in *Many Thousand Gone* (1965), *Jubilee* (1966), and *The Autobiography of Miss Jane Pittman* (1971) provides additional support for Herskovits's concept of the reinterpretation of African kinship networks.

In any event, when Frazier, whose primary interest was in the social structures rather than in the cultural forms, concludes that "Negroes acquired new habits and modes of thought, and whatever elements of African culture were retained lost their original meaning in becoming fused with their experiences in the New World," he is on firm ground. But when he jumps from the premise of an early fusion of African culture with New World experiences to the hasty conclusion that in the "process of adjusting themselves to American civilization, the majority of the Negroes have sloughed off completely the African heritage," he misses the mark. In various ways and degrees the African heritage has influenced the following: such paintings as Lois Mailou Jones's "Les Fetiches" and such drawings as John Bigger's *Ananse, Web of Life in Africa*; such poetry as Countee Cullen's "Heritage" and Bob Kaufman's "African Dream"; such drama as Lorraine Hansberry's *Raisin in the Sun* and Amiri Baraka's *Slave Ship*; and such novels as William Melvin Kelley's *Dunfords Travels Everywheres*, Frank Yerby's *Dahomean*, and Charles Johnson's *Middle Passage*. But the most persuasive contemporary evidence in art history identifying specific Yoruba, Kongo, Dahomean, Mande, and Ejagham influences on the modern art and philosophies of black people throughout the Americas is Robert F. Thompson's landmark *Flash of the Spirit* (1984).[33]

Whereas it is true that the radical shift in their social arenas from Africa to West Indian and Southern plantations, and from sharecropping fields to urban factories and ghettos, resulted in black Americans adopting, adapting, or rejecting the material cultural resources of the larger white society, their symbolic universe (linguistic patterns, cognitive system, interaction rituals, and motor behavior) had its own evolutionary logic and enabled them to develop strategies to cope with their oppression. "The intersubjective context of shared meaning," as literary critic Bernhardt Ostendorf persuasively argues, "is a coherent play world which provides cognitive and emotive alternatives to an oppressive social arena, both therapy for incipient pathology and emancipation of the senses."[34] This, in part, explains the uniqueness of the double consciousness the majority of black Americans experience.

As indicated earlier, W. E. B. Du Bois was the first to describe the sociopsychological experience of black Americans as double consciousness:

> After the Egyptian and Indian, the Greek and Roman, the Teuton and Mongolian, the Negro is a sort of seventh son, born with a veil, and gifted with second-sight in this American world,—a world which yields him no true self-consciousness, but only lets him see himself through the revelation of the other world. It is a peculiar sensation, this double-

> consciousness, this sense of always looking at one's self through the eyes of others, of measuring one's soul by the tape of a world that looks on in amused contempt and pity. One ever feels his twoness,—an American, a Negro; two souls, two thoughts, two unreconciled strivings; two warring ideals in one dark body, whose dogged strength alone keeps it from being torn asunder.

This double vision and double consciousness, as we have seen, is a product of the historical dialectic in American society between black and white cultures. The end of the black American's striving, writes Du Bois, is "to be both a Negro and an American without being cursed and spit upon by his fellows, without having the doors of Opportunity closed in his face . . . to be a co-worker in the kingdom of culture, to escape both death and isolation, to husband and use his best powers and his latent genius."[35] The historical quest of black Americans, their principal canonical story, in short, is for life, liberty, and wholeness—the full development and unity of self and the black community—as a biracial, bicultural people, as Americans of African descent and African Americentric heritage.

The ideological dispute between Du Bois and Booker T. Washington, the black intellectuals who dominated the national scene and influenced the themes and characterization of novels after the death of Frederick Douglass in 1895, crystallized the political, cultural, and economic dichotomy within the black community. After the Atlanta Cotton Exposition speech of 1895 in which Washington, the Southern black leader that white industrial magnates and philanthropists supported as the successor to Douglass, compromised the civil rights of blacks to facilitate their economic growth through industrial training, he became the chief black architect of social accommodationism during the rise of industrialism in the New South. Opposition to Washington's policies and iron-fisted control was led by Du Bois, the principal spokesman of that band of militant middle-class blacks who in 1905 founded the Niagara Movement, the forerunner of the predominantly white-founded National Association for the Advancement of Colored People (NAACP). The conflict between Washington, a dark-skinned mulatto former slave from the Old Dominion, and Du Bois, a free New England–born light-skinned mulatto Brahmin, as to whether industrial training or higher education was the better means for black people to pursue their major objectives seemed irreconcilable.

But the difference between these two leaders was at bottom more a matter of personality and strategy than of principle and genealogy. Both aspired to move their race up from slavery to economic, cultural, and political freedom, literacy, and unity. Washington chose the rural Southern strategy of conciliation and benevolent despotism, inspired by the gospel of menial labor, property ownership, and the toothbrush preached by his New England school teachers. In contrast, Du Bois opted for the urban, aristocratic concept of a "Talented Tenth," his cosmopolitan term for the exceptionally gifted and qualified men and women of the race, the cultural elite, to accept the moral obligation of their good fortune in life to lead the less fortunate masses in the struggle for full American citizenship. At times Du Bois's militancy was nationalistic, and toward the end of his life, in part out of frustration with the betrayal of his countrymen and country, black as well as white, he joined the American Communist Party, renounced his citizenship, and became a citizen of Ghana. But in his more than twenty years of service to blacks through the NAACP, his clarion call was for the "New Negroes" to close ranks to achieve integration and social reform within the American system.

Clearly relative in meaning, the term "New Negro" was introduced into the African American novel by Sutton Griggs, a member of the Niagara Movement. As a student at one of the many missionary-founded black institutions in the South, the hero of Griggs's first novel, *Imperium in Imperio* (1899), leads a militant demonstration against the white administration to dramatize that "the cringing, fawning, sniffling, cowardly Negro which slavery left, had disappeared, and a new Negro, self-respecting, fearless and determined in the assertion of his rights was at hand."[36] Still struggling against racial stereotypes in 1916, William Pickens, a black writer and NAACP officer, published a collection of essays entitled *The New Negro* in which he urged that "every few years should see a book up to date on the general subject of 'The Renaissance of the Negro Race' or 'The New Negro,'" the titles of the first and final essays in his own book.[37] Nine years later Alain Locke, the first black Rhodes Scholar in 1907 and a Howard University philosophy professor, edited a special Harlem issue of *Survey Graphic*, which he subsequently revised and published as *The New Negro* (1925). This anthology heralded the coming-of-age of a new generation of black artists and galvanized support for the spirit of independence and race consciousness that animated the New Negro movement, also known as the Harlem Renaissance, of the 1920s.[38]

The political, economic, and cultural tensions within the race which culminated in the dispute between Washington and Du Bois and in the New Negro movement actually found their way into the early novel in many forms. In theme and character they are most clearly symbolized in the line commonly drawn between radicalism and conservatism, which, contrary to popular opinion, does not follow rigid color and caste lines. In Griggs's five novels, for example, the mulatto character is typically more militant and confrontational than his darker brother, but it is the relative conservatism of the latter, the Washington strategy of conciliatory politics, that is underscored as the wiser course of action. Pauline Hopkins's *Contending Forces* deals with the same intraracial tensions, and the voice calling for rhetoric rather than revolution is that of a black intellectual: "'Brute force will not accomplish anything. We must *agitate*. . . . Appeal for the justice of our cause to every civilized nation under the heavens.' "[39]

Some readers might in retrospect consider Griggs's and Hopkins's bourgeois predilections for accommodationism reprehensible in the face of political terrorism and social exploitation when compared to the revolutionary values of such contemporary novels as *Many Thousand Gone, The Spook Who Sat by the Door,* and *Plan B.* However, the ideology of the Talented Tenth—a reflection of shifting emotions and allegiances fostered by the absurdity of color discrimination and the reality of class distinctions both in the larger society and within the black community—is most lucidly expressed by one of the characters in Griggs's *Pointing the Way* (1908): "Years of development since emancipation have produced a group of cleanly, cultured, aspiring people in the Colored race. The first step in the solution of the race problem is for this group to take charge of and guide the racial thought and life."[40] In other words, to cope with the complexities of their socialized ambivalence, to reconcile the tensions of their double consciousness, the most intellectually capable and economically fortunate middle-class blacks borrowed Eurocentric forms of culture to develop their potential and to lead the masses in their common struggle for self-determination and dignity as a people. In contrast, the black majority, especially the lower class of marginally employed, underemployed, and unemployed, by virtue of their exclusion from full participation in the systems of the larger society, were more inclined toward the alternative of the continuation and revitalization of residually oral Afrocentric forms of culture.

It is certainly no secret that from the birth of the Peculiar Institution to the premature death of the Great Society, black Americans have been restricted in their exposure to the written word, the chief mode of acculturation in Euro-American society. As David Walker declared in his "Appeal" (1829), "for colored people to acquire learning in this country, makes tyrants quake and tremble on their sandy foundation."[41] In the antebellum South, for example, it was a violation of custom and law to teach blacks to read and write; and in the postbellum South nine of ten freedmen were illiterate.[42] "In white America," as cultural historian Charles Keil writes in *Urban Blues,* "the printed word—the literary tradition—and its attendant values are revered. In the Negro Community, more power resides in the spoken word and the oral tradition—good talkers abound, and the best gain power and prestige. . . ."[43] This is not to imply that African Americans are the only group who historically relied on the oral tradition for narrative models to make sense of their world. But as Richard Dorson, the doyen of Euro-American folklorists, has observed: "Only the Negro, as a distinct element of the English-speaking population, maintained a full-blown storytelling tradition. A separate Negro subculture formed within the shell of American life, missing the bounties of general education and material progress, remaining a largely oral, self-contained society with its own unwritten history and literature."[44]

African Oral Narrative Roots

Insofar as African American novelists are the cultural heirs of Western and African narrative traditions, we can more clearly and coherently understand the folk roots of the African American novel by looking first at some of the ancient forms and functions of oral literature, especially narrative, in Africa. In most African institutions, writes literary historian and critic Isidore Okpewho in his classic study *African Oral Literature,* "African oral literature is studied side by side with modern African literature because many modern African writers consciously borrow techniques and ideas from their oral traditions in constructing works dealing essentially with modern life."[45] Although, as literary historian Emmanuel Obiechina states, "the novel . . . has no strict equivalent in the oral tradition of West Africa," its rise and definition are mainly the result of social factors that mark the change of traditional, agrarian, oral cultures to modern, industrial, literate cultures.[46]

Since the pseudo-independence of African Americans in the late nineteenth century, missionaries, linguists, anthropologists, and folklorists have been collecting and publishing African stories. Oral narratives, which anthropologist William Bascom calls "verbal art" and Dorson "folklore,"[47] are an important means of maintaining the continuity and stability of traditional African cultures. For the anthropologist, myths, legends, folktales, and other forms of verbal art have four principal functions. They transmit knowledge, value, and attitudes from one generation to another, enforce conformity to social norms, validate social institutions and religious rituals, and provide a psychological release from the restrictions of society.[48] In *Oral Literature in Africa,* Ruth Finnegan stresses the flexibility of African narratives and the difficulty of establishing clear typologies.[49] For example, myth and legend, the sacred and the profane, are mixed in the story Yoruba kings tell justifying their political authority by claiming direct descent from Odudwa—the creator of the earth in Yoruba tradition. Yoruba diviners also used myth to reinforce belief in the need for making the ritual sacrifices they prescribed to maintain the harmony of the individual and the nation with the rhythms of nature. Instead of stories falling into clear-cut categories, the same story may be told in one society about a god or deity, in another about a trickster figure, and in yet another about a legendary hero; by one people it may be considered sacred truth and by another secular wisdom. Despite this frequent mixing of forms and shifting of the same tale from sacred to profane, depending on the ethnic society and specific context in which the tale is told, most West African societies make some distinction between sacred narratives, which they regard as true, and less serious tales with an entertaining and educational function.

In addition to their pedagogical, anthropological, psychological, and political functions, African oral narratives provided the fertile soil and roots for an indigenous written literature. "Most translations of African literature," writes literary critic Ulli Beier, "are in fact collections of myths, legends and fables."[50] Because of the domination of the structural-functional approach to the study of the oral tradition, however, it is only in recent years that Westerners, particularly folklorists and literary critics, have turned their attention to the relationship of African folklore (i.e., verbal art) to written literature.[51] This is not to say that the folk ideology of Johann Gottfried von Herder—critic, philosopher, and folklorist—did not have a significant impact on the thinking of nineteenth-century European writers in their quest for a national literature. On the contrary, Herder's theory of folk art as the base for a national formal art and of folksongs as the spontaneous, indigenous expression of the collective soul of a people inspired many creative nationalist writers, including the American romantics Ralph Waldo Emerson and Walt Whitman.[52] In the case of West Africans, however, it was not Herderian folk theory so much as the dialectic influence of the oral and literary traditions in societies struggling for independence and industrialization that probably inspired them to draw on their traditional narratives, proverbs, songs, and rituals for themes, structure, and style. Wole Soyinka, for example, frequently deploys the Yoruba god Ogun as a symbol of the revolutionary spirit needed by peoples of African ancestry to combat social evils. Camara Laye's *Dark Child* (1955), Ngugi wa Thiong'o's *Weep Not, Child* (1964), Chinua Achebe's *Things Fall Apart* (1958), and Amos Tutola's *Palm-Wine Drinkard* (1953) are only a few of the modern novels that have their roots in the fertile soil of African folklore. They represent the sophisticated continuation of African storytelling conventions in dialectic tension with the most popular Western form of narrative, the novel.

As for the continuation of the African storytelling tradition by black Americans, Dorson, after a close examination of the tale type and motif indices of black American folktales, concludes that "American Negro tales owed little to Africa and much to Europe and the New World."[53] Although the question of African origins and retentions remains a moot issue, most revisionist scholarship on the question is consistent with historian John Blassingame's conclusion that "however oppressive or dehumanizing the plantation was, the struggle for survival was not severe enough to crush all of the slave's creative instincts."[54] But in *From Trickster to Badman*, Afrocentric critic John W. Roberts overstates his case that "the basis on which African Americans evaluate the actions of their folk heroes as normative is deeply rooted in their African cultural heritage."[55] Rather, residual elements of the oral tradition of Africa, each fulfilling a psychological and social need in the lives of slaves, fused with the dominant white *and* indigenous Native American culture. This syncretistic process created a new system of shared symbols that, even though complementary, was different in pattern and emphases from both its European and its African antecedents. This was particularly true in the slave communities of the Old South.

African American Folk Roots

Digging into the slave past of people of African ancestry in the United States, we discover that the roots of African American folklore, the unique syncretistic blend of a significant number of African survivals with elements of white American culture, are embedded in the Old South, especially the Georgia Sea Islands and the Mississippi Delta. And they bloom perennially in the verbal, musical, and ritualistic expressions—the socially symbolic acts—of rural and urban black Americans. In 1790 when the first census was taken in the colonies, 91 percent of the black population (690,000) lived in the South. As late as 1910, 89 percent (8,900,000) still lived there. With the outbreak of World War I, blacks began pouring into Northern and Western cities: Chicago, Detroit, Philadelphia, Pittsburgh, New York, Boston, and the urban areas of California.[56] As black folks moved from the country to the city, our talk, our walk, our songs, and our stories began to take on a new attitude in expressing the authenticity, authority, and agency of our African American double consciousness. We fled the South for the North, the fields and farms for the shops and factories. We came searching for Canaan. But we found Babylon. The more things changed, the more they remained the same. We suffered contempt and pity because of the color of our skin. We remained the last to be hired and the first to be fired. Consequently, at the turn of the twenty-first century the census report reveals that more than 50 percent of black Americans, about 18,000,000, still live in the South.

It is not surprising that the early African American novel reflects the trauma of this great demographic shift from rural to urban America. Such different novels and romances as Frank Webb's *The Garies and Their Friends* (1857), Pauline Hopkins's *Contending Forces* (1900), Dunbar's *Sport of the Gods* (1902), and William Attaway's *Blood on the Forge* (1947)—in which the basic storylines unfold in Philadelphia, Boston, New York, and Pennsylvania respectively—draw on the romantic machinery of the feudal South as their heroes and heroines search for a place to be somebody and come to grips with the myth of their African American past.

Antiblack racism prevented the full participation of blacks in the dominant culture so that their need for symbols and values had to be filled by the ethnic subculture. This process encouraged the retention, reinterpretation, and syncretism of Africanisms (e.g., hoodoo, conjuring or magic, dance, field holler, work song, and folktale) that would enable eighteenth-century blacks in the United States to cope with the demands of their new life and to express the will of the group to survive. Developed mainly during the slaves' "leisure" time, these modified African cultural resources and the creation of new forms, such as the spirituals, Brer Rabbit fables, and blues, increased in-group cohesion and cultural solidarity. The need to survive the master-slave relationship occasionally led to internalizing antiblack racism and to behavior that symbolically enacted a deep-seated, irrational desire to be white. Most frequently, however, the struggle for survival led to a surface identification with the master's values and a subservient behavior pattern that exploited the disparity between white ideology and black reality. This double consciousness is revealed in the folksaying "Got one mind fuh white folk to see, 'nother fuh what I know's me." In addition, to bridge the many different African languages and to communicate with or "put on" the master, eighteenth- and nineteenth-century blacks developed pidgin and creole languages that combined aspects of African and English grammar, characterized by distinctive physical gestures, semantics, syntax, pitch, and rhythm: the process called creolization by sociolinguists Stewart and Dillard.[57] Thus from the nineteenth century on we have concurrent intraracial and interracial lines of behavioral and linguistic development. By the twentieth century, as black novels of the Harlem Renaissance illustrate, the repertoire of survival strategies and rituals continued to evolve: from Tomming, shucking and jiving, and copping a plea to signifying, sounding, playing the dozens, talking trash, and rapping.[58] Rather than stress the alleged pathological implications of these linguistic and behavioral survival strategies or symbolic acts, Ralph Ellison more appropriately and astutely interprets them as a growing sophistication in overcoming oppressive social circumstances and symbolically expressing "a complex double vision" through the cultural resources of language, music, and dissimulation.[59]

But what is the legacy of African American folk culture to the twentieth and twenty-first centuries? What values does it affirm and reject? What rituals and customs does it seek to preserve? Who are its heroes and heroines? Ellison addresses these questions in general terms when he states that folklore

> offers the first drawings of any group's character. It preserves mainly those situations which have repeated themselves again and again in the history of any given group. It describes those rites, manners, customs, and so forth, which insure the good life, or destroy it; and it describes those boundaries of feeling, thought and action which that particular group has found to be the limitation of the human condition. It projects this wisdom in symbols which express the group's will to survive; it embodies those values by which the group lives and dies. These drawings may be crude but they are nonetheless profound in that they represent the group's attempt to humanize the world.[60]

In her seminal studies of Euro-American culture, Constance Rourke reveals the complex relationship of the first popular indigenous folk characters: the Yankee, the Backwoodsman, and the Negro. Rourke alludes to the popularity of blackface minstrelsy in the 1830s as an example of how "the comic trio tended to merge into a single generic figure," but she carefully points out that "each of the trio remained distinct."[61] Similarly, a close examination of the legends and ballads of Brother Jonathan, Davy Crockett, Daniel Boone, and Paul Bunyan reveals that these narratives derive from a different frame of reference, a different sociocultural context, than those about the legendary black Preacher; John, the trickster slave; Harriet Tubman, the Moses of her people; and John Henry, the steel-driving man.

Drawing on African American folklore for inspiration and material, postbellum black novelists such as Dunbar and Chesnutt were strongly influenced in style by Southern white local colorists like Irwin Russell, Thomas Nelson Page, and Joel Chandler Harris. But the values affirmed by Page's and Harris's fictive uncles are not identical to those affirmed by Chesnutt's, and the white planter's pastoral vision in *Red Rock* (1898) lacks the double-edged irony of the black house servant's vision in *The Sport of the Gods*. Because the difference in consciousness between white American folklore and black American folklore is a difference in response to the New World and the evolution of institutionalized racism, it is not, as some historians argue, the same for all hyphenated ethnic Americans.[62] For unlike the integrationist experience of white ethnic Americans, the total response of Africans to their experience in an alien and hostile antiblack environment not only included the new modes of interaction and communication, especially language, music, and religion, that they developed among themselves for survival. The acculturative response also included those cultural forms forged in the crucible of their experience of double consciousness with whites.

Forged, however, in a society based on the pragmatism of American capitalism and the idealism of the American Creed of social equality, both Euro-American and African American folklore are marked by contradictions. Insofar as both at some level champion the values of the Protestant Ethic and are inspired by the American Dream, they are similar. But insofar as one is the lore of European and English peoples who conquered and controlled the lands and lives of Amerindians and other peoples, the white colonists, colonialists, and their descendants, and the other the lore of the embattled resisters of colonial conquest and control, the enslaved black Africans and their descendants, they are antithetical. Simply stated, traditional white American values emanate from a providential vision of history and of Euro-Americans as a chosen people, a vision that sanctions their individual and collective freedom in the pursuit of property, profit, and happiness. Radical Protestantism, Constitutional democracy, and global industrial capitalism are the white American trinity of values. In contrast, black American values emanate from a cyclical, primarily Judeo-Christian vision of history and of African Americans as a disinherited, colonized people, a vision that sanctions their resilience of spirit and pursuit of social justice. A tragicomic vision of life, a tough-minded grip on reality, an extraordinary faith in the redemptive power of suffering and patience, a highly developed talent for dissimulation, a vigorous zest for life, a wry sense of humor, and a acute sense of timing are basic black American values.[63] These values, mainly the product of the resiliency of the syncretism of African and early American cultural survivals and the resistance to class, color, and gender domination, are the major sources of tension in the themes, characters, and forms of the African American novel.

Residually Oral Forms: Oratory, Myth, Legend, Tale, and Song

"The complexity of a culture," writes British cultural critic Raymond Williams, "is to be found not only in its variable processes and their social definitions—traditions, institutions, and formations—but also in the dynamic interrelations . . . between movements and tendencies both within and beyond a specific and effective dominance."[64] Residual and emergent movements and tendencies are therefore significant in themselves as well as in what they reveal about the characteristics of the dominant system. Cultures in which oral forms compete with the dominant system of print, as in the case of the black American subculture, may thus be classified as residually or largely oral cultures.[65] In contrast to the new meanings, values, practices, and relationships represented by the emergent cultural movement and aesthetic tendencies, Williams explains, "The residual . . . has been effectively formed in the past, but it is still active in the cultural process, not only and often not at all as an element of the past, but as an effective element of the present. Thus certain experiences, meanings, and values which cannot be expressed or substantially verified in terms of the dominant culture, are nevertheless lived and practised on the basis of the residue—cultural as well as social—of some previous social and cultural institution or formation."[66] In contrast to literate cultures, residually oral cultures are basically aural, functional, collective, and direct. Like oral cultures, they stress performance, mnemonics, and improvisational skills. The tendency is to focus on the here and now, to employ some kind of formulaic mode of expression, and to subordinate the individual to the group or type. Whereas an oral culture relies primarily on sound, the spoken word, and a literate culture primarily on sight, the written word, residually oral cultures rely on the interplay or dialectic between the two. Several residually oral forms may be identified in the African American novel: oratory, myth, legend, tale, and song.

"Oratory," writes literary critic F. O. Matthiessen, "moving with the Revolution from the pulpit to the political forum, was . . . the one branch of literature in which America then had a formed tradition."[67] In other words, when the first African American novel appeared seventeen years after Ralph Emerson's call for a national literature, public addresses by both blacks and whites were among the chief means of education and diversion. The political conventions of free blacks, the Fourth of July and *Juneteenth* verbal fireworks, the soul-stirring revival meetings, the radical abolitionist forum, the refined literary societies, the bombastic declamation contests—all of these in one form or another left their mark on the African American novel. For in addition to having their sensibilities shaped by the black dialect or vernacular of their family and friends, their primary speech community, African American romancers and novelists were influenced by the impassioned performances and formal appeals of David Walker, Henry Highland Garnet, and Frederick Douglass, as well as by the grandiloquent speeches of John Q. Adams, Daniel Webster, and William Lloyd Garrison. In these contrasting modes of discourse they found rhetorical models highly suited for their own moral, social, and aesthetic purpose.

In addition to black dialect and formal public addresses, African American novelists employed ritualized black vernacular contests, especially in narratives of the 1920s and 1960s, to establish ethnic atmosphere, to delineate character, and to advance plot. Folklorist Roger D. Abrahams provides helpful insights into the use of narrative forms by modern black men to cope with the pressures of life in their community in South Philadelphia.[68] Through the ritual performance of such verbal contests as toasts, sounding, signifying, and playing the dozens, young blacks in the cities, like their forefathers in rural areas, who had used storytelling or "lying," learn to sublimate their white-provoked feelings of aggression to achieve mastery of words and their world. Whereas black men acquire much of their verbal skill from other men on street corners, in pool rooms, and in barber shops, black women pick up much of theirs from other women in their mother's kitchens, at church gatherings, and the beauty parlor.

The African American narrative most analogous to the Euro-American epic formulaic mode is the modern toast, which is a kind of mock heroic epic, composed "of some sort of picaresque or exciting introduction, action alternating with dialogue . . . and a twist ending of some sort, either a quip, and ironic comment, or a brag."[69] As in the popular black male toasts "Stackolee," "The Signifying Monkey," and "*The Titanic*," their language is highly self-conscious, artful, and frequently profane; and though highly improvisational, their dominant structure is a long sequence of balanced, four-stress-line couplets. Sounding is direct taunting or boastful insult; signifying is a more witty, elaborate, indirect form of goading or insult generally making use of irony, parody, and profanity; and playing the dozens is the explicit hyperbolic sexual insult of another person's parents, particularly the mother. Rhyme, repetition, polyrhythm, irony, parody, hyperbole, and wit are the chief conventions of these ethnic forms of oratory, the black vernacular, which is first developed by boys in play to assert masculinity among themselves and then to achieve a sense of security in their contact with the hostility of the larger society. These ethnic forms of speech are used in a distinctive manner by such different black novelists as Paul L. Dunbar, Charles W. Chesnutt, Rudolph Fisher, Zora N. Hurston, Richard Wright, Ralph Ellison, John O. Killens, John A. Williams, Sarah Wright, Alice Childress, Alice Walker, Gloria Naylor, Gayl Jones, Clarence Major, Trey Ellis, and Ishmael Reed.

A blend of oratory, oral narrative, and song, the chanted sermon, developed primarily by Southern black fundamentalist preachers, also contributes to the distinctive character of some black American novels. "The sermons almost never rhyme," writes Bruce A. Rosenberg in *The Art of the American Folk Preacher*; "they seldom alliterate, the imagery is meager, yet they are poetic. The lines are metrical, the language is ordered, and the effect is often pleasing." Unlike the characteristics of conventional oratory and preaching, in the chanted sermon "the verses are preponderantly formulaic (in the Parry-Lord sense), there are extended passages with parallel syntax, and the constructions are direct with almost no periodicity." It is important to note that the preachers interviewed by Rosenberg rejected, as I suspect most blacks raised in the Baptist, Methodist, and Holiness faiths would reject, his formulaic theory and would hardly agree with his observation about the meager imagery of the sermons. Nevertheless, his definition of the chanted sermon as "groups of words, which, when recited, are metrically and semantically consistent, related in form by the repetition and identical relative placement of at least half the words in the group" is supported by evidence that "the techniques of composition appear to be similar."[70]

More important, as black theologian and preacher Henry H. Mitchell confirms in *Black Preaching*, the major convention of chanted sermons—a highly dramatic, imaginative, improvisational rendering of the Word of God—is the call-and-response.[71] Derived from the African musical practice of alternating improvised lines with fixed refrains, call-and-response in chanted sermons is the spirited, spontaneous antiphonal exchange between the preacher and his congregation as they participate in a profoundly intimate fellowship. Among the major testimonials to the influence of the chanted sermon on black novelists are Hurston's dramatic "The Wounds of Jesus" in *Jonah's Gourd Vine*, Richard Wright's parody "The Death Train to Heaven or Hell" in *Lawd Today*, Ellison's messianic "Let My People Go" story of the life and death of the Founder in *Invisible Man*, Baldwin's fiery text on "The Wages of Sin" in *Go Tell It on the Mountain*, and Morrison's impassioned call in the woods from an unchurched preacher in *Beloved* for black folks to love themselves.

Symbolic representations of crucial life situations that are shared by a people, residually oral African American myths are moral as well as speculative stories that are archetypal in pattern and ethnic in content. They explain the origins of things, activities of gods, and historical human dilemmas. They are therefore generally a fusion of myth and legend that are concerned with the founders of an ethnic group or lineage and that justify the taboos and authority of the group or lineage. The two principal myth-legends that inform the early novel are a messianic delivery from oppression and an eschatological overthrow of white supremacy, rewritten from the oral tradition and the King James Bible.[72] Mainly self-educated and missionary school–trained preachers and teachers fired with a passion for justice and social reform, the first generation of black novelists were frequently concerned with how sanctification and sin, virtue and vice, in this world related to the ultimate destiny of man. And because injustice was the rule rather than the exception for blacks, the hope of future rewards for the racially oppressed and punishment for their oppressors was appealing to many, especially the older generation. Pious, self-effacing types like the Lockleys in George Pryor's *Neither Bond Nor Free* (*A Plea*) (1902) believed "that in the world about them all things worked together for good."[73] Even though for many blacks the hand of Providence assured the triumph of the good eventually, it moved too slowly for some. Rejecting his father-in-law's pious counsel, Martin Delany's young hero in *Blake* (1859) declares:

> "It is not wickedness, Daddy Joe; you don't understand these things at all. If a thousand years with us is but a day with God, do you think that I am required to wait all that time?"
>
> "Don't, Henry, don't! De wud say 'stan still an' see de salbation.'"
>
> "That's no talk for me, Daddy Joe; I've been 'standing still' long enough—I'll 'stand still' no longer."[74]

Sermons, prayers, spirituals, hymns, and sayings are the residual oral forms employed in African American novels by such different novelists as Ellison, Baldwin, Margaret Walker, Toni Morrison, George Bennett, and Randall Kenan to reinterpret, reenact, or reject this Judeo-Christian redemptive view of history.

Whereas in her romance Pauline Hopkins writes: "Surely the Negro race must be productive of some valuable specimens, if only from the infusion which amalgamation with a superior race must eventually bring," Delany ends his with the ominous line: "Woe be unto those devils of whites, I say."[75] Hopkins and Delany illustrate the socialized ambivalence caused by the myth of white supremacy and by the social rituals and color symbolism that justify and perpetuate it. One of the functions of the artist, as Ellison states, is to recognize these social rituals and illumine their deep psychological meanings.[76] It is not surprising, therefore, to discover that the themes, plots, and characterization of the early novels in particular are frequently concerned with the myth and rituals of white supremacy and the omnipresent reality of evil perpetrated by whites. In many cases white and black characters are idealized, but even in these, as well as in the more realistic novels, the attitude of the author and narrator is ambivalence; and irony and parody are frequently at work. "God made us all," says the heroine in Chesnutt's *House behind the Cedars* (1900), "and for some good purpose, though we may not always see it. He made some people white, and strong, and masterful, and—heartless. He made others black and homely, and poor and weak—."[77]

Legends are narratives justifying or protesting the relative social position of ethnic groups, classes, and lineages (e.g., blacks and whites, refined people of color and unrefined black laborers, house servants and field hands, Baptists and Methodists, mulattoes and "pure" blacks). Legends are also integral to the tradition of the African American novel. *Clotel* and Barbara Chase-Riboud's *Sally Hemings* (1979) and *The President's Daughter* (1994), for example, are imaginative rewritings of the legend about Thomas Jefferson's illegitimate daughter by Sally Hemings. The legends of black heroes and heroines such as Toussaint L'Ouverture, Cinqué, Nat Turner, Denmark Vesey, Gabriel Prosser, Harriet Tubman, John Henry, and Booker T. Washington are common leitmotifs in the early novels. But Arna Bontemps's *Black Thunder* (1936) was the first sustained formal retelling of a traditional story by an African American novelist of the self-assertion, the agency, of black slaves for their freedom. Ironically, this historical romance is not about the messianic revolt of Nat Turner in 1831, the most historically and religiously important slave rebellion in America, but about the abortive large-scale plot of Gabriel Prosser in 1800.[78]

Tales are brief, exciting, single-incident narratives about tricksters; about the ubiquitous, sometimes moral, sometimes amoral, black preacher; about the "bad nigger"; and about the "super-bad" hustler. Like legends, tales or "lies," as the pre–World War II generation of black folk called them, have been used in various ways with varying degrees of sophistication by African American novelists. For example, Brown employs several black trickster tales in *Clotel* to illustrate the ingenious strategies and disguises used to escape from slavery. In *Imperium in Imperio* Griggs draws on the traditional tale of the chicken-eating preacher for comic relief. Supernatural and realistic tales are major influences on the themes, style, and structure of the short stories in Dunbar's *Folks from Dixie* and Chesnutt's *Conjure Woman*. Modern and contemporary novelists also reveal the continuity of traditional folktales. Hurston empowers Janie Crawford to liberate herself and her friend Pheoby through storytelling; Wright combines tales about "bad niggers" for his delineation of Bigger Thomas; and Ellison endows Trueblood with the gifts of the traditional storyteller. Such contemporary novelists as John O. Killens, William Melvin Kelley, Ronald Fair, Charles Wright, Ernest Gaines, John E. Wideman, Ishmael Reed, Paule Marshall, Gayl Jones, Gloria Naylor, Toni Morrison, Charles Johnson, Colson Whitehead, and Leon Forrest also experiment with the conventions of legend, tale, and fable.

In addition to oratory, myth, legend, and tale, song or music is a clearly identifiable residual oral form in the tradition of the African American novel. Spirituals, hymns, work songs, patriotic songs, abolitionists songs, ragtime, blues, gospel, and jazz—all, especially the last three, contribute in different degrees of intensity to the thematic and structural concerns of individual novels, from Brown's *Clotel* to Arthur Flowers's *Another Good Loving Blues* (1993), Clarence Major's *Dirty Bird Blues* (1996), and John A. Williams's *Clifford's Blues* (1998). In *Blake*, for example, Aunt Rachel sings:

"In eighteen hundred and twenty-three
They said their people should be free
It is wrote in Jeremiah,
come and go along with me!
It is wrote in Jeremiah
Go sound the Jubilee!"[79]

More recently in *Jubilee*, we hear Vyry often unburdening her soul with song:

"I been buked and I been scorned,
Lord, I been buked and I been scorned,
Lord, I been buked and I been scorned,
I been talked about sho's you borned."[80]

Whether black novelists use them in a manner organic to the development of plot, theme, or character or in a stylistically ornamental manner, these songs of sorrow and joy invariably retain their authentic purpose of decrying oppression and celebrating the possibilities of the human spirit. It is apparently because of these qualities that modern African American music like jazz, which is itself a classical tradition, is rooted in the collective black consciousness and symbolically expressed in spirituals, gospel songs, and blues.

Spirituals, like chanted sermons, are inspired by the Bible, informed by the group experience, and characterized by occasional rhyme, improvised graphic phrases, and dramatic lines delivered in a call-and-response manner. In contrast to spirituals, gospel songs are formal compositions by individuals. But they are also inspired by that old-time religion, especially the emotional fervor of the Holiness church, as best revealed in the novels of Baldwin, especially in *Just Above My Head* (1979). Gospels are the sacred modern continuation in song of the story of the black experience in the city, paradoxically characterized by features of both the spirituals and blues. The strong beat, ambiguous imagery, and wide tonal range of gospel songs were significantly influenced by the pioneer compositions of Thomas A. Dorsey, a convert from the blues tradition. Ellison defines the blues as "an impulse to keep the painful details and episodes of a brutal experience alive in one's aching consciousness, to finger its jagged grain, and to transcend it, not by consolation of philosophy, but by squeezing from it a near-tragic, near-comic lyricism."[81] Structurally, the blues generally takes the form of three-line stanzas rhyming *a a b* with four beats in each line. But because the blues has few absolute features, there are many variations on this form. Stylistically, the blues singer employs formulaic imagistic phrases and interjections like "Oh Baby" and "Yes, Lord"—used in the call-and-response mode with accompanying instrumental improvisation—repetition, and occasional ideophonic moans, growls, and shouts. When performed for nonmembers of the ethnic group or for those with little or no intimacy with the music, it is generally considered mere entertainment; but when performed among black Americans, especially members of the working class, it is a social ritual: a ceremonial, residual oral form whose recurring performance reinforces a sense of order in life and preserves the shared wisdom of the group. As in the themes and style of Major's *Dirty Bird Blues* and Baldwin's *Just Above My Head,* the blues and gospels are secular and sacred lyrical expressions of hard times and the possibility of overcoming personal misery through toughness of spirit.

Structurally and philosophically, in other words, most contemporary African American music is strongly influenced by the blues. Like the blues, for example, jazz uses the call-and-response pattern with the antiphonal relationship occurring between two solo instruments or between solo and ensemble. And in jazz as in blues a traditional melody or harmonic framework serves as the base or point of takeoff for improvisational flights—either solo or collective. Whereas some black novelists recognized the literary potential of these residually oral folk forms as an extension of their social reality, others became aware of their potential as an act of literary discovery. In either case, as probably best demonstrated by Nathaniel Mackey in *Bedouin Hornbook* (1986) and *Djbot Baghostus's Run* (1993), they were still faced with the challenge of developing and mastering a suitable written narrative form in which to express the authenticity, authority, and agency of their particular vision of truth and beauty.

Literary Sources and Branches

Nineteenth-century African American novelists were moved by the dual impulse to stress representative detail and the supernatural. The social conditions and cultural exigencies outlined in the beginning of this chapter compelled most of them to attempt a synthesis of the contrary tendencies toward the novel and romance. "In giving this little romance expression in print," Hopkins writes in her preface, "I am not actuated by a desire for notoriety or for profit, but to do all that I can in a humble way to raise the stigma of degradation from my race."[82] Much of this color stigma was reinforced and perpetuated in the narratives of John P. Kennedy, George Tucker, William G. Simms, Thomas N. Page, and Thomas N. Dixon—to whom I shall return shortly as examples of the plantation tradition school of writing—as well as in James F. Cooper's *Spy,* Edgar A. Poe's *Narrative of Arthur Gordon Pym*, and Herman Melville's "Benito Cereno," where one finds a gallery of Caesars and Babos, black characters who run the gamut from loyal lackeys to diabolic savages. In responding to these white visions of black character and in creating their own images, Hopkins and her fellow novelists were significantly influenced by contemporaneous literary sources, especially abolitionist literature, the Bible, and popular fiction.

ABOLITIONIST LITERATURE

Abolitionist literature—antislavery letters, newspapers, periodicals, journals, pamphlets, verse, and fiction that advocated ending slavery—was by far the most useful tradition for the didactic purposes of black novelists. The formal diction, rhythmic cadences, balanced syntax, stark metaphors, and elevated tone of works like Harriet Beecher Stowe's *Uncle Tom's Cabin* (1852) provided the stylistic blend of matter-of-factness and sentimentality necessary for their initial moral and political antislavery appeals primarily to white readers. By their adaptation of the conventions of abolitionist literature, William W. Brown, Martin Delany, James Howard, Frances E. W. Harper, and others exploited the opportunity to strike a blow at American racism while simultaneously demonstrating their adjustment to and gradual mastery of Euro-American culture.

More important than *Uncle Tom's Cabin* to the neophyte black novelist, however, were the slave or emancipatory narratives, for they provided a natural bridge between the oral and literary traditions. Those pioneers of the African American novel who were neither preachers nor teachers were either former slaves and abolitionist lecturers or the children of free parents and able spokespersons in the Civil Rights movement. In one way or another, they were all familiar with the techniques of the lecture platform and the process for translating this oral performance into literary narratives. Most knew that antislavery meetings would generally begin with introductory remarks by a local abolitionist in preparation for the appearance of a seasoned guest lecturer like Garrison or a fugitive slave like Douglass to provide a dramatic account of life in bondage. This performance would be followed by an impassioned, critical analysis of the evils of the Peculiar Institution and, on occasion, either a few songs or poems. Finally, a collection for the cause would be taken up, abolition publications sold, and the meeting adjourned.[83]

The transformation of personal narrative into romance is a matter of literary history. Highlighting the problems of authenticity, authority, and agency in the African American literary tradition, slave or emancipatory narratives are the personal accounts of physical and psychological bondage and freedom. Some, like *Narratives of the Sufferings of Lewis and Milton Clarke* (1846) and *The Life of Josiah Henson* (1849), were dictated to white amanuenses, but most were written by the fugitive, frequently self-emancipated slaves themselves, who had already told their stories dozens of times from the antislavery platform. The pattern of the written narratives by Frederick Douglass, William W. Brown, J. W. C. Pennington, Solomon Northrup, and William and Ellen Craft begins with the fugitive slave's realization of the evils of the institution, his first attempts at resistance and flight, his cunning victories over oppression, and detailed descriptions of different phases of bondage; it ends with a successful flight North and an activist role in the "true" religion and abolitionist politics.[84] Most of the autobiographies are characterized by moral purpose, Christian values, and emotional fervor. Many read like moral and political allegories. Their style is largely derived from the pulpit, the lectern, and the soapbox, from Scripture and antislavery materials. Even though most of the characters are ostensibly Christian, some narrators are familiar with conjuring, and all narrators carefully distinguish between "true" Christianity and the religion their masters used to justify slavery. And though by and large the narrator's appeals are to the moral conscience of whites, they clearly express a resolute faith in the humanity of blacks and the righteousness of their struggle for freedom, literacy, and fulfillment.

One of the most popular features of agency in the slave narratives was the melodrama and romance of the perilous journey north to freedom. The ingenuity of the escape stratagems and the bold manner in which they were carried out—incidents first passed on by word of mouth in the form of tales and legends among the slaves and then retold from the abolitionist platform—gradually became stock conventions of the form. Some light-skinned slaves passed for white in their flight north, occasionally stopping at the best restaurants and hotels along the way. Some disguised themselves as master and slave, as did the well-known fugitives William and Ellen Craft. Others, like Henry "Box" Brown, employed more elaborate devices, such as shipping themselves north in packing crates or barrels. The courage and imagination of the fugitives won the respect of white abolitionists. "They are among the heroes of our age," wrote Massachusetts Senator Charles Sumner. "Romance has no stories of more thrilling interest than theirs. Classical antiquity has preserved no examples of adventurous trial more worthy of renown."[85]

The heroism of men and women of unusual ability and integrity looms large in the slave narratives. Most of the heroes were skilled, trusted servants (e.g., artisans, drivers, and exhorters) with ambivalent feelings toward whites and blacks alike, particularly the masses. Some were political in character like Frederick Douglass and Harriet Tubman, some intensely religious like Nat Turner and Sojourner Truth, and others self-serving, faithful individualists like Josiah Henson. Regardless of political and personal differences, they were generally articulate activists committed to the struggle for justice and freedom. And the ideals they represent—an indomitable will to be free, unshakable faith in the justice of their cause, extraordinary genius, and irrepressible bravery—are thematically important in the tradition of the African American novel.

THE KING JAMES BIBLE

Equally as important as abolitionist literature in the tradition of the African American novel is the King James Bible. Through sayings, sermons, songs, and stories, its moral lessons were passed on by word of mouth and the printed page from generation to generation. Jean Toomer's *Cane* (1923), Countee Cullen's *One Way to Heaven* (1932), Zora Hurston's *Jonah's Gourd Vine* (1934), Waters Turpin's *O Canaan* (1939), Ralph Ellison's *Invisible Man* (1952), James Baldwin's *Go Tell It on the Mountain* (1953) and *Just Above My Head* (1979), Margaret Walker's *Jubilee* (1966), Hal Bennett's *Lord of Dark Places* (1970), and Leon Forrest's *There Is a Tree More Ancient than Eden* (1973), among others, draw heavily on the Bible for plot and character. Traditionally, African Americans have recognized and creatively utilized the parallels between their oppression and that of the Jews. Aside from allusions to the Hebrew patriarchs and prophets, the most frequent biblical adaptations are of the myth-legends, the hybrid narratives, of Moses and the Second Coming of Christ. "Weevils and wars are pest that God sends against the sinful," says Lewis, one of the central characters in *Cane*. "People are too weak to correct themselves: the Redeemer is coming back. Get ready, ye sinners, for the advent of Our Lord."[86] In the wake of the Civil War, Vyry Brown, the heroine of *Jubilee*, sings joyously of both her earthly salvation and the divine judgment to come. In *Moses, Man of the Mountain* (1939) Hurston rewrites the legend of Moses from the black perspective, foregrounding black dialect, conjuring, and hoodoo. Seth Stanley, the messiah figure in *Appointed* (1894), is white; but Henry Holland in *Blake*, Tucker Caliban in *A Different Drummer* (1962), Jesse Jacobs in *Many Thousand Gone* (1965), Chuck Chaney in *'Sippi* (1967), Dan Freeman in *The Spook Who Sat by the Door*, and most modern-day messiahs in the African American novel are black.

Because of this messianic leitmotif in the tradition of the African American novel, a word or two about the differences between the eschatology of Jews and black Christians is appropriate here.[87] As derived from the Old Testament, the Judaic outlook closely links the coming of the anointed of God with the restoration of the dispersed House of Israel and the peace of Paradise. Early black American converts to Christianity, on the other hand, seem to have derived their eschatological vision mainly from the New Testament, where the end of the world precedes the Second Coming of Christ and the Last Judgment, with its concomitant salvation for the righteous, the just, and damnation for the wicked, the unjust. What was looked for in both redemptive views of history, however, was not an escape from the world, time, and history, but a new world rising out of the ruins of the first. "For, behold," says Is. 65: 17–18, "I create new heavens and a new earth: and the former shall not be remembered, nor come into mind. But be ye glad and rejoice for ever *in that* which I create: for, behold, I create

Jerusalem a rejoicing, and her people a joy." The mediator for this salvation is, of course, the Messiah and his appointed Old Testament messenger, Moses.

In the tradition of the African American novel there is also a significant difference between Pharisaic orthodoxy and apocalyptic visionaries. Converted and educated mainly by white Baptist and Methodist missionaries, the vast majority of early black exhorters, like the Pharisees, preached the gospel of piety and humility in the present age while waiting with hope for the advent of the Messiah, the Day of Judgment, and the Age-to-Come. In contrast, the apocalyptics, like the biblical Daniel and historical Nat, wrote off the present age as irredeemably evil, saw the new age as abruptly replacing, not redeeming, this age, and claimed to have a revealed scheme of things. Historically and biblically, then, the struggle of black Americans for liberation has been essentialist, messianic, eschatological, and apocalyptic. These ideological and strategic tensions became an important leitmotif in the African American novel with the publication of *Blake*, whose protagonist is hailed by his people as the "messenger of light and destruction."

The influence of the Bible is also seen in the tensions between the most common major characters in the African American novel: the preacher and the hustler. Andy, a slave exhorter, is one of the principal organizers of the rebels in *Blake*; and Brother Belden, the folk preacher in James Howard's *Bond and Free* (1886), is a gifted man:

> he was blessed or gifted with a stentorian pair of lungs, a very active and original imagination, and could read the Bible with the lids closed, with as much satisfaction to himself as he could when open, because Brother Belden could not read at all. He had, however, been called to preach and . . . he responded. . . . They were all equally deprived, both the called and the uncalled. . . . In him they confided; him they honored; in him they saw the messenger of the Lord bearing the only consolation which was like balm to their deepest sufferings.[88]

Like the preacher, the hustler is another gifted man who lives by his wits and rap, the power of his oratorical ability. He might be a confidence man, like Sadness, in *The Sport of the Gods*, and belong to that "set which lives, like the leech, upon the blood of others,—that draws its life from the veins of foolish men and immoral women, that prides itself upon its well-dressed idleness and has no shame in its voluntary pauperism."[89] He might be like Mr. Coffin in *Daddy Was a Number Runner*, storyteller, number runner, poker player, and good-hearted family man who deserts his family. Or he might be like Rinehart in *Invisible Man* and become at will "Rine the runner and Rine the gambler and Rine the briber and Rine the lover and Rinehart the Reverend."[90] The list of hustlers in the black American novel—including many musicians and preachers as well as criminals—and the masks they wear to manipulate the ironies and ambivalence of their core identities and lives are legion.

In addition to the dynamic interplay between preacher and hustler types, between religiously or strategically essentialized and socially constructed identities, the tradition of the African American novel reveals a conflict between the stories and supernatural forces of the Bible and the reinterpretations of syncretism of African deities, root doctors, and religious beliefs. Faith in dreams, divine providence, the mysterious powers of the Lord, and a New Jerusalem contend with conjuration, root doctors, hoodoo, and other residual African forces. Having lost the sanctions of religious and social institutions they formally held in Africa, conjuring and hoodoo (the syncretistic blend of Christian and sub-Saharan African, primarily Yoruba, religious traditions in the United States) mingled in time with the witchcraft and ghost lore of European whites and the rituals of the aboriginal peoples.[91] This belief in the mystery, magic, myth, and ritual of residual African religions complements and contends with the paradoxical rationalistic yet Judeo-Christian mode of Western consciousness. That the power of hoodoo, considered mere superstition by most of the literate class, is well established among the black masses can be traced in the African American novel from Brown's *Clotel* to Reed's *Mumbo Jumbo* (1972), Bambara's *Salt Eaters* (1980), Wideman's *Hiding Place* (1981), and Naylor's *Mama Day* (1989).

POPULAR FICTION

Whereas abolitionist literature and the Bible provided many of their most distinctive plots, motifs, symbols, and archetypes based on appeals to "natural law" and a spiritual self, early black novelists also found the popular fiction of nineteenth-century America stylistically useful. Beginning in 1833, the Yankee humor of Seba Smith, the creator of the letters of Jack Downing, and his many followers flourished among the reading public. The popularity of Yankee rustics commenting on political affairs in racy, idiomatic language and awkwardly apt metaphors was not lost on blacks in search of appropriate vehicles for their own satirical commentary on American democracy, Christianity, and racism. Nor were the early novelists beyond the influence of the Southwestern frontier humor of Augustus Longstreet's *Georgia Scenes* (1835) and Joseph Baldwin's *Flush Times in Alabama and Mississippi* (1853). Like the crackerbox philosophy of Yankee types, the sketches of Longstreet and Baldwin were provincial but honest attempts at recording native American humor. Frequently given to caricature and burlesque, they emphasized the common man, oral tale, colloquial speech, local mores, and regional character types. In *Clotel* we see how Brown combines this vein of frontier humor with slave anecdotes when he disguises his fugitive heroine as an Italian gentleman and manipulates her identity with puns on politics and temperance in a burlesqued dialogue among Cincinnati stagecoach passengers.[92] In another episode we overhear a satirical exchange on politics and slavery between Southern and Northern character types that is representative of ironic regional differences. Most critics generally neglect this satirical dimension of the African American novel.[93]

Many point instead to the more common influence of the plantation tradition school of local color and regional writers. Antebellum writers like George Tucker, William A. Caruthers, John P. Kennedy, and Caroline H. Ingraham created idyllic pictures of plantation life and the peculiar endowments of black people. Postbellum local colorists and regionalists such as Harris, Page, and Dixon—the classic literary apologists for slavery—glorified the antebellum Old South even more. Harris's *Uncle Remus: His Songs and Sayings* (1880), a rewriting of black folklore, and *Gabriel Tolliver* (1902), Page's *In Old Virginia* (1887) and *Red Rock*, and Dixon's *Leopard's Spots* (1902) and *The Clansmen* (1905) celebrated the beauty of an orderly, feudal, agrarian society and lamented its destruction by rapacious Unionists and blacks. Although Harris's and Page's extensive use of monologues and tall tales within a framework suggests their debt to the frontier humorists, romance and melodrama were the dominant forms used by the plantation school of writers. The melodramatic conflict was regional, economic, and racial. The "good guys" in this conflict were the chivalrous, white Bourbon aristocrats; their chaste, dazzlingly beautiful belles; and their devoted, contented slaves and freedmen. The "bad guys" were the malevolent white Union Leaguers, carpetbaggers, scalawags, and free black advocates of civil rights. In retrospect, we can see that the moral absolutism of melodrama was highly effective in recording the postbellum schism in the national consciousness and conscience over safeguarding the newly gained rights of black Americans and in contributing to the tide, some might say backlash, of white nationalism that swept the country after Reconstruction.

But melodrama also served the dual psychological, social, and aesthetic needs of early black novelists. According to culture historian David Grimstead, melodrama was basically religious drama, "wherein surface detail, psychological, or social, was firmly subordinated to a world view and 'the real' truth had to be that which affirmed the optimism of tomorrow over the frequent bleakness of today."[94] The last-minute rescues, numerous reunions of long-separated families or lovers, and projected ultimate triumphs of justice over injustice in the early black novels were natural events to those who believed in a universe governed by cosmic yet moral laws. At the same time, viewed from their subjugated economic and political circumstances, the basic goodness of providence, man, nature, and society was being perverted on a grand scale by white devils.

In addition, the dime romances with domestic felicity and female chastity at their matrix seemed heaven-sent for the treatment of illicit relations between black women and white men. Refined heroes and heroines involved in elaborate disguise, mistaken identity, passwords, and violent episodes were keys to the formulaic packaged Beadle dime novels. In developing their forbidden-fruit sexual themes, nineteenth-century black novelists found these melodramatic conventions irresistible. Contrary to popular belief, however, the mulatto heroines of *Clotel* and *Iola Leroy* are not mere carbon copies of Victorian white purity and prudery. True, as Ellen Morton's suicide in *Iola Leroy* indicates, death before sexual dishonor was also the unwritten code for black writers. But—as in the case of Clotel and Althesa—virtue, when frustrated by man-made laws prohibiting interracial marriage, could be satisfied by "a marriage sanctioned by heaven." That both women die before the end of the novel is less important to the plot than their sexual and racial exploitation—Horatio's infidelity and Henry's failure to manumit Althesa—by a perverse, unjust society. In contrast, blue-eyed, near-white Iola survives triumphantly as she reportedly rejects a persistent aristocratic white suitor and selflessly dedicates her life to family and race.

Loyalty to race or region often clashes with loyalty to country in the early African American novel, for patriotism was another cardinal virtue of melodrama. "Faith in the goodness of the United States, its government, and its destiny," Grimstead notes, "was modulated only by association with principles of liberty, justice, and equality, which were assumed to be the birthright of all men."[95] Whereas Belton Piedmont, the protagonist in *Imperium in Imperio*, has faith in white people and chooses patriotism over black nationalism when it comes to armed revolution, Dan Freeman in *The Spook Who Sat by the Door* acts on the principle that blacks must use guerrilla warfare to attain their rights. By and large, the emphasis in the tradition of the African American novel is not on my country right or wrong but, as in *Invisible Man*, on ambivalence toward all men and events, ethnic and national. Moreover, when national values are affirmed over ethnic, it is generally because, despite economic, political, and moral perversions, they are based on principles and ideals common to all: liberty, justice, and equality.

An ostensible ambivalence toward these principles influenced characterization and plot. Convinced that the cause of justice and equality was not served when the birthrights, patriotism, and civil rights of blacks were subordinated to those of poor whites, immigrants, and anarchists, postbellum black novelists depicted this travesty with righteous indignation, parody, and irony. "The Negro is not plotting in beer-saloons against the peace and order of society," we hear a character protesting in *Iola Leroy*. "His fingers are not dripping with dynamite, neither is he spitting upon your flag, nor flaunting the red banner of anarchy in your face."[96] In contrast, Iola is characterized as a black woman whose education and self-respect move her to insist on being self-reliant and gainfully employed in the business world. Understandably, as members of a group that was barred from equal participation in their society during an age when industrialization ran rampant, many black novelists saw middle-class values as the most realistic guarantors of racial justice and equality.

But as the ideological differences and debates between Du Bois and Washington reveal, sobriety, piety, thrift, honesty, hard work, property ownership, and education were often misleadingly portrayed as the keys to freedom, literacy, and fulfillment in a puritan, capitalistic system. "Greater industry, skill, the sticking quality, honesty and reliability will open the way . . ." writes Pryor in support of Washington's accommodationist ideology of stressing dollars over dignity, justice, and the vote. "If we will only cultivate the saving spirit, cut loose from extravagant habits, work the year round, encourage and assist one another in business, we will acquire wealth, and this will effectively dissipate race prejudice."[97] Among other things, the shifting allegiance of early African American novelists was symbolic of the unfulfilled promise of the nation and the unrelenting desire and struggle of black Americans for economic, political, and cultural self-determination.

On the other hand, the double consciousness of African American novelists produced a corresponding ambivalence toward the literary traditions of the day. Influenced by popular fiction and a predominantly white audience, for example, most early novelists masked their authority and agency by including at least one farcical episode and ostensibly minstrel character in their novels. Brown's Sam, the "Black Doctor" with a flair for wearing ruffled shirts and a half pound of butter in his hair, and Griggs's church member, who flings her white charge across the room and swings on the preacher's neck in religious ecstasy, fall into this category. But even here the humor is double-edged, for beneath the minstrel mask is a satirical treatment of color and caste prejudice and practice. The folk, in short, are not simply portrayed from the white perspective of minstrelsy. Indeed, some, like Griggs's Hannah Piedmont, are self-sacrificing black matriarchs; others, like Dunbar's Sadness, are surrogate fathers; and still others, like Chesnutt's Josh Green, are black avengers.

From its inception, then, the African American novel has been concerned with illuminating the experiences of black Americans and the complex double consciousness, socialized ambivalence, and double vision that constitute the distinctive burden and blessing of African American identity. Contributing to the complexity and diversity of the African American novel is the fact that the first generation of novelists relied solely on neither the folk nor literary tradition for creative inspiration and form. Instead, they drew heavily on both in their use of abolitionist literature—in particular emancipatory narratives—the Bible, and popular fiction as literary models of authenticity, authority, and agency. Such diverse sociocultural influences suggest the difficulty of constructing a racial and ethnic theory of the novel.

Nevertheless, I have discovered that from William Wells Brown to Trey Ellis and Gloria Naylor the primary unifying principle in the African American novel is the quest for justice and dignity as a free people of African ancestry and bicultural African American heritage. Integral to this quest for an ethnic identity is the fulfillment of individual potential by merging a divided, alienated self into a truer and better unified, literate self. This quest for authenticity, authority, and agency, derived from the collective experience of black Americans and usually projected with messianic and apocalyptic overtones, begins with bondage, physical or psychological, and leads to some form of deliverance or vision of a new world: moral or political awakening, flight, rebellion, or social reform. Highly rhetorical elements and historical documentation, idealization of character and representative types contended with each other in the novels of the nineteenth and early twentieth centuries. As black novelists sought to achieve the appropriate blend of romance and mimesis for projecting their aesthetic view that true art is moral as well as political, they deployed various strategic combinations of rhetoric, dialectics, and dialogics.

Born in a perversely intransigent social arena where color, class, and gender struggle are the major determinants of consciousness, the novelists are generally ambivalent in their attitude toward both Euro-American and African American values. Their view of history is usually cyclical, but occasionally shifts or spirals between progressive and apocalyptic. In short, the shifting emphases in the African American tradition between the generic tensions of the romance and novel and from the strategies of rhetoric and dialectics to dialogics corresponds to the ever-changing social reality of blacks in America. These shifting emphases also correspond to the symbolic and vernacular patterns of narrative that each novelist appropriates to structure his or her particular vision of reality and the future.

3 / *Mapping the Peaks and Valleys of the African American Novel (1853–1962)*

In order to do justice to their subject matter, in order to depict Negro life in all of its manifold and intricate relationships, a deep, informed and complex consciousness is necessary, a consciousness which draws for its strength upon the fluid lore [vernacular tradition] of a great people, and moulds this lore with the concepts that move and direct the forces of history today.

RICHARD WRIGHT

"Blueprint for Negro Writing"

IN contrast to *The Afro-American Novel and Its Tradition*, which closely examines the symbolic and vernacular patterns of selected novels published between 1853 and 1962, this chapter will primarily map the peaks and valleys of the tradition of the African American novel and highlight its different branches during this time. The first third of the chapter includes the period from the pre–Civil War years through the U.S entry into World War I. The next third, moving from the war years to the early 1950s, covers modernism, the Harlem Renaissance, with its search for new modes of narrative, and the eventual triumph of naturalism spearheaded by Richard Wright. The chapter concludes with a consideration of myth, legend, and ritual in the novels of the fifties.

Early Historical Romance, Social Realism, and Beyond

In tracing the movement of the early African American novel toward social realism and beyond, I have discovered that its history conveniently divides into three periods: antebellum and Civil War novels (1853–65), postbellum, Reconstruction, and post-Reconstruction novels (1865–1902), and pre–World War I novels of the Old Guard (1902–17). With the exception of the novels by Frank Johnson Webb (1828–94) and Harriet E. Wilson (ca. 1824–28–ca. 1863), and the three American editions of *Clotel*, the periods designated also suggest the major thematic shift from slavery to caste, a corresponding shift in setting from rural to urban, and the first experiments with naturalism.

Antebellum and Civil War Novels (1853–1865)

Prior to the Civil War, several novels by Americans of African ancestry were either published in book form or serialized in periodicals after the Fugitive Slave Act of 1850 and the publication of *Uncle Tom's Cabin* in 1852. The four most important of these texts reveal the impact of the burning social issues of the decade on the culture and character of African Americans: abolitionism, education, temperance, women's rights, and commercialism. Despite the laws against teaching blacks, for example, some slaves were receiving education in various parts of the South. Memoirs, diaries, and slave narratives tell of some whites, especially women and children with mixed motives, teaching slaves the rudiments of reading and writing. The cases of Frederick Douglass and William Wells Brown, even though they were largely self-educated, are perhaps the most widely known.

If literacy was a rare pearl that grew slowly among antebellum blacks, books published by blacks were rarer still. The first two novels, Brown's *Clotel; or The President's Daughter: A Narrative of Slave Life in the United States* (1853) and Frank Webb's *The Garies and Their Friends* (1857), were published in London. The second two, Martin R. Delany's *Blake*; or *The Huts of America: A Tale of the Mississippi Valley, the Southern United States and Cuba* (1859), and Harriet E. Wilson's *Our Nig; or Sketches from the Life of a Free Black, In a Two-Story White House, North. Showing That Slavery's Shadows Fall Even There* (1859), are the first novels published by black Americans in the United States. Delany's appeared serially, and Wilson's was printed privately, the first bound novel published in the United States rather than England. Brown's editions of *Clotel* appeared in the United States serially in 1860–61 and in book form in 1864 and 1867.[1]

Of these four narratives, *Blake* is by far the most politically radical, *Clotel* the most romantic, *The Garies and Their Friends* the most novelistic, and *Our Nig* the most original. Whereas *Blake* is messianic in theme and characterization, the protagonist a symbolic response to the calls to rebellion and self-reliance of black abolitionist orators such as David Walker in 1829 and Henry Highland Garnet in 1843,[2] *Clotel* employs realistic details, slave narrative anecdotes, and romantic subplots in the service of historical romance. In verisimilitude, coherence of plot, and delineation of character, *The Garies and Their Friends* reflects the major concerns of the emerging middle-class novel; *Our Nig* individualizes the character and theme of the tragic mulatto. Both *Blake* and *Clotel* end melodramatically with the protagonists or their children finding a haven in another country. Webb's characters also travel to Europe, but their unshakable faith in the myth of the American Dream dictates their eventual return to Philadelphia. Wilson's protagonist settles in Massachusetts.

More important, the rhetorical style, structure, and movement of all four narratives are in the tradition of the slave narratives and sentimental romance.

Families and lovers are separated and reunited; anecdotes about the evils of slavery and race prejudice are sensationally cataloged; tales of seduction of octoroons are sentimentally related; and the villain receives his just retribution while the hero marries the heroine and lives happily ever after, except in *Our Nig*. Again, *Our Nig* and *Blake* are different. *Our Nig* closes ambiguously with the author-narrator's appeal for the sympathy and aid of the reader for the abused and invalid, yet heroically struggling, protagonist who was abandoned as a child by her white mother and as a woman by her husband, a free Northern black confidence man who masqueraded as a fugitive slave lecturer. The truncated version of *Blake* presently available to us closes on an apocalyptic note that is prophetically in tune with the black nationalism of narratives of the late 1960s. In any event, by the end of the Civil War, the tradition of the African American novel clearly revealed a rhetorical and dialectical preoccupation with the struggle of black Americans for freedom from color and caste discrimination as they affirmed their humanity in the process of defining and developing themselves as an ethnic community and as individuals. This quest was symbolically expressed in a mixed narrative form in which rhetorical and romantic elements often dominated social realism.

Postbellum, Reconstruction, and Post-Reconstruction Novels (1865–1902)

The period from the end of the Civil War to the turn of the century saw the rise of American nationalism, industrialism, and imperialism. For white America it was an age of technology, commerce, and finance, while for black America it was an age of short-lived political freedom and long-term peonage, repressive laws, convict labor, and lynchings. In the scramble for wealth and power, Indians, blacks, the poor, and the land were unscrupulously exploited by the captains of industry. Greed and corruption were cloaked under the gospel of progress, and the blessings of civilization were self-righteously and jingoistically imposed on the colored peoples of China, Cuba, and the Philippines. At the same time, social realism was on the rise. In the hands of Bret Harte, Edward Eggleston, Joel C. Harris, Thomas N. Page, George W. Cable, James W. Riley, Mark Twain, and others, folk material, frontier humor, and nostalgia for the days before the war were being popularized in the form of local color and regional writing. With its surface fidelity to regional setting, character, and dialect, local-color writing was the literary bridge between American romanticism and realism.

After the appearance of a fourth version of Brown's novel entitled *Clotelle; or The Colored Heroine: A Tale of the Southern States* in 1867, no new bound African American novel was published until James Howard's *Bond and Free* (1886). In their commitment to liberate and elevate the race from domination and degradation, however, some black writers continued to serialize novels for predominantly black audiences in black periodicals and magazines. Frances E. W. Harper, for example, serialized "Minnie's Sacrifice" (1869), "Sowing and Reaping" (1876–77), and "Trial and Triumph" (1888–89) in the *Christian Recorder*, the official newspaper of the African Methodist Episcopal Church.[3]

Although they were challenged by the many differences between their black and white readers, the major literary dilemma for postbellum and post-Reconstruction African American novelists was how to be true to their vision of reality and still reach their predominantly white readers. Before we explore this dilemma and the anxiety of influence in the novels of Harper, Griggs, Chesnutt, and Dunbar (whose *Sport of the Gods* was published in 1902, at the end of this period), it is important to note that even in the self-authenticating and self-authorizing preface to *Bond and Free* we discover the author seeking indulgence for whatever errors his antiplantation-tradition novel may contain. While affirming the truth of its incidents, he confesses that he has "endeavored to suppress all rancorous feeling" to avoid offending anyone.[4] This may be interpreted as a literary adaptation of the pseudo-apology introduced into black oratory by Frederick Douglass,[5] but, in fact, it would be more than fifty years before such conciliatory attitudes toward white audiences were radically reversed by Richard Wright.

Meanwhile, the black novelists of the period were compelled to have their works printed privately, or to make compromises to appeal to predominantly white readers. Except for Harper, who published three serialized novels in a black church periodical before publishing *Iola Leroy*, and Griggs, whose audience was largely black, most chose to compromise by muting their agency. This usually involved a moderation of militancy while persevering in the artistic attempt to counter the white literary distortions of reality and the experiences of black people. The moral vision of serialized novels like Harper's as well as bound novels like her *Iola Leroy* (1892), Sanda's *Appointed* (1894) and J. McHenry Jones's *Hearts of Gold* (1896), for instance, was unrelentingly shaped by faith in the principles of brotherhood and equality of Christianity and the Constitution. Whereas the humanism and egalitarianism were reinforced by satirical attacks on the corrupt institutions charged with the responsibility of guaranteeing these rights to every man, they were undercut by the paradox that by virtue of color and class some men were more equal than others. According to one of the major characters in *Appointed*, "'the poorer and more ignorant the people—North or South—the deeper rooted are their prejudices.'"[6] In contrast, the more refined and better educated among both races—the quality folks—were generally believed to possess the capacity to alleviate if not to eliminate antiblack racism. Thus the hope and fight for a better world in the novels of Harper, Griggs, Chesnutt, and Dunbar are influenced as much by the material fortunes of man as by the providence of God. And as their novels illustrate, the first task in moving toward social realism in the African American novel was to clear the ground of the lore of antiblack racism and sow the seeds for a more faithful representation of the complexities of black character and culture.

As twenty-first-century readers, we are inclined to forget the tenacity of the tradition of white supremacy with which postbellum and post-Reconstruction black novelists had to contend and the gravity of their dilemma. Confronted by a gallery of mid-nineteenth-century stereotypes of African American character and a deeply prejudiced white audience, Harper, Griggs, Chesnutt, and Dunbar were understandably constrained in their agency and ambivalent in their use of folklore and romance. Only one generation removed from slavery, they felt obliged to put forward the best foot or class of the race to reveal that black Americans were "more human than African." This ambivalence is reflected in their imaginative constructions and reconstructions of such stereotypes of black character as the Tragic Mulatto, Bad Nigger, Contented Servant, and Comic Black, and such myths as the American Dream. The interplay between romance and realism in their narratives thus derives from a conception of narrative art that is social and moral. Like their antebellum predecessors, postbellum and post-Reconstruction black novelists generally acknowledged a dual responsibility: to their race and to their craft. Among other things, this means that the early African American novel was employed as a vehicle for counterattacking white literary distortions of the experiences of blacks and as romances whose characters symbolize the survival strategies and values of African American culture. Frequently, the demands of the white marketplace and the subordination of craftsmanship to moral and social reform resulted in the displacement of such one-dimensional negative stereotypes as Bad Niggers and Sambos by such similarly constructed positive stereotypes as Respectable Mulattoes and Black Messiahs. As the romantic and realistic modes continued to contend for dominance, it was left to future generations to create the social climate in which black novelists could explore the American color, class, and gender conflicts more honestly and powerfully.

The Pre–World War I Novels of the Old Guard (1902–1917)

The years 1902–17, according to cultural historian Vernon L. Parrington, were "a time of extraordinary ferment, when America was seeking to readjust her ideals and institutions to a revolutionary economic order that had come upon her. . . . the old America had been intensely conservative, naively provincial and self-satisfied, compassed by complacence founded on optimism—the gospel of the business man. The new America was eager and hopeful, impatient to square institutions to the new conditions."[7] Whether progressive, moderate, or conservative, those over thirty years old, the Old Guard, were optimistic about the future development of the nation. A major distinction, in addition to that of their ages, between the agency of the Old Guard and the New Negro in their movement up from slavery is the cultural, moral, and economic shift. The New Negro was preparing to shift the focus of the Old Guard from transforming folk culture into "high" culture as the standard of moral and spiritual humanistic achievement to the validation of the moral authority and spiritual wisdom of folk culture itself.

As in the past, however, the movement away from cultural elitism to industrial capitalism and political democracy was primarily for whites. Frustrated by their efforts to participate in the development of white businesses and moved by the desperate plight of millions of black Southerners, black leaders urged their followers to achieve economic independence by organizing their own businesses. In 1899 W. E. B. Du Bois, while director of the Atlanta University Studies Program, convened a conference on the theme "The Negro in Business," which ratified the call for a national league of Negro businessmen. In 1900 Booker T. Washington organized the National Negro Business League, and by 1907 more than 300 local branches had been formed.[8]

Black Americans were hopeful that, as they developed economically, the reign of terror against them would come to an end. But before the outbreak of World War I, over 1,100 blacks across the land had been lynched. And as thousands of blacks began their long march to the cities, an epidemic of racial terrorism began to spread across the nation. White mobs would attack black communities for the largely imaginary or exaggerated offenses of one or two individuals. Contrary to popular opinion, most lynch victims were not accused of rape or attempted rape, but of homicide, robbery, insulting whites, and other violations of the ethics of Jim Crow. In 1904 several blacks were burned alive and their communities terrorized in Statesboro, Georgia; in 1906 several more blacks were massacred in Atlanta, their homes and businesses looted and put to the torch. In November of the same year President Theodore Roosevelt dishonorably discharged three companies of black soldiers for their alleged involvement in the death of a white citizen during the Brownsville, Texas, riot. The denial of civil rights and the pattern of white violence were equally widespread in the North. Among the most infamous were the Illinois lynchings that occurred in 1908 near Abraham Lincoln's home. In reaction to white atrocities, customarily committed with impunity, some progressive black members of the Old Guard, including W. E. B. Du Bois, Monroe Trotter, and Sutton Griggs, in 1905 organized the Niagara Movement. Some joined later with concerned white liberals to found the NAACP in 1910 and the Urban League in 1911. Their purpose was to protect the persons and rights of black citizens. In 1913 eighty-six people were lynched in the United States. Eighty-five were black. Beginning with the Dyer Bill in 1919, the NAACP lobbied vigorously but vainly for many years for a federal anti-lynching law.[9]

In the election of 1912, Woodrow Wilson won many black votes by expressing the desire to have "justice done to the colored people in every matter" and by assurances that should he become president, blacks could count on him "for absolute fair dealing, for everything by which I could assist in advancing the interests of their race in the United States."[10] The death of Booker T. Washington in 1915 and the failure of Wilson's peace gestures in 1917 marked the end of the nation's strained official policy of neutrality toward blacks at home and Germans abroad. In March 1917 the United States joined France in its war against Germany, and the unexpected call went out to blacks from Du Bois and other leaders to close ranks and join the crusade to make the world safe for democracy.

ROMANCE, REALISM, AND NATURALISM

The predominance of romance, realism, or naturalism in the narratives of the Old Guard, the third generation of black novelists, is closely related to the prevailing hope or despair of blacks of ever fully realizing their racial and national identities in America. In Henry Downing's *American Cavalryman* (1917), a melodramatic interracial love story of mistaken identity that examines the social ties between black America and Liberia, this means escape to Africa. In F. Grant Gilmore's *Problem* (1915), another mistaken racial identity love story which, for the first time, celebrates the exploits of the black soldier in the Spanish-American War, it means finding a solution to the color problem in Cuba. But in Oscar Micheaux's *Conquest* (1913), a success story about a prosperous black homesteader, and *Forged Note* (1915), a semi-autobiographical tale of the frustration of a black novelist who is unsuccessful in selling his book to Southern blacks, the refuge is South Dakota. And whereas in Otis Shackelford's *Lillian Simmons* (1915) the solution to the thwarted will of blacks is Booker T. Washington's brand of black capitalism in Chicago, in F. W. Grant's *Out of the Darkness* (1909) the author-narrator prefers Du Bois's program to Washington's. Thus, most of the Old Guard novelists employed stock interracial love plots involving the theme of racial passing and solidarity to stress the strategy of either Washington or Du Bois as the solution to the problem of the color line.

As readers will discover, the distinctiveness of the early subgenres in the tradition of the African American novel is derived from their frequent use of the five African American residually oral forms: oratory (including the vernacular or everyday speech acts), myth (including ritual enactment of belief systems), legend, tale, and song. But eighteenth- and nineteenth-century African American romances and novels were also influenced by the conventions of American popular romances of the period. Sentimentality, sensationalism, seduction, and suicide—psychological, emotional, or physical—these are the general characteristics of popular romance in eighteenth- and nineteenth-century Britain and America. In *Love and Death in the American Novel*, Leslie A. Fiedler more narrowly defines the American romance as "a gothic fiction, nonrealistic and negative, sadist and melodramatic—a literature of darkness and the grotesque in a land of light and affirmation."[11] But the range of Euro-American romances and romancers is actually much broader than this, and their influence on Afro-American romances and romancers was more complex than this definition suggests. For in the Euro-American domestic romances or sentimental novels of William H. Brown, Suzanna Rowson, Susan Warner, and E. D. E. N. Southworth, the Gothic romances of Charles Brockden Brown, the historical romances of James Fenimore Cooper, and the symbolic romances of Hawthorne and Melville, we discover several subgenres in the tradition.[12]

In *The American Novel and Its Tradition,* Richard Chase divides these subgenres of romance into two streams.[13] Cooper and William Gilmore Simms began these two streams, according to Chase, when they adapted European and British narrative conventions to suit the contradictory national culture and the penchant for melodrama of nineteenth-century America. The Cooper stream of romance cultivates the allegorical and moral potential of the form and includes such major authors as Hawthorne, Melville, Twain, and Faulkner. The Simms stream tells a good story, usually stressing the dramatic aspects of the form, but swerves away from the truth of the human heart to escapism, fantasy, and sentimentality. The history of the Euro-American novel for Chase is therefore not only the history of the rise of realism since the Civil War but also the recurring discovery of the power of romance. In agreement with Chase, Fiedler writes: "Our fiction is essentially and at its best nonrealistic, even anti-realistic[;] long before *symbolisme* had been invented in France and exported to America, there was a full-fledged native tradition of symbolism. That tradition was born of the profound contradictions of our national life and sustained by the inheritance from Puritanism of a 'typical' (even allegorical) way of regarding the sensible world—not as an ultimate reality but as a system of signs to be deciphered."[14] The history of the African American novel and its system of signs for representing the experiences of Americans of African descent, however, is different.

As illustrated in the antebellum, postbellum, and post-Reconstruction narratives of Brown, Wilson, Webb, Delany, Harper, Griggs, Chesnutt, and Dunbar, the distinctiveness of the early African American subgenres of the novel is apparent in use of the conventions of oratory, myth, legend, tale, and song. The epistemological and moral authority of these conventions was determined by the shared sociohistorical and sociopsychological ethnic experiences of the authors and the anxiety and ambivalence that characterizes their use of such literary paradigms as slave narratives, the Bible, and popular fiction. The African American subgenres of the romance and novel also combine the themes of love, marriage, and success with the protagonist's struggle for freedom from color and caste discrimination in a cyclical quest to realize fully his or her rights and potential for growth as a person of biracial and bicultural identity. The uniqueness of the tradition of the African American novel, in short, derives from both the double consciousness of its sociocultural and sociopsychological content and the double vision immanent in the pattern of oral and literary conventions of African American and Euro-American sign systems of romance and realism that structure that content.

Realism, as in Cervantes's *Don Quixote* and Twain's *Adventures of Huckleberry Finn,* defines itself against the excesses of romanticism and romance. It displaces metaphysical reality with social reality and substitutes historical, humanistic truth for ahistorical, transcendental truth. Literary realism is a response to the antireferential bias of modern criticism and the deconstructionist theory of the indeterminant meaning of texts. According to literary critic George Levine, literary realism is "a self-conscious effort, usually in the name of some moral enterprise of truth telling and extending the limits of human sympathy, to make literature appear to be describing directly not some other language but reality itself (whatever that may be taken to be); in this effort, the writer must self-contradictorily dismiss previous conventions of representation while, in effect, establishing new ones." Because nineteenth-century realism was a highly self-conscious attempt to explore or create a new reality, the realistic novel persistently questions "not only the nature of artificially imposed social relations, but the nature of nature, and the nature of the novel."[15] As illustrated by the early Twain, Howells, Chesnutt, and Dunbar, who all became less sanguine and more skeptical in their later careers, American realists believed in an empirically shareable world, were generally sympathetic toward democratic principles, and employed the dramatic method as their chief technique. But the authenticity, authority, and agency of Chesnutt and Dunbar, in contrast to Twain and Howells, are most meaningfully assessed by focusing on their narrative use of African American residually oral forms to represent the distinctive double consciousness of African American culture and character. Other major characteristics of nineteenth-century social realism that are deployed differently by white and black realists and naturalists include an analytical observation of ordinary life, a criticism of social problems and the disparity between the practices and principles of democracy, and a psychological exploration of middle- and lower-class characters.

Naturalism, according to critic George Becker, is "in essence and in origin . . . no more than an emphatic and explicit philosophical position taken by some realists, showing man caught in a net from which there can be no escape and degenerating under those circumstances; that is, it is pessimistic materialistic determinism."[16] In *American Literary Naturalism: A Divided Stream,* Charles C. Walcutt describes naturalism as two streams, "partly defying Nature and partly submitting to it," which assume protean forms (clinical, panoramic, slice-of-life, stream of consciousness, and chronicle of despair) and styles (documentary, satire, impressionistic, and sensational).[17] In other words, as illustrated in the novels of Zola and Flaubert, naturalism applies the principles of scientific determinism to fiction, portraying man as circumscribed or victimized primarily by either external forces (economic determinism) or internal drives (biological determinism). The first of these tendencies generally results in sociological studies of the background of many characters; the second fosters psychological studies of individual characters. "The extraordinariness of character and event in the naturalistic novel," as critic Donald Pizer acutely observes, "creates a potential for symbolism and allegory, since the combination of the concrete and the exceptional immediately implies meanings beyond the surface. Naturalism is thus closely related to the romance in its reliance on a sensationalistic symbolism and allegory." Allegorical representations of "how little we are or know, despite our capacity to be and our desire to know" in Euro-American naturalistic novels of the turn of the century are often circular in structure. "The effect of this symbolic structure," Pizer reminds us, "is to suggest that not only are human beings flawed and unfulfilled but that experience itself does not guide, instruct, or judge human nature."[18] During the 1890s while Howells was promoting a literary fidelity to the sunnier details of everyday life, these naturalistic tendencies began to appear in the novels of Stephen Crane *(Maggie*, 1893), Frank Norris *(McTeague*, 1899, and *The Octopus*, 1901), and Theodore Dreiser *(Sister Carrie*, 1900).

Romanticism, realism, and naturalism also began to appear in African American novels during this period. When refracted through the double consciousness and double vision of black American novelists, however, the dual tendencies of romanticism, realism, and naturalism are often suspended in dialectic tension. In naturalism, the sociohistorical source of this tension is the deep-rooted romantic belief of nineteenth-century black Americans in moral responsibility and free will, in a world of purpose and meaning, which contradicted deterministic philosophy and mechanistic despair. As a result, we usually discover a tragicomic vision at the end of African American novels or an ambiguous glimmer of hope beyond despair that concedes life's limitations while celebrating its possibilities. Although we first experience this tragicomic, naturalistic vision in Chesnutt's *Marrow of Tradition* and Dunbar's *Sport of the Gods*, the novels of Du Bois and Johnson are better examples of these dual tendencies and tensions.

LEGACY OF THE OLD GUARD

As in the postbellum period, the post-Reconstruction novels appearing between 1902 and 1917 continued to explore the tragicomic vision and heroic struggle of black Americans. In contrast to the melodramatic terror and pity of the antebellum novels and those by their less well-known contemporaries, however, the vision of Dunbar, Chesnutt, Du Bois, and Johnson is more ironic, especially when reconstructing the ambivalence of characters passing for white. And the representation of the double consciousness of their protagonists, although usually members of the black bourgeoisie, reflects the major internal and external conflicts of blacks during the post-Reconstruction and pre–World War I era. These were the turbulent years when blacks were stiffening their resistance to terror and their determination to realize at all costs their full rights as American citizens. Whether one was a teacher, preacher, porter, or domestic, class lines in the black community were divisive but much less rigid than those in the white community. That many of the protagonists, such as Chesnutt's Dr. Miller and Johnson's nameless musician-narrator, chose the less noble course of agency when confronted by conflicting racial and class interests is, from an aesthetic point of view, salutary. For it reveals that even the most conservative Old Guard novelists were above denying historical fact and psychological truth—however neurotic the parade of pretentious colored folk and their paternalistic white folks—in order to repudiate the stereotypes of Dixon and Page. Whatever their formal shortcomings in conventional literary technique as craftsmen, the most popular and successful novelists of the Old Guard were exceptionally honest and perceptive social critics. But their contributions to the tradition of the African American novel have been receiving the serious, sustained study they deserve only since the 1960s.

Ostensibly, in addition to affirming the possibilities of the romantic vision of black American character, F. W. Grant, Oscar Micheaux, Otis Shackelford, F. Grant Gilmore, and Henry Downing extended the thematic range of the African American novel. Aside from the stark reality and symbolism of ritual lynchings, obligatory Jim Crow episodes, and international intrigue, the most enduring characters to be passed on to novelists of the Harlem Renaissance were the musician and the orator. Also significant intertextually is the use of black church meetings, political councils, public lectures, literary forums, graduation exercises, and cabarets for strengthening group solidarity, expressing ambivalence toward black folklore, and celebrating the unique vernacular gifts of major and minor characters.

Modernism, the Harlem Renaissance, and the Search for New Modes of Narrative (1917–1936)

In 1917 white and black American soldiers went to war to make the world safe for democracy. But when the war ended in 1918, returning black American soldiers soon discovered that their struggle had not done so. Of the more than seventy blacks lynched during the first year of the postwar period, ten were black soldiers in uniform. Eleven were burned alive. And from June 1919 to the end of the year approximately twenty-five race riots erupted. Bitterly disappointed by the efforts of whites to deprive them of gains in jobs and housing made during the war, urban black migrants and war veterans across the nation resisted. Because of a probable conspiracy of silence by white authorities, most Americans were likely unaware of the nation's worst race riot, in Oklahoma in 1921, until "Unearthing a Riot" by Brent Staples appeared in the *New York Times Magazine* in 1999. According to the grim facts gathered by the Tulsa Race Riot Commission in 1997, hundreds of blacks "were shot, burned alive or tied to cars and dragged to death," and thousands were left homeless when deputized white mobs robbed and burned down the black section of Tulsa. This tragic massacre was a response by a lynch mob of thousands of whites to a local newspaper headline that a "Negro" attacked a white girl in an elevator and to the resistance of black male war veterans and homeowners to white terrorism.[19] Rape hysteria and fear of black independence also led to a similar slaughter of blacks and complete destruction of their homes and businesses in Rosewood, Florida, in 1923. Thus the first major period of black resistance to white terrorism began in what J. W. Johnson called the Red Summer of 1919.

The post–World War I years also marked an unprecedented upsurge of world and national interest in Harlem and black culture. European artists—Pablo Picasso, André Gide, Guillaume Apollinaire, and Darius Milhaud, to name a few—reacted to the radical changes resulting from modern industrialism and science by turning to the traditional beauty of African and African American art and incorporating it into their experiments in modernism. Native-born white American writers like Ezra Pound, T. S. Eliot, Gertrude Stein, Ernest Hemingway, e. e. cummings, Sherwood Anderson, Eugene O'Neill, and Waldo Frank, in revolt abroad and at home against the sterility and philistinism of industrial America, led the search for new American values and modes of expression. In the popularization of psychoanalytic theory, especially Freud's concept of the libidinal self, and the European theories of African and African American culture as evidence of the simplicity and beauty of preindustrial, precivilized culture, they found the new vision and direction for white America's salvation. In Stein's "Melanctha" (1909), Vachel Lindsay's "Congo: A Study of the Negro Race" (1914), O'Neill's *Dreamy Kid* (1919) and *Emperor Jones* (1920), Frank's *Holiday* (1923), Anderson's *Dark Laughter* (1925), and Carl Van Vechten's *Nigger Heaven* (1926), we find the nation's vision of the black American and his alleged primitivism. An oversimplification of the resiliency and vitality of black character and culture, literary primitivism exalted instinct over intellect, simple forms of social organization over more complex forms, and nature over art. In their flight from the problems of modern industrialism, many white Americans turned to home-grown varieties of the noble savage and blackface minstrelsy for salvation while maintaining and perpetuating their power and privilege in a national system of antiblack racism.

At the same time, although early signs of a new literary movement were apparent in the 1917 poetry publications of Claude McKay and James Weldon Johnson, the reaction in 1923 of "practically an entire generation of young Negro writers . . . to Toomer's *Cane*," in the words of Arna Bontemps, "marked an awakening that soon thereafter began to be called a Negro renaissance."[20] The Negro renaissance, better known as the Harlem Renaissance and the New Negro movement, was the period of the meteoric rise of such talents as Claude McKay, Jean Toomer, Countee Cullen, Langston Hughes, Bill Robinson, Florence Mills, Josephine Baker, Ethel Waters, Paul Robeson, Roland Hayes, Aaron Douglass, Louis Armstrong, Bessie Smith, and Duke Ellington; it was the second birth of African American culture, highlighting black music, dance, and literature. It was thus also another phase of the complex struggle against white "colonial" rule and cultural domination of nonwhite peoples in America and Africa.

By and large, the New Negro turned to Africa and African American folklore for the authenticity and authority of a usable ethnic past. The nineteenth-century image of Africa as a primitive land, a site of shame and self-hatred for many black Americans, was transformed for many black artists into a symbol of ambivalence or pride by many developments. In addition to the impact of modern science and white artists, some black artists, intellectuals, and cultural workers were influenced by the four Pan-African Congresses convened between 1919 and 1927 by Du Bois[21] and by the pioneer studies on Africa and African American history by Du Bois and Carter G. Woodson.[22] More influential and provocative were the Back-to-Africa movement and Universal Negro Improvement Association (UNIA) of Marcus Garvey, a charismatic Jamaican black nationalist who fired the imagination of the masses with his grand design for the redemption of black people, and the flowering of African American art. On the other hand, the frustration of coping with an alien Northern urban environment and industrial society encouraged many transplanted black Southerners to cling tenaciously to their folk roots.

Seeking to identify politically and culturally with the folk, race-conscious intellectuals and writers began to tap the roots of their ethnic heritage with varying degrees of ambivalence. In the vanguard of the New Negro artists who began their literary careers by looking with mixed emotions to Africa for a usable past and inspiration were Langston Hughes and Countee Cullen. Although Hughes's "The Negro Speaks of Rivers" is less ambivalent than Cullen's "Heritage," both are excellent examples of the function and meaning of Africa to black American writers of the twenties. Both poems reveal the romantic attraction of a place remote in time and space, a place the artists had been taught to reject, a place whose landscape and rhythms of life evoked primitive images and ambivalent passions. In much of their later work, including their novels—Hughes's *Not without Laughter* (1930) and Cullen's *One Way to Heaven* (1932)—both artists reconcile their double consciousness by shifting their concern to the everyday lives of ordinary black folk and the church-centered culture that represents the marrow of the African American tradition.

From the beginning, the thrust of the writers, as Robert Hayden has stated, was "more aesthetic and philosophical—more metaphysical . . . than political."[23] Hughes captured the feeling of aesthetic freedom and ancestralism,[24] the expression and affirmation of the race spirit in black art that characterized the Harlem upsurge in his well-known essay "The Negro and the Racial Mountain."[25] Literary contests and awards sponsored in the 1920s by *Negro World*, Marcus Garvey's weekly UNIA newspaper, and by *The Crisis* and *Opportunity*, the journals of the NAACP and Urban League, were important sources of encouragement for struggling young black artists. These contests and awards were supported by the patronage of wealthy black Harlemites like reputed numbers king Casper Holstein, liberal white publishers like Charles Boni, and Negrophiles and patrons like Carl Van Vechten and Charlotte Osgood Mason.

But the most widely known midwife for the literary birth of the gifted young blacks was Alain Locke, a Howard University professor of philosophy, chronicler of the period, clandestine advisor to Miss Osgood Mason, and editor of the *New Negro*. Containing essays by established black and white men of letters as well as representative selections of creative writing by the younger generation, the *New Negro* celebrates what Locke optimistically viewed as "the attainment of a significant and satisfying new phase of group development" by Americans of African descent. Rejoicing in the new spirit and race consciousness of the age, Locke declares: "The Younger Generation comes, bringing its gifts. They are the first fruits of the Negro Renaissance. Youth speaks, and the voice of the New Negro is heard. What stirs inarticulately in the masses is already vocal upon the lips of the talented few, and the future listens, however the present may shut its ears. Here we have Negro youth, with arresting visions and vibrant prophecies; forecasting in the mirror of art what we must see and recognize in the streets of reality tomorrow, foretelling in new notes and accents the maturing speech of full racial utterance." Writing out of the depths of their group and personal experience, the talented few, Locke was convinced, spoke with a particular representativeness. For "all classes of a people under social pressure are permeated with a common experience; they are emotionally welded as others cannot be. With them, even ordinary living has epic depth and lyric intensity, and this, their material handicap, is their spiritual advantage."[26]

In his enthusiastic efforts to create a wider reception for the New Negro artists, Locke oversimplified the artistic results of sociopsychological tensions and individual expressions of black American double consciousness. For when the New Negro novelist reconstructed the experience of blacks in America, he invariably highlighted those elements of the racial and national past that defined his personal identity and social vision. The result was a wide range of narrative forms and techniques: poetic realism, historical romance, genteel realism, folk romance, folk realism, and satire.

POETIC REALISM AND HISTORICAL ROMANCE

Jean Toomer's *Cane* and Arna Bontemps's *Black Thunder* represent the chronological boundaries and wide spectrum of narrative forms that characterize the flowering of the Harlem Renaissance in the early twenties and its decline in the late thirties. The search for identity, a usable past, and literary form led to poetic realism in *Cane* and to historical romance in *Black Thunder.* The first is essentially a psychological study of a modern black writer in an experimental mode. On the surface, *Cane* is a pastoral work contrasting the values of uninhibited, unlettered black folk with those of the educated, puritanically inhibited black bourgeoisie. On this level Toomer draws on the African American tradition of music as a major structural device. On its lower frequencies, however, *Cane* is the story of a metaphysical quest: a search for the truth about man, God, and America that takes its nameless poet-narrator on a circular journey of self-discovery and self-construction. *Black Thunder,* unlike the apocryphal legend about Jefferson's mulatto daughter in Brown's *Clotel,* is a retelling of a heroic legend in the traditional mode. None of the New Negro writers was more preoccupied with Freudian themes of the repressed self or more innovative in the use of language and form than Toomer. More than any of his contemporaries, he represents a synthesis of the concerns of modernist writers of the Lost Generation and the Harlem Renaissance, and his work embodies the tensions of modern science and folk tradition, of psychoanalytic technique and African American music, of mysticism and African American spirituality.

GENTEEL REALISM: ASSIMILATIONISM, NATIONALISM, OR BICULTURALISM

Harlem was the major base of operation for Marcus Garvey's UNIA, the largest mass movement of blacks ever developed in this country.[27] Garvey brought the organization—founded in Jamaica in 1914—here at a time when the betrayed promises of Reconstruction, World War I, and urbanization had caused the faith of the black masses in themselves and the future to plummet to a new low. A spiritual disciple of Booker T. Washington's economic theory of industrial education, Garvey came to the United States in 1916 with the intent of meeting the founder of Tuskegee Institute, raising funds for the UNIA, and returning to Jamaica to build an institution similar to Tuskegee. Unfortunately, Washington died before Garvey arrived. But Washington's ideas about economic self-determination lived on in the more radical dream of Garvey's black nationalism.

With fiery eloquence and colorful splendor, Garvey advocated the return of Africa to Africans, resurrected the "lost" civilizations of Africa, proclaimed himself provisional president of the continent he had never visited, and organized several ill-fated business enterprises. These included a steamship company to transport American blacks to Africa, the motherland of the human race (a belief since confirmed as fact by modern archaeological research).[28] Romantic, flamboyant, and grandiloquent, Garvey combined the style of the political demagogue and folk preacher to rekindle the pride and win the loyalty of the masses with the message that they were the black and beautiful descendants of a noble race of people. At the same time, Garvey's frequent attacks on middle-class, fair-complexioned leaders like Du Bois, Johnson, and Walter White, NAACP officer and novelist, exacerbated class and color tensions within the black community. From its peak of over a million members between 1920 and 1925, Garvey's movement declined with his imprisonment for mail fraud in 1925 and deportation in 1927.

Although Locke believed that Garveyism was "a transient, if spectacular, phenomenon," he, too, envisioned the New Negro as "the advance-guard of the African peoples in their contact with Twentieth Century civilization" and the younger generation's principal mission as the reestablishment of the pride and prestige of the race in the eyes of the world. And when he stated that the "racialism of the Negro is no limitation or reservation with respect to American life; it is only a constructive effort to build the obstructions in the stream of his progress into an efficient dam of social energy and power,"[29] he was announcing that the major thrust of the artists and intelligentsia was toward cultural dualism, not assimilationism.

As a social concept, assimilationism is the process by which different ethnic groups are absorbed into the larger community by erasing or repressing their ethnic differences. It projects the image of America as a melting pot of nationalities, a myth popularized in 1908 through the Broadway production of Israel Zangwill's *Melting Pot*. But as history and social critics reveal, the myth was and is remote from reality. The reality, as social historian Charles Silberman has noted, is that American politics and American social life are still dominated by the existence of sharply defined ethnic groups. "The WASPS (White Anglo-Saxon Protestants), the Irish-Americans, the Italian-Americans, the Jewish-Americans do differ from each other in essential ways. They vote differently, raise their children differently, have different ideas about sex education, religion, death, etc."[30] On the other side of the tracks, black psychologist Kenneth Clark reminds us, most African Americans still come into the world, live, learn, work, play, pray, and die in ghettos.[31] Thus, with each ethnic group contributing a distinctive flavor to the whole, America is more like a tossed salad, gumbo or, to change the metaphor, a mosaic or quilt than like a melting pot.

This is not to say that the form and content of the African American novel were not influenced by the conflict between nationalism and assimilationism. By family background and education, the New Negro novelists were mainly second-generation members of the middle-class black intelligentsia, a group whose color and class ambivalence, broadened and deepened by their bicultural college and social relationships with whites, was more intense and complex than that of the first generation of lower-middle-class novelists.[32] Even though

Walter White, Jessie Fauset, and Nella Larsen continued to explore the theme of passing, they placed more emphasis on class than color. By focusing on the morals and manners of well-educated members of black high society, they introduced the novel of manners and genteel realism into the tradition of the African American novel. Fauset and Larsen also provided the important perspective of twentieth-century black women toward traditional white middle-class values. Once their characters succeeded in repressing the duality of their identities in order to cross the color line, they would reassess their judgment of the spiritual and cultural virtues of the black experience that transcended the perversity of racial restrictions.

FOLK ROMANCE: PRIMITIVISM, PASTORALISM, AND ANCESTRALISM

Carl Van Vechten played a major role in influencing the literary interpretation of black Harlem life as primitive. As portrayed in his controversial but commercially successful *Nigger Heaven,* the spirit and lifestyle of black Americans were not only atavistic but, in the words of Du Bois, "one damned orgy after another, with hate, hurt, gin and sadism."[33] The self-analysis of Van Vechten's middle-class heroine reveals the major thrust of the novel:

> Savages! Savages at heart! And she had lost or forfeited her birthright, this primitive birthright which was so valuable and important an asset, a birthright that all the civilized races were struggling to get back to—this fact explained the art of a Picasso or a Stravinsky. To be sure, she, too, felt this African beat—it completely aroused her emotionally—but she was conscious of feeling it. This love of drums, of exciting rhythms, this naive delight in glowing colour—the colour that exists only in cloudless, tropical climes—this warm, sexual emotion, all these were hers only through a mental understanding. With Olive these qualities were instinctive. . . . Why, Mary asked herself, is this denied me?

The dominant setting of this primitive birthright in *Nigger Heaven* is Harlem cabaret life: "The music shivered and broke, cracked and smashed. Jungle land. Hottentots and Bantus swaying under the amber moon. Love, sex, passion . . . hate."[34]

As V. Y. Mudimbe reminds us in *The Idea of Africa,* "'savage', from the Latin *silvaticus* . . . is equivalent to marginality and, from a cultural normative space, designates the uncultivated." Etymologically, "'primitive' . . . simply indicates the originary, and, in the strictest sense, Africa is probably the originary locus of human kind."[35] But Van Vechten employs the term in *Nigger Heaven* as the antithetical "Other" of "the civilized race." He thus reduces his black characters to tortured, often grotesque, amoral souls who inhabit an urban jungle of joy in which the good life is symbolized by barbaric orgies, bloodletting fights, and jive talk that requires a "Glossary of Negro Words and Phrases" to decipher.

Although on its surface, Claude McKay's *Home to Harlem* seems to exploit the literary primitivism of Van Vechten, *Home to Harlem* actually moves beyond and beneath the primitivism of *Nigger Heaven*. McKay reveals his more compelling authenticity, authority, and agency by focusing on the double consciousness of his central male characters, Jake, the urban black American worker, and Ray, a deracinated Caribbean black artist, and by probing beneath the surface vitality of their struggle to survive.

Rather than pursue Van Vechten's notion of primitivism, it is more illuminating therefore to describe this romantic phase of modern development in the tradition of the African American novel as a form of pastoralism or, more distinctively, ancestralism. It would be absurd to argue that New Negro artists were not influenced by Freudian theory and white literary interpretations of the African American experience including those of Franz Boas and Horace Kallen's cultural pluralism. Some even succumbed on occasion to the commercial temptation to glorify sexuality and violence for the sake of a white benefactor or audience. In the main, however, the intention of the more committed New Negro artists was to project their vision as honestly as they could: to discover a usable past, to define and explore their culture, not exploit it. Their purpose was to express the historical struggle of black Americans to achieve a dynamic synthesis of their individual and collective double consciousness. Their passion was to reconcile the urban present and future with the rural, occasionally distant and strange, past. And their immediate dilemma was to free themselves from the well-meaning but pernicious influence of whites encouraging them to emphasize the exotic aspects of Harlem life, and from the equally well-meaning but misguided counsel of the black elite criticizing them for literary pandering and for not using their talents to portray the intellectual and social parity of the race.[36]

The term "African American pastoral" draws attention to this historical synthesis of African and Western narrative traditions to which the New Negro novelist was heir. This was no simple fusion of oral and written literature, as German critic Janheinz Jahn points out, but a confluence of styles, patterns of expression, and attitudes.[37] Thus the term stresses continuity and change: a reinterpretation of the past in the light of new experiences and a dialectically evolving consciousness. Based on an implicit moral and social contrast between country and city life, the pastoral tradition is rich in thematic and stylistic variety.[38] It ranges from the classical realism of Theocritus's Sicilian rustics and the allegorical Arcadia of Vergil's eclogues to the modern romantic defenses of a feudal society by the plantation tradition movement and the Southern agrarians; from the Judeo-Christian Edenic myths and West African myth-legends of a past Golden Age to the contrasting urban and rural black havens of McKay and Hurston. Breaking with the traditional distinctions between agrarian and industrial landscapes, the African American pastoral focused on the near rather than remote past for paradigms of the good life, celebrated urban as well as rural settings, elevated social outcasts and plain folk to heroic stature, and attacked the repressive forces of Western civilization, especially social conformity and racism.

The celebration of race consciousness in the novels by New Negroes may also be conveyed by the concept of ancestralism. Out of a sense of loss, a feeling that the times were out of joint and the soul was under siege by destructive forces, a romantic longing for a freer, more innocent time and place was born. This imaginative vision was of a time and place where the rhythms of life were closely linked to nature and one's essential humanity was unquestioned; it invoked a prelapsarian, precolonial time and place that fostered a feeling of harmony and peace with one's ancestors, one's self, and one's progeny. In the crucible of the creative imagination of some black novelists of the Harlem Renaissance, a dimly remembered and romantically constructed past fused with the harsh realities of a sociohistorically demanding present to produce a sociocultural vision of a new, more just and moral social order. More often than not, the realization of this vision in the novels of the period was problematic if not abortive. Their impulse toward social justice and racial progress in response to the violence and indignities of institutional and structural antiblack racism revealed an ambivalence to African American spirituality, Christian myth, and the American Dream.

On one level, the themes were the pretentiousness and repressiveness of Fauset's and Larsen's Northern black bourgeoisie, tragic mulattoes, and city folk; the sensationalism and atavism of McKay's Harlem laborers and street people; and the provincialism and pragmatism of Hurston's down-home lowbrows. On another level, the conflict was largely with white ancestors, as in *There Is Confusion* and *Quicksand,* or with black, as in *Home to Harlem* and *Jonah's Gourd Vine*. Regardless of the level, the quest in the novels of the New Negro was for the resolution of the psychological and social dilemma of the modern black American, for an affirmation of both human spirituality and sexuality over the forces that threatened their integrity and development.

The international scope of the concept of ancestralism is apparent in the *Négritude* movement of Caribbean and Francophone West African writers. Coined in 1939 by Aimé Césaire in "Journal of a Return to My Native Country," a long narrative poem, and popularized in 1948 by Léopold Senghor in *New Anthology of Black and Malagasian Poetry,* the term "Négritude" involves more than what Jean-Paul Sartre called antiracist racism in *Black Orpheus*. Only the most doctrinaire ideologues refuse to concede that peoples of African descent have historically suffered discrimination and oppression because of their color as well as their class. Consequently, Négritude writers not only refused to continue their deference to the white gods of European culture, but also sought with romantic passion and political purpose to reject the myth of white supremacy and to recover and reclaim the ancestral beauty of blackness in order to foster self-pride and respect for cultural pluralism and human equality.

Regarding the relationship between the New Negro movement and the concept of Négritude, Senghor, the former poet-president of Senegal, has acknowledged a great debt to the United States:

> Indeed, with regard to our Négritude, we have depended largely on the teachings of our professors of ethnology, anthropology on the subject of Black African civilizations. But, was it not the "New Negro" movement, the movement of the "Negro Renaissance," with Alain Locke and the others, was it not they who stimulated us to do as they did, to write poetry! In this way, and at this moment, I want to give America that which is due her, that is to say to have been, in a way, the initiator of Négritude.[39]

A shared sense of mixed emotions about ancient African civilizations and experiences with racism and Western economic exploitation was therefore initially a more pragmatic and logical basis for cultural solidarity than political struggle. Rather than being provincial, the character of New Negro art during the Harlem Renaissance stimulated and encouraged corresponding impulses in Caribbean and Francophone West African literary traditions.

The shift toward a biracial, working-class approach to the problems of black Americans during the Great Depression was short-lived. But with the emergence and development of independent African nations in the 1960s and the realization that neocolonial black regimes can be as oppressive as white, a racial analysis of the plight of oppressed peoples is being increasingly challenged in primacy by neo-Marxist economic and feminist analyses. Neither analysis in isolation, however, adequately explains the protracted and complex political, economic, and cultural struggle of blacks for self-determination and social parity.

Except for *Home to Harlem*, the romances and novels of Claude McKay and Zora Neale Hurston were published after the Harlem Renaissance had peaked. With the crash of the stock market in 1929 and the beginning of economic depression in 1930, the Harlem vogue began its rapid decline. The immediate literary reaction of Hurston, who was actually born January 15, 1891, in Notasulga, Alabama, rather than in Eatonville, Florida, as she claimed,[40] and several other novelists was a more intense personal search than in the 1920s for modern forms of ancestralism, of continuity of the folk tradition. George Henderson's *Ollie Miss* (1935) and George Lee's *River George* (1937), for example, also expose the legendary lives of common people who live on the economic and political margins of society. The thematic scope of the folk romances of McKay, Hurston (except for *Their Eyes Were Watching God)*, Henderson, and Lee is narrow. But the lyrical African American vernacular English and unadorned language, the bold explorations of the economic, spiritual, and sexual drives behind the violence of black male-female relationships, and the emphasis on the color and caste problems of black lovers in these folk romances represent a return to rural ethnic roots for aesthetic inspiration. Struggling with the anxiety and ambivalence created by the impact of social crisis on urban life in the mid-1930s, these authors and texts reveal the disrupting undercurrents of social realism and the continuing search for a usable past on which to build a more just, democratic, and humanistic future.

FOLK REALISM: RELIGION, MUSIC, HUMOR, AND LANGUAGE

Unlike the narratives of McKay and Hurston, in which realistic details are used in the service of folk romance, the novels of Langston Hughes and Countee Cullen focus on the everyday life of ordinary churchgoing black folk. These authors' allegiance to folk realism is more in their rendering of representative than marginal or allegorical types. Whether in the big city or a small town, their characters are less idealized, their settings less exotic, and their plots less melodramatic. Their novels strive for the truth of a particular environment and the social rituals of common folk rather than for the truth of the world at large and the lifestyle of street people and migrants. Although each truth has some validity, neither in isolation tells the whole truth of the myriad facets of the experiences of black people in America during the 1920s and 1930s.

During the 1920s Harlem reigned supreme as the cultural capital of the New Negro movement. Between 1900 and 1925 the white neighborhood in the heart of northern Manhattan—roughly from 110th Street to the Harlem River, south to north, and from Fifth Avenue to Morningside and St. Nicholas Avenues, east to west—was transformed into a black metropolis. From all points on the globe people flocked to the city within a city, searching for shelter or stardom or swinging times. There were waves of immigrants from Africa and the West Indies as well as migrants from the South. There were also young, gifted, and black artists from across the land; white blue-collar workers and blue bloods from Europe; and white publishers, dilettantes, and bohemians from downtown Manhattan. Harlem was the cosmopolitan black showcase of the nation, a "Promised Land" for some and "Playland" for others.

But for thousands of transplanted cotton pickers, tobacco choppers, and cane cutters, adjustment to the complexity of an exploitative, industrialized urban environment made the big city a spurious paradise. Exploited as cheap labor and barred by color from full participation in their society, including some of the night clubs (e.g., the Cotton Club) in their own community, the black masses spooled out their lives in an arabesque pattern of hard work and synthetic joy. Some novels of the period stressed "going to meet the man," "slaving for Miss Ann," or "running a game on lames"; others focused on getting down at a houserent party or gin joint with soul food and jumping music on Saturday nights; and a few recalled taking their troubles to the Lord in prayer and song on Sunday. These were the basic rituals of survival for the plain folk of Harlem and, with less intensity and sophistication, Kansas. "The ordinary Negroes," Hughes tells us in *The Big Sea*, "hadn't heard of the Negro Renaissance. And if they had, it hadn't raised their wages any."[41] Hughes and Cullen, as demonstrated in *The Afro-American Novel and Its Tradition*, were more effective than most of their counterparts in providing a realistic portrayal of the ways in which ordinary black folk used religion, music, humor, and language to cope with adversity.

SATIRIC REALISM: THE VICES AND FOLLIES OF THE FOLK AND BLACK BOURGEOISIE

The conventions of satire, particularly irony, were employed by early African American novelists, but it was not until the decline of the Harlem Renaissance that satiric realism fully emerged to compete with other types of realism and naturalism in the tradition of the African American novel.[42] Stripping away the disguise of romantic characters (white knights and fair damsels, black buffoons and savages), oratory (set speeches and stylized conversations), and situations (white paternalism and male domination as eternal laws of nature), several black writers of the Harlem Renaissance turned to comedy and satire for models to represent the ordinary experience of blacks. Whereas comedy, as in Hughes's *Tambourines to Glory*, is basically a humorous representation of the everyday life of lowbrow characters for its own sake, satire, as in Cullen's *One Way to Heaven*, has a clear moral aim. However, because the experiences of black Americans have historically been a mixture of the comic and the tragic, and because the black novelist's audience has been largely white and middle class, Hurston, Hughes, and Cullen generally combined the conventions of both forms in their tragicomic narratives. The most talented black satirists of the period—Rudolph Fisher, George Schuyler, and Wallace Thurman—combined satire and comedy in their novels. Although the era gave license to authors to parade the follies and vices of marginal types as ethnic virtues and cultural truths, the black satirists assumed the role of moralists, revealing the truth beneath the mask of surface reality.

Satire has historically been defended as a moral weapon, and the satirist as a protector of truth, justice, and reason. In *The Power of Satire* Robert C. Elliott traces the development of satire from its ancient origins in magic, myth, and ritual to sophisticated modern literary forms in western Europe and England.[43] Beginning with the improvised invective in Greek phallic songs, Elliott moves quickly to other times and places to describe the use of magical words and ritual phrases by satirical poets in Arabia, Ireland, Africa, and Alaska. These poets use satire to destroy the honor, wealth, health, or lives of personal and public enemies. Although satirists in preliterate cultures relied on the belief of their victims in the efficacy of their apparent preternatural power, the power itself was derived not so much from secret incantations and the mechanics of sympathetic magic as from the satirist's command over the word.[44]

Legends, tales, and sagas in the different cultures reveal the pervasive ancient belief that people actually died from the attacks of satirists. In his definitive study of African oral literature, African critic and novelist Isidore Okpewho reveals that in traditional societies like that of the Igbo of Nigeria moral lapses were "usually denounced by satirical songs or lampoons" in order "to bring shame on the culprits and so discourage future misconduct."[45] As Janie Crawford's destruction of her husband with signifying razor-sharp wit and words in *Their Eyes Were Watching God* illustrates, verbal abuse and ridicule, depending on the valuation placed on the opinion of others, are potent weapons in black American communities and novels for the achievement of social control or liberation.

Using the guilt-shame anthropological model,[46] Elliott describes not only the potency of criticism, shame, and rejection in societies that rely on external sanctions to govern behavior, but also the therapeutic function of ritualized ridicule in releasing pent-up aggressive impulses. Ritualized ridicule, as I explained in the first chapter, takes several forms in black American culture, including signifying, sounding, and playing the dozens. Because satire always contains an implicit or explicit set of normative values, and because the satirist generally represents himself or herself as a responsible critic of men and manners, as a writer who prefers to expose vice and folly through indirection, it is not surprising that the chief device of black satirists is irony. Basically, narrative irony is the result of a disparity of viewpoints among characters, narrator, and reader, and, in more sophisticated works of structural irony, between narrator and author. In *A Rhetoric of Irony* literary critic Wayne C. Booth identifies a fundamental distinction between stable ironies, which intend a precise reconstruction of their surface meanings, and unstable ironies, which imply or assert that all statements and meanings are subject to open-ended undermining.[47] The uses of satire and irony in the African American novel range from the simple effects of Rudolph Fisher, George Schuyler, and Wallace Thurman during the Harlem Renaissance to the extraordinary complexity of modern and contemporary novelists.

Because realism was a means to an end for the satirists and not an end in itself, we find Fisher, Schuyler, and Thurman widely different in their manner of criticizing the people, customs, and institutions of the Harlem Renaissance. Fisher views color prejudice with amusement, whereas Schuyler and Thurman lash out at it with bitter anger. As blacks they realize that color prejudice was not only the cardinal vice of white American society but also the source of much of the tragicomic nature of the African American experience within the black community itself. Moreover, because black folk humor had traditionally been a form of masked aggression, when turned inward on the race it became a form of self-aggression and compensatory relief from discrimination through laughter. It affirmed the humanity of blacks in the face of white society's efforts to deny or destroy that humanity. Consequently, burlesque, sarcasm, exaggeration, invective, and irony were all used in the service of satiric comment on intraracial discrimination and racial chauvinism, sparing neither the man on the street nor the leaders of the race.

The satirists were successful in unmasking the hypocrisy and self-righteousness of the leaders of the race and rejecting idealized images of the race. But they were less successful in avoiding scorn for lower-class urban blacks and their evolving culture. Although they presumed to speak for the lower class, they were actually spokesmen for the black intelligentsia. Their goal was a form of humanism that sought to lift lower-class blacks out of their ethnic community to the spurious perfection of assimilation into the larger white community. Whereas this had long been the goal of the majority of the black middle class, what was advocated now was an alliance with the white working class. But the status, wealth, and power offered by white America and radical black intellectuals before the economic disaster of 1929 were more shadow than substance. As a result, then, of the precipitous decline of the Harlem Renaissance and the onset of the Depression, a more sobering vision of the experiences of urban black Americans began to appear in the naturalistic works of African American novelists.

Richard Wright and the Triumph of Naturalism (1936–1952)

"It was the sociological imagination that was to have its day in the 1930's," writes social historian S. P. Fullinwider, "as the social scientists moved into the position of potential leadership, and as the blues writers, pushed by the logic of the depression, turned to social protest in the tradition of economic radicalism."[48] Although the sociological imagination called for assimilation and personal adjustment, it wanted neither within an exploitative social structure. Influenced by white and black social scientists of the "Chicago School" and by the activities of the Communist Party, Richard Wright and other black novelists of the thirties and forties saw the Great Depression as strong evidence that American society was on the verge of economic collapse. With varying degrees of commitment, they envisioned the solution in terms of biracial working-class solidarity and a restructuring of the American economic system.

The cry for reform had fallen on deaf ears. Although in 1941 President Roosevelt, anticipating our entry into World War II against fascist imperialism and racial genocide in Europe, issued Executive Order 8802 banning discrimination in defense industries and government, racial violence erupted in Detroit, New York, Los Angeles, Chicago, and in the South. These events reinforced the radical belief that only the organized power of the masses could prevail over the power of the wealthy few and the intransigent racism of their middle-class allies. In 1947 President Truman's Committee on Civil Rights issued a report, "To Secure These Rights," recommending improvement in the administration of federal laws protecting the rights of minorities; and in 1948 a similar committee recommended a policy of integration for the armed services. The stark reality of the exploitation of the urban black masses and of the devastating sociopsychological impact of urbanization and institutional racism as well as World War II led to the triumph of a disquieting new naturalistic vision in the African American novel between 1936 and 1952.

WRIGHT AND THE "CHICAGO SCHOOL" OF SOCIOLOGY

In the introduction to *Black Metropolis,* Wright states that "it was from the scientific findings of men like the late Robert E. Park, Robert Redfield, and Louis Wirth that I drew the meanings for my documentary book *Twelve Million Black Voices;* for my novel, *Native Son.*"[49] Park, Redfield, and Wirth were University of Chicago social scientists who broke new ground in the field of urban sociology and race relations with their pioneer studies on the impact of industrialization, urbanization, and social differentiation on "primitive peoples" and ethnic minorities.[50] The "Chicago School" of sociology strongly influenced the thinking and research of many social scientists, including such well-known black sociologists as Charles S. Johnson, E. Franklin Frazier, Horace Cayton, and Oliver C. Cox.

This was especially true of Park's theories on race relations and the city. Park had spent several years (1904–14) at Tuskegee as a ghost writer for Booker T. Washington. Park's theories on "social disorganization" and the "marginal man," even though the latter was defined as a racial and cultural hybrid, a mulatto, seem to be the basis of major studies by some of the black sociologists mentioned above as well as of Wright's conception of African American character and culture in his writings of the 1940s. Although Wright was not a student at the University of Chicago, he was influenced through Wirth and his research assistant, Horace Cayton, whom he first met in 1933. Unable to find work, Wright and his mother were on welfare at the time, and their social worker, Mrs. Mary Wirth, sent him to seek her husband's help in becoming a writer.[51] Over the years, Cayton and Wright became fast friends. More important, drawing on the studies by Park's students and associates in which they attempted to give structure to their own urban experiences with the ethics of Jim Crow during the Great Depression, Wright developed the theory of race relations and black personality that appears in *Lawd Today* and *Native Son.*

THE GREAT DEPRESSION AND THE COMMUNIST PARTY

Wright's hunger for a life that would be freer and fuller than the one he had known in the South led him to Chicago in 1927, but the Depression prolonged his hunger, driving him into the ranks of the underemployed and the unemployed. The Department of Agriculture and the Federal Reserve Board reported that between 1929 and 1933 agricultural prices fell more than 60 percent and industrial production plummeted from an index figure of 120 in 1929 to 57 in 1933. The gross national product declined from $104 billion to $75 billion and, according to the Bureau of Labor Statistics, more than 12 million workers were unemployed in March 1933.[52] While banks and businesses closed in the city and thousands of people stood in bread and soup lines for handouts, the government paid farmers, especially large landowners and planters, millions of dollars to plow under or temporarily not raise wheat, corn, barley, peanuts, hogs, dairy cattle, and beef.

The most disadvantaged and desperate major ethnic group during the Great Depression was black landless farmers and workers. "Negro sharecroppers were found to have an average income of $295 per year as compared with $417 for white sharecroppers; the Negro cash renter averaged $307, the white $568; the Negro wage hand averaged $175, the white $232." The unemployment figures for blacks, according to Urban League reports, were 30 to 60 percent greater than for whites. Not only were whites generally given preference for available jobs, but in some areas blacks were dismissed as elevator operators, bellboys, cooks, waiters, and delivery boys, and replaced by whites. Because of flagrant discrimination by leaders of the Agricultural Adjustment Administration and the National Recovery Administration, as well as the powerlessness of black organizations, "most of the AAA and NRA benefits did not trickle down to the masses of black workers and farmers."[53]

For the intellectuals and black writers of Wright's generation, some of the activities and programs of the Communist Party of the U.S.A. that seemed to meet the social and cultural needs of blacks had strong appeal. Prior to 1928, as Wilson Record points out in *The Negro and the Communist Party,* the Party's efforts to recruit blacks as members or sympathizers were less than successful.[54] Despite their economic exploitation and political disorganization, most black workers of the 1920s were ignorant and frightened of the Communists, and most black intellectuals and writers were skeptical at best of the Party view that racial oppression was simply an expression of economic bondage and that the solution of the "Negro problem" was in the unity of Negroes with all class-conscious workers. After all, there were no guarantees that socialism would provide any more racial equality than a capitalist democracy. But the Party's redefinition in 1928 of the "Negro problem" in the United States as a problem of an oppressed nation, an aspect of the general pattern of imperialism, whose solution—self-determination for the Black Belt—would be the same as that for any other oppressed colonial nation, offered hope of an ally to black nationalists. Because the Party's active support of their self-determination doctrine vacillated after 1934, however, in response to the needs of the Soviet Union's foreign policy, black intellectuals and writers who were sympathetic to the program became increasingly disillusioned. Earlier in the 1930s many had been impressed by the Party's opposition to fascism, and some still supported the activities in behalf of blacks by such front organizations as the industrial unions affiliated with the Trade Union Unity League; the committees and councils of the League of Struggle for Negro Rights, with Langston Hughes, a "fellow traveler," as its elected president; and the International Labor Defense, which played a prominent role in the Scottsboro trials. Some black people saw hope in the Party's running of a black candidate for vice president in the national elections of 1932 and 1936. Of greater interest to black writers were the John Reed clubs and the opportunities their journals provided for publication. But most saw their hopes and their race betrayed in 1939 with the signing of the Stalin-Hitler nonaggression pact and the Party's subordination of the struggle against racial discrimination to the struggle of the Soviet Union for world power.

In 1933 Wright joined the John Reed Club in Chicago and made a full commitment to the Party.[55] In *The God That Failed,* Wright states:

> It was not the economics of Communism, nor the great power of trade unions, nor the excitement of underground politics that claimed me; my attention was caught by the similarity of the experiences of workers in other lands, by the possibility of uniting scattered but kindred peoples into a whole. It seemed to me that here at last, in the realm of revolutionary expression, Negro experience could find a home, a functioning value and role.

As for his own role, he continues:

> The Communists, I felt, had oversimplified the experience of those whom they sought to lead. In their efforts to recruit masses, they had missed the meaning of the lives of the masses, had conceived of people in too abstract a manner. I would try to put some of that meaning back. I would tell Communists how common people felt, and I would tell common people of the self-sacrifice of Communists who strove for unity among them.[56]

For the first time in his life, Wright therefore felt accepted and needed by the white world, and began to articulate his mission as a writer. To his alarm, members of the Party considered him, a junior high school graduate and self-educated man, a suspicious black intellectual. Though they entrusted him with many important duties, his writings were under constant scrutiny for bourgeois consciousness and violations of the Party line. Mutual distrust and Wright's irrepressible individualism finally led to an official break with the Party in 1944, the year before the United States ended World War II by dropping the atomic bomb on Hiroshima and Nagasaki.

THE FEDERAL WRITERS' PROJECT

The New Deal agency that was most beneficial to unemployed black writers was the Federal Writers' Project (FWP). Established in 1935 as a subdivision of the Works Progress Administration and a distinct agency within the Federal Arts Project, which included art, music, and theater, the FWP supported more than six thousand writers of various degrees of talent. Among these were several who were destined to become well-known black novelists: Richard Wright, Claude McKay, Chester Himes, Ralph Ellison, Frank Yerby, Arna Bontemps, William Attaway, Willard Motley, Zora Neale Hurston, and Margaret Walker. The primary task of the FWP was to prepare the *American Guide,* a comprehensive, multivolume guide to the United States. As I indicated at the beginning of the book, in order to ensure that blacks were not neglected in research and publications sponsored by the agency, Sterling A. Brown, with the support of the black leadership, was appointed editor for Negro Affairs. In addition to compiling 378 regional books and pamphlets between 1935 and 1939, white and black writers collected black folk materials, and the most serious and talented of the group were provided with the inspiration and security to continue their own private creative projects.[57] Many of the short pieces written by FWP writers during their spare time, including Richard Wright's "Ethics of Living Jim Crow," appeared in *American Stuff* (1937), a voluminous anthology prepared by directors of the project and published commercially.

THE TRIUMPH OF NATURALISM

Although earlier novels by Dunbar, Du Bois, and Johnson had dealt with the conflict between determinism and the human will, it was the interplay between Freudian psychology and Marxist social analysis in *Native Son* that established the naturalistic model for many black novelists of the forties. Unlike the novels of the New Negro, those influenced by the example of *Native Son* are informed by the belief that the character and history of man can be completely explained by biological and socioeconomic facts. The Wright paradigm of naturalism stresses the violence and pathological personalities that result from racial oppression and economic exploitation. Novelists generally identified as being strongly influenced by Wright include William Attaway (*Blood on the Forge,* 1941); Carl Offord (*The White Face,* 1943); Chester Himes (*If He Hollers Let Him Go,* 1945, and *Lonely Crusade,* 1947); Curtis Lucas (*Third Ward Newark,* 1946); Ann Petry (*The Street,* 1946); Alden Bland (*Behold a Cry,* 1947); Willard Motley (*Knock on Any Door,* 1947); William Gardner Smith (*Last of the Conquerors,* 1948); and Willard Savoy (*Alien Land,* 1949). In an analysis in *The Afro-American Novel and Its Tradition* of selected novels by Attaway, Himes, Petry, and Smith, I demonstrate, however, that the naturalistic vision of these novelists takes such different forms that the concept of a "Wright School" is at best misleading. Attaway's *Blood on the Forge,* for example, is a panoramic study of the destruction of a family and a way of life, whereas Himes's *If He Hollers Let Him Go,* Petry's *Street,* and Smith's *Stone Face* (1963) have more in common with case studies of alienated individuals.

Attaway shares with Wright a pessimistic attitude toward the viability of folk culture in a modern industrial world and a concern for the psychological subtleties of his characters, but Attaway is more sympathetic to a Marxist analysis of the harsh social realities of the working class. Although middle-class and better educated, Himes's characters are at least as much the victims of racial and cultural oppression as Wright's. Also, even though Himes is explicitly at odds with Wright's representation of Bigger's class status as a crucial factor in the injustice and violence of antiblack racism, both the neglect of a viable black vernacular ethos and the assertion of a naive male chauvinism that informs Himes's sociopsychological vision unfortunately restrict the complexity, ironies, and paradoxes of African American character and culture to fear, hatred, powerlessness, and rage, especially sexual, in the black male. In contrast to Bigger Thomas and Himes's Bob Jones, Petry's Lutie Johnson is an intelligent, working-class, commonplace aspiring black single parent, who is driven by the American Dream rather than fear, hatred, and rage even though she is the victim of sexism and antiblack racism. More like Petry's protagonist than Wright's, Smith's Simeon Booker is a black expatriate Philadelphia reporter and amateur painter in Paris who seeks futilely to escape the violence of antiblack racism and to resolve his brooding sense of double consciousness and potential for violent rage and political activism. In style these naturalistic narratives combine objectivity with satire, impressionism, or sensationalism; in point of view, they range from omniscient to first-person narrators with varying degrees of reliability. Their salient themes are color and class violence, and their protagonists are generally victims of forces beyond their control or full understanding.

CONTINUITY AND CHANGE IN THE NOVELS OF THE FORTIES

Of the twenty-eight novels published by black Americans in the forties, excluding the nine by Oscar Micheaux and Frank Yerby,[58] more than a dozen bear traces of the influence of *Native Son* and mark the triumph of naturalism. Even the best of these—*Blood on the Forge, If He Hollers Let Him Go,* and *The Street*—demonstrate that sociological approaches that reduce their naturalistic vision to protest literature risk oversimplifying and misrepresenting the individuality of the novelists' vision of life and aesthetic achievement. This individuality is most apparent in their conceptions and delineations of the dynamics of African American character, which foster ambivalence toward blacks as well as whites, and in their resolutions of the problems of racism and economic exploitation that they portray.

At the same time, the African American novel in the decade from Wright's

Native Son to Smith's *Anger at Innocence* (1950) reveals both continuity and change. The theme of color and class conflict remains dominant, whether in the triumph of the naturalists or the satirists like Dorothy West, whose *The Living Is Easy* (1948) exposes the counterfeit black Brahmins of Boston, and Saunders Redding, whose *Strangers and Alone* attacks the inferiority syndrome of Southern black colleges. West and Redding, like Griggs, Chesnutt, Fisher, Thurman, and Schuyler, reveal that the conflict of color and class is intraracial as well as interracial. Emphasis on external social reality with the conventional closed plot continues, with more documentation of acts of prejudice and discrimination than of black folklore. But there is a corresponding shift, as the novels of Wright and Himes illustrate, to an exploration of the impact of oppression on the feelings and thoughts of the major characters. Although the general tone of naturalistic fiction is objective, pessimistic, and amoral, the black naturalism of the 1940s does not preclude the possibility of an implicit, albeit ironic, reaffirmation of faith in a moral universe and the sanctity of the individual by the implied author.

On one level, for example, Bigger's confession to Max at the end of *Native Son* that he has instinctively rebelled against the morality of a social system that violated his humanity and individuality makes this point: "'I ain't trying to forgive nobody and I ain't asking for nobody to forgive me. I ain't going to cry. They wouldn't let me live and I killed. Maybe it ain't fair to kill, and I reckon I really didn't want to kill. But when I think of why all the killing was, I begin to feel what I wanted, what I am . . .'" (p. 391). Implicit also is the traditional call for social change. By documenting the inherent weaknesses in the social system, what the novels of the forties actually demand, as critic Carl Milton Hughes has pointed out, "is not fundamental change in the social structure; rather they insist on making the letter and spirit of our Constitution and the Declaration of Independence indispensable to American social structure a reality."[59] This is in sharp contrast to some of the revolutionary novels of the 1960s and 1970s, which are more apocalyptic.

Two momentous changes were introduced in the African American novel of the forties. The most obvious and controversial was Wright's creation of Bigger Thomas as the prototypical urban black American, obsessed by a fear and hatred of white people and driven to violence in rebellion against and, paradoxically, in affirmation of his dehumanization. Rejecting the traditional survival strategies offered by black music, the black church, and the extended black family, Wright, probably influenced by the work of Freud, Marx, Park, Dreiser, Dos Passos, and Joyce, depicted the black American as the victim of modern America and as the Bad Nigger incarnate. The unexpurgated editions of *Native Son*, and *Lawd Today* that were edited by biographer and critic Arnold Rampersad and published by the Library of America in 1991 reinforce the authority and authenticity of Wright's initially submitted manuscripts before they were changed to satisfy the racial and sexual prejudices of white Book-of-the-Month Club readers. However, the reincorporation of censored passages such as the theater scene of Bigger and Jack masturbating and expressing sexual interest in Mary Dalton and other white rich girls in *Native Son* and the replacement of deleted experimental passages of songs, wordplay, games, and news headlines in *Lawd Today* also reinforce the character of protagonists Bigger and Jake Jackson. They are still representations of doomed, violent Southern black male victims of modern American racism, urbanization, and industrialism. For novelists like Himes, who tailored Wright's pathological model of African American personality to fit his own better educated protagonists, violence in the form of personal rebellion was the only therapeutic solution to oppression. But for Attaway, Petry, Smith, and those novelists whose vision of African American character affirmed its double consciousness and its multidimensional nature, personal rage and rebellion were neither the only nor necessarily the most politically appropriate or humanistic mode of response and agency to racial oppression and economic exploitation.

The other major change that occurred in the post–World War II period was an increase in the number of black writers who published novels in which the protagonists and the majority of characters were white. In addition to Frank Yerby's white historical romances, these include Ann Petry's *Country Place,* Willard Motley's *Knock on Any Door* and *We Fished All Night,* Zora Neale Hurston's *Seraph on the Sewanee,* and William Gardner Smith's *Anger at Innocence.* Nick Romano in *Knock on Any Door* is perhaps the most sympathetically drawn and memorable of the white protagonists of the decade. As the tradition of the African American novel continued into the fifties, the novelists moved significantly beyond naturalism to the rediscovery of the viability of myth, legend, and ritual as well as modern cultural codes and literary constructs.

Myth, Legend, and Ritual in the Novels of the Fifties (1952–1962)

"The integration that had been inaugurated in the closing years of World War II," as historian John Hope Franklin notes, "was greatly accelerated in the postwar years."[60] One of the dubious honors for black Americans as a result of the climate fostered by the recommendations of President Truman's interracial committees on civil rights and integration is that blacks constituted 30 percent of the United States forces in the Korean War (1950–51) but were only 10 percent of the general population. In 1954 the Supreme Court announced its landmark decision that the doctrine of "separate but equal" in public education was inherently contradictory and unconstitutional. A year later, blacks in Montgomery, Alabama, led by the Reverend Martin Luther King Jr., boycotted the city bus lines to resist racial discrimination and abuse, launching the first postwar direct action movement of the masses organized and led by blacks themselves.

In 1957 Congress passed the first civil rights bill since 1875. It created the Civil Rights Commission, whose hearings in several cities disclosed that Southern white registrars were denying blacks the right to vote. "By 1962 more than thirty cases had been brought by the attorney general," according to Franklin, "to protect blacks in their efforts to vote in Mississippi, Louisiana, Alabama, Tennessee, and Georgia."[61] Also in 1957, President Eisenhower sent federal troops to Little Rock, Arkansas, to protect black school children from the violence of howling white mobs. The winds of social change were also blowing in West Africa, where Ghana achieved independence in the same year. In 1960 four black college students in Greensboro, North Carolina, sat-in at a downtown lunch counter in an effort to desegregate the facility, setting off a chain of nonviolent direct action sit-ins, freedom rides, wade-ins, and freedom marches across the country. The Congress of Racial Equality and the Student Nonviolent Coordinating Committee spearheaded this phase of direct action, but they were soon joined by the Southern Christian Leadership Conference and the National Association for the Advancement of Colored People, which began using the motto "Free by '63." In 1961 political and military intrigue by imperialist countries, following the independence of the Congo, resulted in the execution of Premier Patrice Lumumba. We conclude this thumbnail sketch of 1952–62 with two major acts by President Kennedy to end federal support of racism. In 1961 he intitiated federal equal opportunity policies primarily to redress past racial discrimination against black Americans, Native Americans, Chicanos, and Puerto Ricans; and in 1962 with a stroke of his pen, he ended discrimination in federally supported housing.

BEYOND NATURALISM

From 1952 to 1962 two parallel movements in the tradition of the African American novel can be observed: a movement away from naturalism and nonracial themes, and a movement toward the rediscovery and revitalization of myth, legend, and ritual as appropriate sign systems for expressing the double consciousness, socialized ambivalence, and double vision of the post–World War II experiences of black Americans. Black novelists of the forties, as Carl Milton Hughes illustrates, broadened their perspectives and began experimenting with nonracial themes and white protagonists.[62] This experimenting continued into the fifties with Smith's *Anger at Innocence* (1950), Demby's *Beetlecreek* (1950), Motley's *We Fished All Night* (1951) and *Let No Man Write My Epitaph* (1958), Himes's *Cast the First Stone* (1952), Petry's *Narrows* (1953), Wright's *Savage Holiday* (1954), and Baldwin's *Giovanni's Room* (1956). Most of these have nonwhite minor characters and a third-person undramatized narrator who is sympathetic toward the white protagonist, who, significantly, is a social misfit or outsider.

Baldwin's *Giovanni's Room*, a lyrical story of American and French homosexuality, and Himes's *Cast the First Stone*, a prison novel with homosexual overtones, are largely autobiographical narratives in which the implied authors closely identify with the major events and the first-person narrators. More typical of the novels exploring nonblack themes and communities are Wright's *Savage Holiday,* a melodramatic Freudian tale of the repressed sexuality of Erskine Fowler, "a Mason, a Rotarian, a Sunday School Superintendent, a man of parts"; and Petry's *Narrows,* whose protagonist is black, but whose theme stresses the impact of chance and the historical past on the development of character. Also in this group of experimental novels, Motley's *We Fished All Night* is the story of three Chicagoans who return from World War II as psychological and moral cripples, and the last of these novels, *Let No Man Write My Epitaph,* a sequel to *Knock on Any Door,* traces the criminality and salvation of Nick Romano's youngest brother and illegitimate son.

Motley, Smith, and Demby border on sentimentalism in representing the essential goodness of their white characters. Theodore Hall, in Smith's *Anger at Innocence,* a naturalistic treatment of good and evil, is, for example, a quiet, poetry-loving night watchman with "strange ideas" and "a lot of taboos." Thirty-nine years old, he abruptly leaves his wife of eighteen years and takes up with a nineteen-year-old tramp he wants to marry, but who kills him and herself after he refuses to adopt completely her life of degeneracy. Warned by her neo-Calvinist mother that "Rodina was born evil," Hall, a "good" man, believes just the opposite, but he is unable to redeem her. "She could not change," we learn in Rodina's monologue, "neither could Theodore change. Even if he wanted to. He was what he was. . . . He was good, she was evil."[63] These representations of white characters and communities in several black novels of the 1940s and 1950s in part reveal the impact of the prevailing integrationist movement of the period.

Unsurprisingly, therefore, Bill Trapp, the tragic white victim in *Beetlecreek,* is as much the central character in William Demby's first novel as is Johnny Johnson, the lonely black fourteen-year-old Pittsburgh boy who resettles in Beetlecreek, West Virginia, with his aunt and uncle. David Diggs, Johnny's frustrated, college-educated uncle succumbs to "good-timing" in his efforts to escape the death-grip feeling of being black and trapped in Beetlecreek. Scapegoat for the provinciality, prejudice, and fears of the townspeople, black and white, Trapp has lived between the black and white sections of town as a recluse for fifteen years. He seeks spiritual regeneration and sociability by reaching out to the black community, especially to Johnny and David, who identified with the old man's feelings of neglect and loneliness. Even when he worked in the carnival, "he felt close to them," Trapp reflects. "Watching them secretly as he did he could see that they were always dodging something, were ashamed of something, just as he was; they were the same breed as he."[64]

Critical of what he sees as the philistinism and provincialism of blacks, Demby, an expatriate in Italy from 1949 to the 1960s, is emotionally and morally sympathetic toward Trapp. The well-meaning but naive efforts of Trapp "to reach out and touch people, to love," by giving a picnic in his yard for black and white children result in the malicious rumors that he was a child molester and fiend. Demby is also sympathetic toward Johnny, whose initiation into the Nightriders, a black youth gang, required him to violate his compassion for Trapp by adopting the community's narrow-minded values and burning down Trapp's house. The style and structure of the novel reveal the implied author's equal sympathy toward David, who by leaving Beetlecreek at the end of the book with an old college flame, "stepped outside himself by going with the girl, bringing life to himself when the village had already killed him."[65] Thus we see that the experiment with nonracial themes and protagonists which began in the forties continued in the fifties, when the prevailing political sentiments were integrationist. Contrary to Hughes's contention, however, the parallel tendency of a "break with naturalism and the accompanying philosophy of determinism" did not significantly manifest itself until the fifties.[66]

The gradual movement away from naturalism is apparent in the novels of Lloyd Brown and Frank L. Brown. Lloyd Brown's *Iron City* (1951) is a prison novel that uses black folk history and spirituals to delineate the character of two members of the Communist Party, and newspaper clippings to advance a plot that attacks the legal lynching of Lonnie James, the protagonist, and promotes a Marxist proletarian vision of the weaknesses of American society. Frank Brown's *Trumbull Park* (1959), the first-person story of a black airplane factory worker's courage in resettling his family in a white public housing project in Chicago, also draws on black folklore, especially the songs "We Shall Not Be Moved" and "Every Day I Got the Blues." These conventional narratives celebrate the emerging spiritual as well as political heroism of the working class, a type of critical realism that culminates in the novels of John O. Killens.

The break with naturalism is more pronounced in Wright's *Outsider* (1953) and Gwendolyn Brooks's *Maud Martha* (1953). In *The Outsider* Wright rejects facile color and class explanations of the dilemma of modern man to develop the existential theme that in a godless, meaningless world man must achieve meaning and purpose in the process of creating his own standards and himself. Employing a third-person intimate narrator to probe the consciousness of his protagonist, Cross Damon, Wright relies heavily on indirect interior monologue and Cross's dialogue with Ely Houston, the physically deformed but mentally acute district attorney, to dramatize the sociopsychological depths of his modern theme of alienation. The compelling, controversial theme of *The Outsider* is that by accident of race or birth or chance some men, especially blacks, are outsiders, gifted with a double vision by being inside and outside of American society at the same time and terrified by the psychological knowledge that "man may be just anything at all."[67]

Maud Martha is one of the missing links between the poetic realism of *Cane* in the 1920s and *The Bluest Eye* and *Sula* in the 1970s. Gwendolyn Brooks, a Pulitzer Prize–winning poet, breaks with conventional plot structure and divides her novel into thirty-four impressionistic vignettes or slices-of-life. They outline the growth of Maud Martha from a seven-year-old who found "it hard to believe that a thing of ordinary allurements . . . was as easy to love as a thing of heart-catching beauty" to a post–World War II married woman awaiting her second child. She is doubtful that "the ridiculousness of man would ever completely succeed in destroying the world—or, in fact, the basic equanimity of the least and commonest flower"; and she is thankful that "while people did live they would be grand, would be glorious and brave, would have nimble hearts that would beat and beat."[68] Focusing on Maud, an ordinary black woman whose coming-of-age involves an agonizing struggle with color prejudice, a chauvinistic husband, and an "everydayness" in appearance that she compares to a dandelion, the third-person narrator is intimately involved with the feelings and thoughts of the self-effacing, sensitive protagonist. Her "dearest wish" in life was "to be cherished" by those she loved, especially her husband, whom she criticizes for his insensitivity to her needs and desires. The power of Brooks's lyricism gives poignancy and beauty to the ordinariness of Maud's story, and her use of a commonplace flower as a metaphor for black women was adopted by women novelists of the 1970s like Toni Morrison and Alice Walker.

MYTH, LEGEND, AND RITUAL

The most dramatic break with naturalism occurs in the rediscovery of myth, legend, and ritual by Ralph Ellison and James Baldwin. Because myth, legend, and ritual were discussed at length in the first chapter, I will here only summarize briefly some earlier observations in order to stress the continuing importance of African American folklore, especially the five residually oral vernacular forms, in the modern black American novel. By and large black novelists of the fifties rejected the ahistorical universality of Greco-Roman myth and ritual for a mixture of Christian and social myths and rituals rooted in the particularity of the experiences of black Americans. For example, the myth of white supremacy and the rituals that reinforce and perpetuate the Manichean black and white, evil and good, significations of Western mythology with its overtones of an apocalyptic clash are still a major source for themes, symbols, and images in the novels of the fifties. Ralph Ellison writes in *Shadow and Act*:

> It took me a long time to learn how to adapt such examples of myth into my work—also ritual. The use of ritual is equally a vital part of the creative process. I learned a few things from Eliot, Joyce and Hemingway, but not how to adapt them. When I started writing, I knew that in both *The Waste Land* and *Ulysses* ancient myth and ritual were used to give form

> and significance to the material; but it took me a few years to realize that the myths and rites which we find functioning in our everyday lives could be used in the same way. . . . In any society there are many rituals of situation which, for the most part, go unquestioned. They can be simple or elaborate, but they are the connective tissue between the work of art and the audience.[69]

Because myth, legend, and rituals are cultural codes for communally sanctioned attitudes, beliefs, and behavior, they are ideally suited for novelists in search of appropriate signs and forms to reconstruct the socialized ambivalence—the shifting, conflicting emotions of love and hate, shame and pride fostered by social oppression—of black American life.

Seen in retrospect, then, the most significant development in the tradition of the African American novel between 1952 and 1962 was the rediscovery of myth, legend, and ritual by Ralph Ellison and James Baldwin. Although Petry's *Narrows*, Wright's *Outsider*, and Brooks's *Maud Martha* move beyond naturalism in exploration of new themes, forms, or styles, it is Ellison's *Invisible Man* and Baldwin's *Go Tell It on the Mountain* that most dramatically remind us of the continuity of traditional narrative forms in appropriately modern black contexts. Ellison and Baldwin were both influenced by the achievement in naturalism of Richard Wright, but each chose a different and distinctive approach to the novel. Each became aware of the literary possibilities of his folk tradition as a result of his own personal experiences and his own study of literature.

As in the black American novels of the nineteenth century, however, history and myth, illustrative and representational character types, traditional and personal sign systems are juxtaposed or integrated with each other as Ellison and Baldwin seek the appropriate interplay of realism and modernism for their aesthetic and social purpose. Shaped by the Depression, the Harlem Renaissance, his college background, and his writing apprenticeship, Ellison, the older of the two writers, reveals a more modern sensibility in the literary and vernacular patterns of *Invisible Man* than Baldwin, whose sensibility is poignantly more unconventional, does in *Go Tell It on the Mountain*. As products of institutional racism and the integrationist movements of the 1940s, however, both novelists reveal their own socialized ambivalence and double vision in their themes, plots, characterization, and point of view. As demonstrated in *The Afro-American Novel and Its Tradition*, the novels of both also reveal the qualities of realism and modernism that were to become more pronounced and dichotomous in the 1960s and 1970s.

4 / Forms of Neorealism: Critical and Poetic Realism (1962–1983)

When Black women's books are dealt with at all, it is usually in the context of Black literature, which largely ignores the implications of sexual politics. When white women look at Black women's words they are of course ill-equipped to deal with the subtleties of racial politics. A Black feminist approach to literature that embodies the realization that the politics of sex as well as the politics of race and class are crucially interlocking factors in the works of Black women writers is an absolute necessity.

BARBARA SMITH

"Toward a Black Feminist Criticism"

REBELLION or revolution—that was the burning question of the 1960s. Whether the cry was "We Shall Overcome," "Power to the people!" or "Burn, baby, burn!" black and white voices were raised in protest against racism, poverty, war, corruption, and sexism. Many Americans were deeply disillusioned by the moral bankruptcy of their political and economic system and took radical action to correct or to escape the social injustice of the decade in myriad forms of movements and cults. These radical movements and cults ranged from the Weathermen, a white revolutionary splinter group of Students for a Democratic Society (SDS), who bombed buildings identified as part of the military-industrial complex, to the college students who buried cars as menaces to the ecology, and from the drop-out and turn-on followers of Timothy Leary, the guru of the drug culture and former Harvard professor, to the Charles Manson cult, which committed ritual murders. Eclipsing the first manned U.S. landing on the moon in 1969, a revolution in moral conscience and social consciousness was underway. Spearheading these radical changes and most significant for their impact on the African American novel from 1962 to 1983 were the Black Power and Black Arts movements and, toward the end of the 1960s, the Women's Rights and Black Feminist movements.

The Black Power and Black Arts Movements

The rallying cry "Black Power" was popularized by Stokely Carmichael and Willie Ricks during the continuation by the Student Nonviolent Coordinating

Committee (SNCC) of James Meredith's protest march through the South in 1966. But the phrase is more than a slogan and has a meaning as large as the history of the struggle of black people against antiblack racism in the United States. As a political concept, Black Power expresses the determination of black people to define and liberate themselves. As SNCC leader Stokely Carmichael and political scientist Charles V. Hamilton explain: "The adoption of the concept of Black Power is one of the most legitimate and healthy developments in American politics and race relations in our time. . . . It is a call for black people in this country to unite, to recognize their heritage, to build a sense of community. It is a call for black people to begin to define their own goals, to lead their own organizations and to support those organizations. It is a call to reject the racist institutions and values of this society."[1] Black Power thus has a wide range of meanings, from the development of economic, political, and cultural solidarity and the attainment of full equality as American citizens to the radical reform or, if necessary, revolutionary overthrow of old political, economic, and cultural structures.

The concept also has a long history. In 1954 Richard Wright titled his book about Ghana *Black Power*, but as the essays in Floyd Barbour's *Black Power Revolt* reveal, the concept can be traced back to Benjamin Banneker's epistolary response to Thomas Jefferson's racist comments in *Notes on the State of Virginia* in 1791. The most passionate early statement on Black Power is David Walker's "Appeal to the Colored Citizens of the World" in 1829. On the international level the concept was promoted by the six Pan-African meetings convened between 1900 and 1945. "From the end of World War II through the early 1960's," historian John H. Bracey Jr. writes, "integration was the dominant ideology among Negro protest movements. A few nationalist groups, such as the UNIA splinter groups and the Nation of Islam, persisted but could arouse little mass support."[2] Among the many legal actions, sit-ins, marches, freedom rides, boycotts, demonstrations, and voter registration drives, the most salient civil rights events of the period were the 1954 Supreme Court school desegregation decision, the 1963 March on Washington, the 1964 Civil Rights Act, and the 1965 Voting Rights Act. Among the many civil rights leaders, the two dominant black leaders of the period were vastly different. Martin Luther King Jr. was a charismatic, nonviolent Southern Baptist preacher who rose to national prominence as the guiding spirit of the Montgomery bus boycott in 1955 and of the passive resistance tactics of the Southern Christian Leadership Conference (SCLC), a major civil rights organization. He was also the most dynamic and inspirational speaker at the March on Washington in 1963. In contrast, Malcolm X was the equally charismatic, militant Minister of the Nation of Islam and its chief spokesman until 1964, when he broke with his leader, the Honorable Elijah Muhammad, over irreconcilable doctrinal differences. Assassinated for their activism, Malcolm in 1965 and King in 1968, both men became martyrs of the

Black Power movement and paradigms of heroism in the Black Arts movement, most compellingly re-created in the tradition of the African American novel in John A. Williams's *Man Who Cried I Am* and Charles Johnson's *Dreamer*.

In the early 1960s the example of the emerging free African nations and the Cuban Revolution kindled the latent revolutionary nationalism of many black Americans and spurred the development of Black Studies programs in colleges across the nation. The Black Studies movement inspired the national movement for Ethnic Studies, Women's Studies, and other interdisciplinary programs. Black Power advocates redefined the liberation struggle of black Americans as part of the larger struggle of oppressed peoples against Western imperialism and colonialism. Frustrated by the snail's pace of integration efforts and the tactics of passive resistance, they revived indigenous theories of the colonial relationship of blacks to the dominant culture of the United States. In a cogent explanation of the theory of black Americans as subjects of domestic colonialism, social critic Harold Cruse writes:

> The American Negro shares with colonial peoples many of the socio-economic factors which form the material basis for present day revolutionary nationalism. Like the peoples of the underdeveloped countries, the Negro suffers in varying degree from hunger, illiteracy, disease, ties to the land, urban and semi-urban slums, cultural starvation, and the psychological reactions to being ruled over by others not of his kind. He experiences the tyranny imposed upon the lives of those who inhabit underdeveloped countries. . . . From the beginning, the American Negro has existed as a colonial being. His enslavement coincided with the colonial expansion of European powers and was nothing more or less than a condition of domestic colonialism. Instead of the United States establishing a colonial empire in Africa, it brought the colonial system home and installed it in the Southern states. When the Civil War broke up the slave system and the Negro was emancipated, he gained only partial freedom. Emancipation elevated him only to the position of a semi-independent man, not to that of an equal or independent being. . . . As a wage laborer or tenant farmer, the Negro is discriminated against and exploited. Those in the educated, professional, and intellectual classes suffer a similar fate. Except for a very small percentage of the Negro intelligentsia, the Negro functions in a subcultural world made up, usually of necessity, of his own race only. . . . The only factor which differentiates the Negro's status from that of a pure colonial status is that his position is maintained in the "home" country in close proximity to the dominant racial group. It is not at all remarkable then that the semi-colonial status of the Negro has given rise to nationalist movements. It would be surprising if it had not.[3]

In the revolt against historical exploitation and the many beatings, jailings, and killings of civil rights activists, blacks in the communities across the nation began striking out in rage: in Harlem in 1964, Watts in 1965, Newark and Detroit in 1967, and nearly every city in the nation in 1968 after the assassination of Martin Luther King Jr. Responding to the needs of the black working poor and unemployed, some groups, such as US, promoted the development of an indigenous African-based cultural value system, ritualized in the ceremony of Kwanzaa, a holiday celebrated from December 26 through January 1 to reinforce the spiritual ties of black Americans to Africa. Inspired by leftist ideology, pan-Africanism, and Third World theories, the Black Panther Party, the Revolutionary Action Movement (RAM), the Republic of New Africa, and the League of Revolutionary Black Workers adopted the strategy of achieving black self-determination by any means necessary, including armed struggle.

"Black Art is the aesthetic and spiritual sister of the Black Power concept," writes Larry Neal, a major proponent of the Black Arts movement. "As such, it envisions an art that speaks directly to the needs and aspirations of Black America. In order to perform this task, the Black Arts Movement proposes a radical reordering of the western cultural aesthetic. It proposes a separate symbolism, mythology, critique and iconology."[4] It was launched in the spring of 1964 when LeRoi Jones, whose play *Dutchman* had stunned the theater world, and other black artists opened the Black Arts Repertory Theatre-School in Harlem and took their plays, poetry readings, and concerts into the streets of the black community. Before the end of the summer the Harlem school was forced to close because of violent ideological problems, but black art groups soon sprang up on campuses and in cities across the nation. At the same time, black musicians like Little Richard, Chuck Berry, James Brown, B. B. King, Muddy Waters, Otis Redding, Aretha Franklin, John Coltrane, Stevie Wonder, Jimi Hendrix, Isaac Hayes, and the Supremes became national and international style setters. Black actors and actresses such as Sidney Poitier, James Earl Jones, Cicely Tyson, Ossie Davis, Ruby Dee, Harry Belafonte, Clarence Williams, and Bill Cosby became highly visible in major roles in the movies and on television. And mass periodicals such as *Essence, Encore, Black Collegian, Black Enterprise,* and *Black World;* small presses like Broadside and Third World; and journals like *Umbra, Black Dialogue, Liberator, Journal of Black Poetry,* and *Black Scholar* were born and, in some cases, died early, untimely deaths due to financial and ideological difficulties.

Because the Black Arts and Black Power concepts both relate broadly to the African American's desire for self-determination and nationhood, both are nationalistic. In Neal's words, "One is concerned with the relationship between art and politics; the other with the art of politics."[5] Nevertheless, most black writing of the 1960s, Neal contends, was aimed at the destruction of the double consciousness described by Du Bois in *The Souls of Black Folk.* "It has been aimed at consolidating the African-American personality. And it has not been essentially a literature of protest. It has, instead, turned its attention inward to the internal problems of the group. . . . It is a literature primarily directed at the conscience of black people."[6]

The Women's Rights and Black Feminist Movements

Just as the nineteenth-century struggle for equal rights for women was fired by the struggle to free the slaves, the Women's Rights movement of the 1960s was fired by the Civil Rights and Black Power movements. "The call to that first Woman's Rights Convention came about," as feminist Betty Friedan explains, "because an educated woman, who had already participated in shaping society as an abolitionist, came face to face with the realities of a housewife's drudgery and isolation in a small town."[7] Similarly, participation in the Civil Rights movement, ambivalence about the Black Power movement, especially its male chauvinism, and boredom with their actual or expected lives as suburban housewives spurred many American women more than a century later to renewed activism for women's rights. Most of the leading feminists, of course, were and are middle-class white women. Consequently, the question arises: How relevant are the experiences, truths, and priorities of white women to black women?

Subject to all the restrictions against blacks as well as those against women, the black woman is for many people, as black folk wisdom teaches, "de mule uh de world." Because black men and women struggled equally for liberation during slavery, Reconstruction, and the post-Reconstruction eras, the experience and truths of black women are generally glossed over or ignored when references are made to women and blacks. In *Ain't I a Woman* bell hooks attributes the silence of black women about sexism after the voting rights victory of the Women's Rights movement in the 1920s to the decline of radical reform during World War I and to the patriarchal values of black males. Although black men and women continued to struggle together against antiblack racism during the Civil Rights movement from the 1930s to the 1960s, during the Black Power movement of the 1960s black male activists publicly told black women "that they should take care of household needs and breed warriors for the revolution."[8] Even so, as Gerda Lerner documents in *Black Women in White America,* "black women, speaking with many voices and expressing many individual opinions, have been nearly unanimous in their insistence that their own emancipation cannot be separated from the emancipation of their men. Their liberation depends on the liberation of the race and the improvement of the life of the black community."[9] But with the rise of the women's movement and the internal and external destruction of the Black Power movement, including frequent criticism by black women of black male sexism, public interest began to shift in the late 1960s from the rights of blacks to the rights of women. Consequently, publishers became more receptive to the voices of black women writers. And novels by Margaret Walker, Rosa Guy, Mary Vroman, Louise Meriwether, Paule Marshall, Kristin Hunter, Carlene Polite, Sarah Wright, Alice Walker, Alice Childress, Ellease Southerland, Gloria Naylor, Toni Morrison, Gayl Jones, and Toni Cade Bambara, among the better known, were all published before the end of 1983. Facile generalizations about the parallels between the struggle of blacks and women for status ignore the complexity and distinctiveness of the history of black women, a history that reaches from the legacy of their African past and slave experience to their experience with industrialization and modern corporate America. As author and political analyst Toni Cade Bambara astutely reminds us,

> There is nothing to indicate that the African woman, who ran the marketplace, who built dams, who engaged in international commerce and diplomacy, who sat on thrones, who donned armor to wage battle against the European invaders and the corrupt chieftains who engaged in the slave trade, who were consulted as equals in the affairs of state—nothing to indicate that they were turning their men into faggots, were victims of penis envy, or any such nonsense. There is nothing to indicate that the Sioux, Seminole, Iroquois or other "Indian" nations felt oppressed or threatened by their women, who had mobility, privileges, a voice in governing of the commune. There is evidence, however, that the European white was confused and alarmed by the egalitarian system of these societies and did much to wreck it, creating wedges between the men and women.[10]

In the late sixties, therefore, many African Americans were encouraged by historical circumstances to continue resisting or rejecting Eurocentric models and interpretations of manhood and womanhood.

The most controversial example of these models and interpretations, ironically influenced by studies of social pathology and disorganization in black communities by Kenneth Clark and E. Franklin Frazier, two distinguished black social scientists, was Daniel P. Moynihan's *Negro Family: The Case for National Action*, a 1965 report for the United States Department of Labor which argues from a white middle-class perspective that the inability of black Americans to achieve social equality is due basically to a "tangle of pathology." At the center of the tangle of economic poverty, educational failure, juvenile delinquency, crime, and drug addiction, this sinister study argues, is a weak black family structure of illegitimacy, separation, desertion, and divorce; and at the center of this family disorganization among the black lower class is allegedly black female-headed families or black emasculating matriarchs.[11] In such scholarly studies as Joyce A. Ladner's *Tomorrow's Tomorrow: The Black Woman* (1972), black intellectuals, artists, civil rights leaders, and cultural workers challenged the stereotypes of black female-headed families and the myths of black matriarchy.[12] They turned to non-Western, nonwhite communities and Afrocentric models to discover or create possibilities for autonomous selves and communities through a commitment to the development of a more just, more egalitarian social order, including a neomasculine construction of a less sexist, more responsible black manhood.

This means, then, that the reality of black womanhood is dependent neither on black males first defining their manhood nor on white conceptions of womanhood. At the same time that many black men reject the theory of emasculating black women and have developed a more supportive role in their relationships with women, many black women have rejected the popular notions that their resourcefulness and strength in sharing the responsibility and authority of providing for their families mean that they are superwomen. Nor does the black single mother necessarily believe or feel that she is less of a woman because her family life is different from the imposed norms of a white middle-class family. From another perspective, "The Black Feminist Statement" of the Combahee River Collective declares, "our politics initially sprang from the shared belief that Black women are inherently valuable, that our liberation is a necessity not as an adjunct to somebody else's but because of our need as human persons for autonomy."[13] After identifying the triple oppression of race, class, and sex that black women often experience simultaneously, the statement continues: "we feel solidarity with progressive Black men and do not advocate the fractionalization that white women who are separatists demand. Our situation as Black people necessitates that we have solidarity around the fact of race, which white women of course do not need to have with white men, unless it is their negative solidarity as racial oppressors. We struggle together with Black men against racism, while we also struggle with Black men about sexism."[14] Although drafted in 1977 by a radical group of primarily New York black feminists and lesbians, this statement nevertheless crystallizes the alienation of many black women from the Euro-American Feminist movement.

Elaborating in 1983 on the self-determination of black women, Bambara told an interviewer that black women are defining their movement in ways and terms different from white feminist organizations: "We are more inclined to trust our own traditions, whatever name we gave and now give those impulses, those groups, those agendas, and are less inclined to think we have to sound like, build like, noncolored groups that identify themselves as feminist or as women's rights groups, or so it seems to me."[15] This not only gets to the heart of the differences that many black women have with the priorities and objectives of the Women's Rights movement but also explains in part why Alice Walker adapted the term *womanist* from black folk expression to signify a black feminist or woman of color "who, among other things, is audaciously committed to the survival and wholeness of entire people, male and female."[16] More to the point of my readings of contemporary African American novels by black women, the comments cited above provide the necessary context or subtext for a better understanding of why black women are primarily concerned with how racism, sexism, and classism have influenced the development of love, power, autonomy, creativity, manhood, and womanhood in the black family and community.

In pursuing these themes black women novelists provide a much neglected perspective and chorus of voices on the human experience, but, contrary to the assumptions of some critics, this does not necessarily mean that their works constitute a separate literary tradition. Pointing to the absence, silence, or misrepresentation of black women in literary and nonliterary texts or contexts by black men as well as white men and women had been neither commonplace nor a high priority in texts. "Except for Gwendolyn Brooks, and perhaps Margaret Walker," Calvin Hernton writes in an early black feminist essay by a black male, "the name of not one black woman writer and not one female protagonist was accorded a worthy status in the black literary world prior to the 1970's."[17] Although Hernton overstates his case and overlooks the black women in the anthologies and studies of such poets and literary critics as James Weldon Johnson, Countee Cullen, and Sterling A. Brown,[18] his critique of sexism and support for a critical reassessment of black women in the black literary tradition is one of the significant characteristics of black neo-masculinity. Similarly, black feminist critics such as Mary Helen Washington in her introduction to *Black-Eyed Susans* and Barbara Christian in *Black Women Novelists* applaud the displacement of stereotypic with realistic images by black women writers like Morrison, Meriwether, Marshall, and Bambara. In her essays, Andrea Benton Rushing convincingly illustrates that Eurocentric qualities and categories of stereotypic white women such as the passive female, the submissive wife, and the woman on a pedestal are inappropriately applied in analyses of black women characters, whose historical experiences and cultural imperatives are different from those of white women.[19] As illustrated in the case for a black feminist tradition of criticism by Barbara Smith and Deborah E. McDowell, many black women novelists employ to a greater or lesser degree the following sign and structures: (1) motifs of interlocking racist, sexist, and classist oppression; (2) black female protagonists; (3) spiritual journeys from victimization to the realization of personal autonomy or creativity; (4) a centrality of female bonding or networking; (5) a sharp focus on personal relationships in the family and community; (6) deeper, more detailed exploration and validation of the epistemological power of the emotions; (7) iconography of women's clothing; and (8) black female language.[20] While agreeing with Smith that feminist criticism is "a valid and necessary cultural and political enterprise," McDowell questions the impreciseness of current definitions of lesbianism by black feminists, the possible reductiveness of a lesbian aesthetic, and the vagueness of Smith's analysis in

"Toward a Black Feminist Criticism." McDowell advocates that black feminist critics combine a contextual approach with rigorous textual analysis, including a concern for the issue of gender-specific uses of language.[21]

But many black women writers, including feminists, who acknowledge the influence of male as well as female literary foreparents, underscore the problematics of a completely separate rather than different black female literary tradition. Bambara, for example, says:

> Women are less likely to skirt the feeling place, to finesse with language, to camouflage emotions. But a lot of male writers knock that argument out. . . . Of course, one of the crucial differences that strikes me immediately among poets, dramatists, novelists, storytellers is in the handling of children. I can't nail it down, but the attachment to children and to two-plus-two reality is simply stronger in women's writings; but there are exceptions. And finally, there isn't nearly as large a bulk of gynocentric writing as there is phallic-obsessive writings. I'd love to read/hear a really good discussion of just this issue by someone who's at home with close textual reading—cups, bowls and other motifs in women's writings. We've only just begun . . . to fashion a woman's vocabulary to deal with the "silences" of our lives.[22]

Mary Helen Washington agrees, as she argues for a black female literary tradition in her introduction to *Midnight Birds:* "Black women are searching for a specific language, specific symbols, specific images with which to record their lives, and, even though they can claim a rightful place in the African American tradition and the feminist tradition of women writers, it is also clear that, for purposes of liberation, black women writers will first insist on their own name, their own space."[23] Because there are many intertextual relationships between black male and female novelists as well as between many females of both races on the issue of sexism, readers should examine these relationships to determine the manner and degree of the distinctiveness, consistency, and frequency of their appearance and use in narratives by black women in deciding for themselves whether a separate black female literary tradition exists.

Literary Continuity and Change: Modernism and Neorealism

The novel is a synthetic extended literary narrative which is the product of a complex blend of the social and cultural forces that shape the novelist's attitude toward life and language, especially the imaginative use of oral and literary narrative conventions. It is therefore not surprising that from 1962 to 1983 modernism in the African American novel was characterized by continuity and change. During this period, black American novelists sought structures and styles appropriate for the imaginative reconstruction of their sense of the double consciousness of black people as refracted through their particular vision of a rapidly changing experience of social reality and art. The eruption of the Vietnam and Arab-Israeli wars, the assassinations of major political leaders and civil rights workers, and the profiteering of multinational corporations were cataclysmic signs of a radical new era of American power. The revolutionary impact of the launching of the first manned flight to the moon, the emergence of the Black Power movement, the exposure of the Watergate scandal involving "high crimes and misdemeanors" by President Nixon, and the influence of the pill in radicalizing the Women's Rights movement swept away most of the vestiges of the traditional grounds for confidence in a stable universe, a democratic society, and a mimetic approach to art. Ambivalence toward authority (father, president, God, family, nation, Kingdom of God) with its conflicting attitudes of acceptance and rejection, deepened and spread to all aspects of life and to all fields, resulting often in a crisis of belief for many novelists and readers.

In the past, fact was often stranger than fiction, but in the recent period under discussion here the line between fantasy and reality was nearly invisible. To protect the rights of the Vietnamese people the American military machine destroyed their villages, crops, and countryside with thousands of tons of bombs and deadly toxic chemicals. To preserve law and order the police used clubs, water hoses, electric cattle prods, and snarling dogs on praying, singing civil rights demonstrators. To save the souls of his flock of followers, a contemporary shepherd, the Reverend James Jones, compelled hundreds to drink poisoned Kool-Aid. Challenging the authority and purpose of literature, cultural theorists and literary critics came to celebrate it as a nondiscursive, nonconceptual mode of discourse that has no authority or purpose beyond its symbols, signs, and structure.

How did novelists respond to this moral breakdown, social absurdity, and discrediting of the moral and sociocultural authority of art? More in despair than in hope, more concerned with problems of language than with problems of everyday life, postmodernist Euro-American novelists such as John Barth, William Gass, Donald Barthelme, Kurt Vonnegut Jr., Ronald Sukenick, and Richard Brautigan turned to fantasy and black or gallows humor. Others such as Bernard Malamud, Saul Bellow, and Flannery O'Connor used more traditional techniques of sociopsychological realism and grim comedy to portray more distinctive ethnic and regional visions of urban Jewish and Southern Catholic characters and values.

In contrast, contemporary African American novelists attempted—and still attempt—to displace personal ambivalence and social absurdity with a new order of thinking, feeling, and sharing based on self-determination, a sense of community, and a respect for human rights. Most, like John A. Williams, Alice Walker, Gayl Jones, and Gloria Naylor, continue to experiment in their most compelling narratives with some form of neorealism, especially critical realism.

Some, like Toni Morrison, continue to explore with a gender difference the poetic realism that was introduced into the tradition of the African American novel by Jean Toomer. And others, like Margaret Walker, Ernest Gaines, William Melvin Kelley, Ronald Fair, Hal Bennett, Charles Wright, Clarence Major, John Wideman, Ishmael Reed, and Toni Morrison have experimented with modern and postmodern forms of slave narrative, romance, fable, and satire.

Critical and Poetic Neorealism

Despite the modern formalist view that separates the examination of the language of a literary text from objective reality, the appeal of several types of traditional realism is seen in first novels by the majority of black novelists of the sixties. Many of these, such as Gordon Parks's *Learning Tree* (1963), Kristin Hunter's *God Bless the Child* (1964), Rosa Guy's *Bird at My Window* (1966), Barry Beckham's *My Main Mother* (1969), Louise Meriwether's *Daddy Was a Number Runner* (1970), and Al Young's *Snakes* (1970), are bildungsromans, stories about growing up black in Kansas, Harlem, Maine, and Detroit. Some, such as Nathan A. Heard's *Howard Street* (1968), Robert Dean Pharr's *Book of Numbers* (1969), and George Cain's *Blueschild Baby* (1970), are graphic, naturalistic accounts of the sporting life of hustlers, whores, and addicts. Others, like Cecil Brown's *Life and Loves of Mr. Jiveass Nigger* (1969) and Clarence Major's *All Night Visitors* (1969) are clinically detailed studies of black expatriate and domestic existential stud types. All are essentially mimetic in their tacit common-sense assumption of an intelligible though problematic reality and in their efforts to achieve a close correspondence between their symbolic act of representation and aspects of power relationships that need interrogation, challenge, and reconstruction. As realists the authors, with Major the most striking exception, are generally more pragmatic than idealistic in their quest for truth and their concern for the effect of their work on the reader. Because limitations of space preclude discussing all of these by no means mutually exclusive types of neorealism, I will focus on two that represent the polarities of the continuing tradition of realism—critical and poetic—and ambivalence of African American novelists toward their dual cultural heritage, especially the relationship of language to power in the construction of identity.

But first we should be clear about the meaning of neorealism. Like earlier types of realism in the African American novel, which used the conventional linear, closed plot and combined elements of the slave narrative, historical romance, and genteel realism, and which attacked racial discrimination while embracing middle-class values, neorealism is not only a literary method, but also a philosophical and political attitude toward the human condition. It is in sharp contrast to the implicit nihilism and explicit antimimesis of Alain Robbe-Grillet and Ronald Sukenick, who reject conventional approaches to plot and characterization as inadequate for expressing their perceptions of cultural disintegration and the indeterminacy of language. Although the American tradition foregrounds a more hopeful and playful sense of the world than the French, both Robbe-Grillet and Sukenick prefer to experiment with fantasy and self-reflexional linguistic signs in reconstituting both the novel and reality as fictions. But African American neorealists, like earlier black realists, assume that man is a social being who ought not to be separated from the social and historical context, no matter how alienating and discontinuous, in which he finds his significance and develops his potential as an individual. In short, there is more hope for humanity and the world expressed in African American neorealism and, as the next chapter will demonstrate, modernism and postmodernism than in European and Euro-American postmodernism. However, in contrast to works of traditional social realism such as Frank Webb's *Garies and Their Friends* and Jessie Fauset's *Chinaberry Tree,* which are essentially bourgeois in the truth they express in a documentary, linear manner, neorealism, as John O. Killens's *Youngblood* illustrates, is generally alienated from the old racist, sexist, socioeconomic order and seeks to displace it with new terms of order. Aside from the neoslave narratives of Margaret Walker and Ernest Gaines, which will be examined more appropriately in the next chapter, the most fascinating types of neorealism in the contemporary African American novel are critical realism, which is related to socialist realism, and poetic realism, which uses regional and racial matter in a poetic manner.

CRITICAL REALISM

Influenced by the radical struggles of the age for social change, especially the Black Power, Black Arts, and Women's Rights movements, some contemporary African American novelists explored the flexibility and appropriateness of critical realism for their color, sexual, and class approach to reality. Unlike social realism, a non-Marxist term referring to the generally middle-class life, manners, and truth treated in nineteenth-century realism, critical realism is a Marxist literary concept that is prefigured in the work of Balzac and Flaubert as well as Turgenev and Tolstoy. It is most meaningfully explained by its relationship to socialist realism, which is the antithesis of modernism. The perspective of "socialist realism differs from critical realism," writes Hungarian critic Georg Lukács, "not only in being based on a concrete socialist perspective, but also in using this perspective to describe the forces working towards socialism *from the inside.*"[24] Concreteness involves an awareness of the class and ideological development, structure, and goal of society as a whole. "Socialists," writes Terry Eagleton, "are those who wish to draw the full, concrete, practical applications of the abstract notions of freedom and democracy to which liberal humanism subscribes, taking them at their word when they draw attention to the 'vividly particular.'"[25] Socialist realism, then, is historical and comprehensive in its concrete description of the totality of society, and seeks to identify the human qualities essential for the creation of a new, progressive social order. In contrast, critical realism is not an outright affirmation of socialism so much as it is a negative attitude toward capitalism and a readiness to respect the perspective of socialism and not condemn it out of hand. Whenever such an affirmation is evident though, it will be somewhat abstract, "for even where a critical realist attempts to describe socialism, his is bound to be a description from the outside."[26] The writer using the "outside" method derives exemplary character types from the individual and his personal conflicts; and from this base he works toward wider social significance. But the writer using "the 'inside' method," Lukács explains, "seeks to discover an Archimedian point in the midst of social contradictions, and then bases its typology on an analysis of these contradictions."[27]

Although none of the black neorealists is politically committed to Marxist doctrines of the dominance of class struggle, John O. Killens, John A. Williams, Alice Walker, and Gayl Jones, as I will illustrate, use the indirect, outside method of critical realism as well as other conventions to develop their ambivalence about capitalism, opposition to racism and sexism, and positive typologies for a new social order. Aesthetically, they all seem to believe with Georg Lukács that perspective is of major importance, with Henry James that character is the essence of everything, and with Ralph Ellison that contemporary fiction, despite its technical experimentation, is an ethical as well as a linguistic sign system. Because of their historical ambivalence, contemporary African American novelists, have, in short, tailored critical realism and traditional social realism to fit their consciousness of the interrelated dynamics of capitalism, racism, and sexism. They also affirm that speech acts and dialogue are a bridge between the past, present, and future, as well as that discourse always involves power relationships between individuals and groups.

JOHN OLIVER KILLENS (1916–1987)

If Richard Wright is the spiritual father of critical realism, John O. Killens was probably its contemporary moving force. Born on January 14, 1916, in Macon, Georgia, he was raised and educated primarily in the South. He also attended Howard, Columbia, and New York Universities. A major figure in the Harlem left-wing literary movement of the 1950s, Killens was one of the founders in 1951 of the Harlem Writers' Guild and a contributor to Paul Robeson's *Freedom* newspaper. In the June 1952 issue of *Freedom* he revealed his belief in a rather dogmatic theory of socialist realism by denouncing the modernism of Ralph Ellison's *Invisible Man* as a "vicious distortion of Negro life."[28] His commitment to the tradition of realism was expressed not only in his writings, but also in the creative writing workshops that he taught in the 1960s at the New School for Social Research and at Fisk, Howard, and Columbia Universities, where he encouraged the creative efforts of black women writers like Sarah Wright. Killens died of cancer on October 27, 1987, in Brooklyn, New York.

Although he wrote a couple of screenscripts and plays, a collection of essays, two biographies, a posthumously published biographical novel, *Great Black Russian: A Novel on the Life and Times of Alexander Pushkin* (1989), and numerous uncollected pieces, Killens is best known for his four novels: *Youngblood* (1954), *And Then We Heard the Thunder* (1963), *'Sippi* (1967), and *The Cotillion* (1971). The agency that he declares and represents in all his writing is "to change the world, to capture reality, to melt it down and forge it into something entirely different." Politically, the envisioned something different is socialism, and the method is critical realism. The emphasis in his novels is on telling "as much of the truth as he knows the painful truth to be, and let the flak fall where it may."[29] Believing with Du Bois and Wright that the truth will set us free, he focuses on past and present socioeconomic forces and racial prejudices in America that inhibit and distort the development of dignity and unity among black and working-class people. More important, for him and some other black neorealists the agency, authenticity, and authority of "the hero" are still viable. "At a time when the novel throughout the world celebrates the emergence of the anti-hero," writes Addison Gayle, "Killens reasserts the value of the hero, argues, that is, that heroism lay in the attempt to produce a better world for oneself and his people, and that the telling mark of the hero is his love for people."[30]

Youngblood and *The Cotillion* are the best examples of Killens's preoccupation with color and class, for in them he affirms the potential agency of black people and celebrates the authenticity and authority of their development of black consciousness. In *Youngblood* Killens portrays the life of a black family in a small Southern town during the Depression, when thousands of blacks were fleeing the South in search of a better life and vicariously triumphing over the power of whites with Joe Louis. The novel primarily delineates the character of Robert Youngblood, but it also bares the authenticity and authority of the tough roots of the Youngblood family tree. The accounts of the agency of Robert's parents, Laurie Lee and Joseph Youngblood, for example, foreshadow the heroic spirit of their son, whose experiences, like those of his parents, convince him that the only way for blacks to live with dignity in America is to unite and fight for their human and civil rights.

The title of the novel, the biblical subtitles, and the verses from black spirituals that introduce its four major divisions, together with its episodic structure and realistically drawn characters, all reinforce the authenticity and authority of the theme that a dynamic, assertive new generation of black Americans is coming of age. This new generation continues the struggle of black folks against racial, economic, and sexual exploitation. In documentary fashion, Killens moves from one episode to the next, invariably selecting episodes that reveal the heroic spirit of the Youngbloods while, at the same time, vividly—sometimes melodramatically—depicting the fear, hate, and violence that characterized race relations in the Deep South at the turn of the twentieth century. Laurie's earliest and most indelible impression of white people, for instance, is the terrifying, debasing experience she had at eleven years old with a white man who not only tried to rape her, but also "upped her skirt and peed on her thigh" in utter contempt for her as a black person.

More important than the structure and style of *Youngblood,* however, are its characters, who dramatize the moral and political idea that blacks ought to stay in the South and fight for their rights. As idealized "new Negroes" of the twentieth century, the Youngbloods represent the generation of proud, enlightened people whose sacrifices, unity, and militancy are essential qualities for the progressive society of tomorrow. Laurie, symbolically born in Tipkin, Georgia, at precisely 12:01 a.m. January 1, 1900, is a heroic Southern black mother who passes on the lessons of her grandmother and teaches her children to "fight em every inch of the way, especially the big rich ones."[31] Her husband, Joe, stands as a strong, fiercely proud working-class black who resolves to die a man rather than live a coward. For his determination to end the practice of shortchanging his pay, Joe is shot and killed by the white paymaster. Although the narrator is a disembodied omniscient presence, there is little moral, political, or emotional distance between his agency and the Youngbloods'. He completely embraces their values and encourages our identification with them.

In addition to the parents, there are the Youngblood children, Jenny and Robert, who, in their proud spirit and firm belief in the power of black unity and militancy to achieve economic and social freedom, continue the tradition of their parents. Richard Myles, a black college-educated New Yorker whose tragic love affair motivated him to rebel against his middle-class background and plunge into civil rights work in Georgia, also helps to shape the protagonist's growing black consciousness. More traditional and negative in character are Leroy Jackson and Benjamin Blake, twentieth-century "handkerchief heads": black people who betray their race to the white ruling class for personal gain.

On the other side are several stock white characters. George Cross Jr. is a die-hard conservative Southerner who is irrevocably committed to the exploitative way of life on which his power and privilege are based. Dr. Riley is a Southern liberal who fails to live up to his expressed commitment to social equality when a dying black man needs his help. The ministers Culpepper and Poultry are traditional Southern fundamentalist leaders who pervert the Scriptures to terrorize and control their guilt-ridden followers. And Oscar Jefferson is the obligatory "good" poor white Southerner whose gnawing conscience impels him to volunteer his blood in a futile effort to save Joe Youngblood's life.

At the end of the novel, the progressive color and class consciousness of the Youngblood family prevails. Although Joe Youngblood is killed for his courageous refusal to be cheated by the white paymaster, the success of his son

Robert in organizing fellow workers into a union and the silent display of unity and militancy at Joe's funeral at the close of the book imply victory for the family and a new social order. Predictably, the thematic question of the book—"How do you live in a white man's world?"—is dramatically answered by the indomitable fighting spirit of the Youngbloods themselves.

Revealing an increasing use of the black oral tradition, *And Then We Heard the Thunder* and *'Sippi* also focus on the agency, authenticity, and authority of themes of black consciousness, unity, and resistance. The message in *And Then We Heard the Thunder* is that blacks should neither sacrifice their manhood nor compromise their dignity at any time, place, or price. The Southern setting and dialogue, which sparkles with signifying, folksayings, and ethnic humor, establish the authenticity and authority of the ironic situation and define the agency of the characters. The irony of the plot is that black Americans had to wage a double war for freedom during World War II: one overseas against foreign fascism and the other at home against domestic fascism. The third-person narrator traces the evolving black consciousness of Solomon "Solly" Saunders, an ambitious middle-class soldier who attempts to ignore his color in order to achieve success in the white world, only to discover in an apocalyptic racial war the truth about "all of his individual solutions and his personal assets. Looks, Personality, Education, Success, Acceptance, Security, the whole damn shooting match, was one great grand illusion, without dignity."[32] Through Solly, Killens predicts with authority and authenticity the transformation of many Negroes into blacks during the 1960s. "If I'm proud of me," Solly says after reading Wright's *Twelve Million Black Voices,* "I don't need to hate Mister Charlie's people. I don't want to. I don't need to. If I love me, I can also love the whole damn human race. Black, brown, yellow, white" (p. 372). But love is an ideal state derived from social reality. "Perhaps the New World *would* come raging out of Africa and Asia with a new and different dialogue that was people-oriented. What other hope was there?" (p. 499). Meanwhile, the reality was the racial war that ends the novel and the conviction of the black soldiers who died in that war that it was necessary to beat some sense into the heads of white folks to get their respect. The class struggle does not therefore dominate the struggle for racial justice in Killens's worldview but, as Solly illustrates, it is intertwined with it.

In *'Sippi* Killens explores with more authenticity than authority the human story behind the impact of the Supreme Court school desegregation decision of 1954. With Mississippi and New York as the backdrop of his huge canvas, he outlines the radical changes in attitude and strategy that characterize the increasingly bitter conflict between white power and black power during the 1960s. For the most part, however, the idea that black people must unite and organize their economic and political strength so that they can seize the constitutional rights that whites will not grant them is passionately but less credibly and excitingly rendered in *'Sippi.* At the center of Killens's third novel is the growth of the protagonist into black manhood and an African American version of the tale of two star-crossed lovers of the mid-twentieth century: Carrie Wakefield, the daughter of a wealthy plantation owner and the apotheosis of Southern white womanhood, and Charlie Chaney, the son of Wakefield's faithful black field hand and the prototype of the contemporary militant black prince. A fusion of critical realism and historical romance, the novel opens with a stylized prologue that explains the folkloristic and thematic significance of the book's title. The chain of responses set off by the Supreme Court school desegregation decision begins with Jesse Chaney's wry announcement that there "'ain' no more Mississippi. Ain' no more Mississippi. It's jes' 'Sippi from now on.'"[33] And the conclusion of the book with the assassination of the leader of the black revolution and the protagonist's grim decision to join the Elders for Protection and Defense of Wakefield County heralds a new age of black militancy and self-determination.

In *Youngblood* Killens comes closest to portraying the role that the revolutionary working class plays in the new society; in *The Cotillion,* despite the working-class status of the Lovejoys, this perspective is underdeveloped. In Killens's alienation from the old order, melodramatically illustrated in the apocalyptic battle between white and black American soldiers at the end of *And Then We Heard The Thunder,* class, color, consciousness, and culture are inextricably linked. But class, for Killens, becomes a subordinate element in his writing during the late 1960s, when the struggle for racial and cultural identity was at its peak, and the intended primary audience was the black low-income and middle-class workers. This is particularly true in the satirical typology of *The Cotillion,* which is self-consciously neither comprehensive in its description of society nor objective in its historical vision.

Set in New York, *The Cotillion* is a "Black black comedy," written in "Afro-Americanese" to satirize debutante balls and "other Bourgeois bullshit . . . pulling Black folks in the opposite direction of peoplehood."[34] The representation of the characters, with the exception of the narrator, who possesses authenticity and authority, is flat and one dimensional, the language idiomatic and hyperbolic, the events melodramatic and ironic, the structure loose and freewheeling, and the style vibrant and witty. "White folks invented these debitramp balls," the heroine's father explains, "so that their darling little heifers could git a good shot at the prize bull in the pasture. . . . But colored folks just do these things cause they see white folks doing them" (p. 158). In her quest for agency, authenticity, and authority, Yoruba Evelyn Lovejoy, the heroine, is torn between the urge to whiteness of Daphne, her pretentious Barbadian mother, and the call to black consciousness of her Georgia-born father, Matthew, and her black prince, Ben Ali Lumumba, the jive-talking narrator-writer who turns the Grand Cotillion into a black and beautiful occasion.

Using conventional techniques, Killens was less concerned in his novels with the forces breaking up our society than with those leading toward a new nation, a new social order. Because of his faith in the future and in people, he continued the tradition of conventional plots and of the outsider as hero. But the essential values of the new social order he envisioned are found in his love and respect for the dignity, unity, and potential of black people, his primary audience. The relationship of language to knowledge and power in the journey of his characters to self-esteem and social awareness is predictable. And the characters themselves are more often types than individuals. Consequently, Killens's novels lack the suspense, complexity, and, except for *The Cotillion*, vibrancy, ambiguity, and ambivalence of contemporary life. What they provide in the tradition of the African American novel are inspiring moral and political narratives that reaffirm the revolutionary potential of black history, culture, and youth in creating a better tomorrow for all people.

JOHN A[LFRED] WILLIAMS (1925–)

His parents met and married in Syracuse, New York, but John A. Williams was born on December 5, 1925, in Jackson, Mississippi, his mother's hometown. While he was an infant, the family returned to Syracuse, where he grew up, joined the navy, married, and attended Syracuse University. A childhood interest in reading and early efforts at poetry while in the navy were subsequently cultivated by the discipline acquired in creative writing classes at Syracuse University in 1951. After writing for the *Progressive Herald, Chicago Defender*, and the National Negro Press Association, Williams began his first novel in 1954. "When I began the process of becoming a writer," he says, "it wasn't for the money and it wasn't for fame; it was to keep my sanity and to find some purpose in my life."[35] Although completed in 1956, this first novel, *The Angry Ones*, was not published until 1960. Since then Williams has published more than twenty books, including twelve novels. His post-1983 novels are *The Berhama Account* (1985), an uncompelling narrative of political campaign intrigue, racial conflict, and romantic adventure involving public relations owner Gary Mandarino, a spin-off of Max Reddick in *The Man Who Cried I Am*, on a Caribbean island popular for offshore banking, and *Clifford's Blues* (1999), an epistolary narrative of a black gay jazz musician who survives imprisonment in Dachau by playing and leading a band in a club for Nazi SS officers.

Clearly in the tradition of realism, Williams's novels nevertheless reveal a growing radical consciousness and preoccupation with form. "I suppose I am a realistic writer," he explains. "I've been called a melodramatic writer, but I think that's only because I think the ending of a novel should be at the ending of the book.... In terms of experimenting, I think that I've done some very radical things with form in *The Man Who Cried I Am* and in *Captain Blackman*, which had to be an experimental novel in order to hold the theme of the novel.

What I try to do with novels is to deal in forms that are not standard, to improvise as jazz musicians do with their music, so that a standard theme comes out looking brand new."[36] Thematically and structurally, Williams, unlike Killens, is primarily concerned with the struggle of the individual black American to reconcile his present marginal middle-class status with the past experience of his race.

This and an increasing bitterness at capitalism and antiblack racism are dramatically evident in the pre-1983 novels. In *The Angry Ones,* his first and weakest novel, Steve Hill, the protagonist, triumphs over the anger and frustration of economic and sexual exploitation by white liberal friends, renouncing violence and finding a tenuous, unconvincing security in a new job and marriage to his brother's widow. *Night Song* (1961) is the bittersweet story of the creative yet self-destructive rage of Eagle, a black jazz musician, and the impotent rage of Keel Robinson, his friend, a "black white man." Because it is a more experimental and successful novel than *The Angry Ones,* it will be examined more closely later in this chapter. *Sissie* (1963) is an exploration of the psychic damage suffered by the modern black family and a demythologizing of black matriarchy. In his fourth novel, *The Man Who Cried I Am* (1967), Williams's radical consciousness culminates in the theme of racial genocide and an experiment with time structure.

Except for *Captain Blackman* (1972), Williams's novels of the 1960s and 1970s continue to explore the themes of armed violence and love as alternatives to American racism and to experiment with time structure, but they are less original and effective in their fusion of form and content. In *Sons of Darkness, Sons of Light* (1969) Eugene Browning, a political moderate, triggers a racial Armageddon with his plan to have a white detective killed for his merciless shooting of a black youth. *Captain Blackman*—Williams's most self-conscious experiment with multiple time shifts, flashbacks, dream sequences, and interior monologues—retraces through Abraham Blackman the heroic exploits of black soldiers back down the corridors of American history, from Vietnam to the Revolutionary War. In *Mothersill and the Foxes* (1975), Odell Mothersill, a black social worker, is a modern-day Priapus or Legba, a smooth-talking sower of seeds who discovers that love and manhood involve more than sex. And through the reminiscences of the multiple narrators in *The Junior Bachelor Society* (1976), we discover along with Richard "Bubbles" Wiggins, a frustrated third-string high school halfback and president of the Junior Bachelor Society, that the nostalgia of thirty-year-old boyhood friendships disappears in the face of the harsh truths and painful memories that surface in the manhood rituals of their reunion.

Psychologically, emotionally, and ethically sympathetic to Cato Douglass, the black protagonist and writer in *!Click Song* (1982), Williams considers that work his "very best novel."[37] The title of the book is a wry allusion to the clicking sound of some Bantu languages that have positive expressions in some

South African songs and the speech habits of some contemporary black Americans. The enhancement of this layered cultural allusion with the symbolic significance of the click sound as a negative manifestation of the machine that his book publisher uses to assess a writer's past and future productivity is a possible reason for Williams's high regard for *!Click Song*. Another possible reason is that the retrospective first-person narrative of Cato's soul-trying battles with the antiblack racism and dehumanization of the literary establishment reads like an imaginative reconstruction of Williams's own life both as a black humanist and as a critical realist writer committed to social change and to his interracial family. In contrast, some readers will find *!Click Song* too passionate and discursive a picture of the struggles of black novelists for critical and commercial success in America, which are more compellingly represented in *The Man Who Cried I Am*. Responding to an interviewer's question about whether there are two strains in black American writing, one social reformist or propagandistic and the other formally artistic, Williams states: "It's not so much a question of the writing being political; it's a question of its seeking some humanist level on the basis of clearing the air in terms of oppression and what it does and what would happen if there were no oppression. . . . I've probably become good at mixing both, that is, dealing quite openly with universal problems while achieving some small degree of craftsmanship."[38] Because *The Man Who Cried I Am* is Williams's most thematically provocative and technically masterful novel, I will examine it below more closely.

Looking first more closely at *Night Song*, however, we discover that it is a blues story in the jazz mode. The novel is authentically set in "a world of cool, of arrogant musicians and worrying night club owners . . . a world in which the days were really nights because you lived in the dark and sang your song of life then."[39] The narrative is antiphonal in structure, stressing the call-and-response relationship between Keel and Eagle with a sharp counterpoint provided by David Hillary, a college instructor. The traditional blues theme that life and human agency should be affirmed in the face of disappointment, defeat, and even death is the melodic base for improvisation by the disembodied third-person omniscient narrator.

Basically, *Night Song* is the tragic story of Richie "Eagle" Stokes, a blues riff on the legendary saxophonist Charles "Bird" Parker, and those whose lives he touches and renews through the sacrifice of his own. They include Keel Robinson, a black Harvard Divinity School graduate and converted Muslim (Sadik Jamal) whose moral outrage at the hollowness of bourgeois values, especially institutionalized religion, and at racial prejudice leaves him incapable of consummating his love for his white girl friend; and David Hillary, a morally impotent white liberal, "the kind who do nothing when it counts for everyone" (p. 140), who is guilt-ridden over killing his wife in a car accident. The source of Eagle's blues is that everyone uses him, especially the white world. "'You white,'" he tells Hillary after taking him in off the street. "'It's your world. You won't let me make it in it and you can't. Now ain't that a bitch?'"(p. 67). More viable as a mythic and legendary culture hero than as a conventional realistic character, Eagle is driven by his love-hate feelings. He embodies the paradoxes of African American character and culture, its possibilities and limitations. "'Some people preserve statues and old drawings on cave walls,'" Keel explains to Hillary, "'but we have to have Eagle. He's us. He's fire and brain; he's stubborn and shabby; proud and without pride; kind and evil. His music is our record: blues. . . . Eagle is our aggressiveness, our sickness, our self-hate, but also our will to live in spite of everything. He symbolizes the rebel in us'" (p. 93).

In addition to his significance as an ethnic cultural symbol, Eagle, his music, and the bohemian world are the agents for spiritual redemption for Keel and Hillary. For both, the experience is "like an immersion . . . a baptism" (p. 90). Keel, supported by the patience, understanding, and love of Della, his girlfriend, responds by publicly and frequently reciprocating Eagle's humanitarianism, an act that enables him to rise gradually above the impotence of racial hatred to a renewed faith in himself and life. In contrast, Hillary, who thinks that he has risen above cowardice and bigotry to become "a new man, changed by the people he'd been living with," betrays his "new-found humanitarianism" and Eagle when he fails to come to Eagle's aid as a cop brutally billy-clubs him senseless. "'How could we be unworthy of your love yet worthy of your confession?'" Keel asks him after discovering the betrayal. "'It's not only that you don't know where you are, you don't know where we are. Are you at the top looking down or at the bottom looking up?'" (pp. 142–43).

In the ambiguity and ambivalence of this passage as well as in the thematic structure of the novel, the author-narrator's close philosophical and political identification with Keel Robinson is apparent. Because Keel cannot politically and economically "understand why a white man can't make it in his society" (p. 15), he immediately distrusts and hates Hillary as another white exploiter. The author-narrator's delineation of Hillary as an outsider who knows the surface but not the deeper, ritualistic meaning of jazz foreshadows Hillary's betrayal of Eagle and confirms Keel's suspicion that his friendship for blacks is self-serving and unreliable. Only in "Bohemia, that isolation in time and space which impelled one to act basically" (p. 119), does the author-narrator reveal Hillary cautiously responding to Eagle's charity and acknowledging his potential for moral salvation. For John Williams, then, it was in the apolitical diversity and individualism of Greenwich Village, not the black community, where "people were more like people."

It is also in the Village that Keel, like many alienated and talented blacks and whites of the late 1950s, sought salvation from socialized ambivalence. His problem was "resisting reality" and affirming his love for the white woman who loved him. Middle-class family, money, Protestantism, and Islam did not sustain his faith in himself as a black man, so he turned to the interracial world of the Village where Eagle and Della helped him to reconcile the tensions of his double consciousness. "Della had come, he always said to himself, when he needed her most, almost immediately after he had left the church, and at a time when he felt his obligations to his parents had been paid" (p. 41). But Keel was confused, torn between love and hate, because Della was white, and it is only after Hillary's climactic betrayal of Eagle that Keel is able to express fully and publicly his love for her. Thus racial integration and interracial love, still a radical solution for American racism in 1961, are the cornerstones of Williams's early vision in this underrated novel of a new social and ethical system. But how new, how progressive, is the social system that Williams projects? Actually, the class and color struggles are presented within an apolitical, bourgeois framework with their effects on society being demonstrated indirectly by their personal moral and psychological consequences. Williams explored this vision more deeply and politically in an international historical context in *The Man Who Cried I Am.*

The Man Who Cried I Am, like *Night Song,* is in the realistic tradition, but its plot, which culminates in the discovery of a bold plan of racial genocide and closes ambiguously on an apocalyptic note, is complicated by a shifting temporal and spatial frame and a sardonic use of symbolism. It is the story of the political radicalization and death of Max Reddick, a successful black novelist and former presidential speechwriter. Max's faith in the American Dream is betrayed at every level, and his rectal cancer symbolizes the pain and danger that constantly threaten the lives of American blacks. Realizing that he is dying of advanced carcinoma, Max flies to the Paris funeral of his friend and rival literary lion, Harry Ames, and then takes a train to Amsterdam for a final visit with his estranged Dutch wife, Margrit Reddick. He discovers in Leiden the reason for his friend's death in a letter that Harry leaves, which contains the details about King Alfred, an elaborate government plan to "terminate, once and for all, the Minority threat to the whole of the American society, and, indeed, the Free World."[40]

Divided into three major parts, *The Man Who Cried I Am* is Williams's most compelling and innovative novel. Because of institutionalized racism that the novel intriguingly reveals, the assertion of individuality and independence by black Americans, especially male writers, is painful and dangerous. In the tradition of critical realism, Williams emphasizes the internal contradictions of the authority and agency of characters in an exploitative social system rather than focusing on the forces working toward reconciliation and coexistence in a new system. The existential theme suggested by the title is that the survival of mankind depends on the moral commitment of the individual to self and society in the face of irrationality and death.

The actual time and place of the action are twenty-four hours in May 1964 in the Netherlands, but Williams skillfully manipulates the time through multiple flashbacks, recollections, dreams, and interior monologues to cover nineteen years, 1945–64, and three continents: Europe, Africa, and the United States. Part 1 introduces the cannibalistic theme of white against black and black against black as the white publishing establishment pits black writers against each other in a dog fight for the status of king of the black literary mountain. Part 2 explores the problems of black writers and interracial couples in America and Europe; and Part 3 reveals the ultimate treachery of the American government as black CIA agents, who have infiltrated the black American colony of expatriate artists in Paris, systematically assassinate everyone suspected of having knowledge of King Alfred. Max's decision to marry Margrit Westover is the climactic episode of the existential theme of moral courage implicit in the novel's title. His personal agency in taking a white wife is a paradoxical prelude to his political agency in defending his race, which he expresses by arming himself for a racial war and by calling Minister Q to inform him of King Alfred, the plan of the United States government to confine and eliminate black Americans.

The spirits of the two major black leaders of the sixties and a few of the celebrated modern black male expatriate writers walk the pages of the novel. Minister Q fills the shoes of Malcolm X; the Reverend Paul Durrell, those of the Reverend Martin Luther King Jr.; and Harry Ames, those of Richard Wright. "Where Durrell employed fanciful imagery and rhetoric, Minister Q preached the history, economics and religion of race relations; he preached a message so harsh that it hurt to listen to it" (pp. 209–10). Minister Q and Durrell are one-dimensional characters, but Harry Ames has many of the frailties of the flesh, much of the socialized ambivalence, and the dread of conspiracy, of his historical model, who died mysteriously in Paris. In a dialogue with Max about being a writer, Harry rejects the idea of a "tradition of colored writers" and expresses the view that by writing and publishing a book Max, like himself, became a very special person. This is a cause for pride in producing more books, but it "'also makes you dangerous because they don't burn people anymore, they burn books, and they don't always have bonfires'" (p. 45). In literary achievement and lifestyle, Max Reddick embodies the authority, authenticity, and transgressive individualism of Chester Himes and Williams himself.

The undramatized third-person omniscient narrator enhances the compelling authority and authenticity of the major characters and events in the novel. We move from an intimate view of an estranged interracial couple to a broad view of racial and political conspiracy. The tone is tragic, ambivalent, and sensational. We get sympathetic internal views of Margrit and Harry, but it is Max's double consciousness that predominates and represents the norms of the work. By extensive use of the flashback technique to telescope the past into the present and to reenact Max's memories, Williams minimizes the effects of authorial intrusions and dramatizes his hero's double consciousness and many of the crucial events, both public and private, that led to his radicalization and death. The intimate view we get of Margrit and Max overshadows the intense but brief view we get of Lillian Patch, Max's middle-class black fiancé who dies from a botched abortion. "If there had been no Lillian, would there be a Margrit?" Max wonders after his momentous decision to marry Margrit (p. 281).

Harry's posthumous letter to Max containing information about King Alfred is a short-fused time bomb that enables Max to reflect on his ambivalent relationship with Harry. The letter also serves as an effective device for Williams to shift between internal and external views of the characters and events. "The one alternative left for Negroes," we read with Max at the end of the novel, "would be not only to seek that democracy withheld from them as quickly and as violently as possible, but to fight for their very survival. King Alfred . . . leaves no choice" (p. 304). Because the story is told predominantly through Max's consciousness, there is little moral, philosophical, and political distance between the omniscient author-narrator and his protagonist. Williams thus closely identifies with the values of his central character, and he encourages the reader to do so as well.

Because of his experiment with technique and form, Williams is a critical realist in only the broadest sense of our definition. His critical attitude toward capitalism and its system of privilege emphasizes the exploitation and exclusion of blacks, which may be interpreted as an implicit respect for the socialist perspective. But his title, theme, and central character are romantically individualistic. Borrowing from Malcolm Lowry's telescoping of time in *Under the Volcano* and from Richard Wright, Chester Himes, and Ralph Ellison, among others, in technique, Williams develops the wider social significance of his critical attitude toward America from the personal conflicts and alienation of members of the black middle class, especially male artists. He therefore combines Eurocentric and Afrocentric techniques in continuing the tradition of realism while simultaneously expanding the form of the novel through a reaffirmation of the symbolic importance of the legends and rituals of black music in African American life and literature. "What I try to do with novels," he tells an interviewer, "is to deal in forms that are not standard, to improvise as jazz musicians do with their music, so that a standard theme comes out looking brand new. This is all I try to do with a novel and, like those musicians, I am trying to do things with form that are not always immediately perceptible to most people."[41]

ALICE [MALSENIOR] WALKER (1944–)

Born on February 9, 1944, to sharecroppers in Eatonton, Georgia, Alice Walker was the youngest of eight children. She was a lonely, solitary child as a result of a disfiguring scar she suffered at eight years of age. Educated in local schools and reacting to the cruel insults of her peers and relatives, she "retreated into solitude," she told an interviewer, "and read stories and began to write poems."[42] In 1961 she entered Spelman College, and in her sophomore year was spiritually and politically reborn as an activist in the Georgia voter registration movement of SNCC. She transferred to Sarah Lawrence in 1963 and traveled to East Africa in the summer of 1964, returning to college pregnant, sick, alone, and suicidal. It was during this crisis and before graduating in 1965 that she completed in one week most of the poems in *Once,* her first book of poetry, which was not published until 1968, when the Women's movement began displacing the Black Power movement in the social arena.

Walker has taught at several East Coast colleges and has worked with Head Start in Mississippi and the Department of Welfare in New York City. Her numerous honors and awards include Bread Loaf Writers' Conference Scholar in 1966, Merrill Writing Fellow in 1966–67, McDowell Colony Fellow in 1967, the Rosenthal Award in 1974 for *In Love and Trouble,* the Lillian Smith Award in 1973 for *Revolutionary Petunias,* and the Pulitzer Prize and the American Book Award in 1983 for *The Color Purple.* Walker's publications through 1999 include five volumes of poetry: *Once* (1968), *Revolutionary Petunias* (1973), *Good Night, Willie Lee, I'll See You in the Morning* (1979), *Houses Make a Landscape Look More Beautiful* (1984), and *Her Blue Body Everything We Know* (1991); two collections of short stories: *In Love and Trouble* (1973) and You *Can't Keep a Good Woman Down* (1981); and six novels that illustrate increasingly radical black womanism and narrative experimentation. They are *The Third Life of Grange Copeland* (1970), *Meridian* (1977), *The Color Purple* (1982), *The Temple of My Familiar* (1989), an ambitious multivocal experiment with postmodern romance and magical realism, *Possessing the Secret of Joy* (1992), a boldly didactic thematization of female circumcision in Africa, and *By the Light of My Father's Smile* (1998), another multivocal, antiblack-male celebration of filial spirituality, female sexuality, and "orgasmic freedom," including interracial lesbianism.

"I am preoccupied with the spiritual survival, the survival *whole* of my people," she explains, describing her political agency and thematic concerns to an interviewer. "But beyond that, I am committed to exploring the oppressions, the insanities, the loyalties, and the triumphs of black women. . . . For me, black women are the most fascinating creations in the world. Next to them, I place the old people—male and female—who persist in their beauty in spite of everything." Consistent with this professed concern for the wholeness of both males and females and celebration of "outrageous, audacious, courageous or willful" black women, Walker defines herself as a womanist rather than a feminist. In her fiction as in her life she has an openness to mystery and to animism, which she believes is both the one thing that African Americans have retained of their African heritage and the thing that is "deeper than any politics, race, or geographical locations." She therefore admires women writers who are responsive to mystery: Chopin, the Brontës, Simone de Beauvoir, and Doris Lessing. She admires these writers also because they are "well aware of their own oppression," and "their characters can always envision a solution, an evolution to higher consciousness on the part of society even when society itself cannot."[43] In other words, the class and political authority and authenticity of the struggles explored in Walker's novels are primarily grounded in gender and sexual differences. And the higher consciousness she seeks for society is based on the authority and authenticity of her insider's view of the working-class history and vernacular tradition of blacks in general and the socialized ambivalence and sexuality of black women in particular, as well as on her outsider's view of the conflict of white women with capitalism. Among the many black and white writers who influenced her, she lists Russians, Greeks, Africans, Asians, and such Americans, black and white, as Jean Toomer, Zora Neale Hurston, Arna Bontemps, Emily Dickinson, Robert Graves, William Carlos Williams, e. e. cummings, and Flannery O'Connor. Of these, Hurston is the literary precursor, foremother, and spirit-guide that inspires the audacious ancestralism and autonomy that Walker expresses in her womanist vision.

The Third Life of Grange Copeland, her first novel, is structured like a crazy quilt in that it is disproportionately divided into eleven parts with forty-eight minichapters that outline the three lives of the patriarch of the Copeland clan. Ostensibly about Grange Copeland's rebirth of self-respect after a youth and manhood of dissolution, the novel actually details the social pathology that he passes on to his son, Brownfield. Part 1 briefly outlines the weekly cycles of sweat, fear, and hatred broken on Saturday by the rituals of song, dance, drink, and fighting that characterized the sharecropping life of Grange and, after years of violent abuse, his wife Margaret. When Grange finally deserts the family, Margaret poisons herself and Brownfield's baby brother, whose "father might have been every one of its mother's many lovers." The pace of the narrative picks up in Parts 2 and 3 as Brownfield follows in his father's footsteps from sharecropper to wife-beater. Grange also abruptly and inexplicably reappears to marry Josie, the whore he abandoned but now shares sexually with his son. The eight pages of Part 4 are exclusively reserved for the birth of Ruth, Grange's granddaughter and the agent of his miraculous redemption. Parts 5, 6, and 7 detail Brownfield's malicious treatment of his wife and three daughters with only a brief interlude when his wife, Mem, asserts herself with a shotgun. The novel reaches its violent climax with Brownfield killing Mem and with Ruth going to live on the farm with her grandfather and Josie. In Part 8 Brownfield plots with Josie to take Ruth after his release from prison. Parts 9 and 10 reveal Grange passing on the lessons of his life to Ruth, briefly summarizing his life of hatred in the North. In Part 11 Grange kills Brownfield after he succeeds in getting custody of Ruth, and Grange in turn is killed by the police after returning to Ruth's cottage on their farm.

With more compassion for her female than male characters, with the exception of Grange as an old man, the omniscient author-narrator catalogs episodes in the Copeland family life, especially Brownfield's, to arouse the reader's indignation at the price black women pay as the victims of economic, racial, and sexual exploitation. Margaret Copeland, Brownfield's mother, was like the family dog in some ways. "She didn't have a thing to say that did not in some way show her submission to his father."[44] Grange drives her to drink, degradation, and death. His dreams of escaping the sharecropping system gone, his pride crushed, Brownfield makes his wife quit her teaching job—"Her knowledge reflected badly on a husband who could scarcely read and write," says the editorializing narrator—and begins beating her regularly "because it made him feel, briefly, good. Every Saturday night he beat her, trying to pin the blame for his failure on her by imprinting it on her face" (p. 63). Only Ruth's birth is viewed as a miraculous event. " 'Out of all kinds of shit,' " says Grange, " 'comes something clean, soft and sweet smellin' " (p. 79). But Brownfield felt that his three daughters "were not really human children" and gave them only the dregs of his attention when he was half drunk. " 'You nothing but a sonnabit,' " four-year-old Ruth tells her father after he moves them back into sharecropping. Walker's weaving of character, event, and point of view indicates that she fully agrees with this sentiment. Through Ruth's innocence, Grange learns to love and to accept the responsibility of his life before he dies, but his own son Brownfield goes to his grave blaming white folks and others for the failure of his life. "He felt an indescribable worthlessness," says the author-narrator, "a certain ineffectual *smallness*, a pygmy's frustration in a world of giants" (p. 31).

Although more middle class and less physically violent, the black men of the 1960s in Walker's second novel, *Meridian*, are, with the exception of the father, similarly disloyal and despicable in their abuse of women. Meridian's father was a "dreamy, unambitious" history teacher who grieves over crimes committed against Native Americans and, who gives as restitution the family's sixty acres containing one of their ancient cemeteries to a local Native American. In contrast, Eddie, Meridian's teenaged husband, was "good" because he kept his promise to marry her if she got pregnant and, even though he "cheated" on her and later deserted her and his child, he did not beat her. Truman, her conquering prince, the French-speaking civil rights organizer and painter, impregnated her but betrayed her to marry and then desert a white exchange student and his child. Tommy, a bitter civil rights activist, rapes Truman's wife, Lynne, in revenge for the arm he lost to a white sniper. And Alonzo, the apolitical scrapyard worker, was so grateful for Lynne's invitation to sleep with her that he "licked her from her earlobes to her toes."[45] Like the omniscient narrator, the implied author thus encourages the reader to see most of her black male characters in the limited moral category of the "low-down dirty dog" in the novel who impregnated the thirteen-year-old tragic Wild Child.

Towering over the low-down dirty dogs and moving like a soul possessed through the thirty-four brief chapters of the three-part narrative is the protagonist, Meridian Hill. She shares with her father the legendary peculiar madness of her eccentric paternal great-grandmother, Feather Mae, and is haunted by guilt at her inability to embrace a nurturing role as daughter, wife, and mother. Frail and hallucinatory, Meridian agonizes "for shattering her mother's emerging self," gives away her first child in order to go to college, aborts her second in disillusionment with its unfaithful father, and then, at the suggestion of a callous male gynecologist, has her tubes tied to avoid being further trapped by sex and motherhood while pursuing her commitment in the rural South to community organizing, teaching, and poetry (pp. 40–41). Unlike her mother and grandmothers, we learn from the narrator, Meridian "lived in an age of choice" (p. 123). Despite her unorthodoxy, however, a black Baptist church memorial service for a young civil rights martyr in 1968 lifts her burden of guilt and shame. Affirming the respect she owed her life and the dedication she owed her people, she promises to kill for freedom if necessary, a revolutionary commitment that she had rejected earlier in the novel and that Walker's language implicitly endorses. But the social context and symbolic conclusion resound with personal self-indulgence, for Walker does not describe the revolutionary role of the working class in contemporary society. Nor does the novel end apocalyptically. Instead, Meridian forgives Truman, leaves him in her small religious house, and "returns to the world cleansed of sickness." Wearing her cap and snuggled in her sleeping bag, he wonders if she "knew that the sentence of bearing the conflict in her own soul which she had imposed on herself—and lived through—must now be borne in terror by all the rest of them" (pp. 227–28). The Civil Rights movement, in short, provided a means of spiritual and moral redemption from a guilty past for individuals like Meridian, not a radical new social order in which all could realize their full potential.

In contrast to her most thematically polemical and ambitiously experimental novels—*The Temple of My Familiar, Possessing the Secret of Joy*, and *By the Light of My Father's Smile*—published in the late 1980s and early 1990s, Walker's best novel is *The Color Purple.* Less compelling as critical realism than as folk romance, it is more concerned with the politics of sex and self than with the politics of class and race. Whereas its epistolary form continues with a black and bisexual difference the tradition of Samuel Richardson's *Clarissa Harlowe* (1748) and William H. Brown's *Power of Sympathy* (1789) (the sentimental, sensational tales of seduction that initiated the British and Euro-American traditions of the novel), its unrelenting, severe attack on male hegemony, especially on the violent abuse of black women by black men, is offered as a revolutionary leap forward into a new social order based on sexual egalitarianism. Like Hurston's *Their Eyes Were Watching God, The Color Purple* is stylistically grounded in black folk speech, music, and religion; and its theme is a contemporary rewriting of Janie Crawford's dreams of what a black woman ought to be and do. But rather than heterosexual love, lesbianism is the rite of passage to selfhood, sisterhood, and brotherhood for Celie, Walker's protagonist.

Although rooted in the particularity of the folk experience of some Southern black women, the awakening of the protagonist's consciousness to love, independence, and sisterhood is more romantic than realistic. Rather than portray the growth into womanhood of an average Southern black woman of the 1920s and 1930s, Walker has created a contemporary paradigm of the liberated woman. Covering more than thirty years between the two world wars, the ninety-four letters in which Celie emerges from the brutal domination and abuse of men to a liberated, autonomous self include twenty-three letters to her from Nettie, her younger sister, fourteen from her to Nettie, which came back unopened, and one from Shug Avery, the blues singer who is the moral center of the novel, to Celie. Most of the confusingly undated, often arbitrarily arranged letters are a dramatic monologue to a white, patriarchal God, symbolizing the complexity of metaphysical as well as social oppression for black women in their quest for freedom, literacy, and wholeness. Focused on psychological rather than historical realism, they begin when Celie is fourteen, and they tell more than show her realization of womanist consciousness: from her repeated rape and impregnation by her stepfather; brokered violent marriage to Albert; and rejection of God as a "trifling, forgitful and lowdown" man; to her transforming love for Shug; economic and artistic independence as a seamstress and merchant; and reunion on July 4th with family, friends, and an animistic God that Shug teaches her "ain't a he or she, but a It."[46]

By her handling of the symbolic significance of Shug as a blues singer, of African American religion, and of the black vernacular to develop Celie's long black song of suffering and womanist consciousness, Walker effectively weaves a magic spell that conjures up the socialized ambivalence and double consciousness of African American culture and character between 1914 and 1945. In the tradition of such blues "bad" women as Bessie Smith, Shug embodies and evokes the moral ambivalence of many black Americans toward music and behavior that they feel make the best of a bad situation by being as raw, mean, and wild as human existence itself frequently is. Worldly black folk flock to concerts and jukejoints to see Shug and hear the devil's music, while less worldly and otherworldly folk scorn her as a sinner and sing the Lord's music. Like her "wild sister" in Memphis and the legendary Bessie, Shug, called the Queen Honeybee of the blues, drinks, fights, and "love mens to death" (p. 104). Telling Celie about her earlier love for Albert and how the black community, including her parents and his, condemned her because she moved beyond liberty to license in "taking other women mens" and having three children out of wedlock, Shug says: "I was so mean, and so wild, Lord. I used to go round saying, I don't care who he married to, I'm gonna fuck him. . . . And I did, too. Us fuck so much in the open us give fucking a bad name" (p. 104). Only Albert, the father of her three children, and Celie, who fantasizes about her, honestly and completely love Shug. This socially forbidden love inspires her to create a "low down dirty" blues that she calls Miss Celie's song, which, of course, is Walker's text, and culminates in their lesbian affair. By living the liberated life she sings about without compromising her integrity, Shug, like Bessie, romantically challenges Albert, Celie, and readers to live with boldness and style in the face of adversity, absurdity, and conventional morality.

Shug teaches Celie not only about the sexual importance of her "little button" and "finger and tongue work," but also about the spiritual necessity of conversion to an animistic idea of God. "Just because I don't harass it like some peoples us know," says Shug, "don't mean I ain't got religion" (p. 164). By sympathetically delineating Shug as a blues heroine with religion, who is estranged from the orthodoxy of the Christian tradition, Walker offers her as a contemporary symbol of the ideal pattern of sexual and spiritual liberation and of transgression of traditional African American values and institutions.

Walker, in other words, is morally and politically unsympathetic toward what she considers anachronistic, chauvinistic conventions in the black family and the black church. She ascribes Celie's abject shame and passivity to the dominance of patriarchy, hypocrisy, and otherworldliness in the black church and family. By contrasting the stepfather's incest and the daughter-in-law Sofia's temerity with Celie's timidity, she clearly distances herself from Celie's belief in the biblical injunction to "Honor father and mother no matter what" and to suffering in this world, for "This life soon be over. . . . Heaven last for all ways" (p. 39). In the only church scene that is dramatized, however, the implied author is morally and politically close to both Celie and Shug as "even the preacher got his mouth on Shug, now she down. He take her condition for his text. . . . Talk about slut, hussy, heifer and streetcleaner" (p. 40).

Intertextually, Walker's text is a rewrite and conflation of the legendary and literary lives of women that she respects, beginning with her great-grandmother, "who was raped at twelve by her slaveholding master."[47] The lives of Bessie Smith, Janie Crawford, and Zora Neale Hurston parallel Shug's embedded text of Celie's song, which contrasts with the preacher's embedded text. Finally, in Celie's second letter to Nettie in which she renounces God, Walker implicitly supports Shug's belief that people "come to church to *share* God, not find God" and that because "Man corrupt everything," Celie ought to "conjure up flowers, wind, water, a big rock" (pp. 165, 168). Morally and politically, both Celie and Shug are reliable narrators for the womanist norms of the novel. The sign of these norms is the color purple. "I think it pisses God off if you walk by the color purple in a field somewhere and don't notice it," Shug tells Celie and us (p. 167). The color purple signifies a metaphysical, social, and personal rebirth and a celebration of lesbianism as a natural, beautiful experience of love.

Like her treatment of religion and blues, Walker's encoding of black speech and male characters signifies her sexual, moral, and political closeness to the audacious black women in the narrative. The values and vitality of black American communities, including the socialized ambivalence and quest for wholeness from cradle to grave of its members, are encoded in the sounds, semantics, and syntax of their speech: from "It be more than a notion taking care of children ain't even yourn" (p. 6) to "She look like she ain't long for this world but dressed well for the next" (p. 42). In contrast to the truth of this double vision are the letters in Standard American English from Nettie that tell how the Reverend Samuel and Corrine, the black couple who adopt Celie's kidnapped children and homeless sister, practice their sanctified religion among the Olinka people as token members of a largely white missionary association. These letters do not conjure up for me the texture, tone, and truth of the traditional lives of African peoples.

Equally problematic for many black male readers is the implied author's and protagonist's hostility toward black men, who are humanized only upon adopting womanist principles of sexual egalitarianism. Except for Odessa's Jack, the black men are depicted as dogs or frogs—a rewriting of feminist fictions of male sexuality in general and Hurston's deadly signifying on Jody Starks in particular—with no hope of becoming princes. Gender role reversal or sharing, however, does foster some redemption for them. For example, Harpo not only acquires a love for housekeeping, especially cooking, but also becomes a househusband while his wife works as a storekeeper. Adam, Celie's son, endures the traditional facial scarification initiation rite of Olinka females to prove his love for Tashi. And Albert, whom Celie calls Mr.——, learns not only to make quilts, Walker's symbol for the repressed creativity of women, with Celie, but also to acknowledge her independence and integrity as a person. Guided by the spirit and achievement of Hurston, Walker has Shug to express this theme of the book more poetically in the vernacular when she tells Celie: "You have to git man off your eyeball, before you can see anything a'tall" (p. 168).

In her pre-1983 novels, then, Alice Walker provides a contemporary black womanist's vision of the lives of black Southerners. Although she does not promote socialism as the panacea for the ills of capitalist America, she does stress in *The Third Life of Grange Copeland* the need to change a patriarchal economic system that breeds alienation, exploitation, and the destruction of people's lives, especially black women's. Her characters are uneducated, ignoble young working-class types like Grange and Brownfield Copeland who, except for Grange as an old man, lack the "inner sovereignty" and "embedded strength" of educated, heroic women like Mem and Ruth. In *Meridian* she focuses more sharply on the making of a revolutionary and on living up to what is required by history and economics. Correcting the romantic assumption in the first novel that the mere capacity of people for change and love is sufficient to effect political and economic change, the second novel answers the basic question: "Is there no place in a revolution for a person who *cannot* kill?" (p. 193; Walker's emphasis). Most strikingly, her protagonist is a naive, guilt-ridden visionary for whom the Civil Rights movement is the rite of passage to liberation from guilt and rebirth as a committed community organizer and candidate for political sainthood. Even more revolutionary, the sexual politics of *The Color Purple* and the post-1983 *By the Light of My Father's Smile* also reduce the scale of the struggle for social change to the task of creating a new autonomous self: an androgynous bisexual self and society. Walker's hope for change in the future rests, then, with the young, old, and outrageously bold black woman. By exploring the oppressions and celebrating the triumphs of Southern black wives, mothers, and daughters as they relate intimately, including sexually, more to each other than to working-class black men, she moves intertextually between the narrative conventions of critical realism, folk romance, and black postmodernism as she reinforces the theme of radical black feminism in the African American novel.

GAYL [AMANDA] JONES (1949–)

In an interview with Michael Harper, her mentor at Brown University, Gayl Jones stated that her first stories were hearing "grown-up people talking" and hearing her mother read stories to her that she had written. She therefore thinks that her "language/word foundations were oral rather than written." She also told Harper that she felt "that the best of my writing comes from having *heard* rather than having read."[48] Born on November 23, 1949, in Lexington, Kentucky, to Lucille and Franklin Jones, Gayl Jones attended school to the tenth grade in Lexington, but, as she states, the segregated schools provided "really unfortunate kinds of books" for teaching black children to read.[49]

Although her mother and grandmother introduced her to the oral tradition and storytelling, it was her fifth grade teacher, Mrs. Hodges, who taught her and other students to write stories while listening to music. She and the other students would then have to read the stories aloud to the whole class. After completing high school in 1968, Jones left the South for Connecticut College, where she won a prize for the best original poem in 1969–70. She completed her B.A. in English in 1971 and earned both an M.A. in 1973 and a D.A. in 1975 in creative writing from Brown University under the guidance of Michael Harper and William Meredith.

She then accepted a faculty position at the University of Michigan, which she abruptly resigned in 1983 after her husband, Robert Higgins-Jones, was indicted for a violent confrontation with gay activists. Taking flight to Europe, the couple lived mainly in France during their nearly six years of expatriation before returning to the United States. Subsequently, intermittent conflicts with local Kentucky authorities over alleged racial injustices toward the family culminated in a violent confrontation with the police that resulted in the gory suicide of Robert Higgins-Jones and the brief hospitalization of Gayl Jones for a mental examination.[50]

While still a student at Brown, Gayl Jones published her first novel, *Corregidora* (1975), with the support of Random House editor Toni Morrison. Her other published novels are *Eva's Man* (1976), *The Healing* (1998), and *Mosquito* (1999). She has also published a play, *Chile Woman* (1974), three books of poetry—*Song for Anninho* (1981), *The Hermit-Woman* (1983), and *Xarque and Other Poems* (1985)—a collection of short stories, *White Rat* (1977), and a collection of provocative critical essays tracing the oral roots of African American literature, *Liberating Voices: Oral Tradition in African American Literature* (1998).

Like the blues women in her highly successful early novels, Jones has lived a life of quiet desperation, volcanic desire, male domination, and deep distrust of white Americans. From their tenor, tone, and texture, her writings, especially their orality, seem to be her political liberation and spiritual salvation. Gothically mysterious and shocking, sexually explicit and violent, psychologically dense and disturbing, the language of the vernacular voices that Jones uses to represent the lives of Ursa in *Corregidora* and Eva in *Eva's Man* transgresses thematic and stylistic conventions. In these early novels of gothic and critical realism, Jones fingers the jagged grain (Ellison's descriptive phrase for the blues) of the legacy of slavery and the politics of identity that black women in love and trouble on the margins of society struggle to transform as they tell their own stories and sing their own songs in African American vernacular voices.

The mystery, horror, and revolt of black feminism against male domination and the legacy of slavery, a cornerstone of colonialism and capitalism in the New World, are explored by Jones in *Corregidora* and *Eva's Man* with the authority, authenticity, and agency of the African American vernacular tradition. Because of a hysterectomy following an accident caused by her abusive, drunk husband, blues singer Ursa Corregidora cannot live up to the legacy of three generations of Corregidora women. Their legacy of brutal sexual abuse and economic exploitation compelled them to procreate and perpetuate the incestuous line of tragic witnesses initiated by her slavebreeding Portuguese ancestor, who fathered his own slaves and prostitutes. To avenge the abuse that she and other black women have suffered, Ursa kills her husband with kindness and the implied author's tacit sympathy as the novel closes ambiguously with the act of fellatio. In *Eva's Man* this gothic oral castration motif of a woman's resistance to sexual abuse by men is less ambiguous and more violent. It opens with Eva Medina, the forty-three-year-old, mentally deranged, college-educated protagonist, undergoing psychiatric treatment in prison for poisoning her weekend lover and biting off his penis. The terrible price of liberation from male sexual domination and economic exploitation in both novels is evoked through an emphasis on orality. Flashbacks, reveries, interior monologues, and vernacular voices effectively modulate the tempo, suspense, and horror of these first-person gothic novels of critical realism.

In *Corregidora* "there is no hierarchical relationship between black speech and a separate literary language, no implicit dependency," John Edgar Wideman writes. "The norms of black oral tradition exist full-bodied in the verbal style of the novel. . . . The entire novel flows through the filter of the narrator's sensibility, and Corregidora's sensibility is constructed of blocks of black speech, her own, her men's . . . the voices of her mother and the dead black women keeping alive the memories of slavery."[51] But *The Healing*, especially what Jones calls its confabulatory style and structure, moves beyond her previous blues novels because, as Jones herself states, "they emphasized the narrowest range of subject matter—the man-done-her-wrong-type blues—and even the blues itself has more possibility and range. *The Healing* is meant to be a rejection of those earlier novels."[52]

The Healing and *Mosquito* are more experimental in theme, style and structure, yet less radically black feminist than her earlier fiction. *Mosquito* is a very long, discursively rambling, nonlinear, transcultural, multivocal, metafictional postmodern novel that could just as appropriately be examined under the subheading of fabulation, legend, and neoslave narrative in the next chapter. As critical realism, the novel wryly satirizes racial and ethnic stereotypes as the language of the text moves from AAVE and signifying to SAE and specifying, and from fiction to song and drama in addressing the themes of freedom, literacy, and wholeness, as well as the relationship of language to power and identity formation along the border of Texas and Mexico. The novel unfolds with disruptive and digressive associative and metafictional allusions not only to cultural anthropology, folklore, popular culture, romance, Western classical texts, and detective novels, but also to characters, a song, poem, and play by the author's deceased mother, Lucille Jones. In a mock interview of Monkey Bread by the Daughters of Nzingha, a publishing collective of black women writers, the implied author ironically comments on the style and structure of *Mosquito*:

> At least the Daughters of Nzingha claims they know who I am and that's why I considers y'all along with Nadine to be my primary audience. I don't mix my words or change my words around none. I don't have to explain none of my meanings to y'all. And I don't negotiate my identity with nobody. Even our own peoples. I am who I am. I do writes for peoples who knows how to hear me. I writes with as many words as I wants and digresses as much as I can to get the ideas to the listeners. I think that is so important. Not only to tell the readers what happens in a story but to get your ideas to them, your opinions, and to also tell the reader how you feels about the events in the story.[53]

In short, the implied author invites her primary readers to join her in improvising and interweaving their own stories with hers.

The novel opens with the authority and authenticity of the fascinating but frustratingly rambling African American vernacular voice of the principal narrator and protagonist Sojourner Nadine Jane Johnson, better known as Mosquito, whose "first love is the love of language" (p. 601). Although the protagonist is from Kentucky, and although the novel is a pastiche of literary texts and vernacular voices, the rhythm, idioms, and commonplaces of the dominant voice that we hear have the authentic sound and sense of an African American dialect, but not clearly black Kentuckian. Rather than write stories, Mosquito implicitly comments on the oral and aural style and structure of her book to Ray, "I likes to tell my stories, 'cause then you knows who's hearing them. And all them written books has got a lot of rules. I wouldn't abide by them people's rules. I don't think a Mosquito-crafted novel would abide by any of them people's rules. And then they'd be telling me it weren't no novel" (p. 528).

The driver for and owner of her own truck company, the Mosquito Trucking Company, Mosquito becomes a reluctant activist in the new Underground Railroad, the Sanctuary Movement in the 1980s for Mexican immigrants and undocumented workers. Mosquito unwittingly aids the stowaway and pregnant Maria in eluding immigration authorities on the border road between South Texas and northern Mexico. She becomes a compassionate if not committed agent of social change when she assists in the birth of Maria's child in the truck and transports her to a church sanctuary. More important than this event, however, are Mosquito's endless, often didactic stories and the relationships she develops on her journey with a motley cast of characters, especially Delgadina, the multilingual Chicana bartender and student who is studying to become a creative writer and detective; Monkey Bread, a childhood girlfriend and rival for boyfriends whom she rediscovers as a personal assistant for a movie star in Hollywood and a writer; and Ray, her revolutionary and philosophical lover. Before driving Maria and Journal, her child, back to Mexico at the end of the book, Mosquito underscores its metafictional confabulatory nature: "I's told y'all the true truth about most of the peoples in this story, although I ain't told y'all the whole truth about none of the peoples in this story. Or perhaps I've told y'all the whole truth without telling y'all the real truth" (p. 601).

Although similarly nonlinear, transcultural, and multivocal, *The Healing*, a National Book Award finalist in 1998, is more meaningfully interpreted here as neocritical realism because of its compelling representation of the dynamic role of confabulation and the faith healer in bridging cultural and class differences in contemporary society. It is therefore reasonable to examine the literary merits of its authenticity, authority, and agency by focusing on its confabulation, its imaginative deployment of residual oral forms of religious ritual, vernacular language, and music.

Rather than a blues singer, the central character and principal narrator of *The*

Healing is a faith healer, Harlan Jane Eagleton, who was formerly a beautician who gambled on horses. In the fictive past of the text, she was also the business manager of a not-so-famous black rock-and-roll singer, Joan Savage, who is a bibliophile who "prefers to be called, Savage Joan the Darling Bitch."[54] Harlan immediately establishes her distinctive black identity in the frame story as she eats sardines with an open Bible on her lap while traveling by bus to one of the "little southern and midwestern tank towns" where she performs her healing ritual with a gathering of believers and skeptics. Picked up by a local welcoming committee of women, Harlan reflects in a fluid, nonlinear, oral manner on the relationship of language to knowledge and power that is the primary theme of the novel: "The women in the backseat are still thinking how common I am, how full of chitchat, and my vocabulary sounds elementary, it don't even sound like that preacher-teacher woman that give that lecture, ain't that wondrous and fantabulous vocabulary them healers uses, and if I could really heal, wouldn't I already just know about them trains too? And I don't talk that revelation talk, that prophet passion. Just some ordinary woman, could be one of them, or one of their daughters, one of their own girls" (p. 25).

After establishing the authority and authenticity of the black female faith healer in the initial frame, the dialect becomes more elastic and complex as the story within a story shifts in flashbacks and increasingly shorter chapters to the relationship between Harlan and Joan. The agency and authority of Harlan, the protagonist/narrator, is challenged and contested by other voices in her nonlinear, retrospective narrative movement back from her present calling as healer to her earlier vocations as Joan's beautician and then business manager. Harlan also recalls how her self-healing of a stab wound from a jealous, misguided Joan transformed her from business manager into the healing woman whom we meet in the opening chapter. The frame story closes the forty-six-chapter, five-part novel enigmatically with a two-page epilogue in the black dialect of a local hostess committee that welcomes Harlan, the healing woman, to yet another town. However, instead of Nicholas, her Afro-German lover's black security guard, testifying as usual to her powers, she discovers a male from her past whom she least expected waiting to bear witness to her healing powers. Stylistically and structurally, *The Healing* is thus compellingly and challengingly innovative.

The novel moves beyond the "humorous or pathetic" black dialect of the plantation and minstrel traditions and of the conventional frame structure for representing black American culture and character. Jones filters her novel through the sensibility of the protagonist/narrator, who transgresses the hierarchical relationship between African American Vernacular English and literary language and between foreign languages and Standard American English dialects. For example, after one of her healing rituals, we hear multiple voices filtered through Harlan's limited omniscient voice as Jones strains to encompass both the local and global, the oral and literate modes of knowing and being in the world with others:

> I can already hear 'em talking about me, those flibbertigibbets. She ain't no preacher woman or a teacher woman neither, she a faith healer, one of them others be saying. . . . I seen her heal someone in D.C. I seen her when she healed in Memphis and then again in Kansas City. She even healed folks in Milan, that's over there in Italy. Dottoressa is what they calls her there in that Milan. I seen this picture of her healing over there in Italy and she were surrounded by all these Italians who looked just liked colored people to me. Say she's even healed folks in Brazil. I know they's got colored people in Brazil. Curandera's what they call her in Brazil. (P. 13)

Omitting all quotation marks for direct addresses and dialogue, as well as erasing all specific time markers in identifying specific episodes, Jones constructs a complex text of characters and events whose authority and authenticity are occasionally diminished by anomalous and incongruous repetitions of words, catalogs of books, and sentences in different languages.

Although Harlan was born in New Orleans and raised in Louisville, Kentucky, for example, people say that she has a Geechee or Gullah accent, which is characteristic of the residual African speech behavior of black Americans acculturated on the Georgia and South Carolina Sea Islands. "Don't sound like a accent to me, but other people call it a Geechee accent. Then some people tell me I got a blend of different types of accents" (p. 43). In addition to the elusive voice of the narrator/protagonist, Jones constructs a range of characters and voices whose regional distinctiveness, unusual rhythms, and social variations in the Kentucky setting are more anomalous than authentic. They include Josef Ehelich von Fremd, the Afro-German thorough-bred horse owner and Harlan's lover; Nicholas, his black security guard and the witness to Harlan's first healing; Joan, the well-read, multilingual black college graduate and socially misguided rock-and-roll singer; and James, Joan's ex-husband with whom Harlan has a sexual encounter. More enigmatic and mysterious are the voices of Norvelle, the medical anthropologist in Africa and Harlan's former husband, and Jaboti, the grandmother whose stories about the turtle shell that she was required to wear while performing in a carnival as the Turtle Woman symbolizes the strategies of mask-wearing and tricksterism that enabled black Americans, especially women, to survive the complete domination by others.

In blending fact with fiction, nonstandard with standard English, American with non-American languages, and vernacular with literary voices, Jones moves thematically and stylistically across national, cultural, and linguistic boundaries as she reveals the arrogance of American cultural power. "It's only you Americans who're stingy about language, who believe that your own language is the universal language," Harlan's multilingual Afro-German lover Josef declares (p. 46). Clearly critical of the linguistic limitations of Harlan and the cultural arrogance of Americans in general, Jones, the implied author, is more sympathetic with Harlan's contesting of modern narrative practice and modern ways of knowing and being in the world with others.

Reflecting on the possibility that Nicholas, who observed her "first true healing," would retire as her "confabulatory" witness, and foreshadowing his replacement in the epilogue, Harlan states: "Course there's probably a lot of fakers that hires theyselves witnesses, y'all know like them evangelist fakers . . . and some of them probably do better witnessing than the true witnesses. . . . 'Cause maybe the fake witness got more confabulatory imagination than the true witness that just got a knowledge of the healings" (p. 11). In so far as truth is a fictive or imaginative construction of facts in language that communicates the ideas and feelings of the speaker or writer about the nature of reality to an audience, storytelling or confabulation for Harlan and Jones is both an epistemological and an ontological act.

Nicholas, for example, "usedta tell the tale with more fanfare, more flourish, more confabularooiness. And when he tells about that healing, it sounds like a true tale; it don't sound like no confabulatory tale. Lest the way he usedta tell the tale of that healing. Now he tends to be kinda dry. And those people that come to faith healing most of them want to hear confabulatory-sounding stories, which don't mean they's confabulatory stories they ownself. It's just that when people come to be healed, they just likes to hear them confabulatory-sounding stories" (p. 11). Rather than provide a specific example of Nicholas' "confabulatory" storytelling, the entire text of *The Healing* is Jones's "confabulatory" tale.

By grounding her text in the religious ritual of healing, in the vernacular voices of a black healing woman, and in the music of a college-educated black rock-and-roll singer, Jones moves beyond the ostensible cultural limitations of her blues voice in *Corregidora* and *Eva's Man*. In order to expand the varieties and complexities of agency, authority, and authenticity that mark *The Healing*, Jones explicitly contrasts the notorious Eva of her earlier novel with the identity formation of contemporary Americans of African descent, especially black women like Harlan and Joan Savage who are not "criminally insane." But only Jones's imaginative construction of Harlan bears witness to some of the levels of irony and paradox that mark the political and spiritual struggle of many black women to reconcile the multiple consciousness of their personal and group identities as American women of African descent.

Stylistically and structurally, Jones's contribution to the tradition of the African American novel is most apparent in her representation of that multiple consciousness in the nonlinear, reflexive interplay between the past and present, between the spoken and written language, and between the African Americentric vernacular and Eurocentric cultural forms of her characters. However, the voices in *The Healing* and *Mosquito* displace the authenticity, authority, and agency of a unitary blues construction of black identity that has a distinctive personal and group historical resonance of what cultural historian and novelist Albert Murray calls antagonistic cooperation. For some readers the voices in *The Healing* and *Mosquito* therefore represent a democratic, compelling narrative vision of a fluid, transracial, and transcultural social order that affirms separate but equal ways of knowing, healing, and being black in the world with others. For others the importance of ethnic and racial unity in the struggle against antiblack racism and for social justice is inadequately developed.

[MILTONA] TONI [MIRKIN] CADE BAMBARA (1939–1995)

Like Jones, Toni Cade Bambara had the blessing of Toni Morrison as editor, as well as the inspiration of her mother and the ancestors in committing her life and art to exploring the limitations and possibilities of political and cultural agency in improving social conditions and gender relationships in African American communities. Born in Harlem, New York, on March 25, 1939, Miltona Mirkin Cade was the daughter of Helen Cade and Walter Cade II. She acquired the name Toni while in elementary school and the name Bambara while in Queens College. After graduating in 1959 from Queens with a B.A. in English, she studied in 1961 at the University of Florence and the Ecole de Mime Etienne Decroux in Paris. Subsequently, while working as a social worker, theater manager, and writer, she continued her academic, cultural, and artistic education at several New York institutions. Earning an M.A. in American literature in 1965 from City College of New York, she then began working with black artists Barbara Christian, Audre Lorde, and June Jordan, as well as other black and white administrators, teachers, artists, and cultural workers in the development of the City College SEEK (Search for Education, Elevation, and Knowledge) program. While pregnant and trying to find a name for her daughter Karma in 1970, Bambara told an interviewer in 1994, she was inspired by an African art book to change her name legally to Toni Cade Bambara.[55]

Political activist, cultural worker, and artist, Bambara told an interviewer in 1979 that she could not remember a time when she was not writing, but she did not come to appreciate that writing was "a perfectly legitimate way to participate in struggle" until the early 1970s.[56] Although an avid reader, she felt that her early influences came primarily "off the street rather than from other books" and from other women in the neighborhood, especially the beauty parlors.[57] Writing for her, she told interviewer Beverly Guy-Sheftall, was "an act of language first and foremost.... As an act of language, literature is a spirit informer—an energizer."[58] Her major writings include a classic anthology, *The Black Woman* (1970); two collections of short stories, *Gorilla, My Love* (1972) and *The Sea Birds Are Still Alive* (1977); two novels, *The Salt Eaters* (1980) and *Those*

Bones Are Not My Child (1999); and a posthumously published miscellany, *Deep Sightings and Rescue Missions: Fiction, Essays, and Conversations* (1999), edited by Toni Morrison. Bambara died in 1995 before completing her twelve-year neorealistic project on the murder of more than forty black children in Atlanta, Georgia.

Edited and posthumously published by her friend and former editor, Toni Morrison, *Those Bones Are Not My Child* is a chilling, suspenseful mystery novel and meditation on the history of race, class, sex, and violence in the Deep South. Set in Atlanta and structured as a journal that Marzala Rawls Spencer, the protagonist/narrator, began in September 1979, the novel opens suspensefully on a prologue dated November 16, 1981. The second-person vernacular voice of the prologue's narrator dramatically, authoritatively, and immediately immerses the reader in her mounting anxiety over her daughter's failure to come home from school and her fear that she has become another of the missing and murdered black children. The prologue also reveals how disillusionment with the black and white investigative Task Force and other authorities led to the organization in 1980 of STOP, the Committee to Stop Children's Murders, by mothers of several of the murdered children. Zala, the protagonist, and her estranged Vietnam veteran husband, Spence, join the grassroots investigation for the missing children, especially their son Sonny. The novel closes with an epilogue and a journal entry on July 8, 1987, with the implied author, who is probably the prologue's narrator, writing a letter and packing to leave town.

Sustaining the primary emphasis of the novel on the complex double consciousness and socialized ambivalence of her characters about what they believe to be an official coverup of the serial murders of black children, Bambara defers closure to the narrative by dramatizing Zala's discontinuous, retrospective reflections on the injustice, incompetence, irresponsibility, insensitivity, and inadequacy of the detective and investigative reports by the authorities, media, journalists, and writers. None took "a hard-hitting look at White House-FBI-CIA machinations" in blaming the victims of the crimes, stereotyping the murdered children and their underemployed and unemployed black parents, especially the mothers, as the culpable parties before incredibly closing the case after charging and convicting Wayne Williams, a young black man, for the murders of two adult males. Even though the murders of black children continued after Williams's arrest, the authorities closed the case. Even though Williams "in no way resembled any of the descriptions in the Task Force reports. . . . In no way resembled the descriptions in the reports of STOP's independent investigators, or in the reports of community workers investigating well out of the limelight," the multimillion dollar investigation of Atlanta Missing and Murdered Children's Case ended.[59]

Covering the periods July 20, 1980, through July 11, 1982, the seven major sections of the novel move slowly, speculatively, and suspensefully in journalistic fashion from the bereaved but courageously determined family of Zala Spencer to record the unrelenting assaults on the spirit and lives of black children in Atlanta. Zala and Spence's tireless, desperate investigative search for their son surprisingly and mysteriously culminates with a telephone call from a pediatrics ward in Miami, Florida, on page 512 of the 669-page novel with the news that a badly battered boy was "found wandering in a daze on the highway, barefoot, in khaki shorts and a ragged child's undershirt four sizes too small." Their son was a victim of kidnapping and molestation. At first sight of his emaciated, abused condition, and before nurturing him back to health and speech, Zala protested in disbelief: "Those bones are not my child."[60] The cast of characters includes such actual participants as Commissioner of Public Safety Lee Brown, commander of the Task Force, Maynard Jackson and Andrew Young, black mayors of Atlanta, Vernon Jordan, Urban League leader, Hosea Williams, local civil rights leader, and, of course, Wayne Williams. But the most engaging characters are Zala, Spence, and their children Kenti and Kofi, whose racial representation through cultural references to commonplace sites, smells, sounds, sayings, and signifying seems authentic even though their speech is not clearly marked as Southern African American Vernacular English.

Although Bambara enhances the appeal and amplitude of the tragedy of the black mothers and their sons by ironically comparing their fate to that of Clytemnestra and her son, the authority and agency of the novel are grounded in African American vernacular and literary traditions, from the black church and Bible to the poetry of Gwendolyn Brooks, Maya Angelou, and Alexis DeVeaux. For example, in speaking truth to power and the community of Seven Hills Congregational Church, Zala, wearing a T-shirt with an inscription from a DeVeaux poem, "Question Authority," quotes from a poem by Brooks, "We are all each other's harvest, we are each other's business," and from a poem by Angelou, "Of all the virtues . . . the most important is courage, for without courage none of the other virtues can be practiced with consistency and passion" (p. 658). Because we do not know how extensively Morrison edited *Those Bones Are Not My Child*, and because it is not as compelling as an example of critical realism in its authority, authenticity, and agency as her first novel, let us look more closely at *The Salt Eaters*.

The Salt Eaters is less sensational than Jones's novels and *Those Bones Are Not My Child*, but more dialectical in its representation of the essential forces of cultural progress and radical democracy for Americans of African descent. The novel affirms the viability of traditional divinatory practices that celebrate the mystery and sacredness of life in the post–Civil Rights activist period of the 1970s. With political authority and agency as well as cultural authenticity, it teaches those in search of personal wholeness through the ancestral wisdom of "the mud mothers . . . the difference between eating salt as an antidote to snakebite and turning into salt, succumbing to the serpent."[61] After a suicide attempt, Velma Henry learns through Minnie Ransom, the legendary faith healer of

Claiborne, Georgia, M'Dear Sophie, her godmother, and the community healing and prayer circle that personal and social wholeness and health are "no trifling matter." Philosophically, the implied author and omniscient narrator share the protagonist's conviction "that the truth was in one's own people, and the key was to be centered in the best of one's own traditions" (p. 169).

The retrospective, discontinuous narrative therefore focuses primarily on Velma in the healing session. Mother, wife, sister, computer analyst, community organizer, and civil rights, antinuclear, and women's rights activist, Velma had a nervous breakdown because she was overworked and because her man Obie was unfaithful. She was the principal agent in fostering unity between cultural and political factions in the struggle for Third World solidarity within the militant 7 Arts Academy and with other groups in the Black Belt. Their goal was "to blueprint a sure-fire strategy for mobilizing the people to form and support an independent Black political party before it was too late" for a coalition with such other groups as the Puerto Rican Nationalist Party, the La Raza Unida groups, the American Indian Movement, and the Women for Action (pp. 91, 93). When Velma was not out of town working with computers, she ran the office, did the books, handled the payroll, supervised the office staff, wrote the major proposals, did most of the fund raising, and "saw to it that they were not overlooked as resource people for seminars, conferences and trips" (p. 93). In addition to these activities as a cultural worker and political activist, Obie's demand for "more of a home life" for him and their son and his sleeping with other women drove her over the edge.

During the climatic community Spring Carnival, Velma ritualistically recovers her mental and spiritual balance as she recalls ancestral lessons about the difference between "remedies for snakebite and the bite of the serpent" and as she hears the blues while in the healing and prayer circle:

> She thought she knew that. At some point in her life she was sure Douglass, Tubman, the slave narratives, the songs, the fables, Delaney, Ida Wells, Blyden, DuBois, Garvey, the singers, her parents, Malcolm, Coltrane, the poets, her comrades, her godmother, her neighbors, had taught her that. . . . Thought she knew how to build resistance, make the journey to the center of the circle, stay poised and centered in the work and not fly off, stay centered in the best of her people's traditions and not be available to madness, not become intoxicated by the heady brew of degrees and career and congratulations for nothing done, not become anesthetized by dazzling performances with somebody else's aesthetic, not go under. . . . Thought the vaccine offered by all the theorists and activists and clear thinkers and doers of the warrior clan would take. But amnesia had set in anyhow. Heart/brain/gut muscles atrophied anyhow. (P. 258)

It takes the sound of Minnie and Old Wife playing a recording of "Wiiild women doan worrreee, wild women doan have no bluuuzzzzz" and the memory of Charlie Parker playing "Now Is the Time" on his alto sax finally to restore Velma's sociopsychological balance and wholeness (pp. 262–63).

Although the neorealistic focus of *The Salt Eaters* is on Velma's double consciousness, Bambara also constantly shifts the narrative lens and probes with clinical precision into the internal and external lives of other major and minor characters. Minnie Ransom, for example, "simply placed her left hand on the patient's spine and her right on the navel, then clearing the channels, putting herself aside, she became available to a healing force no one had yet, to her satisfaction, captured in a name" (p. 47). She "daily placed the pots of food and jugs of water for the loa that resided . . . [in the] Old Tree the free coloreds of Claybourne planted in the spring of 1871" (p. 145). As the primary agents of healing and unity in the black community, Minnie and Old Wife complement each other: Minnie with her spiritual powers and psychic energy, and Old Wife with her more traditional black Christian faith, which teaches not only that "The chirren are our glory," but also that "In our extremity is God's opportunity" (p. 47). Equally compelling is the cameo of Campbell, a former student of Mustafa the Magnificent and the freelance writer who, like the implied author Bambara, knew "in a glowing moment that all the systems were the same at base—voodoo, thermodynamics, I Ching, astrology, numerology, alchemy, metaphysics, everybody's ancient myths—they were interchangeable, not at all separate much less conflicting. They were the same, to the extent that their origins survived detractors and perverters." Like his editor and the implied author, readers will be "simply intrigued by Campbell's ability to discuss fission in terms of billiards, to couch principles of thermonuclear dynamics in the language of down-home Bible-quoting folks" (p. 211). Equally intriguing is the multiethnic Seven Sisters of the Grain singing troupe, who, as Iris, from Puerto Rico and New York, reveals, are migrants or immigrants: "transplants all, Inez from farm valley country, Chezia from the Tupercuin hills, Nilda from the contested Black Hills, Mai from the hills of San Francisco they liked to joke, or the paddy fields of Berkeley, Cecile from a maroon community in the hills of Jamaica. Only Palma was at home, and not even, she said it herself. Home was with them or in the studio or with her main man" (p. 238).

Like the ritual of the healing session and prayer circle, the double-edged wit of the black vernacular—for example, the faith healer was "dressed for days," looking "like a farmer in a Halston, a snuff dipper in a Givenchy" (pp. 4, 8)—brilliantly plumbs the depths of African American double consciousness and fosters a sympathetic understanding of Velma. At the same time, the signifying banter between Minnie and Old Wife and among the Seven Sisters of the Grain dramatizes the interrelated roles of ancestral intelligence and political activism in attaining and sustaining unity of self and community and in the process of effecting social change.

Continuity and change in their experiment with vernacular voices and residually oral forms, then, are the chief characteristics of the novels that I have loosely grouped here under the rubric critical realism. John Killens, John Williams, Alice Walker, Gayl Jones, and Toni Bambara, like William Attaway, employ both an insider's and outsider's view in their use of critical realism, responding in different ways to the problems of the past and the modern winds of social and cultural change. Their novels, except for *The Color Purple* and *The Healing*, are generally more historical and mimetic than romantic and didactic. Fidelity to the empirical truth of the actual past and to the psychological truth of the present are their common objectives. They also attempt to develop from the inside the psychic dualism and morality of individuals in search of a better future.

Killens, however, is more direct in style and characterization than Walker, and is more concerned with historical types than individuals. Killens's creation of members of the working class and their middle-class allies heralds the emergence of a bold new world of proud, heroic types like the Youngbloods, Charlie Chaney, and Ben Ali Lumumba. The delineation of his characters also illustrates his anticapitalist position and strong, sometimes polemical, support for the perspective of socialism. Alice Walker's men, on the other hand, are traditional black male chauvinists of both the lower and the middle class, who stereotypically vent their hatred of exploitation by whites on their families, especially the women, and whose only redemptive act is, like Grange Copeland's, to turn from hatred to love and to faith in a new social order based on sexual, economic, and racial equality. In contrast, the struggle—sometimes violent, usually sensational and tragic—by her women characters to reject traditional roles of motherhood, nurturing, and dependence heralds the emergence of a new generation of radical black female protagonists in search of selfhood, security, and power.

The most experimental in technique and structure in this group include Jones, Bambara, Walker, and Williams. In the struggle of their protagonists to retain or recover their mental health, Jones makes use of the blues, castration by fellatio, and healing rituals in her most compelling novels, and Bambara deploys interrelated transcultural belief systems, faith healing rituals, ancestral presences, and grassroots political organization in *The Salt Eaters*. In contrast, Walker weaves the blues, domestic abuse, lesbian eroticism, petit bourgeois female entrepreneurialism, quilting, and epistles into the structure and style of *The Color Purple*. Unlike Bambara, however, Jones and Walker evoke ambivalence in some readers about the authority, authenticity, and private rather than public agency of their contemporary black female protagonists and about the radical feminization or emasculation of black males.

Although equally experimental, John A. Williams's underrated *Night Song* and *The Man Who Cried I Am*, especially their representation of black male identity, occupy the outer boundaries of social and critical realism. They probe the socialized ambivalence of the black male artist, musician, and writer rather than of the working class or the social forces responsible for their alienation and exploitation. *Night Song* experiments with the modalities of black music and the tragic impact of antiblack racism on jazzmen like Charlie Parker. By their talented, usually compelling, occasionally brilliant, use of black residually oral forms, especially music, religion, and speech, Killens, Williams, Walker, Jones, and Bambara deepen our understanding of the distinctive historical limitations and possibilities for empowering the lives of black Americans. These five authors also enrich the vitality and variety of the tradition of the African American novel, including its poetic and Gothic qualities.

POETIC REALISM AND THE GOTHIC FABLE

By combining a concern for the truth of the lives of men and women in actual situations with a concern for the imaginative power, compression, and lyricism of language, poetic realism calls attention to the problems of reality and language while simultaneously insisting that reality is shaped more by consciousness than consciousness is by reality. Like Toomer, contemporary black poetic realists strive more for truth of sensation and environment than for truth of fact, focusing on the supernatural ties of the present to the past and on psychological and sociological concepts for their images of ethical conduct in a world of mystery and unnatural events. In other words, the mystery and terror of atmosphere, events, and character are exploited in the Gothic vision of African American poetic realists. In poetic realism the metaphoric and metonymic qualities of the language—the substitution of figurative for literal expressions—as well as deft, bold strokes of color, distilled experiences, and fleeting but sharp and frequently recurring images of the dominant, often eccentric, traits of the characters and their environment are also usually more meaningful to the author than the photographic representation of external reality. Although occasionally such characters are one-dimensional, static, and grotesque, they are more frequently, as in Toomer's *Cane*, Hurston's *Their Eyes Were Watching God*, and Morrison's *Beloved*, impressionistic and dynamic, with the poetic sensibility of the author-narrator distilling characters and events. Lyrical passages, of course, appear in the narratives of many black novelists. Many others, including Walker, Jones, and Bambara, explore the Gothic aspects of contemporary African American experience. But Morrison began her writing career with two of the best examples of what I call Gothic fables. These are generally short poetic narratives whose celebration of the beauty, truth, and possibilities of life is derived from the exploitation of its magic, mystery, and terror.

[CHLOE ANTHONY] TONI [WOFFORD] MORRISON (1931–)

Born the second of four children to George Wofford, a proud shipyard welder, road construction worker, and car washer, and Ramah Wofford, church choir singer and resourceful homemaker, on February 18, 1931, in Lorain, Ohio, Chloe Anthony Wofford grew up during the Depression in an integrated working-class community of black migrants from the South and white immigrants from Europe. Antiblack white terrorism drove her father north out of Georgia, and white bigotry and injustice dispossessed her maternal grandfather of his land and drove him north out of Alabama, resulting in both men distrusting white people.[62] In contrast, because of their religious faith, Morrison's grandmother and mother were willing to let each experience with whites indicate the possibilities of improved relations between the races. Even so, antiblack racism taught the elders of the family the value of community. Morrison's parents therefore taught their children that "all succor and aid came from themselves and their neighborhood."[63] Remembering her childhood experiences with European immigrants, Morrison told a *Time* interviewer: "In becoming an American, from Europe, what one has in common with that other immigrant is contempt for *me*—it's nothing else but color. Wherever they were from, they would stand together. . . . Every immigrant knew he would not come as the very bottom. He had to come above at least one group—and that was us."[64]

Morrison was also raised in a family of self-reliant storytellers. "There was a comradeship between men and women in the marriages of my grandparents, and of my mother and my father. The business of story-telling was a shared activity between them, and people of both genders participated in it. We, the children, were encouraged to participate in it at a very early age."[65] Her father's specialty and her favorite were ghost stories. "We were always begging him to repeat the stories that terrified us the most," Morrison recalls.[66] On one level, perhaps, this early influence of black folklore, storytelling, and ghost stories explains the Gothic element in her novels. An avid reader of everything from Jane Austen to Russian novels, Morrison graduated in 1949 with honors from Lorain High School, matriculated at Howard University, and changed her name to Toni. At Howard she majored in English, taking her B.A. in 1953 and earning an M.A. from Cornell University in 1955 with a thesis on the theme of suicide in the fiction of Virginia Woolf and William Faulkner. Having traveled to the Deep South with the Howard University Players, she returned there after college to teach at Texas Southern University from 1955 to 1957 and then moved on to a similar post at Howard University from 1957 to 1964. While teaching at Howard, she married a Jamaican, Howard Morrison, in 1958 and had two sons. Following a divorce in 1964, she became an editor, first at a textbook company in Syracuse and then in 1965 at Random House.[67]

As a senior editor at Random House, Morrison guided the production of books by Muhammad Ali, Angela Davis, Toni Cade Bambara, Henry Dumas, and Gayl Jones. "I look very hard for black fiction because I want to participate in developing a canon of black work," Morrison states. "We've had the first rush of black entertainment, where blacks were writing for whites, and whites were encouraging this kind of self-flagellation. Now we can get down to the craft of writing, where black people are talking to black people."[68] In her own novels, "To make the story appear oral, meandering, effortless, spoken—to have the reader *feel* the narrator without *identifying* that narrator, or hearing him or her knock about, and to have the reader work with the author in the construction of the book—is what's important," she states. "What is left out is as important as what is there."[69] Black literature, in other words, is not simply books by and about black people. Nor is it simply "literature that uses a certain mode of language in which you just sort of drop *g*'s." In addition to orality, the chief characteristics of African American literature for Morrison are first, reader participation in the construction of the text; second, a chorus, "the community or the reader at large, commenting on the action as it goes ahead"; and third, the presence of an ancestor, "sort of timeless people whose relationships to the characters are benevolent, instructive, and protective, and they provide a certain kind of wisdom."[70] As an editor, educator, and distinguished writer, Morrison has also taught at such institutions as the State University of New York, Yale, Bard, and Princeton.

Between 1970 and 1999, Morrison published seven novels: *The Bluest Eye* (1970), *Sula* (1973), *Song of Solomon* (1977), *Tar Baby* (1981), *Beloved* (1987), *Jazz* (1992), and *Paradise* (1998). Although *Beloved*, her most awesome book, and the less compelling *Jazz* and *Paradise* could probably more appropriately be analyzed as black postmodern texts in the next chapter, their poetic and Gothic elements also justify their examination here. Among her many honors and awards are the National Book Critics Circle Award and American Academy and Institute of Arts and Letters Award in 1977 for *Song of Solomon*, the Pulitzer Prize in 1988 for *Beloved* and the Nobel Prize for Literature in 1993. In addition, Morrison edited a nonfiction miscellany, *The Black Book* (1974), wrote a drama, *Dreaming Emmett* (1986), and edited *Race-ing Justice, En-Gendering Power* (1992), a collection of essays on the Clarence Thomas and Anita Hill scandal, and Toni Cade Bambara's *Deep Sightings & Rescue Missions* (1999). In 1992 she also published *Playing in the Dark*, a collection of lectures given at Harvard in 1990.

All seven novels continue the poetic and Gothic branches of the African American narrative tradition. Despite its primarily Caribbean setting, occasional Faulknerian sentences, and extended metaphors like the female soldier ant conceit in chapter 10 that reinforces the thematic ambiguity of ensnaring, autonomous black females symbolized in the title, *Tar Baby* is the least poetic and Gothic of the seven. The most ambitious and Gothic is *Song of Solomon*. The two-part novel opens in 1931 in a town near Lake Superior with the mysterious, bizarre suicide flight from a hospital roof of Mr. Robert Smith, a black insurance agent dressed in a blue costume with wide silk wings. On one hand, the symbolic and thematic significance of this leap to death by a commonly named minor character is apparent: it causes the early birth of the uncommonly named black protagonist, Macon "Milkman" Dead, in the historically for-whites-only Mercy Hospital, which blacks sardonically call No Mercy Hospital. On the other hand, the mystery and horror of this event and the fact "that Mr. Smith didn't draw as big a crowd as Lindberg had four years earlier,"[71] despite having announced his suicide plans two days before, are even more richly exploited metaphorically and metonymically by Morrison.

The densely woven, arabesque texture of this opening scene includes the commonplace activities of the daily lives of the absent poor, such as "most of the women were fastening their corsets and getting ready to go see what tails or entrails the butcher might be giving away" (pp. 3–4). The multilayered scene also includes the anecdotal humor of black names (Not Doctor Street, No Mercy Hospital, and Lincoln's Heaven) that wryly reveal cultural and social differences between white and black townspeople; and the mysterious song of the strange black woman wrapped in an old quilt and wearing a knitted cap pulled down over her forehead. We are immediately alerted to the theme that life is precious and that many dead lives and faded memories are buried in the names of places and people in this country: Not Doctor Street, Lincoln's Heaven, Solomon's Leap, Macon Dead, Milkman Dead, Magdalene called Lena Dead, First Corinthians Dead, Pilate Dead, and Sing Dead. But we do not discover until chapter 6 that Robert Smith's suicide is the result of pressures he can no longer endure as a member of the Seven Days, a secret black male vigilante society that avenges the deaths of black victims of white terror. And it is not until chapter 12 of the fifteen-chapter novel that we reconstruct with the protagonist the legendary meaning of the Song of Solomon that Pilate sings as Smith plunges to his death and that the protagonist sings at the end of the novel before plunging to his. Setting, story, and characters thus create a haunting mood of unknown terror.

We move with Milkman through the compressed thirty-two years of his haunted, self-absorbed construction of his black male identity up North in Part 1 and his trip South to his buried family legacy in Part 2. The melodramatic flashbacks and reveries of the characters as well as the digressions of the editorializing omniscient narrator enable us to discover with Milkman the hidden truth about his manhood and his strange family, an ancestral truth which he must recognize and reconstruct in order to become a whole person. With shifting degrees of delight and disgust, we are challenged by the discontinuous dramatic narrative to reconstruct with the protagonist the traumatic events of his past. These include the facts that his mother Ruth continued breast feeding him in a small green room long after he began school; that her husband caught her naked in bed passionately kissing her dead father; and that his maternal "grandfather was a high-yellow nigger who loved ether and hated black skin" (pp. 76–77). We also learn that his father Macon sold his soul to own things and compelled Ruth to attempt repeatedly to abort Milkman's birth; and that his paternal great-grandfather Solomon was an African slave who fathered twenty-one children in Virginia, where legend and a children's song tell of him flying back home to Africa.

Additionally, we learn that Milkman's Aunt Pilate, who wore a brass box earring containing her name, was an unkempt, bootlegging clairvoyant who was miraculously born without a navel after her mother's death. Pilate spoke with the dead—especially her father—and used her supernatural powers to save Milkman's life before he was born. Our moral sympathies are further manipulated by flashbacks revealing that Milkman's paternal grandfather had the top of his head shot off from the back by white Pennsylvanians who wanted his farm, Lincoln's Heaven; and that his friend Guitar became a vigilante because of his conviction that "white people are unnatural" and his fear that "every one of them is a potential nigger-killer, if not an actual one" (pp. 155–56). Because her supernatural birth and powers mark her as a bridge between the living and the dead, Pilate, who has "acquired a deep concern for and about human relationships" (p. 149), is the moral center of the novel. Her death at the end of the novel while she and Milkman are reburying her father Jake's bones on Solomon's Leap moves Milkman to embrace the whole truth of his black male identity in a sacrificial leap down on her assassin, Guitar.

"What is curious to me," Morrison says in her lectures, "is that bestial treatment of human beings never produces a race of beasts." Since her childhood in Lorain, she has been fascinated by the uncommon efforts of common black people to cope with socialized ambivalence. How do they deal with the sexist rules and racist absurdities of life in a small town? Drawing on her family's tradition of telling ghost stories and her long-standing commitment to literature, Morrison began attempting to answer this question and expanding her commitment in 1962 by joining a writers' workshop at Howard. The short story she began in this workshop became the nucleus of *The Bluest Eye.*

Less ambitious in scope and length than *Song of Solomon,* both *The Bluest Eye* and *Sula* are novels of poetic realism and Gothic fables about growing up poor, black, and female in a male-dominated, white middle-class society. In *The Bluest Eye* Morrison contrasts the experience and values of two black families, the poor yet proud MacTeers and the poor, ashamed Breedloves, with those of the Shirley Temple of the white Fisher family. The major focus is on eleven-year-old Pecola Breedlove and the MacTeer sisters, ten-year-old Frieda and nine-year-old Claudia, the narrator. The novel is cleverly structured around an opening story from the standard elementary school Dick-and-Jane readers of the 1940s (the time of the action), which insidiously inculcated an inferiority complex in black children of the inner city by promoting the values of the homogenized white suburban middle-class family. The brief children's story, which Morrison repeats in three different styles—from standard to nonstandard English—provides an ironic contrast to the plot, which is further reinforced by the narrator with a marigold-planting analogy that ingeniously and immediately establishes the lyrical style and tragic mood of the narrative. The novel proper is then divided into the four seasons (autumn, winter, spring, and summer) with the Dick-and-Jane story also broken down into seven headnotes for the minichapters, sharpening the contrast between the ideal experience of the white world and the actual experience of blacks portrayed in the minichapters. After being raped by her drunk father, deceived into believing God had miraculously given her the blue eyes she prayed for, suffering a miscarriage, and being ridiculed by other children, Pecola loses her sanity, and the marigold seeds planted by the MacTeer sisters do not grow. Poetic metaphor and metonomy thus complement each other in their Gothic signification: it is painfully difficult for little black girls to grow into healthy womanhood with a positive self-image when "all the world had agreed that a blue-eyed, yellow-haired, pink-skinned doll was what every girl child treasures."[72]

Progressing from girlhood to womanhood, *Sula,* the most poetic of Morrison's seven novels, focuses on the friendship of two black women and moves into retrospection over a period of forty-six years. Part 1 with six chapters that chronicle the years from 1919 to 1927 distills the legendary qualities of the Bottom, a hilltop black neighborhood in Ohio; of Shadrack, the shell-shocked World War I veteran and founder of National Suicide Day; of Sula Peace, the tough, adventuresome main character; and of her girlhood friendship with Nel Wright, whose wedding ruptures the special relationship they shared. The five chapters of Part 2 (1937, 1939, 1940, 1941, and 1965) continue the chronicle with a worldly-wise, independent Sula returning to the Bottom after a ten-year absence, becoming both a pariah and redeemer of her time and place and people.

Morrison's language throughout *Sula* is even more charged with the beauty, wonder, and pain of the poetry of the black experience than it is in *The Bluest Eye.* Our feelings are stirred and our awareness of the characters' ambivalence about people and events deepened by the irony of such place names as the Bottom (a name derived from the legend or "nigger joke" about the white farmer who kept his promise of freedom and a piece of bottom land to his slave by convincing him to accept infertile land up in the hills as the bottom of heaven), Irene's Palace of Cosmetology, Edna Finch's Mellow House, and the Time and a Half Pool Hall. Equally striking are such metaphorical images as "Grass stood blade by blade, shocked into separateness by an ice that held for days"; and "As Reverend Deal moved into his sermon, the hands of the women unfolded like pairs of ravens and flew high above their hats in the air."[73] But the most clever is Sula's use of a spider conceit to express her disappointment with Nel:

> Now Nel was one of *them.* One of the spiders whose only thought was the next rung of the web, who dangled in dark dry places suspended by

> their own spittle, more terrified of the free fall than the snake's breath below. Their eyes so intent on the wayward stranger who trips into their net, they were blind to the cobalt on their own backs, the moonshine fighting to pierce their corners. If they were touched by the snake's breath, however fatal, they were merely victims and knew how to behave in that role (just as Nel knew how to behave as the wronged wife). But the free fall, oh no, that required—demanded—invention: a thing to do with the wings, a way of holding the legs and most of all a full surrender to the downward flight if they wished to taste their tongues or stay alive. But alive was what they, and now Nel, did not want to be. Too dangerous. Now Nel belonged to the town and all of its ways. She had given herself over to them, and the flick of their tongues would drive her back into her little dry corner where she would cling to her spittle high above the breath of the snake and the fall. (. 120)

Insensitive to Nel's pain at finding her husband, Jude, in bed with her, Sula, as this elaborate analogy reveals, is disappointed at the possessiveness and jealousy of the one person to whom she felt close. No longer, she thinks, is Nel willing to affirm the possibilities of life, to risk rebellion against social conventions and traditional sex roles in order to define herself and assert her independence and vitality.

When they met in 1922, Sula and Nel's friendship was as intense as it was sudden. "Because each had discovered years before that they were neither white nor male, and that all freedom and triumph was forbidden to them, they had set about creating something else to be" (p. 52). Solitary and lonely, they were the only children of distant mothers and incomprehensible fathers—Sula's was dead and Nel's a seaman. Nel's mother, Helene Wright, was attractive, vain, and oppressively class conscious in an effort to escape her creole mother's wild blood. Resisting her mother's attempts to impose distorted middle-class values on her, Nel declares: " 'I'm me. I'm not their daughter. I'm not Nel. I'm me. Me' " (p. 28). Sula's mother, Hannah Peace, was "a kind and generous woman" with "extraordinary beauty and funky elegance," who, like her own mother, Eva Peace, loved all men. Unlike Eva, however, Hannah was promiscuous. Neither Eva nor Hannah showered her daughter with motherly affection. Eva had little time or energy to provide more than the basic necessities for her children's survival, yet she fiercely and ironically demonstrates the depth of her maternal love by burning her drug-addict son to death and throwing herself out of a two-story window in a futile attempt to save Hannah from burning to death. Receiving no sustaining affection from Eva, Hannah is unable or unwilling to show affection to Sula. " 'You love her,' " she tells a friend, " 'like I love Sula. I just don't like her. That's the difference' " (p. 57). Feeling unloved and revealing the evil she embodies, Sula emotionlessly watched Hannah burn to death. Although at twelve years old both were "wishbone thin and easy-assed," Nel "seemed stronger and more consistent than Sula, who could hardly be counted on to sustain any emotion for more than three minutes" (p. 53). Thus, Nel and Sula found in each other the intimacy they needed, and they are equally responsible for the drowning of a small boy, Chicken Little, a secret guilt that seals the bond between them and with Shadrack, who they suspect saw their wicked act.

Morrison intentionally constructs Sula as an ambitious character who evokes ambivalence from all quarters, including the undramatized author-narrator. On one hand, Sula represents a liberated modern black woman, who, in rejecting marriage, declares: "'I don't want to be somebody else. I want to make myself,'" and defiantly tells her grandmother: "'What ever's burning in me is mine. . . . And I'll split this town in two and everything in it before I'll let you put it out'" (pp. 92–93). But Ajax, the handsome, sinister street poet who stirred Sula's girlhood sexual fantasies, becomes her nemesis and the agent for her discovery of the meaning of possessiveness after he responds to her brain as well as her body. On the other hand, Sula represents the actual and imagined force of evil in the black community. When she put her grandmother in a home, they called her a roach; and when she took Jude from Nel and slept with white men, they called her a bitch. The folks of the Bottom, true to their culture, also remembered the "weighty evidence" of Gothic events that proved that Sula was evil: the talk about her watching her mother burn, the plague of robins that announced her return to Medallion, the accidental injury of Teapot and death of Mr. Finley, and the ominous birthmark over her eye. The voice of the omniscient author-narrator is at once sympathetic toward and critical of the black people of the Bottom. She explains their "full recognition of the legitimacy of forces other than good ones" with the awareness and compassion of an insider, affirming their resolve to survive in the face of hard times and evil. But she is critical of the tradition of inferiority implicit in black women's shame of dark complexion, of broad, flat noses, and of coarse, short hair.

Ambivalent about Sula, Morrison ascribes her dangerous behavior to her limited opportunities and alternatives for personal growth as a black woman:

> In a way, her strangeness, her naivete, her craving for the other half of her equation was the consequence of an idle imagination. Had she paints, or clay, or knew the discipline of the dance, or strings; had she anything to engage her tremendous curiosity and her gift for metaphor, she might have exchanged the restlessness and preoccupation with whim for an activity that provided her with all she yearned for. And like any artist with no art form, she became dangerous. (P. 121)

Most important, the author-narrator, like the blacks of the Bottom, sees Sula as both a pariah and a redeemer:

> Their conviction of Sula's evil changed them in accountable yet mysterious ways. Once the source of their personal misfortune was identified, they had leave to protect and love one another. They began to cherish their husbands and wives, protect their children, repair their homes and in general band together against the devil in their midst. In their world, aberrations were as much a part of nature as grace. It was not for them to expel or annihilate it. . . . The presence of evil was something to be first recognized, then dealt with, survived, outwitted, triumphed over. (P. 118)

At the end of the novel, Eva, with a tough-minded understanding of life despite her senility, compels Nel to realize that she and Sula were just alike.

In theme and style Toni Morrison's novels are a fine example of vintage wine in new bottles. Her exploration of the impact of sexism and racism on the lives of black women in her Gothic fables provides a more complex and, perhaps, controversial vision of the personalities and bonding of fiercely alive modern black women than the idealized images of most writers of the 1960s. Particularly in *The Bluest Eye* and *Sula* she distills history and fact with the poetic freedom and Gothic vision of modernist and postmodernist writers. Her sharp eye for the concrete details and telltale gestures that evoke a sense of place and character in the fables and *Song of Solomon* are complemented by a wonderful gift for metaphor and metonymy that are as penetrating in their insightfulness as they are arresting in their freshness and suggestiveness. Her characters are eccentric and maimed as a result of their experience as black men and women in an environment that rigidly defines their humanity by economic, sexual, and racial myths. But still they persevere in their efforts to cope with or triumph over the obstacles in their path to self-esteem, freedom, and wholeness. Thus Pecola is destroyed psychologically, Sula dies an outcast among her own, and Milkman follows the path of his African ancestor. But both Claudia and Nel survive the terror and tragedy of their friends' lives, achieving in the process a precarious adjustment to the worlds of Shirley Temple and the Bottom. Pilate's moral victory is even more Pyrrhic. Because Morrison probes the awesome will to live of her characters in order to suggest the truth of their psychic experience and the complexity of their humanity, her Gothic fables, reminiscent of Toomer's *Cane,* are a quintessential blend of realism and poetry, bizarreness and beauty, revelation and lyricism.

Continuity in the Novel of the Sixties and Seventies

Of the more than one hundred novels by over fifty black American novelists published between 1962 and 1983 that I have examined for this and the following chapter, most continue the synthesis of traditional forms of realism and romance that characterized the beginning of the African American novel in

1853. In this chapter I have focused on twenty-nine novels by six authors that reveal two intriguing trends in realism of the 1960s and 1970s: critical realism and poetic realism. Of the six authors selected on the basis of their contributions both to these trends and to stimulating readers' awareness of the possibilities of life, all are first-generation college-educated individuals who have published two or more novels. In general, the six authors are representative of the educational background, literary productivity, and preferred narrative conventions of contemporary African American novelists. The classifications, it should be remembered, indicate narrative conventions that the authors have employed with distinction in one or more novels, and are not intended as either arbitrary or immutable labels confining the writers or their novels. Rather, the classifications are intended to foster clarity and coherence in understanding the ambivalence of the authors toward all traditions and the contributions they have made to continuity and change in the tradition of the African American novel.

These authors' conflicting emotions and various literary contributions were influenced in part by the radical political and cultural developments of the 1960s—beginning with the March on Washington in 1963, the Black Arts movement in 1964, the accelerated use of paperback books in college classrooms in 1965, and with cultural democratization, the cashing-in on the new vogue in black studies and feminism by publishers and reprint houses in 1969. These developments generated a new, often heated debate in academic circles over the purpose of art, the function of the artist, and the death of the novel. There was, of course, less discussion about black American fiction in the media than about Euro-American and African fiction, and, except for *Negro Digest* (*Black World*), both the black and white media were more interested in promoting black poetry and drama. Nevertheless, there was more than enough ferment in the literary marketplace and writers' workshops for writers like John O. Killens, John A. Williams, Alice Walker, Gayl Jones, Toni Cade Bambara, and Toni Morrison to fulfill their roles as black artists in defining the complexity of African American life and, to paraphrase Ralph Ellison, to realize that in spite of all its technical experimentation, the autonomy of the novel as a system of artificial signs is qualified by its interrelationship with other cultural systems, especially linguistic and ethical.

In their definition of African American life, these writers therefore continue to tap the roots of African American culture and institutions—black music, speech, religion, and the family—repudiating those codes and conventions that impede individual and collective growth and self-determination, and celebrating those that enhance these humanistic objectives. Consistent with recent social developments, there is more emphasis on the importance of music, speech, and religion as the foundations of contemporary African American culture and the principal modalities for expressing the complex double vision of African American character. But there is less importance assigned to the centrality of institutionalized Christianity, which is increasingly criticized and even displaced in importance in the works of some novelists by politics, ancestralism, or other Afrocentric beliefs and rituals. Bambara's *Salt Eaters* is exceptional in its quest for a balance of the spiritual and political, of the traditional and modern; in its representation of the individual striving to ground her subjectivity or identity in the best of her people's traditions.

In Williams's *Sissie,* Alice Walker's *Third Life of Grange Copeland* and *The Color Purple,* and Morrison's *Bluest Eye* and *Sula,* we see a critical exploration of the strengths and weaknesses of the institutions of the black family and church, as well as of the continuing racial and sexual exploitation of black people, especially women. Influenced by the sexual revolution and by the continuing color and class struggle in the American social arena, contemporary African American neorealists are still basically inclined toward a redemptive, paradoxically progressive and apocalyptic view of history even when the surface patterns are dialectical, cyclical, and spiral. Ambivalent in their narrative allegiances to a black aesthetic, they have increased the range of their thematic concerns from the religious or spiritual and political to the economic, psychological, and philosophical aspects of contemporary life.

Because most contemporary black American novelists are college-educated, it is not surprising that the literary and nonliterary influences on their use of narrative conventions have been wide-ranging and varied, indicating the bicultural heritage of African Americans. Many acknowledge the importance of Western and Euro-American writers, some mention Russians, Asians, and Africans, and others include such African Americans as Toomer, Hurston, Wright, Himes, and Ellison. In a national poll of thirty-eight black writers in 1965, more than half named Richard Wright as the most important black American writer of all time; and John A. Williams's *Man Who Cried I Am* and John O. Killens's *And Then We Heard the Thunder* were ranked equally high as the most important novels written by a black American since *Invisible Man.* According to Hoyt Fuller, the managing editor of *Negro Digest,* "The writers were asked no questions dealing with style and technique, partly because these considerations—the editors believe—are more the concern of English teachers and creative writing courses than of readers interested in knowing which writers and which ideas the writers think are important. Style and technique are problems for the individual writer to work out for himself, and his attitude toward style and technique will be reflected in his own work and in the work he admires."[74] Viewed from the historical, anthropological, and formalistic perspectives of this study, however, *The Man Who Cried I Am* is the more successful of the two novels. There are, of course, several novels written since 1965 that are better or at least equally well written, including Ernest Gaines's *Autobiography of Miss Jane Pittman,* Morrison's *Sula,* and Bambara's *Salt Eaters.* In the 1970s Zora Neale Hurston was rediscovered and reassessed as a major voice in the tradition of the African American novel, inspiring the search of many black women writers beyond their mothers' gardens for other literary mothers.

Because of the diverse influences, interests, and talents of contemporary black American novelists, we find a corresponding diversity in their attitudes toward and use of realism and modernism. Even among the neorealists examined in this chapter, we find that most—especially Jones, Williams, Morrison, and Bambara—are inclined on occasions to move beyond realism in their experimentation with form. This suggests that modernism and, for a few, postmodernism are more viable modes for constructing the liberating visions of contemporary African American novelists. As I will reveal in the next chapter, the neoslave narratives of Margaret Walker, Ernest Gaines, Toni Morrison, and Ishmael Reed are outstandingly rich and provocative in their authority, authenticity, and agency, yet diversely experimental and instructive texts. Readers, like novelists, in short, should be as open-minded and responsive to the imperatives of change and the revitalization of earlier forms in the narrative tradition as they are in affirming their identification with historical continuity and enduring ethical values that underlie the distortions and discontinuities of our contemporary culture of narcissism, antiblack racism, and antiessentialism.

5 / Modernism and Postmodernism (1962–1983)

From a woman's point of view, in terms of confronting the problems of where the world is now, black women had to deal with "post-modern" problems in the nineteenth century and earlier. These things had to be addressed by black people a long time ago. Certain kinds of dissolution, the loss of and the need to reconstruct certain kinds of stability. Certain kinds of madness, deliberately going mad in order, as one of the characters says in the book [Beloved], *"in order not to lose your mind." These strategies for survival made the truly modern person. They're a response to predatory Western phenomena. You can call it an ideology and an economy, what it is is a pathology.*

TONI MORRISON
in Paul Gilroy's *Small Acts*

SPEAKING at Gettysburg during the centennial year of the Emancipation Proclamation, Vice President Lyndon B. Johnson said, "Until justice is blind, until education is unaware of race, until opportunity is unconcerned with the color of men's skins, emancipation will be a proclamation but not a fact."[1] Two years after his succession to the presidency following the assassination of John F. Kennedy, President Johnson addressed the Howard University commencement audience and expressed a more radical commitment to interracial reform than any other chief executive. "In far too many ways," he stated, "American Negroes have been another nation: deprived of freedom, crippled by hatred, the doors of opportunity closed to hope." After referring to his role in passing the Civil Rights Act of 1964, the first civil rights legislation in almost a century, and his signing of the Voting Rights Act of 1965 as the beginning of freedom, he continued:

> But freedom is not enough. You do not wipe away the scars of centuries by saying: Now, you are free to go where you want, do as you desire, and choose the leaders you please. You do not take a man who, for years, has been hobbled by chains, liberate him, bring him to the starting line of a race, saying "you are free to compete with all the others," and still justly believe you have been completely fair. Thus it is not enough to open the gates of opportunity. All our citizens must have the ability to walk through those gates. This is the next and the more profound stage of the battle for civil rights. We seek not just freedom but opportunity—not just

> legal equity but human ability—not just equality as a right and a theory, but equality as a fact and a result.[2]

Despite the results of Johnson's Great Society programs in helping African Americans, women, other minorities, and the poor to fulfill their human and civil rights, the modest gains of blacks and the War on Poverty were compromised by the economic and moral drain of the war in Vietnam and reversed by the neoconservative presidencies of Richard Nixon, Gerald Ford, and Ronald Reagan as well as the faint-hearted liberalism of Jimmy Carter. How these and other experiences between 1962 and 1983 influenced the development of modern and postmodern attitudes and conventions by contemporary African American novelists is our chief concern in this chapter.

From Modernism and Structuralism to Poststructuralism and Postmodernism

Even though there are no clear divisions, on the one hand, between modernism, and structuralism, and, on the other hand, between poststructuralism and postmodernism, the relationship among them is most meaningfully and coherently explained in this chapter by outlining them chronologically, by describing some of their chief characteristics, and by identifying some of their major proponents.[3] Commenting on how the impact of Western slavery on Africa and Africans marks the beginning of modernism, Toni Morrison tells an interviewer:

> It's not simply that human life originated in Africa in anthropological terms, but that modern life begins with slavery. . . . Slavery broke the world in half, it broke it in every way. It broke Europe. It made them into something else, it made them slave masters, it made them crazy. You can't do that for hundreds of years and it not take a toll. They had to dehumanize, not just the slaves but themselves. They have had to reconstruct everything in order to make that system appear true. It made everything in World War II possible. It made World War I necessary. Racism is the word that we use to encompass all this. The idea of scientific racism suggests some serious pathology.[4]

Modernism challenges traditional assumptions and conventions about history, science, culture, art, language, and literature. Although modernism can be traced back to the impact of technology, science, and industrialization as well as slavery on different socioeconomic and sociocultural systems, the consensus of opinion of most cultural and literary critics is that Euro-American modernism begins after World War I (1914–18) and culminates between the 1930s and 1950s in American academies with the New Criticism of such Southern literary critics as John Crowe Ransom, who coined the term "New Criticism," Cleanth Brooks, Allen Tate, and Robert Penn Warren.[5] Literary modernism challenges or violates traditional assumptions about what is real, true, and therefore meaningful by separating the literary text from the external world and defining it as an autonomous, self-sufficient world. Shifting their battle from the military and political fields, the Southern New Critics and their disciples focused primarily on poetry for their intellectual, affective, and aesthetic rebellion against the Northern industrialization of the South and the transformation of its traditional agrarian values. Theorists of modernism like I. A. Richards, Thomas Cassirer, Suzanne Langer, T. S. Eliot, Carl Jung, Northrop Frye, Roman Jakobson, and Roman Ingarden argue, as Gerald Graff reveals in his trenchant critique in *Literature against Itself*, that "literature and art deal with experience only as myth, psychology, or language, not as an object of conceptual understanding."[6]

Structuralism is a mode of cultural analysis derived from modern and contemporary linguistics. "The modern structuralist analysis of narrative began," according to British literary critic Terry Eagleton, "with the pioneering work on myth of the French structural anthropologist Claude Lévi-Strauss, who viewed apparently different myths as variations on a number of basic themes." Beginning with *Anatomy of Criticism* in 1957, Canadian literary critic Northrop Frye's theory of literature as an objective system of four fundamental narrative categories (i.e., the comic, romantic, tragic, and ironic) that seem to correspond "respectively to the four *mythoi* of spring, summer, autumn and winter" can be loosely interpreted as similar to structuralism. In the 1960s literary structuralism flourished as an attempt to apply to literature the methods and insights of Ferdinand de Saussure, the founder of modern structural linguistics.[7] In their early work, Roland Barthes and other structuralist critics—those who analyze individual works of literature as signifying systems of hierarchical structures whose meaning, according to Saussure, is the dynamic relationship of the differences from and oppositions to other elements in the system itself—attempt to demystify the modernist concept of literary autonomy. For example, in *Narrative Discourse* (1972) critic Gérard Genette outlines a systematic structuralist theory of narrative that has five central categories: order, duration, frequency, mood, and voice.[8] These categories enable readers to analyze more deeply and precisely the differences between narration, the process of telling a story, and narrative, the events in the story. By theory and practice, they demonstrate "that literary language, linguistic conventions, and 'textuality,' not the imagination or consciousness of the writer, are the constitutive agents of writing."[9]

In "The Fiction of Realism" critic J. Hillis Miller succinctly states the antimimetic, antireferential theory of structuralism:

> One important aspect of current literary criticism is the disintegration of the paradigms of realism under the impact of structural linguistics and

> the renewal of rhetoric. If meaning in language rises not from the reference of signs to something outside words but from differential relations among the words themselves, if "referent" and "meaning" must always be distinguished, then the notion of a literary text which is validated by its one-to-one correspondence to some social, historical, or psychological reality can no longer be taken for granted. No language is purely mimetic or referential, not even the most utilitarian speech. The specifically literary form of language, however, may be defined as a structure of words which in one way or another calls attention to this fact, while at the same time allowing for its own inevitable misreading as a "mirroring of reality."[10]

For Miller and other structuralist critics whose primary analytical focus is on foregrounding language and the internal binary oppositions of narratives, mimetic readings of texts are thus considered misreadings. African American literary critic Robert Stepto's *From Behind the Veil* (1979) is a type of black structuralist study. On the one hand, the book was influenced by the Yale school of deconstruction critics, who in different degrees stressed the ways that literary language undermined its own meaning and whose advocates included Paul de Man, J. Hillis Miller, and Geoffrey Hartman; and on the other hand, it was inspired by Northrop Frye's narrative categories. But, as it will be demonstrated later in this work, most contemporary African American novelists subscribe neither to old theories of mimesis nor to the new ahistorical linguistic and literary laws of intertextuality and self-referentiality.

However, some African American critics and novelists have apparently responded to the appeal of various postmodernists. These include Jacques Derrida's deconstruction criticism in *Of Grammatology* (1976), Roland Barthes's movement from structural criticism in *Mythologies* (1957) to poststructuralism in *S/Z* (1970) and *The Pleasure of the Text* (1976), and Jean-François Lyotard's advocacy of incredulity toward metanarratives as a result of the impact of technological transformations on knowledge in the postmodern age. Deconstruction, as Eagleton notes, is the critical process that undermines or that demonstrates how the text itself undermines "belief in some ultimate 'word,' presence, essence, truth or reality as the foundation of all our thought, language and experience." Metaphysical signs and transcendental meanings are analyzed by deconstruction critics to reveal that they are fictions, "products of a particular system of meaning" and binary oppositions. The movement from structuralism to poststructuralism, according to Barthes, includes a shift from the reader as consumer to that of producer of different playful discourses in the text itself, from reading the poem or novel as a work of stable or determinate meaning to reading it as an open-ended text of indeterminate meaning. The shift is also from focusing on the text as language, "as a chain of signs without a subject," to viewing it as discourse, "as *utterance*, as involving speaking and writing subjects, and therefore also, at least potentially, readers or listeners."[11] Probably the best illustrations of this movement in critical theory and these shifts in narrative practice in the African American literary tradition are Henry L. Gates's critical study *Figures in Black* (1984) and Clarence Major's novel *Reflex and Bone Structure* (1975).

Although the term "postmodern" was "the title given to the 1980 Venice Biennale which marked the institutional recognition of postmodernism in architecture,"[12] it is now present in many fields of cultural production, especially literature, photography, film, painting, video, dance, and music. In *The Politics of Postmodernism* (1989) Canadian critic Linda Hutcheon, one of its most systematic and effective defenders, explains that postmodernism takes the form of "self-conscious, self-contradictory, self-undermining statement. It is rather like saying something whilst at the same time putting inverted commas around what is being said. The effect is to highlight, or 'highlight,' and to subvert, or 'subvert,' and the mode is therefore a 'knowing' and an ironic—or even 'ironic'—one."[13] Like modernism, postmodernism undermines the traditional grounds for the stability and universality of truth and reality; it also compels us to consider that truth and reality are social constructs, that literature has no meaning, that its meaning exists only in our consciousness, or that its meaning is to be found in the indeterminacy of its language. Unlike modernism, postmodernism repudiates the unifying ability of master narratives and the ability to represent Truth through mimetic art. For example, according to Lyotard,

> The grand narrative has lost its credibility, regardless of what mode of unification it uses, regardless of whether it is a speculative narrative or a narrative of emancipation. The decline of narrative can be seen as an effect of the blossoming of techniques and technologies since the Second World War, which has shifted emphasis from the ends of action to its means; it can also be seen as an effect of the redeployment of advanced liberal capitalism after its retreat under the protection of Keynesianism during the period 1930–60, a renewal that has eliminated the communist alternative and valorized the individual enjoyment of goods and services.[14]

As Hutcheon reveals in *A Poetics of Postmodernism* (1988), postmodern culture has a contradictory relationship to modernism and our dominant, liberal humanist culture. Postmodernists thus argue that master narratives, such as myth and metanarratives, may be necessary, but they are nevertheless illusory. Because "knowledge is no longer primarily narrative knowledge of this kind . . . does not mean that knowledge somehow disappears." Rather than deny humanist culture, Hutcheon contends that postmodernism "contests it from within its own assumptions."[15]

Because of the distinctive origins and pattern of their historical experiences and hybrid cultural forms, some African American novelists have experimented with postmodern styles and structures. But most African American readers and most African American novelists have not renounced the faith of their ancestors in a transcendental signifier, in moral truths, in syncretistic African and European ways of knowing, and in social justice for the new gods of postmodernism.[16] "Mus' tek cyear a de root fa' heal de tree." This popular Gullah saying about the importance of ancestral ties probably has more cultural authenticity and moral and political authority among lower-income underemployed and poor black folks with a Southern heritage than do the postmodern theories and texts of white and black academics and intellectuals.

In *Yearning*, bell hooks addresses the challenge to definitions of "authentic" blackness and "the real thing" in postmodernist criticism. She begins by affirming the existence of a very distinctive black culture with Southern agrarian roots that "offers ways of knowing, habits of being, that can help sustain us as a people" and that can be passed on "without essentializing it." She then declares that "current trends in postmodernist cultural critiques devaluing the importance of this legacy by dismissing notions of authenticity or suggesting that the very concept of 'soul' is illusory and not experientially based are disturbing."[17] In locating, defining, and affirming the authenticity of black culture while questioning biological determinism and essentialism, hooks affirms an African American commonplace. The census data for 2000 revealing that the majority of blacks in the United States still live in predominantly black communities in the rural and urban South circumstantially support her position.

Even so, let us examine more closely the kernel of truth in hooks's antiessentialist argument that class mobility fosters multiple varied black identities that challenge "colonial imperialist paradigms of black identity which represent blackness one-dimensionally in ways that reinforce and sustain white supremacy." While opposed to "re-inscribing notions of 'authentic' black identity," she nevertheless argues that "the struggle of oppressed and exploited peoples . . . affords us a privileged critical location from which to speak . . . [and] to construct self and identity that are oppositional and liberatory."[18] Thus hooks paradoxically yet convincingly argues that critical differences which many black people have with postmodernism should not cause us to ignore its useful critique of essentialism in African American reconstructions of anachronistic "notions of universality and overdetermined identity within mass culture and mass consciousness."[19] But, like most postcolonial, cultural studies, and feminist critics, hooks, as *The Contemporary African American Novel* demonstrates, is premature and unpersuasive in her call to abandon all forms of essentialism.

Because the problematics of a postmodern black identity are more fully examined in chapter 6, it is sufficient for clarity here to state that for a major proponent the confusion over the definition and evaluation of postmodernism is best resolved by recognizing the existence of two opposed camps:

> the radically antagonistic and the provisionally supportive. The tone of the former group ranges from sly irony to rabid rage. Curiously, this camp encompasses the opposition of the neoconservative right, the liberal center, and the Marxist left. However positioned politically, the objections seem to be consistently to what are perceived as, on the one hand, the ahistoricism and pastiched depthlessness of the postmodern and, on the other, its crossing of boundaries of genres and discourse once considered discrete and firm. . . . The work of those provisionally or tentatively supportive of postmodernism ranges from descriptive accounts of the postmodern in terms of its incredulity toward grand totalizing narratives to more tendentiously rueful acknowledgments that we are all part of the postmodern, whether we like it or not.[20]

Although illuminating and instructive, Hutcheon's explanation does not resolve all reservations that hooks, I, and most black critics have about postmodernism.

While I am skeptical at best about the apparently infinite varieties of postmodern theory and poststructural practice, my answer to critic Tzvetan Todorov's question in "Race, Writing, and Culture"—"Is there really no middle ground between worshipping dogmas as immutable truth and abandoning the idea of truth itself?"—is a thundering no.[21] The middle ground shifts, however, in different sociohistorical and sociocultural contexts. It shifts as people, individually and collectively, struggle to construct, maintain, or reject in life and literature different varieties and degrees of power, status, and identity. Like Fredric Jameson, I "posit, not the disappearance of the great master-narratives, but their passage underground as it were, their continuing but now unconscious effectivity as a way of 'thinking about' and acting in our current situation."[22] Authors, narrators, and characters in narratives express this struggle for the agency, authenticity, and authority of these buried master narratives, which Jameson calls our political unconscious, in different empowering configurations of rhetoric, dialectics, and dialogics. Because of their struggle in contesting borders and crossing boundaries in their quest for self-definition and self-determination as Americans of African descent and as individual artists, African American novelists employ all three of these modes of discourse in deconstructing and reconstructing sacred and secular master narratives. In the tradition of the African American novel these include the myths of origin and apocalypse in the Books of Genesis and Revelation respectively, the Declaration of Independence, the Constitution of the United States, and the American Dream.

In *A Poetics of Postmodernism,* Hutcheon argues that "there is no dialectic in the postmodern: the self-reflexive remains distinct from its traditionally accepted contrary—the historic-political context in which it is embedded. The result of this deliberate refusal to resolve contradictions is a contesting of what

Lyotard . . . calls the totalizing master narratives of our culture, those systems by which we usually unify and order (and smooth over) any contradictions in order to make them fit." Although I am unconvinced either that the dialectics of Georg Hegel resolve their dynamic tensions in a permanent closure or stasis, or that the hermeneutics of Hans-Georg Gadamer recognizes power conflicts in its view of history as a living dialogue between the past and present, there is apparently some merit to Hutcheon's argument as it applies to her central concern with white Eurocentric postmodernism. In contrast, as I have earlier demonstrated, African American postmodernism is generally more ambivalent and subversive or transgressive in its interrogation and reinscription of master narratives. But some of the parodic, ironic, and metafictional narratives of writers such as Ishmael Reed, Clarence Major, William Melvin Kelley, Toni Morrison, Charles S. Wright, Hal Bennett, and Alice Walker—similar to the white Eurocentric postmodernist narratives that Hutcheon cites, but with a black difference—"challenge the process of meaning-making in the production and reception of art, but also in broader discursive terms: . . . [they foreground] how we make historical 'facts' out of brute 'events' of the past, or, more generally, how our various sign systems grant meaning to our experience." [23]

Even so, white Eurocentric postmodernism moves beyond the modernism of the 1950s in an effort to expand the possibilities of the novel and to reconstruct the liberated lives of the generation of the 1960s. That generation's sensibilities were shaped and misshaped by modern jazz, rock music, drugs, war in Vietnam, political assassinations, Black Power and Women's Rights movements, civil rights and antiwar demonstrations, campus sit-ins and building takeovers—all brought to us daily in black and white or living color by the magic of technology and television. To proclaim the death of art's traditional claims to truth and to herald the birth of a new sensibility, postmodernists employ fantasy, parody, burlesque, and irony. Whether by conscious ironic and parodic reconstruction of ancient myths and rituals or by self-conscious innovativeness that explores the limits of language and the liberating power of the creative process, white postmodernists like John Barth and Ronald Sukenick gave voice to the belief that conventional elements of fiction were exhausted and ineffective in expressing the truth of contemporary life and that the basis of a new fictive reality resided either in the individual perceiving mind or in the act of perception, not in the world outside of the novel.[24]

As illustrated primarily by Ellison and Baldwin, modernism in the African American novel from 1952 to 1962 involved concurrent movements: one away from such earlier forms as realism and naturalism and the other back to a reshaping of such traditional narrative modes as myth and legend. Probably for this as well as for other reasons, critics like Jerome Klinkowitz believe that black modernist and postmodernist novelists are not aesthetically unlike such white contemporary novelists and short story writers as John Hawkes, John Barth,

Donald Barthelme, Richard Brautigan, and Ronald Sukenick.[25] Whereas there is apparently some truth to this line of thought, however, it is not the whole truth. Margaret Walker, Ernest J. Gaines, William M. Kelley, Charles Wright, Ronald Fair, Hal Bennett, John E. Wideman, Clarence Major, Ishmael Reed, Leon Forrest, Toni Morrison, and Toni C. Bambara—to name a few black modernists and even fewer black postmodernists—are definitely influenced by the traditions of Western literature and committed to the freedom of hybrid narrative forms. However, because the legacy of institutional racism and sexism that shaped and continues to shape their consciousness fosters ambivalence about their culture, the struggle for social justice and equality continues. In other words, because many contemporary African American novelists are neorealists or more inclined toward nonrepresentational than antirepresentational narrative theories and practice like many of their nineteenth-century predecessors, they are not inclined to neglect moral, political, and social issues in their narratives. With the possible exception of Clarence Major (who was a member of a white postmodernist fiction collective), they, unlike white postmodernists of what some critics call the antinovel philosophy, are deeply concerned with fictive visions that focus on the truths of the perversity of American antiblack racism and the paradoxes of African American double consciousness. Unlike their white contemporaries, black American postmodernists such as Reed and Major are not merely rejecting the arrogance and anachronism of Western forms and conventions, but also rediscovering and reaffirming the power and wisdom of their own folk tradition: African American ways of seeing, knowing, and expressing reality, especially black speech, music, and religion.

Thus, while insisting on their freedom as individual artists to choose their own subjects, form, and style—widening the range of influences on their novels from literature and music to painting, film, and pop culture—Walker, Gaines, Kelley, Fair, Wideman, Wright, Bennett, Reed, and Major achieve their distinctive voices simultaneously within and against a narrative tradition of continuity and change. This they achieve by experimenting with different combinations of myth, ritual, parable, fable, legend, allegory, and satire in a more often modern than postmodern mode of romance that I join Robert Scholes in calling "fabulation." Scholes, apparently adapting Henri Bergson's term, defines fabulation as "a return to a more verbal kind of fiction . . . a less realistic and more artistic kind of narrative; more shapely, more evocative; more concerned with ideas and ideals, less concerned with things."[26] Although an extraordinary delight in form with a concurrent, self-conscious emphasis on the authority of the shaper of the form distinguishes in part the art of the contemporary romanticist or fabulator from that of the conventional novelist or satirist, the continuing power and wisdom of the traditions of spirituals, sermons, blues, and jazz distinguish on a lower register the possibilities of African American form and style to effect cultural and social change from those of Euro-American.

The following classifications, as I stated earlier, are intended neither to be exhaustive nor to pigeonhole authors or novels, for in the final analysis it is the sincerity, sensitivity, and skill of each author that enable him or her to trust the tenor of the times and the subject of each work to dictate its own appropriate form and style. Consequently, over a period of time the novels of a particular author will more likely than not include any number of variations of different forms and styles. I have nevertheless discovered that some novelists and novels are the best examples of a particular combination of tendencies I have borrowed the term "fabulation" to describe. The classifications are therefore not mutually exclusive but basically descriptive of tendencies in at least one, and usually what I consider the best, of the novels by selected representative authors.

Fabulation, Legend, and Neoslave Narrative

Some contemporary black fabulators combine elements of fable, legend, and slave narrative to protest racism and justify the deeds, struggles, migrations, and spirit of black people. Although the use of black folklore or the vernacular—especially music, speech, and religion—is didactic, contemporary black fabulators like Walker, Gaines, and Kelley rely more on the artifice of the storyteller and humorist than on social realism to stimulate our imagination, win our sympathy, and awaken our conscience to moral and social justice. The power of faith, messianic hope, self-reliance or direct action, and the lynching ritual are central motifs of this hybrid form.

MARGARET [ABIGAIL] WALKER (1915–1998)

The daughter of a fundamentalist music teacher and a Methodist Episcopal minister who lived in a world of books, Margaret Walker was born on July 7, 1915, in Birmingham, Alabama. "I got my love for books and my desire to write from my father," she explains. "He belonged to a family of people who for generations had been interested in culture, in languages, and religions. Books and music, art—that is what I was formed to."[27] She began reading authors like Langston Hughes and Countee Cullen and writing poetry when she was about twelve. Her first poem, "Daydreaming," was published in *The Crisis* when she was nineteen. After early education in the South, she completed her B.A. in 1935 at Northwestern University in Evanston, Illinois.[28] In Chicago during the thirties she developed her poetic voice and control of form, publishing her best-known poem, "For My People," in *Poetry* in 1937. She met many writers in Chicago, including Richard Wright, Arna Bontemps, Fenton Johnson, Willard Motley, and Gwendolyn Brooks. Some she met through Langston Hughes, who introduced her to Wright in 1936 at the National Negro Congress. Others, including several radical white writers, she met at writers' conferences or in such organizations as the Writers' Project of Chicago and the South Side Writers'

Group, a black literary circle organized by Wright, which she joined in 1936. In 1939 she completed her first novel, "Gorse Island," and left the WPA to study in the Writers' Workshop at the University of Iowa, receiving her M.A. in 1940 for the collection of poems *For My People,* which was published in 1942 as winner of the Yale Award for Younger Poets.[29] After marrying, raising four children, and teaching at Livingstone, West Virginia State, and Jackson State Colleges, she returned to the University of Iowa in 1961 for her Ph.D., which she received for *Jubilee* in 1965. As the author of three books of poetry, Walker, who died November 30, 1998 in Chicago, is more widely acclaimed as a poet than for her singular achievement as a novelist in *Jubilee.*

"Long before *Jubilee* had a name," Walker says about the genesis of the novel, "I was living with it and imagining its reality. Its genesis coincides with my childhood, its development grows out of a welter of raw experiences and careful research, and its final form emerged exactly one hundred years after its major events took place."[30] The story of Elvira and Randall Ware, Walker's great-grandparents, and of slave life in Georgia was passed on to Walker in enthralling bedtime stories told by her grandmother, who would indignantly defend their truth, declaring "I'm not telling her tales; I'm telling her the naked truth." Walker was influenced most at Iowa by her adviser Paul Engle, in Chicago by her friend Richard Wright, in New York by historian Lawrence Reddick, then curator of the Schomburg Collection of Negro History on 135th Street in Harlem, and throughout her writing career by Langston Hughes. She was also influenced in the technique and form of historical fiction and folk literature by such authors as Chekhov, Tolstoy, Scott, Faulkner, Steinbeck, and Pearl Buck as well as by Vernon Cassell, Joseph Warren Beach, Robert Lively, and Georg Lukács. Explaining her debt to Lukács in philosophy and point of view, she writes: "I have Lukács to thank for an understanding of the popular character of the historical novel; for the recognition that I was among the first dealing with characters looking up from the bottom rather than down from the top; and for an understanding of Abraham Lincoln as a world historical figure who was always a minor character seen through the mind of the major characters."[31] Margaret Walker's task in *Jubilee,* then, was to create fiction from the oral history of her family and the recorded history of the nation.

As its structure and style reveal, *Jubilee* is a neoslave narrative[32] based primarily on folk material and Vyry's quest for freedom. Set in Georgia, the novel has three main divisions of eighteen to twenty-two sections each and moves chronologically from the antebellum years through the early years of Reconstruction. Each minichapter has a title and epigraph, usually an excerpt from a spiritual, a folksong, or a folksaying which corresponds to the increasingly jubilant mood of the plot. For instance, the first epigraph is from "Swing Low, Sweet Chariot," a sorrow song, and the last from "My Father's House," a joyous song. Most of the section titles are descriptive, like "Cook in the Big House" and "Seventy-five lashes on her naked back," but some are song titles, like "Flee as a bird to your mountain" and "There's a star in the East on Christmas morn." Part I begins dramatically during slavery with two-year-old Vyry, John Dutton's last child by his slave mistress, being brought to see her mother, Hetta, who is dying at twenty-nine years of age after giving birth to her fifteenth child. It ends with Vyry's abortive flight to freedom with her young children. Part II sags under the weight of facts about the Civil War years, often introduced by Walker through a catalog of excerpts from speeches, letters, and newspaper articles. Part III picks up the pace again as the novel ends during Reconstruction with a free, mature, and pregnant Vyry, whom her daughter overhears feeding and calling her own chickens, content with her decision to stay with Innis Brown, her second husband, and raise their family rather than to reunite with Randall Ware, her first husband, after his twelve-year absence. The main plot thus focuses on Vyry's commitment to freedom as expressed in the sermons about Moses, the legendary President Lincoln, and the indomitable will of black folks themselves.

If it is the function of good realistic art to create character types of general appeal, then *Jubilee* is an impressive novel. In the creation of Vyry, Margaret Walker has given us one of the most memorable women in contemporary African American fiction. A pillar of Christian faith and human dignity, Vyry commands our respect first as an individual and then as a symbol of nineteenth-century black womanhood. Shaped by plantation culture, she realistically embodies its strengths and weaknesses. As John Dutton's illegitimate daughter, she could pass as the twin of her master's legitimate daughter, Lillian—"same sandy hair, same gray-blue eyes, same milk-white skin."[33] She thus has a privileged yet precarious status in the caste system of the plantation. Raised in the Quarters of the Big House as a cook, she is neither bitter nor political in her philosophy of life. Her major strengths are integrity, resourcefulness, pragmatism, and songs. Her weaknesses are caste prejudice, fidelity to former white owners, and political naiveté. Torn between loyalty to her first husband and her white family, and loyalty to her second husband and her children, she is guided by her Christian ethics in arriving at a practical rather than radical resolution of the conflict. In contrast to the stereotypic loyal family retainer, she remains on the Dutton plantation after the war because of her promise to Randall Ware that she would wait for him and because of her compassion for her former white mistress. Expanding in the denouement of the novel on the significance of Vyry's character and culture, the author-narrator reveals a close moral and political identification with the protagonist and implicitly invites our similar response: "In her obvious capacity for love, redemptive and forgiving love, she was alive and standing on the highest peaks of her time and human personality. Peasant and slave, unlettered and untutored, she was nevertheless the best true example of motherhood of her race, an ever present assurance that nothing could destroy a people whose sons had come from her loins" (p. 407). Vyry thus evolves as a heroic symbol of the black woman whose Christian faith, humanism, courage, resourcefulness, and music are the bedrock of her survival and the survival of her people. But by limiting Vyry's politics to the domestic and familial, Walker's vision celebrates the black woman of yesterday rather than of tomorrow.

The other characters in the novel are also drawn with knowledge of the times and sympathy for the people. The white characters, particularly the Dutton family, are stock representatives of the planter class of the antebellum and postbellum South. John, Salina, and their children, Lillian and John Jr., were staunch defenders of their privileged color and class position in the plantation tradition. Suffering death or madness but not complete defeat with the collapse of the Confederacy, they foreshadow the rise of white terrorism and intransigence that denied land, education, and the vote to blacks in the New South. The minor black characters are types clearly derived from the oral tradition, revealing Walker's intimate knowledge of black speech and music and the slave narratives. "Brother Ezekiel," for instance, "was a powerfully built, stovepipe-black man. He was neither young nor old. He was the plantation preacher, at least among the slaves" (p. 9). He was in the tradition of those slave exhorters who were gifted speakers and singers who not only admonished their flocks "to have faith in God and He would send them a Moses, a deliverer to free His people," but who also served as a conductor on the Underground Railroad and as a spy for the Union Army. Because of their different backgrounds, the major black male characters, Randall Ware and Innis Brown, are antithetical types. A member of the artisan class of free black laborers who served in the Union Army and a Reconstruction politician, Randall is the voice of black nationalism and radicalism in the novel. It is he who plants the idea of freedom in Vyry's head, giving concrete social reality to the sermons and prayers that God would send a Moses to free her and her people. He is bitter because whites do not respect his rights as a free citizen, and he resists their efforts to cheat, terrorize, and emasculate him. Born a slave, Innis is hard-working and courageous in his protection of Vyry and as naive, conservative, and practical as she is. All he wants in life is a farm of his own where he could raise his own crops and family.

On the problem of verisimilitude and point of view in the novel, Walker explains that her characters "are so real, so intensified, that I become involved with them, so exaggerated that they seem to exact human proportions, and I struggle and suffer with them" (p. 28). The mixture of direct observer and omniscient points of view early in *Jubilee* provides both an opportunity for the reader to participate in the drama of the characters' lives and a wide range of understanding and feeling from a black perspective for the setting and characters. In contrast to the romantic nostalgia of Margaret Mitchell's *Gone with the Wind*, *Jubilee* is realistic and critical. Though the author-narrator is basically omniscient, she is at one with the Christian values of the protagonist, who at the end of the novel distances herself politically and emotionally from her first husband:

> "Well, all I got to say, Randall Ware, is I can't understand you no more'n I can understand evil white peoples what ain't got no shame and ain't got no God. But I ain't gwine try to beat the white man at his own game with his killing and his hating neither. . . . I knows I'm a child of God and I can pray. Things ain't never gwine get too bad for me to pray. And I knows too, that the Good Lawd's will is gwine be done. I has learned that much. I'm gwine leave all the evil shameless peoples in the world in the hands of the Good Lawd and I'm gwine teach my childrens to hate nobody, don't care what they does." (P. 404)

There is Christian faith, hope, and charity in this voice, but no ironic distance here or elsewhere in the novel. In other words, it reveals less of the influence of the critical realism of Lukács than of the social realism of the slave narratives and African American double consciousness.

In *Jubilee,* then, Margaret Walker gives us our first major neoslave narrative: a residually oral, modern narrative of escape from bondage to freedom. (Gaines's *Autobiography of Miss Jane Pittman* would be the second.) As in Brown's *Clotel,* the narrator of *Jubilee* is omniscient and didactic; its structure is episodic; and its subject matter is rooted in black folk history and culture. Unlike the slave narratives, which were told in the first person and *Clotel,* however, *Jubilee* is not romantic in mood, the author-narrator's voice is not ironic, and the plot does not override character. Vyry, although of mixed blood like Clotel, is realistically drawn, yet, at the same time, she has general appeal as a symbol of nineteenth-century black womanhood that challenges historical stereotypes. Although she does not support the political radicalism of Randall Ware, she is nevertheless heroic in her role as nurturer and co-provider of her family. Walker's purpose, unlike Brown's, was not to bring about the abolition of physical slavery but, as she states, "to tell the story that my grandmother had told me, and to set the record straight where Black people are concerned in terms of the Civil War, of slavery, segregation and Reconstruction."[34]

ERNEST J[AMES] GAINES (1933–)

The oldest of twelve children, Ernest Gaines was born on January 15, 1933, on River Lake Plantation, Point Coupee Parish, Louisiana. As a child, he chopped sugar cane for fifty cents a day. When he was fifteen, his family moved to Vallejo, California, where he finished school. At sixteen he wrote his first novel, which was unceremoniously rejected by a New York publisher. In 1953 he was drafted into the army for two years and then attended San Francisco State College, receiving his B.A. in 1957. After publishing two stories in the college magazine, he gave himself ten years to become a writer. In 1958 he won a Wallace Stegner Fellowship in Creative Writing for a year of study at Stanford University, and the following year he received the Joseph Henry Jackson Literary Award. After the publication of *The Autobiography of Miss Jane Pittman,* he won a Guggenheim Fellowship, the California Gold Medal, the Louisiana Library Association Award, and the Black Academy of Arts and Letters Award. His outstanding professional and personal achievements culminated in 1993 when he not only won a MacArthur award but also married Dianne Saulney, a former Florida attorney. By 2001 his major publications included a collection of short stories, *Bloodline* (1968), and six novels: *Catherine Carmier* (1964), *Of Love and Dust* (1967), *The Autobiography of Miss Jane Pittman* (1971), *In My Father's House* (1978), *A Gathering of Old Men* (1983) and *A Lesson before Dying* (1993), which won the National Book Critics Circle Award and was nominated for a Pulitzer Prize. In 1993 Gaines told an interviewer: "My thesis is that black fathers and sons were separated in Africa in the 17th century and have not come back together since. They can eat across the table, but that is not the same as coming together."[35] Nevertheless, *In My Father's House*—the story of a Southern civil rights leader's sins resurfacing in his vengeful, unacknowledged son to shake the father's faith in himself, his community, and his God—is the least compelling of his novels examining the theme of African American male identity. It will be more fruitful, therefore, to focus on the other five novels, especially the memorable lesson of how to live and die with dignity as a black man in the South in the post-1983 *A Lesson before Dying* and the monumental achievement of his best-selling, pre-1983 *The Autobiography of Miss Jane Pittman,* nominated for a Pulitzer Prize.

Before arriving in California and writing what he confesses was "the worst number of pages that anyone could possibly call a novel," Gaines had read little and written less. "I doubt that I read two novels before I went to California," he told an interviewer. "But I came from a long line of storytellers. I come from a plantation, where people told stories by the fireplace at night, people told stories on the ditch bank. . . . I think in my immediate family there were tremendous storytellers or liars or whatever you want to call them."[36] He started to read a lot, especially about the rural South, during the summer of 1949 in the Vallejo public library. That summer he also wrote the first draft of *Catherine Carmier.* At San Francisco State he continued to read novelists like Erskine Caldwell, Faulkner, Steinbeck, Willa Cather, Turgenev, and Hemingway. "When I did not find my people in the Southern writers," he says, "I started reading books about the peasantry in other places. I read [about] the John Steinbeck people of the Selinas [*sic*] Valley, the Chicanos as well as the poor whites. This led me to reading the writers of other countries. Then in some way I went into the Russians and I liked what they were doing with their stories on the peasantry; the peasants were real human beings, whereas in the fiction of American writers, especially Southern writers, they were caricatures of human beings, they were clowns."[37] Surprisingly, rather than George Washington Cable or Kate Chopin, who wrote critically about the complex web of racism and sexism in the creole communities of old Louisiana, the major literary influences on Gaines's early novels are Turgenev and Faulkner.[38]

Turgenev's sense of nihilism and Faulkner's mythic sense of Southern history inform *Catherine Carmier.* "My *Catherine Carmier* is almost written on the structure of *Fathers and Sons,*" Gaines tells us. "As a matter of fact, that was my Bible."[39] Like *Fathers and Sons, Catherine Carmier* treats a young man's return to his rural home and the past from which he and others of his generation have grown alienated in thought, feelings, and values. Unlike Turgenev's nihilistic Bazarov, however, Jackson Bradley, the rebellious black protagonist, is neither as cynical and articulate in his repudiation of the plantation tradition nor as unheroic in his search for truth and dignity in Louisiana. Jackson's former teacher on the Grover plantation, one of several a few miles outside of Gaines's mythic town of Bayonne, old Madame Bayonne is both the spirit of the old Bayou social order and the on-the-scene narrator and elder. Her retrospective account of the stubborn pride and brooding guilt of the creole clan of Raoul Carmier and of the relationship between Jackson and Catherine dominates the omniscient narrative and is reminiscent of the Faulknerian vision of a South doomed to pass on the burden of its sins against God and man from father to son.

In *Of Love and Dust* Faulkner's influence is again apparent. Like *Catherine Carmier, Of Love and Dust* is set on a plantation ten or twelve miles from Bayonne, near Baton Rouge, where, even though the year is 1948, the antebellum social order and value system still shape the lives of blacks, whites, and creoles: a racially mixed people of primarily French or Spanish ancestry. Thus young lovers like Marcus Payne, a citified black convict who is required to serve his five-year sentence on bond working on a local cotton plantation, and Louise Bonbon, the Cajun overseer's wife, who rebel against the old order, are doomed to defeat and death. By their defiance of traditional racial and sexual taboos, they nevertheless represent the forces for social change.

Although the forces for social change are most dramatically represented in Jimmy and Miss Pittman in *The Autobiography of Miss Jane Pittman,* they are as memorably shown in the relationship between the language, knowledge, and power in the drama and characters of the post-1983 *Lesson before Dying.* Grounded, like his pre-1983 novels, in the Jim Crow multiethnic agrarian culture of Louisiana in 1948 and narrated primarily in the language of the black college-educated protagonist Grant Wiggins, Gaines's *Lesson before Dying* is fundamentally a compassionate story about the struggle in the modern South of two young black men for freedom, literacy, and wholeness. Although he is a college graduate and teacher who had been told by a self-hating mulatto teacher, Matthew Antoine, that if he and his peers did not run from the South most of them "would die violently" or "would be brought down to the level of beasts,"[40] Grant has more freedom and a better chance at spiritual and social wholeness than Jefferson, the illiterate laborer and scapegoat. The only freedom and wholeness that Jefferson has is to choose with the help of his elders, teacher Grant Wiggins, and the black community whether he will walk like a man to the electric chair and become a heroic symbol.

Although Gaines told an interviewer that "it's dangerous for writers to think of their audience" and that "he has no particular audience in mind when he writes," he also admits when pressured that he probably writes primarily for "the black youth of the South, to make them aware of who they are."[41] This seems most apparent in *A Lesson before Dying* because it focuses on how young Grant learns to live with dignity by teaching an even younger Jefferson, a black prisoner and former student, how to die with dignity as a man rather than as the boy and beast that he is called in the modern South. Grant is sent to the town jail by his elders Aunt (Tante) Lou and Jefferson's godmother, Miss Emma, to teach Jefferson to die like a man rather than like an illiterate hog (according to his white defense lawyer's plea for mercy) that was not worth the expense of an execution. Caught drinking liquor with money from the cash register in his pocket, the illiterate, destitute, twenty-one-year-old Jefferson, who was raised from the age of six by his godmother Miss Emma, whom he calls "nannan," was convicted of murdering a white storekeeper even though he was an observer of the crime actually committed by the two men whom he innocently accompanied to the store and who were themselves killed by the owner. Confronted by the authority and determination of Miss Emma and his Aunt Lou, Grant, who has returned to the Pinchot plantation to teach after college despite the Jim Crow legacy of love and hate that he has internalized about his manhood, his community, and life in the South, reluctantly accepts the mission of convincing Jefferson to face death like a man so that his godmother can join him in heaven. In the process, Grant learns from Jefferson how to affirm his own manhood, community, and faith.

The dominant thematic, structural, and stylistic dialectics of black redemptive sacrifice and manhood are apparent in the racial, cultural, class, generational, and political conflicts that readers find in the three principal shifts of voice in the novel as Grant moves from mixed emotions about himself, his community, and God to affirmation of his moral responsibility to all three. Code-switching effectively between SAE and AAVE to enhance the authority and authenticity of his text, Gaines develops chapters 1–28 in Grant's voice, chapter 29 exclusively in the nonstandard black Southern dialect of Jefferson's diary voice, and chapter 30 in the third-person omniscient voice of the townspeople responding to the execution, especially the arrival of the electric chair in the town. By setting the main events in the novel between Christmas and Easter of 1948 and by stressing the deep Christian faith of the black elders—Miss Emma, Aunt Lou, and the Reverend Ambrose—the early chapters outline the European American myths of white superiority and black bestiality that inform the antiblack Jim Crow customs and laws that consign black men in general and Jefferson in particular to exploitation, disrespect, dispossession, disillusionment, dissolution, and death at an early age.

On another level, then, *A Lesson before Dying* is an allegorical novel of moral responsibility and redemptive sacrifice in the quest of Grant and Jefferson (1) to reconcile their socialized ambivalence as Southern black men and (2) to bridge the intraracial generational and class conflicts in the black community. Gradually, Grant, with the help of his creole girlfriend Vivian, learns and shares with Jefferson that a man is someone who "would do anything for people . . . because it would make their lives better" (p. 191). Grant also enlists the aid of his students, who send Jefferson a gift of pecans, and the black community, who help to buy him a radio, in reconciling the class difference and initial distrust between himself and Jefferson.

As their relationship becomes psychologically and spiritually closer in the climax of the novel, Grant explains to Jefferson their common double consciousness and mutual need for a friend:

> I want us to be friends . . . Not only you and me, but I want you to be friends with your nannan. I want you to be more than a godson to her. A godson obeys, but a friend—well, a friend would do anything to please a friend. (P. 190)

Grant then explains why Jefferson, unlike himself, has the potential to be a hero and redeemer of his people by standing up, writing in his diary, and showing "the common humanity that is in us all," thus challenging, if not destroying, the myth of white supremacy:

> Do you know what a hero is, Jefferson? A hero is someone who does something for other people. He does something that other men don't and can't do. He is different from other men. He is above other men. . . . I could never be a hero. I teach, but I don't like teaching. I teach because it is the only thing that an educated black man can do in the South today. I don't like it; I hate it. I don't even like living here. I want to run away. . . . That is not a hero. . . . I want you to show them the difference between what they think you are and what you can be. To them you're nothing but another nigger—no dignity, no heart, no love for your people. You can prove them wrong. You can do more than I can ever do. I have always done what they wanted me to do, teach reading, writing, and arithmetic. Nothing else—nothing about dignity, nothing about identity, nothing about loving and caring. . . . I need you much more than you could ever

> need me. I need to know what to do with my life. I want to run away, but go where and do what. I'm needed here and I know it, but I feel that all I'm doing here is choking myself. . . . I need you to tell me, to show me. I'm no hero. . . . You—you can be bigger than anyone you have ever met. (Pp. 191–93)

Symbolically and paradoxically, Jefferson becomes not only a scapegoat for the white townsfolk but also a Christ-figure for the black and white communities. In response to Grant's belief that "it's God that makes people care for people" and that even though "they killed His Son," He never said a mumbling word, Jefferson states: "That's how I want to go, Mr. Wiggins. Not a mumbling word. . . . Me, Mr. Wiggins. Me. Me to take the cross. Your cross, nannan's cross, my own cross. Me, Mr. Wiggins. This old stumbling nigger. Y'all axe a lot, Mr. Wiggins" (pp. 223–24). The redemptive impact on the white community of Jefferson's transformation and sacrifice is represented by the compassion of Paul, the young white deputy sheriff, who not only bears witness to Jefferson's manly death but also delivers the news and Jefferson's notebooks to Grant in the schoolyard. "Allow me to be your friend, Grant Wiggins," Paul says with a profound sincerity that makes Grant cry in the closing episode. "I don't ever want to forget this day. I don't ever want to forget him. . . . I don't know what you're going to say when you go back in there. But tell them he was the bravest man in that room today. I'm a witness, Grant Wiggins, Tell them so" (pp. 255–56).

In contrast to *A Lesson before Dying* and the Euro-American influence on his first two novels, Gaines draws heavily in *The Autobiography of Miss Jane Pittman* on the tradition of the slave narratives for his reconstruction of the life of a venerable old black storyteller whose personal journey from slavery to freedom resonates with the collective struggle of black people for freedom for over a century. Divided into four books ("The War Years," "Reconstruction," "The Plantation," and "The Quarters"), the novel is the story of Miss Jane Pittman's life as told by her and "other people at the house" to the editor, a nameless young history teacher. Over an eight- or nine-month period the teacher interviews and tapes Miss Jane in order to better understand and explain black history to his students. The story unfolds chronologically, from 1864, when Miss Jane (then named Ticey) was a ten- or eleven-year-old slave on a Louisiana plantation, to 1963, when she, now 110 or more, defiantly walks past Robert Samson, the plantation owner, on her way to a civil rights demonstration in Bayonne. In telling her story, Miss Jane, in the traditional manner of storytellers, often digresses as the mood strikes her to elaborate on people and events with acute, frequently colorful, descriptions and mother wit. Late in the novel, for instance, she tells Jimmy, a young civil rights organizer who was born on the plantation but now lives in the city: " 'People and time bring forth leaders. . . .

Leaders don't bring forth people.' "[42] She also follows the folk habit of establishing time by reference to natural or social events. Because other black people in the community at times contribute to the narration, "Miss Jane's story," as the editor states in the introduction, "is all of their stories and their stories are Miss Jane's" (p. viii).

Set in Louisiana, Book 1 opens just before the end of the Civil War at the plantation where the protagonist is renamed Jane by a friendly Ohio soldier. Quickly and episodically the story moves to the end of the war. Jane heads North with other freedmen, who are attacked by patrollers and "Secesh soldiers"; and she and Ned, the young son of an older woman who saved her from rape, are the sole survivors. In Book 2 the tempo slows and the texture of the novel loosens as Jane raises Ned and experiences the federal government's betrayal of blacks with the exodus of the Northern troops in 1877 and the return to power of the Confederates. This is effectively dramatized in the take-over by Colonel Dye of the Bone plantation where she had settled and by the white terrorism that drove Ned into Kansas and killed him when he returned to teach and, in emulation of Frederick Douglass, lead his people. Taking Joe Pittman as her common-law husband, Jane moves to a plantation on the Louisiana-Texas border, where Joe becomes chief horse-breaker and is killed by a black stallion as she had dreamed and a conjure woman had prophesied.

Miss Jane continues her story in Book 3 with descriptive and analytic digressions on the customs, people, and values of the region. Now over fifty years old, she moves to the Samson plantation, joins the church, and becomes the cook at the big house. The suicide of young Tee Bob Samson brings Jane and the reader face to face with the role of her generation in perpetuating the racial taboos responsible in part for the tragedy. Finally, in Book 4 the resilience of African American character and the messianic theme of the novel are reinforced when Jimmy, a fatherless child whom Miss Jane helped to midwife and whom the folks down in the quarters had welcomed at birth as "The One," follows in Ned's footsteps. After Jimmy is murdered while leading a civil rights demonstration in Bayonne, the black community, led now by Jane and Alex, a youthful organizer—a partnership that symbolizes the strength of cooperative leadership by individuals from both the old and young generations in the unending struggle for justice—defies white authority by continuing the demonstration.

Like Margaret Walker's Vyry, Miss Jane Pittman is an extraordinarily credible black woman. She is illiterate, sassy, resourceful, and faithful—particularly to Ned, Joe Pittman, the Samsons, and the folks down in the quarters. In contrast to Vyry's traditionalism, however, Miss Jane's independence, loyalty to blacks, and response to the winds of social change prevail over her loyalty to whites and the past. During the forties she says: "I wanted to move out of the house soon after Tee Bob killed himself, but Robert kept me up there to be with Miss Amma Dean. I stayed five years more and I told them I wanted to get out.

Robert told me I got out when he said I got out. I told him at my age I did what I wanted to do. Miss Amma Dean told me she wanted me up there because I needed looking after much more than she did, but, she said, if I wanted to go, go. I told them I wanted to go, I wanted to move down in the quarters" (p. 201). Rather than a black superwoman, Gaines painstakingly delineates Miss Jane as a complex, dynamic individual. She is barren, yet is surrogate mother to Ned; she claims not to believe in hoodoo, yet consults Madame Gautier about her dreams of Joe's death. She likes fishing, hard work, baseball, and vanilla ice cream. She also "gets religion" late in life, but will give up neither her love of sports nor having the funnies read to her in order to keep her status as mother of the church. Because of her age, her strength, and her wisdom, Miss Jane Pittman towers above her time, bridging past and present, a noble inspiration to all who behold her—just like the oak tree she respects and talks to.

The larger significance of Miss Jane as an individual embodying the basic qualities necessary to bridge the old and new social orders is reinforced by Gaines's delineation of Tee Bob, Joe Pittman, Ned, and Jimmy. Tee Bob, a college student and the plantation owner's only legitimate son, tries to break with the customs of the past by proposing marriage to a creole. But he finds that historical racist attitudes and myths are too deeply rooted to change overnight or for him to endure alone, so he kills himself as much out of protest as defeat. Although he is weak and ineffectual, Gaines, nevertheless, has sympathy for him as a victim. "There will always be men struggling to change," Gaines explains in *Interviews with Black Writers,* "and there will always be those who are controlled by the past. In many cases, those who are controlled by the past can be just as human and sometimes more human than those who try to change conditions; there must always be those who try to break out of the trap the world keeps going in. Man must keep moving."[43]

All of Gaines's heroes seek to fulfill their natural rights and develop their human potential; but because white people have historically sought to deny black men their manhood, attempts by black men to assert themselves frequently result in violence and death. For example, Marcus Payne is killed by the Cajun overseer in *Of Love and Dust*, and Etienne Ray commits suicide in *In My Father's House*. In *The Autobiography of Miss Jane Pittman*, Joe dies attempting to maintain his pride and position as the chief horse-breaker on the Clyde plantation. "'Now, little mama,'" he says, "'man come here to die, didn't he? That's the contract he signed when he was born. . . . Now, all he can do while he's here is do something and do that thing good. The best thing I can do in this world is ride horses'" (p. 89). Ned and Jimmy die because they stand up to whites for their rights as men and citizens. "'Be Americans,'" Ned preaches to the young in his bold sermon at the river. "'But first be men'" (p. 110). Knowing that he would be killed, he tells them, "'You don't own this earth, you're just here for a little while, but while you're here don't let no man tell you the best is for him and you take the scrap'" (p. 108). In seeking the strength and prayers of the old folks on the plantation, the great-aunts and uncles of the black church, Jimmy explains: "'I can't promise you a thing. . . . But we must go on, and the ones already working will go on. Some of us might be killed, some of us definitely going to jail, and some of us might be crippled the rest of our life. But death and jail don't scare us—and we feel that we crippled now, and been crippled a long time, and every day we put up with the white man insults they cripple us just a little bit more" (pp. 226–27). As a contemporary realist, Gaines thus reveals the traits of the men and women of a new social order in the agency and personal and social commitments of individuals. According to his vision of the peculiarly American human condition, the hope of change in the future lies in the courage and pride of the young and the faith and resourcefulness of the old.

Subtly and compellingly, Gaines expresses his social and moral views in *The Autobiography of Miss Jane Pittman* through the manipulation of the distance between himself, the editor, the characters, and the reader in dramatized situations. Because the narrator looks back on the events she relates from the perspective of many years, the editor and implied author immediately address themselves to possible problems for the reader with the verisimilitude of the story and the reliability of the storyteller. The editor not only establishes the historical background and credibility of the storyteller in the introduction, but, as an outsider to the culture and a history teacher, he also heightens the dramatic and historical truth of the narrative through the intellectual and cultural distance between himself, Miss Jane, and the implied author. We perceive this distance in the editor's exchange with Mary Hodges, Miss Jane's friend and companion; in his initial concern about Miss Jane's rambling, repetitious storytelling style; and in how he has tried "not to write everything, but in essence everything that was said" (p. vii). Listening to the first-person narrator's voice, we are drawn emotionally and psychologically closer to her, absorbed by the truth and strength and complexity of her humanity as we relive her experience and come to better understand the values that have sustained black Americans in their historical struggle for freedom and dignity. The creation of this remarkable character and of the second major neoslave narrative (five years after *Jubilee*, the first, and five years before Ishmael Reed's *Flight to Canada*, the third), as well as of the memorable main characters in *A Lesson before Dying* is Ernest Gaines's chief contribution as a fabulator to the tradition of realism in the African American novel.

WILLIAM MELVIN KELLEY (1937–)

William Melvin Kelley was born on November 1, 1937, in New York City. Educated in private schools (Fieldston and Harvard University), he became one of the most talented and innovative postmodern fabulators. As an undergraduate he studied poetry with Archibald MacLeish and fiction with John Hawkes, an important Euro-American fabulator, and won the Dana Reed Prize for creative writing in 1960. In the following two years, he won fellowships to the New York Writers' Conference and the Bread Loaf Writers' Conference as well as a grant from the John Hay Whitney Foundation to work on his first novel, *A Different Drummer* (1962), for which he won the Richard and Hinda Rosenthal Foundation Award. During 1963–64 he and his wife lived in Rome, and during much of the 1970s, in Paris and Jamaica. He has taught at the State University of New York at Geneseo and the New School for Social Research.

In the 1964 preface to *Dancers on the Shore*, his collection of short stories on the black experience, Kelley wrote: "let me say for the record that I am not a sociologist or a politician or a spokesman. Such people try to give answers. A writer, I think, should ask questions. He should depict people, not symbols or ideas disguised as people."[44] But by 1965 he was convinced that the task of the black writer as artist was to address himself to the African American to help him "to find those things that were robbed from him on the shores of Africa, to help repair the damage done to the soul of the Negro in the past three centuries."[45] Actually, from his first short story, "Spring Planting," which appeared in 1959 in *Accent*, to the stories and essays that appeared before 1962 in the *Urbanite, Harvard Advocate*, and the *New York Times Sunday Magazine*, we see Kelley affirming a dual commitment: to his craft and to black people. And in his collection of short stories and four novels—*A Different Drummer, A Drop of Patience* (1965), *dem* (1967), and *Dunfords Travels Everywheres* (1970)—we see his inventive genius at work exploring the African American oral tradition and the complexity of interracial and intraracial color, sexual, and class relationships.

From *A Different Drummer* to *Dunfords Travels Everywheres* Kelley interweaves the histories of the Dunford and Bedlow families and their heritage as African Americans from Africa and the South. Set in a mythical East South Central State in the Deep South, *A Different Drummer* introduces us to "the African," whose heroic spirit and deeds inform the legend of African blood; to Tucker Caliban, his great-great-grandson, whose personal act of liberation sparks the mass exodus of blacks from the South; and to Wallace Bedlow (in the story "Cry for Me"), whose flight to his brother Carlyle in New York culminates in popular acclaim as an authentic blues man. Of the sixteen stories in *Dancers on the Shore*, six focus on the middle-class Dunfords; five on the working-class Bedlows and their relatives; and one on young Peter Dunford and Mance Bedlow. The other four stories trace the fate of General Dewey Willson's black descendants. In *A Drop of Patience*, a fable on American neglect of the creative gift of black jazz musicians, Ludlow Washington, a blind genius of jazz from the mythical town of New Mersails, cracks up after discovering his exploitation and betrayal by the racism and commercialism of New Yorkers, especially the white woman he loved. After his recovery, he turns his back on their belated recognition and finds a small church in need of a good musician. *dem* is a fable on the soap-opera lives of whites in which the sins of the fathers are visited upon their children. Mitchell Pierce, a white advertising executive, suffers the retribution of nonwhites for centuries of violence, injustice, and rape when he is faced with raising a black child, the surviving fraternal twin that his wife delivers after being impregnated within a short time by both him and her maid's black boyfriend, Calvin Coolidge "Cooley" Johnson. And in *Dunfords Travels Everywheres*, Kelley's imaginative and stylistic tour de force of parody and irony, Chig Dunford's quest to discover his own nature and the nature of the world leads him and the reader on a circular journey from European cities to Harlem and from the present world of his struggle with a deadly white consciousness to an awakening black consciousness of his African and Southern past.

Kelley parodies the characters, structure, and style of James Joyce's *Finnegans Wake* and the mythology of the Eddas, one of Joyce's Scandinavian sources, in *Dunfords Travels Everywheres*.[46] Similar to the twins Shem and Shaun in *Finnegans Wake,* Chig and Carlyle, as the fusion of their names to Chiglyle suggests, are blood brothers though they live on different levels of class and color consciousness. Structurally, the adventures of the Harvard-miseducated, racially unawakened Chig Dunford in Europe contrasts with the Harlem adventures of his double, the street-educated racially aware Carlyle Bedlow. Kelley's book, like Joyce's, begins its circular pattern with the protagonist asleep and unaware of the personal, historical, and mythic significance of racism and his alma mater, mother Africa. In chapters 1–7, set in a mythical European country where by law the people are segregated by the blue-red or yellow-red clothing they wear each day, we are introduced to Chig and his five expatriate traveling companions. Wendy, who is believed to be white and is pursued by Chig, and Lane, Wendy's former lover who resents interracial affairs, stand out as the group discusses the recent assassination of John F. Kennedy and the turbulent race relations in the United States. Thus Kelley displaces Joyce's riddle of the universe with the problem of the color line and interracial sex, experimenting with different combinations of several languages to establish the ambiguity and universality of the problem.

Chapters 8 and 9 introduce us to Chig's sleeping black consciousness, dramatized by a lecture on "the foxnoxious bland stimili, the infortunelessnesses of circusdances which weak to worsen the phistorystemical intrafricanical firmly structure of our distinct coresins: The Blafringo-Arumericans,"[47] presented in the professorial voice of Chig's "hId-self." The Aesopian proverb that a fool will cross a female ox (a European woman) with a male elephant (an African man) reinforces the theme that African Americans should not subscribe to racial stereotypes about integration or sacrifice their biological and cultural kinship with Africa and each other for integration or racial mixing with Euro-Americans. In chapters 10–16 the professorial voice continues its efforts to awaken Chig to his "chiltural rackage," relating the sexual adventures of Carlyle with a Harlem dentist's wife to illustrate that Euro-Americans have "lied about everything" and that it is not enough for middle-class blacks to accumulate money; they ought to affirm a commitment to their race, too.

The odd-numbered chapters 17–29 trace Chig's actual and surreal return to New York on a ship he believes is also transporting African slaves, while the even-numbered chapters 18–28 trace Carlyle's success at hustling the devil to save his friend Hondo Johnson's soul. In chapter 30, Carlyle, Hondo, and Chig are all in Jack O'Gee's Golden Grouse Bar and Restaurant, but instead of acknowledging kinship with Carlyle and Hondo, Chig falls asleep listening to a radio program that triggers dreams about the adventures of two African American Texas Rangers, C. Turtom and S. Rabisam. Their daring exploits are fused in sound and sense with elements of the fabled African race between the Turtle and the Hare and the Euro-American children's rhyme "Jack and Jill" ("We vphought t'aFoetofinish, n Jackel O'Chill vrain off wi dPrixpost"), suggesting the need for a historical awareness of the greed and deceit of whites, who seek to destroy the unity and bleach the souls of blacks. Because Chig, "dDreamer boy," will not wake up to the lessons of the collective unconsciousness of his race, "Rabbit" and "Turtle" send him around again to "dProfessay's Lecturall" for lesson thirty-one.

Kelley, like Joyce, manipulates language and standard orthography to express the sound and sense of things on several levels of consciousness. The predominantly standard American English that opens the novel represents the conscious level; and a highly phoneticized form of neoblack English, "d'Tongue o'Now Afreequerquenne," reflects the semiconscious level of both Chig and Carlyle ("seeing z'Mr. Chacallo vbegin tclose dGap in dOwnderstanding o'dFront o'h Experience n tspy dRelayshinship betwin hId-self n dhat"). Equally intriguing, a comic mixture of pidgin English, Spanish, and French that dramatizes the "Languish" of "The Blafringro-Arumericans," the first generation of Africans transported as slaves to the New World, taps Chig's unconscious mind, the dream realm of the black professor, and "the New Africurekey Univercity Family."

Kelley wryly reconstructs the poetic and prose Eddas—the mythology, ethical conceptions, and heroic lore of the ancient North—to contrast with his reconstruction of African mythology and to "telve int'd Relationship betwine weSelfs n d'cold Glareys o'Stunangle" (p. 89). What the Vedas are for India, and the *Odyssey* and *Iliad* are for Greece, the Eddas signify for Scandinavia. Norse and Greek mythologies embody the deepest truths of pagan peoples. From them comes much of the spiritual, ethical, and intellectual Indo-European heritage of white Americans.[48] Allusions to the treachery and fratricide of Odin, the father of the gods, Balder, his son and the most beloved god, who is killed with mistletoe by his brother Hoder in a plot devised by Loki, Odin's foster brother,[49] link the fall or assassination of a beloved American president to the prophecy of the "Iklanders": "the misaltoetumle of the leader of La Colon y de la Thour Yndia Company, Prestodent Eurchill Balderman, preachful as expected, L. Oki to fry" (p. 49). The northern origins and chilling life-destroying values of Odin and his descendants are symbolically contrasted with the equatorial origins and passionate life-giving values of Africa and her descendants:

> The sun beaming the source of all emcergy hit your big, blrown Mamal's tights and heirs and bolleys and moletains most evory afternoun around the pool at the Lake Vik Hotel. There you got your birthbin. There she dalied, darkened by day, greener dang rain, hohonnesbig at the rounded buttem, bowed at the bubberia, pinched in the reygion of her tawny stembuck too. You couldn't wait to get a.m. from school to lay wid-her. You couldn't wait to get the homme to skul so you could run in the strait for her expression in flesh; which deskription inner mind, in contraced to the Momhoo hauting the rocker on the northside of Mudderterrorhanian Aye., N.E.W., bids fire to apall. (Pp. 53–54)

Africans and their descendants, says Chig's dramatized alter ego, should beware that their physical and creative energies not be used for fuel to warm the descendants of "W. Oten-Chiltman," whose legends and lives glorify death and destruction: "Almist since the bin of bawn, he lobbed them to lobe a heart for the frigg of it, unrevel a ball for the yarn of it, burn a barn for the beef of it, but a hut for the strut of it, incise a shoe for the sock of it, heat a sheat for the wick of it. That and Alotoflikkyr and Heshappy, Mr. Chilyle" (p. 54). Unfortunately, many readers will probably find that it takes too much time and effort to understand Kelley's word games and multilevel puns, and will not adequately appreciate the richness of his comic imagination and ironic reconstruction of myth.

More realistic and therefore more accessible, but no less impressive in its fabulation, is *A Different Drummer,* which has a double plot and dual protagonists. The first plot concerns the moral awakening and personal revolt of Tucker Caliban, a reconstruction with a black difference of Shakespeare's Caliban in *The Tempest,* against the control of whites over his life, and the second focuses on the education of whites, especially young Harry Leland and Dewey Willson III, about the nature of racism and the meaning of courage and self-reliance. Divided into eleven chapters, the novel opens in documentary fashion with an excerpt from *The Thumb-Nail Almanac* of 1961, establishing the time of the current action, 1957, and the history of a mythical East South Central State: the home of the Willsons, the most important white aristocrats in the Gulfport area, and the Calibans, their former slaves.

Told predominantly in retrospective narrative and flashbacks through multiple white narrators, the novel proper begins with the ritual gathering of the townsmen of Sutton to hear old Mr. Harper retell the legend of the African as an explanation of Tucker Caliban's radical transformation and the mysterious exodus within three days of most of the blacks in the state. The next two chapters reflect the impact of this development on the consciousness of Harry Leland, a white farmer, and Harold, his eight-year-old son. The fifth chapter, "One Long Ago Autumn Birthday," dramatizes the nature of the modern Caliban-Willson family relationship through the punishment young Tucker unjustly suffers because of the failure of moral courage of his companion Dewey Willson III. The next five chapters then explore the consciousness of the Willsons: Dymphna, the seventeen-year-old daughter who was influenced by the moral example of Tucker's wife, Bethrah; Dewey III, the eighteen-year-old son who grew up with Tucker; Camille, the mother and wife who stood patiently by her husband after his loss of faith and courage; and David, the Southern journalist who lost the courage to continue his struggle against the legacy of racism until Tucker Caliban's methodical destruction of his farm on the old Willson plantation freed them both. The book closes with Mr. Harper consoling Dewey III after his failure to stop the lynching of the Reverend Bradshaw, a West Indian black nationalist leader from the North and his father's former fellow activist against racism. In the final episode young Harold Leland ironically fantasizes that the revelry of the lynching ritual he hears is a party celebrating Tucker Caliban's return to his farm.

A Different Drummer affirms self-reliance and moral courage as the imperatives for social change. The legend of the heroism of Tucker Caliban's African ancestor and the myth of his blood as the explanation for Tucker's personal courage contrast with the failure of courage of the Willsons, whose name is ironic, and society in general to affirm the natural rights of man. The Willson family's story is told primarily through David's diary entries from 1931 to 1957 concerning the Calibans. Tucker's act of conscience in liberating himself and his family from a slave and paternalistic past inspires Dewey and David Willson as well as other blacks to assert their right to dignity and freedom. "Anyone, anyone can break loose from his chains," thinks David, who is morally reawakened after reading how Tucker salted his land, burned down his house, and left for the North with his family. "That courage, no matter how deeply buried, is always waiting to be called out. All it needs is the right coaxing, the right voice to do that coaxing, and it will come roaring like a tiger."[50] The day is coming fast, as the Reverend Bradshaw realizes and his lynching at the end of the novel symbolizes, when the Tuckers of the world will not need leaders to free them, for they will realize that they can and must free themselves.

William Melvin Kelley is clearly less ambivalent toward American individualism than most contemporary black novelists. His most striking theme is that the road to freedom and fulfillment is through self-reliance. For most blacks, as illustrated in *Dunfords Travels Everywheres* and A *Different Drummer,* this means the courage to affirm one's ethnic and personal identity as African American and to trust oneself rather than institutions and organizations to achieve greater independence, growth, and well-being. In giving form to this moral and social vision Kelley is most original in his postmodern adaptation and fusion of traditional narrative modes such as myth, legend, and fable. His skill and sensitivity in filtering Tucker Caliban's story through the consciousness of multiple white narrators, and his dazzling creation of interrelated linguistic and mythological systems in *Dunfords Travels Everywheres* are his chief contributions to the tradition of the African American novel.

RONALD L. FAIR (1932–)

Like Kelley, Ronald Fair is best known for his adaptation of such traditional forms as legend and fable. Born on October 27, 1932, in Chicago to transplanted Mississippi plantation workers who were proud to be black, Fair was educated in the city's public schools. His interest in writing was nurtured by one of his black English teachers. After finishing high school and serving three years as a hospital corpsman in the navy, he returned to Chicago to attend business school and from 1955 to 1966 worked as a court reporter. Influenced by the slave narratives and the example of Richard Wright, he continued to write in his spare time, publishing his first pieces in the *Chicago Daily Defender, Chat Noir Review, Negro Digest,* and *Ebony.* He has taught at Columbia College in Chicago and at Northwestern and Wesleyan Universities. His publications include two novels—*Hog Butcher* (1966) and *We Can't Breathe* (1972)—and three novellas: *Many Thousand Gone* (1965) and "Jerome" and "World of Nothing" in *World of Nothing* (1970), for which he won a National Institute of Arts and Letters Award in 1971.

Hog Butcher and *We Can't Breathe* reveal the continuing appeal of traditional realism and naturalism to some contemporary black novelists. Told by a third-person omniscient author-narrator who closely identifies with the vitality and integrity of his ten-year-old protagonist, *Hog Butcher,* which is set in Chicago in 1965, is the story of Wilfred Robinson's courage in testifying against police who killed his hero, Cornbread, after mistaking him for a burglar and who tried with the collusion of "officialdom" to cover up their mistake. But as the voice of the author-narrator in the intervening critical vignettes that give historical resonance to the novel makes clear, it is also the story of the wave of poor but proud, vibrant black people who migrated to Chicago from the South in the 1940s and 1950s to fulfill their dreams. For Ronald Fair, who borrows the title of his novel from Carl Sandburg's poem "Chicago" and draws heavily on his years as a court reporter to give verisimilitude to his courtroom scene, the white Chicago system is the hog butcher that cuts out the souls of blacks. But the protagonist symbolizes the vitality that the author sees "blossoming among the stone and steel weeds of Chicago. There is, among the young," he says, "among the undeformed, the uncorrupted, the uncompromised, a desire to change the way of life."[51]

Like *Hog Butcher, We Can't Breathe,* a semiautobiographical novel, reveals the bittersweet memories of growing up black in Chicago. The protagonists of both are young black boys who symbolize the author's faith in the future. In contrast, however, to the four-week time span of the events in *Hog Butcher*—which spotlights the friendship of fast-talking Earl, Wilfred, and Cornbread, the shooting of Cornbread, and the coroner's inquest into the shooting—the time span in *We Can't Breathe* is five years in the life of Ernest Johnson, nine years old at the outset, with whom the author closely identifies on all levels. The first-person narrative traces Ernie's childhood efforts to survive with self-respect as he moves into a new neighborhood on the South Side where his friends and extended family are trapped by centuries of injustice and destroyed by racism.

Fair's three novellas are more postmodern than his novels. Although *Many Thousand Gone,* his first and most popular book, is not self-consciously innovative in its exploration of the creative process, it is less realistic and more concerned with ideas and ideals than traditional social realism. Designed primarily for a black general audience during the Black Arts movement, it is explicitly identified in the subtitle as a fable, but the title, borrowed from a black spiritual and folksaying, and internal evidence reveal that it is actually a blend of legend, fable, and slave narrative. Rooted in the historical black experience of slavery and exploitation in the South, it is the brief, simple account of the heroic deeds of Granny Jacobs and Josh Black; its moral and political lessons, ironically dramatized in the closing episode, are that blacks must free themselves. Set entirely in the mythical town of Jacobsville, Mississippi, the plot is melodramatic, episodic, and highly compressed in time, covering the years 1832 to 1963 in fewer than 120 pages. The characters are one-dimensional stock figures with Granny Jacobs, the noble black matriarch, Jesse, the messianic black prince, and Josh Black, the bold black avenger, as the most striking; and the point of view is a mixture of third-person omniscient and dramatic. Although the protagonist is actually the whole black community rather than any single member of that community, the theme and structure of the book, like the slave narratives, are concerned with the journey from bondage to freedom. In Part 1 of the two-part narrative, the emphasis is on the slave past and the legacy of black matriarchy and the hope of being freed by a black messiah like Little Jesse, the last of the "first-borns who were genuinely Negro" and Granny Jacobs's great-grandson. In Part 2 the focus shifts to the radical present, the emergence of black unity and militancy among the young, and the false hope of the older black generation in a white emancipator, the president, whose federal investigators are outsmarted and arrested by the local sheriff.

The catalysts for the emergent unity and militancy in the black community are the arrival of a clandestine subscription to *Ebony,* a popular pictorial black Northern magazine that was scheduled to print a story on Jesse's success in Chicago as an author, and the twenty-five-year-old secret the community shares with Granny Jacobs about how she staged a mock funeral for her great-grandson in order to help him to escape to "God's country" so that he could be free and help his people. By its celebration of the achievements of a growing black urban middle class, *Ebony,* which is essentially conservative and integrationist in its politics, fosters a revolutionary sense of group pride and solidarity among the blacks of Jacobs County. Consequently, when three teenage black girls are raped and butchered to death, the town's 3,000 blacks revolt, burning down the town and killing many of the 400 white men who were on their way to "roast Granny and Preacher Harris alive." Fair ends his American fable ironically as well as apocalyptically with Josh watching the jail holding the federal investigators go up in flames before casually unlocking the door "to set his emancipators free."[52]

Of the short works, "Jerome" and "World of Nothing" are the most innovative in design and ideas. Short and pithy, "Jerome" is a parable of the Black Jesus and an allegorical story of the nature of evil in the modern world, especially the Catholic church. Called "Little Jesus," "Black Night of Christ," and "a true son of God" by the entire neighborhood where he spread the word of God, sometimes just by his presence, five-year-old Jerome is the bastard child of thirteen-year-old Lula and Father Jennings, an ironic twist on the parents of Jesus Christ. Driven by Lula's obsession with devils, by their desecration of the church with their lust for each other, and by Father Jennings's coveting the rector's job, they feel accused by Jerome and see him as the devil. Jerome, who is troubled that he "sensed as much evil in his Father's house," sets fire to the church and is killed by a hysterical Lula and Father Jennings. The reverence of Thelma, the old witch, for Jerome in the prologue, story proper, and epilogue reinforces the meaning of her dramatic scream at the end: " 'They've killed the Black Jesus.' "[53]

In "World of Nothing" Fair returns to his basically naturalistic vision of blacks trapped in the South Side ghetto of Chicago. But this time he is much more imaginative and satirical as he creates a kaleidoscope of sixteen vignettes that capture the pathos and wry humor of place and people. He does this chiefly through the effective use of verbal and situational irony. The first-person anonymous narrator-protagonist, who is a sometime writer and most-of-the-time drunk, tells us he lives in the World of Nothing: "Nothing is a state of black. It's a world where the only white face is an occasional policeman or the peddler or the store owners or those goddamn insurance men. But mostly it's all black. It's even black when the sun beats down on our shiny faces; the rays seem to soak into our world and shatter and form a black cloud that hangs like a gloomy continuation of night symbolic of the segregated quarters wherein we eat and laugh and love and cry and live and die" (p. 65). In this world he shares a two-room apartment in The Place of Peace Hotel with his buddy and fellow wino, Red Top, with whom he once traveled to the white world, a World of Even Less. "It doesn't seem right," says the narrator, "that a people can have so much and still have nothing. We could show them but they don't want any part of us so we'll just keep it to ourselves and have something of real substance from practically nothing of value" (p. 80).

"World of Nothing" is more playful in tone and more artful in construction than Fair's other narratives. This postmodern artifice is apparent in the colorful, wry names and in the two- to three-page descriptions of the places and people in the narrative. As we accompany the narrator, our guide, on his picaresque journey through the World of Nothing, we meet such fantastic people as Junkie Thaddeus Popcorn Jones, the neighborhood junkie who collects $5,000 in an insurance swindle after being pushed in front of a wealthy, drunk white man's car; Miss Joanne Joanne, the whore-house madam's beautiful protégée who likes animals but hates junkies so much that she pushes Junkie Jones in front of a car because he asked her for a nickel; Miss Luhester Homan, a happy, unmarried welfare mother of five children by different men and "one of the most highly respected ladies in the neighborhood"; Preacher Robinson and Sister Grace of the fundamentalist tent church; and Johnnie Sweepstakes, a gambling man who "lost at policy, at horses, at blackjack, at poker, and even at matching and pitching pennies with the kids." At the end of the novella, Red Top, the narrator's friendly, popular roommate, finds meaning in his life through "tent church" religion and leaves the World of Nothing, causing the protagonist anxiety over his own loss to the world of work and conformity until he finds a new roommate. "This guy," he tells us, "is just like me: Buy what you want and beg what you need. It's great to meet someone who is alive. Oh God, it feels good to be alive again. To be free to be alive again" (p. 131). Similar to *Many Thousand Gone* and "Jerome," "World of Nothing" closes on a wry note of regeneration.

Fair's novels, in other words, illustrate that although a wide range of earlier narrative modes are always present in the tradition of the African American novel, certain experiments with combinations of these earlier forms and conventions seem most appropriate to the tenor of the changing times. Whereas *Hog Butcher* and *We Can't Breathe* are evidence of the perennial presence of realism and naturalism, the more intriguing *Many Thousand Gone* is clearly related in structure and tone to the Aesopian fable, the legend, and the slave narrative. By their symbolic tendency toward allegory, "Jerome" and "World of Nothing" involve the reader in a more modern than postmodern process of fabricating the meaning of reality for oneself. "Jerome" draws on both the sacred and profane traditions of the parables of Jesus and the tales of Boccaccio, and "World of Nothing" draws on satiric and picaresque forms.

Fabulation, Romance, and Fantasy

Modern and postmodern blends of romance and fantasy, as in expatriate William Demby's *Catacombs* (1965), stress the artificiality of reality and the reality of artifice. In *The Catacombs,* Demby sets his quasi-autobiographical, nonrepresentational modern narrative in the tomb and womb of Christianity in Rome. He casts himself as an expatriate narrator-writer whose construction of diary entries and newspaper clippings, as well as of baroque allusions to painting, sculpture, and the cinema is designed to make us share in his modernist vision that we are all nothing more than the products of our creative imagination and will to change. Questioning the effectiveness of conventional language and social realism to discover the truth of the apocalyptic tendencies in Western culture and American life, some contemporary black fabulators, like Wideman and Major, have experimented self-consciously with dream visions, stylized characters, and linguistic forms to illuminate the burden and blessing of African American double consciousness. Whereas the quest of some protagonists is for a personal and public wholeness that reconciles conflicting values, including lust and love, the quest of others is for authenticity, authority, and agency in the reconstruction of identity in a physical or spiritual heaven or hell.

JOHN EDGAR WIDEMAN (1941–)

Because the lower frequencies of an African American tradition, oral and literary, were significantly muted in the life and work of John Wideman before the Black Power movement, an examination of authenticity, authority, and agency in his texts reveals the unrelenting struggle to reconcile one's African American double consciousness in an absurd world of antiblack racism. Although he was born on June 14, 1941, in largely black Washington, D.C., and although he was raised and went to school in the predominantly black Homewood section of Pittsburgh, Wideman did not read Richard Wright and other black writers during his youth. Nor did he read them at Oxford University, where as a Rhodes Scholar he was formally trained in English literature. His education in black literature came after his graduation in 1963 from the University of Pennsylvania, where he was awarded both a Ben Franklin Fellowship and a Thouron Fellowship for Creative Writing, and after his acceptance in 1966 of a Kent Fellowship for Creative Writing at the University of Iowa. With this formal academic background, it is not surprising that the early influences on Wideman's craftsmanship were James Joyce and T. S. Eliot, whom he first read in high school, and Henry Fielding and Laurence Sterne, whom he studied at New College, Oxford. It was not until 1967, after the publication of his first novel, *A Glance Away,* and after he started teaching black literature courses at the University of Pennsylvania, that he began to read slave narratives, black folklore, the novels of Wright and Ellison as well as Toomer's *Cane*. The vision and experimentation of these writers, he states in an interview, were important in the development of his Afrocentric aesthetic, for it awakened in him "a different sense of self-image and the whole notion of a third world." He also says: "If there is any single book I learned a hell of a lot from, it's *Tristram Shandy*. . . . I hope that I have learned from the nonrepresentational school about fantasy and playing around with different forms. The novel started out with these two tendencies—realism and fantasy."[54]

Wideman has published three critically acclaimed nonfiction books (*Brothers and Keepers*, 1984, *Fatheralong*, 1995, and *Hoop Roots*, 2001) and three collections of short stories (*Damballah*, 1981, *Fever*, 1989, and *The Stories of John Edgar Wideman*, 1992). But he is most widely respected for the inventive range and depth of his soul-searing black Pittsburgh and Philadelphia family saga in five pre-1983 and four post-1983 novels: *A Glance Away*, 1967, *Hurry Home*, 1970, *The Lynchers*, 1973, *Hiding Place*, 1981, *Sent for You Yesterday*, 1983, *Reuben*, 1987, *Philadelphia Fire*, 1990, *The Cattle Killing*, 1996, and *Two Cities*, 1998. Apparently because of the conflict between his urban ethnic roots and his formal training in Eurocentric literature, Wideman's novels frequently reveal a tension between realistic material and modern experimentation with form and style, especially stream-of-consciousness techniques and the African American vernacular tradition.

The post-1983 novels continue the multivocal urban black family saga of the Homewood trilogy: *Damballah*, *Hiding Place*, and *Sent for You Yesterday*. In *Reuben* the black hunchback dwarf protagonist is a former shoe-shine boy who has become a sage legendary lawyer and mediator between the poor and worse than poor blacks of Homewood and the white authorities downtown. More nonrepresentational than antirepresentational in structure and style, the text and the protagonist rely on a code-switching African American vernacular voice, street smarts, daydreams, reverie, temporal shifts, and West African and Egyptian mythology, as well as on knowledge of the law for their authority, authenticity, and agency.

In *Philadelphia Fire*, *The Cattle Killing* and *Two Cities* Wideman imaginatively deploys myth and symbol to explore the history of the betrayal of the hope and struggle of urban black Americans as individuals and groups for freedom and wholeness. *Philadelphia Fire* is a meditation and lamentation on African American history and communities, especially the 1985 fiery deaths of at least eleven black MOVE members, including children, in their fortified home and headquarters in a black middle-class Philadelphia neighborhood. Following the orders of a self-proclaimed liberal black politician, a predominantly white police force dropped a bomb on the MOVE headquarters. The novel invokes the spirit of John Africa, the radical Afrocentric leader of MOVE, a primitivist countercultural organization, to represent Wideman's vision of the conflicting passions and purposes of contemporary black urban America. In *The Cattle Killing* prophecy, myth, ritual, and symbol dominate the quest of an itinerant black preacher, inspired by the actual antiblack racist scapegoating experience of Richard Allen and Absalom Jones, for survival and wholeness during the 1793 yellow fever epidemic in Philadelphia. Wideman brilliantly deploys this plague as a trope to suggest an analogy to the false prophets and betrayal by whites of the dreams, hopes, and trust of blacks in the tragic cattle-killing ritual in 1853 of the Xhosa people and in the continuing contemporary struggles for social equality in Philadelphia and South Africa. The cattle killing was a desperate act prophesied by Nonqgawuse, a female ethnic priest, to drive away the white colonizers in South Africa. Because cattle were vital to their lives and cultural identity, however, the cattle-killing ritual actually contributed to their tragic self-destruction instead of their redemption

Two Cities is a compelling culmination of the theme of contemporary black urban male double consciousness developed in Wideman's thirteen previous critically acclaimed books. It interweaves a legendary political tragedy of Philadelphia with a blues love story of Pittsburgh. It is a novel that thematically and stylistically explores the boundaries and bridges that paradoxically separate and connect fact and fiction, past and present, places and people, black and white, men and women, young and old. It is an experimental modern novel that linguistically celebrates the resourcefulness and resiliency of the African American blues voice. *Two Cities* is essentially a redemptive, healing story of love between Robert Jones and Kassima, a young, reclusive black widow and mother in mourning for the deaths of her husband, from AIDS in prison, and two sons, from gang violence in the streets of Pittsburgh. After the loss of her husband and sons within the brief period of ten months had resulted in her withdrawal behind an emotional and physical barrier, Kassima lowers the barrier one night to satisfy her sexual urge for a man at Edgar's bar. She is picked up by Jones, a fifty-year-old former family man whose one-night stand turns into a crying, singing day of ecstatic lovemaking, redemptive homecoming to the neighborhood of his youth, and spiritual healing for himself and Kassima. Jones's and Kassima's voices of redemptive and healing love are framed by the blues voice of Mr. Mallory, a college drop-out, eccentric old photographer, and bagman who has migrated from Philadelphia to Pittsburgh to record the continuities and discontinuities in the lives of black families and neighborhoods. A boarder in Kassima's old house on Cassina Way, where Jones was apparently raised into manhood by women, he is a bridge between the implied author, the legendary past of his friend John Africa, and the redemptive love of Jones and Kassima. It is Mallory's and the implied author's code-switching voice between AAVE and SAE, which establishes the moral and political authority and authenticity, that becomes the linguistic norm. This third-person omniscient voice opens and closes the retrospective, discontinuous, fragmented narrative of mainly flashbacks, reveries, and interior monologues.

But the authority, authenticity, and agency of Wideman's imaginative meditation on African American history and urban communities begin in his pre-1983 novels. In *A Glance Away*, Wideman says, "I am going to school to various other writers, using others' techniques, but also trying out some things that I hope are original."[55] Eliot's Eurocentric influence is apparent in the mood, style, and characterization of this first novel, which is a quasi-parable on the resurrection of Edward Lawson, the thirty-year-old black protagonist who returns to

Philadelphia on Easter Sunday, April 20, from a drug rehabilitation center in the South only to suffer the pain and guilt of his mother's death. The person driven by his own painful memories to get him through the night is Robert Thurley, a kindred spirit of T. S. Eliot's J. Alfred Prufrock, a middle-aged white homosexual professor of comparative literature who pursues black lovers and for whom "Eliot was . . . the poet of weariness, of old age."[56] Although Eliot's specter hangs over most of the book, in the final ten pages Wideman displaces dialogue with the alternating inner thoughts of Eddie, Robert, and Brother Small, their albino friend, as they sit in spiritual communion around a small fire in a hobo camp.

Equally Prufrockian in characterization but more nonrepresentational and experimental in time structure and point of view is *Hurry Home.* Whereas Thurley, the ineffectual, suffering intellectual in *A Glance Away,* wanders through the streets and after-hours clubs of Philadelphia, Charles Webb, the guilt-ridden white writer and intellectual of *Hurry Home,* wanders the museums, cafes, and beaches of Spain in a vain search for redemption from the black son he has never seen because he had abandoned his black mistress not knowing she was pregnant. Using interior monologue, letters, journal entries, rapid shifts in time and point of view, surreal vignettes, mythic associations, linguistic puns, and frequent allusions to writers and painters, especially Hieronymus Bosch and his triptych *The Adoration of the Magi,* Wideman is concerned in his second novel with the thin line between reality and fantasy, "between individual and collective experience which permits one to flow into the other."[57] Going to get a haircut for his graduation, Cecil Otis Braithwaite, the protagonist who, aided by the sacrifices of his girlfriend Esther and his scrub-woman mother, is only the second of his race to graduate from the university law school, is symbolically rejected by the black community as a "Humbug magistraitassed uppitty nigger."[58] He, in turn, deserts Esther on their wedding night to go to Spain and Africa, seeking to understand his double consciousness and to accommodate both the gospels and the Easter song, the "St. John Passion," of Heinrich Schutz. The question that Cecil asks throughout the book is, Why did you do that? As he actually and imaginatively travels back in the past for answers, his personal experience is conflated into the collective history of his race. But after three years of wandering through the corridors of time and foreign countries, reconstructing and reliving the journey of his race from Africa to America, he hurries home in the spring to work in a hair straightening parlor, to rejoin his wife, and to dream. "To go back into one's past," Wideman states, "is in fact dreaming. What is history except people's imaginary recreation?"[59] Thus Cecil's actual past and his dream past, like his personal and racial identities, become merged in the course of the novel.

Although the ambiguities of the imagination and of the relationship between blacks and whites in America are common themes in Wideman's first three novels, *The Lynchers* is the most intriguing demonstration of the implied author's authority and agency in the novel's blend of realism and surrealism. Not sharing the antirepresentational and antiessential assumptions of postmodernist texts, the primary theme of the novel is that the historical social realities of race relations in America are driving blacks and whites to apocalyptic attitudes and actions. At the center of the novel is the destruction of the black Wilkerson family—Orin "Sweetman" and Bernice, the parents, and Thomas, their son—and a plan conceived by Willie "Littleman" Hall to lynch a white cop in order to release black people from a fear of death at the hands of whites and to assert a new vision of reality. Introduced by twenty pages of quotations from documents that immerse the reader in the historical record of the use of lynching as a ritual of brutal racial power, the novel proper is divided into three major parts whose chronological time span is less than a month but whose psychological span is years.

Set in the 1960s on the South Side of Philadelphia, Part 1 plunges the reader into a sea of internal and external events that reveal the debris of Orin's and Bernice's lives and the distress that drives Thomas to risk participating in the lynch plan. In Part 2 Wideman continues to experiment with a wide range of modern and postmodern techniques—dream fragments, interior monologue, flashbacks, black vernacular, rapid shifts from third- to first-person narration, and overlapping time frames—to introduce us to the details of the plan, the experiences that led Littleman to conceive it, and the mixture of black history and revolutionary rhetoric he uses to recruit his three irresolute, mutually distrustful accomplices. The plan is to kill a pimping white cop's black whore and to have the community publicly lynch him for her death, symbolically liberating the community from oppression and defining themselves in the process "as fighters, free, violent men who will determine the nature of the reality in which they exist." The "plan's as simple as death," says Littleman. "When one man kills it's murder. When a nation kills murder is called war. If we lynch the cop we will be declaring ourselves a nation."[60] The climax of the external events occurs in Part 2 when Littleman, while making an inflammatory speech on the steps of a black junior high school, is severely beaten by the police. But the internal climax does not come until Part 3 when Wilkerson's consciousness merges with the daughter of the lynchers' intended first victim. Part 3 also reveals how the lynch plan is completely aborted after Wilkerson's father is arrested for killing his best friend. The protagonist himself is shot in a desperate assertion of independence by Rice, an accomplice; and Littleman dies in the hospital after a futile effort to recruit a young black hospital orderly, Alonzo, whose confusion and blind rage represent the disorganized revolutionary potential of the next generation. More important than the failure of the lynch plan, then, are the social realities that impinge on the consciousness of the characters, undermine their political agency, and influence their existential choices. The implied author therefore seems to parody the revolutionary identities forged in political struggle that Frantz Fanon so brilliantly outlines in *The Wretched of the Earth.*

Because Wideman, in other words, is primarily concerned with compelling readers to participate in the reciprocal influence of reality on the imagination and the imagination on the reality of his characters, the novel is more modern than postmodern. The past and present flow together in the bittersweet memories of Wilkerson's parents as they sit across from each other in the kitchen:

> Pocked walls breathing sourly, patient mirrors of everything and if peeled layer by layer paint to paper to paper to paint to paint you would see old lives crowded as saints in the catacombs. Their children's hand prints crawling up the wall. The low border when it was a third leg to hold them up, the grease streaks from the boys' slicked down heads as they leaned back cockily on spindly legged chairs sneaking smokes and trading lies around the kitchen table, up near crease of ceiling and wall, splash of roach where she told Thomas not to squash them even if he could reach that high. Once blue, once yellow, hopelessly white, blue again, now the rosette paper meant for somebody's living room. . . . She realized how easily it could all disappear. Everywhere in the neighborhood buildings were being torn down. (P. 31)

Of the four avenging angels—Graham Rice, a neurotic, spineless janitor; Leonard Saunders, a street-hardened post office worker; Thomas Wilkerson, an ineffectual dreamer and junior high school teacher; and Littleman, the crippled, silver-tongued messenger of historical truth and the mastermind of the lynching plan—Wilkerson and Littleman are Wideman's symbols of the modern intellectual man. In contrast to Wilkerson, Littleman has strong convictions and faith in his plan to change reality. "'Are you still so unconvinced?'" he asks Wilkerson. "'Why is it so much easier for you to doubt than believe?'" (p. 113). But both, as Wideman illustrates by juxtaposing the political and psychological significance of the lynch rope in America, are men of ideas rather than action. Whereas Littleman needs Wilkerson as an intellectual and revolutionary disciple, Wilkerson needs Littleman as a surrogate for the father he loves and hates because his life seemed so accidental and shapeless.

As the omniscient narrator glides in and out of third- and first-person points of view, suggesting the postmodern instability and shifting grounds of authority, truth, and reality, Wideman compels us to become intimately involved with the characters, their frustrations, and their existential choices. Internal and external events merge in Sweetman's mind in the opening domestic scene:

> He would call her but if it is morning she may be asleep and perhaps she slept right through and I can tell her any lie, choose the decent hour I came in just too tired so went to sleep downstairs on the couch. Even as

> he forms a probable fiction he knows she will be sitting in the kitchen, aware of everything. And she is and she asks why did he bother to come home for the hour he did. He wants more from her. He wants her calling him out of his name, calling him *Sweetman,* treating him like he's still in the street or like she wants him gone. (P. 30)

Wideman then quickly shifts to Bernice's thoughts and feelings about the emptiness in her kitchen and her life, about her husband drinking himself to death, ashamed to face her, and her getting "older, tireder and poorer." Next we see and hear Sweetman on his way before sunup to wrestle garbage cans and chase rats, rapping with other sanitation engineers, including his best friend Childress.

Later, Wideman encourages our sympathy for his protagonist, who is reflecting over the pages of his appointment book:

> Were there only two choices? Either cage time in the red lines that marched across the page or like his father in his lost weekends abandon any illusion of control. Littleman believed all men were trapped. No choice existed except to reverse or destroy the particular historical process which at a given time determines the life of individual men. He would see my father and me as equally unredeemable. Perhaps he is right. I believe in his plan. It may free men for an instant, create a limbo between prisons. But can the instant be extended? Can it support life and a society? I don't think Littleman cares. I don't think my father cared when he felt the need to escape. (P. 71)

By the end of the novel the reader's sympathies have shifted several times among the characters, unlike the sharply focused and stable moral sympathies evoked by Vyry and Miss Jane Pittman. And though he sympathizes with Littleman's historical imperatives and existential choices, Wideman, as the tragic denouement illustrates, identifies more closely with his protagonist's disruptive internal changes, especially his moral and political decision to sabotage the plan. The blend of modern and postmodern techniques in *The Lynchers* is representative of continuity and change in the imaginative deployment of myth and ritual by black fabulators like Wideman seeking to reconcile their double consciousness as African American artists.

The Homewood trilogy marks the culmination of Wideman's move from a Eurocentric to a fundamentally Afrocentric and African Americentric tradition, his coming home as it were in the form and style of an extended modernist meditation on history: oral and literary, personal and social. *Damballah,* the collection of twelve stories that the author calls long overdue letters to his imprisoned younger brother, Robby, invokes the ancestral gods of Africa in the New World, especially Damballah Wedo, the venerable serpent god of paternity, as the spirit guides for his mythic ancestral journey. To invoke these gods, says Wideman, is "to stretch one's hand back to that time and to gather up all history into a solid contemporary ground beneath one's feet."[61] From the prefacing texts—letter to Robby, brief note on Damballah, and Begat Chart—and the opening legend of the passing on of the spirit of Damballah to African Americans, the generic distinctions between history and fiction, novel and romance, orality and literariness collapse as Wideman blends epistle, legend, myth, fable, biography, and autobiography in a series of interdependent fictive constructs.

The book concludes cyclically without closure with "The Beginning of Homewood," another letter to his brother. This letter is metafictional in that it is about the creative act of writing. Wideman explains that it began as a literary retelling of the family legend about how the family tree was planted on Bruston Hill in Homewood, the black community of Pittsburgh, Pennsylvania, with the arrival of Sybela Owens, their great-great-great-grandmother, who ran away from slavery with her white master's son, Charles Bell: "her lover, her liberator, her children's father . . ." (p. 197). "This woman, this Sybela Owens, our ancestor," Wideman writes reflectively and ambivalently, "bore the surname of her first owner and the Christian name Sybela, which was probably a corruption of Sybil, a priestess pledged to Apollo. . . . On the plantation Sybela Owens was called Belle. Called that by some because it was customary for slaves to disregard the cumbersome, ironic names bestowed by whites, and rechristen one another in a secret, second language, a language whose forms and words gave substance to the captives' need to see themselves as human beings" (p. 195). Passed on orally by the women in the family, the story of her legendary urge for freedom as a runaway slave, her crime, corresponds in the author-narrator's consciousness to that of his imprisoned brother. Her legend also fosters anxiety and ambivalence about his own freedom and success. Why not me, he asks: "Ask myself if I would have committed the crime of running away or if I would have stayed and tried to make the best of a hopeless situation. Ask if you really had any choice, if anything had changed in the years between her crime and yours" (p. 200).

The two novels, *Hiding Place* and *Sent for You Yesterday*, continue Wideman's blend of fabulation, romance, and fantasy in a meditation on the history of his family, home, and people. Its title borrowed from the black spiritual "There's No Hiding Place Down There," *Hiding Place* expands "Tommy," the imaginative rewriting of the story in *Damballah* that foregrounds Robert Wideman's actual involvement in a robbery attempt and murder, and reweaves it with the story of Mother Bess, the granddaughter of Mother Sybela and the oldest living family member. Through the interweaving of memory, reverie, and interior monologues as well as by the manipulation of black speech, music, and religion, Wideman reveals the sociopsychological process by which the gnarled old roots and wayward young branches of the Owens/Bell family tree strengthen and renew themselves together. Mother Bess, who is hiding from the world in the dilapidated ancestral home on Bruston Hill because of the loss of her only son and blues-singing husband, reluctantly shares her hiding place and spiritual wisdom with her great-grandson Tommy, who is running away from the police because he was an accomplice in a robbery attempt that resulted in murder. Reconciling their mutual ambivalence at the end of the novel, both find the resolve in themselves and each other to come out of hiding and return to confront the blueslike reality of Homewood and the world.

Its title borrowed from the blues song that Jimmy Rushing made popular, and its time structure influenced by the foreshadowing of postmodern metafictional techniques of temporal and spatial discontinuity in Laurence Sterne's eighteenth-century classic, *Tristram Shandy, Sent for You Yesterday* is the long, sad song of Homewood and the contemporary inheritors of its blues legacy. Dividing the novel into three major sections ("The Return of Albert Wilkes," "The Courting of Lucy Tate," and "Brother"), Wideman, who is emotionally, psychologically, and morally close to the surnameless narrator, dances back and forth in time through dreams, memories, and reveries. He artfully yet ambivalently employs the rhythms of black speech and music, especially train symbolism, to reconstruct the blues legacy of Homewood to present and future generations of the French, Tate, and Lawson families. Spanning the years from 1941 to 1970, the novel begins in 1970 with the first-person narrator, christened "Doot" by his Uncle Carl French's best friend Brother Tate, looking back, like Tristram Shandy, to events before he was born. He remembers and affirms through stories he has heard over the years in Homewood that he is "linked to Brother Tate by stories, by his memories of a dead son, by my own memories of a silent scat-singing albino man who was my uncle's best friend."[62] Just as the untrained Brother Tate mysteriously embodies the blues spirit and piano-playing talent of Albert Wilkes, whose return after seven years to a rapidly declining Homewood results in the police blowing his brains out in the Tate home, the narrator, "In Brother's eyes . . . grew up living not only my own life, but the one snatched from Junebug," Brother's son of the same age who died in a fire in 1941.

Brother Tate's sixteen-year silence in mourning for his son, his youthful ritual of playing the death-defying game of chicken with oncoming trains, and his recurring dreams of trains, as well as Lucy Tate's storytelling quilt and the bone fragment from Albert Wilkes's skull that she saves signify, along with the blues, the authentic keep-on-keeping-on lessons that the old Homewood people taught their young by example. As Lucy tells her lover and the narrator's uncle, Carl French, in the closing pages of the book: "'They made Homewood. Walking around, doing the things they had to do. Homewood wasn't bricks and boards. Homewood was them singing and loving and getting where they needed to get. They made these streets. That's why Homewood was real once. Cause they were real. And we gave it all up. Us middle people. You and me, Carl. We got scared and gave up too easy and now it's gone. Just sad songs left. And whimpering. Nothing left to give the ones we supposed to be saving

Homewood for. Nothing but empty hands and sad stories'" (p. 198). Nevertheless, Wideman closes the novel with a ray of hope as his principal narrator, Doot, begins responding to Smokey Robinson's "Tracks of My Tears" on the radio and fantasizing that Brother Tate was signaling to Albert Wilkes to begin playing the piano. Finally, Doot was "learning to stand, to walk, learning to dance" (p. 208).

The major underlying theme, then, in Wideman's novels is that what we think we are is at least as important as what we are. "From the very beginning," he says, "Western civilization has an idea of what black men are, and that idea has come down to us generation after generation, has distorted and made impossible some kinds of very human and basic interaction. The mechanics of that are both very frightening and very fascinating."[63] To explore the interior landscapes of his characters and the conflict between their ascribed and achieved identities as black men, Wideman, who also believes that racial memories exist in the imagination, draws on a wide variety of sources and complex blend of fabulation, romance, and fantasy in his shift from a Eurocentric to a basically Afrocentric tradition. As in Demby's *Catacombs,* his innovative use of legend, myth, music, and painting in *A Glance Away, Hurry Home,* and *The Lynchers* gives resonance to the theme of double consciousness in the tradition of the African American novel. At the same time his use in the Homewood trilogy of Afrocentric terms to reconstruct the anxiety of Eurocentric influences in his experiment with time structure and point of view provides a sharp contrast to Clarence Major's black postmodernist double vision of contemporary African American experiences of reality.

CLARENCE [LEE] MAJOR (1936–)

Clarence Major marches to a different drummer in the tradition of the African American novel. Born on December 31, 1936, in Atlanta, Georgia, he was raised in Chicago. At twelve years old, "while writing crude little novels in school notebooks,"[64] he began exploring the literary landscape to stake out his claim for a writing career. In high school he read everything by Richard Wright and then turned to other black writers like Chester Himes, Willard Motley, and Frank Brown. While a student at the Armed Forces Institute in Wyoming in 1954, he sold his first story, "Ulysses, Who Slept Across from Me," and published his first collection of poetry, *The Fires That Burn in Heaven.* After military service he accepted a fellowship at the Art Institute of Chicago to pursue an equally serious interest in painting. "I think my experience with painting, the way that I learned to see the physical world of lines, color, and composition," Major told an interviewer, "definitely influenced my writing."[65] Since 1958 his poems, short fiction, and essays, all revealing an increasingly postmodernist concern for experimenting with language and form, have appeared in many literary and popular magazines. *Swallow the Lake,* one of his eight collections of poems, won a National Council of the Arts Award in 1970. Moving to New York City in 1966, he became an associate editor of the *Journal of Black Poetry* from 1967 to 1970. He taught literature and creative writing at the Academy of American Poets in 1968, at Brooklyn College in 1968–69, at Sarah Lawrence College in 1972–73, and at Howard University in 1974–76. He then accepted tenured positions at the University of Seattle, the University of Colorado, and the University of California at Davis. In addition to his twelve collections of poetry, Major has edited three anthologies and published a book on African American slang, a collection of essays, and eight novels: *All-Night Visitors* (1969), *NO* (1973), *Reflex and Bone Structure* (1975), *Emergency Exit* (1979), *My Amputations* (1986), *Such Was the Season* (1987), *Painted Turtle: Woman with Guitar* (1988), and *Dirty Bird Blues* (1996).

Even though he has published in black magazines, edited the *Journal of Black Poetry,* and written the frequently anthologized "A Black Criterion," which calls for black poets to destroy the hold of white standards on their minds and work, he claims to have never been a black cultural nationalist.[66] Responding in 1973 to a question about the theme of that 1967 essay, he stated that he now found "repulsive the idea of calling for black writers to do anything other than what they each choose to do. . . . No style or subject should be alien to them. We have to get away from this rigid notion that there are certain topics and methods reserved for black writers. I'm against all that. I'm against coercion from blacks and from whites."[67] Like white Euro-American postmodernists Brautigan, Barthelme, and Sukenick, Major believes that the novel is a linguistic invention that exists on its own terms.[68] He is therefore concerned, he explains to an interviewer, with writing "one that takes on its own reality and is really independent of anything outside itself. . . . You begin with words and you end with words. The content exists in our minds. I don't think that it has to be a reflection of anything. It is a reality that has been created inside of a book. It's put together and exists finally in your mind."[69]

Major's thematic and structural movement beyond racial and political consciousness to a preoccupation with exploring the boundaries of language and imaginative consciousness can be traced in his first four novels. Each is told by a first-person, unreliable, dramatized narrator-protagonist; each is more fragmented and discontinuous in structure than its predecessor; and each engages in linguistic play that blurs the line between the worlds of fantasy and social reality. *All-Night Visitors,* divided into two essentially surreal parts called "The Early Warning System" and "The Intricacy of Ruined Landscapes," is the episodic journey of Eli Bolton, a black, neurotic, twenty-eight-year-old Vietnam veteran. Driven to despair and alienation by his loveless childhood in an orphanage and by witnessing the brutal rape and murder of children and women in Vietnam, Eli seeks to reconstruct his fragmented self and reconcile himself to the bizarre, equally violent reality of life in Chicago and New York. However,

Major's impressionistic, occasionally lyrical celebration of sex, especially fellatio, as the primal expression of the narrator-protagonist's selfhood is predictably chauvinistic and provocative. The emphasis on sexual orgasm is less effective as an iconoclastic assault on puritan morality and the inhumanity of the Vietnam War than as a metaphorical expression of the link between sex and death. As a graphic, phenomenological description of sexual exploits with a series of all-night partners, it also gives a problematic, existential meaning to Eli Bolton's quest for an integrated, responsible self, culminating in his loving and losing a young white VISTA worker. This climactic episode sets the stage for the symbolic resolution of the novel in which a dispossessed, pregnant Puerto Rican mother and her seven small children awaken Eli's will to translate human compassion into socially responsible action. Whether we believe this transformation, marked by a thunderstorm and Eli's declaration that he "had become firmly a man," depends on the degree to which, first, we interpret his experiences as surreal or real and to which, second, we accept the definition of contemporary black manhood that these experiences and the author imply.

NO, as critic John O'Brien states, "moves beyond the first novel in insisting that the self is a phenomenon of language and the imagination rather than of actual experience, time, and place."[70] Divided into three parts whose titles—"influence of the moon," "the witch-burning," and "the mount meru"—suggest the surreal landscape of the novel, it is the retrospective narrative of the narrator-protagonist's growing awareness of his multifaceted, fluid identity, from his first sexual experiences as a child on a farm in Chickamauga, Mississippi, to his full self-awareness as an adult confronting a bull in a bullring in a Latin American country. "I didn't realize," the adult narrator-protagonist states in the opening expository paragraph of the novel, "that I was really trying to crash out of a sort of penal system in which I was born and grew up. Looking back though, I do realize that the activity of my life indicates merely the position of various political, social, and moral incidents."[71] Called such names as Moses Westby, the Boy, Junebug, and Nat Turnips, the protagonist, whom the reader has difficulty distinguishing from the father figure Moses Westby, the prison guard, is not conscious of being on the road to self-determination until after he and other members of the family are shot in a suicidal rage by his father, and after he consummates his marriage to Oni Dunn. Constantly and abruptly shifting nominal, temporal, spatial, and cultural references create a confusing, uninhibited playful linguistic world that contrasts with the protagonist's personal and social sense of living in a prison.

Liberation comes only in the bullring, where touching the bull's head invested life with essence: "In other words I had to give meaning to it," he reflects; "and it had to contain courage. And at the same time I argued with the shallowness of it. With myself—with being." That this crucial event, including the protagonist's subsequent goring by the bull, actually occurred is called into question by the narrator-protagonist's anticlimactic statement: "When I woke up it was a full hour before I began to put the pieces of myself together again."[72] Whether the Hemingwayesque bullring episode of manly courage and grace in the face of danger and death is an actual or imagined experience is less important to the implied author and narrator-protagonist than the shaping influence it has on the ever-changing sense of self. Thus, in the closing line of the novel the narrator-protagonist is flying back to the United States toward what he ambiguously "believed to be a new beginning." For Major, then, as O'Brien notes, "the self is created by and emerges as the product of an imagination that can give it meaning and direction through language."[73]

Unquestionably, the most radically experimental and aesthetically postmodern of Major's eight novels are *Reflex and Bone Structure* and *Emergency Exit.* A composite of everything from a catalog of names from a telephone directory and police report to informational graphics and reproductions of abstract paintings, including a picture of the author in a cow pasture, *Emergency Exit* is a dazzling experiment in collage or montage writing. Major introduces us to the black Ingraham family and their largely white liberal neighbors in Inlet, Connecticut, through an elaborately extended metaphor—the juxtaposing and rapid succession of disparate fragments and images whose principal recurring motif is a doorway—which stresses, as the narrator states, that the ultimate *thingness* of our lives operates as a sort of *extended* metaphor.[74]

Less self-indulgent and more satisfying to the average reader's search for a sense of order is *Reflex and Bone Structure.* Divided into two melodramatically titled parts, "A Bad Connection" and "Body Heat," it is a metafictional mystery novel in what two critics call the antidetective tradition.[75] Major's narrator-protagonist is a fiction writer who discusses the process of constructing a mystery novel while he is simultaneously involved as suspect and detective in a murder mystery. "I want this book to be anything it wants to be," the narrator-protagonist tells us near the end of the first part of the novel, suggesting a close relationship between his aesthetic ideas and those of the implied author. "I want the mystery of the book to be an absolute mystery."[76] Earlier, Cora Hull, a black Greenwich Village actress who is involved in a love quadrangle that results in her murder, tells the nameless narrator-protagonist, "This book you're writing isn't nearly as strange as reality. The only way you're going to make any sense is to stick with the impossible. Any resemblance to the past or present should be purely accidental" (p. 56). From the opening page of the murder mystery, when scattered pieces of bodies are found, to its resolution on the final page when the narrator-protagonist identifies the bodies and himself as the murderer in a burst of short, staccato statements, we are witnesses to and participants in the creative authenticity and authority of Major's fabulation and postmodern linguistic collage.

As the characters are developed in fragments, we are constantly reminded by the narrator-protagonist that he is the self-conscious creator of this murder mystery and that he is "extending reality, not retelling it" (p. 49). In addition to the elusive, promiscuous Cora, who "needs variety, still a child at heart, still dreaming of the prince who won't ever come" (p. 39), and the enigmatic narrator-protagonist, who is not only a writer and a suspect in the murder but also a detective paradoxically "trying to solve a murder. No, not a murder. It's a life" (p. 32), the other characters involved in the love quadrangle are Canada Jackson and Dale. Canada collects guns, seeks to improve the world, and "invents and reinvents the world as he wishes it to be." Because he "sometimes . . . can even handle Canada from the inside out" (p. 31), the narrator-protagonist feels emotionally and psychologically close to him. However, he hates Dale, whom he only vaguely delineates and jealously blows to bits because of his intimacy with Cora: "The fact that Dale really has little or no character doesn't help matters. I cannot help him if he refuses to focus. How can I be blamed for his lack of seriousness. And it isn't that he doesn't talk to me. He talks too much to me, really, and he plots too much, has too many secrets, leaves nothing in the open. Whatever it was about him that attracted Cora shall always remain a mystery to me" (p. 42). Like the protagonist, we are challenged to either solve the mystery of the novel or accept it.

Unlike the structure of traditional detective novels, however, in which the solution of the murder is gradually achieved through the discovery of clues and the construction of a logical, lucid case against a single suspect, *Reflex and Bone Structure* is self-consciously fragmented, bizarre, and ambiguous. Parodying the traditional form of the detective novel and extending its possibilities, Major, like his narrator, is primarily concerned with comparing and contrasting the difficult if not impossible task of the contemporary novelist and the detective in constructing a meaningful sense of self and others, both private and public, out of fragments of an irrational world. As critics McCaffery and Gregory state, "the detective and the antidetective . . . seek different answers which suggest the differing epistemological assumptions of the ages in which they were produced: One looks to eliminate the temporary description of an ordered universe, the other for an arbitrary fictional pattern that will not explain away mystery but will enable him to live with it."[77] The aesthetic bond between Major and his narrator-protagonist is apparent in the experimental style and form of the narrative as well as in the explicit internal references to the title of this novel and to the protagonists of Major's first two novels.

In *Reflex and Bone Structure* Major breaks away from the black detective tradition of Rudolph Fisher and Chester Himes, and in each of his novels he does something new with language and form. Although Ralph Ellison's influence can be seen in the depiction of Moses Westby in *NO* and the nameless narrator-protagonist in *Reflex and Bone Structure,* Major, like Demby in *The Catacombs,* is more clearly influenced by the Euro-American postmodernist approach to writing than other contemporary black American novelists. Rejecting social realism and "militant fictionists," he states, with more disdain and dogmatism than understanding and tolerance, that "the deliberate effort, propaganda, has never helped anyone toward a larger sense of self. It has always been the novel or poem that begins from and spreads all across the entire human experience that ends liberating minds."[78] In defense of his own novels, he argues in "Formula or Freedom" that "the novel *not* deliberately aimed at bringing about human freedom for black people has liberated as many minds as has the propaganda tract, if not more. This does not mean that a wholly human novel by a black writer necessarily becomes assimilable for just anybody. It does mean, though, that a work that takes long root in its author's experience—race being a part of that experience—not only makes sense anywhere in any language but also is likely either to raise hell or to lower heaven."[79] In other words, Major correctly perceives that he and other black novelists who are committed to modernism and postmodernism can at least depend for support on a small, select readership. This readership does not, however, include many blacks, for whom neither the self nor life can be meaningfully or satisfactorily reduced to the blissful, liberating linguistic constructs of structuralist and poststructuralist theory that are advanced in books like Roland Barthes's *Pleasure of the Text.* Many white readers, as Frank Kermode suggests in *The Sense of an Ending,* also "find that there is an irreducible minimum of geometry—of humanly needed shape or structure—which finally limits our ability to accept the mimesis of pure contingency."[80] Nevertheless, judged on their own terms, Major's novels, except the post-1983 neorealistic *Such Was the Season, Painted Turtle: Woman with Guitar,* and *Dirty Bird Blues,* extend the experimental tradition of the African American novel by their subordination of race to a phenomenological exploration of sex and language as a ritualistic rebirth and affirmation of self.

Although Major's three post-1983 novels are more linear in plot and less metafictional, they continue his African Americentric experiments with liberating silenced voices and transgressing narrative boundaries. This is most apparent in his bold assumption of the consciousness and voices of a Navajo guitar player and folksinger in *Painted Turtle,* of a black Southern matriarch in *Such Was the Season,* and of blues singers in *Dirty Bird Blues.* Although more conventional and accessible on the surface for readers than his other novels, *Such Was the Season* is actually an exploration on its lower frequencies of the double consciousness of the implied author and of Dr. Adam North, the estranged nephew whom the narrator/protagonist calls Juneboy, as both return to their Southern black vernacular roots. Rather than expressing uncritical sympathy for his characters, especially Annie Eliza Sommer-Hicks, the black matriarchal narrator-protagonist, Major's voice is characterized by social and cultural ambivalence. Annie Eliza is centered in her racial, ethnic, and regional vernacular culture, but the implied author and Juneboy are respectfully ambivalent about her beliefs, values, and behavior. For example, she is a septuagenarian whose own double consciousness is apparent in her ambivalent reference to Renee, her materialistic daughter-in-law, as a "nigger," in her feeling like a "pickaninny" in the company of some whites, in her confession of telling a "pickaninny" joke to her favorite white employer, and in her disapproval of interracial romance even on television, which she watches compulsively. The illusory character of reality and the reality of illusoriness are dramatized and symbolized by the manner in which television informs Annie Eliza's consciousness and language. The rhythms of her everyday life, like the rhythms of her black vernacular speech, are punctuated by the integration of the technology of television with the traditional morality—the passions, prejudices, and pride—of hard-working, church-going, home-owning lower-middle-class Southern Negro housewives of the 1940s and 1950s. These women helped to support their families by ironing, washing, and cleaning for white folks. Her vibrant, idiomatic dialect illuminates her uncolleged, opinionated, pragmatic, politically conservative character. Thus Major's attempt to reconcile the tensions of African American double consciousness by the subordination of social truth and power for blacks to the expressionistic truth and freedom of the artist also extends the experimental branches of the African American novel.

Fabulation and Satire

Drawing on their sense of the profound ironies and blueslike absurdity of the 1960s and 1970s, some contemporary black novelists, including Charles Wright, Hal Bennett, and Ishmael Reed, employ distinctive combinations of fabulation and satire to spread the news of their tragicomic visions of our times. They have not completely lost faith in the power of satire and laughter as therapy for the ills of the world, but more like George Schuyler and Wallace Thurman than Rudolph Fisher during the Harlem Renaissance, they are much more irreverent, ambivalent, and sardonic about the hypocrisy of Western civilization, Christian orthodoxy, American principles, and black unity.

CHARLES STEVENSON WRIGHT (1932–)

A Southwestern country boy, Charles Wright was born on June 4, 1932, in New Franklin, Missouri, and raised in Sedalia by his grandparents after his mother's death in 1936. An avid reader, he was a regular at the Sedalia Public Library and as a teenager began hitchhiking on weekends to St. Louis and Kansas City to the movies, museums, and libraries. He started writing short pieces in high school, using Hemingway as his model, and for the newspaper *Kansas City Call.* Drafted into the army shortly after his nineteenth birthday, he served a year in this country and a year in Korea. After his discharge in 1956, he settled in St. Louis to write and, like the protagonist in his autobiographical first novel, soon became "the darling of a heterogeneous group of the arty and the literary."[81] Wright's racial wounds, urge to travel, and profound sense of loss plunged him into the bowels of New York life in 1957. He lived in the Bowery and Greenwich

Village while working as a messenger, waiter, dishwasher, and writer. From 1967 to 1973 he wrote a column, "Wright's World," in the *Village Voice.* His publications include two books of poetry, a collection of his journalistic pieces, which are as surreal and ironic as his fiction, and two novels: *The Messenger* (1963) and *The Wig* (1966).

Although he dedicates *The Messenger* to Richard Wright, frequently alludes to other modern novelists in his books, and confesses to having been impressed by Katherine Ann Porter's offbeat style when he was younger, Wright names only Hemingway and Mailer as influences on his writing. Internal evidence in the novels, however, suggests wider influences, including the blues and jazz traditions. As for whether he prefers fantasy or realism, Wright says, "I don't think that one is better than the other. It's whatever suits your purpose."[82] He is disappointed though that most readers of *The Wig* either did not understand or did not appreciate his modernist experiment with fabulation, comedy, and satire.

The Messenger is a picaresque novel which chronicles the desperation and amorality of the protagonist's life in New York's East Village and the nostalgic memories of his ostensibly peaceful youth in a small town in Missouri. In contrast, *The Wig* is a modern fable whose nonconventional, episodic plot satirizes American racial and cultural myths that delude the protagonist into believing at the beginning of the narrative that a good head of hair is the key to success ("'The Wig is gonna see me through these troubled times'")[83] and at the end, that his submission to sterilization will save the nation ("'Having children is the greatest sin in this country . . .'" p. 179). Whereas *The Messenger* overwhelms us with the blues feeling that many if not "most men and women suffer unbearably" (p. 169), *The Wig* is an ironic reflection of the American belief that "'Everybody's got *something* working for them'" (p. 19).

In spite of these differences, the two novels are similar in several respects. Both are set in New York; both have rogues for protagonists; both are told in the first person; both are episodic in structure; both are wry in tone; and both showcase a variety of street people and eccentrics. Excluding the protagonists, the most sympathetically drawn of these characters are Ruby Stonewall and The Deb. Ruby is the "played-out," blues-singing cousin of Charles Stevenson, the beatnik protagonist in *The Messenger;* her blackness teaches her the humility and compassion she tries to pass on to him. The Deb is the prostitute with short, kinky hair in *The Wig,* whom Lester Jefferson, the protagonist, loves and pursues as "an all-American girl"; her death results in Lester's loss of his curls and his manhood. Several of the characters in *The Messenger* bear striking similarities to those in *The Wig*. For example, Mrs. Lee, "an aging, ageless coquette" who has an insatiable appetite for Puerto Rican gigolos in *The Messenger,* seems to reappear in *The Wig* as Nonnie Swift, a degenerate old Southern belle who wants her baby of unknown racial identity to be born in the "unchained slavery" of Harlem. Claudia the Grand Duchess, "a fabulous Negro drag queen" and friend of the protagonist in *The Messenger*, is almost the twin of Miss Sandra Hanover, the Crown Princess, a black homosexual with plucked eyebrows, Chinese-style bangs, and two-inch fake-gold fingernails who in *The Wig* fantasizes about being old movie queens. In short, both novels are first-person narratives whose amoral protagonists take us on a tour of the underground culture and surreal lives of New Yorkers for whom everyday reality and the American Dream are both nightmares.

In comparing the protagonists in the two novels, we discover that Charles Stevenson, a messenger, writer, and beatnik, is the more sympathetically drawn, but Lester Jefferson, an employed blind pursuer of the American Dream, is the more tragic. Living from day to day in quiet desperation on pot, pills, alcohol, and jazz, Charles, as his memories of his grandparents and his friendships with the neighborhood drug addicts, prostitutes, and homosexuals reveal, is a sensitive, aware individual. He "knew and understood loss and loneliness" (p. 68) and could not "don a mask and suck the c——of that sweet secure bitch, middle-class American life" (p. 95). Because the author neither undercuts his narrator nor offers an alternative set of values to those he embraces, we sense no significant racial, political, or moral distance between the two. "They make me an outsider," the apparently reliable narrator says, "A minority within a minority. They called me a dago as a child, before my curls turned to kinks. That sun again! But these kinks form my proud crown. Negro, Negroid, Nigger. Black, brown, and beige. Yellow, shit-colored. Buck, boy. I am the result of generations of bastard Anglo-Saxon, African, Black-creek, and Choctaw Indian blood. Me, the last of the Negro, southwestern, Missouri Stevensons" (p. 144). Semiautobiographical passages such as this reinforce the fictional nature of reality and the reality of fiction.

Less reliable as a narrator is the protagonist of *The Wig*, Lester Jefferson. As "a minority within a minority" he is racially close to Charles and the author, but his norms are radically different from theirs. A twenty-one-year-old, "slightly schizophrenic" Harlemite, he sees himself as "Walter Mitty's target-colored stepson," has faith in the American Dream, and is convinced that processed hair, The Wig,[84] will be his "acquisitional gimmick" for success. As we accompany him on his quest, we are fascinated by Wright's satirical treatment of the thin line between fantasy and reality in American life, ranging from the Uncle Tom masks and gimmicks for making-it used by movie and rock-and-roll stars to the protagonist's battle with rats in a roach-and-rat-infested Harlem apartment. In contrast to the protagonist in *The Messenger*, Lester takes an optimistic, long-range view of life: "I touched The Wig. Yes. Security had always eluded me, but it wouldn't much longer. American until the last breath, a true believer in the Great Society, I'd turn the other cheek, cheat, steal, take the fifth amendment, walk bare-assed up Mr. Jones's ladder, and state firmly that I was too human" (p. 53). Through verbal and situational irony such as this and the chicken man episode, however, Wright repeatedly and wryly undercuts Lester's desperate yet futile attempts to make his "butterscotch-colored dreams" of success, love, and happiness a social reality. "How many people are willing to crawl on their hands and knees, ten hours a day, five and a half days a week?" Lester asks. "For me that was not difficult: I was dreaming, not of a white Christmas, I was dreaming of becoming part of The Great Society" (pp. 140–41). Even after "the necrophilic funeral director," Mr. Fishback, cuts off Lester's hair and sterilizes him, he remains an incorrigible, pathetic optimist, saying with a smile at the end of the novel, " 'I'm beginning to feel better already' " (p. 179).

Wright's novels are a unique blend of satire and ethically controlled fantasy, with *The Messenger* as the more realistic and *The Wig* as the more fantastic. Some white reviewers and critics consider the blend of satire and fantasy in the novels black humor; one reviewer of *The Wig* even proclaimed Wright "the first certified black humorist."[85] Another considers his method phenomenological. Commenting on his bold imagination and bizarre language, Charles Wright states, "I don't know; it's like when everybody is getting *on* a train, I'm going the opposite way."[86] The difficulty in classifying his major structural and stylistic blend of African Americentric fabulation, comedy, and satire is largely due to the wide range of influences on his texts. In addition to Hemingway and Mailer, it is apparent that he draws more on a black modernist than postmodernist interweaving of the picaresque tradition, surrealistic painting, and pop culture in projecting his tragicomic vision of the outsiders in contemporary urban America. His delight in combining the bizarre with the commonplace, illuminating the more surreal, off-beat aspects of bohemian life in Greenwich Village, and experimenting with a blend of the static character, loose structure, and satire of the picaresque tradition with the soulful, self-affirming, inward quest of the blues tradition are his most distinctive contributions to the contemporary African American novel.

[GEORGE HAROLD] HAL BENNETT (1930–)

George Harold Bennett was born on April 21, 1930, in Buckingham, Virginia. Raised and educated in and around Newark, New Jersey, he sold his first story when he was fifteen. His pursuit of a writing career was briefly interrupted by a tour of duty in the air force during the Korean War. After his discharge, he worked as fiction editor from 1953 to 1955 for several African American newspapers. He then moved to Mexico, where he attended Mexico City College and became a fellow of the Centro Mexicano de Escritores. He also won a fellowship in 1966 for *A Wilderness of Vines*, his first novel, to the Bread Loaf Writers' Conference. Called "one of the most original and gifted Black satirists to come along since Wallace Thurman,"[87] he published between 1966 and 1983 four additional novels: *The Black Wine* (1968), *Lord of Dark Places* (1970), *Wait until Evening* (1974), and *Seventh Heaven* (1976).

Employing Christian symbolism and revealing the influence of Faulkner, each of these novels is more irreverent, obscene, and iconoclastic than its predecessor in its satirical demythicizing of American innocence and its black modernist construction of a radically new eschatology. In *A Wilderness of Vines,* about which more will be said below, Bennett introduces us to the racial madness of the pre–World War II black community of Burnside, Virginia, a snake-infested paradise where color prejudice is elevated to a religion, social hypocrisy glorified in the ritual of the Christian tableau, and sex, which is linked to death, celebrated as both the damnation and salvation of its light-skinned and dark-skinned residents. In the more loosely structured *Black Wine,* those who escape the perverted Eden of Burnside, whose social order is in the throes of changing from a color aristocracy to a growing class of chicken raisers, extend the legacy of racial insanity to Decatur, the black community of Cousinsville, New Jersey. There David Hunter, the preadolescent protagonist, is baptized in the primal passion of racial hatred and learns that "life is the dregs, love is the dance. And the wine, the Negro wine? Well, that was a special something, a kind of powerful determination not to die, a kind of hallelujah in the spirit that kept you more or less alive and on an even keel. . . ."[88] Set in Burnside and Cousinsville, *Lord of Dark Places,* the most outrageously profane and morally ambiguous postmodern of the five novels, is a scatological attack on what one critic calls "the phallic myth, the original American folk drama in which the white female virgin and bitch goddess and the Black male as defiler and nigger stud are the two central figures."[89]

As Bennett continues to develop his elaborate modernist personal mythology and postmodern parody of the biblical myths of innocence, carnality, and color in *Wait until Evening* and *Seventh Heaven,* which span the years 1944–71 and 1967–74 respectively, we are once again moved back and forth in time and place between Virginia and New Jersey. Kevin Brittain, the mature black protagonist of *Wait until Evening,* looks back twenty-five years on how he came to embrace the racial and sexual madness of the Reverend Winston Cobb, a recurring symbol of insanity in each novel, and of his Grandma Cora Brittain, who had learned from a witch "how to be as evil and as cunning as white men." Both Cobb and Grandma Brittain have killed black people who threatened or irritated them. *"Isn't the black man who does violence a black hero—a Big Nigger—because he dares to imitate the tactics of the enemy?"* Kevin asks himself during the trial for murder at the end of the novel. "Isn't murder the holiest undertaking for people who have no other way to esteem themselves?" Although Kevin was responsible for the deaths of his brother and father, he was innocent of killing Janet Magee, the crippled white sister of Cop Magee. But the Newark cop was driven by the obsession that Kevin was the "Big Nigger" who killed his sister. Inspired by his grandmother's confession to him that she was responsible for Janet Magee's death and convinced that there were millions of whites like Magee who wanted simultaneously to love and destroy blacks, the protagonist concludes after his case is dismissed that "I had cut my teeth on the dead bodies of my own kin. Now it was time to turn my talents toward *them*."[90]

Despite the apparent authenticity and authority of Bennett's attempt to encourage sympathy for Kevin by filtering the events through his consciousness as a first-person narrator, many readers will still find themselves morally and politically offended by this and Bennett's other novels because of the implied author's moral ambiguity, the narrators' unreliability, and the characters' grotesqueness. But for Bennett, the inversion of traditional color and religious iconography captures the truth of the perversion of contemporary American life and the truth of his vision of the ultimate destiny of black people, American society, and the world. Thus, the Cousinsville, New Jersey, housing project in *Seventh Heaven*, known ironically by its black, Puerto Rican, and Italian residents as Seventh Heaven, breeds desperate men and women. In their desperation they will do anything to survive the obscene American nightmare, including "toying with numbers, shooting drugs, killing each other, and blaming every good or evil act on a colorful magic known as mojo, the juju, the evil eye, la brujeriá, or the United States government, depending on who does the evaluation."[91] Like the modernist perversions of Faulkner's Yoknapatawpha County, the madness of Alcanthia County symbolizes the madness of America and the world.

The authenticity, authority, and agency of Bennett's eschatological vision are most lucidly and strongly expressed in the narrative voice, characterization, structure, and symbolism of *A Wilderness of Vines*. The third-person omniscient, disembodied narrator gives historical and philosophical expansiveness to the significance of the 1930s plantation community of Burnside, Virginia, where the masters are the light-complexioned descendants of antebellum house servants and the modern-day servants are the dark-complexioned descendants of field hands. "Trapped inside a wilderness where only the vines really prospered, and time was said to stand still underneath the talons of the hunter, the people of Burnside, Virginia, in that summer of 1939 exemplified the people of the world."[92] The narrative voice is also freighted with verbal and situational irony as it contrasts the orphanage for dark-skinned girls with that for light-skinned girls. The former, where the girls are taught domestic work, is called "Preacher's Exchange since so many of these good men have tried to insert the Holy Ghost into the black girls, to introduce them to God." The latter, where the girls "are spared this encroachment of the church," is a finishing school for mulatto child brides, providing "enough education to make them harmless, intelligent-appearing listeners" and "good daughters to primarily tobacco farmers" (pp. 9–10). The central characters in Bennett's tragicomic myth of death, judgment, heaven, and hell are Neva Stapleton Manning, a light-complexioned fallen Eve, Charlie Hooker, her black farmhand and redeemer, and Ida Carlisle, "the high priestess" of the light-complexioned faithful former slaves who worshipped and imitated their antebellum masters.

Although the nonlinear narrative opens with Neva, the protagonist, in the metaphorical Edenic garden of the Burnside orphanage during the summer of 1920, and although it focuses primarily on the summer of 1939, foreshadowing the apocalypse of World War II, it flashes back to the Middle Passage of the slave trade as the probable beginning of the color insanity and social unreality of Burnside. It then projects forward to the "larger and more malicious insanity" of Nazism and the war in Europe. Thematically, the plot centers on the sexual repression, spiritual death, and redemption of Neva, the child bride who fears the pain of male domination. Her anxiety is traced back to having witnessed the rape of her mother by a black lover and the violence of a stallion pawing a mare's mattress-covered flanks during coitus. She also suffers guilt about her sexuality because of the catechism of respectability imposed on her by the imperious old man she married. "Being woman," she wondered, "could she also be stallion and vine at the same time, servant and master twined into one?" (p. 24). Throughout the novel sex is metaphorically associated with death and vitality, dark-skinned people with sex and snakes, and vines with entrapment, decay, destruction, and death.

After Neva gives birth to Gene Manning and her dreams of the death of her husband come true when he is trampled by a white mare, she fulfills her fantasies about ravishing a sleeping man with Charlie Hooker. Charlie not only provides Neva's secret release from sexual inhibition but also represents Bennett's symbolic Christ figure and the moral center of the novel. Before being ravished by Neva while he is semiconscious from an accident with a mare, he feverishly cries out to her, "I am the Resurrection and the life. . . . Come unto me all who labor . . ." (p. 151). Compelled by Neva to silence about this episode, Charlie is convinced that "Neva would have to forget respectability and lose her fear of madness before she could become a real woman. . . . As long as she could not admit the truth to him, he could not preach truth to the world" (p. 231). The truth and its source are buried in Charlie's past.

Before he came to Burnside, Charlie's experiences on oil ships, in cotton fields, and at camp meetings had baptized him in the truth of American racism and insanity. If the white man's sin was slavery and his burden, the freed slave, then the black man's "sin was *accepting* slavery; his burden, to demonstrate that he is not a mule, but a man. White had nothing to do with sex. . . . Being a man wasn't all bluster and bellyfugging. It was . . . Feelings. And fire. Fire that no water made can put out" (pp. 139–40). Charlie's marriage to a Jehovah's Witness dramatizes the ironic instability of this truth. While they traveled to sell *Watchtower* magazines to poor Alabamans who could not read, she encouraged him to believe that he was a kind of Black Messiah:

> But then, the more he saw of Alabama—God, sometimes he could cry, those poor bastards with all the life almost squeezed out of them!—and the more he saw, the less he loved Lillie, the less he witnessed for the Lord, he came to believe it was all somehow a brazen lie, it took a lot of lying to yourself to keep on witnessing for the Lord when you found out that He wasn't witnessing for you. And Lillie, in her pretty print dresses, clean as a white woman, was only interested in the three cents for that magazine, not in you or them or God or anybody else but Lillie. (P. 141)

By signifying on the authority and agency of the Bible and Christianity, Bennett challenges readers to consider that because of generations of moral hypocrisy, madness is the psychological norm in contemporary America.

Charlie Hooker's mission, then, is to tell the world about Burnside, to go out and preach the gospel. In preparation for this mission he must purge himself of sin and pledge himself to honesty. "Honest thought, honest action, honest feeling," on one hand, and "The World. America. The Negro" on the other, were his Trinity (p. 216). Charlie wavers in his mission, however, when he discovers that Neva, by confessing their sexual intimacy to her son, has found a more important religion than his own. She had overcome her fear of life, he realizes, whereas "his religion would only talk about the possibility of truth" (p. 276). So his departure by bus for Birmingham to tell people about "understanding" is ambiguous.

Equally ambiguous and more modern than postmodern in challenging metaphysical and social truths is Neva's symbolic rebirth after her sexual repression and spiritual death, confessing to the Reverend Cobb her complicity in her husband's death and leaving Burnside in a heavily painted face and a sexually provocative dress it had taken her ten years to make. Does the implied author agree with Charlie's belief that "only the frustrated are respectable and sane—ladies and virgins and weeping mothers with rape in their hearts? All real women are mad; men require this healthy madness in them" (p. 231). Or does he agree with the conclusions of white Dr. Stanhope, whose participation in the absurd baby vaccination ritual sponsored by Ida Carlisle and in the murder hearing that exposes her madness, moves him to ask himself whether it is true "'that the human soul is callous and warlike by nature, that madness is the animal thing in us which love tries to conquer?'" Stanhope concludes "'that the answer to the problems of Burnside—indeed, of all the world, black and white—lay in the slow conversion of the human heart and mind'" (p. 314). For some readers, as one critic argues, what Bennett gives us in *A Wilderness of Vines is* "the stuff of racial stereotype at that point where stereotype is transformed into archetype."[93] Many African American readers will find the mixture of black modernism and postmodernism morally and politically disturbing.

Bennett's novels thus develop a frequently disturbing, occasionally offensive eschatology that derives its satirical power and symbolic meaning from the experiences, especially the double consciousness, of black Americans. On one hand, his novels are in the satirical tradition of George Schuyler and Wallace Thurman with their caustic criticism of intraracial prejudice and violence. On the other, they are in the modern tradition of William Faulkner, Richard Wright, Ralph Ellison, and James Baldwin. *A Wilderness of Vines,* for example, outlines the mythical Alcanthia County and peoples the town of Burnside, Virginia, with grotesque family lineages like the light-skinned Carlisles and the black-skinned Bartleys to introduce us to America's original sin and eternal burden. The truth and reality of this master narrative and microcosm of the world's rituals of racial and sexual death and rebirth are then deconstructed and destabilized. Blurring the distinction between heaven and hell, *A Wilderness of Vines, The Black Wine, Lord of Dark Places, Wait until Evening,* and *Seventh Heaven* move us from South to North and from the Civil War to the Vietnam War in tracing the search of successive generations of blacks for some place to be somebody and in telling the "good news" of a new coming of Christ in apocalyptic, sardonic, scatological terms. Like Richard Wright, Bennett seems to be primarily and paradoxically concerned with transforming the stereotype of the Big "Bad" Nigger into a modern archetypal Everyman. Like Ralph Ellison and James Baldwin he uses Christian mythology, ritual, and symbolism, although outrageously inverting and parodying them, to structure his personal vision of the world and to affirm the individual's responsibility for constructing his own salvation. In short, Hal Bennett's unique contribution to the tradition of the African American novel is a highly eclectic, irreverent satirical style and scatological mythology of black American color prejudice, sexuality, and messianic hope.

ISHMAEL REED (1938–)

Ishmael Reed is not only one of the nation's most gifted and controversial innovative artists but also one of the leading promoters of multiculturalism as well as of black modernist and postmodernist writing. Born Ishmael Humphrey on February 22, 1938, in Chattanooga, Tennessee, to Henry Lenoir (a YMCA fundraiser) and Thelma Coleman (a salesperson), he moved in 1942 with his mother and stepfather, Bennie Stephen Reed (an auto worker), to Buffalo, New York, where he was raised and educated. Adopting his stepfather's surname, he began writing stories in the second grade, was commissioned to write a birthday poem at the age of fourteen, baffled high school officials with a bizarre satire of the English teacher who hassled him about malapropisms before his graduation in 1956, and wrote a black existential story that made him a celebrity in his English classes at the University of Buffalo. Dropping out of college in 1960 because, among other things, he "just didn't want to be a slave to somebody else's reading lists," he continued experimenting along the lines of writers like Nathanael West, whose style, especially in *The Dream Life of Balso Snell,* began influencing him in high school.[94] Also in 1960, Reed married Priscilla Rose and fathered a daughter, Timothy Bret Reed. From 1960 to 1962 he acquired writing discipline while working as a staff correspondent for the *Empire State Weekly.* Moving with his wife and daughter to New York City in 1962 to become a writer, he wrote visionary poetry like W. B. Yeats until he began hanging out on the Lower East Side with a group of black writers in the *Umbra* Workshop, whose members, including Tom Dent, Calvin Hernton, and David Henderson, he claims "anticipated all of the black cultural directions that were to develop a few years later."[95]

In 1965 Reed founded the community newspaper *Advance* in Newark, New Jersey, publishing original material by many young writers, including some *Umbra* poets. Seeking to destroy the myth "that African American or Black Writing is conformist, monolithic, and dictated by a Committee" and to demonstrate that the new generation of African American writers "will not be consigned to the cultural slaves' quarters as were our geniuses of the past," his anthology *19 Necromancers from Now* showcases the originality and diversity of the contemporary African American novel. In the late 1960s Reed moved to the San Francisco Bay area, divorced his first wife in 1970, married Carla Blank, a modern dancer, and fathered a second daughter, Maria Tennessee. In 1972–73, as principal founder of Yardbird Publishing Company and Reed, Cannon and Johnson Communications, he institutionalized his commitment to promoting artistic freedom and multicultural experimental writing. This broadening of his ethnic and artistic interests probably began in 1967 when he moved to Berkeley to write a Western, but instead became embroiled in the issues of artistic and academic freedom concerning his teaching black studies at Merritt College and the University of California at Berkeley. The unconscious racism of students who would dictate to a black instructor the authors, works, and viewpoint that should be stressed in his course, says Reed,

> is sometimes as rigid as that of their elders. After all, in this country art is what White people do. All other people are "propagandists." One can see this in the methodology used by certain White and Black critics in investigating Black literature. Form, Technique, Symbology, Imagery are rarely investigated with the same care as Argument, and even here, the Argument must be one that appeals to critics' prejudices. Novels that don't have the right "message" are cast aside as "pretentious," for it is assumed that the native who goes the way of art is "uppity."[96]

Uppity, pretentious, pompous, sexist, and sophomoric are the most frequent if not the kindest names hurled by unsympathetic critics at Reed for the Neo-HooDoo aesthetic he develops between 1967 and 2001 in his five books of verse, five anthologies, four collections of essays, four plays, and nine novels.[97]

At the heart of Reed's Neo-HooDoo aesthetic, which is largely constructed from residual elements of syncretistic African religions (Vodun, Pocomania, Candomblé, Macumba, and HooDoo) in the Caribbean and the Americas, especially Haiti, Brazil, and the United States, is a belief in the power of the unknown, particularly as expressed in artistic freedom and originality. In the essay "HooDoo Manifesto #2" Reed tells us that as a modified version of African forms of belief and ritual in the United States and South America, Hoodoo "is multicultural and multiracial; half of its traditional believers in the United States have been European-Americans and in Brazil some European-Americans run temples."[98] In the prose-poem "Neo-HooDoo Manifesto" he tells us that "Neo-HooDoo is a Lost American Church updated," that "Neo-HooDoo borrows from Haiti Africa and South America. Neo-HooDoo comes in all styles and moods," and that "Neo-HooDoo believes that every man is an artist and every artist a priest."[99] An incredibly eclectic mixture of ancient and contemporary techniques and forms of non-Western and Western cultures, Reed's nine novels—*The Free-Lance Pallbearers* (1967), *Yellow Back Radio Broke-Down* (1969), *Mumbo Jumbo* (1972), *The Last Days of Louisiana Red* (1974), *Flight to Canada* (1976), *The Terrible Twos* (1982), *Reckless Eyeballing* (1986), *The Terrible Threes* (1989), and *Japanese by Spring* (1993)—challenge the reader to be as culturally egalitarian and imaginatively bold as the author. His many honors and awards include a Pulitzer Prize nomination for poetry in 1973, being a National Book Award finalist for fiction and poetry in 1973, and receiving the prestigious MacArthur Fellowship in 1998.

As expressionistic satire, Reed's first novel, *The Free-Lance Pallbearers*, attacks the tragic absurdity of the complicity of black nationalists and the black middle class in the political, academic, religious, and artistic bossism, opportunism, hypocrisy, and corruption in Newark, New Jersey. Its narrator-protagonist, Bukka Doopyduk, is a signifying black college drop-out, Nazarene-apprentice-turned-revolutionary-leader who is fatally and ironically betrayed by those whom he seeks to save and rule. *The Last Days of Louisiana Red*, Reed's fourth novel, is a highly innovative West Coast thriller starring PaPa LaBas, the HooDoo detective introduced in *Mumbo Jumbo*. It draws on Greek drama, old newspapers, vaudeville, radio, film, and TV scripts to cast its spell on readers. But the dynamics of black history and culture, especially the heroine of Cab Calloway's song "Minnie the Moocher," are the keys to the mystery of Louisiana Red, symbolic of the complicity of black Americans in their own oppression and death, which is traced back to the legendary deadly conflict between the queen and king of HooDoo, Marie Laveau and Doctor John. *Flight to Canada*, his fifth novel, is an intriguing parody of the slave narrative and *Uncle Tom's Cabin*, as well as a demythicizing, irreverent satire on Abraham Lincoln, Southern culture, and Canada. Interweaving fact with fiction to illustrate that historical truth is as bizarre as imaginative truth, Reed traces the journey of Raven Quicksill—the fugitive slave, narrator-writer—from slavery in Virginia to freedom in Canada: "whether Canada was exile, death, art, liberation or a woman. Each man to his own Canada."[100]

In *The Terrible Twos,* Reed employs the sign of the fantasy world of national leaders in the 1980s who act like two-year-old children to satirize the scandalous manipulation of a gullible, racist electorate by the neoconservative economic policies and racial politics of the wealthy white supporters and unscrupulous government officials of President Dean Clift, a former fashion model and transparent representation of President Reagan. Their grand genocidal conspiracy, "Operation Two Birds," popularly known as the Terrible Twos, is to get rid of surplus people, especially nonwhite people in America and in the African nation that the CIA inaccurately reports has nuclear weapons. The conspiracy and schemes of the Scrooges of corporate America to monopolize Christmas are frustrated only by the bold resistance of Saint Nicholas (Santa Claus), Black Peter (his servant), and the Nicolaites (the followers of Saint Nicholas). *Reckless Eyeballing,* the first of Reed's three post-1983 novels and probably his most controversial novel, is a fiercely sardonic satirical allegory of the actual lynching of Emmett Till, a young black boy from Chicago who was murdered in 1955 in Mississippi for allegedly looking and whistling at a white woman, and of the psychological, spiritual, and cultural lynching of opportunistic middle-class blacks, like the Jamaican playwright Ian Ball and the feminist playwright Tremonisha Smarts, who sell their souls for assimilation into American society. Reed bitterly satirizes the complicity of many blacks, especially Tremonisha, a thinly veiled representation of Alice Walker, in perpetuating the stereotypes and scapegoating of black men in the United States as potential sexual predators and violent criminals.

As its preface reveals, *The Terrible Threes* is a 1990s sequel to *The Terrible Twos* in which the discovery by a Haitian maid of the late Admiral Matthews's letter confessing the conspiracy of the Terrible Twos "to nuke the cities with huge surplus populations, blame it on Nigeria, and then nuke Nigeria"[101] triggers the fear and schemes of the main characters to cover up the failed racial, economic, and political conspiracy in the first novel. But the schemes are unsuccessful in preventing the maid from having the confessional letter published on the front page of the *Washington Sun* on Christmas day. Set during the 1990s cultural and educational wars of the multicultural California university system, *Japanese by Spring* is a sardonic political allegory and bittersweet satire of American cultural and linguistic arrogance, jingoism, opportunism, and neoconservatism. Benjamin "Chappie" Puttbutt III, the opportunistic black educator who aligns himself with whatever movement is in vogue, and Professor Crabtree, the traditionalist Miltonian, become neophyte multiculturalists during their self-serving participation in the take-over of Jack London ("the apostle of Anglo-Saxon superiority") College by Japanese investors and Dr. Yamoto, who rename and reorganize the college according to Japanese cultural standards. "For years, we've been saying that our tradition and our standards were universal," the converted Yoruba-speaking Crabtree confesses, "but Dr. Yamoto has taught us that two can play that game."[102]

Reed's most carefully researched, innovative, and fascinating satires are *Yellow Back Radio Broke-Down* and *Mumbo Jumbo.* The erudition and innovation of *Yellow Back Radio Broke-Down* are most fascinatingly displayed in the multileveled, discontinuous, episodic time structure Reed employs to roam at will through history, parodying popular Westerns, satirizing "Tsars, Monarchs, and their deadly and insidious flunkies," and demythologizing the American cowboy and frontier. On one level, as the title of the novel suggests, Reed draws on the once popular nineteenth-century "lurid sensational yellow kivered books" produced mainly by Eastern dudes for Western frontiersmen.[103] On another level, he has adapted the modern black oral toast to create a black cowboy tall tale: a long, oral narrative of the amazing supernatural feats of an amoral bad man. Its characters are nonrealistic types and caricatures; its language colorful, occasionally obscene, slangy, and hyperbolic; and its techniques borrowed from the black oral tradition, the interlocutor and endman dialogues of vaudeville, the abrupt scene shifts, timing, and symbolism of Western movie, radio, and TV scripts, and from the loose, episodic structure of picaresque novels. Anomalies, incongruities, and anachronisms bombard us for comic effect as radio, TV, ray guns, airplanes, and computerized buses appear in the same time frame as Thomas Jefferson, Doc John, John Wesley Hardin, Meriwether Lewis, William Clark, and Loop Garoo, the protagonist, a black HooDoo cowboy.

Having ransacked the Bancroft Library and yesteryear's newspapers for often neglected or little known Americana, Reed conjures up his irreverent, iconoclastic vision of how the West was really won. In this vision Jefferson, Lewis and Clark, and white cowboys like Drag Gibson are shown to be cultural heroes or gods with cloven feet, and the real folk heroes are the supernatural black cowboy, Loop Garoo, and the super-cool Indian, Chief Showcase, who uses the same tactics on whites that they used on his people: "Foment mischief among his tribes and they will destroy each other" (p. 40). Reed's vision, in short, shows that the perversion of individualism and freedom has its roots in Christianity, the American West and the frontier experience, and that historically oppressed American groups (blacks, Indians, children, and women) will ultimately overthrow this perverted system and replace it with a new social order in which genuine freedom and pluralism prevail. Ironically, the Seven Cities of Cibola that the mob of young and old people rush toward at the end of the novel is "a really garish smaltzy super technological anarcho-paradise" (p. 170).

The fluid, multilevel time structure is an effective technique for the colorful, retrospective introduction by the omniscient, editorializing narrator, who identifies with the norms of the Loop Garoo Kid, gradually revealed to be the apocryphal son of God. Although when we first meet him he is "a desperado so onery he made the Pope cry and the most powerful of cattlemen shed his head to the Executioner's swine," he claims to be the fallen son of God. "Booted out of his father's house after a quarrel, whores snapped at his heels and trick dogs did the fandango on his belly. Men called him brother only to cop his coin and tell malicious stories about his cleft foot" (p. 9). He was the eldest son, "according to what they call apocrypha," Loop tells the Pope. "But I've never cashed in on it like he did. I knew very early that he wasn't the only one, there were others—but his arrogance and selfishness finally got the best of him and he drove them all underground. Now they're making a strong comeback" (p. 164). For Loop, HooDoo, "an unorganized religion without ego-games or death worship," was a richer art form than Christianity. Earlier in the novel in explaining this "American version of the Julu religion that originated in Africa" to Drag Gibson, who has called for his aid to solve the mystery of Loop's power, the Pope recalls that

> when African slaves were sent to Haiti, Santo Domingo and other Latin American countries, we Catholics attempted to change their pantheon, but the natives merely placed our art alongside theirs. Our inspired and uninspiring saints were no match for theirs: Damballah, Legba and other dieties [*sic*] which are their Loa. This religion is so elastic that some of the women priests name Loa after their boyfriends. When Vodun arrived in America, the authorities became so paranoid they banned it for a dozen or so years, even to the extent of discontinuing the importation of slaves from Haiti and Santa Domingo. (Pp. 153–54)

Thus Loop's supernatural powers are doubly potent. And since the Pope has actually been sent by Mary to bring Loop home, at the end of the novel Loop gallops off to catch the "Pope's ship heading towards the horizon," leaving mere mortals to their heaven on earth.

Less fascinating, perhaps, but more revealing of the implied author's approval of the aesthetic values of his protagonist is the exchange early in the novel between Bo Shmo, the leader of the neosocial realist gang, and Loop, who is "always with the avant garde" (p. 165). Bo Shmo is a charismatic con man, an unoriginal confessional writer who writes about the misery of being black, and a "part time autocrat monarchist and guru." Attacking Loop after he is driven out of town by Drag Gibson and left in the desert to die, Bo Shmo calls him a "Crazy dada nigger" who is "given to fantasy and . . . Far out esoteric bullshit . . ." (p. 35). Loop's response is a transparent defense by Reed of his own postmodernist independence, one of the major themes of the novel: "What's your beef with me Bo Shmo, what if I write circuses? No one says a novel has to be one thing. It can be anything it wants to be, a vaudeville show, the six o'clock news, the mumblings of wild men saddled by demons" (p. 36). This satirical unmasking of black cultural nationalist ideologues who argue that "all art must be for the end of liberating the masses. A landscape is only good when it shows the oppressor hanging from a tree," and who threaten to "blast those who don't agree with us," is both comic and deadly serious as Reed closes the aesthetic distance between himself and his protagonist.[104]

Whereas *Yellow Back Radio Broke-Down,* Reed's second novel, is an intellectually provocative but far from sober or conventional Western, *Mumbo Jumbo,* his third and best novel, is a dazzling virtuoso performance of research and improvisation on the conventional detective narrative in the tradition of Rudolph Fisher's *Conjure-Man Dies.* Set in Harlem during the 1920s, the novel ingeniously employs cinematic techniques to juxtapose fact and fiction, ancient and modern history. Readers are challenged to follow the cyclical path of HooDoo detectives PaPa LaBas and Black Herman in tracking down the Western conspiracy to destroy the creative spirit and vitality of man, which Reed calls Jes Grew, and to supplant it with the imitative and repressive aesthetic order of Western civilization, whose museums are Centers of Art Detention for the treasures from Africa, Asia, and South America. First expressed in the ritual dancing and singing of Osiris in Egypt, the spirit of human creativity and vitality spread through Dionysus and the Temples of Osiris and Isis to Greece and Rome. The spirit was then driven underground by the Atonist (Catholic) Church, but it continued in the animism and pantheism of Africa. The liberating spirit of creativity and expressivity resurfaced in Haiti, South America, and finally in the song and dance epidemic of North America. Reed ranges widely over world history, appending to the novel a partial yet impressive bibliography of six pages, to reconstruct the unorthodox tradition of his HooDoo aesthetic, whose cyclical history began in New Orleans in about the 1890s. He satirizes the mission of the Atons, their military arm, the Wallflower Order, and their crusading agents—from the Teutonics, Knights Templars, and Hospitaliers to Hinckle Von Vampton, the Templars' librarian. Hinckle stole the sacred Book of Thoth and became their modern agent assigned to create "a 'spokesman' who would furtively work to prepare the New Negro to resist Jes Grew and not catch it."[105] At the end of the novel PaPa LaBas and Black Herman capture Hinckle Von Vampton, but Jes Grew goes underground again with the burning of the Book of Thoth only to rise once more, we learn in the epilogue, in the 1970s.

In a lecture in the epilogue, where, as in the lengthy denouement of the last quarter of the novel, Reed's authorial presence is most intrusive, although occasionally spellbinding, PaPa LaBas expands on James Weldon Johnson's remark that, like Mrs. Stowe's Topsy in *Uncle Tom's Cabin,* the earliest ragtime songs "jes grew":

> Jes Grew, the Something or Other that led Charlie Parker to scale the Everests of the Chord. Riff fly skid dip soar and gave his Alto Godspeed.

> Jes Grew that touched John Coltrane's Tenor; that tinged the voice of Otis Redding and compelled Black Herman to write a dictionary to Dreams that Freud would have envied. Jes Grew was the manic in the artist who would rather do glossolalia than be "neat clean or lucid".... Jes Grew is the lost liturgy seeking its litany. Its words, chants held in bondage by the mysterious Order "which saved the 2nd Crusade from annihilation by Islamic hordes." Those disgraced Knights. Jes Grew needed its words to tell its carriers what it was up to. Jes Grew was an influence which sought its text, and whenever it thought it knew the location of its words and Labanotations it headed in that direction. (P. 211)

The description of PaPa LaBas as "garrulous gluttonous satirical sardonic but unafraid to march up to the President's Palace and demand tribute" seems also to fit the implied author and disembodied narrator. After identifying the assistant to Osiris as the Black Birdman, for example, the author-narrator sardonically states: "(If anyone thinks this is 'mystifying the past' kindly check out your local bird book and you will find the sacred Ibis' Ornithological name to be *Threskiornis aethiopicus*)" (pp. 211 and 188).

Clearly nonrepresentational, PaPa LaBas, "noonday HooDoo, fugitive-hermit, obeah-man, botanist, animal impersonator, 2-headed man, You-Name-It," like the Loop Garoo Kid of *Yellow Back Radio Broke-Down,* is another black American incarnation of Legba:

> Some say his ancestor is the long Ju Ju of Arno in eastern Nigeria, the man who would oracle, sitting in the mouth of a cave, as his clients stood below in shallow water. Another story is that he is the reincarnation of the famed Moor of Summerland himself, the Black gypsy who according to Sufi Lit sicked the Witches on Europe. Whoever his progenitor, whatever his lineage, his grandfather it is known was brought to America on a slave ship mixed in with other workers who were responsible for bringing African religion to the Americas where it survived to this day. (P. 23)

Because his father ran a successful mail-order root business in New Orleans, it is not surprising that PaPa LaBas was a carrier of Jes Grew, whose powers the people trusted and whose headquarters, where he helps and heals people with "jewelry, Black astrology, charts, herbs, potions, candles, talismans," was derisively called Mumbo Jumbo Kathedral by his critics. PaPa LaBas's prophecy "that before this century is out men will turn once more to mystery, to wonderment" is the Work that Reed, himself a carrier of Jes Grew, brings to the readers of his Hoodoo novels.

When he wrote *The Free-Lance Pallbearers,* Reed tells us, "I wasn't really thinking about writing a novel; I was thinking about telling a story." Storytelling or fabulation, with the emphasis on artifice rather than self-indulgence, also accurately describes the performance and power of *Yellow Back Radio Broke-Down, Mumbo Jumbo, The Last Days of Louisiana Red,* and *Flight to Canada.* "I consider myself a fetish-maker," Reed says, explaining the distinctive power of his conflation of modernism and postmodernism with a black difference. "I see my books as amulets, and in ancient African cultures words were considered in this way. Words were considered to have magical meanings and were considered to be charms." He also tells us, as he reveals a major difference between Eurocentric and Afrocentric postmodernism by wryly confessing his faith in nonlinear metanarratives and stylized characters, that in creating characters he is not interested in rendering a photograph of a person but "in capturing his soul and putting it in a cauldron or in a novel."[106] Thus, despite the extraordinary nonlinear, nonrepresentational, and satirical authenticity, authority, and political agency of *Yellow Back Radio Broke-Down* and *Mumbo Jumbo,* Reed does not consider himself an innovator. Nevertheless, his major contributions to the tradition of the African American novel are clearly twofold. The first is his incomparable African Americentric modernist rather than postmodernist theory and practice of a Neo-HooDoo aesthetic, a reconstruction of the syncretistic African and European, as well as Native American, systems of belief, value, and ritual. The second is his bold demonstrations of the redemptive power of storytelling and satirical truth-telling for the liberation of the minds of black people and for the transformation of the old world order of white Western supremacy into a radical new democracy of multicultural justice and equality.

Change in the Novel of the Sixties and Seventies

Of the nine authors whose novels have been closely examined in this chapter, all but one have published at least two novels, had formal training in writing, and, with the exception of Walker, Gaines, and Reed, lived outside of the United States for an extended period of time. At least six have taught or lectured at the college level, and four have worked as journalists and experienced bohemian lifestyles. These various backgrounds explain, in part, the complex changes in their racial and ethnic double consciousness and in the range of influences that shaped the authenticity, authority, and agency of their aesthetic.

Asked about the differences between white and black contemporary writers, Reed responds: "A black writer sitting down doesn't have all of Europe looking over his shoulder. . . . I think that blacks got over that and are trying to set up their own stuff."[107] Even when exorcising the demons of Eurocentric models, their "own stuff" is fabulously tragicomic and ironic, stressing the hybrid nature of narrative and the contemporary struggle to survive with personal integrity the bizarre disparity between American principles and practices. Despite the differences in their experiments with form and technique, sometimes parodying earlier narrative conventions and sometimes adapting those of earlier black novelists in their attack on racism, Christianity, and debilitating black traditions, African American modernist and postmodernist novelists are similar. Although the few African American postmodernists are ostensibly antirepresentational and the modernists nonrepresentational, they are similar in emphasizing the freedom of the individual more than the group, technique more than message, and psychological and cultural revolution more than social.

Commenting both on William Buckley's perception of the black studies movement as a conflict between the barbarians and the Christians and on the commitment of African American modernist and postmodernist novelists to create their own fictions, Reed states:

> So this is what we want: to sabotage history. They won't know whether we're serious or whether we are writing fiction. They made their own fiction, just like we make our own. But they can't tell whether our fictions are the real thing or whether they're merely fictional. Always keep them guessing. That'll bug them, probably drive them up the walls. What it comes down to is that you let the social realists go after the flatfoots out there on the beat and we'll go after the Pope and see which action causes a revolution. We are mystical detectives about to make an arrest.[108]

Unlike Eurocentric modernism and postmodernism, the more African Americentric modernism and postmodernism change the more their distinctiveness remains the same in grounding the authenticity, authority, and agency of the most aesthetically and commercially successful texts in the core experiences, double consciousness, and five residually oral forms of African American life and culture. Thus the richness, diversity, and vitality of the changing sociohistorical, sociopsychological, and sociocultural same in contemporary African American novels compel readers and critics alike to be as intellectually independent and imaginatively daring in their approach to the narrative tradition of African Americans as the artists are in affirming while reconstructing it.

6 / Continuity and Change in Ethnic Tropes of Identity Formation (1983–2001)

Identity is not as transparent or unproblematic as we think. Perhaps instead of thinking of identity as an already accomplished fact, which the new cultural practices then represent, we should think, instead, of identity as a "production", which is never complete, always in process, and always constituted within, not outside, representation. This view problematises the very authority and authenticity to which the term, "cultural identity", lays claim.

STUART HALL

"Cultural Identity and Diaspora"

BETWEEN 1983 and 2001 African Americans continued their dynamic, dialectic role as agents for change in the identity formation of ethnic Americans and other people around the globe.[1] Although the predominantly middle-class and middle-aged NAACP leadership was deeply divided by ideological, economic, and generational differences over the future political direction of the Civil Rights movement, they were major organizers of and participants in the 1983 march of more than 250,000 people on Washington for jobs, peace, and freedom and in celebration of the anniversary of the 1963 march led by Martin Luther King Jr. Building on his leadership in civil rights groups and community improvement programs in the 1960s and 1970s, Jesse Jackson launched a serious but unsuccessful campaign for the Democratic nomination for president of the United States in 1984 and 1988. As an unofficial ambassador for peace in 1984, he was more successful in securing the freedom of a black American navy pilot in Syria and of twenty-two American prisoners in Cuba. More successful than Jackson as elected black political candidates and agents of change primarily for their middle-class black and white constituents were Douglas Wilder as governor of Virginia in 1989, Carol Moseley Braun as senator from Illinois in 1992, and the mayors of three large cities: Harold Washington in Chicago in 1983, David Dinkins in New York in 1989, and Robert Mosbacher Jr. in Houston in 1997. The landslide reelection of President Reagan in 1984 reinforced the conservative movement of Republicans for traditional American values, including a Strategic Defense Initiative (SDI) popularly called "Star Wars," and against affirmative action policies as a black quota system.

Globally, liberation struggles by various non-Western and frequently nonwhite revolutionaries and radicals continued in the 1980s, including violence against Americans in the United States and abroad, against the imposition of American economic, political, and cultural policies on their nations, especially in Lebanon, Grenada, Nicaragua, Haiti, Somalia, Libya, Panama, Iran, and Iraq. Nevertheless, the radical reforms of Gorbachev in 1987, especially the policy of glasnost or openness, in the Soviet government and economy set the stage for the dismantling of the Berlin Wall in 1989, the collapse of communism in Eastern Europe and Asia, and the first opening of a McDonald's in Moscow in 1990. Equally triumphant, after years of relentless struggle and lobbying by TransAfrica and other organizations in solidarity with freedom fighters in South Africa and around the world to promote anti-apartheid policies in the United States, Nelson Mandela and the African National Congress prevailed in ending the ruthless apartheid system in South Africa in 1991.

Inspired to different degrees and in different directions by the historical struggle for justice and freedom by black Americans, the winds of political and social change blew over the nation and world during the 1980s and 1990s. Fundamental issues of traditional American family values and civil rights, especially religious and sexual freedoms, were heatedly debated by politicians, preachers, pundits, and popular artists. Beginning in the early 1980s with the Reverend Jerry Falwell's Moral Majority and culminating in the Republican landslide victories in 1994 and the popularity of Congressman Newt Gingrich and Rush Limbaugh, the radio talk-show host, reactionary calls by religious fundamentalists and political conservatives for traditional values began to challenge and reverse civil rights reforms that expanded social opportunities for African Americans, women, minorities, and the working class. These attacks involved such economic and political issues as affirmative action programs as well as such moral issues as the sex scandals of televangelists Jim Bakker and Jimmy Swaggart; of the first black Miss America, Vanessa Williams; of androgynous pop music stars such as Michael Jackson, Boy George, Prince, and Grace Jones; of Senator Gary Hart; and in 1998 of President Clinton, who was impeached by the House for lying about his sexual affair with Monica Lewinsky.

The sociohistorical and sociocultural context for post-1983 novels also included the increasing impact in 1984 and 1985 of affirmative action programs on the access to power of the black middle class and white women. During this period African American family values were examined and promoted nationally on television with the phenomenal national success respectively of comedian Bill Cosby's middle-class sitcom, *The Cosby Show*, and Oprah Winfrey's female-empowering talk show and media empire, including the Oprah Book Club founded in 1996. Led by national and community organizations and leaders, especially the controversial and charismatic Minister Louis Farrakhan of the Nation of Islam, the Million Man March on Washington in 1995 was equally phenomenal in its dramatic demonstration of support for strengthening values in African American communities and families. These nonliterary events overlapped with the tradition of the African American novel when, for example, Toni Morrison, the winner of the Nobel Prize for Literature in 1993, appeared on Oprah Winfrey's talk show in 1996 to discuss *Song of Solomon*.

With the mushrooming of such popular national sitcoms and talk shows as those of Cosby, Winfrey, and Roseanne Barr between 1983 and 2001, the media frequently highlighted the issues of power disparities based primarily on racial, ethnic, gender, and class differences that impacted the call for new configurations and representations of authority, authenticity, and agency in life and literature. The responses of many, especially women, to the efforts of the predominantly black Million Man March in 1995 and predominantly white March of the Promise Keepers in 1997 to redefine the traditional roles of males and their responsibilities to themselves and their families were at best anxious and ambivalent. The shocking news in 1987 that Magic Johnson contracted AIDS from heterosexual promiscuity and in 1992 that Arthur Ashe contracted it from a blood transfusion made heterosexuals, especially middle-income blacks, more aware of their vulnerability to the epidemic and the need for safe-sex and safe-health practices. Because in 1983 the United States government declared that finding a cure for AIDS was a top priority, and because in 1985 the World Health Organization launched a global attack on the rapidly spreading fatal disease, especially in African countries, the news in 1998 that the second leading cause of death among African American women between 24 and 44 is AIDS was even more shocking to black communities.[2] African American women suffer increased risk for HIV/AIDS because of disproportionate poverty, inadequate access to quality health care, and unprotected heterosexual encounters, especially with men who do not truthfully reveal their bisexual preferences, which is a recurring motif in the black gay novels of E. Lynn Harris. Less shocking in 1998 to black Americans familiar with the Jefferson and Hemings legend and the national legacy of willful innocence and hypocrisy about interracial unions, sensationalized in the O. J. Simpson murder trial in 1995, was the revelation by DNA evidence that Thomas Jefferson was probably the father of at least one of the children of Sally Hemings, one of his slaves.

Such major sociohistorical, sociocultural, and sociopsychological changes as these in the United States between 1983 and 2001 serve to recontextualize contemporary debates over the role and responsibility of the African American artist and African American literature that began most distinctively in the 1920s. What do African Americans want? Who speaks for them? How should African American artists express their authority, authenticity, and agency in literature? And how should readers assess these qualities in their texts? "There has long been controversy within and without the Negro race," the editors of *The Crisis* declared in a 1926 survey of authors on the Negro in art, "as to just how the

Negro should be treated in art—how he should be pictured by writers and portrayed by artists."[3] This is yet another reminder that the more things change the more they remain the same. For some readers this sounds like nothing more than a clich. For others, especially readers in tune with the distinctive dialectic and cyclical pattern of the historical struggle of African Americans in literature as in life for freedom, knowledge, and power as survivors of antiblack slavery, segregation, sexism, and misrepresentation as a people, it has the ring of proverbial truth. Among other things, the fundamental truth that it calls us to acknowledge is the continuing sociohistorical, sociopsychological, and sociocultural struggle to reconcile the tensions and conflicts of the double or, now more popularly proclaimed, multiple identities of Americans of sub-Saharan black African descent. For this reason, the distinctiveness of the African American novel derives from both the double consciousness of its sociocultural and sociopsychological content and the tragicomic double vision that informs the syncretistic contemporary African Americentric pattern of residually oral forms and the literary conventions of irony, paradox, and parody which frequently structure that content.

The proponents of the New Negro Aesthetic of the 1920s and 1930s, the Black Arts/Aesthetic of the 1960s, and the New Black Aesthetic of the 1980s and 1990s debated the question of the dual responsibility of black artists to their art and their race. The debate also addressed the dominance of a black masculinist, nationalist, and social realistic literary configuration of the five residual vernacular forms of oratory, myth, legend, tale, and song in novels about black American character and culture. In the 1920s survey in *The Crisis* of more than a dozen white and black writers and critics, the responses of Charles W. Chesnutt, from the older generation of middle-class light-complexioned Negroes, and Countee Cullen, from the younger generation of the same class, reveal the sharp differences about the responsibility of the black artist to his or her art and community. Chesnutt writes:

> *The colored writer . . . has not yet passed the point of thinking of himself first as a Negro, burdened with the responsibility of defending and uplifting his race.* Such a frame of mind, however, praiseworthy from a moral standpoint, is bad for art. Tell your story, and if it is on a vital subject, well told, with an outcome that commends itself to right-thinking people, it will, if interesting, be an effective brief for whatever cause it incidentally may postulate.[4]

In light of the paternalistic and negative reviews by "right-thinking" white readers of his turn-of-the-century novels, Chesnutt's response is at best problematic.

In contrast, Cullen writes:

> For Negroes to raise a great hue and cry against . . . misrepresentations [in art] without attempting through their artists, to reconstruct the situation seems futile as well as foolish. *Negro artists have a definite duty to perform in this matter, one which should supersede their individual prerogatives, without denying those rights. We must create types that are truly representative of us as a people, nor do I feel that such a move is necessarily a genuflexion away from true art.*[5]

Yesterday, as today, the question of the rights and responsibilities of the black writer to his or her art and his or her community in the imaginative reconstruction of African American culture and character was central to the debate about aesthetics. Most dramatically demonstrated by the five National Black Writers Conferences inspired by John Killens and convened between 1986 and 2000 at Medgar Evers College of New York City University, these debates continued to engage the political and cultural issues best expressed in the 1930s by Richard Wright.

During the economic and social crisis of the late 1930s, Richard Wright attempted to bridge the Marxist and black cultural nationalist ideologies and aesthetics of the era in his classic essay "Blueprint for Negro Literature." He argued that rarely had the best of African American literature been addressed to the needs, sufferings, and aspirations of the black masses because African American writers seemed to think that they could escape the racial injustice of the masses by denying their racial and ethnic consciousness and by stressing their individual achievement. He was convinced that no theory, including Marxism, could take the place of life experience itself or substitute for technique. Wright therefore cautions the black writer:

> He may with disgust and revulsion, say no and depict the horrors of capitalism encroaching upon the human being. Or he may with hope and passion, say yes and depict the faint stirrings of a new and emerging life. But in whatever social voice he chooses to speak, whether positive or negative, there should always be heard or overheard his faith, his necessity. And this faith and necessity should not be simple or rendered in primer-like terms, for the life of the Negro people is not simple as some dyspeptic intellectuals contend. The presentation of their lives should be simple, yes; but all the complexity, the strangeness, the magic wonder of life that plays like a bright sheen over even the most sordid existence, should be there.

Wright challenged black writers to deploy their dual Western literary and African American folk heritage, to use every "iota of gain in human sensibility and thought," in a synthesis of their social and aesthetic consciousness.[6] The Negro writer, Ralph Ellison argued similarly and persuasively in the collection of cultural essays *Shadow and Act* (1964), has "the task of defining Negro humanity, as this can no more be accomplished by others than freedom, which must be won again and again each day, can be conferred upon another. A people must define itself, and minorities have the responsibility of having their ideals and images recognized as part of the composite image which is that of the still forming American people."[7] In turn, the challenge to and task of readers was and is to respond to the power of the authenticity, authority, and agency of the writers' imaginative reconstruction of their lives with "a complex simplicity."[8]

During the demonstrations of African Americans in the mid-1960s for self-determination and solidarity with the liberation movements of colonized people in Africa and the Third World, Larry Neal and other black cultural nationalists raised the clarion call for a Black, specifically African American, Aesthetic with three basic aims. A Black Aesthetic "speaks directly to the needs and aspirations of Black America," seeks "a radical reordering of the western cultural aesthetic," and strives for "a separate symbolism mythology, critique and iconology."[9] In "The Task of the Negro Writer as Artist: A Symposium," a 1965 survey in *The Negro Digest* of thirty-six famous and not so famous black and white writers, the debate over the role of the writer in relation to his society and art resurged with a new intensity. According to Addison Gayle Jr., a major academic critic and radical proponent of the Black Arts/Aesthetic movement, "To evaluate the life and culture of black people, it is necessary that one live the black experience in a world where substance is more important than form, where the social takes precedence over the aesthetic, where each act, gesture, and movement is political, and where continual rebellion separates the insane from the sane, the robot from the revolutionary."[10] I do not agree with Gayle that one needs to "live the black experience" in order "to evaluate the life and culture of black people." Nor do I agree with Henry Louis Gates Jr. that "Blackness" is only a trope. As an African Americentric vernacular theorist and literary critic by acculturation as well as formal education, I believe that people who live the racial and ethnic experiences about which they write have attained and are capable of expressing not only more subtle ironic and parodic levels of the authenticity and authority of texts as complex sign systems, but also more relentless agency in the struggle for justice for black Americans than those who have not.

With their "gangsta" heroes, the ghetto biographies and residual pulp fiction, also called underground literature, paraliterature, and "blaxploitation novels," of the 1960s and 1970s by Robert Beck (a.k.a. Iceberg Slim) and Donald Goines—such as *Pimp* (1967), *Mama Black Widow* (1969), *Whoreson* (1972), and *Black Gangster* (1972)—are similar in theme and style to the ghettocentric, romanticized "keeping it real," on the one hand, and "livin large," on the other, oral narratives of a new black aesthetic in hip-hop culture, examined more fully below. Books by Iceberg Slim and Goines as well as post-1983 urban pulp fiction by such novelists as Omar Tyree, who calls himself an Urban Griot and wears a kangol hat while versifying in clubs over the rhythms of Alice Coltrane, are popular among young black and Latino men in prison.[11] In contrast, the verbal, gender, and generic shift from the male-dominated black nationalistic poetry and drama of the 1960s and 1970s to the dominant feminist-based new black aesthetic, which preceded Trey Ellis's class-based use of the term New Black Aesthetic (NBA) in African American literature in the 1980s, began with the emergence of commercially and critically successful black womanist and feminist novels of the 1970s. Examined in chapters 4 and 5, these modern and neorealistic written narratives by such black women as Toni Morrison, Alice Walker, Louise Meriwether, Alice Childress, Gayl Jones, and Toni Cade Bambara challenged male dominance, examined stereotypes of black women, empowered the voices and values of women, and moved the language and lives of black women from the margins to the center of the tradition of the African American novel. Based on their commercial and critical success on best-seller lists, in literary awards, in canon reformation in new anthologies, and in college classrooms across the nation, critical and poetic neorealism as well as modern fabulation in novels by primarily black women became the dominant African Americentric aesthetic of the late 1980s.

Because the history of our struggle with the economics of slavery to liberate and define ourselves as Americans of sub-Saharan black African descent and bicultural heritage in black and white institutional sites has been outlined in earlier chapters, it suffices as a context for readers who begin the text in this chapter to affirm that the destiny of African Americans is to function on at least two racial and cultural levels of reality. Our destiny as African Americans began most distinctively in such liminal sites as the Middle Passage and the maroon communities of self-liberated Africans and freedom fighters in South Carolina, Georgia, Virginia, and North Carolina as well as in Jamaica during the seventeenth century. Liminal institutional sites for the identity formation of free blacks include the New York African Free School (1787) and the African Methodist Episcopal Church (1794) during the Age of the Haitian and American Revolutions.

The white nationalism and lynchings of blacks in the post-Reconstruction and World War I eras and the national jingoistic anxieties and disproportionate deaths of blacks during the Cold War with the USSR and the Korean War with North Korea and China frame the founding of major modern and contemporary national civil rights organizations and movements. The origins and leaderships of these organizations and movements chart the complex reality of the struggle of black Americans for self-determination and the dominant tension in the identity formation of African Americans as a biracial and bicultural people of predominantly Southern working-class background. These sites of various degrees of collective agency and power have their modern middle-class origins in the National Association of Colored Women (NACW) in 1896, the five pan-African Congresses between 1900 and 1945, the Niagara Movement in 1905, the NAACP in 1909, the National Urban League in 1911, the Association for the Study of Negro Life and History in 1915, and the United Negro Improvement Association in 1916.

Other important modern and contemporary sites of personal and group empowerment were cultural, political, and economic. The cultural include the New Negro movement (also called the Harlem Renaissance) in the 1920s, the Chicago Negro Renaissance literary movement in 1935, the Committee for the Negro in Arts in the late 1940s, the Harlem Writers Guild in 1951, the *Umbra*-Poets Workshop in 1961, the Free Southern Theatre in 1964, the Black Arts Repertory Theatre/School in 1965, and the Black Studies movement in 1968. The political and economic sites ranged from the National Council of Negro Women (NCNW) and National Negro Congress (NNC) in 1935, the National Congress of Racial Equality (CORE) in 1943, the Montgomery Improvement Association (MIA) in 1955, and the Southern Christian Leadership Conference (SCLC) in 1957, to the Student Nonviolent Coordinating Committee (SNCC) in 1960 and the Black Panther Party in 1966. These institutions, organizations, and movements also illustrate that the attitudes and responses of African Americans to integration and separatism were largely determined by the degree of alienation from or faith in the sincere, systematic implementation by the ruling class of white Americans of fundamental national principles and myths. These fundamental principles and normative values include freedom, individualism, democracy, and capitalism. The fundamental national myths include the purity and supremacy of whites, the cultural assimilationist Melting Pot, the egalitarian American Dream, and the petit bourgeois Horatio Alger story.

The Contemporary Black Aesthetic: Afrocentric and Diasporic Tropes of African American Identity and Community

In the post—Civil Rights and post—Vietnam War era, the achievements of and frustrations with the male chauvinistic Black Power, Black Aesthetic, and Black Studies movements in the mid and late 1960s inspired liberation movements by other minority groups and oppressed neocolonial peoples. The Supreme Court's reversal in 1954 of its 1896 "separate but equal" decision culminated in the triumphant affirmative action policies of 1961,[12] the Civil Rights March on Washington in 1963 and the Civil Rights Act of 1964 and Voting Rights Act of 1965. As quiet as it is kept, especially by white women who are the principal beneficiaries of these political and economic initiatives, white Americans and contemporary immigrants gained as much as, if not more than, black Americans from the Civil Rights movement. This occurred, in part, because ideological and personal differences, exacerbated by antiblack institutional agents and agencies such as the FBI and COINTELPRO, were always integral to the black nationalist formations of the individuals and organizations of the era.

As explained in earlier chapters, the personal and collective construction, as well as the imaginative reconstruction, of a black identity during this era was more than a matter of color and turning the other cheek. In the streets and the arts, authority, authenticity, and agency were defined during the Black Power and Black Aesthetic movements for radical social and cultural change by chromosomes, color, ethnicity, class, gender, geography, age, culture, sexuality, consciousness, commitment, conscience, and choice. The cry was not only "We shall overcome" and "Power to the people," but also "art for people's sake" and "We are an African people." From the Black Panthers and the Deacons of Defense to Askia Toure, Amiri Baraka, Sonia Sanchez, Gil Scott Heron, Nikki Giovanni, Haki Madhubuti (Don Lee) and the Last Poets, the most radical call, echoing the writings of Frantz Fanon, was for personal sacrifice and commitment both to the liberation of peoples of the Third World and to the construction of a more just and egalitarian social order.

Paradoxically, because African American history, especially the relationship between tradition and modernity, is more dialectic and cyclical than linear, the more things changed, the more they remained the same. Although the social focus in the 1980s ostensibly shifted from racial to ethnic difference, the failure of the United States and the United Nations to intervene in the 1990s "ethnic cleansing" and genocide in Africa, especially in Burundi and Rwanda, though they subsequently intervened with not only humanitarian righteousness but also military might in Eastern Europe, is indicative of the fact that race still matters. Racial profiling in the 1980s moved from a general targeting of all black people in public spaces as suspected criminals to subjecting black males in particular to daily risks of brutal assault by policemen and lynching by white male terrorists. The most violent cases of racial profiling and brutality by the police include the relentless clubbing and kicking of Rodney King in California and violent broomstick sodomizing of Abner Louima in a New York precinct house, as well as the deadly bombing of MOVE, a black activist group in Philadelphia, and the deadly volley of bullets that killed Amadou Diallo while he was reaching for a key to his apartment house in New York City. The most horrific evidence of continuing antiblack racism and the most dramatic vindication of a new federal hate crime law was the lynching in 1999 of James Byrd in Texas by three white men, who chained him by his feet behind their truck and dragged his body apart down a country road.

As in the past, however, one of the most dynamic and transformative forces to impact national and global identity formations and political economies is the tradition of African American culture, especially music ranging from the spirituals, blues, and jazz to hip-hop and rap. Resisting the vogue of disco in popular culture, hip-hop culture began in the 1970s in the South Bronx and other

African American and Latino urban communities with contributions from Caribbeans like Clive "Kool DJ Herc" Campbell as a new expressive form of cultural and political authenticity, authority, and agency. Hip-hop culture includes everything from graffiti, dj-ing, mc-ing, rapping, sampling, and break-dancing to clothing fashion, from black hats and leather jackets, unlaced Adidas, and heavy gold chains or sweatsuits and kangol hats to do-rags and jeans and jackets by designers like Tommy Hilfiger and black urban fashion moguls like FUBU and Sean "Puff Daddy" Combs. "As an action and reaction against conservative and liberal backlash," writes cultural critic Davarian L. Baldwin, "at times hip-hop attempts to counter negative notions of blackness with its own 'racial authenticity,' where the position of absolute difference is self-induced. Racial authenticity is best articulated in these instances through the stance that the artistic production is pure and untouched by any means of dilution,"[13] especially by the dominant culture. Historically, a major question in black American communities has centered on who has more authenticity, authority, and agency in representing African Americans and in telling "the truth" about our struggle individually and collectively for freedom, literacy, and wholeness: white people or black, women or men, the black masses or the black bourgeoisie, old folks or young folks?

Because of racial, gender, and class disparities in power, it should be apparent in addressing this question that neither in thought nor in behavior are either black or white Americans a monolithic group. Also, while acknowledging the outstanding achievements of such historical leaders as Frederick Douglass, Ida B. Wells, Booker T. Washington, Mary McLeod Bethune, and Martin Luther King, Jr., we should be mindful that no single leader either speaks for all black Americans or has a corner on truth. Nevertheless, critic Davarian Baldwin is quite perceptive in his class analysis. He exposes the graphic sexuality, sexism, and violence of hip-hop as a threat to American family values. He also reveals the historical and spatial shifts in black authenticity "between the binaries of excess and austerity" in hyperbolic performative representations of the realities of black American urban life:

> In order to combat the "negative" idealizations of blackness, middle-class moral purists (even draped in kente cloth) attack the sexual frankness of hip hop as "excessive" and tend to support what is understood as "positive rap" because of its Afrocentric rhetoric and/or political awareness, where as some "Ghettocentric" advocates defend the explicit lyrics as reality-based and resent the possibilities of censorship as dilutions of the authentic "realness" of black experiences. This position in hip hop is exemplified by the characterization of the "keepin-it-real nigga."[14]

On the one hand, the tropes of romanticized, exaggerated masculinity, promiscuity, criminality, and violence in gangsta rap are often directly related to the norms of American culture and capitalism; and on the other hand, these tropes of power and dominance frequently mask the anxiety and ambivalence of the rappers about their desire for and distrust of women.

Moving from black urban centers to white suburban areas and from independent entrepreneurs (e.g., Russell Simmons, Suge Knight, and Bryan Turner) to multinational corporations, the new black aesthetics of hip-hop and rap spread rapidly by radio, television, videos, CDs, and chronicles (e.g., *The Village Voice, The Source, Vibe, XXL,* and *Blaze*) around the globe in the 1980s and 1990s into a transnational, transcultural economic phenomenon. Cultural critic Greg Tate reminds us that "in concept, hip hop was never anti-capitalist, pro-black or intentionally avant-garde. Up until Public Enemy, hip hop's intent was never to shock the world but to sell the market on its novelty and profitability."[15] In contrast to the 1970s "techno-funk" in the Bronx of Afrika Bambaata's Universal Zulu Nation, Grand Master Flash's and Melle Mel's anticocaine single "White Lines (don't do it)" became a classic rap anthem and international hit in 1983. In 1986 Run-D.M.C.—in their classic black outfits, unlaced sneakers, and heavy gold chains—released a rap version of Aerosmith's "Walk This Way," and rap and hip-hop broke into MTV, the pop charts, and mass media. With the increasing transformation of hip-hop into mainstream popular culture and the increasing upward mobility of many African Americans from black inner cities in the 1980s, the alienation, anxieties, and ambivalences of some hip-hop artists began to stress the imperatives of black political consciousness, nation-building, and Afrocentricity. In 1988 this call for black authenticity, authority, and agency was most apparent in "By All Means Necessary" by KRS-One and "It Takes a Nation of Millions to Hold [Them] Back" by Public Enemy, whose members are from Long Island rather than from the South Bronx. Also in 1988 and from Long Island, but in a different black rap style, De La Soul challenged both the Ghettocentric and Afrocentric dominant hip-hop aesthetic in "Me, Myself and I" as the group moved from clichéd digital samples from James Brown to samples from pop culture like Disney and from wearing sweat suits and gold chains to performing in bohemian flowered shirts, dreadlocks, and African medallions.[16]

Contrasting with Afrocentric urban and suburban New York rap styles, however, N.W.A's (Niggas With Attitude) 1988 album *Straight Outta Compton* sold 500,000 copies, popularizing the "gangsta" school of Los Angeles rap as the authentic black experience. Although in the twentieth century, "Americans of all hues who have been marginalized as ethnic or 'other' have utilized the 'gangsta' as a site of socio-economic mobility,"[17] we find in hip-hop that "the grammar of the gangsta's 'hustle' or 'game' has become the language of the culture industry. Hip-hop artists and other culture workers have become 'playas,' and those who attempt to stop black progress in the game have become dubbed 'playa haters.' "[18] In addition, some artists and cultural critics argue that in gangsta rap "nigga does not mean black as much as it means being a product of the post-industrial ghetto."[19] With the increased appeal of gangsta rap to rebellious white suburban youth, it not only dominated the market of soft, playful rap, but also became the most popular type of hard-core rap music. As the sales of some rappers soared to platinum and multi-platinum, their aesthetic shifted from inventive playful and romantic rhymes and rhythms about black urban life performed in kangol hats, Adidas, and gold chains to defiant, iconoclastic verses about the unrelenting struggle for social and sexual power and respect. Rather than calling for political change, however, new rap performativity increasingly celebrated the conspicuous consumption of extravagant designer clothing and luxury cars, jewelry, boats, and homes, confusing, like the black bourgeoisie in E. Franklin Frazier's famous sociological study of the same name, the glitter (bling, bling) of fool's gold, platinum, and diamonds with the real thing. Two prominent antigangsta rap artists or playa haters are Speech, the leader of Arrested Development, whose family has strong black middle-class roots in Milwaukee, Wisconsin, and whose 1992 video "People Everyday" represents a Southern pastoral alternative, and KRS-One, whose popular 1997 video "Rapture" promotes a nostalgic return to the rhyme, rhythm, and dancing of old-school hip-hop of the South Bronx. Dominating the news about black-on-black violence and the East Coast/West Coast rap war over power and authenticity in the 1990s, however, were the unsolved assassinations of controversial, charismatic platinum star gangsta rappers Tupac Shakur in 1996 and Notorious B.I.G. (Christopher Wallace) in 1997.

Although the intraracial conflict between black independent rappers and record companies is occasionally violent and even deadly, the more relentless and insidious major war to control rap and black music is between white American corporations. According to cultural critic Norman Kelley, the relationship between the "Big Six" record companies is a postmodern form of colonialism.[20] Despite the millions made by black production companies like Def Jam, La Face Records, Uptown Records, Bad Boy Entertainment, and Death Row, and despite the few big black moguls and players like Russell Simmons, Suge Knight, Master P, and Sean Combs, hip-hop and rap, like most other forms of black music, are under the corporate control of whites and purchased mostly by white youths. "With rap, the inner cities have become the raw sites of 'cultural production' and the music is then sold to the suburbs, to white youths who claim they can 'relate' to those dwelling in the urban Bantustans." Norman Kelley argues persuasively in *Black Renaissance/Renaissance Noire*:

> Black music exists in a neocolonial relationship with the $12 billion music industry, which consists of six record companies: Warner Elektra Atlantic (WEA), Polygram, MCA Music Entertainment, BMG Distribution, Sony Music Entertainment, and CEMA/UNI Distribution. These firms, according to New York's *Daily News*, "supply retailers with 90% of the music" that the public purchases (rap accounts for 8.9% of the total, over $1

> billion in 1996 . . .). [they] control a key component of the music-making nexus, namely distribution, and they respond to the major labels' demand for a marketable product. In turn, the major labels respond to a young white audience that purchases 66% of rap music, according to the Recording Industry Association of America (RIAA), as reported by the *Daily News*.[21]

The impact of hip-hop culture and rap music on the tradition of the African American novel is apparent in novels that range from John Edgar Wideman's *Philadelphia Fire* (1990), which is less concerned with white corporate domination than with black intraracial class conflict and police brutality, to Bertice Berry's *Haunting of Hip Hop* (2001), which is more entertaining as a ghost story than engrossing for its style, structure, and characters.

The conflicts in the calls and responses by rappers for cultural and political unity with diversity were also apparent in black arts organizations. These included the *Umbra* Workshop on the Lower East Side of New York (co-founded by such writers as Tom Dent, Calvin Hernton, David Henderson, and Ishmael Reed) and the Black Repertory Theater in Harlem (co-founded by Amiri Baraka). In the Midwest were the Organization of Black American Culture (OBAC) on South Side Chicago (co-founded by Hoyt Fuller, Gerald McWhorter [Abdul Alkalimat], Don L. Lee [Haki Madhubuti], Sterling Plumpp, and Angela Jackson) and the Black River Writers Group, co-sponsored in East St. Louis by Eugene Redmond and Henry Dumas, and on the West Coast in California was the Watts Writers' Workshop (founded by novelist and screenwriter Budd Schulberg). Although the members of these Black Arts/Black Aesthetic organizations were primarily concerned with poetry and drama, they shared a common cynicism about American justice, a disillusionment with the American Dream, and an alienation from the white literary establishment.

Like Reed, Tom Dent believes that *Umbra* was a progenitor of the Black Arts/Black Aesthetic movement: "We might say that the members of *Umbra*, and a few other writers at that time, anticipated the Black Arts Movement, in fact anticipated all of the black cultural directions that were to develop a few years later. Really, we went through every crisis, every form of confrontation over direction, every emotional attitude that black cultural groups went through during the Sixties and Seventies."[22] Oppositional positions concerning race, gender, class, and ethnicity within and between Black Studies, Women's Studies, and Ethnic Studies were intensified by moderate as well as reactionary forces and agents. The conflicts and tensions had their roots in the integrationist ideology of the NAACP, Urban League, CORE, and SCLC on the one side and in the Marxist class ideology of Huey P. Newton and Bobby Seale's Black Panthers, the Afrocentric cultural ideology of Maulana Ron Karenga's United Slaves (US), and the black separatist ideology of the Honorable Elijah Muhammad's and Minister Malcolm X's Nation of Islam on the other. These historical intraracial, political, and cultural differences reveal that the problems of authenticity, authority, and agency did not suddenly emerge in the 1980s or 1990s.

In the post-1983 context, Medgar Evers College of the City University of New York began a National Black Writers Conference series in 1986 with the theme "The Responsibility of the Black Writer to the Community." The inspiration for this conference was twofold. The first was the prize-winning, best-selling novels of black women writers. The second more direct influence was the writer-in-residence John Oliver Killens, the co-founder with Rosa Guy, Julian Mayfield, Maya Angelou, Lorraine Hansberry and others of the Harlem Writers' Guild in 1951 and a distinguished novelist of critical realism who had convened major conferences on black writers in the 1960s at Fisk and Howard Universities. At a gathering of about five hundred general readers, writers, critics, and academics, Killens continued the debate of the 1960s Black Arts/Aesthetic movement that as "the harbingers of truth, black writers have a responsibility to expose to the world the evils of racism, sexism, poverty and ignorance that plague our society."[23] The passionate arguments focused on whether the black writer was a propagandist or artist and on whether black literature was provincial racial protest or universal explorations of the complex humanity of black life and character. These debates were instructive revelations of the hybridity and layers of socialized ambivalence in the identity formations of the panelists and participants.

Although the theme of the most recent National Black Writers Conference in 2000 was "The Impact of Literature by Black Writers on Culture and Values in America," the theme of the conference in 1996 at which prize-winning authors Paule Marshall and Amiri Baraka were the keynote speakers was the nature and direction of the renaissance in black literature of the 1990s. The continuity with a difference of Afrocentric and diasporic tropes in the tradition of the African American novel, including novels by native-born and immigrant writers of Caribbean ancestry, is most apparent in the deployment of African American oratory (including the vernacular), myth (including ritual), legend, tale, and song by such novelists as Paule Marshall, Albert Murray, Gloria Naylor, Al Young, David Bradley, and Leon Forrest.

PAULE [VALENZA PAULINE BURKE] MARSHALL (1929–)

Born Valenza Pauline Burke on April 9, 1929, in Brooklyn, New York, to Samuel and Ada Clement Burke, who immigrated to the United States after World War I, Paule Marshall grew up in a community of immigrants from the West Indies and African American migrants from the South. Life in this community immersed her in the social conflicts and mixed emotions that the ethnic groups expressed about each other and their common African heritage. These social conflicts, especially about the work ethic and property ownership, and cultural differences fostered a mutual ambivalence between black Americans and West Indians. That mutual ambivalence was as important in the construction of Marshall's identity as an African American woman as the antiblack racism of the ruling class of white Americans was in shaping her double consciousness as a black American feminist novelist of Barbadian and African heritage. After a brief enrollment at nine years old in the British school system in Barbados, Marshall completed high school after World War II in Brooklyn, graduated Phi Beta Kappa from Brooklyn College in 1953, and attended Hunter College in 1955. In 1950 she married Kenneth E. Marshall, had a son, Evan, in 1959, divorced her first husband in 1963, and married Nourry Menard, a Haitian businessman, in 1970.

While working as a researcher and staff writer for *Our World*, a small West Indian magazine, from 1953 to 1956, she had assignments in Brazil and the West Indies, where she completed the first novel, *Brown Girl, Brownstones*, of a trilogy. *The Chosen Place, the Timeless People* (1969) and *Praisesong for the Widow* (1983) are the other novels in the trilogy about the quest for personal and collective wholeness of black African Americans and West Indians. *The Chosen Place, the Timeless People* is the only one of her novels with an exclusively West Indian setting. *Soul Clap Hands and Sing* (1961), a collection of four novellas set in Barbados, Brooklyn, British Guiana, and Brazil, is her only book in which black men are the protagonists. *Daughters* (1991) and *The Fisher King* (2000) are her most recent novels. She also published a collection of short stories, *Reena and Other Stories* (1983). Her most outstanding awards include a Guggenheim Fellowship in 1960, a Rosenthal Award in 1962 for *Soul Clap Hands and Sing*, an American Book Award in 1984 for *Praisesong for the Widow*, and a MacArthur Foundation Fellowship in 1992. Marshall has also taught or lectured on creative writing and black literature at such distinguished institutions as Oxford, Columbia, Yale, Michigan State, Cornell, and New York Universities, as well as the University of California in Berkeley and the Commonwealth University of Virginia in Richmond.

The daughter of Barbadian parents and a prize-winning writer, Marshall primarily and compellingly explores in her novels the sociopsychological relationship of West Indian to African American culture in the identity quest of her black female protagonists. Her *Praisesong for the Widow* is probably the most outstanding post-1983 novel published by a native-born African American contemporary feminist novelist of African Caribbean heritage. The vernacular roots of the authenticity, authority, and agency of her literary voice are significantly different from those of three other popular contemporary West Indian women novelists in the United States. The differences in their roots, code-switching language, and primary audience are most apparent. For example, Rosa Guy was born in Trinidad, immigrated at seven to the United States, and writes novels primarily for young adults that include both African American and West Indian vernacular English. Her best known, prize-winning novel is *The Friends* (1973). Maryse Conde, a prolific novelist, playwright, and critic, was born in Guadeloupe, came at the age of forty-eight to the United States as a Fulbright Scholar, and writes primarily in French. Her most celebrated, prize-winning novel is *I, Tituba, Black Witch of Salem* (translation, 1992), the mock-epic story of the hypocritical and racist persecution of a heroic black woman by Puritans. Finally, Jamaica Kincaid was born Elaine Porter Richardson on May 15, 1949, in Antigua, immigrated at seventeen as an *au pair* (nanny) to the United States, and has received critical praise for the mixed British West Indian poetic realism of the intense, detailed mother-daughter ambivalence of her short fiction and three novels: *Annie John* (1985), *Lucy* (1990), and *The Autobiography of My Mother* (1997). Her most critically acclaimed and popular novel is the coming-of-age Antiguan story *Annie John*.

According to interviews with Joyce Pettis and Daryl Dance, the three most indelible memories of Marshall's childhood, which influenced the themes, structure, and style of her fiction, are her father's membership in the quasi-religious organization of Father Divine in Harlem, her first extended visit to Barbados and meeting with her legendary maternal grandmother, affectionately called Da-Duh, and her inspiring experience with the vernacular language and tradition of her mother and other West Indian women who frequently socialized in their Brooklyn kitchen.[24] Mr. Burke's loyalty to Father Divine and the organization's work in kingdom hall in Harlem created an emotional and moral distance between the father and his two daughters. Marshall tells Dance that her father "disappeared out of our lives altogether to go and live in Father Divine's 'kingdom' in Harlem, abandoning us to a cycle of poverty and my mother's rapid decline into bitterness, cancer, and an early death."[25] Marshall seeks to overcome her anger with her father and his failure as a musician and poet in the themes of both *Brown Girl, Brownstones* and *Daughters*.

Equally indelible in Marshall's literary imagination is the memory of her visit at nine years old to Barbados. While attending school in her mother's homeland, she not only acquired a Barbadian accent, but also was awed by the natural landscape and the resiliency and spirit of her very black, small, wiry, quick-stepping maternal grandmother, Da-Duh. "Although my grandmother has been dead for many years now," Marshall says, "she remains an important presence in my life and in my work. She appears in one guise or another in most of my short stories and in *all* of the novels. She embodies for me that long line of unknown black men and women who are my forebears."[26] In *Brown Girl, Brownstones* the elder and ancestor of the community is represented in Mrs. Thompson; in *The Chosen Place, the Timeless People* she is Medford; in *Praisesong for the Widow* both Aunt Cuney and Lebert Joseph represent this presence; and in *Daughters* she is Celestine. The third and most important source of the authenticity, authority, and agency of Marshall's narrative style and structure is her memory of the imagistic, rhythmic, and metaphorical language that her mother and a group of West Indian women friends used in the ritual of their daily kitchen social gatherings. "My mother and a group of her close friends were the principal people in my early life," Marshall said, explaining to Dance why the vernacular and black women are central to her novels. "They were women of great spirit, resourcefulness, and poetry."[27]

As a teenager Marshall recalls spending hours in the library voraciously reading European literature, especially the novels of Thackeray, Dickens, Hardy, Conrad, and Thomas Mann. Although she was not encouraged to read black writers and does not recall reading such West Indian writers and texts as George Lamming's *In the Castle of My Skin* and Jean Rhys's *Wide Sargasso Sea* before adulthood, she does remember the major impact on her of the black dialect of Paul Laurence Dunbar's poems and Gwendolyn Brooks's poetic novel *Maud Martha.* Brooks and Mann were the most important influences on her writing *Brown Girl, Brownstones.*[28] But she calls Ralph Ellison's *Shadow and Act* (1964), a collection of essays on the relationship of American to African American culture and literature, her "literary bible."[29]

Beginning with *Brown Girl, Brownstones,* the story of an urban and modern bicultural black girl growing into womanhood, Marshall's novels are rooted in the autobiographical vernacular traditions of West Indian and African American culture. Born in Brooklyn, Selina, the protagonist, is the daughter of Barbadian immigrants, Silla and Deighton Boyce, who are in conflict over whether to pursue uncritically the promises of the American Dream. The ambitious, transplanted Silla is determined, like other "Bajuns" in the Barbadian Homeowners Association who played "the white man's game in their small way," to assimilate, to save money, to buy the Brooklyn brownstone home that they rented, and to see her children move up the ladder of success in marrying and becoming lighter and brighter every generation.[30] Her charming, but less ambitious husband, Deighton, an alienated and unsuccessful jazz musician, is equally determined to return to Barbados and build a home on land that he unexpectedly inherits. But he is tragically worshipful of Father Peace, and so is rejected, and betrayed to the immigration authorities, by his wife Silla. Her values are rejected, in turn, by the mature Selina in the closing episode of the novel as she leaves Brooklyn and her mother in order to visit Barbados. "'G'long,'" Marshall code-switches to the idioms, grammar, and phonology of Silla's Bajan dialect as she brusquely tells Selina with authenticity and authority, "'You was always too much woman for me anyway, soul. And my own mother did say two head-bulls can't reign in a flock. G'long. . . . If I din dead yet, you and your foolishness can't kill muh now!'"[31] The principal imperative and agency of the characters and the implied author in *Brown Girl, Brownstones* and all of Marshall's novels is to construct "a kind of bridge that joins the two great wings of the black diaspora in this part of world" and to reconcile tensions in the quest for personal and collective freedom, literacy, and wholeness. For Marshall passionately believed that despite differences of culture, color, class, and gender, "All o' we is one."[32]

The Fisher King, Marshall's sixth novel, continues the ethnic trope of the ancestors, the thematic tensions between African Americans and West Indians, the structural centrality of black music as creative expression, and the ritual of sociocultural reconciliation and sociopsychological restoration. The major symbol of the ritual of reconciliation and restoration is nine-year-old Sonny, the biracial, bicultural, and bilingual great-grandson. But the voices of the characters in *The Fisher King* are less authentic and authoritative than those in the more critically successful *Praisesong for the Widow*. The occasional vernacular speech in Brooklyn of Ulene Agatha Payne and Florence Varina McCullum-Jones, the West Indian and African American great-grandmothers in *The Fisher King,* for example, lacks the vitality, rhythms, and legendary spirit of the Gullah patois of great-Aunt Cuney on Tatem Island in *Praisesong for the Widow*. Similarly, the third-person retrospective, fragmented background narrative of the tragic life and death of Sonny-Rhett Payne, a Brooklyn-born black West Indian jazz pianist in Paris, neither engages the reader emotionally with his voice nor directly dramatizes the economics and politics of black musicians in exile in Europe. The most obvious difference in the authenticity and authority of these texts is the Eurocentric allusion in the title and symbolism of the French-speaking grandson in the more recent novel to the quest for spiritual restoration in the romance of the Holy Grail. That literary allusion is less distinctively African Americentric and central to the representation of culture and character in the African diaspora than are the references in *Praisesong for the Widow* to the legend of the enslaved Ibos in South Carolina, who spiritually returned to Africa by walking into the sea, the myth of Legba, and the rituals of music and dance.

Divided into five major sections whose third-person omniscient and retrospective narrative includes intermittent dream sequences, flashbacks, and indirect stream of consciousness monologues, *Praisesong for the Widow* is an extraordinary novel. It celebrates the sociopsychological and sociocultural journey of a fastidiously bourgeois African American widow in the twilight of life to the reconciliation of her double consciousness and attainment of spiritual wholeness as an American of Caribbean African descent and bicultural heritage. In "Runagate," the first section, the title of which echoes the title of Robert Hayden's poem about a self-liberating slave, the reader discovers the sixty-four-year-old protagonist, Avey Johnson, suddenly and secretly repacking her six suitcases after only five days on a cruise to disembark at the next port, Grenada, and to return to Brooklyn by plane. Avey, whose full name, Avatara, symbolizes the reincarnation of ancestral spirits, is abandoning her two-week cruise with her friends because of a dream of her great-Aunt Cuney and the Ibo Landing on Tatem Island in the South Carolina Tidewater, to which the two of them would take ritual walks during her childhood summer visits to the Gullah region near Beaufort.

In a flashback the reader learns that Avey's great-aunt was ordered to leave the island church circle as a young girl because she had crossed her feet while participating in the Ring Shout dance. Rather than return to the authority of the small island church, she began going to Ibo Landing for spiritual communion. At the Ibo Landing, Aunt Cuney would tell Avey about the enslaved Ibos who arrived on Tatem Island, "seen what was to come," turned around singing in their chains, and "just kept walking right on out over the river" back home to Africa. As Avey recalls, " 'They sounded like they was having such a good time my gran' declared she just picked herself up and took off after 'em. In her mind. Her body she always usta say might be in Tatem but her mind, her mind was long gone with the Ibos. . . . ' "[33] After she escapes the symbolically named *Bianca* [white] *Pride*, the cruise ship, and her two female traveling companions, Avey learns from a Grenadan taxi driver that she will have to spend the night in a hotel because she has missed the last flight to New York. He also tells her about the annual Carriacou Excursion, when workers in Grenada from the nearby tiny island of Carriacou go home on a two- or three-day excursion.

The structure and style of the early sections of *Praisesong for the Widow* clearly reveal the wide temporal, cultural, psychological, and class distances between the omniscient narrator and the protagonist as a child, young woman, and widow. These distances are particularly apparent in the code-switching episodes involving the ritual storytelling about the Ibos and the ritual dancing after work to jazz records with her husband. But the distances between the implied author, narrator, and protagonist are closed in the final two sections of the novel in the episodes involving the ritual excursion to Carriacou with the community elder and ancestral Legba figure, Lebert Joseph, who is the mythic mediator for Avey's attainment of psychological, spiritual, and cultural redemption and wholeness. Marshall constructs Avey's dramatic meeting with Lebert in the climax of the penultimate section of the novel, "Lave Tete," when she stops to rest in his rum shop on the beach because of her continuing inexplicable illness.

This section opens with a foreshadowing epigraph from the Haitian *Vodun Introit* that invokes Papa Legba, the mythic trickster figure and messenger of the gods in the Fon and Yoruba belief systems of Africa. Marshall's subsequent sympathetic description of Lebert Joseph as the community elder and ancestor is both compellingly mythic and legendary:

> . . . a stoop-shouldered old man with one leg shorter than the other He was close to ninety perhaps, his eyes as shadowed as the light in the rum shop and the lines etched over his face like the scarification marks of a thousand tribes. . . . He was one of those old people who give the impres-

> sion of having undergone a lifetime trial by fire which they somehow managed to turn to their own good in the end; using the fire to burn away everything in them that could possibly decay, everything mortal. So that what remains finally are only their cast-iron hearts, the few muscles and bones tempered to the consistency of steel needed to move them about, the black skin annealed long ago by the sun's blaze and thus impervious to all other fires; and hidden deep within, out of harm's way, the indestructible will: old people who have the essentials to go on forever. (Pp. 160–61)

The implied author closes the emotional, psychological, and cultural distance between herself and her characters by blending past and present as well as black African, Caribbean, and African American cultural heritages. Sympathetically responding to Avey's illness, Joseph tells her about the annual Big Drum and Beg Pardon ritual bonding of family and ancestors during the Carriacou Excursion, narrates his family genealogy, invites her to join him in the Creole dance of her African ancestors, and insists that she come with him on the excursion: " 'You must come today-self so you can see the Juba done proper' " (p. 181). On Avey's turbulent boat ride to Carriacou, memories of the language of "the presiding mothers of Mount Olivet" and an Easter sermon from the past merge with the Patois language of the women on the boat as the catalysts for Avey's symbolic purgation and purification in a prolonged attack of nausea and diarrhea (pp. 197–207).

In "The Beg Pardon," the final section of the novel, the ritual ceremony of reunion, redemption, restoration, and wholeness for the individual and collective black people of African descent on the Island of Carriacou with the spirits of their ancestors begins with a libation, gifts of food, and prayers of forgiveness to the Old People for personal disruptive and disrespectful acts of disunity. The ritual culminates in the ancestral dances of reunion of each ethnic group to the pulsating rhythmic ceremony of the Big Drum. As the elderly folk danced in a "loose, ever-widening ring," they drew Avey into the circle, and she began to move her feet and body to her memory of the old folk shuffling the Ring Shout back on Tatem Island:

> She had finally after all these decades made it across. The elderly Shouters in the person of the out-islanders had reached out their arms like one great arm and drawn her into their midst. Now, suddenly . . . with her entire life yet to live, she felt the threads streaming out from the old people around her in Lebert Joseph's yard. From their seared eyes. From their navels and their cast-iron hearts. And their brightness as they entered her spoke of possibilities and becoming even in the face of the bare bones and the burnt-out ends. (Pp. 247–49)

After this ritual communion with the souls of the ancestors and the elders, Avey leaves Grenada with a new consciousness and sense of agency to return to Tatem in order to pass on the lesson of the African ancestors and the stories of her great-Aunt Cuney to the estranged souls of the world, especially her own grandsons on annual visits from Brooklyn.

The varying degrees of authenticity, authority, and agency of Marshall's novels are apparent in the continuities and changes in their quasi-autobiographical themes of reconciling African American and Caribbean American womanist double consciousness, their structural experiments with the *bildungsroman*, their stylistic experiments with AAVE, SAE, and Barbadian code-switching, and their celebration of the wit and wisdom as well as the resilience and resourcefulness of the ancestors and the elders of black folks in the African diaspora. According to Marshall: "Some who read my work worry that using the West Indies as a setting, even if in part only, somehow goes against me. That it makes me less 'folks,' less African-American. Very interesting reaction. . . . But I'm afraid I really can't accommodate them because my way of seeing the world has been so profoundly shaped by my dual experience, those two communities, West Indian and African-American. Those two great traditions—they nurtured me, they inspired me. I am fascinated by the interaction of the two cultures, which is really, as I see it, one tradition, one culture."[34] The authenticity, authority, and agency of Marshall's novels are thus most apparent not only in the affirmation of the inspirational legacy and trope of the elders and ancestors of black folks in the African diaspora, but also in the vernacular code-switching that celebrates the bridging of African American and West Indian cultures.

ALBERT [LEE] MURRAY (1916–)

The authenticity, authority, and agency of Albert Murray's novels are different in kind as well as degree from Marshall's because his tropes of ethnic character and culture focus on the omni-American rather than the African and West Indian ancestor and past. Neither Eurocentric nor Afrocentric, Murray derives his cultural theory and practice as a novelist and essayist primarily from his African Americentric Deep Southern roots. When he was around eleven-years old, Murray learned that he was born on June 12, 1916, in Nokomis, Alabama, to John Young, a member of a financially secure middle-class family, and Sadie Graham, a Tuskegee student who worked part-time in the real estate business of John's family. Because his birth parents were unmarried, Murray was adopted as an infant and raised in Magazine Point, a small town near Mobile, Alabama, by Hugh and Mattie Murray, a laborer and housewife. "As far as the Murrays were concerned," the novelist wryly tells an interviewer, "it was a fantastic thing that I finished the ninth grade . . . or that I could read the newspaper."[35] Because of his unconventional family background and the inspiration of the epic heroes he discovered in college in Lord Raglan's *The Hero: A Study in Tradition, Myth, and*

Drama (1936), one of the books most frequently cited in Murray's writings, Murray believed that he was destined after graduating from Mobile Country Training School to realize the early stages of his rites of passage to manhood as an educator, cultural critic, and novelist at Tuskegee Institute. At Tuskegee he became a voracious reader, met fellow student Ralph Ellison in the library around 1935, graduated with a B.A. in 1939, taught there in 1940–43 and 1946–51, and married student Mozelle Menefee in 1941. Murray joined the U.S. Air Force in 1943 and retired as a major in 1962. In 1948 he earned an M.A. in literature, at New York University on the GI Bill.

It was also in New York that Murray developed his friendship with Ellison, whose reading habits in literature, culture, and criticism had been similar in college to Murray's but who had left Tuskegee during his senior year. According to Gates, "Ellison read passages to Murray from a manuscript that would turn into *Invisible Man*. The two men explored the streets and the sounds of Harlem together; over meals and over drinks, they hashed out ideas about improvisation, the blues, and literary modernism."[36] Although they seemed like soul brothers with asymmetrical personalities and reputations to people who knew both of them during the 1960s, when Murray's articles began appearing in periodicals and books, the two friends gradually became estranged after the fire in 1967 that destroyed not only Ellison's summer home in Massachusetts but also the manuscript of his second novel, which had been in progress for many years. With Ellison's apparent anxiety about producing a second novel as good as his first and Murray's star rising as a published cultural critic and novelist, apparently mutual envy and resentment deepened the rift between the two men. In addition to Tuskegee Institute, Murray has lectured or taught at Columbia, Colgate, Emory, and Drew Universities, as well as at the Universities of Massachusetts and Missouri. His publications include six books of cultural and blues criticism, among them *The Omni-Americans* (1970) and *The Blue Devils of Nada* (1996), an autobiography of Count Basie, co-authored with the subject, and three novels: *Train Whistle Guitar* (1974), which received the Lillian Smith Award for Southern Fiction, *The Spyglass Tree* (1991), and *The Seven League Boots* (1995).

The Omni-Americans, his first and most iconoclastic book, is a collection of radical essays written between 1963 and 1969 that not only challenges "the folklore of white supremacy and the fakelore of black pathology," but also represents the manifesto of his authenticity, authority, and agency as a cultural critic and writer. Drawing on his folk roots, especially Duke Ellington and the blues tradition, and such authors as Lord Raglan, Constance Rourke, Andr Malraux, James Joyce, Thomas Mann, and Ralph Ellison, its thesis is that "human nature is no less complex and fascinating for being encased in dark skin."[37] Preferring, like most black folks of his generation, the term "Negro," Murray begins *The Omni-Americans* with the assumption that "all statements are also counter-statements." His provocative propositions are that "identity is best defined in terms of culture," that "American culture . . . is . . . incontestably mulatto," that the fugitive slave's "basic urge to escape was . . . only human . . . but the tactics he employed as well as the objectives he was seeking were *American* not African," and that the blues "affirm not only U.S. Negro life in all of its arbitrary complexities and not only life in America in all of its infinite confusions, [but] they [also] affirm life and humanity itself in the very process of confronting failures and existentialistic absurdities."[38] While art is "a process of stylization; and what is stylized is experience," according to Murray, the "most elementary and hence the least dispensable objective of all serious artistic expression . . . is to make human existence *meaningful*." Consequently, Murray identifies with "the truly serious artist" who feels "a crucial ambivalence in . . . [his] eternal and even infernal involvement with the ironies of *antagonistic cooperation*."[39] He also passionately identifies with the affirmative "exemplary and heroic response" of the "Negro musician or dancer" who swings to the blues:

> Extemporizing in response to the exigencies of the situation in which he finds himself, he is confronting, acknowledging, and contending with the infernal absurdities and ever-impending frustrations inherent in the nature of all existence *by playing with the possibilities that are also there.* Thus does man, the player become man the stylizer and by the same token the humanizer of chaos; and thus does play become ritual, ceremony, and art; and thus also does the dance-beat improvisation of experience in the blues idiom become survival technique, esthetic equipment for living, and a central element in the dynamics of U.S. Negro life style.

It is apparent in his novels that Murray seeks to fulfill the heroic blues mission and style of *The Omni-Americans*: "Perhaps every serious writer proceeds on the assumption that a sufficiently vernacular and revolutionary image can be created to initiate a millennium during his generation."[40]

Many first novels in the African American literary tradition are *bildungsromans*, stories about the education and growth of a child into maturity. In contrast, Murray's first novel begins a trilogy of quasi-autobiographical *kunstleromans,* focused more sharply on the development of the sensibility, consciousness, and language of an artist than on the general education of a young man or woman. *Train Whistle Guitar*, the first novel, is the coming-of-age story of Scooter, a young black boy, in Gasoline Point, Alabama, a predominantly black town near Mobile, in the 1920s. Although, as critic Elizabeth Schultz perceptively observes, Scooter's story on its surface parallels those of such black novels as "Langston Hughes's *Not Without Laughter* (1930), Ralph Ellison's *Invisible Man* (1952), Gordon Parks's *Learning Tree* (1963), Louise Meriwether's *Daddy Was a Number Runner* (1970), and Leon Forrest's *There Is a Tree More Ancient Than Eden* (1973)—they [Murray's novels] differ from them in their consistently upbeat tone."[41] Whether climbing to the top of the tall chinaberry "spyglass" tree in his front yard in order to see beyond his "briarpatch" as far as the horizon or listening to the "singsongsaying," limp-walking, twelve-string-guitar-picking, plucking, strumming, and knuckle-knocking of legendary bluesman Luzana Cholly, Scooter soaks up the music, stories, and lessons of his Southern folk community and culture. The novel closes as he sets his eyes on the prize of college and on the ancestral obligation to make his mama and community proud of him. *The Spyglass Tree*, the second book in the trilogy, continues the life of Scooter in college on a scholarship with fleeting flashbacks to Gasoline Point and vernacular dialogues without enclosing quotation marks in the briar patch that reveal a shift from the various rhythms of a blues style to the liberating tempo and motif improvisations of a jazz style.

But it is *The Seven League Boots* that brings the trilogy of *kunstleromans* to its culmination of cultural literacy and wholeness for Scooter on a national tour that challenges his improvisational powers of reconstructing the "ancestral imperatives" of hometown folks and his personal agency and ethnic identity as a college-educated jazz musician. Scooter's reconstruction of his identity as Schoolboy with band members while traveling as a bass player on the traditional black blues and jazz circuit that was controlled by the Theatre Owners' Booking Agency in the United States provides the background for *The Seven League Boots*, which is divided into three major sections: "The Apprentice," "The Journeyman," and "The Craftsman." In "The Apprentice" the reader is immediately immersed in the authenticity and authority of the code-switching, fluid flowing, unconventionally marked language of the protagonist's first-person stream of consciousness and flashback dialogues with Joe States, the natty-dressing, trash-talking fly drummer from Birmingham, Alabama: "I said I come from Alabama, and he said me and you schoolboy me and you. . . . What he had also said then was So you from down in the Beel, well I'm old Joe States from up in the Ham. Then he had gone on to say now let me tell you something, young fellow. Anybody come asking you some old stuff about where your banjo, you tell them what I tell them. You tell them I got your goddamn banjo swinging down you know where."[42]

Schoolboy was still in college in Alabama when Bossman, the veteran jazz pianist, composer, and bandleader, heard the influence of Old Papa Gladstone, one of the elders around Mobile, in his sound and later hired him to join his band as a temporary replacement for the bassist. In a flashback that reinforces continuing respect for the authenticity and authority of legendary elders and ancestors, Schoolboy, after joining the band, recalls an early dialogue with Bossman: "So it looks like I had you tabbed right away, he said. And I said, You sure did. And he said, That's old Papa Gladness for you. He's got as many children forever turning up somewhere as old Uncle Bud in that old bone knocking rhyme, Giles; and not just children he might have forgotten after all these years, but a whole slew of others like this young fella here that he didn't even know was one of his in the first place" (p. 22). The dominant ethnic identity tropes of ancestors, elders, and musicians in *The Seven League Boots* are apparent in the representation of the protagonist as a college-educated jazz bassist in quest of a graduate degree and in the frequent allusions to such legendary blues and jazz musicians as Luzana Cholly, Doodlebug McMeans, Jelly Roll Morton, Riverboat Shorty, Red Bird, King Velvet, Velma Mackie, Cleo Quitman, Miss Big Money Watkins, and "Ma Rainey and Bessie and all the rest of them red hot Smith mamas" (pp. 22–23).

But Miss Lexine Metcalf at Mobile County Training School, the nameless old roommate from his college years, and Joe States are the bridges between the past and the present, including *Train Whistle Guitar*, the spyglass tree, and Luzana Cholly. They are also the inspiration, especially Miss Metcalf's Windows of the World bulletin board, for the protagonist's dual quest. On the one hand, Schoolboy seeks to reconcile ancestral obligations to bring pride to the old hometown folks by his accomplishments with his personal freedom. On the other hand, he seeks to reconcile his Southern African American vernacular tradition with his literacy as a college graduate to attain wholeness as a cosmopolitan contemporary jazz musician. With no apparent cultural, emotional, and intellectual distance between the narrator, musicians, and himself, the implied author signifies on the band members as they and he riff with succinct ironic comments off the main theme of the protagonist's quest to affirm both the vernacular and the literary traditions: "So you all starting right in trying to teach this college boy bad habits already I see, Ike Ellis said winking at me. And Herman Kemble said, You better watch 'em, Schoolboy. And Joe States said, Who me man? Come on man. Ain't much these college boys ain't already been into these days. Both of y'all know that" (p. 16). In a later flashback, the protagonist contrasts the difference between his obligations and those of the female vocalist with the band: "All I had to do was promise that I would always do my best and if I ever accomplished anything noteworthy it would be something that not only home folks but also others elsewhere could be proud. That was as far as the Early Bird program went. You earned your scholarship to college, and the rest was up to you. But in her case there was an ongoing relationship with her hometown sponsors" (p. 136).

After many discussions of what his old freshman college roommate called "the Scooter Saga or Scooter Cycle to be," Schoolboy reveals a shift in his sense of agency inculcated by Mr. B. Franklin Fisher, the Talented Tenth Early Bird program, and the Mobile County Training School as the Ancestral Imperative when he recalls that even two years later he had not made up his mind on a career field beyond a major in literature: "But my notions about my obligations to hometown expectations had undergone significant modification indeed. They had become more and more a matter of existential implication and less and less obviously a matter of personal social and political progress as such, without becoming any less pragmatic than direct involvement in concrete action as such, precisely because they were concerned with that upon which such action at its best must be predicated" (p. 137). The implied author's ambivalence about the burden of blind adherence to tradition of the ancestors is apparent in his reference to Mr. Fisher's role as social engineer.

It was only after his new roommate raised the question of which ancestor was most inspirational in his identity quest for authenticity, authority, and agency that Schoolboy acknowledges retrospectively his anomalous choice of Miss Metcalf. Rather than a traditional ancestor, she was more of a modern fairy godmother who inspired him to emulate "the seven league stride of the heroes in rocking chair story times" (p. 104). The implied author code-switches between European and African American myths, legends, and tales, as the protagonist recalls that it was she who was to say, "Who if not you, my splendid young man, my splendid young man, who if not you? And who was also to say, Who knows but that you may have to travel far and wide to find out what it is that you are called to do and be" (p. 138). In addition it was she who enabled the legendary Bossman, an allegorical Duke Ellington, to discover Scooter's potential as a musician and who inspired his apprenticeship as Schoolboy with Bossman's band on the road. Schoolboy's successful apprenticeship, which is curiously devoid of the soul-searing violence of antiblack racism, ends when he leaves the band to continue as a journeyman on his own in Hollywood.

The tempos of "The Journeyman" and "The Craftsman," the final major sections of the book, are slower and more nuanced than the rhythm of the first section. In "The Journeyman," the more dramatic of the two, Schoolboy develops his independence as a sideman in jam sessions, studio recordings, and his own new compositions with Eric Threadcraft, and as a ladies' man with Gaynelle Whitlow, the transplanted Mississippi black princess, and Jewel Templeton, a celebrated white movie actress. His new sense of freedom and adventure moves him further from his plans to return to graduate school as he improvises on his music and sexual affairs, especially with Jewel Templeton, who not only takes him into her Beverly Hills home but also takes him to southern France as her companion as this section of the novel closes.

In "The Craftsman," the final section, Murray slows the tempo of the narrative with frequent disruptive flights of stream of consciousness and flashbacks that reveal Schoolboy's motives for leaving Templeton and visiting Paris before returning by plane to New York and ultimately home to Gasoline Point. His chief motive is to complete his ritual initiation into life as a contemporary jazz musician by resolving his ambivalence about the ancestral imperatives of the Talented Tenth, including the expectations of his hometown community, and about his artistic and spiritual impulses. He chooses to continue exploring "horizons of human aspiration" in order to broaden his knowledge of cultural diversity and deepen his authority as a musician. Schoolboy's quest culminates in dialogues about blues and jazz with the Marquis de Chaumienne, the cosmopolitan blues devotee who first introduced Templeton to the blues and jazz, dialogues that have a catalytic impact, similar to that in school of the legendary Mr. Fisher and Miss Metcalf, on the reconstruction of the authenticity and authority of Schoolboy's identity.

Recalling an earlier discussion in Paris with Bossman about blues singers, the Marquis tells Schoolboy that the problem with "idiomatic nuance" for most outsiders, "those not native to it," is twofold:

> First there is the matter of authenticity . . . he [Bossman] said: that the timbre, vibrato, and pulse were no less matters of idiomatic authenticity than slurring and mispronouncing the words *correctly*. . . . Another problem is that all too often the outsider's fascination with the idiomatic is likely to be the same as with the exotic. . . . All too often it is a matter of escape, rejection, or even full blown rebellion and revolution, or in any case a matter of being deliberately unconventional. Whereas when you are native to the idiom you're simply being conventional if you see what I mean. Your basic objective is to measure up and then maybe excel and in some cases also exceed. (Pp. 309 and 369)

The protagonist ends his cyclical journey on a New York plane bound for Mobile after flashbacks as well as dialogues, and stories exchanged between himself as Scooter and Marvin Upshaw, a former classmate who dropped out of Mobile County Training School but who subsequently and proudly earned a high school diploma from night school.

The implied author is in full sympathy with the agency of Scooter's closing caveat to Marvin and readers: "man, they [ancestors] start smiling in their graves the very minute they realize that you realize that nothing less than your personal best is good enough. . . . But man what makes them turn over in their graves is a promising apprentice and journeyman who becomes a qualified but contented craftsman among other craftsman [*sic*] instead of a contender to be reckoned with in the realm of mastercraftsmanship" (p. 367). Albert Murray's thematic, stylistic, and structural improvisations in the Scooter *kunstleromans* illuminate the complex bicultural heritage of the jazz artist and anticipate the provocative innovations of Nathaniel Mackey's jazz trilogy. Murray's *kunstleromans* are the first extended contemporary sociocultural representation and sociopsychological interrogation in a trilogy of the tension between traditional ethnic tropes and imperatives of the ancestors and elders, on the one hand, and personal agency, on the other, in the identity formation of a contemporary African American male blues and jazz musician.

GLORIA NAYLOR (1950–)

In the novels of Gloria Naylor the racial and ethnic tropes of the ancestors and elders shift from the masculinist to the feminist. Born on January 25, 1950, in Queens, New York, to Rossevelt and Alberta McAlpin Naylor, Gloria Naylor is the oldest of three daughters. Her parents were migrants from Robinsonville, Mississippi, where they worked as cotton sharecroppers. In New York, her father worked as a subway motorman, and her mother worked as a telephone operator. Quiet, shy, and precocious as a child, Naylor "seldom talked, read a book a day, and wrote what her third-grade teacher thought was terrifying science fiction."[43] Encouraging her daughter's creativity, Alberta Naylor bought her a diary and later spiral notebooks that she filled with observations, poems, and short stories. After graduating from high school in 1968, Gloria Naylor worked as a Jehovah's Witness missionary in New York, North Carolina, and Florida until 1975. She then gave up missionary work to return to New York City, where she worked in several hotels as a telephone operator and attended Medgar Evers College briefly before having an unsuccessful marriage in 1980 and completing a B.A. in English at Brooklyn College in 1981. In college she first discovered black women writers. "I was 27 years old," she told an interviewer in 1993, "before I knew Black women even wrote books."[44] Receiving a fellowship to Yale University, she earned an M.A. in African American Studies in 1983.

Naylor's first short stories appeared in *Essence* magazine: "A Life on Beekman Place" (March 1979) and "When Mama Comes to Call" (August 1982). These stories were later incorporated as "The Two" and "Kiswana Browne" in *The Women of Brewster Place*. In the 1980s Naylor's literary career blossomed as she began teaching, producing essays in the *New York Times*, *Yale Review*, and *Southern Review*, and publishing novels. She has taught at the University of Pennsylvania as well as at Yale, New York, Princeton, Boston, Brandeis, and Cornell Universities. But she is best known as the author of five novels: *The Women of Brewster Place* (1982), which won the American Book Award for Best First Novel in 1983; *Linden Hills* (1985), which is a revision of her Yale master's thesis; *Mama Day* (1988); *Bailey's Café* (1992); and *The Men of Brewster Place* (1998). Recognition for her literary achievements has included a Distinguished Writer Award from the Mid-Atlantic Writers' Association in 1983, a National Endowment for the Arts Fellowship in 1985, a Guggenheim Fellowship in 1988, and a Lillian Smith Award in 1989.

The consensus of critical opinion is that *The Women of Brewster Place*, the authentic neorealistic code-switching stories of the survival strategies and sisterhood of seven abused and exploited black women who live in a run-down apartment building on a dead-end inner-city street, is Naylor's most successful novel. It was popularized in a 1989 Oprah Winfrey television miniseries. *Linden Hills*, a Dantesque allegorical journey and critique of the crass materialism and spiritual alienation of the black Talented Tenth, reveals her most Eurocentric structural and stylistic influence. *Bailey's Café*, a biblically inspired examination of the Madonna-whore myths and stereotypes of female sexuality that characterize the desperate contemporary lives of the women customers of Bailey's Café, is thematically and stylistically the most-blues inspired of her novels.

But it is in *The Men of Brewster Place*, Naylor's recent stylistically compelling examination of contemporary African American male identity, and in *Mama Day*, Naylor's most authentic and authoritative representation of the black female as elder and ancestor, that readers will find her disturbingly memorable reconstructions of ethnic tropes of identity formation. As the gendered title, several recurring characters, including Ben, Eugene, Jerome, Basil, C. C. Baker, and the Reverend Woods, and a few repeated important episodes indicate, *The Men of Brewster Place* is a sequel to *The Women of Brewster Place*. But the focus shifts in the more recent novel from the representation of the inner lives of the women to that of the men. Brewster Place, readers learn from the principal narrator, with whom the implied author ideologically sympathizes, "gave birth to more than its girl children, ya know. . . . I'm not about to argue was it harder for some than for others: Who's got it worse, the Him with nothing in his pockets, scared to turn the knob on the door; or the Her waiting on the other side to stretch that nothing—once again—for supper?"[45]

Naylor's imaginative construction of the identities of Mattie's son Basil and Ceil's husband Eugene in *The Men of Brewster Place*, for example, moves beyond their flat representation as irresponsible, unreliable, untrustworthy black men in *The Women of Brewster Place*. Although Mattie dies before witnessing her son's neomasculine transformation, Basil is sympathetically represented as a remorseful son who worked two full-time jobs and a part-time one on Sunday for three years in order to pay his mother back for believing in him and putting her house up as collateral for his bail. As he leaves his mother's gravesite, Basil promises her and himself: "I can't undo the past, but I would find some woman somewhere, and make her life happy. I would be the father I never had; I would act like the man I'd finally grown up to be" (p. 46). Although Basil marries Keisha in order to be a father to her two boys, Naylor's adept shifting from his interior anxiety about parenting to his dramatic commitment to it reveals with uncommon sensitivity and sympathy that his sincere efforts to keep his promise of responsible manhood are in vain. Keisha not only begins bringing men home while he is at work but also turns him in to the police for hitting her and jumping bail on the outstanding manslaughter charge. Naylor also provides an exceptionally textured, sensitive, and authentic representation of a gay bar and of Eugene's tragic dilemma as a black bisexual male whose guilt for his wife's abortion and the accidental death of his young daughter drives him into a sadomasochistic relationship.

Unlike the stories of the seven black women in *The Women of Brewster Place*, which share the theme of sisterhood, however, the stories of the eight black men, including Greasy in "The Barbershop," in *The Men of Brewster Place* are not interwoven into a bond of brotherhood. They have in common only the Brewster Place setting, especially the barbershop, the blues, and Ben, the murdered superintendent in *The Women of Brewster Place* whom Naylor resurrects as narrator and witness in *The Men of Brewster Place* in order to enhance the structural and stylistic authenticity and authority of the text as a novel. We meet and hear the tragic story of Greasy, the crack addict who has lost his job, family, friends, and health and who recites only two phrases: "I'm a man. And I'm trying;" in the barbershop, where he desperately seeks to hold on to his manhood and finally slits his own throat.

In contrast, *Mama Day* is Naylor's most ambitious, authentic, and authoritative examination of continuity and change in the vernacular and literary reconstruction of African American ethnic tropes of the ancestors and elders. Introducing the reader to the conflicts between the black Gullah community of Willow Springs and the white developers determined to build neo-plantations, gated white communities and resorts with black servants, on the Sea Islands off the coast of Georgia and South Carolina in the 1980s, Naylor writes:

> Weren't gonna happen in Willow Springs. 'Cause if Mama Day say no, everybody say no. There's 18 & 23, and there's 18 & 23—and nobody was gonna trifle with Mama Day's, 'cause she know how to use it—her being a direct descendant of Sapphira Wade, piled on the fact of springing from the seventh son of a seventh son—uh, uh. Mama Day say no, every-body say no. No point in making a pile of money to be guaranteed the new moon will see you scratching at fleas you don't have or rolling in the marsh like a mud turtle.[46]

As the legendary Southern setting, characters, and vernacular language of this passage suggest, Naylor immediately and compellingly draws on the five African American residual oral forms of oratory, myth/ritual, legend, tale, and song to establish the authenticity, authority, and agency of the novel.

The structure, style, and characters of the novel most impressively and suspensefully develop these elements in Mama Day's transmission of the traditional powers of her racial and ethnic ancestors to her grandniece, Cocoa, the visiting protagonist from the mainland, in her contemporary struggles for personal and communal freedom, literacy, and wholeness. Preceded by the texts of Sapphira Wade's family tree and of her bill of sale as a slave, the prologue of the novel opens in 1999 with the third-person retrospective story and memory of a nameless community narrator telling readers about the local legend of Sapphira Wade and of how black slaves became the owners of Willow Springs. According to the legend, while she was his slave, the African-born Sapphira conjured Bascombe Wade, her former Norwegian master, husband, and the father of her seven sons, into giving the deed to the island to his slaves before she killed him by smothering, stabbing, or poisoning, depending on which version of the 1823 event was passed down by which storyteller in the community. As the granddaughters of the seventh son of the seventh son of Sapphira, Miranda, respected as Mama Day by all in Willow Springs for her second sight, sagacity, resoluteness, and healing powers, and her sister Miss Abigail are the elders of the community.

With a shift in the first of the novel's two major sections to George and Cocoa as alternating and initially mutually alienated narrators of their love story, we learn that the conflict between the Southern African American rural populist traditional way of life in Willow Springs and the Northern African American urban white-collar way of life is at the heart of this refreshingly honest, nonstereotypical, and unsentimental contemporary black love story. The return fourteen years earlier in 1985 to Willow Springs of Cocoa, with her first husband George Andrews, to visit her family generates the nonlinear, suspenseful main plot of the novel. An unexpected couple with nothing ostensibly in common, Cocoa, whose birth name is Ophelia and pet name is Baby Girl to Abigail and Mama Day, is an independent, self-assured black accounts manager and anxious, unsociable New York migrant. George is a mechanical engineer and pragmatic middle-class striver who was raised with a congenital heart condition in an orphanage to have absolutely no illusions about himself and the world and who has "never trusted foods that are mixed together" (p. 54). Because one of the island conjurors, Miss Ruby, believes that her husband is attracted to Cocoa, she uses roots to curse her with a fatal illness that Mama Day can counter only with the assistance of George, who dies while saving the life of his wife on what is his first trip home with her in the four years of their marriage. Since 1985, Cocoa has remarried, had two sons, moved to Charleston, and now in 1999 regularly visits Willow Springs to celebrate her legendary ancestors and affirm her island identity in the annual Candle Walk ritual in August.

Some nonblack readers and black readers with little personal knowledge of the Southern roots of African American culture and less intimacy with living in a predominantly black community will be emotionally and spiritually distant from the authenticity and authority of the African American residually oral style of *Mama Day*. Drawing on her parents' Mississippi experiences and her own experiences as a Jehovah's Witness missionary down south, Naylor constructs a dramatic communal voice that opens the novel with the myth, legend, and tall tale of Sapphira Wade: "A true conjure woman: satin black, biscuit cream, red as Georgia clay. . . . She could walk through a lightning storm without being touched; grab a bolt of lightning in the palm of her hand; use the heat of lightning to start the kindling going under her medicine pot," depending on who in the community is telling the story (p. 3). Although the omniscient narrator tells us that 18 & 23 "was just our way of saying something," the son of a member of the community, "Reema's boy—the one with the pear-shaped head—came hauling himself back from one of those fancy colleges mainside, dragging his notebooks and tape recorder and a funny way of curling up his lip and clicking his teeth, all excited and determined to put Willow Springs on the map" (p. 7).

With a skillful use of irony, signification, call and response, and narrative sequencing that takes the reader and listener on a journey that dramatically weaves around the direct point of the event with word-pictures and concrete observations about life, love, and people before returning to the point, Naylor writes:

> you see, he had come to the conclusion after "extensive field work" (ain't never picked a boll of cotton or head of lettuce in his life—Reema spoiled him silly), but he done still made it to the conclusion that 18 & 23 wasn't 18 & 23 at all—was really 81 & 32, which just so happened to be the lines of longitude and latitude marking off where Willow Springs sits on the map. And we were just so damned dumb that we turned the whole thing around. Not that he called it being dumb, mind you, called it "asserting our cultural identity," "inverting hostile social and political parameters." 'Cause, see, being we was brought here as slaves, we had no choice but to look at everything upside-down. (Pp. 7–8)

The code-switching speech of George and Cocoa reveals the tension in their different notions of freedom, literacy, and wholeness, ranging from dating rituals and literary taste (she seemed to prefer the popular works of Harold Robbins and James Michener while he preferred Hemingway, Ellison, and Shakespeare, especially *The Tragedy of King Lear* and *The Tempest*) to beliefs and values. But the mysterious dust on the letter of thanks for helping her to get a job that Mama Day insisted Cocoa send George from Willow Springs apparently helped to bring the couple together. Even after their marriage, however, George never talked about his feelings and believed in living only in the present, while Cocoa, who ultimately opened up fully to share her feelings, believed that a "person is made up of much more than the 'now'" (pp. 126–27).

Most of Naylor's minor characters are as complex, dynamic, and mysterious as Mama Day, Cocoa, and George. For example, Abigail reads the storms and secrets of Nature like a book, complements in a subdued manner the healing powers of her sister Mama Day, laments the deaths of her three daughters, and with Mama Day raises her granddaughter Cocoa to respect the traditions of her island ancestors and elders. Dr. Buzzard is the island bootlegger and con man at poker and conjuration. Miss Ruby is a conjuring old islander who jealously and malevolently casts fatal spells on women suspected of attracting her younger husband's roving eye. Bernice Duvall is Cocoa's island married friend whose desperation to have children drives her to Dr. Buzzard, fertility drugs, and death's door. And Mrs. Jackson is the severe director who ran the Staten Island orphanage by the rules and who raised George and her other fifty-nine mostly black and Puerto Rican youngsters with tough love to be respectful, responsible, and ever mindful of her frequent admonition: "Only the present has potential, *sir*" (p. 23).

Although the most memorable characters and deployment of ethnic tropes in Naylor's novels focus on the power of female bonding, the black male characters in *Mama Day* and *The Men of Brewster Place* are memorable for being uncommonly and complexly human rather than stereotypic sexist predators and abusers of women. More than other contemporary African American novels *Mama Day* grounds the authenticity, authority, and agency of the identity formation of African Americans in the language, knowledge, and power of the vernacular tradition of the ancestors and elders in the Georgia and South Carolina Sea Islands.

AL[BERT JAMES] YOUNG (1939–)

Prize-winning novelist, poet, short story writer, screenwriter, and editor, Al Young indicates that the authenticity and authority of his literary achievements have their roots in "the black tradition of oral storytelling and versifying and also the black musical tradition with the many facets that entails: different musical idioms—gospel, blues, jazz, pop song and also the idea of additive rhythm and the spirit of improvisation."[47] Albert James Young Jr. was born on May 31, 1939, in Ocean Springs, Mississippi, on the Gulf Coast near Biloxi, the oldest of four sons to Albert James Young Sr., a musician and auto worker, and Mary Campbell Young Simmons. He "grew up in homes where the verbal jam session was a floating and usually festive fixture" in rural Mississippi and urban Detroit, Michigan.[48] Because of his biological father, he also grew up in a home with records and live music. As a pre-schooler he used to sit with his three brothers in front of the family's coal-burning heater and listen to his father's wide-ranging collection of 78-rpm records. Although his family moved to Detroit around 1945 and his mother later remarried, he "was shipped back South" for two years around 1947 and frequently spent summers in Pachuta, Mississippi, on his grandparents' farm with no electricity, cars, or running water.

After intermittent school years in Mississippi, Young graduated from high school in Detroit, majored in Spanish at the University of Michigan at Ann Arbor from 1957 to 1961, and then moved to the West Coast, where he discovered "a sense of belonging as a creative person."[49] In 1963 he married Arlin Belck, with whom he has a son, Michael James; and in 1969 he completed his

B.A. in Spanish with honors at the University of California, Berkeley. While writing and publishing with small presses, Young worked at a variety of jobs, ranging from professional singer and guitarist, disk jockey, and industrial films narrator to medical photographer, clerk-typist, yard clerk for the Southern Pacific Railroad, and college lecturer. Since 1969 he has taught at such institutions of higher education as Stanford University, the University of California, Santa Cruz, the University of Washington, Bowling Green State University, the University of Michigan, the University of Arkansas, and the University of California at Davis.

When he was nine or ten years old, Young decided that his destiny was to be a writer. The residually oral storytelling and music tradition of his family was the major influence in shaping that destiny. In addition to folklore and biblical lore, his reading as a teenager ranged widely from Mark Twain, Ben Franklin, Langston Hughes, Richard Wright, and James T. Farrell to Li Po, the T'ang dynasty Chinese poet, Blaise Cendrars, the Swiss writer, Amos Tutola, René Maran, and Juan Ramon Jimenez. The musicians Louis Armstrong and Charlie Parker were also major influences on Young's literary imagination. Although he started writing science fiction and adventure stories while in the fifth grade, it wasn't until he was around fifteen years old that he began writing seriously and publishing poems, stories, and articles in local newspapers and literary magazines. He has published seven books of poetry: *Dancing* (1969), *The Song Turning Back into Itself* (1971), *Geography of the Near Past* (1976), *The Blues Don't Change* (1982), *Heaven* (1992), *Straight No Chaser* (1994), and *Conjugal Visits* (1996). He has also published four musical memoirs: *Bodies & Soul* (1981), *Kinds of Blue* (1984), *Things Ain't What They Used to Be* (1987), and *Drowning in the Sea of Love* (1995), and is co-author of *Mingus Mingus: Two Memoirs* (1989). In addition, he is the editor of *African American Literature* (1996), co-editor of *Yardbird Lives!* (1972) and *Calafia* (1979), and author or co-author of several screenplays and scripts.

But Young is most widely known and critically respected for his five novels. They include the pre-1983 *Snakes* (1970), *Who Is Angelina?*(1975), *Sitting Pretty* (1976), and *Ask Me Now* (1980), as well as the post-1983 *Seduction by Light* (1988). In these books, "creativity always proceeds from joyousness or fun," rather than alienation and despair. Although he states that he is "not a flagrant experimenter or audacious innovator in the accepted sense," the tragicomic characters in his novels move beyond stereotypes of the 1960s and 1970s. Because he sees himself "fundamentally as a working-class writer geared to a blues esthetic" that is grounded in "a living tradition rather than a literary tradition," his personal hero, Young told an interviewer in 1981, is "the man or woman who is spiritually adventurous and can see around corners and through barriers, so to speak, in their quest for ultimate truth." MC in *Snakes*, Angelina Green in *Who Is Angelina?*, Sidney J. Prettymon in *Sitting Pretty*, Durwood Knight in *Ask Me*

Now, and Mamie Franklin in *Seduction by Light* are protagonists who are "displaced people clinging to intuitive notions of how they really are and pursuing those notions in their lives" and in their quests "to belong and be part of a meaningful whole."[50] Although *Who Is Angelina?* and *Seduction by Light* are imaginatively compelling, authentic constructions of the vernacular voices that illustrate the meditative and mystical as well as realistic quest for freedom, literacy, and wholeness of Angelina and Mamie, the authenticity, authority, and agency of the language and music in *Snakes* challenge the often stereotypic "fist-waving" literary representations of black male identity in the 1960s and 1970s.

Similar to *Train Whistle Guitar,* Albert Murray's first novel, *Snakes* is an upbeat, open-ended black *kunstleroman.* Rejected by one editor as "a little too sweet for a ghetto novel," *Snakes* began as a short story about the impact of black music on the coming-of-age of a young black male artist. Its theme and structure of the quest for sociopsychological wholeness and creative authority are therefore in the tradition of the nameless poet-narrator in Toomer's *Cane,* the nameless musician-narrator in James Weldon Johnson's *Autobiography of an Ex-Colored Man,* and the blind jazz pianist-narrator, Ludlow Washington, in William Melvin Kelley's *Drop of Patience.* Although less experimental than these earlier novels and Murray's *Train Whistle Guitar, Snakes* affirms the power of AAVE and black music in the rites of passage of inner city African Americans, especially young males.

Told in the first-person retrospective narrative voice of the teenage protagonist MC, the novel is divided into three conventional parts. Part One introduces readers to MC and his Detroit neighborhood; to the impact of Claude, his grandmother, and of his family background on MC; and to the influence of Tull, the Mississippi blues pianist, and of Champ, MC's streetwise, modern jazz—loving high school buddy, on the protagonist's ambition to become a musician. Part Two traces the development of the band and its first and only successful recording, "Snakes," which was written by MC the morning after getting high on pot for the first time. Part Three reflects on the break-up of the band, especially in the diary entries in chapter 2, and MC's departure for New York to continue his quest for self-knowledge as a jazz musician. *Snakes* therefore focuses less on the shaping of the sensibility, double consciousness, and skills of a black American writer or musician than on the impact of the fantastic yet fleeting success of a record on the identity formation in the mid 1960s of four inner city young black members of the band, "The Masters of Ceremony." Redheaded James Harris, called Shakes because an aunt had made him as a child read Shakespeare every evening and because he had subsequently developed a smooth rap like the Bard, played the drums, was the co-author with MC of about seventy-five songs with a solid rhythm and blues sound, but was not encouraged by his family to pursue seriously his talents in music. Pipe-smoking, easy-going Jimmy Monday played the bass when he was not working on cars, but ultimately seeks adventure and security in the navy. A little older than the others, blind, and a recent high school graduate, Billy Sanchez, who was already serious about jazz as a career, was the pianist and organist who moved on to become a professional jazz musician. The lead guitarist, composer of their local hit song, "Snakes," and representative of a traditional nonpolitical urban black male of the 1950s was MC.

Both MC and Claude, the grandmother and elder in the novel, are more complex, however, than the frequent stereotypic representations during the 1960s and 1970s of angry black predators and militant revolutionaries on the one hand, and of noble black matriarchs and contemporary African queens on the other. Claudette Moore is no one-dimensional paragon of virtue, no pillar of black female protestant beliefs and rituals. Rather, she is a middle-aged, dark-skinned, hard-working, numbers-playing, resourceful black woman who at fifteen years old ran away from her Mississippi home with a man nearly old enough to be her father. After he impregnated and deserted her in New Orleans, she met her common-law husband Bo. Except for the years during her illness after Bo's death when MC lived with Mississippi cousins, she also raises, loves, supports, and counsels MC in his quest for freedom, literacy, and wholeness after his parents' death in a car accident. Concerned about his spending too much time practicing his guitar and hanging out with Champ, Claude reminds her grandson: "MC, I would so much like for you to go on thru school and make something outta yourself. You speak well. You read a lot. You seem to have the intelligence. I even enjoy your music, what little I can understand, only I wish yall wouldn't play it so loud sometime. You have the ability to make anything out of your life you want to. You could go on to college, go right up here to Wayne State and study to be a lawyer. . . . You could be a teacher or an accountant or anything you choose. . . . I raised you and I love you and I want you to amount to somethin."[51] Worried about being left alone as much as about the dangerous, self-indulgent life of many blues musicians and yet proud of her sixteen-year-old grandson, she tells him "I probly shouldnt tell you this but I think you old enough to make up your own mind about things. You know what you wanna do. People do what they have to do" (p. 94).

The implied author skillfully uses the authenticity, authority, and agency of MC's code-switching from AAVE to SAE and his shift from the blues to jazz to dramatize how the identity formation of the protagonist is an ongoing process. "When I was ten," MC tells us early in the novel in his distinctive voice, "Bo died and Claude took sick and didn't have the means or strength to look after me properly, so I was sent south to live with relatives. They were cousins but I called them Uncle Donald and Aunt Didi. They lived in a small town in Mississippi and were poor as church mice the first year I spent with them" (p. 8). It was after his Uncle Donald turned his house into a beer garden that MC heard and learned by heart blues, rhythm and blues, jazz, and even country and western records. It was also in Mississippi that MC learned to play the blues on the piano and the guitar. But neither he nor the reader learns anything about the antiblack racism of Mississippi beyond Tull's mysterious disappearance and reported imprisonment. Significantly, it was up North in Detroit that young MC and his band had fleeting success with their rhythm and blues record, "Snakes," and Champ, who was hooked on jazz and drugs but played no instrument himself, introduced MC to modern jazz records and *Down Beat*, a popular jazz magazine. In the ostensibly hopeful closing scene of the novel, the implied author is sympathetic with his teenage protagonist's apolitical personal agency in leaving Detroit and the women who love him, Claude, and Donna Lee, for New York and a vocation in music as the construction of his identity continues. But many readers familiar with the civil rights demonstrations and urban violence in Detroit in the late 1960s will find the following apolitical imagined diary entry by MC unrepresentative of the dual personal and collective agency of black urban teenagers of the era in reconciling the tensions of their African American double consciousness: *"For the first time in my life I don't feel trapped; I don't feel free either but I don't feel trapped & I'm going to try & make this feeling last for as long as I can"* (p. 14).

Young's omission in the thematic and structural development of *Snakes*, especially the ending, of the sociohistorical and sociopsychological context of the class and generational tensions between some of the major leaders and members of the Civil Rights and Black Power movements clearly demonstrates the importance of the contemporary debate about the dual responsibility of the black artist to his craft and his community. In avoiding or repressing the development of a social consciousness and political agency in his protagonist, Young affirms the dominant culture's valorization of the individual freedom of an artist to privilege his art over his community, as MC with traditional male insensitively does by leaving for New York with his guitar, sacrificing interpersonal intimacy, and leaving behind the women who love him. Although he effectively deploys irony in the representation of Claude and Champ, Young neglects to heighten the moral, political, psychological, and cultural identity formation of his teenage protagonist with irony as he and MC swim against the political activism of his times, his age group, and his primary black community.

DAVID [HENRY] BRADLEY [JR.] (1950–)

Like Al Young, David Bradley marched to a different drummer during the Black Power and Black Arts movements in his narrative representation of the formation of African American male identity, especially the construction of a neomasculine black identity in his most outstanding novel, *The Chaneysville Incident*. But Bradley is more irreverent, innovative, and iconoclastic as a novelist than Young. Bradley is also more than ten years younger. On September 7, 1950, in Bedford, Pennsylvania, David Henry Bradley Jr. became the only son of David

Henry Bradley Sr., a minister and historian, and Harriette M. Jackson Bradley. Raised in a farm county near the Maryland border with a population of about 100 blacks and 30,000 whites in an area known to blacks as Gravel Hill but to whites as "Niggers' Knob," "Boogie Bend," and "Spade Hollow," Bradley would spend three weeks in the summer every year from 1955 to around 1965 traveling with his father in Virginia and North Carolina, where the Reverend Bradley conducted Christian education workshops.[52] After graduating from Bedford Area High School in 1968, Bradley attended the University of Pennsylvania, where he studied under John Edgar Wideman, and graduated summa cum laude with a B.A. in English and creative writing in 1972. He also received a General Honors Certificate and a Thouron British-American Exchange Scholarship, which enabled him to earn an M.A. at the Institute for United States Studies at King's College of the University of London in 1974. He published both of his novels before 1983: *South Street* (1975) and *The Chaneysville Incident* (1981).

Bradley's father was probably the major influence on his becoming a writer. A graduate of the University of Pittsburgh who pursued a doctoral degree at New York University before settling in Bedford, the elder Bradley "wrote several books on the history of the Methodist Church and published them privately."[53] At nine years old, young Bradley wrote his first work, a science fiction play called "Martian Thanksgiving." Because of his background in a rural, predominantly white area, he felt at the university that he didn't fit in with the urban, politically activist, well-read students of the Black Power and Black Arts movements. But in a bar on South Street in Philadelphia he discovered people with whom he felt comfortable and an environment that confirmed for him that black university students were far less realistic and sincere than the folks on South Street. This experience inspired his first novel, *South Street*, which he wrote while he was an undergraduate.

At the center of the novel is the quest of Adlai Stevenson Brown, a young black Ivy League poet and part-time bartender, to reconstruct his identity as a black man in the 1970s and to find creative inspiration for his poetry. Rejecting the dominant culture's middle-class materialism and respectability advocated by Alicia, his black lover, and moving from her penthouse to a tenement apartment in South Philadelphia, Brown pursues his journey by talking and listening to the working class, underemployed, illicitly self-employed, and unemployed black folks he meets hanging out on South Street in Lightnin' Ed's Bar and Grill. Despite its apparently thin, meandering plot line of the impact of race, class, and gender on identity formation, *South Street* is a probing, satirical examination of the ties that bind the tragicomic lives of black bartenders, janitors, winos, hustlers, numbers runners, prostitutes, pimps, and preachers struggling to get by in the inner city of Philadelphia.

Bradley weaves a narrative of grim yet compellingly authentic vernacular vignettes of a gallery of signifying and parodying characters. They begin with Leo, the overweight "owner-bartender-cashier-bouncer of Lightnin' Ed's Bar and Grill": Big Betsy, a signifying old whore who is still cruising for customers; Rayburn, the bitter janitor and jilted husband of the sexually insatiable Leslie; and Leroy, the bad-ass hustler, numbers runner, and pimp. Most important to the protagonist's construction of a neomasculine black identity that resists the values of the dominant culture are the cautionary tales of Jake, the aging, homeless wino, barroom elder, and affable storytelling male chauvinist. As a wino, he tells Brown, "'You got to give up—bein' reglar. Can't be worryin' 'bout no clothes. Can't be worryin' 'bout no car. Can't get uptight 'bout no house, or no job. Can't be too worried 'bout food. An' women—no women. I tell you, Brown, women's been the downfall a many a good wino. That's why it's hard for a young man to make the grade.'"[54] Jake's antipathy to materialism and women anticipates the traditional sexist attitude of Old Jack Crawley, an elder and surrogate father to John Washington, the protagonist in *The Chaneysville Incident*.

Other dynamic characters in *South Street* include the Reverend Sloan, the lascivious, exploitative pastor of the poor, innocent, and desperate members of The Word of Life Church; Brother Fletcher, the compassionate, faithful associate preacher, husband, and shepherd of the flock in the storefront church; and Vanessa, Leroy's prostitute ex-girl friend and Rayburn's sister-in-law, who becomes Brown's live-in lover and inspiration for him to resume writing poetry. With an acute eye and ear for the authenticity and authority of the sights, sounds, and sense of the rhythms of urban African American culture and character as Brown's primary socializing community, Bradley moves beyond the conventional sociological stereotypes in validating and valorizing Brown's individual and collective agency. "It is not man's skill as a modern warrior, nor his sexual conquests, nor his material wealth that defines 'real' maleness in this novel," Cathy Brigham, one of my most outstanding graduate students, has perceptively written, "it is his ability to produce female pleasure and to decipher female desire."[55] The key, then, to Bradley's construction of his protagonist's neomasculine African American identity is his rejection of Alicia's uncritical black middle-class conformity to the dominant culture's consumerism and his empathy with the vernacular tradition of the black working poor as well as with Vanessa's paradoxical resistance to the commodification of her body.

Whereas many critics have focused on the treatment of history in *The Chaneysville Incident*, only a few, like black feminist Mary Helen Washington and white neo-Freudian Philip J. Egan, have analyzed the theme of misogyny in the novel. Washington defines misogyny as "woman-hating," the popular definition that we find in the tenth edition of *Merriam-Webster's Collegiate Dictionary*. She condemns the book because in Bradley's imaginative reconstruction of the history of African American resistance to slavery and cultural domination, "women are only the hinges connecting one man to his male descendants, where we only know the women's lives as they contribute to the making of another man, in which all the proud, defiant, heroic, gestures are accomplished by men."[56] Whereas the novel clearly reveals extreme dislike and distrust of women by the main male characters, a similar attitude and behavior toward men are apparent in literature, including novels by black women since the 1970s, like Alice Walker's *Color Purple*. Addressing this issue in 1978 in her highly popular and controversial book, *Black Macho and the Myth of the Superwoman*, Michele Wallace wrote, "for perhaps the last fifty years there has been a growing distrust, even hatred, between black men and black women. It has been nursed along not only by racism on the part of whites but also by an almost deliberate ignorance on the part of blacks about the sexual politics of their experience in this country."[57]

Among other things, the history of antiblack racism and social oppression of black Americans has spawned numerous popular and social science negative stereotypes about black men and women that foster socialized ambivalence, if not self-hatred, in many African Americans. These negative stereotypes range from those in plantation tradition literature and blackface minstrelsy to those in Daniel Moynihan's theory of the pathology of black female-headed households in 1965. The two negative stereotypes that are thematically most relevant to the following analysis of *The Chaneysville Incident* are the mythic power of black matriarchy and the complicity of black females with white males in the social emasculation of black males. The extraordinary achievement of the novel, however, is the authenticity, authority, and agency of the intellectual, psychological, and emotional struggle of the neomasculine protagonist to overcome these negative stereotypes and the misogynist legacy of his ancestors and elders by imaginatively reconstructing the love and heroic sacrifice of his great-grandfather C. K. Washington and Harriette Brewer as conductors on the Underground Railroad.

Praising its aesthetic achievement, Egan, in contrast to Washington, is more provocative and illuminating in broadly defining misogyny as "a deep and abiding distrust of women" and analyzing this theme in the novel in relationship to Freud's theory of the Oedipus complex.[58] Drawing on Katharine Rogers's *Troublesome Helpmate*, a historical survey of misogyny in British and American literature, Egan shifts critical attention from the conventional emphasis on the misogyny of Old Jack Crawley to argue intriguingly that in "*Chaneysville* the prominence of both mother and lover (respectively Yvette Washington and Judith Powell) firmly anchors the novel in this tradition."[59] However, both Egan and Mary Helen Washington inadequately assess the role of Harriette Brewer in the novel. Although, as Rogers notes, the "acute fear of female domination which appears in several major modern authors has been intensified and given shape by Freud's emphasis on maternal power,"[60] that is, control over frustration and punishment as well as food, security, and love, it cannot be conclusively established that Freud's Oedipal theories, derived from European myths, Freud's Jewish middle-class identity formation, and the pathology of his European patients, apply universally to contemporary African Americans or that Bradley consciously made use of them.

Nevertheless, the theme of fearing, hating, and distrusting women, which Bradley subtly interweaves with the resistance of John's legendary ancestors to white oppression and which is related symbolically to John's quest for freedom and wholeness as a black man, is most apparent in John's relationship to Judith, the white psychiatrist lover with whom he lives, and Yvette, his mother. While the narrative present (the time of the actual third-person omniscient and first-person telling of the story) ranges from March 3 through 12, 1979, in Bedford County, Pennsylvania, the fictive past (the time of the major legendary events) dates back to the antebellum period in Pennsylvania and the South. The discontinuous, multilayered narrative opens with John, a history professor in Pennsylvania, receiving a call to the death bed of Old Jack Crawley, a legendary storyteller and outdoorsman, as well as John's surrogate father. In response to this call back to his black community and to the traditional male values of hunting, John increasingly overcomes his distrust of Judith Powell and his antipathy for Yvette.

The relationship of language to knowledge, power, and identity is established in the opening episode with John's unwillingness to share his thoughts and feelings with Judith. "'Someday,' she said, 'you're going to talk to me. And when you do I'm going to listen to you. I'm going to listen to you so Goddamn hard it's going to hurt'" (p. 4). In chapter 7 she challenges John for lying to her. "'I know why you do it,' she said. 'You do it because you don't trust me. I don't know why, but I know that. And I know I can't take any more of it. I need you to share with me. Now. I need that'" (p. 261). Rejecting his lurid details and local color stories, Judith exposes John's double consciousness during the climactic episodes: "'I know. You can hate me and love me at the same time. But you see, that's not what I want. I don't want you to hate me at all. I don't want to live like that. If I have to, in order to be with you, then I will, for as long as I can. But if I'm going to do that, I have to know more about the hate, about where it comes from. Because you're talking about hating me'" (p. 275). This dialectic process involves John shifting from an exclusive reliance on the authority of facts and cognition to a synthesis of these powers with the imagination and emotions, knowledge acquired from the stories by and hunting rituals with Old Jack Crawley, in explaining the mysterious deaths of his father (Moses Washington), grandfather (Lamen Washington), and great-grandfather (C. K. Washington). Bradley thus demonstrates that one's neomasculine identity formation is a dynamic process rather than a static product as John's growing knowledge and power enable him to ascertain the truth of his family legacy, to reconstruct his hatred of whites and women, and to achieve a provisional psychological wholeness.

Overcoming the earlier hatred of whites and women that is apparent in his youthful rape of a white female acquaintance, John reconstructs his neomasculine identity from memories, legends, rumors, stories, dreams, and family recorded facts about thirteen mysterious graves which he gradually shares with Judith in a pseudo-psychoanalytic manner. By addressing questions about the reliability of the narrator and protagonist with shifts from third-person omniscient to first-person narrative strategies, this process enables John not only to overcome his deep-seated hatred of whites and women, but also to understand more fully the resistance to slavery and antiblack racism by both the male and female ancestors, especially the heroism of Harriette Brewer, and elders of his African American family and community. Among other things, Bradley risks the reliability of his narrator and protagonist by combining rumors, memory, and legend as John reconstructs the legacy of his ancestors and elders while climbing the Hill to Old Jack's cabin. He recalls that Jack, Josh White, who was nearly lynched during a love affair with a white woman, and Moses Washington, legendary ruffian, hunter, bootlegger, and highly decorated Korean veteran, were hunting, fishing, and drinking buddies for forty years before Moses married Yvette, the haughty daughter of a Howard University professor, in 1946. John's fear and hatred of women are mainly instilled by Jack, who believes that women are dangerous. According to John's recall of Jack's story, Moses, in anticipation of something happening to him, had asked his old friend to take his son and " 'teach him to hunt, an' teach him to fish, an' drink whiskey an' cuss. Teach him to track' " (p. 36). Jack therefore introduces nine-year-old John to whiskey toddies with the warning that " 'women do more harm to a man than whiskey ever did' " (p. 32). He teaches him that a good woman is dangerous on " 'accounta she don' try to change a man, she jest makes him think he oughta change' " (p. 69). Condemning the church " 'biddies' " for gossiping about Josh White courting a white girl in a nearby Ku Klux Klan county, Jack says: " 'Them bitches'd spread anything 'ceptin' their legs for their husbands' " (p. 84).

In a flashback to his first visit in the middle of the night as a child to Jack's cabin, thirty-year-old John recalls his surrogate father's lessons about the four things necessary for being a real man: air, land, water, and sun. He learns that not only man but also mankind needs air to breathe, water to drink, land to stand on, and the sun for power: " 'Now, them's the four things a man needs, but he don't need them on accounta he's a man, he needs 'em on accounta he's an animal. An' if he stops when he's got 'em, he won't never be nothin' but an animal. He won't be a man. He won't be a man on accounta he can't make none a them things. So he ain't got no say. If he don't have no say over the things he needs to live, he ain' got no say over whether he lives at all, an' if he ain't got no say over that, he ain't no man. A man has to have say'" (pp. 40–41). According to Jack, it is fire that gives man the final say because it enables him to destroy anything. He admits, however, "'that ain't much say, an' it ain't the best kinda say, but it's bettern havin' no say at all. Because a man with no say is an animal. So a man has to be able to make a fire, has to know how to make it in the wind an' the rain an' the dark. When he can do that, he can have some say'" (p. 42). Bradley thus affirms the complex relationship of language to knowledge and power in the human agency of resisting oppression and the process of identity formation, which clearly includes the power of violence.

Readers also hear that John has recurring dreams in which his mother's ostensible caring for him while he was sick and feverish turns into a cold, murderous intent that he struggles to escape. "I had asked her to stop," he recalls retrospectively, "but she had kept on bathing me, and I realized that she was trying to kill me."[61] John's hatred of his mother has its origin in her hitting and verbally emasculating him in front of the white principal for fighting another boy who called him a "nigger." Leaving the school, she explains her ostensible complicity with whites and misguided effort at protecting him from antiblack racism: "'John, don't you forget, don't ever forget that white people are the ones that say what happens to you. Maybe it isn't right, but that's just exactly the way it is. And so long as you're going to their school, so long as they're teaching you what you need to learn, you have to be quiet, and careful, and respectful. Because you've got your head in the lion's mouth'" (p. 119). John's blend of fear and dislike of his mother intensifies with her ostensible false piety in erecting a shrine in their home for his brother Bill after she contributed to his death by convincing him to join the army to avoid a jail sentence instead of following John's advice and escaping to Canada. Although Freud's theory of castration anxiety generally focuses on a son's competition with the father over the mother's love, as Egan notes, John's hatred of his father and anxiety revert to Yvette, his mother, after his father's mysterious death.

In fact, beginning with his mother's "brisk, efficient, and dry-eyed" manner at Moses' funeral in 1958 (p. 22) and with drunken Old Jack Crawley's attempt to keep his promise to Moses to raise his son, John, at nine years old, "increasingly finds his mother an oppressive presence, and he subsequently associates her with images of engulfment typical of a castration fear."[62] Listening to Old Jack on his dying bed in 1979, John has a flashback to his first visit to Jack's shack and learns that Moses was "'a real hateable man'" who "'didn't give a good God damn about anybody in the world'" (p. 35), except probably John. Because he distrusted the appropriateness of Yvette's "uppity" color, class, and gender beliefs and values to raise John into manhood, Moses designated Old Jack, his closest friend and hunting buddy, to teach his son how to become an independent black man in an antiblack white rural Pennsylvania community.

Bradley dramatically reveals this to readers early in the first chapter in one of Old Jack's legendary stories. Jack told young John: "'Said you was too much your mamma's child. Said he was worried you was gonna end up bein' a preacher or a sissy or somethin', on account a the way that woman carried on around you, fussin' with your clothes an' fixin' you food an' things that a man oughta be able to do for hisself. . . . He said there was a lot a woman in you. He didn't mean nothin' bad by that—jest meant that you was the kind that trusted people. Kind that believed there was always gonna be somebody to help you get through things'" (p. 34). The dramatic irony during this flashback is that as an adult John had become psychologically, emotionally, and culturally distant from the cultural legacy, especially the misogyny, of his rural black male ancestors and elders like Moses and Jack not only by becoming an urbanized professor of history in a white institution but also by sharing an apartment with a white lover.

Although in his interracial affair with Judith he struggles with his ambivalence about whites and women, John does not significantly move beyond his misogyny for his mother until she surprisingly demonstrates respect for Jack Crawley in her testimonial at his funeral. "'This man was a brother to my husband,'" she says. "'Walked with him, and talked with him. Saved his life, more than once. Saved him for me. I owe this man for that. . . . And this man was a father to my boy. Taught him things I couldn't teach him. Showed him things I couldn't show him. . . . I didn't like that. It made me fear. . . . But he loved my son. And he taught him the things he taught him because that was what he believed a man should know'" (pp. 217–18). After discovering in the closing episode of chapter 7 that his father actually committed suicide, John finally develops sympathy for his mother as he realizes that she does not know this: "But then I realized that it made no difference what she knew, because for a dozen years she had lived with a man who was so crazy that one day he was going to walk twenty-two miles just to find a nice spot in which to blow his brains out, and so preoccupied as not only to do it, but not to care enough about the effect of it on his wife—and his children—to try and make it look like an accident; a man who showed her no mercy" (p. 307). Before leaving with Judith to continue his quest, John asks his mother whether marriage to his father was worth it. In response, she silently turns her radio on in an ambivalent act of moral indignation and resignation. The discovery of his father's suicide also fosters sensitivity and trust for Judith, whom he allows to aid him in the exclusively male ritual of preparing his toddy. She also participates in dialogues with him to answer the enigma of the death of C. K., his legendary great-grandfather, a conductor on the Underground Railroad. In addition, her dialogues help him to solve the mysterious deaths of the eleven slaves that C. K. and Harriette Brewer, his partner in love and the Underground Railroad, were helping to escape a relentless legendary slavecatcher. During this ritual, John acknowledges to Judith that he had underestimated his mother, and "had done it in a way that cheated us both" (p. 411).

With the imaginative reconstruction of the heroic courage, resolve, and sacrifice of Harriette Brewer in violently resisting slavery, bravely conducting slaves to freedom, and resolutely choosing death with C. K. and the other slaves rather than reenslavement when trapped by Pettis, the slavecatcher, John concludes the narrative of his family's legacy and reconciles the ambivalence of his double consciousness about black women. As filtered through John's account of her story, Harriette grew up in a privileged class of free people of color, but she began hating her mother, whites, and men after discovering that her mother was the mistress of a white man. Feeling guilty in 1850 about her privileged life, she was inspired by the dedication of abolitionists, like William Still and C. K., helping slaves to escape on the Underground Railroad, and she not only joined the movement but also fell in love with C. K. In time C. K. " 'had come to accept her, to respect her, and the plans [for escaping slaves] were no longer his plans amended by her, but plans created by both of them' " (p. 419). While carrying C. K.'s child and while assuming personal responsibility for helping slaves in the South to escape, she was betrayed, enslaved, and ultimately impregnated with two daughters. When the slave father of her children threatened to betray the escape that she had organized, she cut his throat and led her three children and the group of slaves to South County, Pennsylvania, where she unexpectedly reunited with C. K. to lead them to freedom.

Surrounded by Pettis and his posse of slavecatchers, inspired by the ancestral myth-legend chanted by Azacca, the elder of their group, that " 'Death, was not an ending of things, but a passing on of spirit,' " and influenced by teenage Juda's act of infanticide, the slaves, led by C. K. and Harriette, chose death rather than reenslavement: "For a moment he was not sure that he [C. K.] could lead them, was not sure that they would follow, but then he saw Harriette Brewer take her knife from beneath her shawl and hold it high, and he heard her, heard her singing softly, then louder, heard the others join in, the words of the song growing, rising from the hilltop, floating down the incline . . . 'And before I'll be a slave I'll be buried in my grave, and go home to my God, and be free.' " (pp. 428, 430) As the last voice to fall silent when she takes her own life, Harriette joins the other slaves in resolutely demonstrating the power of what Old Jack called final say by their acts of parricide and suicide. It is John's imaginative reconstruction of this final act of authority and agency by C. K. and Harriette, as well as of the probability that the slaves were buried as families by the white miller, Iiames, that represents the dynamic process of continuity and change in his neomasculine African American identity formation, especially the transformation of his hatred of whites and women.

Like Ishmael Reed in *Mumbo Jumbo*, David Bradley boldly and innovatively creates an unreliable narrator to interrogate the complex impact of the legacy of colonialism, antiblack racism, slavery, and sexism on the relationship of language to knowledge and power in imaginatively reconstructing a viable African American past and challenging contemporary stereotypes of neomasculine identities in *The Chaneysville Incident*. Although the novel problematizes the universality of historical and scientific truth, it is neither antirepresentational nor antiessentialist like most postmodern novels. Instead, the themes, structure, and style of *The Chaneysville Incident* affirm the fundamental humanism of empathy and love, as well as the transhistorical value of freedom, literacy, wholeness, orality, myth, legend, tale, and song in the construction of contemporary African American human identities. In the narrative tradition of Margaret Walker, Ishmael Reed, Toni Morrison, Alice Walker, Albert Murray, Gayl Jones, and Gloria Naylor, Bradley experiments with modern literary uses of the African American vernacular tradition in the contemporary novel. In *The Chaneysville Incident* the core beliefs and values of black legendary male and female ancestors and elders are represented as equally enduring symbols and tropes that many contemporary African American novelists deploy to reconstruct imaginatively our tragicomic, often ironic and paradoxical, struggle for authority, authenticity, and agency as individuals and as a people.

LEON [RICHARD] FORREST (1937–1997)

Novelist, short story writer, and essayist, Leon Forrest also experimented with the African American residually oral forms of oratory (including vernacular voices), myth/ritual performances, legend, tale, and song in the contemporary novel. The only child of Leon Forrest Sr., a recorded lyricist and bartender on the Sante Fe Railroad, and Adeline Green, a short story writer and fan of jazz singers, Leon Richard Forrest was born January 8, 1937, in Chicago.[63] Raised on the city's South Side, he was heavily influenced by the myths and rituals of both the Catholicism of his mother's family and the Protestantism of his father's, as well as by the musical interests of his parents. As a young boy he became familiar with the language, myths, characters, and drama of the Bible by reading it to his great-grandmother. This influence, reinforced by the rituals of the Black Baptist church that he attended with his father, informs the themes, structure, and style of his novels.

As a student at Hyde Park High School from 1951 to 1955, Forrest developed an interest in creative writing and journalism, winning several poetry and essay contests. He also served as a reporter on the school newspaper. After graduation from high school, he attended Wilson Junior College (1955–56), Roosevelt University (1957–58), and the University of Chicago (1959–60), where he was mentored by fiction writer Perrin H. Lowrey. While serving in the army between 1960 and 1962, Forrest wrote for the newspaper *Spearhead*. Returning to the University of Chicago from 1962 to 1963, he continued pursuing his interest in creative writing and journalism. In 1964 he began working with community newspapers, becoming a non-Muslim reporter and later managing editor with *Muhammed Speaks*, the newspaper of the Nation of Islam, in 1969. Forrest taught in the African American Studies Program at Northwestern University from 1973 until his death in 1997. He also lectured at Yale and Wesleyan Universities as well as at the Rochester Institute of Technology. His honors include the Carl Sandburg Award (1985) and the Society of Midland Authors Award (1985), as well as the *Chicago Sun-Times* Chicago Book of the Year Award (1992) and the *New York Times* Notable Book of the Year (1993) for *Divine Days*. He has published two collections of essays, two musical plays, and four novels: *There Is a Tree More Ancient Than Eden* (1973), *The Bloodworth Orphans* (1977), *Two Wings to Veil My Face* (1984), and *Divine Days* (1992).

In the trilogy formed by the first three of those novels, Forrest draws heavily on the symbolic language of the Bible, folk sermon, and code-switching between AAVE and SAE for the authority and authenticity to reveal the trials and tribulations of bearing witness to the sorrows of life, the pains of death, and the promise of rebirth for the people of Forest County, the imaginative setting for all four of his novels. The most compelling and dramatic examples of African American code-switching voices are "The Epistle of Sweetie Reed" and the sermon "Oh Jeremiah of the Dreamers," two episodes added in 1988 to the end of *There Is a Tree More Ancient Than Eden*.[64] Addressing the confrontational politics of politicians and activists of the Civil Rights and Black Power movements, the first is a letter of mother wit, wry social criticism, and sage advice about the War on Poverty and generation gap from a centenarian of the Black community to the President of the United States. The second is an early morning sermon, passionately preached in a tavern by the Reverend Pompey C. J. Browne, that celebrates the legacy of the Reverend Martin Luther King Jr.

Steeled to the challenge of life that "Each man must re-create himself"[65] and of "finding a way out of no way," primarily by the folk wisdom of his family elders, Aunt Hattie Breedlove Wordlaw and surrogate grandmother Great-Momma Sweetie Reed Witherspoon, Nathaniel Witherspoon, the principal narrator in the trilogy, bears witness to the saga of the Bloodworths and the Witherspoons. This saga is highlighted by nightmarish rituals of rape, miscegenation, bastardy, incest, parricide, abortion, abandonment, adoption, and death. "We ought to rise above being scandalized and shamefaced because of our past" is the hard-learned lesson, the personal and collective agency, of the trilogy and *Divine Days*. Because "we all orphans of the wreckage," we ought to accept the frailty of the flesh and act on the faith that "you make of your name what you make of your center being and life."[66] Of the four novels, the first is the most enigmatic because its authority relies heavily on interior monologues, and the last is the most encyclopedic and engaging in deriving its authenticity and authority from an extraordinary exploration of the rich diversity of African American culture and character. These novels plumb the depths of the surreal lives of their combined cast of more than three dozen characters, several of whom appear in all the books, to chart an allegorical journey of black Americans from hell to heaven, from the Salem Cup-Overflowing Tabernacle to the River Rock of Eden Baptist Church and the storefront church Divine Days, from Southern Trees Bearing Strange Fruit to the Tree of Knowledge and the Tree of Life. Because Forrest's manipulation of points of view among several apparently unreliable narrators, and because his improvisational, multivocal, historically and mythically allusive structure and rapturous, surrealistic African Americentric modernist style overwhelm all but the most patient and discerning serious readers, we will examine more closely the artifice and achievement of his magnum opus: *Divine Days*.

Divine Days has received critical acclaim as "the *War and Peace* of the African-American novel," as "the black *Ulysses*," as "an enormous comic epic," and as an "epic detective story."[67] Set on the South Side of Chicago during the compressed period of seven days, this monumental 1,135-page African Americentric modernist novel is written in the form of a journal of fifteen entries dated from February 16 to 23, 1966, by Joubert Antoine Jones, the narrator and protagonist. A seven-time college drop-out, writer, and aspiring playwright, Jones returns home to Forest County after two years in the army in Germany in order to resume work as a bartender and manager in his Aunt Eloise's Night Light Lounge and journalist with her for the *Forest County Dispatch*. He also begins writing a play based on two legendary members of the community: Sugar-Groove, the street-wise cunning hustler, lady's man, and "mythic soul of Forest County, whose early memory was forged mainly in Mississippi,"[68] and W. A. D. Ford, the charlatan cult leader and bamboozling trickster of poor, gullible, desperate seekers of salvation. A year earlier Joubert completed *Divine Days*, a one-act play on Ford, which is rejected by a theater company and returned to him by mail with disappointing criticism. It draws heavily on the charismatic leadership of such historical cult leaders as Father Divine, Daddy Grace, W. A. Ford, and the Honorable Elijah Mohammad. When the novel opens, Joubert is gathering stories for a play about Sugar-Groove. Although these two legendary characters are central to the thematic, structural, and stylistic vernacular authenticity, authority, and agency of the novel, the wide range of tragicomic characters that Joubert Jones and readers meet in (Oscar) Williemain's Barbershop and Eloise's Lounge reveals the rich diversity, double consciousness, resilience, resourcefulness, and wry humor of the survival strategies and storytelling developed by urban African Americans in their quest for freedom, literacy, and wholeness.

From the opening episode of the discontinuous, multivocal narrative, the emphasis is on the memory, names, and imaginative reconstruction of the voices of the Forest County black community. "I've been hearing voices all of my life . . . since before I can remember," the protagonist says:

> Sometimes these incantations overtake me, speaking not only to me, but through me and rendering me up frazzled and daffy. . . . I'm too hypersensitively attuned to the sound of voices, babblings, other-worldly and worldly tongues. I never forget the nuances of sounds within voices. . . . Not reverie, nor nostalgia, nor melancholia, nor that most misused term, dj vu, none of these explain from where the voices within me hail. In certain cases I've assigned these voices surnames. Names as concepts, over-lines to captions for voices that appear when I dream, awake or sleeping. (Pp. 10–11)

Filtered through Joubert's memory of and stories about the importance of the vernacular culture and characters of the barbershop to the identity formation of African American men, we encounter the distinctive lives of (Oscar) Williemain, the barber, "fabulous liar," and founder of "The Mainly-Manly Club" and the Righteous Rites and Royal Ramblings Club that meets in the back of the barbershop; of Manford MacDuff, the retired, stuttering Red Cap who is nearly shot for signifying on Williemain's first name and mother; of Galloway Wheeler, the barber and Shakespearean scholar; and of the three professors.

When he is inducted as a Fellow into the Club, Joubert explains the relationship of language to knowledge and power in the status and bonding of black men across class lines:

> There were three major black professors who came into Williemain's and each held a place of respect and honor . . . accorded them absolutely nowhere else in the Negro Community. Of the three, it was the Historian who was best known outside the barbershop. But Professor Jamesway was Williemain's favorite. . . . The third Professor had the greatest vocabulary, it was rumored, in the Western World. He was in literature and religion. When he spoke even Galloway Wheeler shut-up. Only these three professors could have corrected Williemain out loud in a barbershop full of people and not been referred to as a *louse*. (P. 844)

But it was as a shoe-shine boy in Williemain's barbershop that Joubert first met and heard the legendary stories about Sugar-Groove, a "Negro hustler and drifter" who lived a fast, wild life before being converted on his deathbed by his grand-aunt. Like the character Rinehart in Ellison's *Invisible Man*, Sugar-Groove had multiple identities but they were all based in Sugar: "There was Sugar-Ditch, for his home town, but the only others that I was aware of (Sugar-Dripper, Sugar-Dipper, Sugar-Groove, Sugar-Grove, Sugar-Spook, Sugar-Goose, Sugar-Sack, Sugar-Shank, Sugar-Stroke, Sugar-Splib . . . Sugar-Dick, Sugar-Stud, Sugar-Loaf, Sugar-Smoke, Sugar-Shit, Sugar-Eyes, and Sugar-Shark) referred to various tributes paid to his revealed sexual merriment and moxie and prowess; or his cunning at dice, cards, gambling tables and other games of chance" (pp. 97–98). As Joubert gathers the stories to write the play on Sugar-Groove, he is culturally and psychologically challenged to reconcile his ambivalence about the social and religious impact of Sugar-Groove and W. A. Ford, whose identity is also fluid, on his life and the life of blacks in Forest County.

Ford and a parade of drunks, pimps, prostitutes, preachers, number runners, cab drivers, barbers, teachers, physicians, and thespians were all regular or occasional customers of the Night Light Lounge, which was owned by Eloise and her husband Hickles. Although not as extensively developed as Ford, many of these characters are distinctively and memorably captured in brief, improvisational vignettes. They include the comic, Chivas Regal–drinking drunk Ratcliffe Shackleford and the alcoholic policemen Daniel Conway and Prescott Willoughby, as well as the barmaid La Dorrestine Conway, who "played the gullible innocent, yellow-girl role to the hilt" (p. 35), and the "celebrated oddity, Miss Daisy Dawes" (p. 44), who nearly shoots Joubert for signifying on the sexuality of her minister, the Reverend Honeywood "Swet-Briar" Cox. But it is Wizard Alpha Decathalon Ford, also known as Bishop St. Palm, who first appeared in *The Bloodworth Orphans*, who is the religious contrast to Sugar-Groove as the symbolic force of linguistic power and spiritual transcendence. Ford is "a white-headed, yet ageless evangelist, with a baby soft, high yellow complexion (with reddish brown undertones)" who is the mythic and legendary religious showman who rented the large storefront on East 79th Street three months before it became the site of Eloise's Lounge. Ford conducted "mysterious ritual services" and "fantastic ceremonies in which lizards were deployed in a tortuous disciplining act" before his followers in the church he called "Divine Days" (pp. 37–38). Although Ford mysteriously disappears seven weeks after filling out a rental application for "Divine Days," Joubert attended at least three services in the storefront church and took notes for a news column and a one-act play before Ford vanished.

In the long last journal entry of the novel, Mister Wilkerson, an elder of the community, tells Joubert, whom he calls Brer Bear Jones (the African American nickname given to him by his Aunt Eloise), the mythic story of the final symbolic confrontation on the mountaintop between Ford and Sugar-Groove. Ford is now unmasked as the diabolic Seer and shape-shifting Evil One, and Sugar-Groove is like Legba, "the African trickster God, who was a magician," defiantly breaking taboos and struggling to rediscover "'a form of his manhood,'" "'that inner core of spirituality,'" and that "'one identity with a centered down wholeness; and probably, a wholeness with the energies of the Universe'" (pp. 1046, 1056, and 1066). Ford is determined to blind and destroy Sugar-Groove "'out of revenge, and vengeance. . . . Because he believed that Sugar-Groove had come to see too much about existence, about nature . . . into the other world. . . . Thought Sugar-Groove might possess certain powers beyond those of mere mortals; therefore must be cut down'" (pp. 1066–67). But before he dies, Sugar-Groove, dramatizing the wry humor of the novel, shoots Ford "'seven different places in his low-life ass'" (p. 1044). In the closing paragraphs of the novel Joubert morally, spiritually, and creatively understands and identifies with Sugar-Groove: "I understand now that is why Sugar-Groove went up into the mountains, not only to find his soul and to renew it; to discover something of the meaning of existence and his relationship to it, within the sources of creation . . . the radiance amid the rapture, which is surely what I seek as a playwright" (p. 1134). Joubert's completed play on Ford sat in the dead letter section of the post office before being returned to him in a soiled, rejected condition early in the novel, but the play-in-progress on Sugar-Groove has much more potential for success: "I know that I shall take the memory of Sugar-Groove and fling it with my arrow of fire out into new stars of Heaven with a wondrous (if not perfect) light of illumination" (p. 1134). Reinforcing the improvisational code-switching of idioms and grammar between SAE and AAVE, Forrest returns to Williemain's mythic story at the opening of the novel. He compares Sugar-Groove's creative boldness in heaven to the legendary story of the resourceful, bold black angel who "had to fly around heaven with one wing on the right, roped off and tied behind him" as he "reinvented himself out of all of that so much so that St. Peter himself was startled to amazement" (p. 1134). In *Divine Days* Forrest thus celebrates with imaginative and improvisational power and virtuosity "the Negro-American's will to transform, reinvent, and stylize until Hell freezes over" (pp. 1127–28).

While Afrocentric tropes dominate the African Americentric residual oral forms in Marshall's *Praisesong for the Widow* and Naylor's *Mama Day*, the reverse is true in Murray's trilogy, especially *The Seven League Boots*, Young's *Snakes*, Bradley's *Chaneysville Incident*, and Forrest's trilogy and *Divine Days*. The authenticity, authority, and agency of each text as fundamentally African American, however, are generally most effectively illuminated by the imaginative deployment of code-switching black voices, particularly of the community ancestors and elders. These voices, emanating especially from bars, clubs, barbershops, kitchens, and the church, affirm the dynamic relationship of language to knowledge and power in the continuing struggle, individually and collectively, against antiblack racism and for a new world order of freedom, literacy, and wholeness for all people.

7 / The New Black Aesthetic: Eurocentric Metafiction and African Americentric Tropes of Transcultural Identity and Community (1983–2001)

This New Black Movement . . . somehow synthesizes the last two black art revivals, the Harlem Renaissance and the Black Arts Movement. In the Twenties blacks wanted no part of dominant culture at all. In the Sixties we wanted no part of dominant culture at all. Today the NBA wants to dominate it. We feel "separate but better."

TREY ELLIS

"Response to NBA Critiques"

THE national census of 2000 confirms the growing potential power shift in the demographics of the United States to immigrants and native-born people generally called Latinos (i.e., citizens and noncitizens from North, Central, and South American nations of Spanish and various ethnic mixtures) as the largest ethnic political coalition in the nation. Internationally, the cataclysmic ethnic conflicts, migrations, drug wars, or genocidal wars in the former Union of Soviet Socialist Republics, the Congo, and the former Yugoslavia, as well as in Colombia, South Africa, India, Sri Lanka, and Burundi tragically reveal that the struggle of peoples to reconcile the tension between their national or political and ethnic or cultural identities is a major disruptive problem in the emerging new world order. These demographic shifts and cataclysmic global events explain in part the recent popularity of discourses on multiculturalism as well as of the stylistic and structural experimentation in narratives with magical realism and postmodernism. These developments have fostered a corresponding shift in power and popularity in the academy away from African American Studies, vernacular theories of art, and neorealism to Postcolonial and Cultural Studies as well as postmodern theories and practices of art and literature. In their belated search in the 1980s and 1990s for a pan-American comparative theory and methodology for American Studies, most critics have neglected to acknowledge the legacy of a similar search in the 1960s and 1970s for a pan-African movement in Black Studies and an African Americentric as well as an Afrocentric aesthetic in art, especially Amiri Baraka's momentous transformation of consciousness and cultural productions during the Black Arts movement and Ishmael Reed's culturally specific Neo-HooDoo aesthetic and geographically diverse multiculturalism.

The post-1983 theory of Anglo-Jamaican critic Paul Gilroy about the culture of the Black Diaspora, the transatlantic sites in the Americas to which dispossessed sub-Saharan nonwhite Africans were dispersed, outlines modern themes of identity formation and double consciousness techniques grounded in black contemporary music that transcend specific nationalities and ethnicities to produce a shared hybrid black Atlantic culture. In contrast to Gilroy's affirmation of double consciousness in his cultural theory, white American proponents of cultural hybridity and multiculturalism such as Myra Jehlen, Amy Kaplan, Frederick Crews, and Gregory S. Jay reject Du Bois's trope of double consciousness and displace Frederick Jackson Turner's theory of the frontier as the defining space for the development of a distinctive white ethnic American culture and character.[1] Theories and tropes of border crossing and multiple consciousness like Gloria Anzaldua's autobiographical celebration of cultural hybridity in *Borderlands/La Frontera: The New Mestiza* (1987) are provided as the most democratic and liberating contemporary American identity formations. In many modern and contemporary novels, however, African Americans are ironically and paradoxically relegated to the margins of the dominant postindustrial, neocolonial social order of the United States as expendable cheap labor yet inexpendable consumers who are represented as either invisible men and women or outsiders.

In the quest for a better life and a more just social order, each generation has developed a new aesthetic to meet the challenge of survival and fulfillment in an ever changing world of difference and diversity. Code-switching and code-mixing language in her book "from English to Castillian Spanish to the North Mexican dialect to Tex-Mex to a sprinkling of Nahuatl to a mixture of all of these," Anzaldua, for example, describes herself as a bicultural subject: "I am a border woman. I grew up between two cultures, the Mexican (with a heavy Indian influence) and the Anglo (as a member of a colonized people in our own territory). I have been straddling that *tejas*-Mexican border, and others, all my life. It's not a comfortable territory to live in, this place of contradictions. Hatred, anger and exploitation are the prominent features of this landscape."[2] Because Anzaldua speaks in her text from and for multiple subject positions, including the lesbian, postcolonial theorist Homi Bhabha and Americanist Cyrus R. K. Patell argue that her hybridity creates a new "Third Space of enunciation" and provides a solution to the assumed binarism of double consciousness and the hyphenated American.[3] As this book attempts to demonstrate, however, African Americans were, to borrow a postmodern phrase, always already marginal people of mixed biological and cultural heritage, writing bidialectally from the distinctive social and linguistic position of being paradoxically at both the margins and center of modern American society.

The shifting cyclical pattern of residual, emerging, and dominant aesthetic movements in literature continues among some artists and cultural workers in the twenty-first century as a New Black Aesthetic (NBA) that stresses racial, class, gender, and sexually transgressive hybridity and multiculturalism. It emerged in response to the residual African Americentric aesthetic of the slave narratives, including neoslave narratives, and the neo-Hoodoo aesthetic that informs novels at different levels from Reed's *Mumbo Jumbo* to Arthur Flowers's Vietnam War novel *De Mojo Blues* (1985), as well as to the dominant Afrocentric Black Arts vernacular aesthetic of the 1970s and the Black Womanist political and aesthetic movement of the early 1980s. The most recent movement for an NBA began in the late 1980s with a new generation that novelist Trey Ellis calls "cultural mulattoes," "blacks who grew up in white neighborhoods" but "now live in black neighborhoods"[4] and "alienated (junior) intellectuals . . . educated by a multi-racial mix of cultures."[5] Many were influenced by the African Americentric tropes, transcultural characters, and avant garde styles of novelists like Ishmael Reed, Clarence Major, John Edgar Wideman, and Toni Morrison, as well as nonblack writers like Twain, Joyce, and Faulkner.

Assuming that African American literature is fundamentally a socially symbolic linguistic construct, I find that the aesthetics of Charles Johnson, Nathaniel Mackey, Trey Ellis, Percival Everett, and Colson Whitehead seek in different ways to displace rather than complement and expand African American proletarian and vernacular tropes of core black personal and collective identity with African American middle-class satirical tropes that privilege individualism and indeterminate multiculturalism and sexuality. Even so, the five residual oral forms—oratory (including everyday speech acts), myth/ritual performance, legend, tale, and song—as well as satire, irony, and paradox continue to inform the authenticity of the complex dualism and cultural ambivalence of the most engaging contemporary novels and novelists, including those in the NBA movement. Although represented with a parodic and satiric difference, the legendary black ancestor and elder, the gifted and often rebellious orator, the musician, the artist, the spiritual leader, and the messianic figure are equally enduring symbols and tropes. Contemporary African American novelists deploy these characters and symbols to reconstruct imaginatively our tragicomic struggle as individuals and as a people for authority, authenticity and agency. Nevertheless, many contemporary antiessentialist critics and readers who seek to move beyond the label of racial provincialism seem obsessed with validating and valorizing transcultural literary relationships while neglecting or rejecting an acknowledgment of the core vernacular roots of intracultural relationships and identities in the African American narrative tradition.

For example, at a 1999 academic conference in Pennsylvania, entitled "Afro-American Literature at the End of the Twentieth Century," a distinguished African American literary critic reproachfully raised the question why all the books under examination were by black Americans. On the one hand, the question was an implied criticism both of the ostensible academic and literary provincialism of the conference program for focusing primarily on the intertextuality among black texts, and of the apparent anachronism of Afrocentric African American Studies programs in general. On the other hand, it was a call for more ethnic and racial diversity in examining our national identities as Americans. Even though Jewish, Chicano, Puerto Rican, and Asian Studies programs and conference organizers are rarely if ever criticized for generally not including African American students, faculty, and books, neither the criticism nor the call was a new issue for African Americans. In fact, in coalition with progressive whites, the struggles of African Americans for civil rights and self-determination have historically expanded and extended the power not only of other minority groups, but also of all national and indirectly many international liberation groups.

How, then, does this assumed new hybridity relate to the lived and imagined literary identities of such different biracial and bicultural African American novelists as Jean Toomer, Langston Hughes, Rudolph Fisher, Zora Neale Hurston, Ralph Ellison, John Oliver Killens, William Melvin Kelley, Ishmael Reed, Toni Morrison, Charles Johnson, Gloria Naylor, Nathaniel Mackey, Trey Ellis, Percival Everett, and Colson Whitehead? Like such writers as Van Wyck Brooks and Waldo Frank in their quest for a new mythic American, Toomer celebrated himself in modern literature and life as an essentialist, a poetic realist, and as a New American, rather than as a New Negro in the 1920s. As illustrated earlier in this study, these novelists construct the double consciousness of their imagined characters and their own social and literary identities in narratives with code-switching and a hybridized language from what Bhabha calls a "Third Space" and what black critics of my generation call desegregated predominantly white suburban areas. In the novel, according to Mikhail Bakhtin, hybridization is "a mixture of two social languages within the limits of a single utterance, an encounter, within the arena of an utterance, between two different linguistic consciousnesses, separated from one another by an epoch, by social differentiation or by some other factor."[6] The hybridized language and identities in pre-1983 African American novels were compelling constructions of the imagined communities in which the struggle for authenticity, authority, and agency by the authors and their characters unfolded. This exploration of hybridized language and identity continues with a difference in the struggle for authenticity, authority, and agency in the post-1983 narratives by such novelists as Johnson, Mackey, Ellis, Everett, and Whitehead. Unlike Ellis, Everett, and Whitehead, with their multicultural NBA, however, Johnson and Mackey create new transgeneric and transcultural, yet fundamentally authentic African American philosophical and post-bebop improvisational music or new jazz aesthetics respectively in their novels.

CHARLES [RICHARD] JOHNSON (1948–)

Born on April 23, 1948, in Evanston, Illinois, at the all-black Community Hospital because neither black doctors nor their patients were welcome in the segregated Evanston Hospital, the multitalented Charles Johnson grew up in a community that was like an extended black family. It laid the foundation for not only his life but also his new black aesthetic in philosophical fiction. His father, Benjamin Lee Johnson, was a shy, proud, church-going, conservative Republican, who occasionally worked three jobs to provide for his family. He discontinued his education in the fifth grade while growing up with eleven siblings on a farm near Abbeville, South Carolina, before reluctantly moving in the 1940s to Chicago to work for one of his older brothers in the construction business. In contrast, Charles Johnson's mother, Ruby Elizabeth Jackson, who occasionally worked as a cleaning woman for a Northwestern University sorority, was the pious, chaste, yet open-minded only child of transplanted Georgians. According to Johnson, she was "emotional, moody, a high school graduate who believed in integration, belonged to three book clubs, and always voted for Democrats." Raised, baptized, and married in Ebenezer A. M. E. Church, Johnson and his parents, relatives, and neighbors were "all quietly pioused" Methodists who frowned on the "'shouting' and 'getting happy'" black Baptists, but who played active roles in their church and were watchful of the welfare of their neighbors and their neighbors' children.[7]

As an only child, Johnson turned to drawing and reading for adventure and enjoyment and was praised in elementary school for his drawing. His first ambition was to become a cartoonist. Before entering high school, he was an avid reader of science fiction and comic books. His mother, who was also an avid reader, would bring home boxes of books that sorority students would throw away at the end of the semester. Among the wide range of titles and topics was a book on yoga, which introduced him to the philosophy that would later become invaluable for his life and literary aesthetic. After enrollment at the integrated Evanston Township High School, Johnson wanted to become a commercial artist and began a schedule of reading one book a week, ranging from collections of early comic art and James Bond novels to Plutarch's *Lives of the Noble Grecians*. After a correspondence course in cartoon drawing with mystery writer and cartoonist Lawrence Lariar and after working during the summers as a garbage man, Johnson became a published cartoonist on his high school, university, and local newspapers before he began hosting in 1968 a drawing series called *Charlie's Pad* on a PBS local station. The show ran for ten years.

Although his mother first interested him in writing by encouraging him to keep a diary or journal, it was Johnson's creative writing teacher who submitted two of his short stories, "Man Beneath Rags" and "50 Cards 50," for publication in his high school newspaper. Following his art and photography teacher's advice, Johnson decided in his senior year of high school in 1966 to attend Southern Illinois University for a degree in journalism rather than going to art school. Rekindling an early fascination with Eastern philosophy, he took almost as many classes in philosophy as he took in his major. It was while reading Eastern and Western philosophical fiction writers in 1967 that he was overwhelmed by Hermann Hesse's *Siddhartha* and felt challenged to respond to it in a novel of his own. After six early unpublished apprentice novels that were even more influenced by the Black Arts movement of the late 1960s, he published *Faith and the Good Thing* in 1974. The source of its narrative authenticity and moral authority is the engrossing black and white folktale, allegory, and myth of the quest of Faith Cross for the Good Thing. His second novel, *Oxherding Tale* (1982), a wry modern philosophical blend of a neoslave narrative and eighteenth-century English novel with Eastern parable, is Johnson's response to *Siddhartha*. In his quest for liberation and the Good Thing (Selfhood), its half-white protagonist, Andrew Hawkins, embodies the tensions between Eastern (Zen) and Western (phenomenology) philosophy, as well as between black and white racial and cultural traditions. It was also during this time that Johnson began the serious study and practice of kung fu. Equally momentous for him was the 1968 awakening of his consciousness to black cultural nationalism in response to Amiri Baraka's poetry reading, lecture, and call for black students to take their talents back to the black community. "I walked home from Baraka's lecture in a daze," Johnson writes. "I sat down before my drawing board, my inkwell, my pens. I started to sketch. I worked for a solid week, cutting my classes. The more I drew and took notes for gag-lines, the faster the ideas came."[8] In seven days he produced *Black Humor*, but it was not published until 1970 after he had worked the previous summer as an intern reporter on the *Chicago Tribune*.

After his marriage in 1970 to Joan New, an elementary school teacher, Johnson began seriously writing novels. In two years he completed six novels under the influence of black cultural nationalism and, in his words, "in the style of naturalistic black authors . . . Richard Wright, James Baldwin, and John A. Williams." Thus, the authenticity, authority, and agency of Johnson's core values were African Americentric. But from the start, he was more interested in the "philosophical novel" by such writers as Sartre, Malraux, Hesse, Mann, Ellison, Voltaire, and Melville, "the world-class authors who understood instinctively that fiction and philosophy were sister disciplines." So he enrolled in a professional writing course with John Gardner, the novelist, critic, medievalist, and moralist, who became his mentor and friend during the production of his first novel, *Faith and the Good Thing*.

In all of his philosophical fiction, Johnson explores the phenomenological foundation or aboriginal faith of his central characters. Through detailed descriptions, metaphors, and similes, he encourages the reader's mystical understanding of the basic unity of our lives. The major transcultural narrative and ideological impulses that inform the quest for unity of Being in the content and form of Johnson's African American philosophical fiction are phenomenological. Because for many African American readers human consciousness and self-awareness are more than the sum of discrete sensory experiences, it is imperative to acknowledge and valorize other ways of knowing and being in the world with others besides the legacy of science and reason to the relationship of race to culture during the Age of Enlightenment. As Johnson indicates in *Being and Race* (1988), his literary manifesto and phenomenological study of black writing since 1970, "writers begin their lifelong odyssey in art with expression or experience interpreted by others, not with . . . an ensemble of events that already mean something."[9] For his new black aesthetic, Johnson thus draws on Eurocentric ancient and modern philosophers from Socrates to Merleau-Ponty and on modern white symbolic and moralistic novelists like André Malraux and John Gardner, as well as on modern African Americentric writers from Richard Wright and Ralph Ellison to John A. Williams. *Native Son* "remains one of our most phenomenologically successful novels," Johnson contends, because of its "construction of a consistent, coherent, and complete racial universe—Southside Chicago—that is fully shaped by a sensitive if seared black subjectivity." Even more than with his meticulous attention to sociological details, says Johnson, "Wright reminds us through his method here—eidetic description, or presenting things in their lived essence (meaning) for a historical subject—that the world we live in is, first and foremost, one shaped by the mind." Responding to *Native Son*, Ellison's *Invisible Man*, according to Johnson, is "something of the modern Ur-text for black fiction."[10] As in Melville's *Billy Budd*, *Moby Dick*, and "Benito Cereno," the moral vision and symbolic form of the nature of good and evil in the world in these fictions are calls to which Johnson feels that he and other African American and minority writers are challenged to respond. In addition to two cartoon collections, several television scripts, a collection of short stories, and a book of criticism on contemporary black writing, Johnson has published the two already noted pre-1983 and two post-1983 novels: *Middle Passage* (1990) and *Dreamer* (1998).

Although *Dreamer* is a bold, intriguing, imaginative use of the Conradian doppelganger and the biblical myth of Cain to thematize the authority, authenticity, and agency of Martin Luther King Jr., the most outstanding African American preacherman, moral philosopher, and dreamer in the twentieth century, *Middle Passage*, which won the National Book Award, remains Johnson's most critically and commercially successful philosophical novel. Intertextually, *Middle Passage* is in the philosophical and symbolic literary tradition of not only *Billy Budd* and *Moby Dick*, but also accounts of actual slave mutinies, especially those aboard the *Amistad* in 1839 and the *Creole* in 1841. Its ancestral roots may be found in pioneering liberation narratives and fiction like Olaudah Equiano's *Interesting Narrative of the Life of Olaudah Equiano* (1789) and *The Heroic Slave* (1853) by Frederick Douglass. Based on the successful mutiny of Madison Washington and 134 slaves who were being shipped from Hampton, Virginia, to New Orleans aboard the *Creole, The Heroic Slave* is the first novella in African American literature.

The characters, structure, and style of the slave revolt in *Middle Passage* most strikingly mark it as a contemporary rewrite of Douglass's *Heroic Slave* and Melville's "Benito Cereno." As moral agents and symbols, Babo, Francesco, and Atufal, Melville's African mutineers, reappear as self-liberators in the code-switching language of Johnson's narrative of the psychological impact of slavery and oppression on human beings—especially the newly freed Illinois bondman Rutherford Calhoun, slave ship captain Ebenezer Falcon, and the legendary Allmuseri people. In contrast to Madison Washington, Douglass's heroic, humanistic, married orator and slave protagonist, Rutherford is a nonheroic, free, philosophizing petty thief and parasite. Through the code-switching language of this unreliable narrator-protagonist, readers learn that in 1830 he becomes a cook's helper on a New Orleans slave clipper to escape a mobster's enforcer and a shotgun marriage to a dark yet innocent, transplanted, cat-loving Boston schoolteacher.

Falcon, the dwarfish philosopher-buccaneer captain of the *Republic*, bound for the Guinea coast to transport peace-loving, highly prized Allmuseri captives and their deity back to New Orleans, is the demonic antithesis of Melville's captains Benito Cereno and Amaso Delano. "He was the Devil," Rutherford discovers near the end of his voyage. "Who else could enslave gods and men alike?" As First Mate Cringle reinforces in his explicit allusion to Delano, the prototypical symbol of what Baldwin called the willful innocence of white Americans, in a self-sacrificial speech to his starving crew, all of these white slave traders tragically blind themselves to the common humanity, intelligence, and resolve for freedom of blacks. The infamous, erudite, multilingual Captain Falcon, "empire builder, explorer, and imperialist," plundered the religious shrines of the Hottentots, Tibetans, and Allmuseri in his missionary and profiteering zeal "to Americanize the entire planet." In one of several prolix philosophical conversations with the protagonist, Falcon expounds pompously on dualism as "a bloody structure of the mind. Subject and object, perceiver and perceived, self and other . . . We cannot think without them. . . . They are signs of a transcendental Fault, a deep crack in consciousness itself. . . . Slavery, if you think this through . . . is the social correlate of a deeper, ontic wound."[11] After the mutiny of the polyglot crew is preempted by the revolt of the captive Allmuseri, who ironically prohibit the speaking of English by the survivors, Captain Falcon's dying charge to Rutherford, his "eyes and ears," is to write the truth of their voyage in the ship's log. " 'Not just Mr. Cringle's side . . . or the story the mutineers will spin,' he says, 'but things I told you when we met alone in secret'" (p. 146). Rutherford, who has learned to speak the language of the Allmuseri, promises himself "that even though I'd tell the story . . . it would be, first and foremost, as I saw it since my escape from New Orleans" (p. 146).

The frequent literary and linguistic allusions (e.g., "as the hag in the Wife of Bath's Tale had loved her fickle knight," p. 17), anachronisms ("she and her sisters had no one to teach them to think like independent, menless Modern Women," p. 18; "a love letter from their black chambermaid that was worthy of James Cleveland," p. 48), and anomalies ("He was . . . the very Ur-type of Gangster," p. 13) result from filtering the narrative of the slave revolt through Rutherford's educated bicultural consciousness. Before manumitting Rutherford, his biblical-scholar master, the Reverend Peleg Chandler, educated him to be a preacher. The Reverend not only taught him to read, write, count, and play the piano but also instructed him in "disquisitions on Neoplatonism, the evils of nominalism, the genius of Aquinas and the work of such seers as Jakob Bhme" (p. 3). But after seeing his brother, who is "shackled to subservience," decline to accept their master's deathbed reward of personal wealth, Rutherford rejects the life of a "gentleman of color" to become "a lecher for perception and the nerve-knocking thrill, like a shot of opium, of new 'experiences'" (p. 3).

Such poetic similes as "[the] wind off the water was like a fist of fresh air" (p. 4) evoke the reader's sense of wonder at the commonplace experience. But figures of speech and tropes that yoke the commonplace to disparate Eastern and Western religions (as in "an evening sky as blue as the skin of heathen Lord Krishna" (p. 5) and "She was . . . as out of place in New Orleans as Saint Teresa would be at an orgy with de Sade" (p. 5) suggest more about the syncretistic cultural dualism and wit of Charles Johnson than they do about Rutherford Calhoun. The authenticity, authority, and agency of the configuration of these tropes do not effectively evoke or conjure up the sense of a unity of Being that the implied author and unreliable narrator seek. Rutherford's belated discovery of the relativity of historical truth, of the horrific impact of the transatlantic slave trade on the culture and character of all aboard the *Republic*, a parody of Plato's ideal society and an ironic symbol of American social and cultural diversity, transforms or destroys his life and the lives of others, especially the Allmuseri. The sobering truth of his ironic role in enslaving his African ancestors does not begin to dawn on him until he is warned of the danger of Arab traders' stealing him off the ship and selling him back into slavery with the Allmuseri. Physically, the Allmuseri "seemed a synthesis of several tribes, as if longevity in this land had made them a biological repository of Egyptian and sub-Saharan eccentricities or—in the Hegelian equation—a clan distilled from the essence of everything that came earlier. Put another way, they might have been the Ur-tribe of humanity itself" (p. 61). According to their oral history, they were once a seafaring people who had sailed to India and Central America, had developed an elegant fighting art similar to the Brazilian *capoeira*, spoke a gnomic language "that dovetailed articles into nouns, nouns into verbs," and wrote in pictograms. "Eating no meat, they were easy to feed. Disliking property, they were simple to clothe. Able to heal themselves, they required no medication. They seldom fought. They could not steal. They fell sick, it was said, if they wronged anyone" (pp. 76–78).

Like Equiano, the Allmuseri panicked at the sight of "the great ship and squalid pit that would house them sardined belly-to-buttocks in the orlop, with its dead air and razor teethed bilge rats" (p. 65). Like him, they thought the white sailors were barbarians shipping them to America to be eaten. Cannibalism, as Johnson dramatizes it with detailed relish in the parodic eating of First Mate Cringle's body by Rutherford and the crew, was not uncommon for men at sea. Cringle's New England gentility, innocence, and sacrifice parody the Christ-figure character of Billy Budd and Amasa Delano. In the Allmuseri mythology, "Europeans had once been members of their tribe—rulers even, for a time—but fell into what was for these people the blackest of sins. The failure to experience the unity of Being everywhere was the Allmuseri vision of Hell. . . . That was where we were taking them—into the madness of multiplicity—and the thought of it drove them wild" (p. 65). Until he sees the stolen Allmuseri god stored in a crate in the ship's hold, Rutherford also fails to experience the unity of Being.

Transformed by his participation in the brutal, dehumanizing enslavement of a people in whom, unlike the diverse white ethnic sailors, he sees himself and his own blighted history, Rutherford sits with his hair turning white as he asks himself: "How could I feel whole after seeing it? How could I tell my children of it without placing a curse on them forever? How could I even dare to have children in a world so senseless?" Later, after helping to throw overboard the rotting corpse of an African man about his own age of twenty-three, he discovers that rather than pure essence the lives and culture of the Allmuseri were "process and Heraclitean change, like any men, not fixed but evolving and as vulnerable to metamorphosis as the body of the boy we'd thrown overboard" (p. 124). Rutherford also realizes that the horrors of slavery on board the *Republic* have reshaped the souls as well as the bodies of the Africans, so that they were "no longer Africans, yet not Americans either" (p. 125).

When Rutherford descends into the hold to feed the omnipotent Allmuseri deity, who is believed to sustain everything in the universe and to assume the image of all things, the god 543 appears as his fugitive-slave father, Riley Calhoun, whom Rutherford hates for abandoning him in slavery. In "a seriality of images" the god reconciles Rutherford to his father by delivering "the complete content of the antecedent universe to which my father, as a single thread, belonged. . . . He seemed everywhere, his presence, and that of countless others, in me as well as the chamber, which had subtly changed. Suddenly I knew the god's name: Rutherford" (p. 171). One of few survivors of the mutiny and storm-wrecked ship, Rutherford is a changed man at the end of the novel. He returns to New Orleans and his Boston schoolteacher with Baleka, the Allmuseri girl with whom he has bonded as surrogate father. As he recounts, "The voyage had irreversibly changed my seeing, made of me a cultural mongrel, and transformed the world into a fleeting shadow play I felt no need to possess or dominate, only appreciate in the ever extended present" (p. 187).

More like Ellison's modern naive nameless protagonist than antebellum slave narrators, Charles Johnson's contemporary protagonist comes to terms with the cultural dualism of his past by writing it down. Thus the thematic significance of freedom, literacy, and wholeness in the tradition of the African American novel continues. But after his fleeting consciousness of personal and cosmic wholeness, the absence of closure at the end of *Middle Passage* suggests that the narrator's quest for unity of Being remains open. By his thematic and stylistic blend of Western and Eastern philosophy, Johnson intellectually and aesthetically distances himself and the authority and authenticity of his text not only from other African American novels but also from everyday working-class black American readers. Equally philosophical and didactic, Nathaniel Mackey's trilogy of novels—*Bedouin Hornbook, Djbot Baghostus's Run*, and *Atet, A.D.*—provides an even more challengingly erudite and radically different avant-garde musical and linguistic improvisation on continuity and change in the quest of black Americans of African descent for a usable past in constructing the authority, authenticity, and agency of their complex transcultural African Americentric identities.

NATHANIEL [ERNEST] MACKEY (1947–)

Born on October 25, 1947, in Miami, Florida, to Sadie Jane Wilcox from Georgia and Alexander Obadiah Mackey, the son of Bahamian parents from the Panama Canal Zone, Nathaniel Mackey moved with his mother, two brothers, and sister to northern California when his parents separated in 1951.[12] In 1958 the family moved to Santa Ana, California, where he grew up with a fascination for math, science, and music before graduating from high school in 1965. But math and science were no match for his earliest experiences around eight years old with the dynamic spiritual power of music, which he witnessed in the ritual singing, shouting, dancing, and trances of black members of his family's Baptist church. After he began reading poetry in high school, especially the modernists William Carlos Williams and Amiri Baraka, he fell under the influence of their poetic use of music and varieties of American vernacular speech. Overcoming an initial alienation from jazz in his early teens, he also began in high school to discover a similar affinity between music, spirituality, and alternative ways of knowing in the authority and authenticity of the post-bebop improvised music of Miles Davis, John Coltrane, and such "outside" players as Ornette Coleman,

Don Cherry, Archie Shepp, and Cecil Taylor. In his own quest for authority, authenticity, and agency as a contemporary African American artist, Mackey later realized parallels between the ritual relationship of music and spirituality in the Baptist church and Haitian vodun and Cuban Santer "a, and he began to reconstruct them imaginatively in his own serial transgeneric, transcultural poetry and novels.

Mackey did not begin a serious study of writing, however, until entering Princeton University in 1965. Ambivalent about Jones's repudiation of his earlier white Eurocentric modernist aesthetic and his militant advocacy of a new Black Aesthetic grounded in the lives and vernacular culture, especially everyday speech and music, of working-class African Americans, Mackey investigated this shift in aesthetics and identity in his senior thesis, "The Conversion of LeRoi Jones." Fundamentally a poet in sensibility, style, and structure, Mackey was strongly influenced by the Black Mountain or Projectivists poets Charles Olson, Robert Creeley, and Robert Duncan, as well as by the Black Arts movement and the quest for a new Black Aesthetic, especially the tension in the innovative vernacular language used in the search for identity and a usable past in the two emerging aesthetics as expressed in the pre-1965 poetry and theory of LeRoi Jones.

Explaining the significance of the "new thing" in jazz in his 1978 essay "The Changing Same: Black Music in the Poetry of Amiri Baraka," Mackey writes: "This tendency involved a departure from—even outright abandonment of—bebop's reliance on the recurring chords referred to as 'the changes' of a particular piece. . . . To listeners accustomed to recurrent reminders of a tune's head [or melody] in the form of the soloist's confinement to the changes, the new music seemed structureless and incoherent. . . . The players were frequently said to sound *lost*."[13] As Mackey began to write and study contemporary literature seriously while an undergraduate at Princeton, post-bebop improvised music and musicians, especially John Coltrane, became his core African Americentric trope as he moved centrifugally across and beyond language, cultural, and generic boundaries in developing his authority and authenticity as a poet and novelist. In 1974, while pursuing a Ph.D. in English and American literature at Stanford University, he was one of the editors of *Hambone*, a single-issue literary magazine that published African American writers and artists; he reorganized it as the sole editor in 1982 and began publishing eclectic, experimental, esoteric "Cross-cultural work emphasizing the centrifugal."[14] After receiving his Ph.D. in 1975, Mackey taught at the University of Wisconsin-Madison and the University of Southern California, and since 1979 has been at the University of California, Santa Cruz. In 1991, after developing his cultural and academic capital, including hosting *Tanganyika Strut*, a world music radio show, he married Pascale Gaitet and became the father of a stepson, Joe, and a young daughter, Naima. His publications include seven chapbooks and books of poetry;

Discrepant Engagement, a collection of critical essays on contemporary black and white cross-cultural experimental writers; the critical journal *Hambone*; a coedited book on jazz in poetry and prose; a special issue of *Callaloo* on his favorite Caribbean writer, Wilson Harris; and *From a Broken Bottle Traces of Perfume Still Emanate*, a trilogy of novels: *Bedouin Hornbook* (1986), *Djbot Baghostus's Run* (1993), and *Atet, A.D.* (2001).

Mackey's trilogy provides an erudite philosophical and didactic avant-garde musical and linguistic improvisation on continuity and change in the quest of black Americans of African descent for a usable past in constructing the authority, authenticity, and agency of their complex identities. The metaphorical title of the trilogy refers to the transgeneric style of his writing and a major theme of both his poetry and his prose. The title thematizes Mackey's investigation of why and how "the past, that is, one's origins," as literary critic Mark Scroggins notes, "is available only as 'traces,' as momentary, unresolved glimpses and intuitions."[15] The dominant structure and style of his writings is epistolary and resembles African American improvisational post-bebop music. "The African-American improvisational legacy in music has been instructive way beyond the confines of the venues in which it takes place and the particular musical culture in which it takes place, way beyond music itself," he tells an interviewer in 1996. "It's become a metaphor for all kinds of processes of cultural and social revaluation, cultural and social critique, cultural and social change."[16] The cultural, literary, and moral authenticity, authority, and agency of his novels are developed first in multivocal poetry that draws on erudite, mythic, and mystical African, Haitian, Cuban, Arabic, Western, and African American transcultural sources. These sources include the sage Dogon elder Ogotemmeli's religious text, the religious rituals of vodun and Santeria, the Koran, the Pyramid Texts of Unas, the Book of Revelation, and the post-bebop music of such jazz musicians as John Coltrane, Pharaoh Sanders, and Don Cherry.

For example, the Arabic-entitled *Bedouin Hornbook*, the first of the novels, opens with the poem "Song of the Andoumboulou: 6," which was inspired by a Dogon funeral song and which is the first of a series of letters dating from 14.VI.78 to 2.VI.81 from N., an African American composer and multi-instrumental jazz musician, to the Angel of Dust, an imagined spirit. Published first in chapbooks and little magazines, as well as by small independent presses like Sun & Moon Press, sympathetic to experimental writing, the code-switching poetic letters in *Bedouin Hornbook*, *Djbot Baghostus's Run* and *Atet, A.D.* a highly philosophical, transcultural, and disruptive, yet wryly playful exploration and examination, according to Mackey, of "the spiritual vocation of music, the spiritual vocation of art, [and] the spiritual vocation of poetry."[17] His subsequent publication of a collection of poetry with the University of Illinois Press and of a collection of critical essays with Cambridge University Press confirms that the primary intended audience for Mackey's novels and poetry is a highly restricted circle of readers with the extensive intellectual and transcultural knowledge, competences, or dispositions necessary to decode his texts.

"Settling neither for the shattered I of postmodernity or the autotelic I of the Enlightenment," writes critic Paul Naylor, "Mackey's works consistently present the I as ensemble—as a band of multi-instrumentalists who sometimes harmonize and sometimes don't, yet who are bound together by the hope of creating a beautiful, albeit discrepant engagement with one another."[18] *Djbot Baghostus's Run*, the second novel in his trilogy, is probably the most compelling example of this conflated linguistic and musical trope of community with diversity. The origin and meaning of the title of the book and the principal character's name are revealed by a grasshopper, the ghost of the narrator's father, in N.'s appendix to the novel: "E PO PEN or, The Creaking of the Word: After-the-Fact Lecture/Libretto." Sustaining the complex improvisational dream series, mystical events, plays on words, and tributes primarily to legendary black musicians and music throughout the novel, the grasshopper whispers in Djbot Baghostus's ear while he is lying on his back reflecting on the song or speech he would perform the next day: "Tell them your father is a wealthy man, that he sang with The Ink Spots before they made it big. . . . Tell them that's why he named you Djbot. Spell it out for them if you have to: d as in dot, j as in jot, b-o-t as in bottle. Tell them it relates to ink, eponymous ink, namesake ink. Tell them you're not from here, even that you're not really here. Tell them it relates to ink, invisible ink. You can never make too much of it. Tell them you're a ghost."[19] In his "mind's eye" N. frequently remembers that when he was four years old he killed a grasshopper, and that his father not only scolded him about his insensitivity, but also scared him later that night by awakening him dressed in a sheet as the ghost of the grasshopper seeking revenge. "His whole life since then," N. tells us as he expands his "namesake testimony" to include allusions to the post-bebop aesthetics of Charles Mingus and the cosmology of the Dogon, ". . . had been one long sprint, an ongoing after-the-fact flight. It was as if, unable to run then, he'd been running ever since" (p. 189).

In the penultimate letter of the novel dated 14.II.82, N.'s explanation of the origin and meaning of "Baghostus" ranges widely from "an Osirian play on Malachi Favor's 'Maghostus' (*Ba* being what the Egyptians called the soul)" to a song "Come For Your Dinner" that N. frequently played on the album *The Real Bahamas*. The name "Bynassy" is associated with the Bahamian song and probable folkloric allusions to "the trickster-hero B'Anansi (also known as Nansi, Boy Nasty and Gulumbanasi)" (p. 184). In the Bahamas as the prefix to a name, B', Ba, Be, Ber, Bioh, Bra, B'Bra, Brer, Bro, Bra, Bu, Bul and Bulla indicate "brother" or friend. Thus, N. tells Angel of Dust and readers, "B'Ghostus and Baghostus both, a B'-*Ba* conjunction whose Egypto-Bahamian harmonics plumb the tie between 'brother' and 'soul'" (p. 185).

Although the epistolary, surreal, self-reflexive text with letters that date from

11.VIII.81 to 15.II.82 is clearly nonlinear in structure, the letters to Angel of Dust from N.—the composer, multi-instrumentalist, and narrator—just as clearly identify a double quest: N.'s open-ended composition of an antithetical opera and the search of his jazz band, The Mystic Horn Society, for a drummer. The members of the ensemble are three men (N., Penguin, and Lambert) and two women (Djamilaa and Aunt Nancy). The authority and authenticity of the opening letter dramatically demonstrate the grounding of the novel in the aesthetics of song and legend, especially African American music and musicians, as the ensemble prepares to achieve a missing quantitative and qualitative balance by auditioning a drummer, SunStick, who riffs on the thematic, structural, and stylistic concerns of the novel with the complex relationship between time and truth in culture, music, and literature with the claim, "I've never played time, I play truth" (p. 8). N., who had heard him play before, was particularly impressed by SunStick's approach to time: "He tends . . . to pit the bass drum against the cymbal in such a way as to rescind the punctuality of time, exacting a feeling for the tenuous, uninsured continuum the so-called beat thereby allows or is made to admit itself to be." What struck N. most was "his playing's apparently absent yet all the more convincing regard for linearity, his having collapse and consolidation, qualm and quanta, find their way to one another" (p. 8). Although N. indicates that this style is similar to that initiated by Milford Graves, Sunny Murray, and Rashied Ali, Mackey actually invokes and evokes the legendary bassist Charles Mingus as the principal post-bebop experimental percussionist with shifting tempos. But N. demonstrates his authority, agency, and early commitment to "I as ensemble" when he discovers that the two women in the ensemble were more interested in the harmony and absence of sexual equality in the numbers and sound of the band.

As critic David C. Kress observes in a different context,[20] Djamilaa and Aunt Nancy indirectly voice their objection to the prospective new member of the ensemble. They come late to the audition dressed in identical white outfits, give the men in the band business cards that read "Halve Not, Will Travel," and play in shifting tempos a Kashmiri drum called the *not* ("a clay pitcherlike affair with a narrow mouth and a big belly," p. 10). Aunt Nancy also plays with "resonant hollowness" an Iranian flute called the *nay*: "Each beat was a hoof to one's head, driving home a point. It was more than appropriate, one was made to admit, that the band, on the verge of becoming a sextet, address and take the issue of sexual equality into account. No women had been considered for the new position, the nots reminded us. Here was our chance to even things up, yet here we were, blowing it" (p. 11). By overcoming his initial resistance to the performance of a musical and dialectic opposition by the women in the ensemble, N. opens himself, the ensemble, and the novel to the possibilities of reconciliation and to the attainment of resonance rather than resolution in composing his after-the-fact lecture/libretto.

"Jarred Bottle's I made of opera glass dropped out," the narrator effortlessly shifts from "I" as subject to "eye" as object as he begins the composition with a Platonic/Pythagorean pun. "Orb and vessel both (i.e., glass eye, reading glass and wine glass rolled into one), it dropped out, fell to the floor and shattered, having turned lower-case and taken the place of Aunt Nancy's u. . . . Jarred Bottle had begun his lecture by reading a quote: 'Some clever fellow, making a play with words, called the soul a jar, because it can easily be jarred by persuasive words into believing this or that'" (p. 50). As readers experience throughout the novel, especially in the concluding "E PO PEN or, The Creaking of the Word: After-the-Fact Lecture/Libretto," the narrator thus achieves polyphonic resonance in his performance with the synaesthetic language of the implied author that blends sensory perceptions with concrete objects and abstract concepts, as well as with the presence and sound of Drennete, the new female drummer who is foreshadowed in the dreams of the narrator and other band members as the genie Djeannine, Jeannie, and the recording "Jeannine" (pp. 20–47). Ironically, because of the historical, cultural, intellectual, and spiritual density of specific African American vernacular references to music and transcultural resonances, the authority, authenticity, and agency of Mackey's novels are neither primarily intended for nor accessible to general readers, particularly African Americans. This is most apparent in the dreams, monologues, dialogues, and dialectics on the titles, themes, structures, and styles of songs by legendary black blues, post-bebop and reggae musicians as illustrated, for example, in "Three M's and an H": The Mystic Horn Society's tribute to Charles Mingus, Bob Marley, Thelonius Monk, and Lightnin' Hopkins at the news of Monk's death. But some readers will be frustrated by the absence of political agency in a novel that addresses social change in the lives of ordinary African Americans beyond the jazz community. Even readers who dig out and play old albums and recent CDs by the relevant bebop and post-bebop musicians—especially Gillespie, Parker, Monk, Mingus, Roach, Coltrane, Davis, and Shepp—while reading Mackey's novels may find themselves overwhelmed and frustrated by the sustained, intense richness of transcultural tropes and ethnomusicological details that so intricately informs the fusion of theme, structure, and style of the trilogy of novels, particularly *Djbot Baghostus's Run.*

TREY ELLIS [WILLIAM ARTHUR ELLIS III] (1962–)

On October 14, 1962, William Arthur Ellis III, novelist and screenwriter whose pen name is Trey Ellis, was born in Washington, D.C., to William A. Ellis, a psychiatrist, and Pamela Fern Ellis, a psychologist. While his mother and father attended the University of Michigan and Yale, young Ellis "grew up in the predominantly white, middle and working-class suburbs around Ann Arbor, Michigan, and New Haven, Connecticut."[21] After attending public elementary school in Hamden, Connecticut, he went to private schools in New Haven and graduated in 1980 from Phillips Academy in Andover, Massachusetts. While at

Phillips Academy, he was influenced by the novelist Alexander Theroux. At Stanford University, it was primarily Gilbert Sorrentino, another novelist, who guided him in earning a B.A. in creative writing in the Department of English in 1984. From 1982 to 1983 Ellis worked as a journalist-intern for *Newsweek,* and he has subsequently contributed articles to such magazines and newspapers as *Playboy,* the *Village Voice, Washington Post Book World,* and the *Los Angeles Times.* Multilingual, Ellis has traveled widely in Africa, Europe, and Japan, as well as in South and Central America. He is the author of several television movies, including *Tuskegee Airmen,* and three novels: *Platitudes* (1988), a metafictional story-within-a-story about the contrasting aesthetics of a black female and a black male writer; *Home Repairs* (1993), a satirical coming-of-age diary of a TV show handyman; and *Right Here, Right Now* (1999), an elaborate parody, with tape recordings as narrative devices, of evangelical cults and motivational speakers that won the American Book Award.

In his three novels and the essays "The New Black Aesthetic" and "Response to NBA Critiques," Ellis boldly defines, defends, and promotes a New Black Aesthetic (NBA) for his generation. But his NBA is as problematic as the radical black cultural nationalist aesthetic which it seeks to displace. After confessing that he is "a bourgie black boy" who had not lived in a black community other than his family before moving as a freshman "into Ujamaa, Stanford's black dorm," Ellis writes: "Just as a genetic mulatto is a black person of mixed parents who can often get along fine with his white grandparents, a cultural mulatto, educated by a multi-racial mix of cultures, can also navigate easily in the white world. And it is by and large this rapidly growing group of cultural mulattoes that fuels the NBA. We no longer need to deny or suppress any part of our complicated and sometimes contradictory cultural baggage to please either white people or black."[22] Actually, Ellis's advocacy of shifting the thematic, stylistic, and structural focus of African American novels from neorealistic representations of working-class black Americans' vernacular responses to the reality of antiblack racism, to the multicultural experiences of the black bourgeoisie is nothing new. The tradition of the African American novel begins in the antebellum and postbellum periods by focusing primarily on the lives of mulattoes, especially women, whose phenotype, especially color, is a dominant factor in their class and cultural status, as well as their double consciousness and socialized ambivalence. Also, a major debate between artists and the publishing industry, black and white, during the Harlem Renaissance was about the celebration of the lives of rural folk, the economically uprooted, and the urban industrial working class as the authentic African American experience, to the neglect of the transcultural lives and achievements of the black bourgeoisie.

In his 1989 literary manifesto, "The New Black Aesthetic," Ellis argues that Lisa and Kellie Jones, the biracial, bicultural daughters of Amiri Baraka and

Hettie Jones, and "many other members of the NBA are the children of Civil Rights workers or black nationalists" are cultural mulattoes who not only have inherited from their parents a "postliberated aesthetic,"[23] but also have chosen to construct a black middle-class identity for themselves. But the trope cultural mulattoes is a misnomer that unfortunately resurrects and reinforces the pejorative nineteenth-century association of first-generation biologically half-black and half-white persons with the sterility of mules and the trope of tragic mulattoes who agonize over being neither white nor black. The writers that Ellis identifies as members of the NBA are primarily second- and third- rather than first-generation progeny of exogamous, often interracial, couples who are college graduates of predominantly white private and elitist academic institutions and who raised their children in predominantly white middle-class communities. Anthropologically, then, because the beliefs and values of Ellis's cultural mulattoes were fundamentally shaped by immersion during their formative years in predominantly white middle-class communities, their acculturation and identity formation could be reasonably viewed as less authentically black than those of contemporaries who were raised in predominantly black communities. Some NBA novelists, however, are also the children or descendants of disaffected black cultural nationalists; of black urban professionals and bourgeois social climbers; or of reactionary black avant-garde artists. How do the ironies, paradoxes, and stark contradictions of the biologically, socially, and culturally mixed backgrounds of this emergent group of artists and writers constitute a new black literary movement and aesthetic that Ellis feels is "separate but better"?

Despite making no suggestion in his initial declaration "that a 'cultural mulatto' has an edge over a black artist more traditionally raised," Ellis claims in his response to critics of his manifesto that "what is new and interesting now . . . is that we have a flood of both types." He considers the NBA "an anti-aesthetic that defies definition" and "an attitude of liberalism rather than a restrictive code." Because "today we can be more honest and critical of ourselves than ever before," he argues, ". . . this open-minded far-sightedness may very well produce some of the greatest works of art the world has ever known, because, like Newton, we stand on the shoulders of giants."[24] Rather than a synthesis of the principles, poetics, and politics of the Harlem Renaissance and the Black Arts movement, Ellis's NBA, as he admits, is "fueled by nave exuberance and . . . [an] unshakable belief that our youthful black power can perfect society and perfect the soul."[25] Although he ascribes a "leftist, neo-Nationalist politic" to the NBA artists who "castigate their buppie contemporaries,"[26] moving up from the poverty of the majority of the black working poor to the prosperity of the black professional and middle class and moving out of black ghettoes to predominantly white and racially mixed suburbs seem to be primarily matters of personal choice for Ellis. Personal choice and freedom, like lifting yourself up by your own bootstraps even when you do not have boots, are thus the dominant factors in the middle-class values of Ellis's naive new Talented Tenth and in their African Americentric transcultural identity formations.

Although all of Ellis's novels are semi-autobiographical experimental narratives about the transcultural identity formation of young black middle-class men, *Platitudes* is the most compelling thematically, structurally, and stylistically. The novel is primarily a satirical attack on monolithic and stereotypic representations of authentic African American culture and character that argues ironically for transcultural middle-class values as the norm for African American identities. According to critic J. Martin Favor, "Ellis moves in *Platitudes* to create a heteroglossic structure which, in a Bakhtinian sense, allows competing languages of African American identity to 'be juxtaposed to one another, mutually supplement one another, contradict one another and be interrelated dialogically.'"[27] While this is certainly a valid way of reading the text, it subordinates an African Americentric reading that privileges its signifying style to a Eurocentric reading of its dialogism. But this type of interpretation fails to address the fallacious assumption of Bakhtin's dialogism that various diverse languages are or will be equally and mutually respected epistemological and ontological modes of identity formation in hierarchically constructed heteroglossic communities and texts such as those indigenous to the United States. As students who are criticized for "talking white" discover, phenotypical African Americans who are unfamiliar with AAVE and speak or write exclusively SAE are often perceived as culturally white by speakers whose primary speech community is AAVE. Since the dynamics of the interaction between the languages of primary and wider speech communities reveal a struggle for status and power between speakers of standard and nonstandard modes of language, readers, like auditors, should be aware of and attuned to the culturally specific criteria, especially vernacular experiences and voices, by which the proficiency, power, and identity of the speaker and writer—that is, his or her authenticity, authority, and agency—are ascertained and assessed. *Platitudes,* in other words, is most meaningfully read and appreciated as an African Americentric metafictional and satirical story-within-a-story about the quest in life and literature of black American writers and artists to reconstruct and reconcile with authenticity, authority, and agency the double consciousness and diverse voices of African Americans.

The linguistic code-switching, wry humor, parody, and culturally specific tropes memorably illuminate the authenticity, authority, and agency of Ellis, the implied author, and the major characters, Dewayne Wellington, black experimental novelist, and Isshee Ayam, a militant womanist novelist, in constructing a distinctively African American novel. Rather than the conventional frame of a story-within-a-story, the implied author opens *Platitudes* with two realistic, dull fragments of a novel about black characters that Dewayne has difficulties in constructing with authenticity and authority. So *Platitudes* is actually a composite of three stories. The first is the novel by Trey Ellis with embedded stories by a black male and female writer. The second is the coming-of-age story of sixteen-year-old Earle, a Northern and urban materialistic child of the middle—class, whose interracially dating black mother and integrationist social life are wryly parodied in code-switching language: "She is neither fat (her breasts don't swell the lace top of the apron she has never owned), nor has she any gold teeth. She cannot sing, nor is she ever called 'Mama' (though that is what she calls her own mother). She does not, not work in public relations and her two-handed backhand is not, not envied by her peers."[28] Earle's mother dates Solomon Levitt, and her son fantasizes about Janey Rosenbloom at "the B'nai B'rith/NAACP dance at the Copa" (pp. 4–7). Both Ellis and Dewayne are satirizing the historical relationship, including personal intimacy and political coalitions, between African Americans and Jewish Americans as being more stereotypic than authentic.

Advised by a friend in the publishing industry that "black women *sell*," Dewayne begins a second narrative about the Northern and urban black working-class life of sixteen-year-old Dorothy, who attends a Catholic school for girls and whose mother, Darcelle, is "one of those fundamentalist, tough-as-nails black women who, underneath, are pussycats," and who "can be so street sometimes" (pp. 11–13). In response to Dewayne's request for help from readers about which story is better, including which characters, witticisms, and grammatical devices he should kill for authenticity, Isshee Ayam—a punning parody of African American naming customs, the burning bush episode in the Bible, and the yam episode in Ralph Ellison's *Invisible Man*—provides her authentic versions of Dewayne's stories. She shifts the gender perspective, cultural setting, and characters from a black masculinist urban North to a black womanist rural South. "No," Isshee writes to Dewayne, "we women of color do not need your atavistic brand of representation, thank you" (p. 15). Ellis's novel is thus composed of three embedded stories.

Even though satire and parody are at work in the stories by both Dewayne and Isshee, the implied author reveals by the pattern and intensity of his language and imaginative critique less class and aesthetic distance between himself and Dewayne Wellington than between himself and Isshee Ayam. In addition to the names of the writers, the names of Maylene, Nadine, and Lurlene, the sisters; I. Corinthians, the "cardboard colored" rent collector; Mr. Wyte, the Georgia landlord; and Abe, Moses, and Jesus, the family dogs; are parodies of the vernacular representation of African American culture and character that Isshee provides in her rewrite of Dewayne's story in chapter 1. A wryly and sexually exaggerated, even farcical, representation of Earle's Mama as a legendary black matriarch undercuts the intended authenticity of Isshee's chapter:

"Yes, from out of those wide Baptist thighs, thighs that shook with the centuries of injustice and degradation, thighs that twitched with the hope of generations yet unplanted, thighs that quivered with the friction of jubilant, bed-thumping, and funky-smelling lovemaking, emerged Earle" (p. 16). In ironic response to Isshee's sassy and sexy African American vernacular reconstruction of the oppressive legacy of slavery absent in Dewayne's story, a literary representation which Ellis is clearly parodying as stereotypic rather than authentic, Dewayne writes: "I'm speechless, Ms. Ayam. How can I thank you for dragging my meager tale back to its roots in Afro-American glory-stories?" (p. 19). "To the tune of John Coltrane's 'My Favorite Things,'" a jazz arrangement of a Rodgers and Hammerstein song, Dewayne (and indirectly Ellis) then seeks to validate the authenticity of his urban, middle-class representation of African American culture and character by offering a long, diverse list of "a few of Earle's favorite things." They range widely and randomly from tanks, Janey Rosenbloom, Cream of Wheat, and Slurpees to Christmas, World War Two, "not this restaurant, not Lenox Avenue, but a double helping of chicken livers and gravy and grits and rolls" (pp. 19–20).

In reconciling the tension between Dewayne and Isshee over which is an authentic literary representation of African American culture and character, Ellis not only ideologically sympathizes with Dewayne but also aesthetically displaces the marginally employed, working-class culture of the majority of African Americans with the white-collar, middle- and upper-class culture of the minority of African Americans. This pattern of reconciliation begins with the exchange of correspondence between Isshee and Dewayne dated December 26 and 31, 1984. Although still critical of Dewayne's "unforgivable penchant for pornography" and "misogynistic belches," Isshee writes on December 26: "I must admit that this latest passage on Dorothy is not altogether without merit. The dialectic between class struggle and cultural assimilation, the mental anguish of rising (???!) from a middle-class Harlem household to the rich, white, New York, controlled-substance-abusing elite is almost interestingly handled" (pp. 108–9). She closes her letter by warmly extending "a most merry Kwanzaa and a Happy New Year" to Dewayne and his family.

Equally conciliatory, Dewayne, in turn, writes on December 31: "You are absolutely correct. My prose and my thoughts have changed, tightened, and—if I may be so bold—improved. Isshee—may I call you that—for after just having read and thoroughly enjoyed your *Chillun o' de Lawd, Hog Jowl Junction,* and *My Big Ol' Feets Gon' Stomp Dat Evil Down*, I feel a real intimacy between us" (p. 110). He also closes warmly with "your colleague and fan"(p. 111). Their reconciliation culminates in Isshee's letter of January 20, 1985. As Trey Ellis sustains the satiric and metafictional relationship among the stereotypic or monolithic representations of racial and cultural authenticity in the three versions of *Platitudes*, which is the title of the narratives by Dewayne and Isshee as well as by Ellis, Isshee writes: "after reading your last letter, I feel nothing but shame over my past conduct. I was catty and cruel because I believed you to be yet another misogynistic, insensitive cretin with a penchant for child molesting. I had no idea you were merely another heartbroken human being. . . . I believe *Platitudes* is now coming along rather well. The two-completely-different-types-fall-in-love Love Story is a time-honored favorite" (pp. 148–49). Isshee is also conciliatory to Dewayne's experimental style, which Ellis, like Dewayne and Isshee, fallaciously assumes is antithetical to African American neorealism. "I have never been a fan of you experimentalists, *per se*, and often find that school a bit too sure of itself and arch, yet I must admit that I sometimes envy your stylistic liberty" (p. 149). Ironic and parodic to the end, the *Platitudes*, the insipid yet wryly humorous stories-within-a-story of Earle and Dorothy and of Dewayne and Isshee close in romantic, melodramatic love-making scenes.

Although, as critic Favor insightfully observes, "Ellis challenges the notion of a single authenticity by foregrounding the processes of reading and writing, (re)construction and revision," he reconciles the African American double consciousness in his essays and *Platitudes* by displacing urban black working-class culture with the culture of the black bourgeoisie and the NBA of cultural mulattoes. The representation of agency in *Platitudes* is therefore neither leftist nor neo-Nationalist. Furthermore, historically and anthropologically, as a racially and ethnically mixed people acculturated in an antiblack racist society, African Americans have always biologically, culturally, socially, politically, and ideologically manifested different shades and degrees of blackness as authentic. This explains, in part, the African American intraracial signifying name of "Oreo" for people who look black but act white with its multivalent ironic and parodic meanings. For example, in *Our Nig*, an 1859 landmark African American novel, Jim, an African character, proposes marriage to Mag Smith, a white woman who was ostracized and poor because she had a child out of wedlock. " 'I's black outside, I know, but I's got a white heart inside,' " says Jim. " 'Which you rather have, a black heart in a white skin, or a white heart in a black one?' "[29] As this study demonstrates, the actual and literary constructions of an authentic African American identity are more complex and complicated than merely a matter of color and class. More often than not, when individuals, groups, or organizations are metaphorically and socially called "white," since all racial categories are unscientific, they are actually considered not really black or not black enough, rather than not black at all. Conferred from without and from within the rites of passage of one's life or lived experience, as I stated earlier, authenticity is attained by transcending restrictive material conditions and transgressing social and moral boundaries while both discovering and constructing a usable past and a viable, more just future. This is the challenge and call to which Percival L. Everett responds in his eleven novels.

PERCIVAL L[EONARD] EVERETT (1956–)

Born on December 22, 1956, in Fort Gordon, Georgia, an army base near Augusta, to Sergeant Percival Leonard Everett, who became a dentist after his discharge from the service, and Dorothy Stinson Everett, young Percival grew up in a black middle-class family in Columbia, South Carolina, during the turbulent sixties, graduated from A. C. Flora High School in 1973, and has become a highly versatile and prolific African American novelist.[30] After earning a bachelor's degree in philosophy from the University of Miami in 1977, he pursued graduate study between 1978 and 1980 at the University of Oregon and earned a master's degree in creative writing from Brown University in 1982. A peripatetic ranch worker, high school teacher, jazz musician, and novelist, Everett writes on a wide range of topics and sets many of his narratives, especially his early novels *Suder* and *Walk Me to the Distance*, in stark, isolated, spacious, nonblack landscapes of the American West. Although he was married from 1985 to 1991 to Shere Coleman, a costume designer and painter, he is currently married to Francesca Rochberg, a professor of ancient history at the University of California, Riverside. Since 1985, Everett has been an associate professor of English and creative writing at various universities, including the Universities of Kentucky, Notre Dame, Wyoming, and California at Riverside, and he is currently a professor at the University of Southern California.

Like Clarence Major, Percival Everett is not only an expressionistic painter, but also a prolific and versatile writer of fourteen books. Although he was raised in the South, most of Everett's novels and short stories are primarily Eurocentric nonlinear modernist texts that range in structure and style from neorealism and antirealism to poststructuralism and whose black characters seek their freedom and wholeness in the West in isolation from black communities. The authority, authenticity, and agency of his novels are therefore most apparent in his modernist movement beyond African American neorealism to experiments with expressionism and poststructuralism. For example, *Suder* (1983) is a neorealistic and expressionistic blend of a declining black baseball player's obsession with a Charlie Parker recording of "Ornithology," a saxophone, an abused circus elephant, and a runaway little white girl. These multiple obsessions drive Suder, the disturbed protagonist, to take flight figuratively and literally from his personal and professional failures in life. Since his zany examination of a modern black male mid-life identity crisis in this first novel, Everett has published two collections of short stories, *The Weather and Women Treat Me Fair* (1987) and *Big Picture* (1996), a children's book, *The One That Got Away* (1992), and ten additional novels, including the science fiction narrative *Zulus* (1990). *For Her Dark Skin* (1990) and *Frenzy* (1997) are adaptations of the ancient Greek myths of Medea and Dionysus. The post-1983 novels include *Walk Me to the Distance* (1985), *Cutting Lisa* (1986), *God's Country* (1994), *The Body of Martin Aguilera*

(1994), *Watershed* (1996), *Glyph* (1999), and *Erasure* (2001). His awards include the New American Writing Award in 1990 for *Zulus* and the Pen/Oakland—Josephine Miles Award for Excellence in Literature in 1996 for *Big Picture*.

A provocative satire on the impact of the publishing industry on the authority, authenticity, and agency of autonomous, nonconventional contemporary African American novelists in particular and on the double consciousness of middle-class African Americans in general, *Erasure* is probably Everett's most wryly humorous and disturbingly semiautobiographcal and metafictional novel. Like Thelonius "Monk" Ellison—the avant-garde novelist who reworks Greek myths, the college professor who parodies Roland Barthes's poststructuralist criticism in *S/Z*, and the protagonist whose name is a conflation of the highly innovative black modernist bebop musician Thelonius Monk, and the expressionist novelist Ralph Ellison—Everett chooses to erase or nullify his African American identity in his transgressive quest for transcultural freedom and wholeness as an artist. In contrast, white publishers paradoxically erase his individuality by rejecting his books as not black enough. "Monk's experience is very much my own," Everett tells an interviewer, "though he of course is not me at all. Yes, I have been hit with the 'not black enough' complaint, but always from white editors and critics."[31]

Because his own most recent experimental novel has been rejected by publishers as not black enough, Monk is outraged at the national success of Juanita Mae Jenkins, an amateur black middle-class writer with little knowledge and less actual experience of living in an urban black community, and her exploitative first novel in the neorealistic tradition of the ghetto and gangster pulp fiction of Robert "Iceberg Slim" Beck and Donald Goines, *We's Lives in Da Ghetto*. With self-righteous indignation, Monk, under the pen name Stagg R. Leigh and with little or no intellectual, aesthetic, and ethical distance between himself and Everett, the implied author of *Erasure*, writes *My Pafology*, an outrageously scurrilous parody in eye dialect whose authenticity and authority are acclaimed by white editors and critics as well as a popular black TV talk-show hostess as a commercial and critical prize-winning success. In contrast to Monk's judgment of the parody, whose title he has under the alias of Stagg R. Leigh blatantly insisted that the publishers change to *Fuck*, as "offensive, poorly written, racist and mindless," the white judges on the Book Award Committee consider it "the truest novel" that they had ever read. "It could only have been written by someone who has done hard time. It's the real thing."[32] Ultimately, the huge commercial success of the parody and the pseudonymous Stagg R. Leigh, engineered by a multimillion-dollar movie contract and the Book Club of Kenya Dunston, a nationally popular TV talk-show hostess, results in Monk's complicity with the media in the erasure of his individuality.

The structure and style of the paradoxically double-voiced satirical attack in *Erasure* on African American double consciousness, African American neorealism, Eurocentric poststructuralism, and popular culture in the United States are both a clever and crude imaginative construction of the disturbing socialized ambivalence and identity crisis of the implied author and protagonist of the novel. Before readers begin the double-voiced story-within-a-story narrative, they are struck by the stark photo on the book cover of a smiling little black boy in a multicolored shirt and suspenders-supported jeans pointing a gun at his head in what is ostensibly a mock suicide with the book title in lower case letters and the sign of a red "x" under the photo, suggesting the child's violent self-erasure. Following six hyperbolic blurbs by white and black writers and the title page, readers are alerted to the satirical structure and style of the novel by an epigraph from Mark Twain's ostensibly misanthropic book *Following the Equator*: "I could never tell a lie that anybody would doubt, nor a truth that anybody would believe." The frame story begins as a wryly humorous, metafictional first-person journal with the structural irony of abruptly shifting, alternating subsections of flashbacks and retrospective narrative that reveal in various lengths separated by three "x's," rather than specific dates, his childhood ambition to become a serious writer and his modernist literary aesthetic. The chapter divisions and all of the letters, except "A," in the title that is included on odd-numbered pages are also marked with "x," the sign of erasure.

The ironic voice of the narrator and protagonist sustains the tragicomic mood of the pretextual signs and paradoxical motif of the self-erasure of one's racial identity and existence as an artist in the opening sentence of the frame story. "My journal is a private affair," Monk wryly introduces himself, "but as I cannot know the time of my coming death, and since I am not disposed, however unfortunately, to the serious consideration of self-termination, I am afraid that others will see these pages" (p. 1). On the basis of his biological appearance and slave ancestry, the beliefs and values of the dominant white society and popular culture racially classify him as black. But he immediately challenges this apparently stereotypic classification and affirms his individuality by describing himself as "no good at basketball," a music fan of "Mahler, Aretha Franklin, Charlie Parker and Ty Cooder," and a *summa cum laude* graduate of Harvard who cannot dance. Most important, in a classic example of the tragic irony of the protagonist's identity crisis, the implied author erases or nullifies the geographical and class foundations of the cultural identity of most African Americans by proudly declaring that he "did not grow up in any inner city or the rural south" and that not only were his grandfather, father, and two siblings doctors, but his family also owned a summer bungalow near Annapolis. The dramatic irony is reinforced by his response to a book agent's advice that he could sell many books if he would "forget about writing retellings of Euripides and parodies of French poststructuralists and settle down to write the true, gritty real stories of black life" (p. 2). Some black readers will merely shake their heads and exclaim in exasperation, "My people! My people! My people!" at the willful innocence of his response: "I told him that I was living a *black* life, far blacker than he could ever know, that I had lived one, that I would be living one" (p. 2).

The satirical events that dominate the frame story of Monk's new expressionist aesthetic as a writer and college professor and that reveal his intellectual arrogance and alienation as an African American artist are disrupted periodically. Flashbacks to his childhood fascination with woodworking and fly fishing with his father illuminate the origins of his existential angst, his exaggerated sense of intellectual difference, and the subsequent emotional estrangement and psychological alienation from his siblings and acquaintances fostered by his father, who committed suicide, and his mother. "'You're not like your brother and sister,'" his father told him as a child. "'. . . You have a special mind. The way you see things. If I had the patience to figure out what you were saying sometimes, I know you'd make me a smarter man'" (p. 9). Monk's bold declaration when he was nearly twelve that he would become a serious writer is validated by his father's pronouncement: "'Lisa, you and Bill will be doctors. But Monk will be an artist. He's not like us'" (p. 143). Even though the death of his gynecologist sister and divorce of his gay plastic surgeon brother confronted him with the responsibility of moving from Los Angeles to the District of Columbia to care for his mother, whose health has rapidly declined due to Alzheimer's, the family relationship, like his professional relationship to other writers and his sexual relationship with Linda Mallory and Marilyn Tilman, is intellectually, psychologically, and emotionally estranged.

As the metafictional and satirical structure and style of the novel reveal, both Everett and his protagonist, Monk, parody the gangsta pulp fiction of Iceberg Slim, Donald Goines, and Omar Tyree, the naturalism of Richard Wright, the vernacular novels and romances of Terry McMillan, and the popular TV book club of Oprah Winfrey, as well as the poststructuralism of Roland Barthes and Jacques Derrida. Monk ultimately erases his own integrity and individuality by succumbing ironically to the commercial values of the publishing industry and popular culture, especially TV, that he bitterly disdains by becoming Stagg R. Leigh. Reflecting disturbingly on suicide while viewing paintings by Mark Rothko and Antoine de Saint-Exupéry in the National Gallery of Art, Monk thinks to himself: "My self-murder would not be an act of rage and despair, but of only despair and my artistic sensibility could not stand that. Throughout my teens and twenties I had killed myself many times, even made some of the preparations, stopping always at the writing of the note. I knew that I could manage nothing more that [*sic*] a perfunctory scribble and I didn't want to see that, have my silly romantic notions shattered by a lack of imagination" (p. 139). Monk's artistic sensibility and standards thus dominate and erase other aspects of his identity. At the close of the novel, as the other judges on the committee are looking for Stagg R. Leigh to present him the Book Award for *Fuck*, Monk, who was unsuccessful as one of the judges in attacking the aesthetics of the book, discovers: "The faces of my life, of my past, of my world became as real as the unreal. . . . Then there was a small boy, perhaps me as boy, and he held up a mirror so that I could see my face and it was the face of Stagg Leigh. 'Now you're free of illusion,' Stagg said. 'How does it feel to be free of one's illusions?' " (p. 264).

The framed novella, *My Pafology* by Stagg R. Leigh—Monk's and Everett's pun on the name of the legendary black vernacular character Stagger Lee—takes up only 68 of the 265 pages of the novel. Van Go Jenkins, the protagonist of the novella and parody of Bigger Thomas, is a nineteen-year-old urban, unemployed, unmarried, irresponsible, self-hating, violent black male rapist, killer, and father of four children—Aspireene, Tylenola, Dexatrina, and Rexall—by four different women. Self-consciously fictional, the African American dialect in the parody is largely restricted to the misuse of the durative verb "to be" and to gross phonetic distortions for comic effect of eye dialect; the protagonist's black idiolect is reduced basically to variations of three vulgarities and epithets: "fuck," "muthafucka," and "nigger." The parody in which intraracial class and cultural differences dominate racial differences ends with Van Go's capture in the glaring TV lights of the evening news as he gloats: " 'Hey, Mama . . . Hey, Baby Girl. Look at me. I on TV' " (p. 131). Disappointingly, the novel evades issues of political agency.

So where does Percival Everett stand on the issue of the authenticity of racial and ethnic identities in *Erasure* and life in the United States? "I am a writer. I am a man. I am black man in this culture," Everett tells an interviewer. "Of course my experience as a black man in America influences my art; it influences the way I drive down the street. But certainly John Updike's work is influenced by his being white in America, but we never really discuss that. I think readers, black and white, are sophisticated enough to be engaged by a range of black experience, informed by economic situation, religion (or lack thereof) or geography, just as one accepts a range of so-called white experience."[33] Everett is apparently unfamiliar with critical responses by some Jews, especially Cynthia Ozick, to the novels of Updike, a gentile, about Henry Bech, a Jewish writer, as well as with articles about Saul Bellow, Philip Roth, and Bernard Malamud that discuss the impact of their racial and ethnic identities on their aesthetics, but such studies do exist.[34] Also, even though the sociohistorical, sociopsychological, and sociocultural dynamics of the legacy of the economics of slavery are fundamental to the authenticity and authority of the identity formation of African Americans, their racial and cultural identities include more elements than class, religion, and geography. "Far from being grounded in a mere 'recovery' of the past, which is waiting to be found, and which, when found, will secure our sense of ourselves into eternity," writes cultural theorist Stuart Hall, "identities are the names we give to the different ways we are positioned by, and position ourselves within, the narratives of the past."[35] Despite the popularity in the academies of antiessentialist arguments by postmodern critics, the authority, authenticity, and agency of the identities of African Americans emanate not only from the particularity of our historical struggle against slavery and its legacy of antiblack racism in the United States. They also emanate from the shared cultural codes and language of our individual and collective political agency to reconcile our unique double consciousness and to control the dynamic relationship of our chromosomes, color, ethnicity, class, gender, geography, age, culture, sexuality, consciousness, commitment, conscience, and choice in the open-ended process of constructing our identities and reconstructing a new world order.

COLSON WHITEHEAD (1969–)

Born on November 6, 1969, in New York City to Arch and Mary Ann Whitehead, the owners of an executive recruiting firm, Colson Whitehead, a journalist and prize-winning novelist, is the third of four children.[36] Raised in an upper-middle-class family on the Upper West Side of Manhattan and educated exclusively in private schools, he admits spending much of his time as a boy reading and watching television. He was so fascinated by Stephen King's novels, comic books, and science fiction during his youth that he initially planned on a career in these popular genres. He graduated from Trinity Preparatory School in 1987 and from Harvard, where he studied English and comparative literature but was unsuccessful in enrolling in a creative writing class, in 1991. He then married Natasha Stovall, a writer and photographer, and worked for several years as a popular culture critic for the *Village Voice*, advancing from intern and editorial assistant for the literary supplement to TV editor. "I wanted to become one of those ambidextrous pop culture critics who started to abound in the late eighties and early nineties," he tells an interviewer.[37] Although he wrote an unpublished novel while working at the *Village Voice*, his two published novels, *The Intuitionist* (1999), winner of the Whiting Award for emerging writers, and *John Henry Days* (2001), have received outstanding critical praise.

Inspired both by a television program about defective escalators and by hard-boiled detective novels, *The Intuitionist* is an allegorical mystery novel about the dual search of Lila Mae Watson, the first black female elevator inspector. On one level, her search is for the guilty parties who caused the free-fall crash of an elevator in her skyscraper office building. On another level, she searches for the missing notebooks and blueprints for a foolproof skyscraper elevator that would end the union rivalry in the city between two groups of inspectors: the Intuitionists, Watson's group, who use intuition in their examinations of elevator systems, and the Empiricists, who rely exclusively on scientific facts and mechanical examinations in their work. Despite the originality of its theme, the characters in *The Intuitionist* are less memorable, and its structure and style are less experimental in using African American residually oral forms than *John Henry Days*.

The authenticity, authority, and agency of *John Henry Days* emanate from the challenging metafictional shifts in the theme, structure, and style of the satirical novel. The dominant African American residually oral forms deployed in the novel are song and legend, especially ballads. Is John Henry, the nineteenth-century legendary black "steel-driving man" who raced and beat a machine before dying while building the C&O Railroad, the center of the novel, or is J. Sutter, the twentieth-century freeloading freelance journalist for the information superhighway? Although they all have some claim to authenticity and authority, readers must determine which representation of John Henry is the most authentic and authoritative: the historical record, the memorata, the myth, the legend, the ballad, or the novel? Whitehead's fourth-grade teacher during the 1970s introduced him to John Henry in a cartoon film presented as a lesson on multiculturalism. Anthropologically, the predominantly white epistemological context, text, and modes of popular culture by which Whitehead first acquired the germ of the idea for the novel also mark their centrality in his subsequent identity formation as an NBA artist.

To establish the ambiguous ironic tone and the dialectic tension between fact and fiction, myth and legend, folk culture and popular culture, the oral and literary traditions that inform the theme, structure, and style of the novel, Whitehead opens *John Henry Days* with a prologue containing fourteen variants of the ballad of John Henry as remembered in testimonials by different people of different ages from different states along the East Coast. Because the phonology, morphology, and syntax of most of the voices are in SAE, and because the voices include such lexical terms as "dusky sex," "nigger," and "the negro element," the majority of the informants are probably white working-class Americans. "I am a steam shovel operator or 'runner' and have heard steel drivers sing 'John Henry' all my life," says one informant, "and there are probably lots of verses I never heard as it used to be that every new steel driving 'nigger' had a new verse to 'John Henry.' "[38] In "Terminal City," the first of the five major sections of the book, we meet J. Sutter, the hack writer and junketeer, on assignment in Talcott, West Virginia, in 1996 to report for a new travel Web site on the first annual "John Henry Days" festival, which coincides with release of the U.S. Postal Service's Folk Heroes stamp series of four legendary figures, including John Henry. Whitehead then traces in discontinuous narrative fragments of different lengths the impact of the idea of John Henry as a man, story, and song on the lives of Sutter and several characters while satirizing the triumph of technology over humans and celebrating the relativity of truth in the representation of reality.

"John Henry was killed by the Industrial Age; Sutter suffers the insidious effects of the Information Age," writes one astute reviewer.[39] Like Whitehead, for whom contemporary American popular culture and media are central to his personal and professional life as a writer, Sutter, who first heard of John Henry in a cartoon film while in the fifth grade, constructs his identity primarily from the beliefs and values of his postindustrial, capitalistic, multicultural, technological antiblack racist social system. Sutter, we learn from the omniscient narrator in the beginning of the book, "likes the new sound of cash registers, no more chimes: Instead this novel theater of validating purchases, the electronic scrying [*sic*] of purple ink across paper, that tiny pulse that reaches out to the network testing the credibility of credit cards" (p. 11). We also discover that Sutter "possesses the standard amount of black Yankee scorn for the South, a studied disdain that attempts to make a callus of history. It manifests itself in various guises: sophisticated contempt, a healthy stock of white trash jokes, things of that nature, and instinctual stiffening to the words County Sheriff. One look at the cannibals massing at the arrival gate and his revulsion rubs its paws together and hisses. . . . (None of this is true, of course, but perception is all; to and from each his own dark continent)" (pp. 14–15). Unlike the implied author, however, Sutter has become so seduced by the tawdry spectacle and hype of popular culture and the petty cost effectiveness of technology that he has reduced his life to breaking the record for journalistic coverage of an unbroken, uninspiring line of crass public relations events. But in the closing pages of Part Five, "Adding Verses," Sutter is spiritually awakened by joining with Pamela Street, the daughter of the most devoted and tragic collector of John Henry memorabilia and artifacts, in burying her father's ashes in the legendary Talcott Mountain site of John Henry's grave. When Pamela asks Sutter if he got his story, he replies yes. "He has a story but it is not the one he planned. . . . It is not the kind of thing he usually writes. It is not puff. It is not for the website. He does not know who would take it. . . . He does not even know if it is a story. He only knows it is worth telling" (p. 387).

J. Sutter and Pamela Street are not the only characters in the novel whose lives change dramatically as a result of John Henry legends and songs. Mr. Street, Pamela's father, whose obsessive hobby of collecting John Henry artifacts alienated his family and drove him to a lonely death after establishing a John Henry Museum in his apartment that never had a single visitor, is the most tragic character influenced by the legacy of John Henry. In addition, Whitehead traces the evolution of the legend of John Henry as a black folk hero from the worksongs and ballads of such minor characters as black laborers and railroad men to the songs of a bluesman, Tin Pan Alley songwriter, and Broadway actor. In his field study interviews in the 1930s to discount the theory that the outlaw John Hardy and steeldriving John Henry were the same person, black folklorist Guy Johnson concluded that "the Hardy songs are confined to the Appalachia area, and sung by whites, whereas the Henry songs have been disseminated all over by itinerant Negro workers, who carried the song from construction camp to construction camp; the song traveled the rails with the men who laid the rails, from state to state, accruing texture from all who came to hear and sing it" (p. 159). But while some informants told him and Louis Chappell, a white scholar of John Henry, that neither John Henry nor the contest between him and the machine existed, others said that it did. Ironically, in their studies Chappell concludes that the contest happened, but Johnson contends that there wasn't enough proof. Whitehead, disappointingly, neglects to examine adequately either the economic or political impact of industrialization on the lives of ordinary African Americans.

On the South Side of Chicago with its rapid increase of black migrants from the South during the 1920s, Moses, an itinerant bluesman, accepts the exploitative offer of forty dollars for each side from Andrew Goodman to cut his first record, starting with John Henry. "Moses felt the natural thing would be to sing about what the man felt waking up in his bed on the day of the race. Knowing what he had to do and knowing that it was his last sunrise. Last breakfast, last everything. Moses could relate to that, he figured most everyone could feel what that was like" (p. 260). Shifting to Jake, a Tin Pan Alley songwriter in New York, Whitehead outlines how on a late, snowy night a Bowery assault and encounter with an ostensibly drunk homeless man singing "John Henry" become the catalyst for the modern copyrighting and commodification of the folksong. "Jake looked it up and no one had published a version of the ballad. . . . Jake thought with everybody chasing after the latest fashion, a ballad was going to sneak through. . . . This John Henry isn't going to be a million-seller, but it'll show the old man he has initiative. A fellow's got to start somewhere" (p. 205). Also in New York in 1940, black singer and actor Paul Robeson plays John Henry in an unsuccessful musical that white author Roark Bradford adapted from his 1931 novel. "The dialogue is terrible, the characters racist, the situation appalling," says the narrator of *John Henry Days*, "but in John Henry, a man of the land, Paul Robeson sees the folk. The masses. He wants to represent the experiences of the common man. Out of this folktale, even if diverted down ruined streams, flows the truth of men and women. They sacrifice and give" (p. 229). The disruptive sequence and frequency of these and other fragmentary vignettes in *John Henry Days* vary widely in length and intensity depending ostensibly on the kind and degree of impact that John Henry had or has on the working-class lives of their subjects. Nevertheless, most of the vignettes are more intriguing than the vapid middle-class lives of J. Sutter and his fellow media agents, who have no genuine altruistic interest in memorializing the life, legends, and songs of John Henry for the present and future generations.

In retrospect, the most striking characteristics of the agency and hybridity of language, culture, and identity in the novels of Johnson, Mackey, Ellis, Everett, and Whitehead are the shifts in primary audience to the intellectually elite, in theme to a valorization of the lives of the African American middle class, and in structure and style to a wider range of experimentation with satire, parody, and irony in their imaginative—some readers claim postmodern—visions of Eurocentric, Afrocentric, and African Americentric culture. In the quest for authenticity, authority, and agency in their novels, they seek in different ways to expand and enrich the African American novel and its tradition, to take them in a new direction. But for many readers the satirical and parodic styles of Johnson, Mackey, Ellis, Everett, and Whitehead not only question the authenticity and agency of African American rural and urban working-class vernacular tropes of core black cultural identity. Their styles also replace core biracial, bicultural, working-class vernacular tropes with transcultural African American middle-class tropes that celebrate individualism and an unproblematized multiculturalism as more authentic representations of a usable past and desirable new world order. However, as stated earlier in this chapter, the five African American residual oral forms of oratory, myth, legend, tale, and song, as well as the rhetorical conventions of satire, irony, and paradox continue to inform the authenticity, authority, and agency of the complex dualism and cultural ambivalence of the most engaging contemporary novels and novelists in the NBA movement. Also, the legendary biracial, bicultural ancestor and elder—gifted and often militant, if not radical, orator, musician, artist, spiritual leader, and messianic figure—continue to be enduring distinctive symbols and tropes in contemporary African American novels, revealing that some are more fundamentally African Americentric than others.

8 / Contemporary African American Paraliterature: Science/Speculative Fiction, Gay/Lesbian, and Detective/Mystery Novels and Romances (1983–2001)

Chester Himes has said that the black people in this country are the only new race in modern times and I think that's probably true. Nothing in history quite happened like it happened here. I think that the young black writer draws from this experience instead of looking over his shoulder to Homer or to the Latins as white writers do, at least many of them. I think that's the difference.

ISHMAEL REED

In John O'Brien, *Interviews with Black Writers*

THE 1980s and 1990s marked a renaissance in the tradition of the African American novel. On one hand, we witnessed the extraordinary critical success of Alice Walker, Gloria Naylor, Charles Johnson, and Toni Morrison for their experiments with nonrepresentational modernism and antirepresentational postmodernism.[1] On the other hand, with the overwhelming response of black and crossover white readers, especially women, we saw the astounding commercial success of contemporary representational African American romances and paraliterature. Paraliterature ranges from pulp fiction and formulaic adventure stories to extraterrestrial journeys and apolitical romances. It includes the transgeneric novels of science/speculative fiction by Samuel Delany and Octavia Butler and the detective/mystery novels by Walter Mosley, as well as the gay novels by E. Lynn Harris and straight romances by Terry McMillan. On the *New York Times* bestseller list for thirty-eight weeks, McMillan's 1992 romance *Waiting to Exhale* sold 700,000 copies in hardcover and 3 million in paperback. Due in part to the Oprah Winfrey Book Club, black American authors and books, especially novels and romances by women, had astounding success in the marketplace and unprecedented impact on the lives of readers. According to the American Booksellers Association, 90 percent of the 9.9 million black adults who were regular buyers of fiction in 2000 were women.[2]

But what is the relationship of the success of popular, mass market representational and vernacular literature and what Samuel Delany calls "paraliterature," which is generally derived from "pulp magazines, outside the traditional realms of literature,"[3] to literary art? This relationship is complicated when the meaning of paraliterature is extended to include some radically sensational, anti-establishment, sexually and morally transgressive underground and counterculture literature published by little magazines and small presses for limited target audiences. But the central question remains: Can both paraliterature and critically acclaimed serious and experimental novels become popular, commercially successful best-sellers? Of course, some representatives of each, like Harris's *Just as I Am* and Walker's *Color Purple*, have; others, like Larry Duplechan's *Eight Days a Week* and Reed's *Mumbo Jumbo*, have not. How does the representation of race, class, gender, and sexuality, especially the problems of the color line and identity formation, in African American science/speculative, gay/lesbian, and detective/mystery novels and romances influence the type and degree of success they achieve? How significant are the residually oral forms of oratory (including the vernacular), myth (including ritual), legend, tale, and song to the distinctiveness of these extended narratives? How are the issues of narrative authenticity and authority as well as political and moral agency addressed by authors and received by audiences in these subgenres? How is the relationship among language, knowledge, and power represented in them? These questions about the production and reception of literary genres and standards are still very important for many readers—especially students, writers, and literary critics—even as we enter the third millennium. This chapter will therefore explain the manner and degree to which some of the black authors of paraliterature create a space for themselves within the tradition of the African American novel.

In contrast to the formal, traditional standards established by literary institutions and academies for canonical literature, the standards of the parallel tradition of popular, mass market, vernacular literature and paraliterature are governed by formulaic, commercial, and practical interests. Many readers of paraliterature are more interested in whether a book is readable, exciting, and entertaining, than whether it is authentic, authoritative, and empowering. However, if we assume that literature is writing highly valued by different audiences, and if we interpret specific genres of narrative by focusing on the deployment of rhetorical and discursive practices in texts, then we should be concerned with how both canonical and paraliterary narratives are organized and developed. We should also be concerned with the specific kinds of effects that the deployment of different forms and devices have on the authenticity, authority, and agency of particular authors and characters, as well as on the response of particular audiences in actual situations.

Historically, rhetoric has examined the way discourses or sign systems and signifying practices in our society are constructed to achieve certain effects, especially in influencing the relationship between knowledge and power. The horizon of rhetoric, as critic Terry Eagleton states, "was nothing less than the field of discursive practices in society as a whole, and its particular interest lay in grasping such practices as forms of power and performance."[4] Language does not merely reflect reality, it also influences our construction and perception of it. Assuming that literature has the power to influence social change and even to make us better people, then the transformative effect of literature should be concrete and practical, which involves people's political consciousness and situation as a whole, and not merely abstract moral arguments and immediate interpersonal relations.

The difference between a conventional critic who speaks of the chaos of experience in Twain, Faulkner, Ellison or Morrison, and the African Americanist critic—whether Afrocentric, Eurocentric, Americentric, or African Americentric—who examines not only the representations of race, class, and gender by those writers, but also the assumptions behind those representations, is not a distinction between nonpolitical and political criticism. "It is," as Eagleton argues convincingly, "a distinction between different forms of politics—between those who subscribe to the doctrine that history, society and human reality as a whole are fragmentary, arbitrary and directionless, and those who have other interests which imply alternative views about the way the world is. . . . It is not a question of debating whether literature should be related to 'history' or not: it is a question of different readings of history itself."[5] In this context of the historical relationship of language to knowledge and power, let us examine how African American science/speculative fiction, gay/lesbian, and detective/mystery novels not only construct different world orders, but also continue to demonstrate the viability of African American residual oral forms of oratory, myth, legend, tale, and song in validating the authenticity, authority, and agency of different literary texts.

Science Fiction and Speculative Fiction Novels

According to science fiction writer and historian Brian W. Aldiss, "Science fiction is the search for a definition of mankind and his status in the universe which will stand in our advanced but confused state of knowledge (science), and is characteristically cast in the Gothic or post-Gothic mode."[6] Although the term "science fiction" was not used to designate the narrative form as a genre until it was applied to the stories in American pulp magazines, as it was to *Amazing Stories* in 1926, Aldiss argues that the inspiration for science fiction has its origin in the rise of the Industrial Revolution and Gothic fantasy outside of the United States. "Only in an epoch when a power source more reliable than ocean currents or the wind, faster than the horse, has been developed," he reminds us, "can we expect to find a literature that will concern itself with problems of power, either literal or metaphorical. Such problems lie at the heart of SF [science fiction], the fiction of a technological age. . . . Shall we increase technology until the whole surface of the planet is covered by concrete and steel? Is all religion an aberration? Is war inevitable? Will artificial intelligence take over our governance, and is that desirable? Do we need to conquer space? How would utopia come about? What of our immortal souls?"[7]

The rise of industrialization, cities, and the middle class in the eighteenth and nineteenth centuries fostered questions, problems, hopes, fears, and obsessions that were addressed by both the Gothic romance, relying on suspense and mystery, and the social novel, relying on realistic details and working-class characters. A blend of fantasy and fact, the structure and theme of the Gothic often involve the voluntary or involuntary descent or journey of the protagonist from the natural to a supernatural world in search of a secret, an identity, or a relationship. For example, because it involved the quest of a strange scientist for the secret to human life, Mary Shelley's *Frankenstein* (1818) is believed by some readers to mark the beginning of SF. Because of the space race between the Soviet Union and the United States, the first walk on the moon by an American astronaut, and the popularity of the *Star Trek* television program and the *Star Wars* movies between the 1960s and 1980s, it is difficult to separate science fact from science fiction. Consequently, the term "hard science fiction" adheres more to the "science" end of the spectrum and is therefore different from science fantasy, which in its narrowest sense "generally implies a fiction leaning more towards myth or the mythopoaeic than towards an assumed realism."[8] In a more general sense, however, SF can also be imagined to stand for science fantasy or speculative fiction. In fact, since the 1960s, Samuel Delany and some literary critics have preferred the term speculative fiction as a more formal generic classification for SF.

Unlike African American gay/lesbian and detective/mystery novels, as the subsequent sections of this chapter reveal, African American SF to my knowledge has not yet inspired a book-length critical study. However, in *The Oxford Companion to African American Literature* under the broader term of speculative fiction, Sandra Govan, a highly perceptive black SF critic, provides an extended, informative, and provocative general discussion of African American SF that builds on earlier definitions. Although the term was coined by Robert Heinlein in the 1950s, critic Darko Suvin defines speculative fiction as "a literary genre whose necessary and sufficient conditions are the presence and the interaction of estrangement and condition, and whose main formal device is an imaginative framework alternative to the author's empirical environment."[9] Govan provides a more rhetorical classification of speculative fiction "as the umbrella genre that shelters the subgenres of fantasy, science fiction, utopian and dystopian fiction, supernatural fiction, what has come to be called by some critics fabulative fiction or fabulation."[10] This specific list of subgenres enables Govan to contest the domination by white authors and a white audience by identifying many African American writers and books that have included rhetorical elements of speculative fiction in their texts. These range from Martin R. Delany's *Blake, or the Huts of America* (1859), Sutton E. Griggs's *Imperium in Imperio* (1899), Charles Waddell Chesnutt's *Conjure Woman* (1899), and George S. Schuyler's *Black No More* (1931), to John A. Williams's *Captain Blackman* (1972), Ishmael Reed's *Yellow Back Radio Broke-Down* (1971), and, most surprisingly, Virginia Hamilton's Justice trilogy of juvenile books: *Justice and Her Brothers* (1978), *Dustland* (1980), and *The Gathering* (1981).

However, even though my research reveals that the SF genre is still dominated by white male authors and a white audience, I prefer to interpret African American SF as moving beyond realism toward the residual oral form of myth in its exploration of the relationship of language to knowledge and power in past, present, and future world orders. I have located only six well-known African American writers who have published SF novels: Samuel R. Delany, Octavia E. Butler, Steven E. Barnes (*Street Lethal*, 1983, *The Kundalini Equation*, 1986, *Gorgon Child*, 1989, *Fire Dance*, 1993, *Blood Brothers*, 1996, *Iron Shadows*, 1997, *Saturn's Race*, 1998, and five co-authored books with his SF mentor Larry Niven), Jewelle Gomez (*The Gilda Stories*. 1991), Tananarive Due (*The Between*, 1995, and *My Soul to Keep*, 1997), and Walter Mosley (*Blue Light*, 1998). The most successful and celebrated African American SF novelists are Samuel Delany and Octavia Butler. The winner of several Nebula and Hugo Awards, the two most prestigious prizes in SF, Delany is one of the field's preeminent authors. Working in a genre long dominated by whites, he brings to his speculative worlds the authority of self-authenticating black and racially mixed characters who are more mythic than realistic in their representation of the relationship of language to knowledge and power.

SAMUEL [RAY] DELANY [JR.] (1942–)

Born on April 1, 1942, to Samuel R. Delany Sr., a prosperous Harlem funeral director, and Margaret Carey Boyd Delany, a funeral director and a librarian in the New York Public Library, Samuel Ray (Chip) Delany was raised in Harlem. His privileged childhood included visits to the family summer home in upstate New York and enrollment in the progressive, predominantly white Dalton Elementary School further downtown in Manhattan. His friends in Harlem were the children of the black poor and working class; his Dalton peers and playmates were the children and grandchildren of the white political and cultural elite. "The dichotomies in his daily life," according to Govan, "affected young Sam's emotional stability and his behavior; he ran away from home several times between the ages of five and seventeen, and eventually he was referred to a child-guidance center for psychotherapy because of his 'deep maladjustment.'"[11]

Delany's problems with alienation, ambivalence, and anxiety in growing up black and middle class were compounded by his dyslexia and homosexuality. While at Dalton, Delany not only struggled with his homosexuality and met the poet Marilyn Hacker, whom he married in 1961, but also was assigned to remedial classes by misguided, patronizing teachers who neglected to discover his dyslexia. Nevertheless, he pursued his passion for reading and writing before graduating in 1956 and moving on to the Bronx High School of Science. He was particularly fascinated by such well-known SF writers as Robert Heinlein, Theodore Sturgeon, Alfred Bester, Isaac Asimov, and Ray Bradbury. As a teenager, Delany also read black American literature, ranging from Paul Laurence Dunbar to LeRoi Jones. In 1958–59 he won first place for a short story and second place for an essay in the Scholastic Writing Awards contest. In addition, he continued to develop his interest in math, physics, music, and the arts, completing a violin concerto in 1956–57, receiving a fellowship to the Bread Loaf Writers' Conference in 1960, attending City College of New York in 1961, and producing several apprentice literary projects between 1954 and 1963.[12]

Beginning with *The Jewels of Aptor* (1962), relating the adventures of the poet Geo, Delany's principal publications include novels, short stories, critical essays, and memoirs. Before suffering a nervous breakdown in 1964, he completed four novels: *The Fall of the Towers* trilogy (*Captives of the Flame*, 1963; *The Towers of Toron*, 1964; and *City of a Thousand Suns*, 1965), a "space opera" that deploys traditional science fiction technology in the mythic struggle of good and evil in the decline and rise of civilizations; and *The Ballad of Beta-2* (1965), which features mythmaking and a university honors student of galactic anthropology, Joneny Horatio T'wabaga, as the protagonist. Both *Babel-17* (1966), featuring Rydra Wong, an Asian poet, and the mysterious language called Babel-17, and *The Einstein Intersection* (1967), whose protagonist, Lobey, is a black musician who is half man and half beast, explore the relationship between language, knowledge, and power. Both also won Nebula Awards. Delany's first major cycle of SF novels ends with *Empire Star* (1966), a short novel that traces young Comet Jo's journey from a simple to complex understanding of the cyclical nature of history; and *Nova* (1968), his most critically acclaimed interplanetary space opera and romance.

Many of his novels and romances published in the 1970s and 1980s, when the space race between the United States and the Soviet Union culminated in President Reagan's "Star Wars" missile defense program and in the popular success of *Star Trek* and *Star Wars* movies, were equally, if not more, transgressive in crossing racial, cultural, sexual, and language boundaries. For example, Delany's *Tides of Lust* (1973) is an orgiastic carnival of sexual expression and experimentation. *Dhalgren* (1975) is one of the most controversial, experimental, and sensational SF books of the decade because of its labyrinthine structure, its self-authenticating, amoral protagonist (the poet Kid), and its graphic, sympathetic treatment of homosexual and heterosexual desire. In *Triton* (1976), the authority of Bron Hellstrom, the alienated white protagonist and male prostitute, to construct a viable bisexual identity in a new world order of forty to fifty different sexes is frustrated by the confusion of sexual license with freedom that fosters mass chaos rather than individual choice on Earth and Mars. As stated by the character Steiner in the preface to the 1993 edition of *Tales of Neveryon*, the "Return to *Neveryon*" series is a fascinating "narrative hall of mirrors, an intricate argument about power, sexuality, and narration itself."[13] Thematically, stylistically, and structurally concerned with the adventures of Gorgic, the barbarian protagonist, and the reversal of conventional hierarchical, oppositional relationships, the series includes: *The Tales of Neveryon* (1979), *Neveryona; or, The Tale of Signs and Cities* (1983), *Flight from Neveryon* (1985), and *The Bridge of Lost Desire* (1987). Delany's other novels are *Distant Stars* (1981), *Stars in My Pocket Like Grains of Sand* (1984), and *Mad Man* (1994), which is more sexually detailed than *The Tides of Lust*, and probably his most provocative and graphic homoerotic narrative of uninhibited, impersonal sexual entanglements among contemporary social and sexual outsiders.

In addition to Nebula Award–winning "Aye and Gomorrah . . ." (1967), "We, in Some Strange Power's Employ . . ." (1968), and "Time Considered as a Helix of Semi-Precious Stones" (1969), Delany published a collection of short stories, *Driftglass: Ten Tales of Speculative Fiction* (1971). He also published five collections of erudite SF criticism: *The Jewel-Hinged Jaw: Notes on the Language of Science Fiction* (1977), *The American Shore* (1978), *Starboard Wine: More Notes on the Language of Science Fiction* (1984), *Straits of Messina* (1988), and *Wagner/Artaud: A Play of Nineteenth and Twentieth Century Critical Fictions* (1988). His memoirs include *Heavenly Breakfast* (1979) and *The Motion of Light in Water: Sex and Science Fiction Writing in the East Village, 1957–1965* (1988).

Of Delany's nearly two dozen novels, the relationship of language to power, racial heredity, and ethnic heritage, as well as to authenticity, authority, and agency, are most apparent and essential to the characters and multilayered plots of *Nova* and *Dhalgren*. Aesthetically, Delany, notes critic Peter Alterman, "considers the totality of the story, plot, character, language, etc. to be a *textus*, or web of meaning, within which the text proper resides. The manner in which *textus* translates into text he alludes to with the term metonymy, the concept of language as connotative rather than denotative."[14] Katin, the narrator of *Nova*, is a novelist whose dictation of notes for *Nova* is interwoven with the actual events of the quest novel as well as the metafictional commentary on the historical authority and authenticity of the Grail quest from Chretien de Troyes to Charles Williams by both Katin and his musician friend, Mouse. To avoid the fate of the Grail authors, who usually died before completing their romances, Katin and Delany, the implied author, end *Nova* in mid-sentence. This gives an African American ironic, reflexive twist to the satiric and allegorical meaning of the narrative and the social unity achieved in the medieval Grail tradition. Unlike the medieval quest, as critic Jeanne Murray Walker notes, *Nova* develops a social system based on the exchange of material commodities similar to the capitalist exchange system in which the struggle of individuals in competition with each other for the ownership of material goods divides rather than unites people.[15]

In *Nova*, as Govan trenchantly observes, "a black man moves from the role of strong support to that of hero proper; but . . . most of the critical response to the novel concentrates on Delany's wedding of form to theme; space opera to the mythic quests for power, for art, for meaning, for free will."[16] On the level of romance or space opera, then, human alienation from work and the universe in *Nova* is resolved by Delany's invention of a technology that enables his crew to function as cyborgs. They have neural devices on their arms and backs that plug into the sockets of computers on board the starship, empowering the crew to work freely and to achieve communion among themselves, the machines, and the cosmos. On another level, however, Delany has declared that in "most of my futures the racial things have changed and changed for the better. As a young writer I thought it very important to keep an image of such a possibility before people. I don't ever remember subscribing to the idea that 'being black doesn't matter.' I wanted to write about worlds where being black mattered in different ways from the ways it matters now."[17]

On this level, Captain Lorq Von Ray, the protagonist of *Nova*, dramatically asserts his authority and agency as the grandson of a space pirate who settled on Pleiades and the son of a Senegalese mother and Norwegian father. Lorq, who is ironically in love with Ruby Red, the white daughter of his family's chief economic and political rivals, courageously demonstrates his agency by embarking on a quest to discover new sources of illyrion, the valuable fuel that is the key to economic power, with a crew from the three diverse, economically competing sectors of the galaxy. They are the Draco Federation, including Earth, the oldest, most conservative, capitalistic sector, which is controlled by the powerful Reds family; the Pleiades Federation, settled by adventurers and political radicals like the Von Ray family, beginning with Lorq's grandfather; and the Outer Colonies, the newly emerging political and economic sector of workers and mines. These sectors and families are analogous to the historical blocs of capitalist, communist, and Third World nations. The quest has layers of mythic and spiritual ties to the Holy Grail as dramatized by the different speech and cultural behaviors of Lorq and the crew that seek to avoid economic chaos and achieve social unity.

On the surface level, Lorq must find sufficient quantities of the extremely valuable fuel illyrion on a nova, a burned-out star, in order to defeat the efforts of the Red-Shift Company of Draco Federation. Led by Prince and Ruby Red, the Draco Federation conspires to control the use of illyrion and dominate the Outer Colonies, the sector with the largest and richest natural resources of illyrion, and the Pleiades. Instead of fostering familial and interstellar unity by his successful quest, Lorq destroys the incestuous Prince and Ruby Red, Draco's economy, and one third of the galaxy by finding and dumping tons of illyrion on the world market. Lorq and the implied author thereby dramatize an ambivalence about Lorq's power as a black hero and about the economic superiority of Pleiades. On a deeper level, however, Lorq ultimately succumbs to the tragic irony of the loss of his sight from the brilliant light of the dying star and of his responsibility for creating an economic exchange system that perpetuates unbridled individualism and violence, unrelenting ambition and acquisitiveness, and interstellar disunity instead of unity.

While Delany uses a more traditional and romantic SF genre of the space opera to explore socioeconomic and mythical issues in *Nova,* some critics believe that *Dhalgren* is not only his most controversial and experimental novel, but also not even SF. This critical response is primarily due to *Dhalgren*'s nightmarishly violent setting, schizophrenic narrator and poet/protagonist, multilayered structure, sexually explicit and transgeneric style, and multiple themes. Named after the Roman goddess of war, Bellona, the setting is a mysterious, lawless, dangerous, near-future American city of devastation, decay, and death. Bellona has suffered a cataclysmic civil war in the wake of the assassination of Paul Fenster, who is black, by white terrorists and the rape of June, who is white, by George Harrison, who is black. "'Where is this city?'" asks the black evangelist minister Reverend Amy Tayler. "'Stuck out of time! Where is it builded [*sic*]? On the brink of truth and lies.'"[18] In this borderland of paradoxes, the authority of Delany, the implied author, and Kid, "the psychologically wounded poet/protagonist," is undermined by the close psychological, sexual, and artistic relationship between them. Unlike Delany, though, the Kid is half-Indian and half-white, not black, but he becomes the leader of a gang called the Scorpions, most of whose male and female membership is black.[19] Although the Scorpions are three-fourths black, Bellona is a racially divided city where blacks are still the targets of terrorism by white arsonists and snipers. Ironically, the agency and authority of the major black character, George Harrison, are dramatized in his sexual exploits with white women and homosexuals, including rape, and are symbolically and ritually celebrated by the Bellonians over the spiritual and mythic explanations by Reverend Tayler of the miraculous appearance of an awesome sun and two moons. The Bellonians even perversely name one of the moons George.

Because Kid is dyslexic (like Delany, he has problems with right-left orientation and visual reversal of letters and objects), suffers from amnesia and epilepsy, and undergoes many disorienting changes, his political agency and moral authority as narrator/protagonist are problematic. Lacking a clear, coherent, linear narrative structure, *Dhalgren* compels multileveled or multiplexed readings. For example, the narrative opens with the narrator/protagonist not even remembering his name and being named Kid by Tak Loufer, a member of a Bellonian commune. "Kid clearly is responsible for writing the journal, and therein perhaps the novel," Alterman notes, "but there are many Kids. There is Kidd, the confused immigrant, Kid the Poet, who also may be Ernest Newboy, Kid the Scorpion leader, and finally, the Michael Henry."[20] Because of his occasional temporal and spatial disorientation and the changes that he undergoes in Bellona, Kid is an unreliable narrator, and the narrative is temporally discontinuous and highly ironic in structure and development. Kid's dyslexic disorientation is apparent in such events as his confusion about time sequence, about the direction of the rising sun, and about the location of the bridge.

Beginning with the title of the first chapter, the frequent references to prisms, mirrors, and lenses throughout the novel are symbolic of multiple points of view of reality as expressed by the artist and fostered primarily by racial, ethnic, class, sexual, physical, and psychological difference. As critic Jane Branham Weedman perceptively writes:

> Delany creates disorientation in *Dhalgren* to explore the problems which occur when reality models differ from reality. By illustrating these occurrences he is able to approach two problems in our society: prejudice and insanity. Since American blacks exist in two cultures, both of which have their own reality models, they necessarily have some conflicting reality models. The reality models of both cultures may also conflict with what they actually observe. . . . The second area Delany explores is our hesitancy to accept that others perceive differently than we do. . . . We are afraid to question our perceptions because we fear what will happen to our minds if we are stripped of our familiar patterns. We designate, because of our fear, that those who differ are wrong and therefore less acceptable than we are, or we label them as insane.[21]

By using a biracial, bicultural, dyslexic, epileptic narrator/protagonist, Delany validates and valorizes multiple points of view in *Dhalgren*. Moving beyond double consciousness, he interrogates the fear which we feel when our own reality models are questioned and when we perceive a difference between what we have been taught is true and what we perceive is real.

The explicit descriptions of heterosexual and homosexual acts by Kid and George with Lanya, June, and Tak are developed in the four different styles of *Dhalgren*: two different types of journal entries; the book of poems, *The Brass Orchids*; and the text of *Dhalgren* itself. The different styles of the journal entries are not only the product of Kid's dyslexia, amnesia, and epilepsy, but also his ambidexterity. He writes with his right and left hands when he is fully conscious of what he is doing, and he writes in another manner with both hands during periods of his amnesia. Commenting metafictionally on the two types of writing in the journal, Kid tells us:

> Re-reading, I note the entries only ghost chronological order. Not only have I filled up all the free pages, but all the half and quarter pages left

> around the poems or at the ends of other entries. . . . Sometimes I cannot tell who wrote what. That is upsetting. With some sections, I can remember the place and time I wrote them, but have no memory of the incidents described. Similarly, other sections refur [*sic*] to things I recall happening to me, but kne/o/w [*sic*] just as well I never wrote out. Then there are pages that, today, I interpret one way with the clear recollection of having interpreted them another at the last re-reading. Most annoying is when I recall an entry, go hunting through, and not find it [*sic*] find it or half of it not there. (P. 759)

As Kid observes and records his experiences in his poems, journal, and novel, the complexity of the style and authority of *Dhalgren* is further compounded by the close aesthetic correlation between the implied author and the narrator/protagonist writing about themselves in both the first and third person.

Thus, the authenticity, authority, and agency of *Dhalgren* are best interpreted through the structural irony of the multiple responses of racially and culturally mixed Kid and Delany to the crucial question of the novel: What happens when patterns of perception are changed, when we are forced to accept the fact that our reality models are different from others? The authenticity of their multilayered answer is apparent in the creative originality of its opposition to traditional binary linguistic, generic, and social codes. But the moral authority and political agency of Kid and Delany are highly problematic because of their shared schizophrenic values and style. Delany's multiplex answer in *Nova* and *Dhalgren*, as critic Weedman succinctly states, is "that you become an artist, a criminal, an artist/criminal, or insane."[22] This answer radically challenges the viability of African American double consciousness and traditional Eurocentric social, psychological, and aesthetic standards of knowing and being in the world with culturally diverse others.

OCTAVIA [ESTELLE] BUTLER (1947–)

Octavia E. Butler is the first and only major critically successful African American female SF writer. The only child of Laurice and Octavia M. Butler, a shoeshine man and a maid, she was born on June 22, 1947, in Pasadena, California. Because her father died when she was a baby, she was raised by her poor, strict Baptist mother, grandmother, and other relatives. Shy, unworldly, bookish, dyslexic (like Delany), and taller than her classmates, she grew up an outsider to her peer group in a racially mixed area and felt more comfortable with older people.

To escape boredom and loneliness, she began writing at ten years old, and at twelve she became interested in writing SF. She received an Associate of Arts degree in 1968 from Pasadena City College and attended California State University at Los Angeles, but dropped out because she was unable to major in creative writing. In 1969–70, while working at various jobs during the Black

Power and Black Arts movements, she attended evening writing classes at UCLA. Inspired by a different muse than the Black Arts writers, she also participated in the Open Door Program of the Writers Guild of America, West, a program for aspiring authors, where she received encouragement from writers Sid Stebel and Harlan Ellison. In the summer of 1970 she was a student of Delany, Joanna Russ, Fritz Leiber, Kate Wilhelm, Damon Knight, and Robin Scott Wilson at a six-week session of the Clarion Science Fiction Writers' Workshop. She also continued formal training as an SF writer with Harlan Ellison and Theodore Sturgeon at UCLA.

Like Delany, Butler has received the prestigious Nebula and Hugo Awards. She is the author of a collection of short stories, *Bloodchild and Other Stories* (1995), and eleven novels. In her stories and novels the implicit struggle for agency, authority, and power revolves around explicit conflicts of will and the survival of a heroine in a community of racial and gender equality. Butler's most outstanding transracial novels are *Kindred* (1979), a neoslave fantasy; the Patternist saga—*Patternmaster* (1976), *Mind of My Mind* (1977), *Survivor* (1978), *Wild Seed* (1980), and *Clay's Ark* (1984)—which traces the community or pattern formed by the mentally linked descendants of Doro, a 4,000–year-old Nubian vampire psychic; and the Xenogenesis trilogy—*Dawn* (1987), *Adulthood Rites* (1988), and *Imago* (1989)—which examines the struggles of humans with war and gene-transplanting extraterrestrials. "In Octavia Butler's Xenogenesis trilogy," cultural critic Walter Benn Michaels argues persuasively, "human beings of different races are forcefully reminded of the irrelevance of their phenotypical differences by the fact that they are being asked to breed with aliens who look like sea slugs with limbs and tentacles. The difference between black and white skin looks pretty insignificant compared to the difference between humans and walking mollusks."[23] Her most recent Earthseed series—*Parable of the Sower* (1993) and *Parable of the Talents* (1998), for which she received her second Nebula Award in 1999—follows the visions and religious philosophy of Lauren Oya Olamina, a black hyperempathetic prophet who creates a Californian religious community in a twenty-first-century dystopian world. In 1995 Butler received a prestigious MacArthur Foundation Fellowship.

Unlike Delany, who repeats SF conventions with a radically experimental difference, Butler repeats SF conventions with a black feminist difference. Delany's thematic interest lies in the relation of language, knowledge, and power in the liberation of male and female sexuality. In contrast Butler is more concerned with the struggle for human agency, authenticity, and authority of nonwhite women and the evolution of a world of racial and gender equality. Exploring the impact of race and gender on humans in the future on Earth and other planets, she creates speculative fiction in which the rulers include women and nonwhites whose power is based on extrasensory abilities and egalitarianism rather than on racial, sexual, or national domination. "I began writing about power," Butler tells an interviewer, "because I had so little."[24] In her essay "Why I Write," Butler states: "I began to write consciously, deliberately, about people who were afraid and who functioned in spite of their fear. People who failed sometimes and were not destroyed. . . . Every story I write adds to me a little, forces me to reexamine an attitude or belief, causes me to research and learn, helps me to understand people and grow. . . . Every story I create creates me. I write to create myself."[25] Butler is therefore as interested in constructing egalitarian communities in her novels as she is in representing independent, intelligent black women leaders. "Community is so precious to me," she explains, "that my characters, no matter what book they are in, tend to build communities around them if they don't have it in the first place. Now they don't all do it the same way. And they don't all come to the same sort of end, and they are not all the same kind of communities. But they all value community."[26]

The seven major black women characters in Butler's eleven novels represent a wide range of personal and collective identity formations. In *Patternmaster*, set in an agrarian community in the distant future of California, Amber is the golden brown, complex, bisexual healer and killer who mentors Teray in developing his humanity with compassion in the struggle for power with his older brother, Coransee. In *Mind of My Mind*, set in a suburb of Los Angeles in the near future, Mary is Doro's authentically gifted daughter whose extrasensory powers and capacity for aggression rival his. Mary is able to overthrow Doro when these abilities are combined with the extraordinary feminist nurturing powers acquired from Emma, Mary's foster mother and Doro's equally god-like hundred-year-old associate. Butler thus suggests that the relationship between sexuality and power is not only diverse, but also changes with time, place, and social conditions.

In *Survivor*, set in the future on an alien planet of racial and religious conflict, Alanna, the young earthling daughter of an Asian woman and an African man, survives as a wild child after the death of her parents. Adopted and taken to another planet by a family of bigoted white American missionaries who were servant mutes to the Patternists, she escapes the plague spread by the nonhuman Clayarks on earth. After being kidnapped by, married to, and impregnated by a leader of the alien color-changing, furry race of Tehkohns, Alanna grows to love her husband and his culture. Rather than a static state of being in the world with others, the dynamic state of becoming is at the center of Butler's speculative vision of identity formation in the future. In *Parable of the Sower*, set in a futuristic religious community in Northern California, Butler examines the agency and authority of Olamina, a black Baptist preacher's visionary daughter. Olamina suffers the pains of others, escapes the terror of homeless gangs, leads survivors to a new community in the wilderness, and records her philosophy of life in her journals, *Earthseed: The Books of the Living*. At the center of *Parable of the Talents* is Olamina's daughter of the same name, who was separated in infancy from her mother. The daughter discovers that the alienation from the mother she never knew and the philosophical tenets of the Earthseed faith that she collects after her mother's death frustrate her own efforts to rebuild a viable community in the twenty-first century. Butler therefore suggests that racial and sexual politics in future social systems will be based on the reconstruction and reconciliation of oppositional cultural differences.

Butler's most engaging major black women of authenticity, agency, and authority, however, are in *Kindred* and *Wild Seed*. Unlike her other futuristic novels, both *Kindred* and *Wild Seed* are set primarily in the past, respectively in the nineteenth-century antebellum American South and in seventeenth-century precolonial Africa. Although these books may also be read as traditional fantasy or historical romance, their cognitive impulse has a stronger relationship to speculative fiction. The realism and authenticity of *Kindred* and *Wild Seed* are influenced by Butler's extensive, diligent research. The research for *Kindred* included slave narratives, especially Frederick Douglass's autobiography of 1845, and a visit to Talbot, Maryland, the site of the novel.[27] Although the extraordinarily insightful and detailed representation of the Igbos and their culture in Chinua Achebe's *Things Fall Apart* and the ethnography of Richard Henderson's *King in Every Man* were major influences in the construction of *Wild Seed*, this influence is not apparent in the language of the novel.[28] Rather than stressing a rigorous application of the principles and technology of such natural sciences as physics and astronomy to fiction, both novels are more concerned epistemologically with the social sciences of cultural anthropology, sociology, and psychology. Although *Kindred* is an experimental imbrication of slave narrative and time-travel travelogue, and although *Wild Seed* is a blend of historical romance and parapsychological realism, Butler's classification of *Kindred* as "a grim fantasy" is equally appropriate for highlighting the dominant tropes of *Wild Seed*.[29] In *Kindred*, Dana Franklin, the unpublished twenty-six-year-old black writer and narrator/protagonist, is telekinetically and psychokinetically called back to the past whenever her white great-grandfather, Rufus Weylin is in mortal danger and needs her help. During this time travel, she unwittingly mitigates the rape and facilitates the impregnation of her black great-grandmother, Alice Greenwood. Sometimes Dana is alone in her time travels and sometimes with Kevin, her white husband, when he is physically close to her. But when she is threatened periodically with death by her white ancestors, ultimately killing Rufus to avoid being raped by him, she returns from the pre–Civil War era to the twentieth century and the bicentennial year of the Declaration of Independence.

Although the first-person narrator tells the story in retrospection from her hospital bed in Los Angeles in 1976, the fictional time when and setting where Dana directly experiences slavery are during the antebellum years on a plantation in Maryland, beginning in 1815. But the focus of the narrative is not on the realistic technological, biological, and psychological details of time travel. Nor is it on fidelity to the black vernacular speech and culture of the antebellum South. When told by a slave that the white master did not like her because she talked "More like white folks than some white folks," Dana naively responds that she talked the way her mother, a school teacher, taught her. Because she "wasn't good at accents," Dana, with the tacit approval of the implied author, also dangerously and "deliberately decided not to assume one."[30]

As Butler and Dana follow Rufus in his development from childhood to adulthood in Dana's six trips into the past, the narrative focus is on Dana's agency and authority as she experiences the ambivalence of moral responsibility and disgust for the role of guardian for Rufus and slave to the Weylins that she feels compelled to play. "A black to watch over him in a society that considered blacks subhuman," she reflects on the ironies of her dual identity, "a woman to watch over him in a society that considered women perennial children" (p. 68). She is distrusted by both the black and the white characters because she talks like she is white and dresses like she is a man. Although Butler represents Dana more as an agent than as a victim who merely endures suffering, Dana's political accommodationism with slavery and moral complicity in the sexual violation of her great-grandmother are disturbing imaginative truths about the legacy of American racism and slavery. Although Dana develops a kinship with both racial communities with her medical care and literacy skills, the primary focus is on Dana's white great-grandfather, who "loved," raped, and impregnated the black great-grandmother whom Dana resembles.

At the end of the novel, Dana is psychokinetically called back by Rufus to the Weylin plantation on July 4, 1976, to bear witness to Rufus's grief over Alice's suicide in 1831. Rufus had fathered two children with Alice, who hated him. While defending herself from the attempt of her white great-grandfather to rape her because she was so much like her dead black great-grandmother, Dana kills Rufus. In the process she loses her left arm as she ironically liberates herself and transmigrates back to Los Angeles and her white husband on the bicentennial anniversary of American independence. More consistent with fantasy than realism, the relationship between the language, knowledge, and power of the characters in *Kindred* is more representative of twentieth-century Northern racial and sexual politics than those of the Southern antebellum era.

Even though the modern standard American English of *Wild Seed* is also inconsistent with its seventeenth-century Igbo and eighteenth-century American settings, the authenticity and authority of Anyanwu, the female protagonist, is more compelling than Dana's in *Kindred*. Anyanwu, like Amber in *Survivor*, is an example of Butler's strong, authentic black women with authority who use power with compassion. Anyanwu is a three-hundred-year-old female "wild seed" and Onitsha priestess of the Igbo people who uses her powers of prophecy, healing, shape-shifting, and nurturance to protect herself, her children, and her people from the domination and destruction of strangers like Doro. He is a four-thousand-year-old psychic vampire, form-shifter, and progenitor of a race of psychically sensitive and telepathic beings. Anyanwu, Doro, and other major characters are reportedly multilingual. Their cultural differences are most apparent in the contrasting European and non-European mythologies and references to cannibalism that ostensibly distinguished the civilized from the savages. In her African seed village, Anyanwu grew herbs "as medicines for healing. . . . Often she needed no medicines, but she kept that to herself. She served her people by giving them relief from pain and sickness . . . [and] by allowing them to spread word of her abilities to neighboring people." She was also an oracle who was well paid for her services. Her people feared and obeyed her. "But now and then one of them overcame his fear and found reason to try to end her life."[31]

Despite allusions to Job and other books of the Bible, Butler therefore relies most significantly on a thematic exploration of residually oral African mythic, ritual, gender, and kinship systems in *Wild Seed* for narrative authenticity, authority, and audience appeal. Although both Anyanwu and Doro are mutant immortals who physically transform themselves into different human forms, Anyanwu, unlike Doro, also has the power to transform herself into animal forms and birds that Doro cannot track. When Doro uses his tracking powers for his first meeting with Anyanwu in an African village in 1690, they feel a mutual attraction that their names ironically foreshadow. His name means the east, the direction of the land of Kush from which his people come and the direction from which the sun rises; and hers signifies the sun. Their names are thus a sign of their destiny to complement each other. Although both have tremendous physical strength and ability to kill, Doro, unlike Anyanwu, is ruthless. "People's morals rarely survived confrontations with him," the omniscient narrator explains, describing Doro's response to Anyanwu's cry of abomination at the suggestion that her sons and daughters marry each other. "For now, though, gentleness. This woman was valuable. . . . She was descended from people whose abnormally long lives, resistance to disease, and budding special abilities made them very important to him. . . . Nothing must happen to this one survivor, this fortunate little hybrid. Above all, she must be protected from Doro himself. He must not kill her out of anger or by accident" (p. 14).

By threatening her people and children, Doro demonstrates his power to take Anyanwu with him to one of his more secure seed towns in the New World to breed a strong new race of people. But on a slave ship to America and during the development of his seed village in Wheatley, Massachusetts, and subsequently in Louisiana in 1840, Anyanwu frustrates Doro's efforts to kill her by changing into a bird. Resisting Doro's domination, Anyanwu succeeds in using her moral authority, nurturing, and love to change his ruthless killing. By influencing him to kill neither her close relatives nor those whose useful service to him has ended, Govan writes perceptively, "Anyanwu makes Doro salvage what humanity he has remaining, and that is no small victory."[32] Butler's speculative/science fiction narratives are therefore less concerned with the relationship of language, knowledge, and power than Delany's. Instead, they are more concerned with the struggle for human agency, authenticity, and authority of nonwhite women, a possible reason for their negligible use of African American vernacular English, and the evolution of a world of racial and gender complementarity if not equality.

Gay/Lesbian Novels and Romances

"That 'modern' American era from 1880 to 1950, in which the 'homosexual' and 'heterosexual' made their social debuts," Jonathan Ned Katz writes in *Gay/Lesbian Almanac: A New Documentary*, "was an age whose ideologies and citizens were obsessed with the relation of eroticism, 'femininity,' and 'masculinity.' That dominant 'modern' preoccupation with lust and gender differed from the central concern of the early colonists, whose main worry was about lust, procreation, and the failure to so produce."[33] The term "homosexual" first appeared in American medical books and journals in the early 1890s and came into popular use in the 1920s. *The New York Times* first used the words "homosexuality" in 1926 and "homosexual" in 1930. Although the word "gay" as a secret code for self-identification was common in the homosexual subculture in the United States before the 1960s, gay as a name for homosexuals was first used by the *New York Times* in 1963. "Since the mid-1970s," Katz states, "the common use in the political subculture of the terms 'lesbian' and 'gay,' to stress the different social experience of women-loving women and men-loving men, reflects the historical existence of a vocal lesbian feminist movement."[34] Katz broadly and vaguely defines lesbian and gay as "all manifestations of female-female and male-male eroticism."[35]

The Stonewall Rebellion of June 1969, the violent resistance of white gays and lesbians to harassment by New York policemen in the Stonewall Inn in Greenwich Village, marks the birth of the contemporary gay and lesbian liberation movement. But it was as early as 1961 that Frank Kemeny, the founder of the Washington, D.C., branch of the Mattachine Society, the pioneer activist homosexual organization founded in 1948, began advocating the idea that, contrary to custom and law, homosexuality was not a sickness.[36] Prior to 1973 in the United States, the social disapproval and moral rejection of homosexuality as a normal expression of sexual desire was reinforced by the American Psychiatric Association's classification of homosexuality as a disease or sickness. Despite its declassification by specialists as a pathology, however, many black social scientists, humanists, writers, and readers still believe that homosexuality is socially and morally unacceptable behavior in the black community.

Rooted in the tradition of moral conservatism of most black Baptist and Methodist churches, especially fundamentalist and pentecostal denominations, strict sexual proscriptions are among the many controversial and contradictory aspects of black American belief and value systems. In contrast to postmodern critical theory and jargon that dismisses "transcendental signifiers," God and His master plan or teleology, as inscribed in the Bible, still reign supreme in the hearts and souls of many ordinary working-class black folk over forty years old. As preached by zealots and punished by death in some cases during the colonial period and until recently by various state laws in the twentieth century, sodomy (i.e., nonprocreative anal penetration or genital contact between members of the same sex) is primarily a sin against God. In contrast, for many progressive black readers of my generation it is probably acceptable when performed in private between consenting partners. For some the issue is a transgression against nature, the family, and the community, rather than involving a sin or prejudice against homosexuals. And for others sodomy by black preachers, deacons, ushers, and choir directors, as narrated in the novels of James Baldwin, E. Lynn Harris, Larry Duplechan, and Randall Kenan is a tragic violation of the moral principles they preach and of the community they serve or lead.

In advocating a more progressive view of homosexuality in the African American community, gay activist and critic Ron Simmons writes in "Some Thoughts on the Challenges Facing Black Gay Intellectuals":

> In the African American community, "homophobia" is not so much a fear of "homosexuals" but a fear that homosexuality will become pervasive in the community. Thus, a homophobic person can accept a homosexual as an individual friend or family member, yet not accept homosexuality. This is the attitude that predominates in the African American community. The motivation for homophobia is "heterosexism"—the belief that heterosexual sex is good and proper, and homosexual sex is bad and immoral. . . . Homophobic and heterosexist viewpoints are espoused by some of our most respected leaders, writers, and scholars, such as Nathan Hare, Jawanza Kunjufu, Robert Staples, Louis Farrakhan, Molefi Asante, Haki Madhubuti, Amiri Baraka, and Yosuf Ben-Jochannan.[37]

In the effort to move from invisibility to visibility, from object to subject, in his advocacy of gay liberation and pride, Simmons flips the script—reverses the definitions, classifications, and perpetrators of morally and socially acceptable behavior—to assert political agency and moral authority for his voice and radical argument that "Black men loving black men is indeed a sacred act."[38]

"Because of the heterosexism among African American intellectuals and the racism in the white gay community," gay critic Charles I. Nero also argues in "Toward a Black Gay Aesthetic: Signifying in Contemporary Black Gay Literature," "black gay men have been an invisible population."[39] In "The Black Lesbian in American Literature: An Overview," Ann Shockley compares the black lesbian in American literature "to Ralph Ellison's 'invisible man,' . . . seen but not seen because of what the eyes did not wish to behold."[40] Despite recent changes in federal and state laws expanding and protecting the rights of homosexuals, Simmons and Nero lament, most black social scientists, humanists, writers, and readers disapprove of homosexuality, especially in the black community. This disapproval ranges from compassion for transgressors of the code of the community to condemnation of the sinnerman as well as the sin.

In addition to Asante, Baraka, and Hare, Nero lists Frantz Fanon, Alvin Poussaint, Eldridge Cleaver, and Toni Morrison as antihomosexual. In *Black Skin, White Masks*, for example, Fanon declares erroneously that in the Caribbean "there is no homosexuality, which is, rather an attribute of the white race, Western civilization."[41] In *The Autobiography of a Runaway Slave* Esteban Montejo reveals that during and after the abolition in 1880 of slavery in Cuba some men "had sex between themselves and did not want to know anything of women. This was their life—sodomy. The effeminate men washed the clothes and did the cooking too, if they had a 'husband.' . . . It was after Abolition that the term 'effeminate' came into use, for the practice continued. I don't think it can have come from Africa, because the old men hated it. They would have nothing to do with queers. To tell the truth, it never bothered me."[42] As the two cases of sodomy by blacks cited in Jonathan Katz's two documentary books reveal, the evidence of homosexuality among black males during the colonial period and slavery in the United States is as scarce as that in the Caribbean.[43]

Attributing black homosexuality mainly to the prison system, Asante argues in *Afrocentricity*, on the one hand, that "we must demonstrate a real antagonism toward those gays who are as unconscious as other people." But he also argues in the same text that homosexuality "can be and must be tolerated until such time as our families and schools are engaged in Afrocentric instructions for males."[44] In *Soul on Ice* Eldridge Cleaver declares that black homosexuality is a "racial death wish"; it is "the product of the fissure of society into antagonistic classes and a dying culture and civilization alienated from its biology."[45] In *The Endangered Black Family* black clinical psychologists Nathan and Julia Hare see black gay and lesbian people as a threat to the black family and community. "What we must do," they write, "is offer the homosexual brother or sister a proper compassion and acceptance without advocacy."[46]

Although sympathetic to the challenge of gay narratives to the normative authority of heterosexuality, some readers contest the new orthodoxy of negatively labeling heterosexuality. In contrast to the old orthodoxy that judged homosexuality a sin or sickness, the new orthodoxy of radical gay theorists and critics reverses the normative group by labeling heterosexuals "homophobic and heterosexists," sick oppressors who disapprove of homosexuality yet accept individual homosexuals as friends or family members. The new orthodoxy has also popularized the rhetorical and juridical use of "homosexual panic." As used by critic Eve Kosofsky Sedgwick the phrase names "the most private, psychologized form in which many twentieth-century Western men experience their vulnerability to the social pressure of homophobic blackmail," while as a defense strategy "homosexual panic" is "commonly used to prevent conviction or to lighten sentencing of gay-bashers."[47] What does this rhetorical and oppositional forensic strategy say about the complex relationship of language to knowledge and power in general and of the moral authority and political agency of master narratives and sociocultural codes in the formation of our identities in particular?

Responding to the rapid development of techniques and technologies since World War II, Lyotard and his followers argue that the grand or master narrative is no longer credible, "regardless of what mode of unification it uses, regardless of whether it is a speculative narrative or a narrative of emancipation."[48] On one level, this discrediting of master narratives is consistent with the challenges and deconstruction in African American literature of the myths of white supremacy and black inferiority. On another level, however, many African American novelists and readers still find master narratives important in our quest to construct and affirm unified, yet diverse and complex spiritual, existential, and cultural identities as gendered subjects in political communities. Contemporary African American novelists who fashionably devalue and deconstruct master narratives generally displace political agency with language games and other sorts of play in their imaginative constructions of a postindustrial world of social contingency and linguistic indeterminacy. But how do ordinary white and black working-class Americans, in contrast to white and black intellectuals and media pundits, construct a reasonable and ethical balance between their natural and civil rights in democratic communities of mutually respectful and responsible human beings?

For example, in the wake of the liberation movements of blacks, women, gays, and others, advocates of gay rights have boldly used the declassification by American psychiatrists of homosexuality as a mental illness in an effective political tactic. This tactic attributes a Freudian phobia (i.e., an exaggerated, irrational fear of sexual intimacy with someone of the same sex) to all people who subscribe to heterosexuality as the norm *and* who morally object to homosexuality. Sexual discrimination in public affairs is illegal, and for many people the idea of different strokes for different folks in their private affairs includes understanding and acceptance of sexual difference. But neither in most black narratives, except as demonstrated in the anger, frustration, defiance, and celebration of homoeroticism in gay novels, nor in most black communities do this law and folksaying translate into sanctioning homosexuality as the social and moral equivalent of heterosexuality. Nor do traditional black communities, despite the way they are depicted in some black gay novels, generally confuse or conflate lust with love and eros (romantic love) with agape (familial and humanistic love) in moral judgments about men loving men and women loving women. Even though all facets of our racial, ethnic, gender, class, and sexual identities are important, all are not generally stressed equally in our everyday lives. Nor are the many facets of our identities stressed equally in understanding and transforming the politics of difference in power relations in the United States to create a more just, peaceful, and productive democratic social order for all peoples.

Addressing the politics of sexual and racial difference, Nero writes: "Given their invisibility by both black heterosexism and white gay racism, two questions emerge: How have black gay men created a positive identity for themselves and how have they constructed literary texts which would render their lives visible, and therefore valid?"[49] In the 1980s, novels by black lesbians and gays expanded the boundaries of the tradition of the African American novel. But even in a white gay literary critic's construction in 1998 of a canon of gay fiction from 1945 to 1995, black gay novels, except for Baldwin's raceless *Giovanni's Room* and Delany's dissolute *Mad Man*, remain invisible and ignored.[50] In *Mad Man*, Delany not only celebrates the consumption of bodily fluids during sexual activity, but also glorifies sexual fetishes and sadomasochism, including the consumption of human excrement. Black lesbian novels were also invisible in the pre-1983 era. Ann Shockley's imaginative reconstruction of a transracial affair between women in *Loving Her* (1970) is, as far as I have discovered, the first contemporary black American novel with a lesbian protagonist. Rosa Guy's *Ruby* (1976), a novel for young adults, examines with restraint the lesbian relationship between the teenage West Indian protagonist and her high school classmate. But Alice Walker's *The Color Purple* (1982), which also celebrates homoeroticism, is the most notable African American novel in which a lesbian relationship is central to the development of the narrative.

As demonstrated in a previous chapter, *The Color Purple* is less compelling as critical realism than as folk romance, for it is stylistically and structurally more concerned with the politics of sex than the politics of class and race. Its epistolary form rewrites from a black womanist vantage point the seminal texts of the eighteenth-century heterosexual and sentimental tradition of British and European American novels. Walker not only gives prominence to the epistolary form in the tradition of the African American novel, but also uses it for an unrelenting attack on the dominance of black males in their primary racial communities, especially their violent abuse of black women. Grounded in the African American vernacular tradition (especially rural Southern black dialect, the blues, and fundamentalist Baptist and Methodist religion), its major theme is a celebration of the independence of modern Southern black women and black sexual egalitarianism. But rather than heterosexual love, lesbianism is the rite of passage to selfhood, sisterhood, and brotherhood for Celie, Walker's protagonist. Even though it fails to address the political and racial issues of gay communities, the popular and critical success of *The Color Purple* marks it as the most celebrated lesbian novel in the tradition of the white ethnic American novel as well as in the African American novel.

Go Tell It on the Mountain (1953) expanded the boundaries of the African American novel with its subtle, poignant treatment of black homosexuality and spiritual redemption. *Giovanni's Room* (1956) was a thematically and stylistically bold and compassionate critique of the willful innocence of a white American, his American fiancée, and his tragic homoerotic relationship with an Italian in Paris. But *Another Country* (1962) was even more transgressive in its fascinating exploration of the agony and ecstasy of transracial, transnational heterosexual and homosexual relationships. These texts mark James Baldwin as the outstanding novelist of black gay moral anxiety in not only modern African American but also, for some readers, Anglo-American literature. Canonized in 1998 by the Library of America book series, Baldwin has been an inspiration, even when not the model, for the more recent achievements and popularity of the representation of homoerotic desire and sexual identity in gay novels with both gay and straight audiences.

It should be self-evident that novels by gays, about gays, and for gays engage the issues of narrative authenticity, moral authority, and political agency in a different, often more radical and sexually explicit manner than novels written by gays for a crossover or general audience. Stylistically and thematically, novels by black gays for gays are even more diverse in their representation of the impact of the politics of race and class as well as of the politics of sexuality on their African American double consciousness. On the one hand, many black gay texts focus on coming out of the closet in nongay interracial communities and coping with the AIDS epidemic—as in Larry Duplechan's *Eight Days a Week* (1985), *Blackbird* (1986), *Tangled Up in Blue* (1989), and *Captain Swing* (1993). On the other hand, many stress a defiant, transgressive celebration in gay communities of extreme forms of sexual activity and liberation from social conventions as in Samuel Delany's *Mad Man* (1994).

More grounded in African American residual oral forms and generally less explicit sexually in their appeal to a general audience, black gay crossover novels and romances range from Steven Corbin's *No Easy Place to Be* (1989), Melvin Dixon's *Trouble the Water* (1989), and Randall Kenan's *Visitation of Spirits* (1989) to the bestsellers of E. Lynn Harris: *Invisible Life* (1991), *Just as I Am* (1994), *And This too Shall Pass* (1996), *If This World Were Mine* (1997), *Abide with Me* (1999), and *Not a Day Goes By* (2000). Set in a Southern rural town, Kenan's only novel is a highly nuanced, intriguing, authentic rewriting of Baldwin's *Go Tell It on the Mountain* with a tragic ending. Because of the contrast in their sites of publication, primary audience, and critical success, therefore, a closer look at the novels and romances of Duplechan and Harris is more illuminating about the variety of black gay paraliterature.

LARRY DUPLECHAN (1956–)

Larry Duplechan was born on December 30, 1956, in Panorama City, California, and grew up in predominantly white sections of Los Angeles and Sacramento. After graduating from high school in 1974, he went on to earn a degree in English from the University of California at Los Angeles. Although Alfred O. Guzman and Joan Robbins, his high school and college teachers, encouraged him to become a writer, Duplechan actually began his career as a musician, singing for six years around Los Angeles after graduating from college. Writing during the evenings and on weekends while working for a Los Angeles law firm, he published four homoerotic romances and novels between 1985 and 1993. Beginning with *Eight Days a Week*, which was published at his own expense, all are the products of gay publishing outlets. The 1985 and 1993 novels were published by Alyson Publications in Boston, and the 1986 and 1989 novels were published in the Stonewall Inn editions of St. Martin's Press in New York. Because these books were not only published outside of the traditional sites of literature but were also significantly influenced by formulaic, commercial, and pornographic as well as political interests, they may be read as paraliterature.

Although the sites of publication clearly indicate that the primary audience were gays, *Tangled Up in Blue* and *Captain Swing*, Duplechan's most recent novels, were widely reviewed in the straight press. Inspired by the announcement that Rock Hudson was dying of AIDS, *Tangled Up in Blue* is a sensitive treatment of the devastating impact of the epidemic on the lives of a white married couple whose gay friend, Crockett, reveals that he not only has been diagnosed HIV-positive, but also was once a lover of the husband, Daniel Sullivan. *Captain Swing* reintroduces the quest for love, sex, and happiness of the irrepressible and irresponsible black gay protagonist of Duplechan's earlier novels, Johnnie Ray Rousseau. But *Eight Days a Week* and *Blackbird*, which were unnoticed by the straight media even though generally praised for their treatment of gay black experience by the gay press, are more critically distinctive for their narrative authenticity, political agency, and moral authority.

Duplechan occupies these critical positions in his earliest two novels by contesting heterosexual norms and affirming assimilationist goals in his representation of the homoerotic desire of black men. A vanity publication, *Eight Days a Week* derives its authenticity from its semi-autobiographical style and structure. Like Duplechan, the protagonist is a gay black nightclub singer, Johnnie Ray Rousseau, who has a sexual obsession with white male lovers. Stylistically and structurally, the novel is grounded primarily in specific allusions to black R&B songs and singers even though the 1979 setting is in the disco era. The initial chapters have epigraphs from songs by the Shirelles and the Shangri-las, and all of the chapter numbers are inscribed in treble clef bars of music.

Paradoxically, Duplechan most formulaically yet distinctively develops the emotional and sexual themes of his gay love story by references to black music. For example, Johnnie Ray describes his feelings for Keith, his white lover, as analogous to an R&B song: "Great song. 'Sweet Was The Wine,' by Jerry Butler and the Impressions. It's the flip side of 'For Your Precious Love,' which was their first chart hit, back in 1959. A dynamite single if you can get your paws on it. It always reminds me of Keith, but for an entirely different reason than does Donna Summer's 'I Feel Love.' When Keith kissed me, it was sweeter than anything I know" (p. 86).

The narrowly personal rather than broadly political agency of both Duplechan and Johnnie Ray is apparent in the language that constructs their assimilationist beliefs and values as self-liberating gay individuals. "My gay identity is much more important to me [than my black identity]," Duplechan candidly tells an interviewer. "But more than that, I am very much an assimilationist. By that I mean, I have no desire to set myself apart from the white gay men . . . or from black gays or white heterosexuals or Native American bisexual leather dominatrixes, for that matter."[51] Johnnie Ray similarly and repeatedly affirms his gay identity and individuality even in the Los Angeles law firm where he works. But the authenticity and authority of his rapturous language in graphically describing the delights of uninhibited interracial gay love, especially sex with Keith and others, most dramatically reveals that his pride and passion do not extend to agency beyond satisfying his desires within the gay community.

By graphically detailing specific acts of gay lust and love, including oral sex and sodomy, Duplechan constructs his subjectivity and that of his protagonist by implicitly rather than stridently repudiating conventional morality and celebrating homoerotic desire. "True, I do tend to fall in lust two or three times a day," Johnnie Ray confesses to his friend Snookie; "And . . . I am prone to temporary spasms of galloping romanticism following just about any satisfactory sexual experience. . . . But, as to falling in love, I had up to that point, in what I can only snickeringly refer to as my adult life, fallen in love, but really head-over-teacup fall-down-go-boom in love, exactly once before. . . . Anyway, I'd been in love, and I knew good and well what it felt like. Like an itchin' in my heart. Like a heat wave. Like I can't do nothin' but love, Babe, eight days a week. Like nothing else" (pp. 106–7). The moral distance between the implied author, his protagonist, and his primary audience of gay readers in this and similar ecstatically detailed homosexual episodes is probably minimal. Nevertheless, many heterosexual or straight readers in the larger audience may find this type of cloying homoerotic sentimentality morally objectionable and aesthetically weak in gay as well as straight texts.

The homosexual episodes and language in *Blackbird* dramatically illustrate that its implied author is also morally and politically empathetic to his protagonist and gay readers. This empathy is apparent in the novel's title, which is symbolic of the tragicomic coming-out-of-the-closet of Johnnie Ray, at that point a black gay seventeen-year-old and a talented singer whose favorite song is "Blackbird." Beginning with the protagonist's wet dream about Sal Mineo on the opening page of the first chapter to his participation in the final chapter in "the World's biggest homecoming" at the first Gay Students' Union meeting at UCLA, Duplechan paints a graphic, wryly humorous, sentimental picture of growing up gay and black in a largely white community. Much of the authenticity of the representation of adolescent gay life is grounded in Johnnie Ray's frequent interpretation of his life by allusions to popular movies, music, and books. Smoking pot with his first male lover, the part Cherokee Marshall Two-Hawks McNeill, for example, Johnnie Ray muses: "I looked around the room. The light seemed not so much light as a glow. It looked as if the evening had been shot in Technicolor by Twentieth Century-Fox, circa 1944. I suddenly thought of *The Gang's All Here*, with Alice Faye and Carmen Miranda, and Bennie Goodman (and his orchestra), who performed a silly song called 'Pa-dooka': 'If you want to, you can rhyme it with Bazooka'" (p. 125).

The racism and conservatism, both political and moral, of the predominantly Mormon and Baptist white town, located ninety miles from Los Angeles, cloud the protagonist's desire for a part in a school comedy revue, "Hooray for Love," that his peers and white teacher know his audition earned him. These antiblack, antihomosexual forces also rain bitter disappointment on his rejection for a role that would have probably required him, he states, "to nuzzle some flower of white womanhood right there on stage" (p. 9). When he isn't cast for the part, Johnny Ray explodes at the drama teacher: "'There's one reason and only one reason why I wasn't cast. And you know what it is as well as I do. Why couldn't you go against this goddamn town just once? Just once? 'Cause you're a god-damn racist, just like most of this town, that's why . . .'" (p. 48). In this melodramatic act of self-identification, Johnnie Ray is verbally responding to his experience of racial rather than sexual discrimination.

But Duplechan satirizes the antihomosexual forces more than the antiblack. On the one hand, this is apparent in Johnnie Ray's parents naming him after the white singer of "The Little White Cloud That Cried." The racial preference of his parents and of the family of the black girl who seduces him to attend the all-white Baptist church instead of the church in the black community more directly demonstrates his family's assimilationist values. On the other hand, the antihomosexual acts of Johnnie Ray's parents and the Christian community are represented as more destructive than racism to the protagonist's life and the lives of his white peers. The community also indirectly drives to suicide the "extremely decorative dude" for whom Johnnie Ray has an obsessive sexual desire. But the community's hypocrisy is most effectively dramatized in Duplechan's satire of the Christian ritual of exorcism to purge Johnnie Ray of his homosexuality. After the youth minister to whom he had confessed his homosexuality betrays his trust by telling the Rousseaus and by arranging an exorcism, Johnnie Ray fakes the effectiveness of "deliverance from unclean spirits" to relieve the fear of his parents that he is a pervert (p. 156). However, actual deliverance for Johnnie Ray comes only with his graduation from high school and his first Gay Students' Union meeting at UCLA.

Although *Eight Days a Week* and *Blackbird* are both authentic representations and celebrations of the experiences of a young black gay Californian that challenge middle-class Christian sexual morality in the post-Stonewall period, *Blackbird* is stylistically and structurally more effective as a novel for straight readers. Like *Eight Days a Week, Blackbird* luxuriates in the detailed descriptive language and power of homoerotic desire. But its wryly humorous focus on the agony and ecstasy of the coming-out-of-the-closet stage of the construction of black adolescent gay identity, especially Johnnie Ray's power to control his frequent erections by reciting the Twenty-third Psalm, mitigates the possible moral distance created by homosexual fantasies, wet dreams, masturbation, and sodomy for sympathetic straight readers. Engaging some of the issues in politically combating antihomosexuality in the protagonist's hometown would have enhanced the appeal of Duplechan's novels.

E[VERETTE] LYNN HARRIS (1957–)

As indicated by his books on the *New York Times* bestsellers list, the most commercially successful contemporary African American gay writer, especially among blacks, is E. Lynn Harris. Born in 1957 in Flint, Michigan, Harris was raised with three younger sisters in Little Rock, Arkansas—where federal troops were sent to desegregate Central High School in 1957—by his mother, Etta W. Harris, an AT&T factory worker, and a stern stepfather. Harris did not meet his biological father until a year before the latter's death around 1970. During high school, he repressed his homosexuality and dated female cheerleaders. After graduation in 1972 or 1973, he entered the University of Arkansas at Fayetteville. With the political encouragement of several black members of the predominantly African American football team, he became in his senior year the school's first African American male cheerleader. "Looking back," Harris writes, "I realize it was a wonderful year. For one thing, I met my first lover—a football player. And though our squad never truly bonded, our challenges to prejudice worked out."[52]

After graduating with honors from the University of Arkansas in 1977, Harris went to work as a sales executive for IBM. In 1991, he quit his job, paid $25,000 to publish his first novel, *Invisible Life*, and sold it primarily in black beauty salons, bookstores, and book clubs. In 1994 Doubleday published the Anchor paperback edition, and it, along with *Just as I Am*, quickly soared to number one on the Blackboard Bestseller List of African American titles, a further indication of Harris's increasing popularity with black middle-class women readers. His first three novels sold over 500,000 copies. Success skyrocketed even more when *And This Too Shall Pass*, *If This World Were Mine*, *Abide with Me*, and *Not a Day Goes By* became the *New York Times* bestsellers, indicating Harris's widening popularity with white and heterosexual crossover readers. His honors and awards include the SBC Magazine Brother of the Year in Literature, Harlem Y Mentor Award, and Gay Men of African Descent Angel Award. In 1997 *If This World Were Mine* was a finalist for the NAACP Image Award and won the James Baldwin Award for Literary Excellence. And in 2000 *Not a Day Goes By*, his sixth novel, was listed second on the *New York Times* bestseller list with a first printing of 152,000 copies.[53]

Thematically, stylistically, and structurally Harris's six books display a varying degree of narrative tension between the sentimentalism of contemporary popular romances and the neorealism of contemporary novels. They are all positive, sensitive, vivid, episodic, tragicomic stories of love, lust, and loss that focus primarily on the everyday lives of black gay and bisexual middle-class, urban professional men and their families, friends, and lovers during the AIDS epidemic of the 1980s. "Over the ten years ending in June 1991," black gay cultural critic Philip Brian Harper writes, "some 179,694 persons in the United States were diagnosed as having Acquired Immune Deficiency Syndrome. Of that number of total reported cases, 41,179—or roughly 23 percent—occurred in males of African descent, although black males accounted for less than 6 percent of the total U.S. population."[54] Although he neglects to dramatize the pain and suffering of black AIDS victim Kyle in *Just as I Am*, the central theme of all of Harris's books is the healing power of faith and the love of family and friends, as unforgettably embodied in the ancestral faith, love, wisdom, and moral authority of MamaCee in *And This Too Shall Pass*. But the black gay and bisexual dual identities of Raymond Tyler Jr. and John Basil Henderson in *Invisible Life*, *Just as I Am*, *If This World Were Mine*, *Abide with Me* and *Not a Day Goes By* are at the center of the paradoxes and ironies in what Harris calls "the saga of the tragic sexual mulatto."[55]

Harris establishes the sociocultural authenticity of post–Black Power, post–Black Arts, and post-Stonewall era black middle-class life in his texts by code-switching. He compellingly and convincingly crosses group and class boundaries by switching between the idioms, sayings, rhythms, and vernacular allusions of African American English and Standard American English, especially in the conversational idiolects of Basil and Kyle. Harris interweaves their ethnic responses to their experiences in the dominant white social arena with those in black universities (e.g., Howard and Hampton), Greek organizations (e.g., AKA and Deltas), social organizations (e.g., Links and NAACP), and music (e.g., R&B and popular). He also enhances the tragicomic, ironic tone and texture of this authenticity by effectively interweaving the ambivalent responses of his middle-class ethnic insiders with his own as the implied author. With this strategy, Harris demonstrates how his knowledge of black urban professional and gay life enhances the authority and power of his narrative reconstruction of black bisexuality. By challenging the conventional negative stereotypes of homosexuality as a choice of lifestyles rather than as a natural, God-given sexual identity, he foregrounds the contemporary issues of political agency in the affirmation of an essential identity or the construction of sociolinguistic personal and collective subjectivities. And by judiciously rejecting the antihomosexual attitudes and behavior of the traditional black church and community while passionately affirming the healing power of spirituality, love, and friendship, the implied author and his major characters challenge the normative moral authority of his texts in a nonpolemical manner. Because these qualities are best represented in *Just as I Am*, we will examine it more closely after briefly outlining Harris's displacement of the moral authority and political agency of the trope of the tragic mulatto with the saga of the tragic sexual mulatto in the other books.

In Harris's four interrelated narratives of the complex sociocultural and sociopsychological identity of African Americans, the focus is shifted from the tragic plight of racial hybridity, even though most of the major characters are light-skinned African Americans, to the moral and political issues of agency involving sexual hybridity. At the heart of *Invisible Life, Just as I Am, If This World Were Mine,* and *Abide with Me* are two soap opera–handsome bisexual men: the light-skinned, green-eyed, athletically built, attorney, Raymond Tyler Jr., who is represented by only a name in *Not a Day Goes By*, and his sexually irresistible and irresponsible lover, the "honey-colored," gray-eyed, muscularly built pro-football player, John Basil Henderson. When we first meet Raymond and Basil in *Invisible Life*, both are closet bisexuals who generally conceal from partners and others their passion for men and women. Although both are equally dishonest, anxious, and guilty about their bisexuality after beginning their intimacy in *Just as I Am*, Raymond, unlike Basil, becomes more honest and responsible as the soap opera saga progresses in acknowledging the duality of his identity and in striving for the perfect world of unconditional love from family, friends, and partners. This shift in Raymond's character begins in the final chapters of *Invisible Life* after a series of entangling interpersonal relationships and traumatic events: witnessing the death of Candance, a friend, from the probable contraction of AIDS from his first bisexual lover, Kelvin; admitting his gayness to the main heterosexual love of his life, Nicole; losing his best gay friend, Kyle, to AIDS; undergoing psychiatric therapy; and finding a devoted male lover in Trent Walters, a fraternity brother and architect.

Just as I Am, the second book in the series, is probably the most fascinating, provocative primer for straight and crossover readers, especially black women. Its lessons in the three major sections of the book about lust, love, loss, and life move beyond the authenticity of such gay language as "snow queens," black gays with a passion for white homosexuals, "tea rooms," the restrooms in subways, and "trade," men who had sex with other men for money or other compensation, that were introduced in *Invisible Life*. One of the major themes of the multiple narrators in *Just as I Am* is that the invisible or secret lives of post-Stonewall, post-Soul era gay and bisexual BUPPIES, black urban professionals, and BAPS, black American Princesses and Princes, are full of joy and pain. This rather obvious knowledge of sexual and social desire culminates in the AIDS deaths of Candance and Kyle, which, in turn, belatedly empower their black friends to transform their private pain into the public collective agency of support for minority AIDS patients. This theme also resonates with the actual AIDS deaths in 1988 of the possibly bisexual former ABC news anchor Max Robinson and in 1993 of the straight tennis champion Arthur Ashe. Another more politically and morally problematic theme is that black gay and bisexual "orientation was not a belief or choice," according to Raymond Jr., the protagonist, and the implied author, "but a fact of my birth. And just like the color of my skin and eyes, these things could not be changed, at least not permanently" (p. 1). The moral authority and political agency of the text emanate from the successful efforts of the implied author, protagonist, and other major characters to show sensitively rather than shout sensationally why "the majority of black gay and bisexual men lived their lives in the closet" and how this secrecy ironically endangered the health and happiness of themselves and others (p. 33).

Although Harris is ambivalent about whether unconditional love and spirituality are more likely found in the hearts of women than men, he is unequivocal that both have the capacity to respect and understand that, as the Reverend Jesse Jackson sermonizes, gay, straight, red, black, brown, and white, we're all precious in God's sight. In addition to his lustful relationship with Basil, Raymond's relationships with his parents, friend and betrayed lover Nicole, straight male friend Jared, best gay friend Kyle, and gay lover Trent most consistently and compassionately reveal the tragicomic personal quest for self-definition and self-determination in this saga of romance and realism. Born and raised in the newly integrated Birmingham, Alabama, Raymond in *Just as I Am* is a thirty-two-year-old attorney with a black female-owned firm that specializes in sports and entertainment law. He is the older son of Raymond Winston Tyler, an attorney and state senator, and Marlee Allen Tyler, an elementary school teacher.

In his first-person retrospective summary of the major interpersonal relationships in *Invisible Life*, Raymond tells readers in the opening pages of *Just as I Am*: "I wasn't forced into the closet, it was just a choice I'd made out of respect for my family, especially my pops" (pp. 2–3). His parents knew about and tried to accept his sexuality, but they did not want to discuss it around the dinner table or with his little brother because of their traditional moral convictions. However, the death of his openly gay friend Kyle and the advice he leaves in a letter influence Raymond to challenge his parents' moral authority with the determination to talk about his homosexuality and to live his life on his own terms. His father responds angrily: "'We've talked about this, Raymond. . . . We love you but do you have to push this stuff in our face?'" (p. 309). After telling his parents about being in therapy to work out his own moral and psychological ambivalence about being bisexual, or, as Raymond calls himself "a sexual mulatto" (p. 4), they express their willingness to join him in some therapy sessions. Also, his father reaffirms that they love him just the way he is, and his mother later calls Parents and Friends of Lesbians and Gays (PFLAG) for help in understanding homosexuality. Nevertheless, the father's mixed expression of pain, anger, sympathy, and love dramatically demonstrates that he does not morally approve of his son bringing a man home as a lover (p. 309).

Many black readers, especially men with traditional Baptist, working-class backgrounds, will probably find understandable both the father's behavior and the respect he expects from his son for their differences in moral principles and sexual practices. Earlier in therapy, Raymond acknowledges his father's tough love and respects their moral differences. "'My father knows that I like men,'" he admits, "'but I don't think he wants to see me being affectionate with a man in his presence. I think it's okay as long as I don't throw it in his face. . . . I owe him that'" (p. 289). Rather than wallow in self-pity and self-hatred as a victim of social stereotypes and prejudice, Raymond moves from the personal agency of efforts to reconcile his own sexual ambivalence to the collective agency of his friends Nicole, Jared, and Kyle effecting social change that benefits the lives of black AIDS victims.

With her trust betrayed and her health endangered by Raymond's secrecy and dishonesty about his sexuality, Nicole Springer's love for Raymond shifts from romantic to sisterly, from eros to agape, as she inspires him and others by her resurgent faith and friendship. The insecure, dark-skinned, thirty-year-old daughter of cotton farmers, Nicole is a former Miss Arkansas beauty queen and Broadway actress who "had been taught and for the most part believed that prayer and faith could solve any problems . . . [she] faced" (p. 24). The loss of her father to a heart attack, of her best friend Candance to AIDS, of her dream man Raymond to another man, and of her special friend Kyle to AIDS inspired her to begin a daily morning phone prayer partnership with Sheila, another actress.

Framed by Harris's prayerful thanks to Jesus Christ in the Acknowledgments and his thematic contrast of lust and love, which probably enhances his moral authority for many black women readers, Nicole's call-and-response telephone prayers and faith reinforce the authenticity and moral authority of the narrative. The implied author's sympathy with Nicole's moral position is apparent when Sheila's antihomosexual belief that Satan, not Christ, made men gay ruptures her prayer partnership with Nicole. Ironically, although Harris has Nicole, Raymond, and even Kyle insist that homosexuality is a gift from God rather than a curse from Satan, a congenital condition rather than a chosen lifestyle, the implied author represents psychiatric counseling as a valid and viable mode of therapy for problems of sexual identity. For example, because Nicole also felt that during her crisis she needed someone to talk to that she could see, she sought psychiatric therapy. "I'd started seeing Dr. Vanessa Huntley shortly after Candance died," Nicole confesses. "The first year we worked on my grief about Candance's death, but then slowly turned to my relationships with men, my shaky relationship with my mother, and my own lack of self-confidence" (p. 24). After assisting Raymond in providing care for Kyle during the terminal stage of his AIDS and witnessing Raymond's depression in the wake of Kyle's death, Nicole recommends that he, too, seek help from a psychiatrist, as well as God. In addition, Raymond successfully encourages Basil to undergo psychiatric therapy in *Abide with Me*.

Perhaps Harris's most compelling achievement in *Just as I Am* is his construction of Raymond's deep friendship and love for Jared, Kyle, and Trent, which complicates and enriches Raymond's struggle to reconcile his double consciousness as a tragic sexual mulatto. The "oldest child and the only son of a devoted mother who had raised him and his two sisters alone in southwest Atlanta," Jared Taylor Stovall was a tall, smart, good-looking, "biscuit-brown" political consultant who graduated at the top of his class at Morris Brown College in 1983 and earned an MBA at Clark-Atlanta University (p. 3). Raymond met Jared back in Birmingham when he was hired to run the senior Tyler's political campaign for state senator. "Our relationship wavered between brotherly love and romantic love," says Raymond in the retrospective narrative bridge from *Invisible Life* to *Just as I Am*, "though it was a romance without sex. A romance in my mind only, at least as far as I knew," even though Jared, who is straight, often calls him, " 'my niggah' " (p. 3). The implied author thus constructs a melodramatic, yet realistic network of intense interpersonal relationships. After Raymond belatedly confesses his bisexuality, Jared's unconditional brotherly love for him continues. It even expands to include both a concern for Kyle that leads to his successful search for Kyle's father and a rekindled erotic love for Nicole that had been sparked initially when they were both college students in Atlanta in the early 1980s.

Kyle Alexander Benton is the most memorable construction of an authentic, morally paradoxical, self-liberated, tragicomic sexual mulatto in *Just as I Am*. With "cornbread brown skin, deep-set brown eyes, thin black curly hair that was starting to recede, and a smile that could dilute darkness," Kyle, we learn from Nicole, is Raymond's best friend. He is also "openly gay and didn't pull any punches" with his honesty, quick wit, and African American English (p. 7). For example, with a snap of his fingers in the air, he wryly responds to Nicole's entreaty to give his life to the Lord: " 'I've got that under control. I have a prayer cloth from Reverend Ike'" (p. 212). Contesting the normative value of heterosexuality, Harris constructs Kyle as the moral center of the narrative. A Princeton graduate whose indomitable spirit sustains him in his struggle with AIDS, drugs, and prostitution in a male escort service, Kyle is the mentor and guide to black gay life not only for Raymond and Nicole, but also for the reader. From Nicole, whom Kyle calls "Miss Thang," we learn that Kyle believes that he has a personal relationship with Christ and that he is certain he is going to heaven. He also believes "that as a little boy, he'd realized that he was different and that that difference was being gay. He felt Christ was the only one who understood him and loved him just the way he was . . . [and that] he got AIDS not because he was gay or promiscuous, but because Christ knew he could handle it. That maybe Christ needed him" (p. 246). In spite of his personal faith and false claims of practicing safe sex, Kyle's life is a dramatic example of how the unconditional love of his mother and close friends Nicole, Raymond, and Delaney helps him to struggle with his unrestrained lust. "'Ray, I don't have any qualms about how I've lived my life,'" Kyle declares. "'I learned early on that the kids are too fickle to trust your feelings with, so I've relied on friends for my emotional support'" (p. 225).

In addition to Kyle's personal faith and values, which include financial support for his mother and sick grandfather, Harris stresses two major lessons of Kyle's life. As Kyle earnestly tells Nicole, the first is "'that no man black or white chooses to be gay. That goes for women too'" (p. 246). A corollary issue concerning the origin or nature of homosexuality, which Kyle raises with Nicole, is whether she believes that "'gay men are less than whole'" (p. 245). For Nicole, Raymond, and many black readers, the subconscious or conscious belief that homosexuals are not "true men" and "true women" is a legacy of Victorianism. According to Katz's documentary history: "The 'sexual pervert' was the late Victorian descendant, the degenerate cousin, of the early Victorian 'true woman' and 'true man.'"[56] This Victorian legacy for contemporary African Americans was refracted through the historical, cultural, and class prism of slavery, the tragic mulattoes, W. E. B. Du Bois's Talented Tenth, and E. Franklin Frazier's black bourgeoisie.

The second lesson of Kyle's life, especially for his primary audience of black readers, is that "the African American community had a long way to go in the areas of education and support of minority AIDS patients" (p. 205). Even black gays shunned him once the rumors of his illness spread. Except for his mother Peaches, a single parent, and friends such as Nicole, Raymond, and Jared, all the support that Kyle received came from the white gay community, especially the Gay Men's Health Crisis. "Friendship turned out to be the one thing in the gay lifestyle that I could depend on," Kyle wrote in his deathbed letter to Raymond (p. 305). This condition inspired Kyle's economic, moral, and political agency to provide in one of his insurance policies for Raymond to establish a foundation, More Than Friends, that would give support on a regular basis to minority AIDS patients, regardless of their gender and sexuality.

Finally, Kyle's wryly humorous promise that once he is "assigned to . . . [his] angel troop up in heaven" he will send a special love for Nicole and Raymond is ironically fulfilled in Part Three of the book. Just as she "was preparing to give up on straight black men and fairy tale endings," Nicole tells us, "a shining ebony prince, namely Jared Stovall," declares his love and proposes marriage (pp. 354 and 356). Similarly, Raymond develops a homoerotic relationship with Trent Carlton Walters, a fraternity brother and, as Raymond reflects, "someone who was already deeply in love with me and who knew me fairly well. A relationship based on truth and honesty" (p. 359). Kyle's and the implied author's paradoxical moral and male authority is reinforced in Nicole's final therapy session with her affirmation of advice from Kyle, her father, and, intertextually, Shug in Walker's *The Color Purple*: " 'I'm finally living a life that wouldn't piss God or His newest angel off. I'm listening to my heart again' " (p. 368).

Like Walker in *The Color Purple*, Harris and Duplechan are morally and politically critical of the traditional antihomosexual principles in the Christian church. Whereas Duplechan satirizes Christian sexual hypocrisy and the misguided use of the ritual of exorcism in *Blackbird*, Harris rewrites Walker's celebration of lesbianism, symbolized by the color purple, as a natural, beautiful experience of love sanctioned by God. Like Shug, who says, "I think it pisses God off if you walk by the color purple in a field somewhere and don't notice it" in *The Color Purple*,[57] Kyle affirms the naturalness and essentialism of sexual difference by telling Nicole in *Just as I Am*: "God only gets mad at us when we come down here and pretend to be something we're not. That really pisses Him off" (p. 368). While watching a movie with Kyle about black drag queens, Raymond reflects on his own feelings of superiority to gays who were overly effeminate. "I thought if I ever could create a perfect world, I would want everyone to be equal," we learn from his indirect interior monologue. "A world where the only rule would be respect, respect for each individual to live life the way he or she saw fit" (p. 252).

Although Harris stresses honesty (a refusal to lie, steal, or deceive) and respect (the state of being worthy of high regard) as essential for genuine friendship and love, he morally and politically distances himself from characters and presumably readers whose honesty compels a rejection or questioning of unconditional love for homosexuality as a lifestyle. Some of the characters, like many black readers, believe that to be worthy of high regard or esteem from others is to acknowledge limitations on public and private behaviors that violate moral and social codes established to safeguard the lives, liberty, health and general welfare of the individual and his or her community. However, one of the lessons of the ancestors, the black church, and the Bible to which Raymond alludes is that "we are all equal in the sight of Christ," which encourages tolerance and even respect for difference (p. 252). Another lesson, which the text subordinates to unconditional love, is that the respect of others begins with the love of God and self-respect. Rather than unconditional love, the moral authority and political agency of the characters in *Just as I Am* are more effective in dramatizing the importance of friendship based on mutual honesty and respect in overcoming the ambivalence and anxiety in the African American community about homosexuality.

As Harris's fictive construction of Raymond's and Kyle's mothers, as well as of Raymond, Nicole, and Jared suggests, unconditional love is a rare quality, perhaps even a blessing from God, more likely demonstrated by women, especially mothers, than by men, especially fathers. As the fundamental principle or imperative of an ideal moral and social community, unconditional love has its roots in ancient myths and folktales, its branches in modern legends, tales, and romances, and its mixture of flowers of different colors in contemporary soap operas, popular romances, and other forms of paraliterature. By rewriting the tragic plight of the racial hybrid as the tragic saga of the sexual mulatto, Harris offers *Just as I Am* as a purple rose in the garden of African American gay romances and novels that celebrate sexual license as sexual liberty.

Detective/Mystery Novels

In the 1980s and 1990s the African American detective novel, another form of paraliterature, experienced a resurgence of popularity and critical acclaim which began with the inspirational impact of the life and work of Chester Himes on many established black writers during the Black Arts movement of the 1970s. Julius Lester, Charles Wright, Ishmael Reed, and John Williams admired the naturalistic power of Himes's early novels and the originality of the Coffin Ed and Grave Digger detective novels. Himes "taught me the essential difference between a Black detective and Sherlock Holmes," Reed declares.[58] The film adaptation of *Cotton Comes to Harlem* and his autobiographies, *The Quality of Hurt* and *My Life of Absurdity*, published in the 1970s, were also popular successes that reinforced the fallacious assumption of many readers that Himes was the first African American detective novelist.

The first edition of *The Afro-American Novel and Its Tradition* misleadingly states that Rudolph Fisher's *Conjure-Man Dies* (1932) was "the second detective novel by a black American." More egregiously, Stanley Ellin, a former president of Mystery Writers of America, claims in his introduction to the 1971 reprint of the novel that "there had been no Negro writer who utilized this [mystery] technique as a means of literary expression until Fisher came along."[59] But the research and analysis by Stephen Soitos, mystery writer, critic, and teacher, of serialized black detective/mystery novels by Pauline Hopkins and J. E. Bruce sets the record straight.

The Conjure-Man Dies is actually the first unserialized detective novel published as a book, rather than in a magazine, by an African American. It is also the first black detective novel to rely completely on a black environment and all-black cast of characters for the authenticity and authority of its themes, style, and structure. However, with the invaluable archaeological recovery of texts in the 1970s and 1980s by Henry Louis Gates's Black Literary Periodical Project and Maryemma Graham's Black Fiction Project, several serialized mystery stories and novels have been discovered in independently published black local papers and magazines. For example, magazine editor and author Pauline Hopkins's serial novel *Hagar's Daughter* (1901–2), which appeared under the pen name of Sarah A. Allen, was published in the *Colored American Magazine* in Boston, and J. E. Bruce's *Black Sleuth* (1907–9) was published in *McGirt's Magazine* in Philadelphia. Because her serialized mystery novel appeared in print before *The Conjure-Man Dies*, some feminist critics consider Hopkins "the foremother of African American mystery fiction."[60] As Soitos argues in his prize-winning study of African American detective fiction, "The terms 'detective' and 'mystery' are almost interchangeable when applied to genre works. Generally, the term 'detective' connotes a work in which a detective is actually part of the cast of characters. 'Mystery' is a more universal term for genre works that use the typical conventions of suspense, action, physical danger, and intrigue; a detective may or may not be part of the plot."[61] He further notes that "detective writers such as Pauline Hopkins and J. E. Bruce initiated the use of distinctive African American cultural tropes in four areas: alteration of detective personas, double-conscious detection, black vernaculars, and hoodoo. Furthermore, these writers signify on the conventions of detective fiction by use of these tropes, establishing a tradition of black detection that extends over the twentieth century" (p. 52).

The consensus of major critics of the detective novel is that Edgar Allan Poe created the detective story in the nineteenth century with such classic tales of ratiocination as "The Murders in the Rue Morgue" (1841), "The Mystery of Marie Roget" (1842), and "The Purloined Letter" (1845). In *The Puritan Pleasures of the Detective Story*, critic Erik Routley defines the detective story as "a story involving crime, a police force, a detective (who may or may not be a member of the force) and a solution. It must evoke a major interest in the finding of the solution. Without these properties any story that appears to be 'detection' is so called only by analogy" (quoted in Soitos, p. 16). Poe's fascination with the Gothic romance and other popular forms probably influenced his creation of detective fiction. The conventions of the detective genre that he invented include "the amateur detective who is both highly rational and curiously intuitive and eccentric, the first-person narrator who is usually a friend or associate of the detective, the baffled and thick-headed police, the analytical examination of clues and details, the locked-room mystery, and the cleverly hidden object or clue needed for the investigation" (p. 17).

There were many milestones in the development of the tradition of the detective novel between Poe and the hardboiled school of Dashiell Hammett and Raymond Chandler in America in the 1920s and 1930s. The forerunners in the tradition include Charles Dickens's *Bleak House* (1853) and Wilkie Collins's *Woman in White* (1860) and *The Moonstone* (1868) in England and Emile Gaboriau's *L'Affaire Lerouge* (1866) in France. The American forerunners are two novels by women: Seeley Regester's (pen name Metta Victoria Fuller Victor) *The Dead Letter* (1864) and Anna Katherine Green's *The Leavenworth Case* (1878). Dime novels, "poorly written adventure and Western tales published on inferior yellow paper stock, with a stiff illustrated cover" and popular during the Civil War, began the Old Sleuth series in 1885 (pp. 18–19).

In 1887 Arthur Conan Doyle's classic detective Sherlock Holmes, who became famous for his pipe, hat, and cloak, as well as his outstanding powers of reason and character analysis, first appeared in *A Study in Scarlet*. Poe and Doyle established seven basic elements for the conventional detective plot: "1) the crime occurs; 2) the investigator, often a bit eccentric, takes on the case; 3) the finger of suspicion points at several characters; 4) mystery and confusion abound; 5) the seemingly guilty are proven innocent; 6) the seemingly innocent are proven guilty; 7) the detective provides an explanation at the denouement clarifying what has happened and revealing how she/he has arrived at the discovery."[62] Literary historians generally mark the publication in 1913 of E. C. Bentley's *Trent's Last Case* as the beginning of the modern classical detective story in Europe and associate its popularity in England with the publications of Agatha Christie, Dorothy Sayers, and others (p. 20).

In contrast to the Poe and Doyle classical detective fiction of Europe and America, the hardboiled pattern of detective fiction was established by American writers, especially Dashiell Hammett, Carroll John Daly, and Raymond Chandler, for the magazine *Black Mask*. Although *Black Mask* was established in 1920 by H. L. Mencken and George Nathan, it was Captain Joseph T. Shaw who encouraged the development of the hardboiled school of fiction after assuming the editorship in 1926. In general, hardboiled fiction was terse, direct, and violent. It reflected the worldview of a white middle-aged man who was self-educated and extremely disillusioned by the conditions of urban life, especially the inefficient police and government. The hardboiled detectives were fatalistic in their cynicism toward the police and government, as well as in their chauvinism toward women. They were working-class professionals "who spoke and acted with American vernacular crudeness." In contrast, the classical detectives were upper-class amateurs "who spoke and acted with aristocratic grace." The stories in the classical school were told either in limited omniscience by a sidekick of the detective's or from the third-person omniscient point of view. But the hardboiled school used direct first-person narration, which made the action much more dramatic and the style equal in importance to the plot.[63] Three of the most important hardboiled novels are Hammett's *Red Harvest* (1929) and *Maltese Falcon* (1930) and Chandler's *Big Sleep* (1939).

Published in African American magazines primarily for a black audience, the serial detective novels of Pauline Hopkins and John Edward Bruce reconfigured the conventions of detective fiction for criticism of the racial, political, and cultural climate in the post–Civil War (1865–1902) and pre–World War I (1902–17) eras. Like the serial novels published in *The Christian Recorder* by Frances Ellen Watkins Harper, they are forerunners in the development of an African American tradition of popular fiction. By signifying on the traditional conventions of detective and mystery fiction, the serialized novels of Hopkins and Bruce are also a bridge to the detective novels of Rudolph Fisher and Chester Himes.[64] Similarly, Fisher's experiment with African American residual vernacular forms in *The Conjure-Man Dies* and Himes's examination of racial, class, and gender issues in the ten detective novels in which he created the hardboiled black detectives Coffin Ed Johnson and Grave Digger Jones inspired the postmodern antidetective novels *Mumbo Jumbo* by Ishmael Reed and *Reflex and Bone Structure* by Clarence Major.

More recently, however, black detective and mystery authors, including women, and black detectives, especially women, have proliferated. Some of the most popular detective and mystery novels by black women authors are Dolores Komo's *Clio Brown, Private Investigator* (1988); Barbara Neely's *Blanche on the Lam* (1992), *Blanche among the Talented Tenth* (1994), *Blanche Cleans Up* (1998), and *Blanche Passes Go* (2000); Eleanor Taylor Bland's *Dead Time* (1992), *Slowburn* (1993), *Gone Quiet* (1994), *Done Wrong* (1995), *Keep Still* (1996), *See No Evil* (1998), and *Scream in Silence* (2000); Nikki Baker's *In the Game* (1991), *The Lavender House Murder* (1992), and *The Long Goodbyes* (1993); and Valerie Wilson Wesley's *When Death Comes Stealing* (1995) and *Devil's Gonna Get Him* (1996). In contrast to the detective novels by men, all of the detective protagonists in these novels are women, including some single parents and, in Baker's three books, a lesbian businesswoman. But let us look more closely at Barbara Neely and Walter Mosley, arguably the most popular and critically distinctive black American detective and mystery novelists of the 1980s and 1990s.

BARBARA NEELY (1941–)

Born the oldest of three children to Ann and Bernard Neely, a homemaker and a hotel owner who was once a construction worker, Barbara Neely was the only black student in her Catholic elementary and high school in Lebanon, Pennsylvania.[65] But she more closely identified with the children of black Bethlehem Steel workers and iron-ore miners in her hometown. After graduating from high school, she moved to Jamestown, New York, and enrolled in business school. In the 1960s during the Black Power movement, she relocated to Pittsburgh, earned a degree in urban planning from the University of Pittsburgh in 1971, and organized a suburban community home, Shady Side, for female ex-convicts. With the emergence in the 1970s and 1980s of a black feminism movement that challenged the racial and class hegemony of the white middle-class women's rights movement, she was a community activist who worked with black homeless women, teenage mothers, and women on welfare in North Carolina, Massachusetts, and New York, as well as in Pennsylvania.

At the same time, Neely was a writer for *Southern Exposure* and producer of radio shows for the African News Service, as well as the author of short stories, publishing her first, "Passing the Word," in *Essence* in 1981. Although a fan of Agatha Christie, P. D. James, Chester Himes, and Walter Mosley, she was inspired most by Toni Morrison in celebrating the lives of ordinary black women in fiction. With the encouragement of an editor and agent, Neely began writing and publishing her Blanche novels in the 1990s. Her awards and prizes in detective and mystery writing include the "Go on Girl," the Agatha, the Anthony, and the McCavity, all in 1992 for the best first mystery novel, and the Women of Conviction Award for Arts and Literature in 1994.

More structurally and stylistically mystery than detective novels, Neely's *Blanche on the Lam*, *Blanche among the Talented Tenth*, *Blanche Cleans Up*, and *Blanche Passes Go* are contemporary neorealistic reconfigurations of Hopkins's *Hagar's Daughter*. Each features a black maid as a reluctant amateur detective whose color, class, culture, and gender are stressed over the rational solution of a crime in order to enhance the authenticity, authority, and agency of the protagonist and the telling of the story. Blanche White, Neely's protagonist, is a professional domestic who cleans up the homes and lives of upper-class white families. Like other mystery novels by contemporary white and black women, Neely's subvert the male genre by challenging sexist assumptions as she reconstructs the plot and hero from a feminist perspective primarily for a black audience. But unlike the professional and amateur female detectives of her contemporaries, Blanche possesses authenticity, authority, and agency grounded in the African American vernacular tradition and the double consciousness of a dark-skinned, full-bodied, middle-aged, working-class, self-taught single mother of her dead sister's two children. Blanche is a uniquely sassy, smart, sensitive black feminist amateur detective.

In *Blanche on the Lam* Blanche escapes a jail sentence in North Carolina for cashing bad checks by accepting a temporary job as housekeeper at the country home of a wealthy white family who mistake her for the summer replacement sent by a domestic agency. She becomes a reluctant detective as a result of her compassion for Mumsfield, the white boy with Down's syndrome whose inheritance his relatives plot to embezzle, and Nate, the black gardener at the country estate, who is murdered. Blanche invokes the resilient spirit of her ancestors, her knowledge as a maid of the ways of wealthy white folks, and her tough-minded pursuit of social justice in order to reconcile her double consciousness and to solve the murders of Emmeline and Nate. Unconsciously revealing her socialized ambivalence to the reader, Blanche states:

> For all his specialness and their seeming connectedness, Mumsfield was still a whiteman. She didn't want to shower concern on someone whose ancestors had most likely bought and sold her ancestors as though they were shoes or machines. Would she always find some reason—retardation, blindness, sheer incompetence—to nurture people who had been raised to believe she had no other purpose in life than to be their "girl"? Had the slavers stamped mammyism into her genes when they raped her great-grandmothers? If they had, she was determined to prove the power of will over blood. (P. 182)

Like most ordinary working-class black folks, Blanche uses wry humor to express her tragicomic vision of life, which the implied author suggests provides the moral authority and political agency for solving the crimes.

That vision of life and her double consciousness as an African American also frame the radio news of Nate's murder.

> A thick, hot rage began to roil in her stomach at the thought of the deaths of all the poor black Nates and, yes, Blanches at the hands of the privileged white Everetts of the world. Nowadays, people wanted to tell you class didn't exist and color didn't matter anymore. Look at Miss America and the chairman of the Joint Chiefs of Staff. But Miss America and the chairman were no more black people than Mother Teresa was white people. Men like Nate and women like her were the people, the folks, the mud from which the rest were made. . . . They ought to have been appreciated for being the wattle that held the walls together. Instead, they were expendable, interchangeable, rarely missed, hardly regarded, easily forgotten. Not this time! (Pp. 148–49)

Relying more on the epistemological significance of radio news reports and overheard conversations in her own life and that of the black community than on the relentless pursuit of the truth and the physical danger of tracking down the perpetrator of a crime, Neely's detective persona will be less engaging for readers uninterested in the character's personal attempt to challenge, if not reverse, negative stereotypes about African American culture and character. In contrast to the standard detective persona, Blanche and the implied author reveal that her primary social responsibility and agency are to the black community as she uses the money that she receives from the white family for solving the crime and maintaining silence about the skeletons in the family's closet to send her adopted niece and nephew to private school up North.

The problems of double consciousness and the color and class divisions within the black community that are the legacy of white American racism are even more central to the plot and characters in *Blanche among the Talented Tenth*. Concerned about the color and class attitudes that her adopted children were learning from private school classmates whose parents invited them for a summer vacation, Blanche joins her children to share childcare responsibilities with their hosts, the Crowleys, at Amber Cove, an exclusive Maine resort for the African American elite. After he was refused admittance to a wealthy white Cape Cod resort, a black tycoon, Josiah Coghill, who made his fortune on skin lightening cream and lye-based hair straightener for black men, founded Amber Cove in 1898. He then created his own exclusive resort by building spacious cottages on the grounds and selling them to friends and business associates. Blanche White, whose name is an ironic contrast to her dark color, wanted to see how her children acted toward her in their friends' community. "She wanted a glimpse of how and why being among people who had everything could make a child or a fool look down on those who didn't have a pot" (p. 18).

At Amber Cove—probably Neely's ironic reference to Oak Bluffs, the formerly exclusive summer resort for blacks on Martha's Vineyard—Blanche soon discovers the truth of her girlfriend Ardell's belief that "well-off blacks were even more color prejudiced than the everyday fools who'd tormented Blanche all of her life" (p. 21). The "light-bright prejudice" of the "hincty . . . bunch of Talented Tenths," Du Bois's term for the most exceptionally qualified potential black leaders whom Neely scathingly unmasks, is most apparent to Blanche in the Insider and Outsider seating arrangement in the dining room of Amber Cove Inn (pp. 68 and 65). As far as Blanche could see, however, "the things, beside color, that made a person black were either missing or mere ghosts of their former selves" at Amber Cove (p. 58).

Neely identifies the major source of Blanche White's cultural authenticity and moral authority as her belief in the mystery, magic, myth, and ritual of residual African syncretic religions. Blanche, for example, was told by Harlem conjurer Madame Rosa to go to a place with the letters AC to honor and praise Mother Water for help in understanding her dreams about the major crossroads and connections in her life that she was approaching. Because of their association with slavery and male domination, Blanche has avoided Christianity and Islam all her life. Instead of looking for a place to worship, "she turned her tendency to talk to her dead grandmothers into ancestor worship. She began collecting pictures of all her dead relatives and built an altar for them. . . . Every morning, she lit the candles and incense and talked to her ancestors about her problems and dreams, her wishes for her children, her hopes. She accepted as correct her childhood perception that she was somehow connected to the tree she climbed, the water she swam in and the air that filled her lungs. She routinely called on all the forces in the universe for power" (p. 61). Guided by the spirits of her ancestors, Blanche makes a connection with Mattie Harris, a celebrated black feminist writer, "fierce old bitch," and grand old diva of the Insiders, that results in her solving the mysterious deaths of two Amber Cove Insiders (p. 44).

Despite the suspense of her quest for revenge for an earlier rape and her search for the killer of a woman in her North Carolina hometown, the plot of *Blanche Passes Go* is neither as suspenseful nor as ambitious as that of *Blanche Cleans Up*. Like *Blanche on the Lam* and *Blanche among the Talented Tenth, Blanche Cleans Up* derives its distinctive narrative, political, and moral agency, authenticity, and authority from the residually oral African American forms with which the implied author and limited omniscient narrator construct their black feminist identities. As in Neely's other novels, the close racial, class, political, and gender relationship between the implied author and Blanche is apparent in the code-switching between SAE and AAVE in the development of Blanche's knowledge and power as a black feminist domestic and amateur detective.

Beginning with the opening page of the novel, Blanche's faith in ancestral guidance and her experience as a domestic enable her to understand how much houses had to say about themselves. "Understanding houses was part of how she made her living," the omniscient narrator says sympathetically. "Just like a good surgeon didn't open up a patient without an examination, she didn't clean or cook in a house until she'd done the same" (p. 1). Blanche's "uneasy feeling" about the house, the job, and the Brindle family immediately establishes the suspense that is intensified by the dramatic irony of the regular cook Inez's "tiresome talk about her wonderful white employers and their best-in-the-world son" (p. 2). The suspense is heightened by the ambitiousness of the plot. For attempting to expose Allison Brindle as a political and moral hypocrite in his campaign for governor as a champion of family values, Inez's son, Ray-Ray, is killed. In pursuing the killers, Blanche, her adopted children, and the black community of Roxbury are entangled in a dangerous web of scandalous secrets that Felicia Brindle, Allison, and Marc, their son, have spun and that Blanche must disentangle with the assistance of members of the black community.

Pursuing Ray-Ray's killer while standing in for Inez as a favor to her own Cousin Charlotte, Blanche constructs her moral authority and political agency as a black feminist amateur detective by subverting the moral and political authority of the Brindles and the Reverend Maurice Samuelson, Allison Brindle's shameless partner in crime and perversions. The founder in Roxbury of the Temple of the Divine Enlightenment, "a new kind of African-American religion where Christian, Jewish, and Muslim holy books and beliefs were mixed together," Samuelson conspires to deliver what he calls the "Aunt Jemima and Uncle Ben" vote in Allison Brindle's conservative campaign for governor. Overhearing Samuelson's "promise to keep the Darkies in line for Massa" while she was serving cocktails, Blanche is so outraged that she accidentally on purpose knocks the "butt-sucking maggot" off balance with a sharp elbow to his spine (pp. 18–19). In the course of her shrewd detective work, Blanche, with the aid of her family and other members of the black community, also exposes the good Reverend as a greedy, unscrupulous, incestuous lecher, gangster, and ghetto landlord of lead-poisoned housing in Roxbury.

Among other things, Blanche's religious and political beliefs foster a sympathy for sexual difference that is critical of the Christian values of Carrie, the housemaid, who morally distances herself from Mick Harper, Felicia Brindle's openly lesbian masseuse. "'I don't get it,'" Blanche responds to Carrie's antihomosexuality. "'You Christians say God made everything and everybody, which has gotta include lesbians. But then you say lesbians are ungodly. Seems to me that you, your pastor, or your God is very confused, honey'" (p. 22). Blanche and the implied author further demonstrate their support of sexual difference when Blanche first meets Mick Harper. In response to Mick's "mannish haircut, bone-crushing handshake . . . butch walk" and "purple T-shirt" emblazoned with "I CAN'T EVEN THINK STRAIGHT," Blanche says approvingly, with the implied author's implicit agreement, "'Love that shirt'" (p. 53). Reinforcing the boldness of her lesbian pride and the limited omniscient narrator's challenge to traditional moral authority, Mick also wears a black T-shirt that reads: "DYKES DO IT BETTER in big white letters inside a pink triangle" (p. 125). Unlike Blanche, Mick's family and Carrie morally distance themselves in various degrees from homosexuality and, in some cases, homosexuals.

Although "not simply open-minded but a cheerleader for people who were different from what the rule-setters said was the way to live, behave, or feel" (p. 173), Blanche, the limited omniscient narrator, and the implied author draw the line at the apparent sexual deviancy of the Brindles. Blanche fantasizes about sex, considers herself horny, and even spends a day of passionate lovemaking with Leo, her married former lover. But she, the narrator, and the implied author are far less tolerant of Felicia's adulterous relationship with her personal trainer, Saxe, who is also having a homosexual relationship with Marc Brindle, her son. A twisted triangle of lust, love, and intrigue results in the murder of Ray-Ray, Marc's earlier homosexual lover, the murder of Ms. Barker, Ray-Ray's self-appointed godmother, the murder of Saxe, and the suicide of Marc. But the mysterious video tape that is the source of most of the suspense and murders in the novel reveals that Allison Brindle, the conservative political champion of family values, is even more sexually and morally reprehensible. While viewing the tape, Blanche is tolerant of Allison Brindle's kinky passion for being spanked with a hairbrush while dressed as a little girl and even for being sodomized by a large German shepherd dog. Consistent with the opinion of some feminists, Blanche concludes that Allison's behavior was "kinky, maybe, but no more so than men who went out on football and rugby fields to get kicked and gouged for so-called fun" (p. 271). But the morally and legally outrageous episode of Allison's sexual activities with three little girls under eight makes Blanche vomit.

For some black women readers Blanche's most authentic and compelling feature is her primary role as a working-class single mother. Unlike most conventional mystery novels, Neely's weave Blanche's parenting of her adopted pre-teenaged children, Malik and Taifa, and of Shaquita, the sixteen-year-old granddaughter of Cousin Charlotte who is also briefly living with Blanche, into the main plot. Racial, generational, class, gender, cultural, and political differences provide a multifaceted view of the rite of passage of black children into manhood and womanhood in Boston during the 1980s. Raising her children in a cooperative housing development in Roxbury and providing them with the best education that she can since taking them out of private school, Blanche contends with the problems of children killing children, hair and dress styles, Ebonics, teen-age pregnancy, and the deadly impact of lead poisoning on black children.

For example, after transferring to public school, Taifa and Malik apparently code-switched from SAE to Ebonics or AAVE with their family and peers. Rather than condemning Taifa for saying " 'I seen these new kinda curlers they be better than the . . . ,' " Blanche tacitly acknowledges that Taifa is bilingual. "She also knew Taifa was trying to out hood girls who'd spent their entire lives in this community. It was Taifa's way of making up for having been a private-school girl her first year in Boston" (p. 37). But the subplot of Shaquita's pregnancy and Blanche's moral authority, including personal anecdote, in counseling her about a woman's right to control her own body marks a more important stage in the rite of passage of children having children. More central to the main plot and the Reverend Samuelson's crimes as a black ghetto landlord, however, is the development of Malik's social agency and moral consciousness while he works on a school and community project concerning the relationship of lead poisoning to violence in black communities. That Blanche overcomes her initial resistance to Malik's involvement in a collective community action that contrasts with her personal activism as a feminist is an affirmation of the importance of organized movements for social change.

Blanche White is an authentic amateur black detective. Guided by the moral and spiritual authority of her ancestors and by the political and gendered agency of her everyday experience as a black feminist, working-class single mother, she signifies on the traditions of black and white mystery novels by women and men in her personal mission to reconstruct a more just and moral social order. Neely's Blanche White series thus rewrites the traditional mystery novel as a dynamic and critical examination of the complex web of racial, political, class, and sexual circumstances that influence the effectiveness of personal and community actions in shaping the lives of working-class contemporary African American men and women. Neely's Blanche White series also provides a fascinating contrast to Walter Mosley's Easy Rawlins series of mystery novels.

WALTER [ELLIS] MOSLEY (1952–)

"I'd like to be remembered in the canon of genre writers in this field," Walter Mosley told an interviewer in 1994. "I'd like my name to be mentioned with Raymond Chandler, Hammett, Ross McDonald, people like that. If people mention my race, I wouldn't be unhappy."[66] Born in 1952, the first year in more than seventy that no lynchings were recorded in America, to Leroy and Ella Mosley, a black school custodian and a Jewish housewife, Mosley was raised and educated in South Central Los Angeles, the setting of his first four mystery novels. After completing high school, he attended Goddard College and Johnson State University in Vermont, earning a bachelor degree in political science in 1975. Moving to Manhattan in 1981, he worked as a freelance computer programmer for several years before enrolling in a creative writing program at the City College of New York. Under the guidance of novelists Frederic Tuten and Jerome Charyn, Mosley apparently worked on his first Easy Rawlins novel, *Gone Fishin'*, which was not published until 1997 (by Black Classic Press), and completed *Devil in a Blue Dress*. With the assistance of Tuten, who submitted *Devil in a Blue Dress* to his agent without Mosley's knowledge, Mosley acquired Gloria Loomis as an agent and W. W. Norton as the publisher of the Easy Rawlins series.[67]

Mosley is the best-selling, prize-winning author of six mystery novels. *Devil in a Blue Dress* (1990) was nominated for the Edgar Allan Poe Award for the best first mystery novel of the year and won both the Shamus Award in America and the John Creasey Award in Great Britain for best first novel. It was released as a feature film starring Denzel Washington as Easy Rawlins and Don Cheadle as Mouse in 1995. *A Red Death* (1991) was nominated for the Golden Dagger Award. *White Butterfly* (1992) was nominated for the Edgar Allan Poe and Golden Dagger Awards. *Black Betty* (1994) was also nominated for the Edgar Allan Poe Award. Set in 1963, *A Little Yellow Dog* (1996) charts Easy's search with an abandoned yellow dog to find the murderer of two people, including the beautiful teacher who owned the dog. Completing the cycle of Easy Rawlins novels, *Gone Fishin'* (1997) traces the friendship between Easy and Mouse back to southern Texas, where Mouse killed his stepfather in 1939. In addition, Mosley published a blues novel inspired by the legendary bluesman Robert Louis Johnson, *RL's Dream* (1995), a science fiction novel, *Blue Light* (1998), a collection of short stories featuring the ex-con philosopher Socrates Fortlow, *Always Outnumbered, Always Outgunned* (1998), and the novel introducing another street-smart, bad-ass amateur detective like Easy Rawlins in *Fearless Jones* (2001). A former member of the Executive Board of the PEN American Center and former president of the Mystery Writers of America, Mosley has also served as a member of the board of directors of the National Book Awards.

Although he states that his audience is primarily "the African American men of his father's generation who migrated from the South to Los Angeles to escape racism and to search for economic opportunity," his popularity crosses all boundaries; in 1992 Bill Clinton said that Mosley is his favorite mystery writer.[68] Mosley's national and international popular appeal and critical success derive mainly from the authenticity, authority, and agency of his narrative voice.

"If the story rings true to them [the men who grew up in his father's generation in Texas and Louisiana], if they say, 'Yeah, that's the way it was,' that's like a tuning fork for me," Mosley has said.[69]

Like Raymond Chandler's detective novels, Mosley's are set primarily in the realistically described mean streets of Los Angeles. Unlike Chandler, however, Mosley focuses on the relationship of an amateur black detective to the black community of Watts from 1948 to 1963 and, in a flashback narrative (*Gone Fishin'*), that of Houston and Pariah, Texas, in 1939. The series traces the self-construction and moral authority of Ezekiel "Easy" Rawlins as a streetwise, self-educated, compassionate, hardworking property owner and amateur black detective with a legendary Staggerlee sidekick, Raymond "Mouse" Alexander. Unlike Chandler's and Hammett's detectives, Easy, as his domesticity indicates, does not have a static identity. In the first novel in the series Easy is a bachelor who becomes the surrogate father of a sexually abused Mexican boy. But by the third novel he has a wife, infant daughter, and another adopted child.

Set during the congressional witchhunt for Communists in the 1950s, *A Red Death*, the second novel in the Rawlins series, dramatically demonstrates Easy's authenticity as a World War II veteran and amateur tough-guy detective by his compassion and his parenting skills. A real estate owner disguised as a janitor who still does favors for black neighbors as a detective, Easy is intimidated by the IRS for tax evasion into joining a black church in order to inform on a suspected Jewish traitor, Chaim Wenzler. As the plot unfolds we discover that Easy not only formally becomes the godfather of Jesus, the sexually abused Mexican boy he rescues in *Devil in a Blue Dress*, but also changes a baby's diaper and prepares dinner for a young woman, Juanita Barnes, while she sews his clothes before making love to him.

In *White Butterfly*, the third novel in the Rawlins series, Easy is still a home-owner and landlord masquerading as a janitor in the 1950s. In contrast to traditional hardboiled and classic detectives, however, he now has a more stable, responsible, and nurturing male identity, surrounded by a beautiful wife of two years, Regina Riles, an infant daughter, Edna, and an eight-year-old godson, Jesus. He is not only sensitive to the emotional needs of Jesus, who is speechless from the trauma of his earlier sexual abuse, but also shows himself a loving father in preparing his daughter's formula and changing her diaper. "I washed her with a soft chamois towel, saying little nonsense things and kissing her now and again," the narrator tells us. "By the time she was clean all the tears were gone. The bottle was ready and I changed her fast. I held her to my chest again and gave her the bottle" (p. 35). Because of his more settled life, Easy futilely resists the pressure of the local police to help them to find a serial killer of women.

But as the plot thickens, he not only helps to solve the murders, but also loses his wife and baby daughter in the process. Easy's wife leaves him because she feels that he "likes criminals and bein' in the street." Regina, voicing the complaints of many contemporary women readers about men in general, is also unhappy that Easy does not show her his "weak parts" and that he does not seem to need her strength. "'A woman don't care but that you need her love,'" she tells him. "'You know I got a job an' you ain't ever even asked me fo' a penny. . . . You change the baby and water the lawn and even sew up yo' own clothes. You know you ain't never asked me for a thing, Easy. Not one damn thing'" (pp. 180–81). With both the confusion and guilt of many male readers, Easy responds: "I always thought that if you did for people they'd like you; maybe even love you. Nobody cared for a man who cried. . . . I knew that a lot of tough-talking men would go home to their wives at night and cry about how hard their lives were. I never understood why a woman would stick it out with a man like that" (p. 181). The subsequent desertion of his wife and baby with a former friend, Dupree, a subtle allusion to the legendary folk character in "Dupree and Betty Blues," is relieved only by two events in the closing pages of *White Butterfly*. The first is Easy's tearful memory of his abrupt loss as a child of his parents. The second is his adoption of Feather, the mixed-race baby of the white college strip-dancer, White Butterfly, who is the final and most sensational victim in the serial murder case that Easy helps to solve.

It is Mosley's trustworthy, vibrant use of the African American vernacular and, in the laudatory words of Ernest Gaines, "tremendous ear for dialogue,"[70] however, that most compellingly enhance the authenticity and authority of the Rawlins series. Inspired by the existential dilemmas of Albert Camus's *Stranger* and the vernacular voices of black writers like Langston Hughes and Zora Neale Hurston, Mosley constructs his characters as resilient, resourceful subjects or agents struggling with moral and social issues rather than as flat pathetic or tragic victims. "I've tried to write about Black people as Black people," he declares. "Not as black people in relation to white people, not as victims of whatever, but Black people living their lives."[71]

Because of the authenticity and authority of its black vernacular post–World War II urban setting, two unique black detective personas, and double consciousness detection, *Devil in a Blue Dress* is arguably the best of the Rawlins series. The novel is grounded in the past, looking back to the impact of racism on blacks despite President Roosevelt's 1941 Executive Order 8802 prohibiting discrimination in defense industries and government and President Truman's 1948 order to desegregate the armed services. The opening chapters immediately immerse the reader in the sights, sounds, and smells of transplanted Southern unemployed, underemployed, and illicitly employed working-class African Americans coping with a dream deferred in the bars, nightclubs, and churches in the promised land of Watts, California. This cityscape and the double consciousness it fosters are more suggestive of the Harlem of Chester Himes's novels than the Los Angeles of Raymond Chandler's.

The main plot is simple enough. Laid off from his aircraft factory job by his racist supervisor, Easy, a World War II veteran, hangs out in Joppy's, a small bar for "Negro butchers" on the second floor of a butchers' warehouse, and John's Place, a former speakeasy in the back of a market that now functions as a private black nightclub for business and good times. Because he is well known in the black community and needs money to pay the mortgage on his home, Easy cautiously accepts the job offered by a tough, ostensibly white mobster, DeWitt Albright, to find Daphne Monet, a beautiful, racially mixed, light-skinned woman. Daphne is passing for white and " 'has a predilection for Negroes' " and " 'likes jazz and pigs' feet and dark meat' " (p. 19).

As the main plot develops and the bodies pile up in Easy's search for Daphne Monet, several minor plots are intertwined in the nonlinear main narrative. The most significant of these concerns Easy's guilt about his irresponsible past and his ambivalent relationship with Mouse, his homicidal friend and occasional partner in dangerous cases. The second involves Daphne's theft of $30,000 dollars from her jilted white lover and investment broker, Todd Carter, for whom Albright works. The third concerns the sexual abuse of a young Mexican boy by Matthew Teran, a white politician and pedophile who is also searching for Daphne. The fourth deals with the deadly competition between Albright and Mouse to recover the $30,000 dollars from Daphne for themselves. And the fifth significant minor plot reveals that Daphne Monet is actually Ruby Hanks, the sister of the black hijacker Frank Green, who is one of several men that Mouse kills while assisting Easy to rescue Ruby and while convincing her to split the money with him and Easy.

More like Himes than Chandler and Hammett, Mosley creates a heavily layered black vernacular atmosphere of double consciousness in *Devil in a Blue Dress* that realistically and mythically demonstrates why Easy was hired by Albright for his first detective adventure. Beginning his search for Daphne in John's Place, Easy tells us reflectively,

> When I opened the door, I was slapped in the face by the force of Lips' alto horn. I had been hearing Lips and Willie and Flattop since I was a boy in Houston. All of them and John and half the people in that crowded room had migrated from Houston after the war, and some before that. California was like heaven for the southern Negro. People told stories of how you could eat fruit off the trees and get enough work to retire one day. The stories were true for the most part but the truth wasn't like the dream. Life was still hard in L.A. and if you worked every day you still found yourself on the bottom. But being on the bottom didn't feel so bad if you could come to John's now and then and remember how it felt back home in Texas, dreaming about California. (P. 27)

In a distinctive hardboiled tone, Mosley thus constructs Easy as one of the postwar transplanted black migrants who express their distinctive tragicomic worldview in improvisational forms of music, speech, and wry humor in segregated communities.

In these communities they struggle to reconcile the double consciousness of their past Southern values and oral myths of the North as the Promised Land with their present grim realities of racial and class discrimination and injustice. For example, Easy tells us that "a job in a factory is an awful lot like working on a plantation in the South. The bosses see all the workers like they're children, and everyone knows how lazy children are. So Benny thought he'd teach me a little something about responsibility because he was the boss and I was the child. The white workers didn't have a problem with that kind of treatment because they didn't come from a place where men were always called boys" (p. 62). Even in the army, he tells us, "I never minded that those white boys hated me, but if they didn't respect me I was ready to fight" (p. 96). Even though his boss was not required to give him his job back, Easy insisted that he be treated with respect and called Mr. Rawlins just as he respected the boss by calling him Mr. Giacomo. Earlier in the book Easy confesses his rural working-class roots and urban middle-class ethics. "I love going home," he says. "Maybe it was that I was raised on a sharecropper's farm or that I never owned anything until I bought that house, but I loved my little home. . . . that house meant more to me than any woman I ever knew. . . . Working for Joppy's friend [DeWitt Albright] was the only way I saw to keep my house" (p. 11). Mosley's narrative genius in *Devil in a Blue Dress* thus enables readers to bear witness to Easy's transformation from a sharecropper and factory-worker to a property owner and businessman.

Mosley's introduction of the amateur detective Easy and his partner Mouse in *Devil in a Blue Dress* is an original reconfiguration of the black detective persona that moves beyond Himes's deadly dynamic duo of Coffin Ed and Grave Digger. Although Coffin Ed and Grave Digger express the pride, anger, and frustration of urban blacks through violence at the racism responsible for social injustice and poverty in Harlem, the major feature of Easy's character is not violence. Rather, it is the moral authority with which he constructs his male identity within the black community by developing personal relationships that enable him to reconcile the color, class, and cultural tensions of his African American double consciousness.

We first hear about these tensions in Joppy's ironic tale of Easy's working-class values and middle-class aspirations. Easy demonstrates his patriotism and courage as a black man by volunteering to serve with General Patton during the war. He lost his aircraft factory job because he defended his personal work ethic, rejected his white supervisor's negative stereotype of lazy blacks, and demanded respect as a man. He affirmed a belief in the value of education not only by acquiring his high school equivalency papers from night school, but also by planning to go to college. These color, class, and cultural tensions are primarily experienced by the reader in the black dialect, dialogue, and flashbacks of the story, especially Easy's code-switching from SAE to AAVE when he dramatically tells his own version of these events. "Yeah, well, Mouse is a lot like Mr. Albright," Easy says, explaining to Joppy his reluctance to become an amateur detective for Albright. "He's smooth and a natty dresser and he's smilin' all the time. But he always got his business in the front'a his mind, and if you get in the way you might come to no good. I always tried to speak proper English in my life, the kind of English they taught in school," Easy declares, as he directly addresses his readers and reveals his ambivalence about bidialectalism; "but I found over the years that I could only truly express myself in the natural, 'uneducated' dialect of my upbringing" (p. 10).

The relationship between Easy and Mouse in *Devil in a Blue Dress* is uniquely ambivalent and dangerous. When Mouse and Easy were young men in Texas, they were best friends. "We fought in the streets side by side and we shared the same women without ever getting mad about it," Easy says, revealing the sexual objectification of women by many black men as well as in the hardboiled detective tradition. "What was a woman compared to the love of two friends? But when it came time for Mouse to marry Etta Mae Harris things began to change" (p. 47). Mouse was "a small, rodent-faced man" with gold rimmed teeth who dressed flashily and was deadly confident. Easy was both "free from fear" when he ran with Mouse and fearful of Mouse's cold-hearted power. He "was barely five-foot-six but he'd go up against a man Dupree's size [a muscular six-two] and you know I'd bet on the Mouse to walk away from it," Easy recalls with ambivalence. "He could put a knife in a man's stomach and ten minutes later sit down to a plate of spaghetti" (p. 48). Threatened by Albright and the police in chapter 16, Easy calls down to Texas for Mouse's help even though he is worried about him being an evil killer and not following orders. Mouse arrives at a critical moment in "a plaid zoot suit with Broadway suspenders . . . spats on over his patent leather shoes and the biggest pistol" that Easy had ever seen. Mouse saves Easy from having his throat cut by Frank "Knifehand" Green and ultimately helps him to solve the case in a bloody shootout, more for a share of the $30,000 dollars than for their friendship.

Although he sleeps with Coretta and Etta Mae, the girl friend and wife respectively of his best friends, Dupree and Mouse, Easy wrestles with his conscience about his moral lapses and struggles with uneven success through this and other novels in the series to become a responsible, sensitive, proud, compassionate, virile man. He has killed men in war and still considers himself "a killing machine." But he is not a heartless killer like Mouse and Albright, even when threatened by young white toughs on a Santa Monica pier. As an adventurous young man, Easy drove his best friend Mouse to Pariah, Texas, in a stolen car so that Mouse could get his inheritance from his stepfather. But Easy is haunted by guilt and fear because he accepted bribe money from Mouse even though he did not know that Mouse was going to kill and rob his stepfather and another man.

"I ran away from Mouse and Texas to go to the army and then later to L.A.," Easy reflects on his identity formation. "I hated myself. I signed up to fight in the war to prove to myself that I was a man. Before we launched the attack on D-Day I was frightened but I fought. I fought despite the fear. The first time I fought a German hand-to-hand I screamed for help the whole time I was killing him" (p. 48). Easy is guided in the construction of his manhood by an inner voice he first hears in Normandy after his buddies are killed by a German sniper. "'You cain't let him do that to you. Even if he lets you live you be scared the rest'a yo' life. Kill that motherfucker,' he told me. And I did. The voice has no lust. He never told me to rape or steal. He just tells me how it is if I want to survive. Survive like a man. When the voice speaks, I listen" (p. 99).

In *A Red Death* Easy has a wife and infant daughter, Edna, and in *White Butterfly* he becomes the foster parent of the mixed race daughter, Feather, of a murdered white college stripper. The first significant signs of Easy's growing responsibility and compassion are apparent in *Devil in a Blue Dress*. Easy's compassion for the people in Texas that Mouse kills in cold blood, for the tragic death of a pre-teenage Jewish refugee from a Nazi concentration camp, and for the sexually molested Mexican boy, Jesus, foreshadow the moral sensitivity and choices that he displays in subsequent books in the series. In response to Easy's disapproval of Mouse's killing Joppy and Frank to intimidate Daphne into splitting the stolen $30,000 dollars with them, Mouse compares the color, class, and cultural double consciousness of Daphne and Easy in the closing pages of the novel. "That's just like you, Easy," he says in AAVE. "You learn stuff and you be thinkin' like white men be thinkin'. You be thinkin' that what's right fo' them is right fo' you. She look like she white and you think like you white. But brother you don't know that you both poor niggers. And a nigger ain't never gonna be happy 'less he accept what he is" (p. 205). These ironic and paradoxical qualities also reveal the uniqueness of Mosley's African American detective personas.

Blurring the traditional generic boundaries between the popular romance and novel, postmodern African American science fiction, gay, and detective paraliterature created a black, gay, and white crossover audience and an expanding space for itself in the tradition of the African American novel. The narrative, political, and moral agency, authority, and authenticity of African American romances and novels of the 1980s and 1990s moved from the margins to the center and from lowbrow to middlebrow commercial and critical status. Even so, these postmodern romances and novels continue to derive their most distinctive power from the language, epistemology, and ontology of residual oral forms of African American oratory, myth, legend, tale and song. Also, highly experimental novels such as those by Samuel Delany continue to be more critically than commercially successful.

Conclusion

STORYTELLING is nearly as old and fundamental to our human identity as life itself. Historically, the human quest of peoples around the globe to tell their own stories and sing their own songs is consistent with their desire to affirm the importance of the relationship between language, knowledge, and power in personal and collective self-determination and identity formation. "American fiction," James W. Tuttleton writes in "Tracking the American Novel into the Void," "is among other things a self-conscious enterprise intent on nothing less than appropriating the liberty claimed in the great political and social declarations so as to remake afresh the fictive forms of representation."[1] As black American authors develop their distinctive voices within and against the larger tradition of fiction, this intent is also implicit in the various constructions and reconstructions of identity and double consciousness that are encoded in the modern and contemporary literary branches of the African American novel. As literary theorist Northrop Frye reminds us, "the purpose of criticism by genres is not so much to classify as to clarify such traditions and affinities, thereby bringing out a large number of literary relationships that would not be noticed as long as there were not context established for them."[2] Stylistically and structurally, therefore, from the nineteenth-century narratives of Brown and Wilson to the twenty-first-century narratives of Reed, Morrison, Delany, Butler, Duplechan, Harris, Neely, Mosley, Johnson, Mackey, Ellis, Everett, and Whitehead, the dual tradition of the African American novel is distinctively characterized by the dialectic tension between residually African Americentric oral forms of vernacular and Eurocentric formal literary traditions. Thematically, these shifting blends of the possible and probable experiences in the romance and novel frame the personal and collective odysseys of black folks to realize the full potential of our mixed heritage and complex identity.

Looking back on the journey from Africa and slavery to liberation, literacy, and wholeness in the tradition of the contemporary African American novel, we notice the saliency of the tragicomic paradox of African American culture and character: the more things change, the more they remain the same. Raised up South by a single mother as a manchild of the Depression and World War II in de jure and de facto racially segregated urban and rural communities of the nation's capital in the District of Columbia, Norbeck, Maryland, and the South Bronx; inspired by the example and spirit of such ancestors and elders as my paternal grandfather, uncles, and intellectual mentors; and seasoned by my experience as an activist and revisionist scholar in the Black Studies movement, I read life and literature through the lenses of a neomasculine postcolonial African Americanist. As the Reverend Martin Luther King Jr. used to intone in the tradition of my grandfather and the Southern black Baptist preachers who chanted sermons at revival meetings I participated in as a boy at Vermont Avenue Baptist Church in the District of Columbia: "We ain't what we wanna be. We ain't what we gonna be. But thank God Almighty, we ain't what we was!"

As this book reminds readers, Africa and her progeny, especially in the United States, fell victim to the myth of an ignoble past. Africans and other nonwhites were cast by Europeans, the British, and European Americans alike in their conquest of Africa and the Americas as archetypal sons and daughters of darkness on a Manichean world stage. Allegorically, we black people of African and mixed biological descent and cultural heritage represented for them the embodiment of absolute spiritual, cultural, and moral truths such as Rousseau's Noble Savage, Melville's diabolical Babo, and Conrad's nameless, voiceless primitives. These archetypes and allegories of blacks were used to reinforce the myth of white racial purity and cultural superiority, as well as to sanction the mission of whites to Christianize, civilize, and colonize nonwhite peoples. It is in this context that black Americans of African descent and mixed heritage began asserting our own authenticity, authority, and agency as we resisted or rejected in various ways with uneven success the imposed identities of others. We resisted mainly by our double-voiced manner of speaking truth to power and to our own people, of telling our own stories and singing our own songs, and of representing in life and literature our own selves to frequently hostile audiences in antiblack cultural and political sites in the United States.

Although ostensibly fascinating and informative, challenges to authenticity as a valid criterion for assessing the distinctive blackness in contemporary African American culture and literature are advanced basically by three groups of critics. The first group is primarily non–African American intellectuals and deracinated or assimilated members of the Talented Tenth who are defensive about having little or no experience living and working with underpaid, underemployed, and unemployed black workers about whom they claim intellectual authority and for whom they advocate political agency. Their major argument seems to be that the racial and ethnic identity of an artist cannot be accurately discerned from the text without the intervention of such graphic assistance as a book blurb or photograph. However, this book demonstrates how the language of the text, its style and structure, is a reasonable and conventional, though clearly unscientific, means of ascertaining cultural traits and patterns peculiar to a writer, group, or movement.

The second group is composed primarily of postmodernists and postcolonialists who assume that the principle of authenticity innately, invariably, and narrowly restricts the freedom and diversity of artists and texts to essential, static, stereotypic constructions and interpretations of black life and art. Drawing primarily on philosopher Charles Taylor's *Ethics of Authenticity*, I have revealed the fallaciousness of this assumption by defining authenticity in texts as a complex principle that is conferred from without as well as within the dialectic process of one's life. Rather than necessarily promoting a fixed, monolithic construction of reality, identity, truth, and beauty, authenticity, especially when operating in a matrix with authority and agency, manifests the ability to transcend restrictive material conditions and to transgress social and moral boundaries. As the analysis of novels in this book illuminates, authority, because it has the power to influence thought and behavior, differs from authenticity and derives its legitimate power from traditional values, legal prerogatives, and special expertise relevant to the situation. As defined earlier, agency is the sociocultural and sociopsychological process by which the individual assumes a responsible political position in maintaining or changing the systems of language and power by which he or she constructs and represents a personal and group identity of authenticity and authority. For example, even though as an African American intellectual I have for many years lived and worked in predominantly white areas, I have worked primarily as a mentor, advisor, teacher, and scholar in empowering the next generation of young, gifted black and nonwhite leaders as well as many others in predominantly white state universities and international institutions. My various awards indicate that I have had some success in effecting radical democratic changes in their academic, intellectual, cultural, and political programs and lives while keeping in touch with the spiritual strivings and providing some of the everyday needs of the ordinary black working poor in my own extended family. This means that for some readers with a primary commitment to the transformative spiritual and political legacy of the language, knowledge, and power of African American working-class communities and vernacular codes, the celebration in novels of existential angst, personal desire, and buppy lifestyles is an inadequate, problematic performance of agency.

The third and final group of possible critics are well-meaning ideologues whose explicit or implicit arguments against my theoretical matrix of authenticity, authority, and agency as a valid and viable criterion in assessing the manner and degree to which Blackness is manifested in a text are problematic. This occurs because they generally rely exclusively on the 1980s Afrocentric vernacular narrative theories of the two domiinant African American critics and texts: Houston Baker's *Blues, Ideology, and Afro-American Literature* and Henry Louis Gates's *Signifying Monkey.* Most anti–Black Arts and anti–Black Power ideologues neglect to examine closely and judiciously such 1960s and 1970s vernacular theories and criticism as LeRoi Jones's "How You Sound," Carolyn M. Rodgers's "Black Poetry—Where It's At," Don L. Lee's *Dynamite Voices: Black*

Poets of the 1960s, Stephen Henderson's *Understanding the New Black Poetry*, and my own *Folk Roots of Contemporary Afro-American Poetry*. Consequently, they misrepresent the range, richness, diversity, and legacy of the politics and aesthetics of the identity formations, neorealism, and modernism in the vernacular and literary tradition of African American literature in general and the novel in particular.

The major problem begins with the ambiguous trope of Blackness, which in the 1960s was an affirmative sign of pride in the struggle for liberation and pan-African unity of peoples of sub-Saharan black racial and cultural heritage in Africa as well as those who were dispersed by the Atlantic slave trade and are acculturated in the Atlantic diaspora. Because the trope of Blackness lacks cultural and geographic specificity in examining the process and representation of identity formations in the United States, I have invoked African American double consciousness in this book as the more appropriate and most dynamic contemporary sign for the core beliefs and values of African Americans. Du Bois did not stress class and gender in his use of double consciousness because, in part, he believed profoundly and prophetically that the primary problem of the twentieth century, which subsumed and dominated all others, was racial. Responding to the winds of change in our postindustrial and postmodern age, my revised use of the trope of double consciousness examines the complex interrelationship of thirteen overlapping variables of chromosomes, color, ethnicity, class, gender, geography, age, culture, sexuality, consciousness, commitment, conscience, and choice in the constructions and representations of the identity formation of African Americans in life and literature. In short, ontogeny recapitulates phylogeny; the more things change, the more they remain the same. Despite the complications of racism owing to the resurgency of feminism and multiethnicity during the 1970s and 1980s, especially the increasing displacement of race by ethnicity, for example intraracial ethnic genocide in Africa and Eastern Europe, as the primary global problem of the twenty-first century, racial prejudice and discrimination still have the most dominant impact on the lives of most black Americans. Double consciousness still marks the most distinctive racially and culturally mixed, yet primarily biracial and bicultural, identity of black Americans of African descent and their vernacular and literary tradition in the United States.

Of course, on some level European Americans and African Americans share a belief in the principles and promise of freedom, democracy, capitalism, and individualism as expressed in the Declaration of Independence, Constitution of the United States, Protestant Ethic, and American Dream. However, as I argue in chapter 2 of this book, core African American beliefs and values, which derive from the unique historical journey of black Americans from Africa and slavery to freedom in the United States, include a tragicomic vision of life, a tough-minded grip on reality, an extraordinary faith in the redemptive power of suffering and patience, a highly developed talent for dissimulation, a vigorous zest for life, a wry sense of humor, and an acute sense of timing. I also identify five residually oral forms by which these beliefs and values are transmitted from generation to generation and mark in a variety of combinations and degrees the distinctiveness of the African American novel: oratory (especially irony, parody, and signifying), myth (including ritual enactments), legend, tale, and song (especially blues and jazz).

Political and philosophical arguments of some multiculturalists and postmodernists against the centrality of white and black issues as anachronistic binarisms gloss over the profoundly ironic and paradoxical history of racial and cultural mixing. In making a case for other groups that have suffered discrimination and injustice, they also ignore the continuing social and economic impact of antiblack racism, de facto racial segregation, and racial discrimination in the United States. Some contemporary African American novelists and critics who are influenced by vested interracial personal interests as multiculturalists and by postmodern theories and practice of antiessentialist, antirepresentational, transcultural narratives, celebrate self-reflexive navel gazing and obscure language games in novels. Some of these novelists and critics stress middle-class strivings, multiculturalism, and, like Charles W. Chesnutt at the turn of the twentieth century and Harvard sociologist Orlando Patterson more recently in *The Ordeal of Integration* (1998), interracial marriage and children as the last best hope for racial and ethnic integration, peace, and justice in the new millennium. But the majority of contemporary African American novelists are not antirepresentational postmodernists. Some are commercially successful popular romantic and realistic novelists such as Terry McMillan, Walter Mosley, Octavia Butler, E. Lynn Harris, Eric Jerome Dickey, Connie Briscoe, and Bebe Moore Campbell. The most critically acclaimed novelists and their best novels, however, are either experimentally neorealistic or nonrepresentational modernist like John A. Williams, Alice Walker, Toni Cade Bambara, Toni Morrison, Ernest J. Gaines, William Melvin Kelley, John Edgar Wideman, Ishmael Reed, Paule Marshall, Gloria Naylor, David Bradley, and Leon Forrest. As Americanist critic Michael Berube insightfully states, "every attempt to define postmodern fiction in stylistic terms—as a form of writing that defeats readers' expectations of coherence, as experimental narrative that plays with generic conventions, as fiction that dwells on ambiguity and uncertainty—winds up being a definition of modernist fiction as well."[3] In short, most contemporary African American novelists continue their imaginative linguistic experimentations with extended modernist narratives and their explorations of the limitations and possibilities of reconstructing a more just social order. As culturally and socially symbolic acts, their novels generally enhance mutual respect for the rights of all people to self-determination, political representation, and personal security in realizing with dignity their full human potential.

Therefore, the consensus of contemporary specialists in the fields of African American literary history and criticism is that the African American literary tradition is best understood and appreciated by interpreting its merits within the context of its own indigenous nature and function. "Major attempts by Afro-American academicians and artists to identify the strengths of Afro-American folk art and its potentialities for a Black American tradition of high art," I argued in 1974, "have been strikingly similar to the spirit if not the letter of Herder's folk ideology."[4] Circumstantial evidence indicates that Du Bois, Locke, Johnson, Wright, Ellison, and Jones were familiar with Johann Gottfried von Herder's theory that folk art is the foundation of high art and that folksong represents "a spontaneous, indigenous expression of the collective soul of a people."[5] The three contemporary vernacular theories of reading and understanding the distinctiveness of African American culture and literature that I believe are most exciting and enlightening are by Houston A. Baker Jr., Henry Louis Gates Jr., and, so I have been led to understand by colleagues and students, me. Baker's *Blues, Ideology, and Afro-American Literature* focuses on the blues as the key black vernacular trope; and Gates's *Signifying Monkey* privileges signifying and pastiche as the prototypical black vernacular and literary tropes. In contrast, this book and its predecessor, *The Afro-American Novel and Its Tradition*, interpret the African American novel as a socially symbolic act that formally encodes and wryly illumines five fundamental biracial, bicultural residually oral forms of African American literature: oratory, myth, legend, tale, and song.

The major difference therefore in the 1980s vernacular theories of Baker, Gates, and myself is that Baker focuses on music (which in the 1970s I also privileged in *The Folk Roots of Contemporary Afro-American Poetry*), Gates on language, and I more broadly on oratory, myth, legend, tale, and song as the principal residually oral forms that generate the distinctive dialectic tension between oral and written African American literature. As this book demonstrates, I remain committed to and convinced of two ancestral legacies. The first is that a systematic, rigorous inquiry into the use of African American vernacular forms by novelists offers readers the most illuminating, challenging, and effective method of assessing the complex relationship of language, power, and knowledge in their interrogations of the distinctive correlations of literature to life, fiction to fact, and myth to reality in the tradition of the contemporary African American novel. The second is that despite the liberating advances of the Civil Rights, Black Power, Black Arts, and the Black Feminist movements, antiblack racism and our struggle against it continue as we remember to keep faith with our ancestors and our God: "We ain't what we wanna be. We ain't what we gonna be. But thank God Almighty, we ain't what we was!"

Notes

Memoir: On Becoming an African American Scholar Activist

1. James Baldwin, *The Fire Next Time* (New York: Dial Press, 1963), p. 119.

2. According to the introduction to political theorist Antonio Gramsci's *Selections from the Prison Notebooks*, "organic intellectuals are distinguished less by their profession, which may be any job characteristic of their class, than by their function in directing the ideas and aspirations of the class to which they organically belong." Gramsci writes: "When one distinguishes between intellectuals and non-intellectuals, one is referring in reality only to the immediate social function of the professional category of the intellectuals, that is, one has in mind the direction in which their specific professional activity is weighted, whether towards intellectual elaboration or towards muscular-nervous effort. This means that, although one can speak of intellectuals, one cannot speak of non-intellectuals, because non-intellectuals do not exist. . . . Each man, finally, outside his professional activity, carries on some form of intellectual activity, that is, he is a 'philosopher', an artist, a man of taste, he participates in a particular conception of the world, has a conscious line of moral conduct, and therefore contributes to sustain a conception of the world or to modify it, that is, to bring into being new modes of thought. . . . In the modern world, technical education, closely bound to industrial labour even at the most primitive and unqualified level, must form the basis of the new type of intellectual." Antonio Gramsci, *Selections from the Prison Notebooks*, trans. and ed. with an Introduction by Quintin Hoare and Geoffrey Nowell Smith (London: Lawrence and Wishart, 1971), pp. 4, 9.

3. For the anthropological meanings and significance of rites of passage, see Arnold van Gennep, *The Rites of Passage*, trans. Monika B. Vizedom and Gabrielle L. Caffee (Chicago: University of Chicago Press, 1960), chap. 1; and Victor W. Turner, *The Ritual Process: Structure and Anti-Structure* (Middlesex, England: Penguin Books, 1974), chap. 3.

4. Henry Louis Gates Jr. and Cornel West, *The Future of the Race* (New York: Alfred A. Knopf, 1996), pp. 18–19.

5. Floyd B. Barbour, ed., *The Black Power Revolt: A Collection of Essays* (Boston: Collier Books, 1968), p. 42.

6. Joseph E. Holloway, "The Origins of African-American Culture," in *Africanisms in American Culture*, ed. Holloway (Bloomington: Indiana University Press, 1991), pp. 1–18.

7. W. E. B. Du Bois, *The Souls of Black Folk: Essays and Sketches* (New York: Crest Books, 1965), pp. 17 and 55–64. David Levering Lewis, *W. E. B. Du Bois: Biography of a Race, 1868–1919* (New York: Owl Books, 1994), p. 143.

8. Alain Locke, ed., *The New Negro* (New York: Atheneum, 1968), pp. 3, 4, 15; and Langston Hughes, *The Big Sea* (New York: Hill and Wang, 1993), p. 228.

9. *The Compact Edition of the Oxford English Dictionary II* (Oxford: Oxford University Press, 1971), p. 3614. See also Houston A. Baker Jr., *Blues, Ideology, and Afro-American*

Literature: A Vernacular Theory (Chicago: University of Chicago Press, 1984), p. 2; and Barbara E. Johnson, "Response," in *Afro-American Literary Study in the 1990s*, ed. Houston A. Baker Jr. and Patricia Redmond (Chicago: University of Chicago Press, 1989), p. 42.

10. "The Blues reflects earlier developments of an African-American speech and continuing musical experience now given new forms as reflection of the post–Civil War African-American culture that was no longer limited as severely to religious reference or the social restraints of slavery. . . . By the nineteenth century the diverse Africans had become African Americans and the Blues, from spiritual and work song, through hollers and shouts and arhoolies, jumped out to celebrate black entrance into a less repressive, less specialized world—less harsh, more uncertain, but still tragic and depriving in too many ways." Amiri Baraka, "The 'Blues Aesthetic' and the 'Black Aesthetic': Aesthetics as the Continuing Political History of a Culture," *Black Music Research Journal* (Fall 1991): 101–2.

11. Diana Fuss, *Essentially Speaking: Feminism, Nature, and Difference* (New York: Routledge, 1989), p. 6.

12. Paul Gilroy, *The Black Atlantic: Modernity and Double Consciousness* (Cambridge: Harvard University Press, 1993), p. 3.

13. I have adapted this term from Stephen Soitos's neologism "Euro-Americentric" in *The Blues Detective: A Study of African American Detective Fiction* (Amherst: University of Massachusetts Press, 1996).

14. Randal Johnson, "Editor's Introduction: Pierre Bourdieu on Art, Literature, and Culture," in Pierre Bourdieu, *The Field of Cultural Production: Essays on Art and Literature*, ed. Randal Johnson (New York: Columbia University Press, 1993), p. 7.

15. Johnson, "Editor's Introduction," p. 9.

16. Quoted in Norman R. Yetman, *Life under the "Peculiar Institution": Selections from the Slave Narrative Collection* (New York: Holt, Rinehart and Winston, 1970), p. 1.

17. Yetman, *Life under the "Peculiar Institution,"* p. 341.

18. Ulrich Bonnell Phillips, *American Negro Slavery: A Survey of the Supply, Employment, and Control of Negro Labor as Determined by the Plantation Regime* (Baton Rouge: Louisiana State University Press, 1966), p. 8.

19. Stanley M. Elkins, *Slavery: A Problem in American Institutional & Intellectual Life* (New York: Universal Library, 1959), p. 82.

20. Yetman, *Life under the "Peculiar Institution,"* pp. 341–45.

21. John B. Cade, "Out of the Mouths of Ex-Slaves," *Journal of Negro History* 20 (1935): 294–337.

22. Yetman, *Life under the "Peculiar Institution,"* p. 348. For an antiessentialist interpretation of the Slave Narrative Collection that highlights the biases of the national administrators, state editors, and white interviewers that influenced the authenticity, authority, and agency of the interviews, see Sharon Ann Musher, "Contesting 'The Way the Almighty Wants It': Crafting Memories of Ex-Slaves in the Slave Narrative Collection," *American Quarterly* 53 (March 2001): 1–31.

23. Sterling N. Brown, *My Own Life Story* (Washington, D.C.: Hamilton Printing, 1924), p. 6.

24. Joanne V. Gabbin, *Sterling A. Brown: Building the Black Aesthetic Tradition* (Westport, Conn.: Greenwood Press, 1985), p. 70.

25. Gabbin, *Sterling A. Brown*, p. 72.

26. Gabbin, *Sterling A. Brown*, p. 73.

27. Kenneth M. Stampp, *The Peculiar Institution: Slavery in the Ante-Bellum South* (New York: Vintage Books, 1956), p. vii.

28. See, for example, Thomas Sowell, *Black Education: Myths and Tragedies* (New York: David McKay, 1972); Nick Aaron Ford, *Black Studies: Threat-or-Challenge?* (Port Washington, N.Y.: Kennikat Press, 1973); and Perry A. Hall, *In the Vineyard: Working in African American Studies* (Knoxville: University of Tennessee Press, 1999).

29. Barbour, *Black Power Revolt*, p. 42.

Introduction

1. Bernard W. Bell, *The Afro-American Novel and Its Tradition* (Amherst: University of Massachusetts Press, 1987), p. xii.

2. Bell, *Afro-American Novel*, pp. xii–xiii.

3. In the earlier study I examine "the formal text as a rewriting of the survival strategies, especially the use of the vernacular, music, and religion, by which black Americans as an ethnic group . . . [struggled for] consciousness of themselves and celebrated their quest for personal and social freedom, literacy, and wholeness." Bell, *Afro-American Novel*, p. xii.

4. Clyde W. Franklin II, "Men's Studies, the Men's Movement, and the Study of Black Masculinities: Further Demystification of Masculinities in America," in *The American Black Male: His Present Status and His Future*, ed. Richard G. Majors and Jacob U. Gordon (Chicago: Nelson-Hall, 1994), p. 12. According to many experts in men's studies, the most important book in the field is J. H. Pleck, *The Myth of Masculinity* (Cambridge: M.I.T. Press, 1981). Although Pleck's analysis of literature on the traditional definition of masculinity and its assumed normative constituent elements revealed no support for the hegemonic definition, its focus was white American males, not black.

5. Quoted in Jonathan Ned Katz, *Gay/Lesbian Almanac: A New Documentary* (New York: Carroll and Graf, 1994), n. 34, pp. 667–68.

6. Michel Foucault, *The History of Sexuality*, Volume I: *An Introduction*, trans. Robert Hurley (New York: Vintage Books 1990), p. 103.

7. Maulana Karenga, "Black and Latino Relations: Context, Challenge, and Possibilities," in*Multi-America: Essays on Cultural Wars and Cultural Peace*, ed. Ishmael Reed (New York: Penguin Books, 1998), pp. 196–200.

8. Reed, *Multi-America*, p. xxi.

9. For the most persuasive argument for this neo-Marxist interpretation of the distinctiveness of African American culture and consciousness, see Baker, *Blues, Ideology, and Afro-American Literature*, chap. 2.

10. As sociologist Mary C. Waters notes, in 1978 "the Office of Management and Budget (OMB) issued a federal directive (Number 15) designating the standards for reporting race and ethnic data. This directive established five federal reporting categories: American Indian or Alaska Native, Asian or Pacific Islander, Black, Hispanic, and White. . . . In October 1997 it was announced that the Asian and Pacific Islander category would be separated into two categories—"Asian," and "Native Hawaiian or Other Pacific Islander." Although the OMB also approved a proposal to allow people to identify themselves with more than one racial/ethnic category, it rejected the proposal to establish a separate

multiracial category. Mary C. Waters, "Multiple Ethnicities and Identity in the United States," in Reed, *Multi-America*, pp. 14–15.

11. Joe Chung Fong, "Ethnic Conflict and Harmony between African and Asian Americans in the United States," in Reed, *Multi-America*, p. 312.

12. Ana Castillo, "A Countryless Woman: The Early Feminista," in Reed, *Multi-America*, p. 268.

13. "'Hispanic' as the ethnic label for all people who reside in the United States with some distant connection with the culture brought by the Spaniards during the conquest of the Americas is a gross misnomer." Castillo, "A Countryless Woman," p. 266.

14. Orlando Patterson, "Race by the Numbers," *New York Times*, May 8, 2001, p. A31.

15. Castillo, "A Countryless Woman," p. 268.

16. Blaustein and Zangrando, *Civil Rights and the American Negro*, pp. 294–311, 418, and 437.

17. John Langston Gwaltney, *Drylongso: A Self Portrait of Black America* (New York: Random House, 1980), pp. 96–97.

18. For a convenient, brief, informative introduction and guide to the genealogy of racial discourse by such representative Enlightenment thinkers on race as Carl von Linne, George Louis Leclerc Buffon, David Hume, James Beattie, Immanuel Kant, Johann Gottfried von Herder, Johann Friedrich Blumenbach, Thomas Jefferson, Georges Leopold Cuvier, and Georg Wilhelm Friedrich Hegel, see Emmanuel Chukwudi Eze, ed., *Race and the Enlightenment: A Reader* (Cambridge: Blackwell, 1997). See also Thomas F. Gossett, *Race: The History of an Idea in America* (New York: Schocken, 1965).

19. Wayne C. Booth, *The Rhetoric of Fiction* (Chicago: Phoenix Books, 1967), pp. 149–65.

1. *Mapping the Rhetoric, Politics, and Poetics of Representation*

1. See Roland Barthes, "The Death of the Author," in *The Rustle of Language*, trans. Richard Howard (New York: Hill and Wang, 1986); *Image, Music, Text: Roland Barthes*, ed. and trans. Stephen Heath (New York: Hill and Wang, 1977); *The Pleasure of the Text*, trans. Richard Miller (New York: Hill and Wang, 1975); and *S/Z: An Essay*, trans. Richard Miller (New York: Noonday Press, 1974). In contrast to Barthes, Foucault acknowledges the continuing authority and agency of the author. See Michel Foucault, "What Is an Author?," in *The Foucault Reader*, ed. Paul Rabinow (New York: Pantheon Books, 1984).

2. LeRoi Jones, *Home: Social Essays* (New York: William Morrow, 1966), p. 105.

3. See Gregory S. Jay, *American Literature and the Culture Wars* (Ithaca: Cornell University Press, 1997), p. 8.

4. Majors and Gordon, *The American Black Male*, p. 14.

5. C[larence] Hugh Holman and William Harmon, *A Handbook to Literature*, 5th ed. (New York: Macmillan, 1986), p. 233.

6. Alice Walker, *The Color Purple* (New York: Washington Square Press, 1983), p. 179.

7. Linda Hutcheon, *A Poetics of Postmodernism: History, Theory, Fiction* (New York: Routledge, 1988), p. 12.

8. Linda Hutcheon, *The Politics of Postmodernism* (New York: Routledge, 1989), p. 17.

9. Hutcheon, *Poetics of Postmodernism*, pp. x–xi.

10. Hutcheon, *Poetics of Postmodernism*, p. x.

11. Ludwig Wittgenstein, *On Certainty* (Oxford: Blackwell, 1969), p. 73; Ferdinand de Saussure, *Course in General Linguistics*, 1915, trans. Wade Baskin (New York: McGraw-Hill, 1966), p. 14; Gramsci, *Selections from the Prison Notebooks*, pp. 55–58 and 81–82; Wolfgang Iser, *The Act of Reading: A Theory of Aesthetic Response* (Baltimore: Johns Hopkins University Press, 1978), p. 34; Barthes, *S/Z*, pp. 4–6; Jacques Derrida, *Of Grammatology*, trans. Gayatri Chakravorty Spivak (Baltimore: John Hopkins University Press, 1974), pp. 70–75, 23, 62; Jean-François Lyotard, *The Postmodern Condition: A Report on Knowledge*, trans. Geoff Bennington and Brian Massumi (Minneapolis: University of Minnesota Press, 1984), pp. xxiv and 31–32; Roman Ingarden, *The Cognition of the Literary Work of Art*, trans. Ruth Ann Crowley and Kenneth Olson (Evanston: Northwestern University Press, 1973), pp. 13–14; Frantz Fanon, *The Wretched of the Earth*, trans. Constance Farrington (New York: Grove Press, 1963), pp. 41, 233–34, 1; Gayatri Chakravorty Spivak, "Subaltern Studies: Deconstructing Historiography," in her *In Other Worlds: Essays in Cultural Politics* (New York: Methuen, 1987), pp. 202–7; Spivak, "Poststructuralism, Marginality, Postcoloniality, and Value," in *Literary Theory Today*, ed. Peter Collier and Helga Geyer-Ryan (Cambridge: Polity Press, 1990), p. 220; Hutcheon, *Poetics of Postmodernism*, p. 11; Michel Foucault, *The Archeology of Knowledge and the Discourse on Language*, trans. A. M. Sheridan Smith (New York: Pantheon Books, 1972), pp. 3–17, 25–30, 233; Mikhail Bakhtin, "Discourse and the Novel," in *The Dialogic Imagination: Four Essays*, trans. Caryl Emerson and Michael Holquist (Austin: University of Texas Press, 1981), pp. 273, 263; Jacques Lacan, "The Mirror Stage," in his *Ecrits: A Selection*, trans. Alan Sheridan (New York: W. W. Norton, 1977), pp. 1–7; Gilles Deleuze and Félix Guattari, "What Is a Minor Literature?," in *Kafka: Toward a Minor Literature*, trans. Dana Polan (Minneapolis: University of Minnesota Press, 1986), pp. 16–27; Edward Said, *Culture and Imperialism* (New York: Alfred A. Knopf, 1993), pp. 228–30; and Homi Bhabha, *The Location of Culture* (New York: Routledge, 1994), pp. 36–39, 66.

12. Lyotard, *Postmodern Condition*, pp. xxiii, 3, 37.

13. As paraphrased succinctly in Terry Eagleton, *Literary Theory: An Introduction* (Minneapolis: University of Minnesota Press, 1983), p. 131. See Derrida, *Of Grammatology*, pp. 10–26.

14. Jonathan Culler, *On Deconstruction: Theory and Criticism after Structuralism* (Ithaca: Cornell University Press, 1983), p. 86.

15. Said, *Culture and Imperialism*, p. 228.

16. Said, *Culture and Imperialism*, p. 307.

17. In an explicit, but ironic, disclaimer, Spivak writes, "I was born in India and received my primary, secondary, and university education there, including two years of graduate work. My Indian example could thus be seen as a nostalgic investigation of the lost roots of my own identity. Yet even as I know that one cannot freely enter the thickets of 'motivations,' I would maintain that my chief project is to point out the positivist-idealist variety of such nostalgia. I turn to Indian material because, in the absence of advanced disciplinary training, that accident of birth and education has provided me with a *sense* of the historical canvas, a hold on some of the pertinent languages that are useful tools for a *bricoleur*, especially when armed with the Marxist skepticism of concrete experience as the final arbiter and a critique of disciplinary formations. Yet the Indian case cannot be taken as representative of all countries, nations, cultures, and the like that may

be invoked as the Other of Europe as Self." Gayatri Chakravorty Spivak, "Can the Subaltern Speak?," in *Marxism and the Interpretation of Culture*, ed. Cary Nelson and Lawrence Grossberg (Urbana: University of Illinois Press, 1988), pp. 281, 296–308.

18. Spivak, "Can the Subaltern Speak?," p. 296.

19. E. San Juan, *Beyond Postcolonial Theory* (New York: St. Martins Press, 1998), pp. 6–7. Also, see Bhabha, *Location of Culture*, p. 5.

20. For a valuable contemporary study of the development of African American Studies and an explanation of the transformative approach to the field, see Hall, *In the Vineyard*, pp. 72–80. By "transformationist," Hall refers "to a range of alternative perspectives that maintain critical scrutiny of both conventional epistemological approaches and the emergent Afrocentrist alternative" (p. 66).

21. Ania Loomba, *Colonialism/Postcolonialism* (New York: Routledge, 1998), pp. 2, xiii.

22. Quoted in San Juan, *Beyond Postcolonial Theory*, pp. 5–6. Also see Aijaz Ahmad, "The Politics of Literary Postcoloniality," *Race and Class* 36, no. 3 (Jan.–Mar. 1995): 1–20.

23. Loomba, *Colonialism/Postcolonialism*, p. 7.

24. Loomba, *Colonialism/Postcolonialism*, p. 12.

25. See Molefi Kete Asante, *Afrocentricity* (Trenton: Africa World Press, 1988), *The Afrocentric Idea* (Philadelphia: Temple University Press, 1987), and *Kemet, Afrocentricity, and Knowledge* (Trenton: Africa World Press, 1990).

26. Asante, *Afrocentricity*, p. 6.

27. Asante, *Afrocentric Idea*, p. 9.

28. See Wilson Jeremiah Moses, *Afrotopia: The Roots of African American Popular History* (New York: Cambridge University Press, 1998) p. 2, chap. 1 n. 2, chap. 2 n. 1; Asante, *Afrocentricity*, p. 16.

29. Hall, *In the Vineyard*, p. 51.

30. Joseph E. Holloway, "The Origins of African-American Culture," in *Africanisms in American Culture*, ed. Holloway (Bloomington: Indiana University Press/Midland Books, 1991), p. 2.

31. Ann duCille, "Postcolonialism and Afrocentricity: Discourse and Dat Course," in *The Black Columbiad: Defining Moments in African American Literature and Culture*, ed. Werner Sollors and Maria Diedrich (Cambridge: Harvard University Press, 1994), p. 30.

32. duCille, "Postcolonialism and Afrocentricity," p. 31.

33. See Manning Marable, *How Capitalism Underdeveloped Black America: Problems in Race, Political Economy, and Society* (Boston: South End Press, 1983), and "We Need New and Critical Study of Race and Ethnicity," *Chronicle of Higher Education*, February 25, 2000, pp. B4–B7; James Stewart, "Reaching for Higher Ground: Toward an Understanding of Black/Africana Studies," *The Afrocentric Scholar* 1 (May 1992): 1–63; and Michael Eric Dyson, *Reflecting Black: African American Cultural Criticism* (Minneapolis: University of Minnesota Press, 1993).

34. Maulana Karenga, *Kwanzaa: A Celebration of Family, Community, and Culture* (Los Angeles: University of Sankore Press, 1998).

35. Moses, *Afrotopia*, p. 33.

36. See Allan Bloom, *The Closing of the American Mind: How Higher Education Has Failed Democracy and Impoverished the Souls of Today's Students* (New York: Simon and Schuster, 1987); Lynne Cheney, *Telling the Truth: Why Our Culture and Our Country Have Stopped Making Sense—and What We Can Do about It* (New York: Simon and Schuster,

1995); Arthur M. Schlesinger, *The Disuniting of America: Reflections on a Multicultural Society* (New York: W. W. Norton, 1991); and Mary Lefkowitz, *Not Out of Africa: How Afrocentrism Became an Excuse to Teach Myth as History* (New York: Basic Books, 1996).

37. See Werner Sollors, *Beyond Ethnicity: Consent and Descent in American Culture* (New York: Oxford University Press, 1986); Barbara E. Johnson, "Response [to Henry Louis Gates Jr.]," *Afro-American Literary Study in the 1990s*, ed. Houston A. Baker and Patricia Redmond (Chicago: University of Chicago Press, 1989); Lefkowitz, *Not Out of Africa*; and George Hutchinson, *The Harlem Renaissance in Black and White* (Cambridge: Belknap Press, 1995).

38. Sollors, *Beyond Ethnicity*, pp. 12–13.

39. Sollors, *Beyond Ethnicity*, p. 11.

40. David Lionel Smith, "The Black Arts Movement and Its Critics," *American Literary History* (Spring 1991): 93.

41. B. Johnson, "Response [to Henry Louis Gates Jr.]," p. 42.

42. Hutchinson, *Harlem Renaissance*, pp. 14–15.

43. Sollors and Diedrich, *Black Columbiad*, p. 11.

44. bell hooks, *Yearning: Race, Gender, and Cultural Politics* (Boston: South End Press, 1990), p. 8.

45. Ann duCille, *Skin Trade* (Cambridge: Harvard University Press, 1996), pp. 105–12.

46. hooks, *Yearning*, p. 9.

47. Robert Blauner, *Racial Oppression in America* (New York: Harper and Row, 1972), pp. 12–13.

48. Blauner, *Racial Oppression*, p. 52.

49. Harold Cruse, *Rebellion or Revolution?* (New York: Apollo Editions, 1969), chap. 7; Blauner, *Racial Oppression*, p. 82.

50. Natalie Angier, "Do Races Differ? Not Really, Genes Show," *New York Times*, August 22, 2000, pp. D1, D6.

51. See, for example, John W. Blassingame, *The Slave Community: Plantation Life in the Antebellum South* (New York: Oxford University Press, 1972), pp. 82–85; Eugene D. Genovese, *Roll, Jordan, Roll: The World the Slaves Made* (New York: Vintage Books, 1976), pp. 413–31; Angela Y. Davis, *Women, Race, and Class* (New York: Vintage Books, 1983), pp. 3–29; Frederick Douglass, *The Life and Times of Frederick Douglass* (New York: Collier Books, 1962), chaps. 5 and 6; Harriet A. Jacobs, *Incidents in the Life of a Slave Girl, Written by Herself*, ed. Jean Fagan Yellin (Cambridge: Harvard University Press, 1987); Gayl Jones, *Corregidora* (Boston: Beacon Press, 1975); and Carolivia Herron, *Thereafter Johnnie* (New York: Vintage Books, 1991).

52. Davis, *Women, Race, and Class*, p. 18.

53. Gilroy, *Black Atlantic*, p. 191.

54. Gilroy, *Black Atlantic*, p. 15.

55. Albert P. Blaustein and Robert L. Zangrando, eds., *Civil Rights and the American Negro: A Documentary History* (New York: Washington Square Press, 1968), pp. 42–44 and 47–50. See also Charles C. Tansill, ed., *Documents Illustrative of the Formation of the Union of the American States* (Washington, D.C.: U. S. Government Printing Office, 1927), especially pp. 508, 588–89, 616–18, 631, and 719; and Max Farrand, *The Framing of the Constitution of the United States* (New Haven: Yale University Press, 1913; rpt. 1970), pp. 91–112 and 149–52.

56. Shakespeare, *The Tempest*, I.2. Also see Roberto Fernandez Retamar, *Caliban and Other Essays*, trans. Edward Baker (Minneapolis: University of Minnesota Press, 1989). For an ambitious, provocative study of phallocentric and Calibanic discourse in novels by contemporary black male novelists, see James W. Coleman, *Black Male Fiction and the Legacy of Caliban* (Lexington: University Press of Kentucky, 2001).

57. Trudier Harris, *Exorcising Blackness: Historical and Literary Lynching and Burning Rituals* (Bloomington: Indiana University Press, 1984), p. 7.

58. Quoted in *Race and the Enlightenment*, ed. Emmanuel Chukwudi Eze (Cambridge: Blackwell, 1997), pp. 102–3.

59. See Martin R. Delany, *The Condition, Elevation, Emigration, and Destiny of the Colored People of the United States* (Philadelphia: The Author, 1852; rpt. New York: Arno Press and *The New York Times*, 1969), p. 13; Alexander Crummell, "The Social Principle Among a People," in *The Greatness of Christ and Other Sermons* (New York: Thomas Whittaker, 1882), p. 290; and W. E. B. Du Bois, "An Essay toward a History of the Black Man in the Great War," *Crisis* 18, no. 2 (1919): 64. Also see Kenneth B. Clark, *Dark Ghetto: Dilemmas of Social Power* (New York: Harper Torchbooks, 1967); Stokely Carmichael (Kwame Toure) and Charles V. Hamilton, *Black Power: The Politics of Liberation in America* (New York: Vintage Books, 1967); Cruse, *Rebellion or Revolution?*; Robert L. Allen, *Black Awakening in Capitalist America* (New York: Doubleday, 1970); and Blauner, *Racial Oppression*.

60. Benjamin B. Ringer and Elinor R. Lawless, *Race-Ethnicity and Society* (New York: Routledge, 1989), pp. xiii–xiv, chap. 5.

61. Michel Foucault, *Power/Knowledge: Selected Interviews & Other Writings, 1972–1977*, ed. Colin Gordon, trans. Colin Gordon, Leo Marshall, John Mepham, and Kate Soper (New York: Pantheon Books, 1980), p. 69.

62. Quoted in Kevin K. Gaines, *Uplifting the Race: Black Leadership, Politics, and Culture in the Twentieth Century* (Chapel Hill: University of North Carolina, 1996), p. xiii.

63. Ringer and Lawless, *Race-Ethnicity and Society*, p. 108.

64. Richard Poe, "Negro: by Definition," *Negro History Bulletin* 40 (1977): 668. See Poe's brief yet cogent article for a clearly and persuasively illustrated inventory of state miscegenation laws.

65. Pauline Hopkins, *The Magazine Novels of Pauline Hopkins*, ed. Hazel Carby (New York: Oxford University Press, 1988).

66. See, for example, Derrick Bell, *Faces at the Bottom of the Well: The Permanence of Racism* (New York: Basic Books, 1992); Richard Delgado, ed., *Critical Race Theory: The Cutting Edge* (Philadelphia: Temple University Press, 1995); and Kimberle Crenshaw, Neil Gotanda, Gary Peller, and Kendall Thomas, eds., *Critical Race Theory: The Key Writings That Formed the Movement* (New York: New Press, 1995).

67. Elaine K. Ginsberg, "Introduction" to Ginsberg, ed., *Passing and the Fictions of Identity* (Durham: Duke University Press, 1996), p. 13.

68. Patricia Hill Collins, *Black Feminist Thought: Knowledge, Consciousness, and the Politics of Empowerment* (New York: Routledge, 1991), pp. 164–65.

69. Steven Goldberg, *The Inevitability of Patriarchy* (New York: William Morrow, 1974), p. 33. Goldberg argues that "(a) the different hormonal development of males and females engenders different male and female behavior, and (b) patriarchy and male dominance (and the relevant social values and socialization) are conformations to (and exaggerations of) this different behavior of males and females" (p. 245).

70. See Collins, *Black Feminist Thought*, chap. 8; Angela Y. Davis, "Rape, Racism, and the Capitalist Setting," *Black Scholar* 9, no. 7 (1978): 24–30; and Davis, *Women, Race, and Class*.

71. See Majors and Gordon, *American Black Male*, pp. ix–xi; and Jacob U. Gordon, comp., *The African-American Male: An Annotated Bibliography* (Westport, Conn.: Greenwood Press, 1999), p. x.

72. Fox Butterfield, "Racial Disparities Seen as Pervasive in Juvenile Justice," *New York Times*, April 26, 2000, pp. A1, A18.

73. Majors and Gordon, *American Black Male*, pp. ix–xi; and Gordon, *African-American Male*, p. x.

74. Dorian Sagan, "Gender Specifics: Why Women Aren't Men," *New York Times*, June 21, 1998, sec. 15, pp. 1, 20.

75. See Nicholas Wade, "Taking New Measurements for Jefferson's Pedestal," *New York Times*, March 7, 1999, p. 20; Wade, "DNA Backs a Tribe's Tradition of Early Descent from the Jews," *New York Times*, May 9, 1999, sec. 1, p. 1; and *60 Minutes* Video Report, "The Lemba Jews," April 23, 2000.

76. John Edgar Wideman, "Frame and Dialect: The Evolution of the Black Voice in Fiction," *American Poetry Review* 5 (1976): 36.

77. Ronald Wardhaugh, *An Introduction to Sociolinguistics*, 3rd ed. (Malden, Mass.: Blackwell, 1998), pp. 21–53, 86–129; Peter Trudgill, *Sociolinguistics: An Introduction to Language and Society* (New York: Penguin Books, 1987), pp. 51–77; and Geneva Smitherman, *Talkin and Testifyin: The Language of Black America* (Boston: Houghton Mifflin, 1977), pp. 31, 173, 207–9.

78. Lionel Trilling, *Sincerity and Authenticity* (Cambridge: Harvard University Press, 1971), p. 134.

79. J. Martin Favor, *Authentic Blackness: The Folk in the New Negro Renaissance* (Durham: Duke University Press, 1999), p. 153, n. 5.

80. Charles Taylor, *The Ethics of Authenticity* (Cambridge: Harvard University Press, 1991), p. 66.

81. Max Weber, *The Theory of Social and Economic Organization*, trans. A. M. Henderson and ed. Talcott Parsons (New York: Free Press, 1964), p. 152.

82. Marvin E. Olsen, "Power as a Social Process," in his *Power in Societies* (New York: Macmillan, 1970), p. 7.

83. Charles Taylor, *Human Agency and Language* (Cambridge: Cambridge University Press, 1985), pp. 3–5.

84. Taylor, *Human Agency and Language*, p. 8.

85. Asante also notes, "That which the speaker expresses by the extreme dimensions of his media of words, tones, fables, myths, legends, and sounds is a sort of word subtlety, intended to subvert the established order by guerrilla rhetoric tactics." Asante, *Afrocentric Idea*, p. 116.

86. Chinweizu, Onuwuchekwa Jemie, and Ihechukwu Madubuike, *Toward the Decolonization of African Literature* I (Washington, D.C.: Howard University Press, 1983), p. 12.

87. Geneva Smitherman, "'What Is Africa to Me?'; Language, Ideology, and AFRICAN AMERICAN," *American Speech* 66, no. 2 (Summer 1991): 117.

88. Michel Foucault, *The Order of Things: An Archaeology of the Human Sciences* (New York: Random House, 1970), p. 380.

89. Bakhtin, *Dialogic Imagination*, pp. 293–94.

90. Eagleton, *Literary Theory*, p. 210.

91. See Smitherman, *Talkin and Testifyin;* Salikoko S. Mufwene et al., eds., *African American English: Structure, History and Use* (New York: Routledge, 1998); Theresa Perry and Lisa Delpit, eds., *The Real Ebonics Debate: Power, Language, and the Education of African American Children* (Boston: Beacon Press, 1998); and Robert L. Williams, ed., *Ebonics: The True Language of Black Folks* (St. Louis: Robert L. Williams and Associates, 1975).

92. John Russell Rickford, *Spoken Soul: The Story of Black English* (New York: John Wiley and Sons, 2000), p. 130; and John McWhorter, *The Word on the Street: Fact and Fable about American English* (New York: Plenum Trade, 1998), p. 185. Also see Smitherman, *Talkin and Testifyin*, pp. 1–15; Mufwene, *African American English*, pp. 154–225; Perry and Delpit, *Real Ebonics Debate*; and Williams, *Ebonics*.

93. Harold Cruse, "Revolutionary Nationalism and the Afro-American," in *Black Fire: An Anthology of Afro-American Writing*, ed. LeRoi Jones and Larry Neal (New York: Apollo Editions, 1969), p. 41. Cruse's essay first appeared in *Studies on the Left* 2, no. 3 (1962).

94. Larry Neal, "And Shine Swam On," in *Black Fire*, ed. Jones and Neal, p. 654.

95. Henry Louis Gates Jr., *Figures in Black: Words, Signs, and the "Racial" Self* (New York: Oxford University Press, 1987), p. 44.

96. Dexter Fisher and Robert Stepto, eds., *Afro-American Literature: The Reconstruction of Instruction* (New York: The Modern Language Association of America, 1979), p. 2.

97. Saussure was more interested in "langue," the objective structure of signs that made speech possible, than "parole," the individual utterance of actual speakers separate from social dialogue. See Saussure, *Course in General Linguistics*. Also see Eagleton, *Literary Theory*, pp. 97–118.

98. Eagleton, *Literary Theory*, p. 115.

99. Eagleton, *Literary Theory*, p. 117.

100. Foucault, *Power/Knowledge*, pp. 112–13.

101. Foucault, *Power/Knowledge*, p. 114.

102. See Michel deCerteau, *The Practice of Everyday Life*, trans. Steven F. Randall (Berkeley: University of California Press, 1984), pp. xix, 30; and Michel Foucault, "The Subject and Power," *Critical Inquiry* 8, no. 4 (1982): 793.

103. Frederick Douglass, "No Progress Without Struggle!, 1849," in Barbour, *Black Power Revolt*, p. 42.

104. Gwaltney, *Drylongso*, p. xxiii.

105. Gwaltney, *Drylongso*, p. xiii.

106. Fuss, *Essentially Speaking*, p. 20.

107. Fuss, *Essentially Speaking*, p. xii.

108. Quoted in Katya Gibel Azoulay, "Experience, Empathy, and Strategic Essentialism," *Cultural Studies* 11, no. 1 (1997): 102–3. See also Fuss, *Essentially Speaking*, p. xii; and Gayatri Chakravorty Spivak, *Outside in the Teaching Machine* (New York: Routledge, 1993), p. 162.

109. Stuart Hall, "Cultural Identity and Diaspora," in *Identity, Community, Culture, Difference*, ed. Jonathan Rutherford (London: Lawrence and Wishart, 1990), p. 224.

110. Hall, "Cultural Identity and Diaspora," p. 223.

111. Hall, "Cultural Identity and Diaspora," p. 223.

112. Gaines, *Uplifting the Race*, pp. xv.

113. Gwaltney, *Drylongso*, p. 5.

114. Benedict Anderson, *Imagined Communities: Reflections on the Origin and Spread of Nationalism*, rev. ed. (New York: Verso, 1996), p. 6.

115. Hall, "Cultural Identity and Diaspora," pp. 222–25.

116. bell hooks, *Feminist Theory: From Margin to Center* (Boston: South End Press, 1984), p. ix.

117. Toni Morrison, *Sula* (New York: Alfred A. Knopf, 1974), pp. 4–5.

118. Hazel Carby, "The Multicultural Wars," *Radical History Review* 54 (Fall 1992): 12.

119. bell hooks, "Representing Whiteness in the Black Imagination" in *Cultural Studies*, ed. Lawrence Grossberg, Cary Nelson, and Paul A. Trechler (New York: Routledge, 1992), pp. 339–40.

120. hooks, "Representing Whiteness," p. 338.

121. Tzvetan Todorov, "Race, Writing, and Culture," trans. Loulou Mack, in *"Race," Writing, and Difference*, ed. Henry Louis Gates Jr. (Chicago: University of Chicago Press, 1986), p. 379.

122. Fredric Jameson, Foreword to Lyotard, *Postmodern Condition*, p. xii.

123. Foucault, *Power/Knowledge*, p. 114.

124. Don Bialostosky, "Dialogics as an Art of Discourse in Literary Criticism," *PMLA* 101, no. 4 (September 1986): 788–97.

2. *The Roots of the Contemporary African American Novel*

1. Nathan Glazer and Daniel P. Moynihan, *Beyond the Melting Pot: The Negroes, Puerto Ricans, Jews, Italians, and Irish of New York City* (Cambridge: M.I.T. Press, 1964), p. 53.

2. See, for example, Charles A. Valentine, *Culture and Poverty: Critique and Counter-Proposals* (Chicago: University of Chicago Press, 1968); Norman E. Whitten Jr. and John F. Szwed, eds., *Afro-American Anthropology: Contemporary Perspectives* (New York: The Free Press, 1970); Blassingame, *Slave Community*; Herbert G. Gutman, *The Black Family in Slavery and Freedom, 1750–1925* (New York: Pantheon Books, 1976); Lawrence W. Levine, *Black Culture and Black Consciousness: African American Folk Thought from Slavery to Freedom* (New York: Oxford University Press, 1977); Alan Dundes, ed., *Mother Wit from the Laughing Barrel: Readings in the Interpretation of African American Folklore* (Englewood Cliffs: Prentice-Hall, 1973); John Lovell Jr., *Black Song: The Forge and the Flame; The Story of How the African American Spiritual Was Hammered Out* (New York: Macmillan, 1972); Dell Hymes, ed., *Pidginization and Creolization of Languages: Proceedings of a Conference Held at the University of West Indies Mona, Jamaica, April 1968* (London: Cambridge University Press, 1974); J. L. Dillard, *Black English: Its History and Usage in the United States* (New York: Random House, 1972); and Bernhardt Ostendorf, *Black Literature in White America* (Totowa, N.J.: Barnes and Noble Books, 1982).

3. Robert Blauner, "Black Culture: Myth or Reality?," in Whitten and Szwed, *Afro-American Anthropology*, p. 352.

4. David Theo Goldberg, *Racist Culture: Philosophy and the Politics of Meaning*, (Cambridge: Blackwell, 1993; rpt. 1994), p. 98.

5. Michael Omi and Howard Winant, *Racial Formation in the United States from the 1960's to the 1990's*, 2nd ed. (New York: Routledge, 1994), pp. viii, 162 n. 2.

6. Omi and Winant, *Racial Formation*, p. 72.

7. Omi and Winant, *Racial Formation*, p. 81.

8. Alvin M. Josephy Jr., *The Indian Heritage of America* (New York: Alfred A. Knopf, 1968), p. 351.

9. Omi and Winant, *Racial Formation*, p. 81.

10. Ralph Ellison, *Shadow and Act* (New York: Signet Books, 1966), pp. 136–37. I am indebted to this collection of essays for the seminal idea of this critical study.

11. Melville J. Herskovits, *The Myth of the Negro Past* (Boston: Beacon Press, 1958), chaps. 5–7. See also Whitten and Szwed, "Introduction," pp. 27–28.

12. Holloway, *Africanisms in American Culture*, p. x.

13. Sidney Mintz and Richard Price, *An Anthropological Approach to the African American Past: A Caribbean Perspective* (Philadelphia: Institute for the Study of Human Issues, 1977), pp. 22–24.

14. John Hope Franklin, *From Slavery to Freedom: A History of Negro Americans*, 3rd ed. (New York: Alfred A. Knopf, 1967), p. 28.

15. Carl N. Degler, "Slavery and the Genesis of American Race Prejudice," *Comparative Studies of Society and History* 2 (October 1959): 49–66; Winthrop D. Jordan, *White over Black: American Attitudes toward the Negro, 1550–1812* (Chapel Hill: University of North Carolina Press, 1968), pp. 73–75. See also George M. Frederickson, "Toward a Social Interpretation of the Development of American Racism," in *Key Issues in the African American Experience*, ed. Nathan I. Huggins, Martin Kilson, and Daniel M. Fox, 2 vols. (New York: Harcourt Brace Jovanovich, 1971)1: 240–54.

16. Quoted in Franklin, *From Slavery to Freedom*, pp. 101–2.

17. Quoted in Elkins, *Slavery*, p. 40.

18. Benjamin Quarles, *The Negro in the American Revolution* (Chapel Hill: University of North Carolina Press, 1961), p. 42; and Franklin, *From Slavery to Freedom*, p. 130.

19. Max Farrand, *The Framing of the Constitution of the United States* (New Haven: Yale University Press, 1961), pp. 148–52; and Franklin, *From Slavery to Freedom*, pp. 142–44.

20. Franklin, *From Slavery to Freedom*, p. 144.

21. Although the congressional bill of March 1865 creating the Bureau of Refugees, Freedmen, and Abandoned Lands explicitly instructed General Oliver O. Howard, the head of the bureau, to "'set apart for the loyal refugees or freedmen, such tracts of land . . . as shall have been abandoned' in lots 'not more than forty acres' and rent them, at a modest percent of their value, to freedmen and their families," President Andrew Johnson subverted this plan by issuing his Amnesty Proclamation in May 1865 pardoning most former Confederates and restoring to them their abandoned lands. See William McFeely, "Unfinished Business: The Freedman's Bureau and Federal Action in Race Relations," in Huggins, Kilson, and Fox, *Key Issues*, 2: 11–12.

22. Gunnar Myrdal, *An American Dilemma: The Negro Problem and Modern Democracy* (1944; rpt. New York: Harper and Row, 1962), pp. 927–30; E. Franklin Frazier, The Negro in the United States (1949; rev. ed. New York: Macmillan, 1957), pp. 687-706.

23. Raymond Williams, *Culture and Society, 1780–1950*. (1958; rpt. New York: Harper and Row, 1966), p. xiv.

24. Clifford Geertz, *Interpretation of Cultures: Selected Essays* (New York: Basic Books, 1973), p. 89; and Sidney Mintz, Foreword to Whitten and Szwed, *African American Anthropology*, p. 10.

25. Valentine, *Culture and Poverty*, p. 3.

26. Herbert G. Gutman, "Work, Culture, and Society in Industrializing America, 1815–1919," *American Historical Review* 78 (1973): 542–43.

27. Mintz, Foreword to Whitten and Szwed, *African American Anthropology*, p. 10.

28. Peter L. Berger and Thomas Luckman, *The Social Construction of Reality: A Treatise in the Sociology of Knowledge* (Baltimore: Penguin Books, 1966), p. 86. For this and other useful insights into contemporary European perceptions of black American culture, I am indebted to Bernhard Ostendorf's criticism of an early draft of this chapter and his "Black Poetry, Blues, and Folklore: Double Consciousness in African American Oral Culture," an unpublished manuscript.

29. Whitten and Szwed, *African American Anthropology*, p. 351.

30. See Robert E. Park, "Mentality of Racial Hybrids," *American Journal of Sociology* 36 (January 1931): 534–51.

31. Melville J. Herskovits, *Life in a Haitian Valley* (New York: Alfred A. Knopf, 1937), pp. 295–96.

32. Albert J. Raboteau, *Slave Religion: The "Invisible Institution" in the Antebellum South*, (New York: Oxford University Press, 1980), pp. 55–59.

33. E. Franklin Frazier, *The Negro in the United States*, rev. ed. (New York: Macmillan, 1957), p. 21. Robert Farris Thompson, *Flash of the Spirit: African and African American Art and Philosophy* (1983; rpt. New York: Vintage Books, 1984).

34. Ostendorf, "Black Poetry, Blues, and Folklore," p. 6. See also J. Huizinga, *Homo Ludens* (London: Routledge and Kegan Paul, 1949).

35. Du Bois, *Souls of Black Folk*, pp. 16–17.

36. Sutton E. Griggs, *Imperium in Imperio: A Study of the Negro Race Problem, A Novel* (1899; rpt. Miami: Mnemosyne, 1969), p. 62.

37. Williams Pickens, *The New Negro: His Political, Civil, and Mental Status and Related Essays* (1916; rpt. New York: Negro Universities Press, 1969), p. 15.

38. Given the different temporal and spatial contexts in which they used it, the phrase "New Negro" obviously meant different things to Griggs, Pickens, and Locke. See Robert A. Bone, *The Negro Novel in America*, rev. ed. (New Haven: Yale University Press, 1965), pp. 32–35. For a discussion of the ubiquitousness of the phrase, see Lawrence Levine, "The Concept of the New Negro and the Realities of Black Culture," in Huggins, Kilson, and Fox, *Key Issues*, 2: 128–29. See also Hugh Gloster, "Sutton Griggs: Novelist of the New Negro," *Phylon* 4 (1943): 335–45; rpt. in *The Black Novelist*, ed. Robert Hemenway (Columbus: Charles E. Merrill, 1970), pp. 11–23; Hugh Gloster, *Negro Voices in American Fiction* (1948; rpt. New York: Russell and Russell, 1965), pp. 56–67; and Patricia D. Watkins, "Sutton Griggs: The Evolution of a Propagandist" (master's thesis, Howard University, 1970).

39. Pauline Hopkins, *Contending Forces: A Romance Illustrative of Negro Life North and South* (1900; rpt. Miami: Mnemosyne, 1969), p. 272.

40. Sutton E. Griggs, *Pointing the Way* (Nashville: Orion, 1908), p. 101.

41. Herbert Aptheker, ed., *A Documentary History of the Negro People in the United States*, 3rd ed., 4 vols. (New York: Citadel Press, 1965), 1: 95.

42. According to Lawrence Levine, "at the time of emancipation at least 93 percent of the adult Negroes in the United States were illiterate. In 1870 the number had been reduced to about 80 percent; by 1890, 56 percent; 1900, 44 percent; 1950, 10 percent. . . . When freedom first came, more than nine out of ten blacks had been illiterate; by the mid-

twentieth century nine out of ten were literate." He defines literacy as "the minimal ability to read and write" (*Black Culture and Black Consciousness*, pp. 156–57).

43. Charles Keil, *Urban Blues*, (Chicago: University of Chicago Press, 1966), p. 17.

44. Richard Dorson, *American Negro Folktales* (Greenwich, Conn.: Fawcett Premier Books, 1967), p. 12.

45. Isidore Okpewho, *African Oral Literature: Backgrounds, Character, and Continuity* (Bloomington: Indiana University Press, 1992), p. 18. This outstanding comprehensive study supersedes Ruth Finnegan's *Oral Literature in Africa* (London: Oxford University Press, 1970).

46. Emmanuel Obiechina, *Culture, Tradition, and Society in the West African Novel* (London: Cambridge University Press, 1975), p. 34.

47. Because the term "folklore" was first used in England in 1846 to describe the body of material and nonmaterial culture that distinguishes the intellectual from the tradition-bound classes, it is of questionable value in discussing ethnic or mythic societies in which all is oral and most is traditional. But with the emergence of African national states in the 1960s and the appearance of a Westernized African elite, the use of the term makes more sense. See Richard Dorson, "Africa and the Folklorist," *African Folklore* (Bloomington: Indiana University Press, 1972), pp. 3–67.

48. For an informative outline of the forms and functions of folklore, see William Bascom, "The Forms of Folklore: Prose Narratives," *Journal of American Folklore* 78 (1965): 3–20, and "The Folklore and Literature," *The African World* (New York: Frederick Praeger, 1965), pp. 459–90.

49. Finnegan, *Oral Tradition in Africa*, pp. 315–88. See also Melville J. Herskovits and Frances S. Herskovits, *Dahomean Narrative* (Evanston: Northwestern University Press, 1958).

50. Ulli Beier, quoted in Janheinz Jahn, *Neo-African Literature: History of Black Writing*, trans. Oliver Coburn and Ursula Lehrburger (New York: Evergreen, 1969), p. 62. This is an ambitious, provocative study of the relationship of contemporary African literature to its oral tradition. See also Jahn, *Muntu: An Outline of the New African Culture*, trans. Marjorie Gree (New York: Grove Press, 1961), pp. 185–215.

51. For a model study of an African writer's use of folklore, see Bernth Lindfors, "Amos Tutuola: Debts and Assets," *Cahiers d'Etudes Africaines* 10 (1970): 306–34. See also Lindfors, "Critical Approaches to Folklore in African Literature," in Dorson, *African Folklore*, pp. 223–34. For a useful discussion of the methods for determining the presence of folklore in literature, see Richard M. Dorson, "The Identification of Folklore in American Literature," *Journal of American Folklore* 70 (1957); rpt. in Dorson, *American Folklore and the Historian* (Chicago: University of Chicago Press, 1971), pp. 186–203. For an insightful model study of an African American writer's use of folklore, see Robert Hemenway, "Are You a Flying Lark or a Setting Dove?" in Fisher and Stepto, *African American Literature*, pp. 122–52.

52. For an intriguing examination of this subject, see Gene Bluestein, *The Voice of the Folk: Folklore and American Literary Theory* (Amherst: University of Massachusetts Press, 1972); and Bernard W. Bell, *The Folk Roots of Contemporary African American Poetry* (Detroit: Broadside, 1974).

53. Dorson, *American Negro Folktales*, p. 66.

54. Blassingame, *Slave Community*, p. 41. By making use of slave narratives as well as

the records of white planters and travel accounts, Blassingame's book not only breaks with the tradition of American historiography but also reveals the influence of African retentions on antebellum African American life and provides a more reliable account of the shaping of African American identity than the Sambo thesis advanced by Stanley Elkins. Studies by several white and black social scientists and historians have uncritically applied Elkins's thesis to modern-day African Americans: Glazer and Moynihan, *Beyond the Melting Pot*; Charles Silberman, *Crisis in Black and White* (New York: Vintage Books, 1964); Eugene D. Genovese, *The Red and the Black: Marxian Explorations in Southern and African American History* (New York: Panther Books, 1968); Thomas Pettigrew, *A Profile of the Negro American* (Princeton: Van Nostrand, 1964); and William H. Grier and Price M. Cobbs, *Black Rage* (New York: Bantam Books, 1968). See also the invaluable anthology of challenges to Elkins's controversial thesis in Ann J. Lane, ed., *The Debate over Slavery: Stanley Elkins and His Critics* (Urbana: University of Illinois Press, 1971).

55. John W. Roberts, *From Trickster to Badman: The Black Folk Hero in Slavery and Freedom* (Philadelphia: University of Pennsylvania Press, 1989), p. 14.

56. On the migration of blacks to Northern cities and the impact of urbanization, see Arna Bontemps and Jack Conroy, *Anyplace but Here* (New York: Hill and Wang, 1966); Claude McKay, *Harlem: Negro Metropolis* (1940; rpt. New York: Harvest Books, 1968); Roi Ottley and William J. Weatherby, *The Negro in New York: An Informal Social History, 1626–1940* (New York: Praeger, 1969); Richard Wright, *Twelve Million Black Voices: A Folk History of the Negro in the United States* (New York: Viking Press, 1941); and St. Clair Drake and Horace R. Cayton, *Black Metropolis: A Study of Negro Life in a Northern City*, rev. ed., 2 vols. (New York: Harbinger Books, 1962).

57. William A. Stewart, "Sociolinguistic Factors in the History of American Negro Dialects," *Florida Foreign Language Reporter* 5 (1967): 11–29; and Dillard, *Black English*, pp.73–185. See also Hymes, *Pidginization and Creolization of Languages*.

58. A useful cultural history that examines black minstrelsy in the 1920s is Nathan I. Huggins, *Harlem Renaissance* (New York: Oxford University Press, 1971). The standard works are Carl Wittke, *Tambo and Bones: A History of the American Minstrel Stage* (1930; rpt. Westport, Conn.: Greenwood Press, 1968); Hans Nathan, *Dan Emmett and the Rise of Early Negro Minstrelsy* (Norman: University of Oklahoma Press, 1962); and Robert C. Toll, *Blacking Up: The Minstrel Show in Nineteenth-Century America* (New York: Oxford University Press, 1974). For varieties of black speech, see Thomas Kochman, ed., *Rappin' and Stylin' Out: Communication in Urban Black America* (Urbana: University of Illinois Press, 1972); Langston Hughes and Arna Bontemps, eds., *The Book of Negro Folklore* (New York: Dodd, Mead, 1958), pp. 477–97; John Dollard, "The Dozens: The Dialect of Insult," *American Imago* 1 (1939): 3–25; and Roger D. Abrahams, "Playing the Dozens," *Journal of American Folklore* 75 (1962): 209–20.

59. Ellison, "The World and the Jug," *Shadow and Act*, pp. 136–37. See also Levine, *Black Culture and Black Consciousness*, pp. 5–55; and the exchange on the relationship of folklore to literature: Stanley E. Hyman and Ralph Ellison, "The Negro Writer in America: An Exchange," *Partisan Review* 25 (Spring 1958): 197–222.

60. Ellison, *Shadow and Act*, p. 172.

61. Constance Rourke, *American Humor: A Study of the National Character* (New York: Harcourt, Brace, 1931), pp. 88–89.

62. See, for example, Michael Kammen, *People of Paradox: An Inquiry Concerning the*

Origins of American Civilization (New York: Alfred A. Knopf, 1972), esp. chap. 4. According to Kammen and Huggins, as Ostendorf notes, "everyone, white or black, was socialized into a pervasive national ambivalence, due to the 'biformity' or 'split nature' of the American 'national style.' This integrationist gesture, which forces a variety of socio-cultural conflicts into an all-American norm and which domesticates current anxieties by americanizing their genesis, belittles the 'wounds' of socialization and embezzles the 'bow' of black cultural resources. Black double consciousness is more than an existential constant; it has both a deeper historical and anthropological dimension, the first defined by slavery and segregation along a color line, the second by African cultural retentions" (Ostendorf, *Black Literature in White America*, p. 19).

63. See Ellison, *Shadow and Act*, pp. 39–40, 42–43, and 136–37; and George E. Kent, "Ethnic Impact in American Literature: Reflections on a Course," *College Language Association Journal* 11 (September 1967): 24–37.

64. Williams, *Marxism and Literature*, p. 121.

65. For an exegesis of the history of the word and the tyranny of print in the Judeo-Christian tradition, see Walter J. Ong, *The Presence of the Word: Some Prolegomena for Cultural and Religious History* (New Haven: Yale University Press, 1967); and Marshall McLuhan, *The Gutenberg Galaxy: The Making of Typographic Man* (1962; rpt. New York: Signet Books, 1969).

66. Williams, *Marxism and Literature*, p. 122.

67. F. O. Matthiessen, *American Renaissance: Art and Expression in the Age of Emerson and Whitman* (1941; rpt. New York: Oxford University Press, 1979), p. 18.

68. Roger D. Abrahams, *Deep Down in the Jungle: Negro Narrative Folklore from the Streets of Philadelphia*, rev. ed. (Chicago: Aldine, 1979); and *Positively Black* (Englewood Cliffs: Prentice-Hall, 1970).

69. Abrahams, *Deep Down in the Jungle*, p. 97.

70. Bruce Rosenberg, *The Art of the American Folk Preacher* (New York: Oxford University Press, 1970), pp. 5, 10, 53.

71. Henry H. Mitchell, *Black Preaching* (New York: J. B. Lippincott, 1970), p. 167.

72. According to black theologian Benjamin E. Mays, "the ideas of God in Negro literature are developed along three principal lines: (1) Ideas of God that are used to support or give adherence to traditional, compensatory patterns; (2) Ideas, whether traditional or otherwise, that are developed and interpreted to support a growing consciousness of social and psychological adjustment needed; (3) Ideas of God that show a tendency or threat to abandon the idea of God as a 'useful instrument' in perfecting social change." See *The Negro's God as Reflected in His Literature* (1938; rpt. New York: Atheneum, 1968), p. 245.

73. George Pryor, *Neither Bond Nor Free (A Plea)* (New York: J. S. Oglive, 1902). The title of the novel is borrowed from Gal. 3:28.

74. Martin Delany, *Blake; or The Huts of America* (Boston: Beacon Press, 1970), p. 21.

75. Hopkins, *Contending Forces*, p. 87; and Delany, *Blake*, p. 313.

76. Ellison, *Shadow and Act*, p. 175.

77. Charles Chesnutt, *The House behind the Cedars*, (1900; rpt. New York: Collier Books, 1969), p. 163.

78. The tragedy of Nat Turner's rebellion was fictionalized by William Styron, a white Southern novelist, as a "meditation on history." Despite the criticism of many black read-

ers that Styron manipulated history to perpetuate stereotypes of African American character, the book was awarded the Pulitzer Prize in 1968. See *The Confessions of Nat Turner* (New York: Random House, 1967). For the reaction of some black scholars and critics, see John Henrik Clark, ed., *William Styron's Nat Turner: Ten Black Writers Respond* (Boston: Beacon Press, 1968); and Bernard W. Bell, "Styron's Confessions," *Michigan Quarterly Review* 7 (Fall 1968): 280–82.

79. Delany, *Blake*, p. 91.

80. Margaret Walker, *Jubilee* (1966; rpt. New York: Bantam Books, 1967), pp. 363–64.

81. See Ellison, *Shadow and Act*, pp. 78–79.

82. Hopkins, *Contending Forces*, p. 13.

83. For a useful description of the Brown lectures and those by William and Ellen Craft, see Williams E. Farrison, *William Wells Brown: Author and Reformer* (Chicago: University of Chicago Press, 1969), pp. 136–37.

84. See Frederick Douglass, *Narrative of the Life of Frederick Douglass: An American Slave*, ed. Benjamin Quarles (Cambridge: Belknap Press, 1967); Gilbert Osofsky, ed., *Puttin' on Ole Massa: The Slave Narratives of Henry Bibb, William Wells Brown, and Solomon Northup* (New York: Harper Torchbooks, 1969); Arna Bontemps, ed., *Great Slave Narratives* (Boston: Beacon Press, 1969); and William Loren Katz, ed., *Five Slave Narratives* (New York: Arno Press and *The New York Times*, 1969). See also Charles Nichols, *Many Thousand Gone: The Ex-Slaves' Account of Their Bondage and Freedom* (1963; rpt. Bloomington: Indiana University Press, 1969); George P. Rawick, *The American Slave: A Composite Autobiography*, 19 vols. *From Sundown to Sunup: The Making of the Black Community*, 1 (Amherst: University of Massachusetts Press, 1974); and Frances Smith Foster, *Witnessing Slavery: The Development of Ante-Bellum Slave Narratives* (Westport, Conn.: Greenwood Press, 1979).

85. Charles Sumner, *The Liberator*, October 22, 1852; quoted in Osofsky, *Puttin' on Ole Massa*, p. 29.

86. Jean Toomer, *Cane* (1923; rpt. New York: Perennial Classics, 1969) p. 199.

87. The subsequent information is condensed from the following sources: James Hastings, ed., *A Dictionary of the Bible*, 5 vols. (New York: Charles Scribner's Sons, 1908), 1:. 734–57; "Eschatology," *Encyclopedia Britannica* (1965), 8: 694–97; John S. Mibiti, *African Religions and Philosophy* (Garden City: Anchor Books, 1970), pp. 1–119, 195–216, 266–81, and 299–342; E. Franklin Frazier, *The Negro Church in America* (New York: Oxford University Press, 1970), pp. 62–85; and Mays, *Negro's God*, pp. 245–55.

88. James H. W. Howard, *Bond and Free: A True Tale of Slave Times* (1886; rpt. Miami: Mnemosyne, 1969), pp. 24–25.

89. Paul Laurence Dunbar, *The Sport of the Gods* (1902; rpt. Miami: Mnemosyne, 1969), p. 150. Subsequent references to this novel will be in the text.

90. Ralph Ellison, *Invisible Man* (1952; rpt. New York: Signet Books, 1964), p. 326. Subsequent references to this novel will be in the text.

91. See Charles W. Chesnutt, "Superstitions and Folklore of the South," *Modern Culture* 13 (1901): 231–35; rpt. in Dundes, *Mother Wit*, pp. 369–76. As this article and his short stories illustrate, Chesnutt was not only a talented novelist but also, even though not formally trained in the discipline like Hurston, a serious, sensitive student of folklore.

92. William Wells Brown, *Clotel; or The President's Daughter: A Narrative of Slave Life in the United States* (1853; rpt. New York: Collier Books, 1970), p. 155. Subsequent references to this novel will be in the text.

93. A notable exception is Jean Fagan Yellin, *The Intricate Knot: Black Figures in American Literature, 1776–1863* (New York: New York University Press, 1972), pp. 172–77.

94. David Grimstead, "Melodrama as Echo of the Historically Voiceless," in *Anonymous Americans*, ed. Tamara K. Hareven (Englewood Cliffs: Prentice-Hall, 1971), pp. 82–83.

95. Grimstead, "Melodrama as Echo," p. 87.

96. Frances E. W. Harper, *Iola Leroy; or Shadows Uplifted* (Boston: James H. Earle, 1892), p. 223. Subsequent references to this novel will be in the text.

97. Pryor, *Neither Bond Nor Free*, p. 81.

3. *Mapping the Peaks and Valleys (1853–1962)*

1. Brown wrote three revisions of *Clotel* for American publication, each time changing titles, plot details, and the names of characters. *Miralda; or, The Beautiful Quadroon: A Romance of American Slavery Founded on Fact* appeared as a serial in the *Weekly Anglo-African* during the winter of 1860–61. The second version, *Clotelle: A Tale of the Southern States*, was published in 1864, and the final American edition, *Clotelle; or, The Colored Heroine: A Tale of the Southern States*, in 1867. For a reprint of the 1864 edition and an excellent introduction, see J. Noel Heermance, *William Wells Brown and Clotelle: A Portrait of the Artist in the First Negro Novel* (Hamden, Conn.: Archon Books, 1969). Less perceptive and reliable are the introductions to reprints of *Blake* and *Clotelle* in Ronald T. Takaki, ed., *Violence in the Black Imagination: Essays and Documents* (New York: Putnam, 1972).

2. See David Walker, "Walker's Appeal in Four Articles: Together with a Preamble, to the Coloured Citizens of the World, . . ." and Henry Highland Garnet, "An Address to the Slaves of the United States" in *A Documentary History of the Negro People in the United States*, ed. Aptheker, 1: 93–97, 226–33.

3. Frances Smith Foster, "Introduction," to *Minnie's Sacrifice/Sowing and Reaping /Trial and Triumph: Three Rediscovered Novels by Frances E. W. Harper*, ed. Frances Smith Foster (Boston: Beacon Press, 1994), pp. xi–xii.

4. Howard, *Bond and Free*, pp. 3–4.

5. "I have nothing to commend me to your consideration in the way of learning, nothing in the way of education to entitle me to your attention," Douglass would say in his opening remarks to white audiences. "But I will take it for granted that you know something about the degrading influences of slavery, and that you will not expect great things from me this evening, but simply facts as I may be able to advance immediately in connection with my own experience of slavery." This mock apology became an effective prefacing device for fugitive orators and early novelists. Quoted in Heermance, *William Wells Brown*, p. 44.

6. Walter H. Stowers and William H. Anderson [Sanda, pseud.], *Appointed; an American Novel* (Detroit: Detroit Law, 1894), p. 270.

7. Vernon L. Parrington, *Main Currents in American Thought: The Beginnings of Critical Realism in America 1860–1920*, (New York: Harbinger Books, 1930), 3: 346.

8. Franklin, *From Slavery to Freedom*, pp. 294–95.

9. Between 1882 and 1927, 4,951 people were lynched in the United States. Of the victims 3,513 were black and 1,438 were white; 76 black women and 16 white women are included in these numbers. "The number of victims each year has sharply decreased, but

the savagery with which the smaller number of victims are tortured by American mobs is proportionately greater than at the turn of the century. From the days when one John Malcolm was 'genteely Tarr'd and Feather'd' at Pownalborough, Massachusetts, in 1773, mobbism has inevitably degenerated to the point where an uncomfortably large percentage of American citizens can read in their newspapers of the slow roasting alive of a human being in Mississippi and turn, promptly and with little thought, to the comic strip or sporting page. Thus has lynching become an almost integral part of our national folkways." Walter Francis White, *Rope and Faggot: A Biography of Judge Lynch* (1929; rpt. New York: Arno Press and *The New York Times*, 1969), pp. ix–x; see also pp. 227–69.

10. Quoted in Franklin, *From Slavery to Freedom*, p. 334.

11. Leslie Fiedler, *Love and Death in the American Novel*, rev. ed. (New York: Delta Books, 1966), p. 29.

12. See Fiedler, *Love and Death*, pp. 23–38; and Edwin M. Eigner, *The Metaphysical Novel in England and America: Dickens, Bulwer, Melville, and Hawthorne* (Berkeley: University of California Press, 1978), pp. 1–13.

13. Richard Chase, *The American Novel and Its Tradition* (Garden City, N.Y.: Doubleday, 1957), p. 20.

14. Fiedler, *Love and Death*, pp. 28–29.

15. George Levine, *The Realistic Imagination: English Fiction from Frankenstein to Lady Chatterley* (Chicago: University of Chicago Press, 1980), pp. 8, 20–21.

16. George Becker, "Introduction: Modern Realism as a Literary Movement," in *Documents of Modern Literary Realism*, ed. Becker (Princeton: Princeton University Press, 1963), p. 35.

17. Charles C. Walcutt, *American Literary Naturalism: A Divided Stream* (Minnesota: University of Minnesota Press, 1956), pp. vii–viii, 20–23.

18. Donald Pizer, *Twentieth-Century American Literary Naturalism: An Interpretation* (Carbondale: Southern Illinois University Press, 1982), pp. xi, 8–9.

19. Brent Staples, "Unearthing a Riot," *New York Times Magazine*, December 19, 1999, p. 64. See also "Tulsa Burning," *60 Minutes II* news segment online summary, aired July 10, 2001, accessed July 12, 2001, http://cbsnews.com/now/story/0,1597,69603-412,00.shtml.

20. Arna Bontemps, in "Introduction" to *Cane*, by Toomer, p. x. The first flowering of African American literature occurs in the antebellum slave narratives of Douglass and Brown, and culminates in the 1890s poetry, fiction, and essays of Dunbar, Chesnutt, and Du Bois. The seeds of the Harlem Renaissance, according to Bontemps, were planted in 1917 with the publication of McKay's "Harlem Dancer" and Johnson's *50 Years and Other Poems*. See "The Black Renaissance of the Twenties," *Black World*, November 1970, p. 7.

21. There were actually six international Pan-African meetings. The first was organized by Henry S. Williams, a Trinidad lawyer, in 1900, and the sixth was convened by George Padmore, also from Trinidad, and Du Bois in 1945. Because the first meeting was called a "Conference" and the subsequent meetings "Congresses," some students of pan-Africanism do not include it in their discussions. Richard B. Moore, "Du Bois and Pan Africa," *Freedomways*, First Quarter 1965, pp. 166–87.

22. See W. E. B. Du Bois, *The Negro and The Gift of Black Folk: The Negroes in the Making of America* (Boston: Stratford, 1924); and Carter G. Woodson, *The Negro in Our History* (Washington, D.C.: Associated Publishers, 1922).

23. Robert Hayden, Preface, *The New Negro*, ed. Alain Locke (1925; rpt. New York: Atheneum, 1968), p. ix.

24. I am indebted to Professors Richard Long and Wilfred Cartey for this concept. But I have expanded and radically modified it. See Richard Long, "Alain Locke: Cultural and Social Mentor," *Black World*, November 1970, pp. 87–90; and Wilfred Cartey, Introduction, *Negritude: Black Poetry from Africa and the Caribbean*, ed. and trans. Norman R. Shapiro (New York: October House, 1970), pp. 17–37.

25. Langston Hughes, "The Negro Artist and the Racial Mountain," *Nation*, June 23, 1926, p. 694.

26. Locke, *New Negro*, p. 47.

27. See Edmund D. Cronon, *Black Moses: The Story of Marcus Garvey and the Universal Negro Improvement Association* (1955; rpt. Madison: University of Wisconsin Press, 1968); Amy Jacques-Garvey, *Garvey and Garveyism* (New York: Collier Books, 1970); and *Philosophy and Opinions of Marcus Garvey*, ed. Amy Jacques-Garvey (New York: Atheneum, 1970).

28. In this sense, whether black, white, yellow, or brown, we are all peoples of African descent. See for example, L.S.B. Leakey, *The Progress and Evolution of Man in Africa* (New York: Oxford University Press, 1961), pp. 1–3; Robert W. July, *A History of the African People* (New York: Scribner and Sons, 1970), pp. 8–10; and John G. Jackson, *Introduction to African Civilizations* (New York: University Books, 1970), pp. 40–50.

29. Locke, *New Negro*, pp. 14–15, 12.

30. Silberman, *Crisis in Black and White*, p. 165.

31. Kenneth B. Clark, *Dark Ghetto: Dilemmas of Social Power* (New York: Harper Torchbooks, 1967).

32. Toomer, McKay, Hughes, Cullen, Bontemps, Hurston, Fauset, Larsen and most of the younger New Negroes attended college, and their parents were "55 percent professionals and 45 percent white collar" (Bone, *Negro Novel*, p. 56 n. 5).

33. W. E. B. Du Bois, "Review of *Nigger Heaven*," in Carl Van Vechten, *Nigger Heaven* (1926; rpt. New York: Harper Colophon, 1971), p. ix.

34. Van Vechten, *Nigger Heaven*, pp. 89–90, 281.

35. V. Y. Mudimbe, *The Idea of Africa* (Bloomington: Indiana University Press, 1994), p. 27.

36. See, for example, James Weldon Johnson, "Dilemma of the Negro Author," *American Mercury*, December 1928, p. 480.

37. Jahn, *Neo-African Literature;* pp. 15–24; and Robert A. Bone, *Down Home: A History of Afro-American Short Fiction from Its Beginnings to the End of the Harlem Renaissance* (New York: Capricorn Books, 1975), pp. xiii–xxii.

38. For intriguing modern studies of this topic, see Raymond Williams, *The Country and the City* (New York: Oxford University Press, 1973); Leo Marx, *The Machine in the Garden: Technology and the Pastoral Idea in America* (1964; rpt. New York: Galaxy, 1967); and Bone, *Down Home*.

39. Senghor, quoted in Abraham Chapman, "The Harlem Renaissance in Literary History," *College Language Association Journal* 15 (September 1967): 57 n. 31.

40. See Carla Kaplan, ed., *Zora Neale Hurston: A Life in Letters* (New York: Doubleday, 2002), p. 37.

41. Langston Hughes, *The Big Sea* (1940; rpt. New York: Hill and Wang, 1968), p. 228.

42. Bone is in error when he writes: "Satire as a literary attitude was out of the question for the early Negro novelist. The social struggle in which he was engaged was too compelling, and humor too keen a blade for his blunt needs. Self-satire, moreover, could hardly be expected of those whose first impulse was to defend their race against the slanderous attacks of white authors" (Bone, *Negro Novel*, p. 89).

43. Robert C. Elliott, *The Power of Satire: Magic, Ritual, Art* (Princeton: Princeton University Press, 1969). See also Ronald Paulsen, *Satire and the Novel in Eighteenth-Century England* (New Haven: Yale University Press, 1967), pp. 11–22.

44. Elliott, *Power of Satire*, pp. 14–15.

45. Okpewho, *African Oral Literature*, p. 118.

46. For an illuminating analysis of this controversial theory, see Gerhart Piers and Milton B. Singer, *Shame and Guilt: A Psychoanalytic and A Cultural Study* (Springfield, Ill.: Charles C. Thomas, 1953). See also Ruth Benedict, *The Chrysanthemum and the Sword* (Boston: Houghton Mifflin, 1946), pp. 222–24.

47. Wayne C. Booth, *A Rhetoric of Irony* (Chicago: University of Chicago Press, 1974), pp. 240–41.

48. S. P. Fullinwider, *The Mind and Mood of Black America: 20th Century Thought* (Homewood, Ill.: Dorsey Press, 1969), p. 172.

49. Richard Wright, Introduction to St. Clair Drake and Horace Cayton, *Black Metropolis: A Study of Negro Life in a Northern City* (New York: Harcourt, Brace and World, 1945), p. xviii.

50. Citing the work of Alfred Adler, Park was perhaps the first to develop the theory that feelings of inferiority are related to the pathological behavior that results from a disorganized community. Robert E. Park, "Community Organization and Juvenile Delinquency," in Park, Ernest W. Burgess, and Roderick D. McKenzie, *The City* (Chicago: University of Chicago Press, 1925), pp. 99–112. According to Park's theory of "social disorganization," the impersonal, industrial life of the city breaks down the community mores of transplanted migrants and ethnic minorities. With the breakdown of the family unit, the most important social structure for controlling interpersonal relationships, the usual result is antisocial behavior on the part of the individual. Another key concept developed by Park involves the man caught between two cultures, the "marginal man." Unlike Du Bois's concept of double consciousness, which stresses cultural fusion as well as conflict as the common fate of African Americans, Park's concept of marginal man refers to the conflict of cultures and social roles of only mulattoes, racial hybrids. Drawing on Park and others, Everett V. Stonequist defines the marginal man as "the individual who through migration, education, marriage, or some other influence leaves one social group or culture without making a satisfactory adjustment to another [and] finds himself on the margin of each but a member of neither." See Robert E. Park "Mentality of Racial Hybrids," *American Journal of Sociology* 36 (January 1931): 534–51; and Everett V. Stonequist, *The Marginal Man: A Study in Personality and Culture Conflict* (New York: Charles Scribner's Sons, 1937), pp. 2–3. See also Robert E. Park and Ernest W. Burgess, *Introduction to the Science of Sociology* (Chicago: University of Chicago Press, 1921); Robert Redfield, *Tepoztlan* (Chicago: University of Chicago Press, 1930); and Louis Wirth, *The Ghetto* (Chicago: University of Chicago Press, 1928). For a highly informative discussion of the "Chicago School," see Fullinwider, *Mind and Mood of Black America*, pp. 72–122.

51. Herbert Hill, "Reflections on Richard Wright: A Symposium on an Exiled Native Son," in *Anger, and Beyond: The Negro Writer in the United States,* ed. Hill (1966; rpt. New York: Perennial Library, 1968), p. 197.

52. Raymond Wolters, *Negroes and the Great Depression: The Problem of Economic Recovery* (Westport, Conn.: Greenwood Press, 1970), pp. 3, 83.

53. Wolters, *Negroes and the Great Depression,* pp. 8, xi–xiii.

54. Wilson Record, *The Negro and the Communist Party* (1951; rpt. New York: Atheneum, 1971), pp. 25–26.

55. Michel Fabre, *The Unfinished Quest of Richard Wright,* trans. Isabel Barzun (New York: William Morrow, 1973), p. 103. Wright's early Communist affiliation was mainly responsible for his surveillance and harassment by the FBI, the CIA, and the State Department, an ordeal that Addison Gayle believes probably contributed to the anxiety and stress responsible for his sudden death in a French clinic. Addison Gayle Jr., *Richard Wright: Ordeal of a Native Son* (Garden City, N.Y.: Doubleday Anchor Books, 1980), pp. x–xv, chaps. 16 and 17.

56. Richard Crossman, ed., *The God That Failed* (1950; rpt. New York: Bantam Matrix, 1965), pp. 106, 107–8.

57. Harvey Swados, ed., *The American Writer and the Great Depression* (New York: Bobbs-Merrill, 1966), pp. xi–xxxvi; Norman R. Yetman, ed., *Life under the "Peculiar Institution": Selections from the Slave Narrative Collection* (New York: Holt, Rinehart and Winston, 1970), pp. 339–55; and Bone, *Negro Novel,* pp. 113–14.

58. The novels published in the forties by Micheaux and Yerby are not discussed because both authors are unique cases. Both were influenced by pulp and historical fiction, but whereas Micheaux displays more creative imagination as a filmmaker than as a novelist and published his novels through his own company, Yerby was a highly talented and popular creator of historical romances with white heroes that were primarily designed for pure entertainment. His first novel with a black protagonist, *Speak Now,* was not published until 1970. See Carl Milton Hughes, *The Negro Novelist: A Discussion of Writing of American Negro Novelists, 1940–1950* (1953; rpt. New York: Citadel Press, 1979), pp. 130–33, 149–59.

59. C. Hughes, *Negro Novelist,* p. 252.

60. Franklin, *From Slavery to Freedom,* p. 464.

61. Franklin, *From Slavery to Freedom,* p. 477.

62. C. Hughes, *Negro Novelist,* p. 20.

63. William G. Smith, *Anger at Innocence* (1950; rpt. Chatham, N.J.: Chatham Bookseller, 1973), p. 273.

64. William Demby, *Beetlecreek* (1950; rpt. New York: Avon Books, 1967), p. 46.

65. Demby, *Beetlecreek,* p. 148.

66. C. Hughes, *Negro Novelist,* p. 20.

67. Richard Wright, *The Outsider* (1953; rpt. New York: Perennial Library, 1965), pp. 128–36.

68. Gwendolyn Brooks, *Maude Martha* (1953); rpt. in *The World of Gwendolyn Brooks* (New York: Harper and Row, 1971), pp. 128, 305.

69. Ellison, *Shadow and Act,* pp. 174–75.

4. *Forms of Neorealism (1962–1983)*

1. Stokely Carmichael and Charles V. Hamilton, *Black Power: The Politics of Liberation in America* (New York: Vintage Books, 1967), p. 44.

2. John H. Bracey Jr., "Black Nationalism since Garvey," in *Key Issues in the Afro-American Experience*, ed. Huggins, Kilson, and Fox, 2: 266–67.

3. Cruse, *Rebellion or Revolution?*, pp. 75–77.

4. Larry Neal, "The Black Arts Movement," in *The Black Aesthetic*, ed. Addison Gayle Jr. (1971; rpt. Garden City, N.Y.: Anchor Books, 1972), p. 257.

5. Neal, "The Black Arts Movement," p. 257.

6. Larry Neal, "And Shine Swam On," in *Black Fire*, ed. Jones and Neal, pp. 643–48.

7. Betty Friedan, *The Feminine Mystique* (New York: Dell Books, 1975), p. 85.

8. bell hooks, *Ain't I a Woman: Black Women and Feminism* (Boston: South End Press, 1981), p. 4.

9. Gerda Lerner, ed., *Black Women in White America: A Documentary History* (New York: Vintage Books, 1973), p. xxv. See also hooks, *Ain't I a Woman*, pp. 119–96.

10. Toni Cade, "On the Issue of Roles," in *The Black Woman: An Anthology*, ed. Cade (New York: Signet Books, 1970), pp. 103–4.

11. Lee Rainwater and William L. Yancey, *The Moynihan Report and the Politics of Controversy* (Cambridge: MIT Press, 1967), pp. 1–45.

12. Joyce A. Ladner, *Tomorrow's Tomorrow: The Black Woman* (Garden City, N.Y.: Anchor Books, 1972), pp. 15–54. See also Collins, *Black Feminist Thought*, pp. 70–78.

13. Combahee River Collective, "Black Feminist Statement," in *All the Women Are White, All the Blacks Are Men, But Some of Us Are Brave*, ed. Gloria T. Hull, Patricia Bell Scott, and Barbara Smith (Old Westbury, N.Y.: Feminist Press, 1982), p. 15.

14. Combahee River Collective, "Black Feminist Statement," p. 15.

15. Toni Cade Bambara, cited in *Black Women Writers at Work*, ed. Claudia Tate (New York: Continuum, 1983), p. 34.

16. Alice Walker, *In Search of Our Mothers' Gardens: Womanist Prose* (New York: Harvest/HBJ Books, 1984), p. xi.

17. Calvin Hernton, "The Sexual Mountain and Black Women Writers," *Black American Literature Forum* 18 (Winter 1984): 139.

18. See Sterling A. Brown, *Negro Poetry and Drama and The Negro in American Fiction* (New York: Atheneum, 1969); Countee Cullen, ed., *Caroling Dusk: An Anthology of Verse by Negro Poets* (New York: Harper and Brothers, 1927); and James Weldon Johnson, ed., *The Book of American Negro Poetry*, rev. ed., (New York: Harbrace Paperbound Library, 1959).

19. Andrea Benton Rushing: "Images of Black Women in Afro-American Poetry," in *The Afro-American Woman: Struggles and Images*, ed. Sharon Harley and Rosalyn Terborg-Penn (Port Washington, N.Y.: Kennikat, 1978), pp. 74–84; "Images of Black Women in Modern African Poetry: An Overview," in *Sturdy Black Bridges: Visions of Black Women in Literature*, ed. Roseanne P. Bell, Bettye J. Parker, and Beverly Guy-Sheftall (Garden City, N.Y.: Anchor Books, 1979), pp. 18–24; and "Family Resemblances: A Comparative Study of Women Protagonists in Contemporary African-American and Anglophone-African Novels" (Ph.D. diss., University of Massachusetts, Amherst, 1983).

20. Barbara Smith, "Toward a Black Feminist Criticism," in *The New Feminist Criticism: Essays on Women, Literature, and Theory*, ed. Elaine Showalter (New York: Pantheon Books,

1985), pp. 168–85; and Deborah E. McDowell, "New Directions for Black Feminist Criticism," in *The New Feminist Criticism*, ed. Showalter, pp. 186–99.

21. McDowell, "New Directions for Black Feminist Criticism," pp. 190–95.

22. Bambara, *Black Women Writers at Work*, pp. 19–20.

23. Mary Helen Washington, ed., *Midnight Birds: Stories of Contemporary Black Women Writers* (Garden City, N.Y.: Anchor Books, 1980), p. xvi.

24. Georg Lukács, *Realism in Our Time: Literature and the Class Struggle*, trans. John Mander and Necke Mander (1963; rpt. New York: Harper Torchbooks, 1971), p. 93.

25. Eagleton, *Literary Theory*, p. 208.

26. Lukács, *Realism in Our Time*, p. 94.

27. Lukács, *Realism in Our Time* pp. 93, 94. Emphasis in original.

28. John O. Killens, quoted in Harold Cruse, *The Crisis of the Negro Intellectual* (1967; rpt. New York: Apollo Editions, 1968), p. 235. Cruse's critique of the failure of the Harlem Left is highly informative despite his personal attacks on individuals. On Killens, see pp. 206–52.

29. John O. Killens, "The Black Writer vis-à-vis His Country," in his *Black Man's Burden* (New York: Trident Press, 1965), pp. 34, 31.

30. Addison Gayle Jr., *The Way of the New World: The Black Novel in America* (Garden City, N.Y.: Anchor Books, 1975), p. 276.

31. John O. Killens, *Youngblood* (1954; rpt. New York: Pocket Books, 1955), p. 9.

32. John O. Killens, *And Then We Heard the Thunder* (1963; rpt. New York: Pocket Books, 1964), p. 496. Subsequent references to this novel will be in the text.

33. John O. Killens, *'Sippi* (New York: Trident Press, 1967), p. xiii. For an informative discussion on Killens's use of folklore, see William H. Wiggins Jr., "Black Folktales in the Novels of John O. Killens," *Black Scholar: Journal of Black Studies and Research* 3 (November 1971): 50–58.

34. John O. Killens, *The Cotillion; or One Good Bull Is Half the Herd* (New York: Pocket Books, 1972), p. 171. Subsequent references to this novel will be in the text.

35. John A. Williams, "Career by Accident," in his *Flashbacks: A Twenty-Year Diary of Article Writing* (Garden City, N.Y.: Anchor Press/Doubleday, 1973), p. 394.

36. John A. Williams quoted in John O'Brien, ed., *Interviews with Black Writers* (New York: Liveright, 1973), p. 230.

37. John A. Williams, "John A. Williams," *Contemporary Authors Autobiography Series*, Vol. 3, ed. Adele Sarkissian (Detroit: Gale Research Co., 1986), p. 432.

38. John O'Brien, "Seeking a Humanist Level: Interview with John A. Williams," *The Humanist Alternative* (Spring–Summer 1973): 95.

39. John A. Williams, *Night Song* (1961, *Sweet Love Bitter;* rpt. New York: Pocket Books, 1970), p. 41. Subsequent references to this novel will be in the text.

40. John A. Williams, *The Man Who Cried I Am* (1967; rpt. New York: Signet Books, 1968), p. 308. Subsequent references to this novel will be in the text.

41. "Nobody has really influenced me," Williams tells an interviewer. "This is because I read without discrimination when I was a great deal younger. In terms of form, my single influence has been Malcolm Lowry in *Under the Volcano.* I tried to emulate him in *Sissie* and improve on what he did with the telescoping of time. But I think I did it much better in *The Man Who Cried I Am*" (O'Brien, *Interviews*, pp. 233, 230).

42. O'Brien, *Interviews*, p. 187.

43. O'Brien, *Interviews*, pp. 192, 193.

44. Alice Walker, *The Third Life of Grange Copeland* (1970; rpt. New York: Avon Books, 1971), p. 12. Subsequent references to this novel will be in the text.

45. Alice Walker, *Meridian* (New York: Harcourt Brace Jovanovich, 1976), p. 167. Subsequent references to this novel will be in the text.

46. Alice Walker, *The Color Purple* (New York: Harcourt Brace Jovanovich, 1982), p. 167. Subsequent references to this novel will be in the text.

47. Trudier Harris, "On *The Color Purple,* Stereotypes, and Silence," *Black American Literature Forum* 18 (Winter 1984): 157.

48. "Interview: Gayl Jones and Michael S. Harper," *Chant of Saints: A Gathering of Afro-American Literature, Art, and Scholarship*, ed. Michael S. Harper and Robert B. Stepto (Urbana: University of Illinois Press, 1979), pp. 352–75.

49. Michael Harper, "Gayl Jones: An Interview," *Massachusetts Review* 18 (Winter 1977): 692–715.

50. Rick Bragg, "Author's Downward Spin Rivals Tragedies in Her Novels of Black America," *New York Times*, March 2, 1998, p. A11.

51. John Edgar Wideman, "Frame and Dialect: The Evolution of the Black Voice in Fiction," *American Poetry Review* 5 (1976): 36.

52. Quoted in Veronica Chambers, "The Invisible Woman Reappears—Sort Of," *Newsweek*, February 16, 1998, p. 68.

53. Gayl Jones, *Mosquito* (Boston: Beacon Press, 1999), p. 433. Subsequent references to this novel will be in the text.

54. Gayl Jones, *The Healing* (Boston: Beacon Press, 1998), p. 148. Subsequent references to this novel will be in the text.

55. Louis Massiah, "How She Came by Her Name," in *Deep Sightings and Rescue Missions: Fiction, Essays, and Conversations*, ed. Toni Cade Bambara (New York: Vintage Books, 1999), pp. 205–6.

56. Bell, Parker, and Guy-Sheftall, *Sturdy Black Bridges*, p. 232.

57. Bell, Parker, and Guy-Sheftall, *Sturdy Black Bridges*, p. 234.

58. Bell, Parker, and Guy-Sheftall, *Sturdy Black Bridges*, p. 236.

59. Toni Cade Bambara, *Those Bones Are Not My Child* (New York: Vintage Books, 1999), p. 7.

60. Bambara, *Those Bones Are Not My Child*, p. 517.

61. Toni Cade Bambara, *The Salt Eaters* (New York: Random House, 1980), p. 8. Subsequent references to this novel will be in the text.

62. Ray Brown, ed., *Contemporary Heroes and Heroines* (Detroit: Gale Research Co., 1990), p. 384.

63. Susan Blake, "Toni Morrison," *Dictionary of Literary Biography,* vol. 33: *Afro-American Fiction Writers after 1955*, ed. Thadious M. Davis and Trudier Harris (Detroit: Gale Research Co., 1984), p. 188.

64. Quoted in Brown, *Contemporary Heroes and Heroines*, p. 385.

65. Nellie McKay, "An Interview with Toni Morrison," in *Conversations with Toni Morrison*, ed. Danielle Taylor-Guthrie (Jackson: University Press of Mississippi, 1994), p. 141.

66. Quoted in Brown, *Contemporary Heroes and Heroines*, p. 385.

67. Blake, "Toni Morrison," pp. 187–99.

68. Blake, "Toni Morrison," p. 188.

69. Toni Morrison, "Rootedness: The Ancestor as Foundation," in *Black Women Writers (1950–1980):A Critical Evaluation*, ed. Mari Evans (Garden City, N.Y.: Anchor Books, 1984), p. 341.

70. Morrison, "Rootedness," pp. 341–43.

71. Toni Morrison, *Song of Solomon* (New York: Alfred A. Knopf, 1977), p. 3. Subsequent references to this novel will be in the text.

72. Toni Morrison, *The Bluest Eye* (1970; rpt. New York: Pocket Books, 1972), p. 20.

73. Toni Morrison, *Sula* (New York: Alfred A. Knopf, 1973), pp. 152, 65. Subsequent references to this novel will be in the text.

74. Hoyt W. Fuller, "A Survey: Black Writers' Views on Literary Lions and Values," *Negro Digest* 16 (January 1968): 21.

5. Modernism and Postmodernism (1962–1983)

1. Quoted in Franklin, *From Slavery to Freedom*, p. 482.

2. Blaustein and Zangrando, *Civil Rights and the American Negro*, pp. 559–61.

3. Major sources for the explanation of the terms that follows include M. H. Abrams, *A Glossary of Literary Terms*, 5th ed. (New York: Holt, Rinehart, and Winston, 1985); Jonathan Culler, *Structuralist Poetics: Structuralism, Linguistics, and the Study of Literature* (Ithaca: Cornell University Press, 1976), and *On Deconstruction*; Eagleton, *Literary Theory*; Holman and Harmon, *A Handbook to Literature*; and Hutcheon, *Poetics of Modernism* and *Politics of Modernism*.

4. Paul Gilroy, *Small Acts: Thoughts on the Politics of Black Cultures* (New York: Serpent's Tail, 1993), p. 178.

5. Eagleton, *Literary Theory*, p. 46.

6. Gerald Graff, *Literature against Itself: Literary Ideas in Modern Society* (Chicago: University of Chicago Press, 1979), p. 48.

7. Eagleton, *Literary Theory*, pp. 103 and 91–96,

8. Gérard Genette, *Narrative Discourse: An Essay in Method*, trans. Jane E. Lewin (Ithaca,: Cornell University Press, 1983).

9. Genette, *Narrative Discourse*, p. 18.

10. Quoted in Graff, *Literature against Itself*, p. 19.

11. Eagleton, *Literary Theory*, pp. 115 and 130–145.

12. Hutcheon, *Poetics of Postmodernism*, p. 4.

13. Hutcheon, *Politics of Postmodernism*, p. 1.

14. Lyotard, *The Postmodern Condition*, pp. 37–38.

15. Hutcheon, *Poetics of Postmodernism*, p. 6.

16. While transcendental signifiers include God, Messiah, Spirit, and Soul, examples of moral truths include God is great; Jesus saves; Faith is the answer; Love conquers all; We're all God's children; and We are our brothers' keepers. Syncretistic belief systems and epistemologies in the African diaspora include Conjuring, Hoodoo, Vodun, Santeria, Pocamania, Macumba, and Candomble.

17. hooks, *Yearning*, p. 38.

18. hooks, *Yearning*, pp. 28–29.

19. hooks, *Yearning*, p. 28.

20. Hutcheon, *Politics of Postmodernism*, p. 17.

21. Todorov, "Race, Writing, and Culture," p. 379.

22. Foreword, Lyotard, *The Postmodern Condition*, 1993, p. xii.

23. Hutcheon, *Poetics of Postmodernism*, p. x.

24. Jerome Klinkowitz, *Literary Disruptions: The Making of a Post-Contemporary American Fiction*, 2nd ed. (Urbana: University of Illinois Press, 1980), pp. 3–11.

25. Klinkowitz, *Literary Disruptions*, pp. 175–89.

26. Robert Scholes, *The Fabulators* (New York: Oxford University Press, 1967), p. 12. According to Gregg Lambert, who traces the term to Gilles Deleuze's attribution of it to Bergson, "The concept of 'fabulation' first appears in *Bergsonism* . . . and then disappears almost entirely until it is highlighted in the later writings, particularly in *Cinema 2: The Time-Image* . . . and again in the interviews conducted between 1972 and 1990 that appear in the English edition under the title of *Negotiations* . . . where Deleuze makes the following pronouncement: 'Utopia is not a good concept, but rather a "fabulation" common to people and to art. We should return to the Bergsonian notion of fabulation to provide it with a political sense' . . ." See Gregg Lambert, "On the Uses and Abuses of Literature for Life," in *Deleuze and Literature*, ed. Ian Buchanan and John Marks (Edinburgh: Edinburgh University Press, 2000), pp. 147–48.

27. Nikki Giovanni and Margaret Walker, *A Poetic Equation: Conversations between Nikki Giovanni and Margaret Walker* (Washington, D.C.: Howard University Press, 1974), p. 3.

28. Most biographical sketches erroneously cite 1937 as the year she graduated from Northwestern, but she reveals that it was actually 1935. See Margaret Walker Alexander, "Richard Wright" in *Richard Wright: Impressions and Perspectives*, ed. David Ray and Robert M. Farnsworth (1971; rpt. Ann Arbor: University of Michigan Press, 1973), p. 49.

29. Giovanni and Walker, *Poetic Equation*, pp. 91–92. Margaret Walker, *How I Wrote "Jubilee"* (Chicago: Third World Press, 1972), pp. 13–14.

30. Walker, *How I Wrote "Jubilee,"* p. 11.

31. Walker, *How I Wrote "Jubilee,"* pp. 12, 27.

32. Although Ishmael Reed coined the term "Neo-Slave Narrative" in 1969 to satirize the growing popularity of black confessional autobiographical writing in the 1960s, I adapted the term in 1987 in *The Afro-American Novel and Its Tradition* to classify contemporary hybrid novels influenced by the structure and style of fables, legends, and slave narratives, beginning with Margaret Walker's *Jubilee* (1966). See Ishmael Reed, ed., *19 Necromancers from Now* (New York: Anchor Books, 1970), pp. xv–xvi.

33. Walker, *Jubilee*, p. 13. Subsequent references to this novel will be in the text.

34. Charles Rowell, "Poetry, History, and Humanism: An Interview with Margaret Walker," *Black World* 25, no. 2 (December 1975): 10.

35. Bob Summer, "Ernest J. Gaines," *Publishers Weekly*, May 24, 1993, pp. 62–64.

36. Ruth Laney, "A Conversation with Ernest Gaines," *Southern Review* 10 (January 1974): 3.

37. John O'Brien, *Interviews with Black Writers* (New York: Liveright, 1973), p. 83.

38. Some critics believe that Gaines "succumbs to the power and achievement of Hemingway and Faulkner" in *Catherine Carmier* and *Of Love and Dust*, but achieves his own distinctive style in *Bloodline* and *The Autobiography of Miss Jane Pittman*. See, for example, Jerry Bryant, "From Death to Life: The Fiction of Ernest J. Gaines," *Iowa Review* 3, no. 1 (Winter 1972): 106–20.

39. Laney, "Conversation with Gaines," p. 6.

40. Ernest J. Gaines, *A Lesson before Dying* (New York: Alfred A Knopf, 1993), p. 62. Subsequent references to this novel will be in the text.

41. Summer, "Ernest J. Gaines," p. 64.

42. Ernest J. Gaines, *The Autobiography of Miss Jane Pittman* (1971; rpt. New York: Bantam Books, 1972), p. 228. Subsequent references to this novel will be in the text.

43. O'Brien, *Interviews*, p. 84.

44. William Melvin Kelley, *Dancers on the Shore* (1964; rpt. Chatham, N.J.: Chatham Bookseller, 1973), preface.

45. William Melvin Kelley, quoted in Hoyt W. Fuller, "The Task of the Negro Writer as Artist: A Symposium," *Negro Digest* 14, no. 6, (April 1965): 78.

46. For much of the following discussion of Joycean parallels, I am indebted to Grace Eckley, "The Awakening of Mr. Afrinnegan: Kelley's *Dunfords Travels Everywheres* and Joyce's *Finnegans Wake*," *Obsidian: Black Literature in Review* 1 (Summer 1975): 27–40.

47. William Melvin Kelley, *Dunfords Travels Everywheres* (Garden City, N.Y.: Doubleday, 1970), p. 49. Subsequent references to this novel will be in the text.

48. See Edward O. G. Turville-Petrie, *Myth and Religion of the North: The Religion of Ancient Scandinavia* (New York: Holt, Rinehart, and Winston, 1964); *The Poetic Edda*, 2nd rev. ed., trans. Lee H. Hollander (Austin: University of Texas Press, 1962); *The Prose Edda of Snorri Sturluson; Tales from Norse Mythology*, trans. Jean I. Young (Berkeley: University of California Press, 1973); and Edith Hamilton, *Mythology* (New York: Mentor Books, 1969), pp. 300–315.

49. See *Prose Edda*, pp. 80–86.

50. William Melvin Kelley, *A Different Drummer* (Garden City, N.Y.: Anchor Books, 1969), p. 151. Subsequent references to this novel will be in the text.

51. Ronald L. Fair, *Hog Butcher* (New York: Harcourt, Brace and World, 1966), p. 161.

52. Ronald L. Fair, *Many Thousand Gone* (New York: Harcourt, Brace and World, 1965), pp. 111 and 119.

53. Ronald L. Fair, *World of Nothing: Two Novellas* (New York: Harper and Row, 1970), p. 62. Subsequent references to these novellas will be in the text.

54. O'Brien, *Interviews*, pp. 216, 217.

55. O'Brien, *Interviews*, p. 214.

56. John Edgar Wideman, *A Glance Away* (1967; rpt. Chatham, N.J.: Chatham Bookseller, 1975), p. 54. For an informative analysis of Eliot's influence and the relationship between history and imagination, see Kermit Frazier, "The Novels of John Wideman," *Black World* 24, no. 8 (June 1975):. 18–38.

57. O'Brien, *Interviews*, p. 219.

58. John Edgar Wideman, *Hurry Home* (New York: Harcourt, Brace and World, 1970), p. 33.

59. O'Brien, *Interviews*, p. 220.

60. John Edgar Wideman, *The Lynchers* (1973; rpt. New York: Dell Books. 1974), pp. 114–15. Subsequent references to this novel will be in the text.

61. John Edgar Wideman, *Damballah* (New York: Bard Books. 1981), p. 7. Subsequent references to this book will be in the text.

62. John Edgar Wideman, *Sent for You Yesterday* (New York: Bard Books, 1983), p. 17. Subsequent references to this novel will be in the text.

63. O'Brien, *Interviews*, p. 218.

64. Clarence Major, *The Dark and Feeling: Black American Writers and Their Work* (New York: Third Press, 1974), p. 12.

65. O'Brien, *Interviews*, p. 138.

66. Major, *Dark and Feeling*, p. 150.

67. O'Brien, *Interviews*, p. 127.

68. Klinkowitz, *Literary Disruptions*, pp. 183–85.

69. O'Brien, *Interviews*, p. 130.

70. O'Brien, *Interviews*, p. 126.

71. Clarence Major, *NO* (New York: Emerson Hall, 1973), p. 3.

72. Major, *NO*, pp. 204, 205.

73. O'Brien, *Interviews*, p. 126.

74. Clarence Major, *Emergency Exit* (New York: Fiction Collective, 1979), p. 55.

75. Larry McCaffery and Linda Gregory, "Major's *Reflex and Bone Structure* and the Anti-Detective Tradition," *Black American Literature Forum* 13 (Summer 1979): 39–45.

76. Clarence Major, *Reflex and Bone Structure* (New York: Fiction Collective, 1975), p. 61. Subsequent references to this novel will be in the text.

77. McCaffery and Gregory, "Major's *Reflex and Bone Structure*," p. 40.

78. Major, *Dark and Feeling*, p. 128.

79. Major, *Dark and Feeling*, pp. 24–25.

80. Frank Kermode, *The Sense of an Ending: Studies in the Theory of Fiction* (New York: Oxford University Press, 1967), p. 132.

81. Charles Wright, *The Messenger* (New York: Manor Books, 1974), p. 174. Subsequent references to this novel will be in the text.

82. O'Brien, *Interviews*, p. 250.

83. Charles Wright, *The Wig: A Mirror Image* (New York: Farrar, Straus and Giroux, 1966), p. 13. Subsequent references to this novel will be in the text.

84. One white critic misinterprets this black slang expression or misreads the novel, erroneously stating that "Lester even buys a wig because the salesman guarantees him that it will help" (O'Brien, *Interviews*, p. 246).

85. Victor Navasky, *New York Times*, February 27, 1966, sec. 8, p. 5. See also Max F. Schulz, *Black Humor Fiction of the Sixties: A Pluralistic Definition of Man and His World* (Athens: Ohio University Press, 1973), pp. 99–101, 108–14, 119–22.

86. O'Brien, *Interviews*, pp. 246, 257.

87. Ronald Walcott, "The Novels of Hal Bennett," Part 1, *Black World* 23, no. 8 (June 1974): 37.

88. Hal Bennett, *The Black Wine* (New York: Pyramid Books, 1968), p. 300.

89. Ronald Walcott, "The Novels of Hal Bennett," Part 2, *Black World* 23, no. 9 (July 1974): 79.

90. Hal Bennett, *Wait until Evening* (Garden City, N.Y.: Doubleday, 1974), pp. 250, 256 (italics in the original), 258.

91. Hal Bennett, *Seventh Heaven* (Garden City, N.Y.: Doubleday, 1976), p. 13.

92. Hal Bennett, A *Wilderness of Vines* (New York: Pyramid Books, 1967), p. 85. Subsequent references to this novel will be in the text.

93. Walcott, "Novels," Part 1, p. 48

94. O'Brien, *Interviews*, pp. 167–68. This biographical information was gleaned

mainly from Reginald Martin, "Ishmael Reed," in *Black Writers*, ed. Linda Metzger (Detroit: Gale Research Inc., 1989), pp. 478–84; and Jeffrey Louis Decker, ed., "The Black Aesthetic Movement," in vol. 8 of *Dictionary of Literary Biography Documentary Series*, (Detroit: Gale Research Inc., 1991), pp. 254–312.

95. O'Brien, *Interviews*, p. 167; Reed, *19 Necromancers from Now*, p. xxiv; and Tom Dent, "*Umbra* Days," *Black American Literature Forum* 14 (Fall 1980): 107. The last is a highly informative essay on this generally neglected, historically important group of new black artists. Besides Dent, Hernton, and Henderson, the *Umbra* Workshop included Joe Johnson, Askia Muhammad Toure, Alvin Haynes, Lloyd Addison, Charles Patterson, Lorenzo Thomas, Leroy McLucas, Archie Shepp, Norman Pritchard, Ishmael Reed, Lennox Ralphael, James Thompson, Oliver Pitcher, Art Berger, and Steve Cannon.

96. Reed, *19 Necromancers from Now*, pp. xxiv, xiii.

97. See, for example, Houston Baker Jr., review of *The Last Days of Louisiana Red*, by Ishmael Reed, *Black World* 24, no. 8 (June 1975): 51–52, 89.

98. Ishmael Reed, "Hoodoo Manifesto #2: The Baker-Gayle Fallacy," *Umnum Newsletter* 4, no. 3–4 (1975): 8–11.

99. Ishmael Reed, *Conjure: Selected Poems, 1963–1970* (Amherst: University of Massachusetts Press, 1972), pp. 20–22.

100. Ishmael Reed, *Flight to Canada* (New York: Random House, 1976), p. 88.

101. Ishmael Reed, *The Terrible Threes* (New York: Atheneum, 1989), p. 30.

102. Ishmael Reed, *Japanese by Spring* (New York: Atheneum, 1993), p. 154.

103. Ishmael Reed, *Yellow Back Radio Broke-Down* (Garden City, N.Y.: Doubleday, 1969), p. 128. Subsequent references to this novel will be in the text. See also O'Brien, *Interviews*, p. 172; and Ishmael Reed, "The Writer as Seer: Ishmael Reed on Ishmael Reed," *Black World* 23, no. 8 (June 1974): 25.

104. See, for example, Ron Karenga, "Black Art: A Rhythmic Reality of Revolution," *Negro Digest* 17, no. 3 (January 1968): 5–9.

105. Ishmael Reed, *Mumbo Jumbo* (Garden City, N.Y.: Doubleday, 1972), p. 190. Subsequent references to this novel will be in the text.

106. O'Brien, *Interviews*, pp. 172, 177.

107. O'Brien, *Interviews*, pp. 18–82.

108. O'Brien, *Interviews*, p. 179.

6. Continuity and Change in Ethnic Tropes of Identity Formation (1983–2001)

1. The following sources provided the major facts for this chapter's sociohistorical and sociocultural framework: *The World Almanac and Book of Facts* (Mahwah, N.J.: Almanac Books, 2001), for the years 1984–2001; Lois Gordon and Alan Gordon, *American Chronicles: Year by Year through the Twentieth Century* (New Haven: Yale University Press, 1999).

2. According to the Center for Disease Control, "Women of color—particularly African-American women—bear a disproportional burden of HIV/AIDS in the United States. In 1998, an estimated 6,600 African American women were diagnosed with AIDS, representing 62% of all estimated AIDS cases among women in that year. Since the AIDS epidemic began in the U.S., more than 64,000 African American women have been diagnosed with AIDS. It is now the second leading cause of death for African-American women between 25 and 44 years of age." United States, "AIDS and African American

Women," *Communication at CDC*, Center for Disease Control, 6 Aug. 2001, 27 June 2002, http://www.cdc.gov/communication/tips/aids.htm.

3. "The Negro in Art: How Shall He Be Portrayed, A Symposium," *The Crisis* 31, no. 4 (February 1926): 165. The piece that begins the symposium ("A Questionnaire") was drafted by W. E. B. Du Bois but not credited to him. See Herbert Aptheker, *Annotated Bibliography of the Writings of W. E. B. Du Bois* (Millwood, N.Y.: Kraus-Thomson Organization Limited, 1973), p. 266.

4. Charles W. Chesnutt, *The Crisis* 33, no. 1 (November 1926): 9. My italics.

5. Countee Cullen, *The Crisis* 32, no. 4 (August 1926): 193. My italics.

6. Richard Wright, "Blueprint for Negro Writing," *New Challenge* 2 (Fall 1937): 60.

7. Ellison, *Shadow and Act*, pp. 43–44.

8. Wright, "Blueprint for Negro Writing," p. 60.

9. Neal, "The Black Arts Movement," p. 272.

10. Gayle, *The Way of the New World*, pp. xi–xii.

11. See Gwendolyn Osborne, "The Legacy of Ghetto Pulp Fiction," *Black Issues Book Review* (September–October 2001): 50–52; Tracy Grant, "Why Hip-Hop Heads Love Donald Goines." *Black Issues Book Review* (September—October 2001): 53; Gwendolyn Osborne, "Old School Masters of Blaxploitation Lit," *Black Issues Book Review* (September—October 2001): 54–56; Anthony Davis, "The New Sons of Iceberg Slim," *Black Issues Book Review* (September–October 2001): 56–57; and Brett Johnson, "Omar Tyree: Raw and Uncut," *Black Issues Book Review* (July—August 2002): 40–43.

12. Black lawyer Hobart Taylor Jr. coined the phrase "affirmative action" in his draft of Executive Order 10925, which banned discriminatory hiring by federal contractors. In March 1961 President Kennedy issued Executive Order 10925, which established his Committee on Equal Employment Opportunity.

13. Davarian L. Baldwin, "Black Empires, White Desires: The Spatial Politics of Identity in the Age of Hip Hop," *Black Renaissance/Renaissance Noire* 2, no. 2 (Summer 1999): 140.

14. Baldwin, "Black Empires, White Desires," p. 140.

15. Greg Tate, "Funking Intellect," *Vibe* (June/July 1997): 70.

16. Baldwin, "Black Empires, White Desires," p. 144.

17. Denning, *The Cultural Front*, p. 248.

18. Baldwin, "Black Empires, White Desires," p. 142.

19. Robin D. G. Kelley, *Race Rebels* (New York: Free Press, 1994), p. 210.

20. "In classic colonialism (or neocolonialism), products were produced in a 'raw periphery' and sent back to the imperial 'motherland' to be finished into commodities and sold in the metropolitan centers or sent back to the colonies, resulting in the stunting of the colony's economic growth due to it being denied the ability to engage in manufacturing products for its own needs and for export. Blacks in the inner cities, if not as an aggregate, share some of the classic characteristics of a colony: low per capita income; high birth rate; high infant mortality rate; a small or weak middle class; low rate of capital formation and domestic savings; economic dependence on external markets; labor as a major export; a tremendous demand for commodities produced by the colony but consumed by wealthier nations; and with most of the land and business owned by foreigners." Norman Kelley, "Rhythm Nation: The Political Economy of Black Music," *Black Renaissance/Renaissance Noire* 2, no. 2 (Summer 1999): 10.

21. Kelley, "Rhythm Nation," pp. 9–10.

22. Tom Dent, "*Umbra* Days," *Black American Literature Forum* 14, no. 3 (Autumn 1980): 107–8.

23. Quoted in Elizabeth Nunez and Brenda M. Greene, eds., *Defining Ourselves: Black Writers in the 1990s* (New York: Peter Lang, 1999), p. 1.

24. Joyce Pettis, "A *MELUS* Interview: Paule Marshall," *MELUS* (Winter 1991–1992): 117–29; and Daryl Cumber Dance, "An Interview with Paule Marshall," *Southern Review* 28 (January 1992): 1–20.

25. Dance, "Interview," p. 8.

26. Dance, "Interview," p. 7.

27. Dance, "Interview," p. 19.

28. Pettis, "A *MELUS* Interview," p. 120; and Dance, "Interview," p. 18.

29. Henry Louis Gates Jr. and Nellie Y. McKay, gen. eds., *The Norton Anthology of African American Literature* (New York: W. W. Norton, 1997), p. 2051. See also Paule Marshall, "Shadow and Act," *Mademoiselle*, June 1974, pp. 82–83.

30. Paule Marshall, *Brown Girl, Brownstones* (New York: Avon Books, 1970), p. 217.

31. Marshall, *Brown Girl, Brownstones*, p. 252.

32. Dance, "Interview," p. 15.

33. Paule Marshall, *Praisesong for the Widow* (New York: Putnam, 1983), pp. 38–39.

34. Dance, "Interview," p. 17.

35. The following two articles were most helpful for the subsequent biographical information. Henry Louis Gates Jr., "King of Cats," *New Yorker*, April 8, 1996, p. 74; and Elizabeth Schultz, "Albert L. Murray," in *Afro-American Writers after 1955: Dramatists and Prose Writers, Dictionary of Literary Biography*, vol. 38., ed. Thadious M. Davis and Trudier Harris (Detroit: Gale Research Co., 1985), pp. 214–24.

36. Gates, "King of Cats," p. 75.

37. Albert Murray, *The Omni-Americans: Some Alternatives to the Folklore of White Supremacy* (1970; rpt. New York: Vintage Books, 1983), pp. 4 and 7.

38. Murray, *The Omni-Americans*, pp. 18, 22, and 147.

39. Murray, *The Omni-Americans*, pp. 54, 58, and 151.

40. Murray, *The Omni-Americans*, pp. 58 and 226.

41. Schultz, "Albert L. Murray," pp. 220–21. In addition to the coming-of-age novels identified by Schultz and by me earlier in this book are Harriet Wilson's *Our "Nig"* (1859), W. E. B. Du Bois's *Quest of the Silver Fleece* (1911), J. W. Johnson's *Autobiography of an Ex-Colored Man* (1912), Owen Dodson's *Boy at the Window* (1951), James Baldwin's *Go Tell It on the Mountain* (1953), John O. Killens's *Youngblood* (1954), Richard Wright's *Long Dream* (1958), Rosa Guy's *Bird at My Window* (1966), Kristin Hunter's *God Bless the Child* (1967), Barry Beckham's *My Main Mother* (1969), Toni Morrison's *Bluest Eye* (1970), and Alice Childress's *Short Walk* (1979).

42. Albert Murray, *The Seven League Boots* (New York: Pantheon Books, 1995), p. 3. Subsequent references to this novel will be cited parenthetically in the text.

43. Vashti Crutcher Lewis, "Gloria Naylor," *American Novelists since World War II*, 5th series, *Dictionary of Literary Biography*, vol. 173, ed. James R. Giles and Wanda H. Giles (Detroit: Gale Research Co., 1996), p. 171. This biographical sketch draws primarily on Lewis; Kristine A. Yohe, "Gloria Naylor," *Oxford Companion to African American Literature*, ed. William L. Andrews, Frances Smith Foster, and Trudier Harris (New York: Oxford University Press, 1997), pp. 527–29; Gloria Naylor and Toni Morrison, "A Conversation,"

Southern Review 21 (July 1985): 567–93; and Henry Louis Gates Jr. and K. A. Appiah, eds., *Gloria Naylor: Critical Perspectives Past and Present* (New York: Amistad Press, 1993).

44. Quoted in Lewis, "Gloria Naylor," p. 171. See also Naylor and Morrison, "A Conversation," p. 570.

45. Gloria Naylor, *The Men of Brewster Place* (New York: Hyperion, 1998), p. 3. Subsequent references to this novel will be cited parenthetically in the text.

46. Gloria Naylor, *Mama Day* (New York: Vintage Books, 1989), p. 6. Subsequent references to this novel will be cited parenthetically in the text.

47. William J. Harris, "'I Write the Blues:' An Interview with Al Young," *Greenfield Review* 10 (Summer/Fall 1982): 1–19. Additionally helpful for the biographical sketch of Young were the following: O'Brien, *Interviews*, pp. 259–69; William J. Harris, "Al Young," in *Afro-American Fiction Writers after 1955*, *Dictionary of Literary Biography*, vol. 33., ed. Thadious M. Davis and Trudier Harris (Detroit: Gale Research Co., 1984), pp. 300–306; Al Young, *Drowning in the Sea of Love: Musical Memoirs* (New Jersey: Ecco Press, 1995); and James P. Draper, ed., *Black Literature Criticism*, vol. 3 (Detroit: Gale Research Co., 1992), pp. 2032–47.

48. Young, *Drowning in the Sea of Love*, p. 139.

49. Harris, "I Write the Blues," pp. 2–3.

50. Harris, "I Write the Blues," pp. 4–10.

51. Al Young, *Snakes* (New York: Holt, Rinehart and Winston, 1970), pp. 71–72. Subsequent references to this novel will be cited parenthetically in the text.

52. This biographical sketch draws mainly on the following sources: Mel Watkins, "Thirteen Runaway Slaves and David Bradley," *New York Times Book Review*, April 19, 1981, pp. 7, 20–21; Patricia Holt, "PW Interviews: David Bradley," *Publishers Weekly*, April 10, 1981, pp. 12–14; Susan L. Blake and James A. Miller, "The Business of Writing: An Interview with David Bradley," *Callaloo* 7 (Spring—Summer 1984): 19–39; Valerie Smith, "David Bradley," in *Afro-American Fiction Writers after 1955*, *Dictionary of Literary Biography*, vol. 33., ed. Thadious M. Davis and Trudier Harris. (Detroit: Gale Research Co., 1984), pp. 28–32; and Frances Brailsford, "David (Henry, Jr.) Bradley," *Contemporary Authors: New Revision Series*, vol. 26, pp. 71–73.

53. Watkins, "Thirteen Runaway Slaves and David Bradley," p. 7.

54. David Bradley, *South Street* (New York: Scribner and Sons, 1986), p. 235.

55. Cathy Brigham, "Dissenting Fictions: Identity and Resistance in the Contemporary U.S. Novel," Diss., Penn State University, 1995, p. 151. See also Brigham, "Identity, Masculinity, and Desire in David Bradley's Fiction," *Contemporary Literature* 36, no. 2 (1995): 289–316.

56. Mary Helen Washington, "Black History: His Story or Hers," *Washington Post Book World*, April 12, 1981, pp. 3 and 13.

57. Michele Wallace, *Black Macho and the Myth of the Superwoman* (1979; rpt. New York: Verso, 1990), p. 13.

58. Philip J. Egan, "Unraveling Misogyny and Forging the New Self: Mother, Lover, and Storyteller in *The Chaneysville Incident*," *Papers on Language & Literature* (Summer 1997): 266.

59. Egan, "Unraveling Misogyny," p. 266.

60. Katharine M. Rogers, *The Troublesome Helpmate: A History of Misogyny in Literature* (Seattle: University of Washington Press, 1966), p. 237. Deleuze and Guattari challenge

Freud's theory of universal oedipalization in their argument that "psychic repression depend[s] on social repression," which is a product of middle-class family structure rather than a universal psychic formation. See Deleuze and Guattari, *Anti-Oedipus*, pp. 118–20.

61. David Bradley, *The Chaneysville Incident* (New York: Harper and Row, 1981), p. 147. Subsequent references to this novel will be cited parenthetically in the text.

62. Egan, "Unraveling Misogyny," p. 268.

63. The following biographical sketch draws mainly on the following sources: Johnanna L. Grimes, "Leon Forrest," *Dictionary of Literary Biography*, Gale Research, 25 Feb. 2002, 20 Nov. 2002, http://www.galenet.com; and John G. Calwelti, ed., *Leon Forrest: Introductions and Interpretations* (Bowling Green, Ohio: Bowling Green State University Popular Press, 1997), pp. 1–74.

64. See Calwelti, *Leon Forrest*, p. 72, n. 18.

65. Leon Forrest, *Two Wings to Veil My Face* (Chicago: Another Chicago Press, 1983), p. 5.

66. Leon Forrest, *The Bloodworth Orphans* (New York: Random House, 1977), pp. 185–86.

67. Book blurb solicited from Henry Louis Gates by publisher. This was confirmed in telephone conversation with W. W. Norton staff (January 28, 2002). Martin Brady, "Out of Chicago, A Black 'Ulysses,'" *Chicago Sun-Times*, July 19, 1992, p. 12; John Calwelti, "Leon Forrest: The Labyrinth of Luminosity: An Introduction," Calwelti, *Leon Forrest*, p. 57; and Stanley Crouch, "The Soul of Joubert Jones," *New York Times Book Review*, July 25, 1993, p. 14.

68. Leon Forrest, *Divine Days* (New York: W. W. Norton, 1993), p. 9. Subsequent references to this novel will be cited parenthetically in the text.

7. *The New Black Aesthetic (1983–2001)*

1. See Myra Jehlen, "Introduction," *Ideology and Classic American Literature*, ed. Sacvan Bercovitch and Myra Jehlen (Cambridge: Cambridge University Press, 1986); Amy Kaplan, "'Left Alone with America': The Absence of Empire in the Study of American Culture," *Cultures of United States Imperialism*, ed. Amy Kaplan and Donald E. Pease (Durham: Duke University Press, 1993), pp. 3–21; Frederick Crews, *The Critics Bear It Away: American Fiction and the Academy* (New York: Random House, 1992); and Gregory S. Jay, *American Literature and the Culture Wars* (Ithaca: Cornell University Press, 1997).

2. Gloria Anzaldua, "Preface," *Borderlands/La Frontera: The New Mestiza* (San Francisco: aunt lute books, 1987), n.p.

3. Homi Bhabha, *The Location of Culture* (New York: Routledge, 1994), p. 37; and Cyrus R. K. Patell, *Negative Liberties: Morrison, Pynchon, and the Problem of Liberal Ideology* (Durham: Duke University Press, 2001), p. 177.

4. Trey Ellis, "Response to NBA Critiques," *Callaloo* 0, no. 38 (Winter 1989): 250–51.

5. Trey Ellis, "The New Black Aesthetic," *Callaloo* 12, no. 1 (Winter 1989): 234–35.

6. Bakhtin, *The Dialogic Imagination*, p. 358.

7. Rudolph P. Byrd, ed., *I Call Myself an Artist: Writings by and about Charles Johnson* (Bloomington: Indiana University Press, 1999), pp. 4–5. My biographical sketch relies primarily on Charles Johnson's autobiographical sketch, "I Call Myself an Artist," in this book.

8. Byrd, *I Call Myself an Artist*, p. 19.
9. Charles Johnson, *Being and Race* (Bloomington: Indiana University Press, 1988), p. 4.
10. Johnson, *Being and Race*, pp. 14–15.
11. Charles Johnson, *Middle Passage* (New York: Atheneum, 1990), pp. 120, 29, 30, and 98. Subsequent documentation for this novel will be included parenthetically in the text.
12. The subsequent biographical sketch draws mainly on Mark Scroggins, "Nathaniel Mackey," *American Poets since World War II: Fifth Series*, ed. Joseph Conte, *Dictionary of Literary Biography* (Detroit: Gale Research Co., 1996), pp. 179–91.
13. Quoted in Scroggins, "Nathaniel Mackey," p. 181.
14. Scroggins, "Nathaniel Mackey," p. 182.
15. Scroggins, "Nathaniel Mackey," p. 187.
16. Peter O'Leary, "An Interview with Nathaniel Mackey," *Chicago Review* 43, no. 1 (Winter 1997): 40.
17. O'Leary, "An Interview with Nathaniel Mackey," p. 36.
18. Paul Naylor, ed., *Nathaniel Mackey: A Special Issue, Callaloo* 23, no. 3 (Spring 2000): 501.
19. Nathaniel Mackey, *Djbot Baghostus's Run* (Los Angeles: Sun and Moon Press, 1993), p. 188. Subsequent references to this novel will be cited parenthetically in the text.
20. "Middle Voice Moves in Nathaniel Mackey's *Djbot Baghostus's Run*," *Callaloo* 23, no. 3 (Spring 2000): 772–73.
21. This biographical sketch draws on Ellis, "The New Black Aesthetic," pp. 233–51, esp. 235.
22. Ellis, "The New Black Aesthetic," p. 235.
23. Ellis, "The New Black Aesthetic," pp. 234–35.
24. Ellis, "Response to NBA Critiques," p. 251.
25. Ellis, "Response to NBA Critiques," p. 250.
26. Ellis, "Response to NBA Critiques," p. 250.
27. J. Martin Favor, "'Ain't Nothin' Like the Real Thing, Baby': Trey Ellis' Search for New Black Voices," *Callaloo* 16, no. 3 (Summer 1993): 695.
28. Trey Ellis, *Platitudes* (New York: Vintage Books, 1988), p. 4. Subsequent references to this novel will be cited parenthetically in the text.
29. "Our Nig" [Harriet E. Wilson], *Our Nig: or, Sketches from the Life of a Free Black, In a Two-Story White House, North, Showing that Slavery's Shadows Fall Even There* (New York: Vintage Books, 1983), p. 12.
30. The subsequent biographical sketch draws on the following informative sources: S. Thomas Mack, "Percival L. Everett," *Cyclopedia of World Authors*, vol. 2, 3rd rev. ed, ed. Frank N. Magill and associate eds. McCrea Adams and Julianne Brand (Pasadena, Calif.: Salem Press, 1997), pp. 654–55; Carolyn See, "*Suder*," *Los Angeles Times Book Review*, July 31, 1983, pp. 1 and 8; and "Percival L. Everett," *Contemporary Authors*, February 25, 2002, November 20, 2002, http://www.galenet.com.
31. "An Interview with Percival Everett," University Press of New England, October 16, 2002, 22 Nov. 2002, http://www.dartmouth.edu/acad-inst/upne/features/Everett Q&A.html.
32. Percival Everett, *Erasure* (Hanover, N.H.: University Press of New England, 2001), p. 261. Subsequent references to this novel will be cited parenthetically in the text.
33. "An Interview with Percival Everett."
34. See, for example, Cynthia Ozick, "Literary Blacks and Jews," *Art and Ardor* (New

York: Alfred A. Knopf, 1983), pp. 90–113; and Sanford Pinsker, "John Updike and the Distractions of Henry Bech, Professional Writer and Amateur American Jew," *Modern Fiction Studies* 37, no. 1 (Spring 1991): 97–111.

35. Hall, "Cultural Identity and Diaspora," p. 225.

36. This biographical sketch relies primarily on the following sources: Dan Cryer, "The Evolving Ballad of Colson Whitehead, Writer," *Los Angeles Times*, June 17, 2001, p. E4; Dave Welch, "Post Office to Unveil Colson Whitehead Stamp," *Powells.com*, 14 June 2001, 22 Nov. 2002, http://www.powells.com/authors/whitehead.html; "Colson Whitehead," *Contemporary Authors* 4 Oct. 2002, 22 Nov. 2002, Gale Literary Databases, http://www.galenet.com; and Kevin Larimer, "Industrial Strength in the Information Age: A Profile of Colson Whitehead," *Poets & Writers Magazine* (July/August 2001): 21–25.

37. Larimer, "Industrial Strength in the Information Age," p. 22.

38. Colson Whitehead, *John Henry Days* (New York: Doubleday, 2001), p. 5. Subsequent references to this novel will be cited parenthetically in the text.

39. Larimer, "Industrial Strength in the Information Age," p. 24.

8. Contemporary African American Paraliterature (1983–2001)

1. Alice Walker received the Pulitzer Prize and the American Book Award in 1983 for *The Color Purple*; Gloria Naylor received the American Book Award in 1982 for *The Women of Brewster Place*; Charles Johnson received the National Book Award in 1990 for *Middle Passage*; and Toni Morrison received the American Book Award and the Pulitzer Prize in 1988 for *Beloved*. She received the Nobel Prize in Literature in 1993.

2. Brett Johnson, "Omar Tyree: Raw and Uncut," *Black Issues Book Review* (July–August 2002): 41.

3. Charles Johnson, "Interview with Samuel Delany," *Callaloo* 7, no. 3 (Fall 1984): 27–35. Rpt. in Draper, *Black Literature Criticism*, p. 538.

4. Eagleton, *Literary Theory*, p. 205.

5. Eagleton, *Literary Theory*, p. 209.

6. Brian Aldiss with David Wingrove, *Trillion Year Spree: The History of Science Fiction* (New York: Atheneum, 1986), p. 25. The subsequent historical overview of science fiction draws mainly on this book and the studies of black critic Sandra Y. Govan.

7. Aldiss, *Trillion Year Spree*, pp. 13–15, 27.

8. Aldiss, *Trillion Year Spree*, p. 26.

9. Darko Suvin, *Metamorphoses of Science Fiction: On the Poetics and History of a Literary Genre* (New Haven: Yale University Press, 1979), pp. 7–8.

10. Andrews, Foster, and Harris, eds., *The Oxford Companion to African American Literature*, p. 683. "I prefer Robert Scholes's definition of fabulation as the shift from realism to a more verbal, shapely, and evocative kind of narrative." (*The Fabulators*), p. 12.

11. Govan, *Dictionary of Literary Biography*, 33, p. 53.

12. Govan, *Dictionary of Literary Biography*, 33, p. 53.

13. Delaney, *The Tales of Neveryon* (Middletown, Conn.: Wesleyan University Press, 1993), p. 14.

14. Peter S. Alterman, "The Surreal Translations of Samuel R. Delany," *Science-Fiction Studies* 4, no. 11 (March 1977): 25–34.

15. Jeanne Murray Walker, "Reciprocity and Exchange in Samuel Delany's *Nova*," *Extrapolation* 23, no. 3 (Fall 1982): 221–34.

16. Sandra Govan, "The Insistent Presence of Black Folk in the Novels of Samuel R. Delany," *Black American Literature Forum* 18, no. 2 (Summer 1984): 43–48.

17. Quoted in Michael W. Peplow and Robert S. Bravard, *Samuel R. Delany: A Primary and Secondary Bibliography, 1962–1979* (Boston: G. K. Hall, 1980), pp. 54–55.

18. Samuel Delany, *Dhalgren* (New York: Bantam Books, 1975), p. 524.

19. Govan, "The Insistent Presence of Black Folk in the Novels of Samuel R. Delany," p. 47.

20. Alterman, "The Surreal Translations of Samuel R. Delany," pp. 26–27.

21. Jane Branham Weedman, *Samuel R. Delany* (Mercer Island, Wash.: Starmont House, 1982), pp. 61–69.

22. Weedman, *Samuel R. Delany*, p. 69.

23. Walter Benn Michaels, "Political Science Fictions," *New Literary History* 31, no. 4 (2001): 649.

24. Quoted in Sandra Y. Govan, "Connections, Links, and Extended Networks: Patterns in Octavia Butler's Science Fiction," *Black American Literature Forum* 18, no. 2 (Summer 1984): 82.

25. Quoted in Rosemary Stevenson, "Octavia Butler," *Black Women in America: An Historical Encyclopedia*, vol. 1, ed. Darlene Clark Hine, Elsa Barkley Brown, and Rosalyn Terborg-Penn (Bloomington: Indiana University Press, 1993), p. 210.

26. Quoted in Susan McHenry, "Octavia's Mind Trip into the Near Future," *Black Issues Book Review* (January–February 1999): 18.

27. Robert Crossley, in "Introduction," *Kindred*, by Octavia Butler (Boston: Beacon Press, 1979) pp. xii and xx.

28. Margaret Anne O'Connor, "Octavia E. Butler," *Dictionary of Literary Biography*, pp. 33, 40; and Govan, "Connections . . ." fn 6, p. 87.

29. Crossley, "Introduction," *Kindred*, p. xii.

30. Butler, *Kindred*, p. 74. Subsequent references to this novel will be cited parenthetically in the main text.

31. Butler, *Wild Seed* (New York: Popular Library, 1980), pp. 4–5. Subsequent references to this novel will be cited parenthetically in the main text.

32. Govan, "Connections . . . ," p. 83.

33. Jonathan Ned Katz, *Gay/Lesbian Almanac: A New Documentary* (1983; rpt. New York: Carroll & Graf, 1994), p. 16.

34. Katz, *Gay/Lesbian Almanac*, pp. 15–16.

35. Katz, *Gay/Lesbian Almanac*, p. 11. Also see Eve Kosofsky Sedgwick, *Epistemology of the Closet* (Berkeley: University of California Press, 1990), pp. 16–18.

36. Jonathan Ned Katz, *Gay American History: Lesbians & Gay Men in the U.S.A* (New York: Meridian, 1972; rev. ed 1992), pp. 406–20, 427.

37. Ron Simmons, "Some Thoughts on the Challenges Facing Black Gay Intellectuals," in *Brother to Brother: New Writings by Black Gay Men*, ed. Essex Hemphill (Boston: Alyson Books, 1991), pp. 211–12. "In reviewing African American literature," Simmons argues, "one finds that black homophobic and heterosexist scholars believe homosexuality in the African American community is the result of: (1) the emasculation of black men by white oppression (e.g., Staples, Madhubuti, Asante, Farrakhan, and Baraka); (2) the breakdown

of the family structure and the loss of male role models (e.g., Kunjufu, Madhubuti, Farrakhan, and Hare); (3) a sinister plot perpetuated by diabolical racists who want to destroy the black race (e.g., Hare); and (4) immorality as defined by biblical scriptures, Koranic suras, or Egyptian 'Books of the Dead' (e.g., Farrakhan and Ben-Jochannan)."

38. Simmons, "Some Thoughts," p. 225.

39. Charles I. Nero, "Toward a Black Gay Aesthetic: Signifying in Contemporary Black Gay Literature," in *Brother to Brother*, ed. Hemphill, p. 229.

40. Ann Allen Shockley, "The Black Lesbian in American Literature: An Overview," in *Home Girls: A Black Feminist Anthology*, ed. Barbara Smith (New York: Kitchen Table: Women of Color Press, 1983) p. 83.

41. Fanon, *Black Skin, White Masks*, p. 84.

42. Esteban Montejo, *The Autobiography of a Runaway Slave*, trans. Jocasta Innes, ed. Miguel Barnet (New York: Vintage Books, 1973), p. 41.

43. Katz, *Gay American History*, 35–36; Katz, *Gay/Lesbian Almanac*, p. 61.

44. Asante, *Afrocentricity*, p. 57.

45. Eldridge Cleaver, *Soul on Ice*, (New York: McGraw-Hill, 1968), p. 177.

46. Nathan Hare and Julia Hare, *The Endangered Black Family: Coping with the Unisexualization and Coming Extinction of the Black Race* (San Francisco: Black Think Tank, 1984), p. 65.

47. Sedgwick, *Epistemology of the Closet*, pp. 19–21.

48. Lyotard, *The Postmodern Condition*, p. 37.

49. Nero, "Toward a Black Gay Aesthetic," p. 229. Also see Melvin Donaldson, ed., *Cornerstones: An Anthology of African American Literature* (New York: St. Martin's Press, 1996), pp. 971–89.

50. See Reed Woodhouse, *Unlimited Embrace: A Canon of Gay Fiction, 1945–1995* (Amherst: University of Massachusetts Press, 1998).

51. Christopher Davis, "CS Interview with Larry Duplechan," *Christopher Street* 10 (1987): 60–62. Quoted in John H. Pearson, "Larry Duplechan," *Contemporary Gay American Novelists: A Bio-Bibliographical Critical Sourcebook*, ed. Emmanuel S. Nelson (Westport, Conn.: Greenwood Press, 1993), p. 117.

52. E. Lynn Harris, *The Advocate*, November 24, 1998, p. 67.

53. Martin Arnold, "In the Art of the Craft," *New York Times*, July 27, 2000, p. B3.

54. Philip Brian Harper, *Are We Not Men? Masculine Anxiety and the Problem of African-American Identity* (New York: Oxford University Press, 1998), p. 3.

55. E. Lynn Harris, *Just as I Am* (New York: Anchor Books, 1995), p. 148. Subsequent references to this novel will be cited in the main text.

56. As described by historian Barbara Welter, "the prophets of 'The Cult of True Womanhood: 1820–1860' posited a 'true woman' with four cardinal virtues: piety, purity, submissiveness, and domesticity. Those ideal 'female' characteristics translated into a feminine temperament whose emotional components were love of God and devotion to morality, a controlled, procreation-focused sexuality, a family-centered love, nurturing desires, and feelings of dependency. . . . The characteristic virtues of the true man were devotion to hard work and material success, a 'pure,' controlled (though insistent) sexuality, assertiveness, and the attributes of the benevolent, patriarchal ruler. These translated into a 'male' temperament comprising love of this-worldly rewards, and the struggle to obtain them, an ideally sublimated, procreative-focused lust, a desire for independence,

and an authoritarian, protective feeling for wife and family." Katz, *Gay/Lesbian Almanac*, p. 139.

57. Walker, *The Color Purple*, p. 167.

58. Ishmael Reed, *Shrovetide in Old New Orleans* (New York: Discus Books, 1979), p. 115.

59. Ellin, "Introduction" to Rudolph Fisher, *The Conjure-Man Dies* (1932; rpt. New York: Arno Press and *The New York Times*, 1971), n.p.

60. See Paula L. Woods, ed., *Spooks, Spies, and Private Eyes: Black Mystery, Crime, and Suspense Fiction* (New York: Doubleday, 1995), fn. 2, p. xv.

61. Stephen Soitos, *The Blues Detective: A Study of African American Detective Fiction* (Amherst, Mass.: University of Massachusetts Press, 1996), fn. l, p. 237. The subsequent historical overview of the tradition of detective and mystery fiction draws mainly on this standard study.

62. Quoted in Soitos, *The Blues Detective*, 19. Gloria A. Biamonte, "Detection and the Text: Reading Three American Women of Mystery," Diss., University of Massachusetts, Amherst, 1991, p. 24.

63. Soitos, *The Blues Detective*, pp. 20–21.

64. Soitos, *The Blues Detective*, chaps. 2 and 3. See also Carby, "Introduction" to *The Magazine Novels of Pauline Hopkins* (New York: Oxford University Press, 1988), pp. xxix–xxxvi.

65. This biographical sketch relies primarily on Rebecca Carroll, "Interview with Barbara Neely," in *I Know What the Red Clay Looks Like: The Voice and Vision of Black Women Writers*, ed. Carroll (New York: Crown Trade Paperbacks,1994), pp. 174–84; and Sandra Govan, "Barbara Neely," *Oxford Companion to African American Literature*, ed. Andrews, Foster, and Harris, pp. 530–31.

66. Bob McCullough, "Walter Mosley," *Publishers Weekly*, May 23, 1994, p. 67.

67. McCullough, "Walter Mosley," p. 67; Kristina L. Knotts, "Walter Mosley," *Contemporary African American Novelists: A Bio-Bibliographical Critical Sourcebook*, ed. Emmanuel S. Nelson (Westport, Conn.: Greenwood Press, 1999), pp. 350–54.

68. Knotts, "Walter Mosley," p. 351.

69. Peter Hogness, "How Walter Mosley Discovered His Audience—And the Voice of His Fiction," *Writer's Digest* 76 (March 1996): 8.

70. Ernest Gaines, "Easy Rawlins, Just a Little Older," *Los Angeles Times Book Review*, June 5, 1994, p. 3.

71. Quoted in Knotts, "Walter Mosley," p. 351.

Conclusion

1. James W. Tuttleton, "Tracking the American Novel into the Void," *The World & I* (May 1989): 456.

2. Frye, *Anatomy of Criticism*, p. 247.

3. Michael Berube, "Teaching Postmodern Fiction without Being Sure That the Genre Exists," *Chronicle of Higher Education*, May 19, 2000, B4.

4. Bell, *The Folk Roots of Contemporary Afro-American Poetry*, p. 20.

5. Bell, *The Folk Roots of Contemporary Afro-American Poetry*, p. 21.

Selected Bibliography

I have not included here all of the primary and secondary sources that I consulted in writing this book. Instead, I list first the 74 novels published between 1962 and 2001 that I have examined closely, by 32 authors for whom I provide background information. I also include a list of 238 other novels by those authors and 79 others, as well as the secondary sources that should be most useful to the reader who wants to pursue further study and research on interdisciplinary approaches to the folk roots and modern literary branches of the African American novel.

Primary Novels (1962–2001)

Bambara, Toni Cade. *The Salt Eaters*. New York: Random House, 1980.

———. *These Bones Are Not My Child*. New York: Vintage Books, 1999.

Bennett, Hal. *The Black Wine*. New York: Pyramid Books 1968.

———. *Lord of Dark Places*. New York: Bantam Books, 1971.

———. *Seventh Heaven*. Garden City, N.Y.: Doubleday, 1976.

———. *Wait until Evening*. Garden City, N.Y.: Doubleday, 1974.

———. *Wilderness of Vines*. New York: Pyramid, 1967.

Bradley, David. *The Chaneysville Incident*. New York: Harper and Row, 1981.

———. *South Street*. New York: Scribner and Sons, 1986.

Butler, Octavia. *Kindred*. Garden City, N.Y.: Doubleday, 1979.

———. *Wild Seed*. Garden City, N.Y.: Doubleday, 1980.

Delany, Samuel. *Dhalgren*. New York: Bantam Books, 1968.

———. *Nova*. Garden City, N.Y.: Doubleday, 1968.

Duplechan, Larry. *Blackbird*. New York: St. Martin's Press, 1986.

———. *Eight Days a Week*. Los Angeles: Alyson Books, 1985.

Ellis, Trey. *Platitudes*. New York: Vintage Books, 1988.

Everett, Percival. *Erasure*. Hanover: University Press of New England, 2001.

———. *Suder*. New York: Viking Press, 1983.

Fair, Ronald L. *Many Thousand Gone*. New York: Harcourt Brace and World, 1965.

Forrest, Leon. *Divine Days*. 1992. Reprint. New York: W. W. Norton, 1993.

———. *There Is a Tree More Ancient Than Eden*. New York: Random House, 1973.

Gaines, Ernest J. *The Autobiography of Miss Jane Pittman*. 1971. Reprint. New York: Bantam Books, 1972.

———. *A Gathering of Old Men*. New York: Vintage Books, 1992.

———. *In My Father's House*. New York: Alfred A. Knopf, 1978.

———. *A Lesson before Dying*. New York: Alfred A. Knopf, 1993.

———. *Of Love and Dust*. 1967. Reprint. New York: W. W. Norton, 1979.

Harris, E. Lynn. *Invisible Life*. Atlanta: Atlanta Consortium Press, 1991.

———. *Just as I Am*. New York: Doubleday, 1994.
———. *Not a Day Goes By*. New York: Doubleday, 2000.
Johnson, Charles. *Faith and the Good Thing*. New York: Viking Press, 1974.
———. *Middle Passage*. New York: Atheneum, 1990.
———. *Oxherding Tale*. Bloomington: Indiana University Press, 1982.
Jones, Gayl. *Corregidora*. New York: Random House, 1975.
———. *Eva's Man*. New York: Bantam Books, 1978.
———. *The Healing*. Boston: Beacon Press, 1998.
———. *Mosquito*. Boston: Beacon Press, 1999.
Kelley, William Melvin. *A Different Drummer*. Garden City, N.Y.: Anchor Books, 1969.
———. *Dunfords Travels Everywheres*. Garden City, N.Y.: Doubleday, 1970.
Killens, John O. *And Then We Heard the Thunder*. 1963. Reprint. New York: Pocket Books, 1964.
———. *The Cotillion; or One Good Bull Is Half the Herd*. New York: Pocket Books, 1972.
———. *Youngblood*. 1954. Reprint. New York: Pocket Books, 1955.
Mackey, Nathaniel. *Bedouin Hornbook*. Lexington: University of Kentucky Press, 1986.
———. *Djbot Baghostus's Run*. Los Angeles: Sun and Moon Press, 1993.
———. *Atet, A.D.* San Francisco: City Lights, 2001.
Major, Clarence. *All Night Visitors*. New York: Olympia Press, 1969.
———. *Dirty Bird Blues*. San Francisco: Mercury House, 1996.
———. *Emergency Exit*. New York: Fiction Collective, 1979.
———. *NO*. New York: Emerson Hall, 1973.
———. *Painted Turtle: Woman with Guitar*. Los Angeles: Sun and Moon Press, 1988
———. *Reflex and Bone Structure*. New York: Fiction Collective, 1975.
———. *Such Was the Season*. San Francisco: Mercury House, 1987.
Marshall, Paule. *Praisesong for the Widow*. New York: Putnam, 1983.
Morrison, Toni. *The Bluest Eye*. 1970. Reprint. New York: Pocket Books, 1972.
———. *Song of Solomon*. New York: Alfred A. Knopf, 1977.
———. *Sula*. New York: Alfred A. Knopf, 1973.
Mosley, Walter. *Devil in a Blue Dress*. New York: W. W. Norton, 1990.
Murray, Albert. *The Spyglass Tree*. New York: Pantheon Books, 1991.
———. *Train Whistle Guitar*. New York: McGraw–Hill, 1974.
Naylor, Gloria. *Mama Day*. New York: Vintage Books, 1988.
———. *The Men of Brewster Place*. New York: Hyperion, 1998.
Neely, Barbara. *Blanche among the Talented Tenth*. New York: Penguin Books, 1994.
———. *Blanche Cleans Up*. New York: Penguin Books, 1998.
———. *Blanche Passes Go*. New York: Viking Press, 2000.
Reed, Ishmael. *Japanese by Spring*. New York: Atheneum, 1993.
———. *Mumbo Jumbo*. Garden City, N.Y.: Doubleday, 1972.
———. *The Terrible Threes*. New York: Atheneum, 1989.
———. *The Terrible Twos*. New York: St. Martin's Press, 1982.
Walker, Alice. *The Color Purple*. New York: Harcourt Brace Jovanovich, 1982.
———. *The Third Life of Grange Copeland*. 1970. Reprint. New York: Avon Books, 1971.
Walker, Margaret. *Jubilee*. 1966. New York: Bantam Books, 1967.
Whitehead, Colson. *The Intuitionist*. New York: Anchor Books, 1999.
———. *John Henry Days*. New York: Doubleday, 2001.

Wideman, John Edgar. *The Cattle Killing*. Boston: Houghton–Mifflin, 1996.
———. *Damballah*. New York: Bard Books, 1981.
———. *A Glance Away*. 1967. Reprint. Chatham, N.J.: Chatham Bookseller, 1975.
———. *Hiding Place*. New York: Bard Books, 1981.
———. *Hurry Home*. New York: Harcourt Brace and World, 1970.
———. *The Lynchers*. 1973. Reprint. New York: Dell Books, 1974.
———. *Philadelphia Fire*. New York: Holt, 1990; London: Viking, 1991.
———. *Reuben*. New York: Holt, 1987; London: Viking, 1988.
———. *Sent for You Yesterday*. New York: Bard Books, 1983.
———. *Two Cities*. Boston: Houghton Mifflin, 1998
Williams, John A. *Clifford's Blues*. Minneapolis: Coffee House Press, 1999.
———. *The Man Who Cried I Am*. 1967. Reprint. New York: Signet Books, 1968.
———. *Night Song*. 1961. *Sweet Love Bitter*. Reprint. New York: Pocket Books, 1970.
Wright, Charles. *The Messenger*. New York: Manor Books, 1974.
———. *The Wig: A Mirror Image*. New York: Farrar, Straus and Giroux, 1966.
Young, Al. *Snakes*. New York: Holt, Rinehart, and Winston, 1970.

Secondary Novels

Achebe, Chinua. *Things Fall Apart*. 1958. Reprint. New York: Alfred A. Knopf, 1992.
Attaway, William. *Blood on the Forge: A Novel*. 1941. Reprint. New York: Collier Books, 1970.
Baker, Nikki. *In the Game*. Tallahassee: Naiad Press, 1991
———. *The Lavender House Murder*. Tallahassee: Naiad Press, 1992.
———. *The Long Goodbyes*. Tallahassee: Naiad Press, 1993.
Baldwin, James. *Another Country*. New York: Dell Books, 1963.
———. *Giovanni's Room*. 1956. Reprint. New York: Apollo Editions, 1962.
———. *Go Tell It on the Mountain*. 1953. Reprint. New York: Grosset's Universal Library, 1961.
———. *Just Above my Head*. 1979. Reprint. New York: Dell Books, 1980.
Barnes, Steven A. *Blood Brothers*. New York: St. Martin's Press, 1996.
———. *FireDance*. New York: Tor Books, 1993.
———. *Gorgon Child*. New York: Tor Books, 1989.
———. *Iron Shadows*. New York: St. Martin's Press, 1998.
———. *The Kundalini Equation*. New York: Tor Books, 1986.
———. *Saturn's Race*. New York: Tor Books, 1998.
———. *Streetlethal*. New York: Ace Books, 1983.
Beckham, Barry. *My Main Mother*. 1969. Reprint. New York: Signet Books, 1971.
Bentley, E. C. *Trent's Last Case*. 1913. Reprint. New York: Alfred A. Knopf, 1929.
Bland, Eleanor Taylor. *Dead Time*. New York: St. Martin's Press, 1992.
———. *Done Wrong*. New York: St. Martin's Press, 1995.
———. *Gone Quiet*. New York: St. Martin's Press, 1994.
———. *Keep Still*. New York: St. Martin's Press, 1996.
———. *Scream in Silence*. New York: St. Martin's Press, 2000.
———. *See No Evil*. New York: St. Martin's Press, 1998.
———. *Slowburn*. New York: St. Martin's Press, 1993.

Bontemps, Arna. *Black Thunder*. 1936. Reprint. Boston: Beacon Press, 1992.
Brooks, Gwendolyn. *Maud Martha*. 1953. Reprinted in *The World of Gwendolyn Brooks*. New York: Harper and Row, 1971.
Brown, Cecil. *Life and Loves of Mr. Jiveass Nigger*. 1969. Reprint. New York: Crest Books, 1971.
Brown, Frank. *Trumbull Park*. Chicago: Henry Regnery, 1959.
Brown, Lloyd. *Iron City*. New York: Masses and Mainstream, 1951.
Brown, William Wells. *Clotel; or the President's Daughter. A Narrative of Slave Life in the United States*. 1853. Reprint. New York: Collier Books, 1970.
Bruce, John Edward. *Black Sleuth*. 1907–9. Reprint, edited by John Cullen Gruesser. Boston: Northeastern University Press, 2002.
Butler, Octavia. *Adulthood Rites*. New York: Warner Books, 1988.
———. *Clay's Ark*. New York: St. Martin's Press, 1984.
———. *Dawn*. New York: Warner Books, 1987.
———. *Imago*. New York: Warner Books, 1989.
———. *Mind of My Mind*. Garden City, N.Y.: Doubleday, 1977.
———. *Parable of the Sower*. New York: Four Walls Eight Windows, 1993.
———. *Parable of the Talents*. New York: Seven Stories, 1998.
———. *Patternmaster*. Garden City, N.Y.: Doubleday, 1976.
———. *Survivor*. Garden City, N.Y.: Doubleday, 1978.
Cain, George. *Blueschild Baby*. 1970. Reprint. New York: Dell Books, 1972.
Chase-Riboud, Barbara. *The President's Daughter*. New York: Crown, 1994.
———. *Sally Hemings*. New York: Viking Press, 1979.
Chesnutt, Charles W. *The Conjure Woman*. Boston: Houghton Mifflin, 1898.
———. *The House behind the Cedars*. 1900. Reprint. New York: Collier Books, 1969.
———. *The Marrow of Tradition*. 1901. Reprint. Ann Arbor: Ann Arbor Paperbacks, 1969.
Childress, Alice. *A Short Walk*. 1979. Reprint. New York: Avon Books, 1981.
Conde, Maryse. *I, Tituba, Black Witch of Salem*. 1992. Reprint. New York: Ballantine Books, 1994.
Corbin, Steven. *No Easy Place to Be*. New York: Simon and Schuster, 1989.
Cullen, Countee. *One Way to Heaven*. New York: Harper and Brothers, 1932.
Delany, Martin R. *Blake*; or *The Huts of America: A Tale of the Mississippi Valley, the Southern United States and Cuba*. 1859. Reprint. Boston: Beacon Press, 1970.
Delany, Samuel. *Babel-17*. New York: Ace Books, 1966.
———. *The Ballad of Beta-2*. New York: Ace Books, 1965.
———. *Bridge of Lost Desire*. New York: Arbor House, 1987.
———. *Captives of the Flame*. New York: AceBooks, 1963.
———. *City of a Thousand Suns*. London: Sphere Books, 1965.
———. *Distant Stars*. New York: Bantam Books, 1981.
———. *The Einstein Intersection*. New York: Ace Books, 1967.
———. *Empire Star*. New York: Ace Books, 1966.
———. *Flight from Neveryon*. New York: Bantam Books, 1979.
———. *The Jewels of Aptor*. New York: Ace Books, 1962.
———. *The Mad Man*. New York: Masquerade Books, 1996.
———. *Neveryona; Or the Tale of Signs and Cities*. New York: Bantam Books, 1983.
———. *Stars in My Pocket Like Grains of Sand*. New York: Bantam Books, 1983.

———. *The Tides of Lust*. New York: Lancer Books, 1973.
———. *Towers of Toron*. New York: Ace Books, 1964.
———. *Triton*. New York: Bantam Books, 1976.
Demby, William. *Beetlecreek*. 1950. Reprint. New York: Avon Books, 1967.
———. *The Catacombs*. New York: Pantheon Books, 1965.
Dixon, Melvin. *Trouble the Water*. Boulder, Colo.: Fiction Collective Two, 1989.
Dodson, Owen. *Boy at the Window: A Novel*. 1951. Reprint. Chatham, N.J.: Chatham Bookseller, 1972.
Downing, Henry F. *The American Cavalryman; A Liberian Romance*. New York: Neale, 1917.
Du Bois, W. E. B. *The Quest of the Silver Fleece*. 1911. Reprint. Miami: Mnemosyne, 1969.
Due, Tananarive. *My Soul to Keep*. New York: Harper Collins, 1997.
———. *The Between*. New York: Harper Collins, 1995.
Dunbar, Paul Laurence. *Folks from Dixie*. New York: Dodd, Mead,1898.
———. *The Sport of the Gods*. 1902. Reprint. Miami: Mnemosyne, 1969.
Duplechan, Larry. *Captain Swing*. Boston: Alyson Books, 1993.
———. *Tangled Up in Blue*. New York: St. Martin's Press, 1989.
Ellis, Trey. *Here and Now*. New York: Simon and Schuster, 1999.
———. *Home Repairs*. New York: Simon and Schuster, 1993.
Ellison, Ralph. *Invisible Man*.1952. Reprint. New York: Signet Books, 1964.
Everett, Percival. *The Body of Martin Aguilera*. Seattle: Owl Creek Press. 1994.
———. *Cutting Lisa*. New York: Ticknor and Fields, 1986.
———. *For Her Dark Skin*. Seattle: Owl Creek Press, 1990.
———. *Frenzy*. Saint Paul: Graywolf Press, 1997.
———. *Glyph*. Saint Paul: Graywolf Press, 1999.
———. *God's Country*. Boston: Faber Press, 1994.
———. *Walk Me to the Distance*. New York: Ticknor and Fields, 1985.
———. *Watershed*. Saint Paul: Graywolf Press, 1996.
———. *Zulus*. Sag Harbor, N.Y.: Permanent Press, 1990.
Fair, Ronald L. *Hog Butcher*. New York: Harcourt Brace and World, 1966.
———. *We Can't Breathe*. New York: Harper and Row, 1972.
———. *World of Nothing: Two Novellas*. New York: Harper and Row, 1970.
Fauset, Jessie. *The Chinaberry Tree: A Novel of American Life*. 1931. Reprint. College Park, Md.: McGrath, 1969.
———. *There Is Confusion*. New York: Boni and Liveright, 1924.
Fisher, Rudolph. *The Conjure-Man Dies*, 1932. Reprint. New York: Arno Press and *The New York Times*, 1971.
Flowers, Arthur. *Another Good Loving Blues*. New York: Viking Press, 1993.
Forrest, Leon. *The Bloodworth Orphans*. New York: Random House, 1977.
———. *Two Wings to Veil My Face*. Chicago: Another Chicago Press, 1983.
Frank, Waldo David. *Holiday*. New York: Boni and Liveright, 1923.
Gaines, Ernest J. *Catherine Carmier: A Novel*. 1964. Reprint. New York: Vintage Books, 1993.
Gilmore, F. Grant. *"Problem": A Military Novel*. Rochester: Press of Henry Connolly Co., 1915.
Gomez, Jewelle. *The Gilda Stories*. New York: Firebrand Press, 1991.
Grant, J. W. *Out of the Darkness; or, Diabolism and Destiny*. Nashville: National Baptist Publishing Board, 1909.

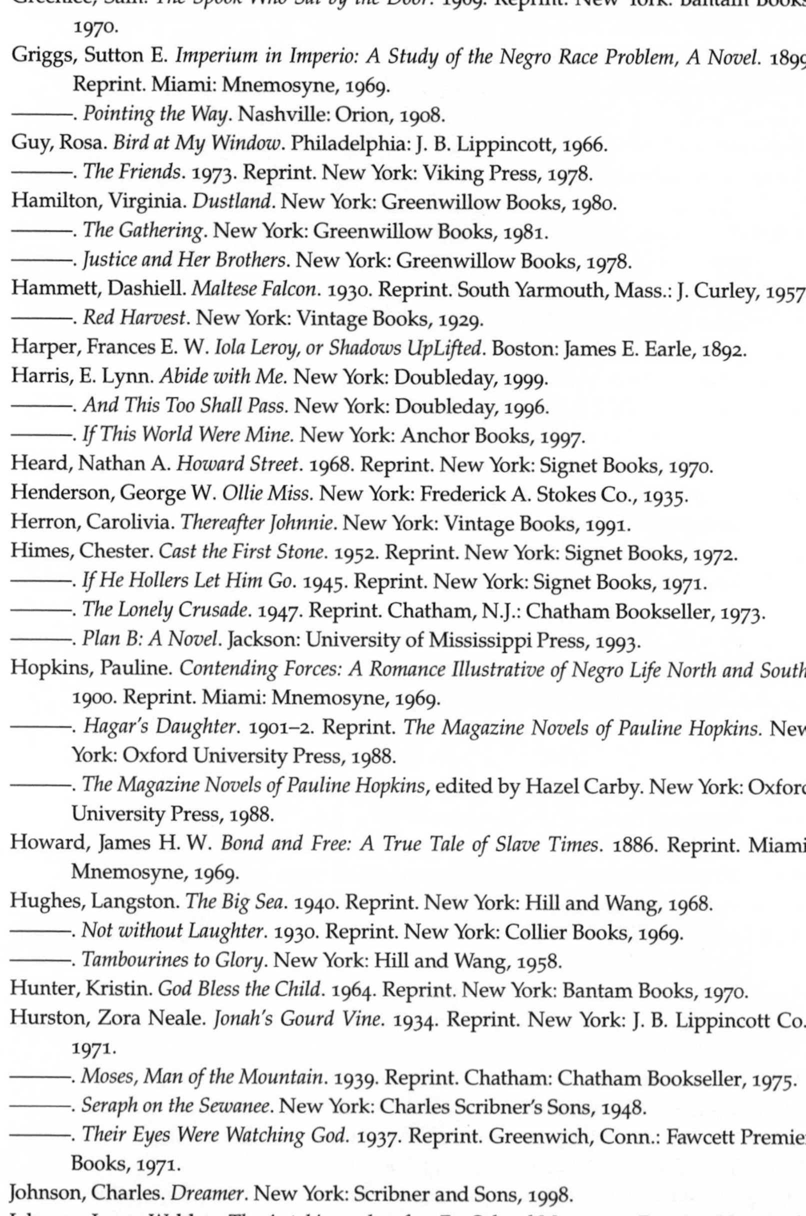

Greenlee, Sam. *The Spook Who Sat by the Door.* 1969. Reprint. New York: Bantam Books, 1970.

Griggs, Sutton E. *Imperium in Imperio: A Study of the Negro Race Problem, A Novel.* 1899. Reprint. Miami: Mnemosyne, 1969.

———. *Pointing the Way.* Nashville: Orion, 1908.

Guy, Rosa. *Bird at My Window.* Philadelphia: J. B. Lippincott, 1966.

———. *The Friends.* 1973. Reprint. New York: Viking Press, 1978.

Hamilton, Virginia. *Dustland.* New York: Greenwillow Books, 1980.

———. *The Gathering.* New York: Greenwillow Books, 1981.

———. *Justice and Her Brothers.* New York: Greenwillow Books, 1978.

Hammett, Dashiell. *Maltese Falcon.* 1930. Reprint. South Yarmouth, Mass.: J. Curley, 1957.

———. *Red Harvest.* New York: Vintage Books, 1929.

Harper, Frances E. W. *Iola Leroy, or Shadows UpLifted.* Boston: James E. Earle, 1892.

Harris, E. Lynn. *Abide with Me.* New York: Doubleday, 1999.

———. *And This Too Shall Pass.* New York: Doubleday, 1996.

———. *If This World Were Mine.* New York: Anchor Books, 1997.

Heard, Nathan A. *Howard Street.* 1968. Reprint. New York: Signet Books, 1970.

Henderson, George W. *Ollie Miss.* New York: Frederick A. Stokes Co., 1935.

Herron, Carolivia. *Thereafter Johnnie.* New York: Vintage Books, 1991.

Himes, Chester. *Cast the First Stone.* 1952. Reprint. New York: Signet Books, 1972.

———. *If He Hollers Let Him Go.* 1945. Reprint. New York: Signet Books, 1971.

———. *The Lonely Crusade.* 1947. Reprint. Chatham, N.J.: Chatham Bookseller, 1973.

———. *Plan B: A Novel.* Jackson: University of Mississippi Press, 1993.

Hopkins, Pauline. *Contending Forces: A Romance Illustrative of Negro Life North and South.* 1900. Reprint. Miami: Mnemosyne, 1969.

———. *Hagar's Daughter.* 1901–2. Reprint. *The Magazine Novels of Pauline Hopkins.* New York: Oxford University Press, 1988.

———. *The Magazine Novels of Pauline Hopkins*, edited by Hazel Carby. New York: Oxford University Press, 1988.

Howard, James H. W. *Bond and Free: A True Tale of Slave Times.* 1886. Reprint. Miami: Mnemosyne, 1969.

Hughes, Langston. *The Big Sea.* 1940. Reprint. New York: Hill and Wang, 1968.

———. *Not without Laughter.* 1930. Reprint. New York: Collier Books, 1969.

———. *Tambourines to Glory.* New York: Hill and Wang, 1958.

Hunter, Kristin. *God Bless the Child.* 1964. Reprint. New York: Bantam Books, 1970.

Hurston, Zora Neale. *Jonah's Gourd Vine.* 1934. Reprint. New York: J. B. Lippincott Co., 1971.

———. *Moses, Man of the Mountain.* 1939. Reprint. Chatham: Chatham Bookseller, 1975.

———. *Seraph on the Sewanee.* New York: Charles Scribner's Sons, 1948.

———. *Their Eyes Were Watching God.* 1937. Reprint. Greenwich, Conn.: Fawcett Premier Books, 1971.

Johnson, Charles. *Dreamer.* New York: Scribner and Sons, 1998.

Johnson, James Weldon. *The Autobiography of an Ex-Colored Man.* 1912. Reprint. New York: Hill and Wang, 1960.

Jones, J. McHenry. *Hearts of Gold.* Wheeling, W. Va.: Daily Intelligencer Steam Job Press, 1896.

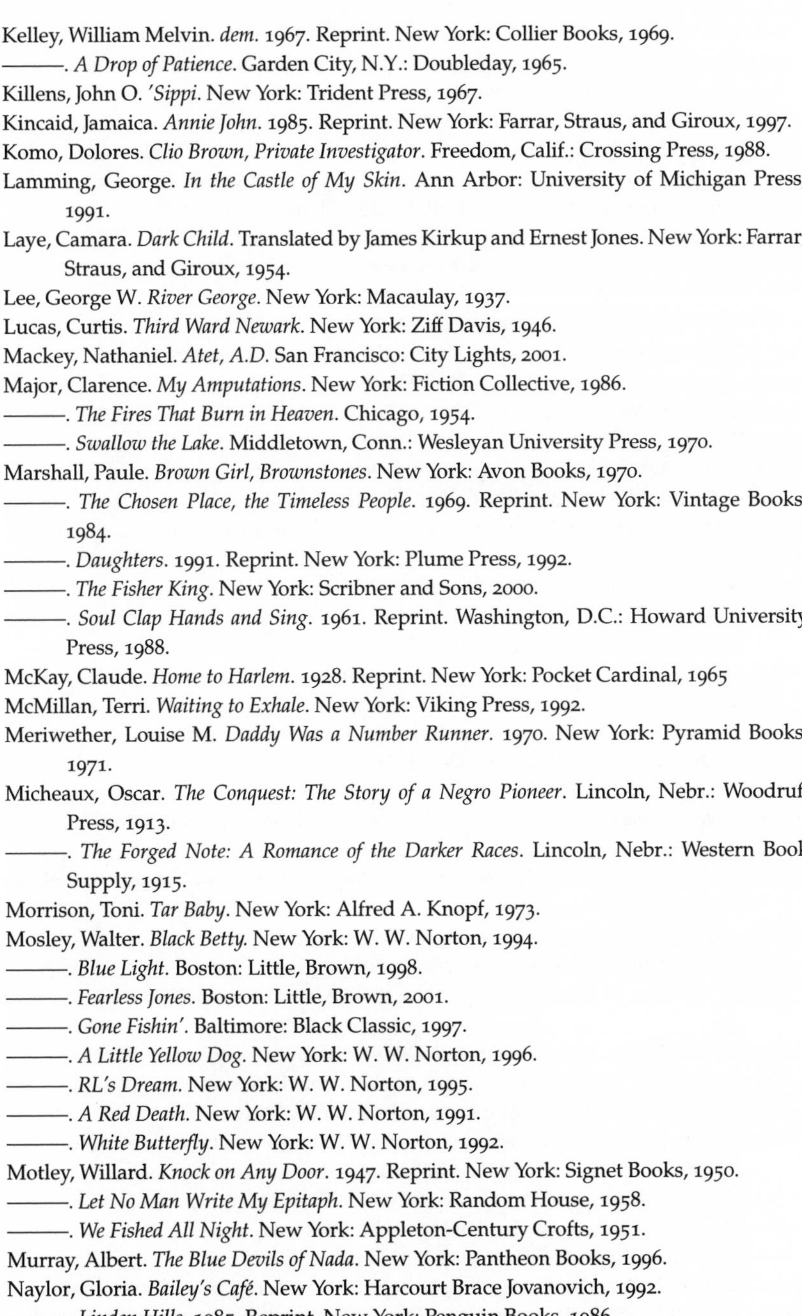

Kelley, William Melvin. *dem.* 1967. Reprint. New York: Collier Books, 1969.
———. *A Drop of Patience.* Garden City, N.Y.: Doubleday, 1965.
Killens, John O. *'Sippi.* New York: Trident Press, 1967.
Kincaid, Jamaica. *Annie John.* 1985. Reprint. New York: Farrar, Straus, and Giroux, 1997.
Komo, Dolores. *Clio Brown, Private Investigator.* Freedom, Calif.: Crossing Press, 1988.
Lamming, George. *In the Castle of My Skin.* Ann Arbor: University of Michigan Press, 1991.
Laye, Camara. *Dark Child.* Translated by James Kirkup and Ernest Jones. New York: Farrar, Straus, and Giroux, 1954.
Lee, George W. *River George.* New York: Macaulay, 1937.
Lucas, Curtis. *Third Ward Newark.* New York: Ziff Davis, 1946.
Mackey, Nathaniel. *Atet, A.D.* San Francisco: City Lights, 2001.
Major, Clarence. *My Amputations.* New York: Fiction Collective, 1986.
———. *The Fires That Burn in Heaven.* Chicago, 1954.
———. *Swallow the Lake.* Middletown, Conn.: Wesleyan University Press, 1970.
Marshall, Paule. *Brown Girl, Brownstones.* New York: Avon Books, 1970.
———. *The Chosen Place, the Timeless People.* 1969. Reprint. New York: Vintage Books, 1984.
———. *Daughters.* 1991. Reprint. New York: Plume Press, 1992.
———. *The Fisher King.* New York: Scribner and Sons, 2000.
———. *Soul Clap Hands and Sing.* 1961. Reprint. Washington, D.C.: Howard University Press, 1988.
McKay, Claude. *Home to Harlem.* 1928. Reprint. New York: Pocket Cardinal, 1965
McMillan, Terri. *Waiting to Exhale.* New York: Viking Press, 1992.
Meriwether, Louise M. *Daddy Was a Number Runner.* 1970. New York: Pyramid Books, 1971.
Micheaux, Oscar. *The Conquest: The Story of a Negro Pioneer.* Lincoln, Nebr.: Woodruff Press, 1913.
———. *The Forged Note: A Romance of the Darker Races.* Lincoln, Nebr.: Western Book Supply, 1915.
Morrison, Toni. *Tar Baby.* New York: Alfred A. Knopf, 1973.
Mosley, Walter. *Black Betty.* New York: W. W. Norton, 1994.
———. *Blue Light.* Boston: Little, Brown, 1998.
———. *Fearless Jones.* Boston: Little, Brown, 2001.
———. *Gone Fishin'.* Baltimore: Black Classic, 1997.
———. *A Little Yellow Dog.* New York: W. W. Norton, 1996.
———. *RL's Dream.* New York: W. W. Norton, 1995.
———. *A Red Death.* New York: W. W. Norton, 1991.
———. *White Butterfly.* New York: W. W. Norton, 1992.
Motley, Willard. *Knock on Any Door.* 1947. Reprint. New York: Signet Books, 1950.
———. *Let No Man Write My Epitaph.* New York: Random House, 1958.
———. *We Fished All Night.* New York: Appleton-Century Crofts, 1951.
Murray, Albert. *The Blue Devils of Nada.* New York: Pantheon Books, 1996.
Naylor, Gloria. *Bailey's Café.* New York: Harcourt Brace Jovanovich, 1992.
———. *Linden Hills.* 1985. Reprint. New York: Penguin Books, 1986.
Neely, Barbara. *Blanche on the Lam.* New York: Penguin Books, 1992.

Offord, Carl. *The White Face*. New York: Robert M. McBride, 1943.
Petry, Ann. *Country Place*. 1947. Reprint. Chatham, N.J.: Chatham Bookseller, 1971.
———. *The Narrows*. Boston: Houghton Mifflin, 1953.
———. *The Street*. 1946. Reprint. New York: Pyramid Books, 1961.
Pharr, Robert Dean. *Book of Numbers*. 1969. Reprint. New York: Avon Books, 1970.
Pryor, George. *Neither Bond Nor Free*. New York: J. S. Oglive, 1902.
Reed, Ishmael. *Flight to Canada*. New York: Random House, 1976.
———. *The Free-Lance Pallbearers*. 1967. Reprint. New York: Bantam Books, 1969.
———. *The Last Days of Louisiana Red*. New York: Random House, 1974.
———. *Reckless Eyeballing*. New York: St. Martin's Press, 1986.
———. *Shrovetide in Old New Orleans*. New York: Discus Books, 1979.
———. *Yellow Back Radio Broke-Down*. Garden City, N.Y.: Doubleday, 1969.
Savoy, Willard. *Alien Land*. New York: E. P. Dutton, 1949.
Shackelford, Otis M. *Lillian Simmons; or The Conflict of Sections*. Kansas City: R. M. Rigby Printing Co., 1915.
Shockley, Ann. *Loving Her*. 1974. Reprint. New York: Avon Books, 1978.
Schuyler, George. *Black No More*. New York: Macaulay, 1931.
Smith, William G. *Anger at Innocence*. 1950. Reprint. Chatham, N.J.: Chatham Bookseller, 1973.
———. *Last of the Conquerors*. New York: Farrar, Straus, 1948.
Stowers, Walter H., and William H. Anderson [Sanda, pseud]. *Appointed; an American Novel*. Detroit: Detroit Law Printing Co., 1894.
Thiong'o, Ngugi wa. *Weep Not, Child*. 1964. Reprint. London: James Currey/Heinemann, 1987.
Toomer, Jean. *Cane*. 1923. Reprint. New York: Perennial Classics, 1969.
Turpin, Waters. *O Canaan!* New York: Doubleday, 1939.
Tutola, Amos. *Palm-Wine Drinkard*. New York: Grove Press, 1953.
Walker, Alice. *By the Light of My Father's Smile*. New York: Random House, 1998.
———. *Meridian*. New York: Harcourt Brace Jovanovich, 1976.
Webb, Frank. *The Garies and Their Friends*. 1857. Reprint. New York: Arno Press and *The New York Times*, 1969.
Wesley, Valerie Wilson. *Devil's Gonna Get Him*. New York: Putnam, 1996.
———. *When Death Comes Stealing*. New York: Putnam, 1995.
West, Dorothy. *The LivingIs Easy*. 1948. New York: Arno Press and *The New York Times*, 1969.
Wideman, John Edgar. *Brothers and Keepers*. New York: Holt, Rinehart and Winston, 1984.
———. *Fatheralong*. New York: Pantheon, 1994; London: Picador, 1995.
———. *Fever*. New York: Holt, 1989; London: Penguin Books, 1991.
Williams, John A. *Captain Blackman*. 1972. Reprint. New York: Bantam Books, 1974.
———. *!Click Song*. Boston: Houghton Mifflin, 1982.
———. *The Junior Bachelor Society*. Garden City, N.Y.: Doubleday, 1976.
———. *Mothersill and the Foxes*. Garden City, N.Y.: Doubleday, 1975.
———. *Sissie*. 1963. Reprint. Garden City, N.Y.: Anchor Books, 1969.
———. *Sons of Darkness, Sons of Light*. 1969. Reprint. New York: Pocket Books, 1970.
Wilson, Harriet E. "Our Nig," pseud. *Our Nig; or, Sketches from the Life of a Free Black, In a*

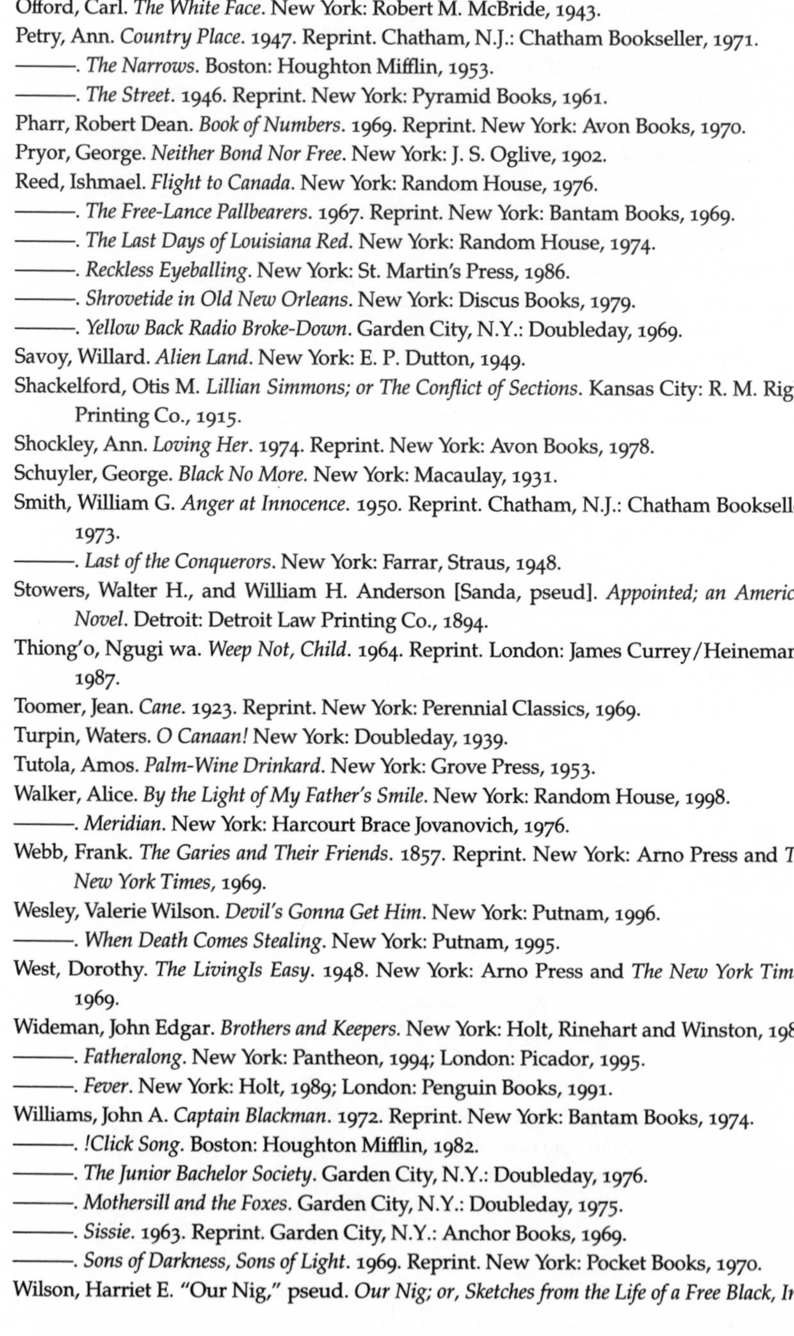

Two–Story White House, North Showing That Slavery's Shadows Fall Even There. 1859. 2nd ed. New York: Vintage Books, 1983.
Wright, Richard. *Lawd Today*. New York: Avon Books, 1963.
———. *Long Dream*. Garden City, N.Y.: Doubleday, 1958.
———. *Native Son*. 1940. Reprint. New York: Perennial Classics, 1966.
———. *The Outsider*. 1953. Reprint. New York: Perennial Library, 1965.
———. *Savage Holliday*. 1954. Reprint. New York: Award Books, 1965.
Young, Al. *Seduction by Light*. New York: Delta Fiction, 1988.
———. *Sitting Pretty: A Novel*. New York: Holt, Rinehart, and Winston, 1976.
———. *Who Is Angelina?* 1976. Reprint. Berkeley: University of California Press, 1996.

Secondary Sources

Abrahams, Roger D. *Deep Down in the Jungle: Negro Narrative Folklore from the Streets of Philadelphia*. Rev. ed. Chicago: Aldine, 1979.
———. "Playing the Dozens." *Journal of American Folklore* 75 (1962): 209–20.
———. *Positively Black*. Englewood Cliffs, N.J.: Prentice-Hall, 1970.
Abrams, M. H. *A Glossary of Literary Terms*, 5th ed. New York: Holt, Rinehart and Winston, 1985.
Ahmad, Aijaz. "AIDS and African American Women." *Communication at CDC*. 6 Aug. 2001. Center for Disease Control. 27 Mar. 2002, http://www.cdc.gov/communication/tips/aids/htm.—
———. "The Politics of Literary Postcoloniality." *Race and Class* 36, no. 3 (Jan–Mar 1995): 1–20.
Aldiss, Brian, with David Wingrove. *Trillion Year Spree: The History of Science Fiction*. New York: Atheneum, 1986.
Alexander, Margaret Walker. "Richard Wright." In *Richard Wright: Impressions and Perspectives*, edited by David Ray and Robert M. Farnsworth, 47–67. Reprint. Ann Arbor: University of Michigan Press, 1973.
Alterman, Peter S. "The Surreal Translations of Samuel R. Delany." *Science-Fiction Studies* 4, no. 11 (March 1977): 25–34.
Anderson, Benedict. *Imagined Communities: Reflections on the Origin and Spread of Nationalism*. Rev. ed. New York: Verso, 1996.
Andrews, William L., Frances Smith Foster, and Trudier Harris, eds. *The Oxford Companion to African American Literature*. New York: Oxford University Press, 1997.
Angier, Natalie. "Do Races Differ? Not Really, Genes Show." *New York Times:* August 22, 2000: D1+.
Anzaldua, Gloria. "Preface," *Borderlands/La Frontera: The New Mestiza*. San Francisco: Aunt Lute Books, 1987.
Aptheker, Herbert. *Annotated Bibliography of the Writings of W. E. B. Du Bois*. Millwood, N.Y.: Kraus-Thomson, 1973.
———., ed. *A Documentary History of the Negro People in the United States*. 4 volumes. 3rd ed. New York: Citadel Press, 1965.
Arnold, Martin. "In the Art of the Craft." *New York Times:* July 27, 2000: B3.
Asante, Molefi Kete. *The Afrocentric Idea*. Philadelphia: Temple University Press, 1987.

———. *Afrocentricity.* Trenton: Africa World Press, 1980.

———. *Kemet, Afrocentricity, and Knowledge.* Trenton: Africa World Press, 1990.

Attaway, Richard. *Blood on the Forge.* 1941. Reprint. New York: Collier Books, 1970.

Azoulay, Katya Gibel. "Experience, Empathy and Strategic Essentialism." *Cultural Studies* 11, no. 1 (1997): 89–110.

Baker, Houston, Jr. *Blues, Ideology, and Afro-American Literature: A Vernacular Theory.* Chicago: University of Chicago Press, 1989.

———. Review of *The Last Days of Louisiana Red,* by Ishmael Reed. *Black World* 24, no. 8 (June 1975): 51–52, 89.

Bakhtin, Mikhail. *The Dialogic Imagination.* Translated by Caryl Emerson and Michael Holquist. Austin: University of Texas Press, 1981.

Baldwin, Davarian L. "Black Empires, White Desires: The Spatial Politics of Identity in theAge of Hip Hop." *Black Renaissance/Renaissance Noire* 2, no. 2 (Summer 1999): 140.

Baldwin, James. *The Fire Next Time.* New York: Dial Press, 1963.

Baldwin, Joseph. *The Flush Times of Alabama and Mississippi: A Series of Sketches.* New York: D. Appleton, 1854.

Bambara, Toni Cade. "On the Issue of Roles." In *The Black Woman: An Anthology,* edited by Toni Cade, 101–10. New York: Signet Books, 1970.

Baraka, Amiri. "The 'Blues Aesthetic' and the 'Black Aesthetic': Aesthetics as the Continuing Political History of a Culture." *Black Music Research Journal* (Fall 1991): 101–9.

Barbour, Floyd. *The Black Power Revolt.* New York: Collier Books, 1968.

Barthes, Roland. "The Death of the Author." In *The Rustle of Language.* Translated by Richard Howard. New York: Hill and Wang, 1986.

———. *Mythologies.* Translated and edited by Annette Lavers. New York: Noonday Press, 1972.

——— *The Pleasure of the Text.* Translated by Richard Miller. New York: Hill and Wang, 1975.

———. *S/Z.* Translated by Richard Miller. New York: Noonday Press, 1974.

Bascom, William. "The Folklore and Literature." In *The African World: A Survey of Social Research,* edited by Robert A. Lystod, 459–90. New York: Frederick Praeger, 1965.

———. "The Forms of Folklore: Prose Narratives." *Journal of American Folklore* 78 (1965): 3–20.

Becker, George J. "Introduction: Modern Realism as a Literary Movement." In *Documents of Literary Realism,* edited by George J. Becker, 3–38. Princeton: Princeton University Press, 1963.

Bell, Bernard W. *The Afro-American Novel and Its Tradition.* Amherst: University of Massachusetts Press, 1987.

———. *The Folk Roots of Contemporary African American Poetry.* Detroit: Broadside, 1974.

———. "Styron's Confessions." *Michigan Quarterly Review* 7 (Fall 1968): 280–82.

Bell, Derrick. *Faces at the Bottom of the Well: The Permanence of Racism.* New York: Basic Books, 1992.

Bell, Roseanne P., Bettye J. Parker, and Beverly Guy-Sheftall, eds. *Sturdy Black Bridges: Images of Black Women in Literature.* Garden City, N.Y.: Anchor Press, 1979.

Benedict, Ruth. *The Chrysanthemum and the Sword.* Boston: Houghton Mifflin, 1946.

Berger, Peter L., and Thomas Luckman. *The Social Construction of Reality: A Treatise in the Sociology of Knowledge*. Baltimore: Penguin Books, 1966.

Bhabha, Homi. *The Location of Culture*. New York: Routledge, 1994.

Bialostosky, Don. "Dialogics as an Art of Discourse in Literary Criticism." *PMLA* 101, no. 4 (September 1986): 788–97.

Blake, Susan. "Toni Morrison." In *Dictionary of Literary Biography (Afro-American Fiction Writers after 1955)*, Vol. 33, edited by Thadious M. Davis and Trudier Harris, 187–99. Detroit: Gale, 1984.

———, and James A. Miller. "The Business of Writing: An Interview with David Bradley." *Callaloo* 7 (Spring–Summer 1984): 19–39.

Bland, Alden. *Behold a Cry*. New York: Charles Scribner's Sons, 1947.

Blassingame, John W. *The Slave Community: Plantation Life in the Ante-Bellum South*. New York: Oxford University Press, 1972.

———, ed. *Slave Testimony: Two Centuries Of Letters, Speeches, Interviews, And Autobiographies*. Baton Rouge: Louisiana State University Press, 1977.

Blauner, Robert. "Black Culture: Myth or Reality?" In *Afro-American Anthropology: Contemporary Perspectives*, edited by Norman E. Whitten Jr. and John F. Szwed, 347–66. New York: The Free Press, 1970.

———. *Racial Oppression in America*. New York: Harper and Row, 1972.

Blaustein, Albert P., and Robert L. Zangrando. *Civil Rights and the American Negro: A Documentary History*. New York: Washington Square, 1968.

Bloom, Allan. *The Closing of the American Mind: How Higher Education Has Failed Democracy and Impoverished the Souls of Today's Students*. New York: Simon and Schuster, 1987.

Bluestein, Gene. *The Voice of the Folk: Folklore and American Literary Theory*. Amherst: University of Massachusetts Press, 1972.

Bone, Robert A. *Down Home: A History of Afro-American Short Fiction from Its Beginnings to the End of the Harlem Renaissance*. New York: Capricorn Books, 1975.

———. *The Negro Novel in America*. Rev. ed. New Haven: Yale University Press, 1965.

Bontemps, Arna. "The Black Renaissance of the Twenties." *Black World* (November 1970): 5–9.

———, ed. *Great Slave Narratives*. Boston: Beacon Press, 1969.

———. "Introduction." In *Cane*, by Jean Toomer, vi–xvi. 1923. Reprint. New York: Harper and Row, 1969.

———, and Jack Conroy. *Anyplace but Here*. New York: Hill and Wang, 1966.

Booth, Wayne C. *The Rhetoric of Fiction*. 1961. Reprint. Chicago: Phoenix Books, 1967.

———. *A Rhetoric of Irony*. Chicago: University of Chicago Press, 1974.

Bourdieu, Pierre. "The Field of Cultural Production on Art, Literature, and Culture." In *The Field Of Cultural Production: Essays on Art and Literature*, edited by Randal Johnson, 22–73. New York: Columbia University Press, 1993.

Botkin, B. A., ed. *Lay My Burden Down*. Chicago: University of Chicago Press, 1945.

Bracey, John H., Jr. "Black Nationalism since Garvey." In *Key Issues in the Afro-American Experience*. Vols. 1 and 2, edited by Nathan I. Huggins, Martin Kilson, and Daniel Fox, 259–79. New York: Harcourt Brace Jovanovich, 1971.

Brady, Martin. "Out of Chicago, A Black 'Ulysses.'" *Chicago Sun-Times*, July 19, 1992: 12.

Brailsford, Frances. "David (Henry Jr.) Bradley." In *Contemporary Authors: New Revision Series*, Vol. 26, edited by Hal May and James G. Lesniak, 71–73. Detroit: Gale, 1989.

Bragg, Rick. "Author's Downward Spin Rivals Tragedies in Her Novels of Black America." *The New York Times:* March 2, 1998, A11.

Brigham, Cathy. "Dissenting Fictions: Identity and Resistance in the Contemporary U.S. Novel." Ph.D. diss., Pennsylvania State University, 1995.

———. "Identity, Masculinity, and Desire in David Bradley's Fictions." *Contemporary Literature* 36, no. 2 (1995): 289–316.

Brown, Ray, ed. *Contemporary Heroes and Heroines.* Detroit: Gale Research, 1990.

Brown, Sterling A. *Negro Poetry and Drama and the Negro in American Fiction.* New York: Atheneum, 1969.

Brown, Sterling N. *My Own Life Story.* Washington, D.C.: Hamilton Printing Company, 1924.

Brown, William H. *Power of Sympathy.* 1789. Reprint. New York: Penguin Books, 1996.

Bryant, Jerry. "From Death to Life: The Fiction of Ernest J. Gaines." *Iowa Review* 3, no. 1 (Winter 1972): 106–20.

Buchanan, Ian, and John Marks. *Deleuze and Literature.* Edinburgh: Edinburgh University Press, 2000.

Butterfield, Fox. "Racial Disparities Seen as Pervasive in Juvenile Justice." *New York* Times, April 26, 2000, A1+.

Byrd, Rudolph P., ed. *I Call Myself an Artist: Writings by and about Charles Johnson.* Bloomington: Indiana University Press, 1999.

Cade, John B. "Out of the Mouths of Ex-Slaves." *Journal of Negro History* 20 (July 1935): 294–337.

Calwelti, John. *Leon Forrest: Introductions and Interpretations.* Bowling Green: Bowling Green State University Popular Press, 1997.

Carby, Hazel. "Introduction." In *The Magazine Novels of Pauline Hopkins,* xxix–l. New York: Oxford University Press, 1988.

———. "The Multicultural Wars." *Radical History Review* 54 (1992): 7–18.

Carmichael, Stokely, and Charles V. Hamilton. *Black Power: The Politics of Liberation in America.* New York: Vintage Books, 1967.

Carroll, Rebecca. "Interview with Barbara Neely." In *I Know What the Red Clay Looks Like: The Voice and Vision of Black Women Writers,* edited by Rebecca Caroll, 174–84. New York: Crown Trade Paperbacks, 1994.

Cartey, Wilfred. "Introduction." In *Negritude: Black Poetry from Africa and the Caribbean,* translated and edited by Norman R. Shapiro, 17–37. New York: October House, 1970.

Castillo, Ana. "A Countryless Woman: The Early Feminista." In *Multi-America: Essays on Cultural Wars and Cultural Peace,* edited by Ishmael Reed, 261–78. New York: Penguin Books, 1998.

Césaire, Aimé. "Journal of a Return to My Native Country." 1939. Reprint. *Return to My Native Land.* Translated by Émile Snyder. Paris: Présence Africaine, 1971.

Chambers, Veronica. "The Invisible Woman Reappears—Sort Of." *Newsweek,* February 16, 1998: 68.

Chandler, Raymond. *Big Sleep.* 1939. Reprint. New York: Vintage Books, 1976.

Chapman, Abraham. "The Harlem Renaissance in Literary History." *College Language Association Journal* 11, no. 1 (September 1967): 38–58.

Chase, Richard. *The American Novel and Its Tradition.* Garden City, N.Y.: Doubleday, 1957.

Cheney, Lynne. *Telling the Truth: Why Our Culture and Our Country Have Stopped Making Sense—and What We Can Do about It*. New York: Simon and Schuster, 1995.

Chesnutt, Charles W. Response. "The Negro in Art: How Shall He Be Portrayed, A Symposium." *The Crisis* 33, no. 1 (November 1926): 28–29.

———. *The Marrow of Tradition*. 1901. Reprint. Ann Arbor: Ann Arbor Paperbacks, 1969.

Christian, Barbara. *Black Women Novelists: The Development of a Tradition, 1892–1976*. Westport, Conn.: Greenwood Press, 1980.

Chinweizu, Onuwuchekwa Jemie, and Ihechukwu Madubuike. *Toward the Decolonization of African Literature*. Vol. 1. Washington, D.C.: Howard University Press, 1983.

Clark, John Henrik, ed. *William Styron's Nat Turner: Ten Black Writers Respond*. Boston: Beacon Press, 1968.

Clark, Kenneth. *Dark Ghetto: Dilemmas of Social Power*. New York: Harper Torchbooks, 1967.

Clark, Lewis Garrard. *Narratives of the Sufferings of Lewis and Milton Clarke*. 1846. Reprint. New York: Arno Press and *The New York Times*, 1969.

Cleaver, Eldridge. *Soul on Ice*. New York: McGraw-Hill, 1968.

Collins, Patricia Hill. *Black Feminist Thought: Knowledge, Consciousness, and the Politics of Empowerment*. New York: Routledge, 1991.

"Colson Whitehead." *Contemporary Authors*. 4 Oct. 2002, 22. Gale Literary Databases. 22 Nov. 2002, http://www.galenet.com.

Combahee River Collective. "Black Feminist Statement." In *All the Women Are White, All the Blacks Are Men, But Some of Us Are Brave*, edited by Gloria T. Hull, Patricia Bell Scott, and Barbara Smith, 13–22. Old Westbury: Feminist Press, 1982.

Crenshaw, Kimberlé, et al., eds. *Critical Race Theory: The Key Writings That Formed the Movement*. New York: New Press, 1995.

Crews, Frederick. *The Critics Bear It Away: American Fiction and the Academy*. New York: Random, 1992.

Cronon, Edmund D. *Black Moses: The Story of Marcus Garvey and the Universal Negro Improvement Association*. 1955. Reprint. Madison: University of Wisconsin Press, 1968.

Crossly, Robert. "Introduction." In *Kindred*, by Octavia Butler, x–xxiii. Garden City, N.Y.: Doubleday, 1979.

Crossman, Richard, ed. *The God That Failed*. 1950. Reprint. New York: Bantam Matrix, 1965.

Crouch, Stanley. "The Soul of Joubert Jones." *New York Times Book Review*, July 25, 1993: 14.

Crummell, Alexander. "The Social Principle among a People." In *The Greatness of Christ and Other Sermons*, 254–68. New York: Thomas Whittaker, 1882.

Cruse, Harold. *The Crisis of the Negro Intellectual*. 1967. Reprint. New York: Apollo Editions, 1968.

———. *Rebellion or Revolution?* New York: William Morrow, 1969.

———. "Revolutionary Nationalism and the Afro-American." In *Black Fire: An Anthology of Afro-American Writing*, edited by LeRoi Jones and Larry Neal, 39–63. New York: Apollo Editions, 1969.

Cryer, Dan. "The Evolving Ballad of Colson Whitehead, Writer." *Los Angeles Times*, June 17, 2001: E4.

Cullen, Countee, ed. *Caroling Dusk: An Anthology of Verse by Negro Poets.* New York: Harper and Brothers, 1927.

———. "Heritage." 1925. Reprint. In *Modern and Contemporary Afro-American Poetry*, edited by Bernard W. Bell, 47–50. Boston: Allyn and Bacon, 1972.

———. Response. "The Negro in Art: How Shall He Be Portrayed, A Symposium." *The Crisis* 32, no. 4 (August 1926): 193–94.

Culler, Jonathan. *On Deconstruction: Theory and Criticism after Structuralism.* Ithaca: Cornell University Press, 1983.

———. *Structuralist Poetics: Structuralism, Linguistics, and the Study of Literature.* Ithaca: Cornell University Press, 1976.

Dance, Daryl Cumber. "An Interview with Paule Marshall." *Southern Review* 28, no. 1 (January 1992): 1–20.

Davis, Angela Y. "Rape, Racism, and the Capitalist Setting." *Black Scholar* 9, no. 7 (1978): 24–30.

———. *Women, Race, & Class.* New York: Vintage Books, 1983.

Davis, Christopher. "CS Interview with Larry Duplechan." *Christopher Street* 10 (1987): 60–62.

deCerteau, Michel. *The Practice of Everyday Life.* Translated by Steven F. Randall. Berkeley: University of California Press, 1984.

Decker, Jeffrey Louis, ed. "The Black Aesthetic Movement." In *Dictionary of Literary Biography Documentary Series*, Vol. 8, 254–312. Detroit: Gale Research, Inc., 1991.

Degler, Carl N. "Slavery and the Genesis of American Race Prejudice." *Comparative Studies of Society and History* 2 (October 1959): 49–66.

Delany, Martin R. *The Condition, Elevation, Emigration and Destiny of the Colored People of the United States.* Philadelphia: The Author, 1852; Reprint. New York: Arno Press and *The New York Times*, 1969.

Deleuze, Gilles, and Félix Guattari. *Anti-Oedipus: Capitalism and Schizophrenia.* Translated by Robert Hurley, Mark Seem, and Helen R. Lane; preface by Michel Foucault. Minneapolis: University of Minnesota Press, c1983.

———. "What Is a Minor Literature?" In *Kafka: Toward a Minor Literature*, translated by Dana Polan. Minneapolis: University of Minnesota Press, 1986.

Delgado, Richard, ed. *Critical Race Theory: The Cutting Edge.* Philadelphia: Temple University Press, 1995.

Denning, Michael. *The Cultural Front: The Laboring of American Culture in the Twentieth Century.* London: Verso, 1996.

Dent, Tom. "Umbra Days." *Black American Literature Forum* 14, no. 3 (Autumn 1980): 105–8.

Derrida, Jaques. *Of Grammatology.* Translated by Gayatri Chakravorty Spivak. Baltimore: John Hopkins University Press, 1974.

Dillard, J. L. *Black English: Its History and Usage in the United States.* New York: Random House, 1972.

Dollard, John. "The Dozens: The Dialect of Insult." *American Imago* 1 (1939): 3–25.

Donaldson, Melvin, ed. *Cornerstones: An Anthology of African American Literature.* New York: St. Martin's Press, 1996.

Dorson, Richard. "Africa and the Folklorist." In *African Folklore*, edited by Dorson, 3–67. Bloomington: Indiana University Press, 1972.

———. *American Negro Folktales*. Greenwich, Conn.: Fawcett Premier Books, 1967.

———. "The Identification of Folklore in American Literature." 1957. Reprint. In *American Folklore and the Historian*, edited by Richard M. Dorson, 186–203. Chicago: University of Chicago Press, 1971.

Douglass, Frederick. *Narrative of the Life of Frederick Douglass: An American Slave*. 1845. Reprint, edited by Benjamin Quarles. Cambridge: Belknap Press, 1967.

———. "No Progress Without Struggle!, 1849." In *The Black Power Revolt*, edited by Floyd B. Barbour, 36–37. Boston: Extending Horizons Books, Porter Sargent, 1968.

Downing, Henry F. *The American Cavalryman; A Liberian Romance*. New York: Neale, 1917.

Draper, James P., ed. *Black Literature Criticism*. Vol. 3. Detroit: Gale, 1992.

Drake, St. Clair, and Horace R. Cayton. *Black Metropolis: A Study of Negro Life in a Northern City*. Rev. ed. New York: Harbinger Books, 1962.

Du Bois, W. E. B. *Black Reconstruction in America*. New York: Russell and Russell, 1935.

———"An Essay Toward a History of the Black Man in the Great War." *Crisis* 18, no. 2 (1919): 63–87.

———. *The Negro and the Gift of Black Folk: The Negroes in the Making of America*. 1924. Reprint. New York: Washington Square Press, 1970.

———. Review of *Nigger Heaven* by Carl Van Vechten. 1926. Reprint. New York: Harper Colophon, 1971.

———. *The Souls of Black Folk*. 1902. Reprint. Greenwich, Conn.: Crest Books, 1965.

duCille, Ann. "Postcolonialism and Afrocentricity: Discourse and Dat Course." In *The Black Columbiad: Defining Moments in African American Literature and Culture*, edited by Werner Sollors and Maria Diedrich, 28–41. Cambridge: Harvard University Press, 1994.

———. *Skin Trade*. Cambridge: Harvard University Press, 1996.

Dundes, Alan, ed. *Mother Wit from the Laughing Barrel: Readings in the Interpretation of African American Folklore*. Englewood Cliffs: Prentice–Hall, 1973.

Dyson, Michael Eric. *Reflecting Black: African American Cultural Criticism*. Minneapolis, University of Minnesota Press, 1993.

Eagleton, Terry. *The Illusions of Postmodernism*. Malden, Mass.: Blackwell, 1996.

———. *Literary Theory: An Introduction*. Minneapolis: University of Minnesota Press, 1983.

Eckley, Grace. "The Awakening of Mr. Afrinnegan: Kelley's *Dunfords Travels Everywheres* and Joyce's *Finnegans Wake*." *Obsidian: Black Literature in Review* 1 (Summer 1975): 27–40.

Egan, Philip J. "Unraveling Misogyny and Forging the New Self: Mother, Lover, and Storyteller in *The Chaneysville Incident*." *Papers on Language & Literature* (Summer 1997): 265–87.

Eigner, Edwin M. *The Metaphysical Novel in England and America: Dickens, Bulwer, Melville, and Hawthorne*. Berkeley: University of California Press, 1978.

Elkins, Stanley M. *Slavery: A Problem in American Institutional & Intellectual Life*. NewYork: Universal Library, 1959.

Elliot, Robert C. *The Power of Satire: Magic, Ritual, Art*. Princeton: Princeton University Press, 1969.

Ellis, Trey. "The New Black Aesthetic." *Callaloo* 12, no. 1 (1989): 233–51.

———. "Response to NBA Critiques." *Callaloo* 0, no. 38 (Winter 1989): 250–51.

Ellison, Ralph. "Eschatology." *Encyclopedia Britannica* 8 (1965): 694–97.

———. *Shadow and Act*. 1964. Reprint. New York: Signet Books, 1966.

Eze, Emmanuel Chukwudi, ed. *Race and the Enlightenment: A Reader*. Cambridge, Mass.: Blackwell, 1997.

Fabre, Michel. *The Unfinished Quest of Richard Wright*. Translated by Isabel Barzun. New York: William Morrow, 1973.

Fanon, Frantz. *Black Skin, White Masks*. Translated by Constance Farrington. New York: Grove Press, 1963.

———. *The Wretched of the Earth*. Translated by Constance Farrington. New York: Grove Press, 1963.

Farrand, Max. *The Framing of the Constitution of the United States*. New Haven: Yale University Press, 1961.

Farrison, Williams E. *William Wells Brown: Author and Reformer*. Chicago: University of Chicago Press, 1969.

Favor, J. Martin. "'Ain't Nothin' Like the Real Thing, Baby': Trey Ellis' Search for New Black Voices." *Callaloo* 16, no. 3 (Summer 1993): 694–705.

———. *Authentic Blackness: The Folk in the New Negro Renaissance*. Durham: Duke University Press, 1999.

Fiedler, Leslie A. *Love and Death in the American Novel*. New York: Delta Books, 1966.

Finnegan, Ruth. *Oral Literature in America*. London: Oxford University Press, 1970.

Fisher, Dexter, and Robert Stepto, eds. *Afro-American Literature: The Reconstruction of Instruction*. New York: The Modern Language Association of America, 1979.

Fong, Joe Chung. "Ethnic Conflict and Harmony between African and Asian Americans in the United States." In *Multi–America: Essays on Cultural Wars and Cultural Peace*, edited by Ishmael Reed, 309–18. New York: Penguin Books 1998.

Ford, Nick Aaron. *Black Studies: Threat-or-Challenge*. Port Washington, N.Y.: Kennikat Press, 1973.

Foster, Frances Smith. "Introduction." In *Minnie's Sacrifice/Sowing and Reaping/Trial and Triumph: Three Rediscovered Novels by Frances E. W. Harper*, edited by Frances Smith Foster, xi–xii. Boston: Beacon Press, 1994.

———. *Witnessing Slavery: The Development of Ante–Bellum Slave Narratives*. Westport, Conn.: Greenwood Press, 1979.

Foucault, Michel. *The Archeology of Knowledge*. Translated by A. M. Sheridan Smith. New York: Pantheon Books, 1972.

———. *The Order of Things: An Archaeology of the Human Sciences*. New York: Random House, 1970.

———. *Power/Knowledge: Selected Interviews and Other Writings, 1972–1977*. Translated and edited by Colin Gordon. New York: Pantheon Books, 1980.

———. "The Subject and Power." *Critical Inquiry* 8, no. 4 (1982): 777–95.

———. "What Is an Author?" *The Foucault Reader*. Translated and edited by Paul Rabinow. New York: Pantheon Books, 1984.

Franklin, Clyde W., II. "Men's Studies, the Men's Movement, and the Study of Black Masculinities: Further Demystification of Masculinities in America." In *The American Black Male: His Present Status and His Future*, edited by Richard G. Majors and Jacob U. Gordon, 3–19. Chicago: Nelson-Hall, 1994.

Franklin, John Hope. *From Slavery to Freedom: A History of Negro Americans*. 3rd ed. New York: Alfred A. Knopf, 1967.

Frazier, E. Franklin. *The Negro Church in America*. New York: Oxford University Press, 1970.

———. *The Negro in the United States*. Revised ed. New York: Macmillan, 1957.

Frazier, Kermit. "The Novels of John Wideman." *Black World* 24, no. 8 (June 1975): 18–38.

Frederickson, George M. "Toward a Social Interpretation of the Development of American Racism." In *Key Issues in the Afro-American Experience*, Vols. 1 and 2, edited by. Nathan Huggins, Martin Kilson, and Daniel Fox, 240–54. New York: Harcourt Brace Jovanovich, 1971.

Friedan, Betty. *The Feminine Mystique*. 1963. Reprint. New York: Dell Books, 1975.

Frye, Northrop. *Anatomy Of Criticism: Four Essays*. Princeton: Princeton University Press, 1957.

Fuller, Hoyt W. "A Survey: Black Writers' Views on Literary Lions and Values." *Negro Digest* 16 (January 1968): 10–48.

———. "The Task of the Negro Writer as Artist: A Symposium." *Negro Digest* 14, no. 6 (April 1965): 54–70, 72–83.

Fullinwider, S. P. *The Mind and Mood of Black America: 20th Century Thought*. Homewood, Ill.: Dorsey Press, 1969.

Fuss, Diana. *Essentially Speaking: Feminism, Nature & Difference*. New York: Routledge, 1989.

Gabbin, Joanne V. *Sterling A. Brown: Building the Black Aesthetic Tradition*. Westport, Conn.: Greenwood Press, 1985.

Gaines, Ernest. "Easy Rawlings, Just a Little Older." *Los Angeles Times Book Review*, June 5, 1994: 3, 12.

Gaines, Kevin K. *Uplifting the Race*. Chapel Hill: University of North Carolina Press, 1996.

Garnet, Henry Highland. "Address to the Slaves of the United States." 1843. Reprint. In *A Documentary History of the Negro People in the United States*, edited by Herbert Aptheker, 1: 226–33. 3rd ed. New York: Citadel Press, 1965.

Gates, Henry Louis, Jr. *The Future of the Race*. New York: Alfred A. Knopf, 1996.

———. "King of Cats." *New Yorker*, April 8, 1996: 70–81.

Gates, Henry Louis, Jr., and Cornel West. *Figures in Black: Words, Signs, and the "Racial" Self*. New York: Oxford University Press, 1987.

Gates, Henry Louis, Jr., and K. A. Appiah, eds. *Gloria Naylor: Critical Perspectives Past and Present*. New York: Amistad Press, 1993.

Gates, Henry Louis, Jr., and Nellie Y. McKay, gen. eds. *The Norton Anthology of African American Literature*. New York: W. W. Norton, 1997.

Gayle, Addison, Jr. *Richard Wright: Ordeal of a Native Son*. Garden City, N.Y.: Doubleday / Anchor Books, 1980.

———. *The Way of the New World: The Black Novel in America*. Garden City, N.Y.: Anchor Books, 1975.

Geertz, Clifford. *The Interpretation of Cultures: Selected Essays*. New York: Basic Books, 1973.

Genette, Gérard. *Narrative Discourse: An Essay in Method*. Translated by Jane E. Lewin. Ithaca: Cornell University Press, 1983.

Genovese, Eugene D. *The Red and the Black: Marxian Explorations in Southern and African American History*. New York: Panther Books, 1968.

———. *Roll, Jordan, Roll: The World the Slaves Made*. New York: Vintage Books, 1976.

Gilroy, Paul. *The Black Atlantic: Modernity and Double Consciousness.* Cambridge: Harvard University Press, 1993.

———. *Small Acts: Thoughts on the Politics of Black Cultures.* New York: Serpent's Tail, 1993.

Ginsberg, Elaine K. "Introduction." In *Passing and the Fictions of Identity*, edited by Elaine K. Ginsberg. Durham: Duke University Press, 1996.

Giovanni, Nikki, and Margaret Walker. *A Poetic Equation: Conversations between Nikki Giovanni and Margaret Walker.* Washington, D.C.: Howard University Press, 1974.

Glazer, Nathan, and Daniel P. Moynihan. *Beyond the Melting Pot: The Negroes, Puerto Ricans, Jews, Italians, and Irish of New York City.* Cambridge: M.I.T. Press, 1964.

Gloster, Hugh. *Negro Voices in American Fiction.* 1948. Reprint. New York: Russell and Russell, 1965.

———. "Sutton Griggs: Novelist of the New Negro." *Phylon* 4 (1943): 335–45. Reprint. *The Black Novelist*, edited by Robert Hemenway, 11–23. Columbus: Charles E. Merrill, 1970.

Goldberg, David Theo. *Racist Culture: Philosophy and the Politics of Meaning.* Cambridge: Blackwell, 1993.

Goldberg, Steven. *The Inevitability of Patriarchy.* New York: William Morrow, 1973.

Gordon, Jacob U., comp. *The African-American Male: An Annotated Bibliography.* Westport, Conn.: Greenwood Press, 1999.

Gordon, Lois, and Alan Gordon. *American Chronicles: Year by Year through the Twentieth Century.* New Haven: Yale University Press, 1999.

Gossett, Thomas F. *Race: The History of an Idea in America.* New York: Schocken Books, 1965.

Govan, Sandra. "Barbara Neely." In *The Oxford Companion to African American Literature*, edited by William Andrews, Frances Smith Foster, and Trudier Harris, 530–31. New York: Oxford University Press, 1997.

———. "Connections, Links, and Extended Networks: Patterns in Octavia Butler's Science Fiction." *Black American Literature Forum* 18, no. 2 (Summer 1984): 82–87.

———. "The Insistent Presence of Black Folk in the Novels of Samuel R. Delany." *Black American Literature Forum* 18, no. 2 (Summer 1984): 43–48.

———. "Samuel Delany." In *Dictionary of Literary Biography*, Vol. 33: 52–58. Detroit: Gale Research Co., 1984.

Graff, Gerald. *Literature against Itself: Literary Ideas in Modern Society.* Chicago: University of Chicago Press, 1979.

Gramsci, Antonio. *Selections from the Prison Notebook.* Translated and edited by Quintin Hoare and Geoffrey Nowell Smith. London: Lawrence and Wishart, 1971.

Grant, J. W. *Out of the Darkness; or, Diabolism and Destiny.* Nashville: National Baptist Publishing Board, 1909.

Grier, William H., and Price M. Cobbs. *Black Rage.* New York: Bantam Books, 1968.

Griggs, Sutton E. *Pointing the Way.* Nashville: Orion, 1908.

Grimes, Johanna L. "Leon Forrest." *Afro-American Fiction Writers After 1955.* In *Dictionary of Literary Biography*, Vol. 33, edited by Thadious M. Davis and Trudier Harris, 77–83. University of North Carolina at Chapel Hill: Gale, 1984.

Grimstead, David. "Melodrama as Echo of the Historically Voiceless." In *Anonymous Americans*, edited by Tamara K. Hareven, 80–98. Englewood Cliffs, N.J.: Prentice-Hall, 1971.

Gutman, Herbert G. *The Black Family in Slavery and Freedom, 1750–1925*. New York: Pantheon Books, 1976.

———. "Work, Culture, and Society in Industrializing America, 1815–1919." *American Historical Review* 78 (1973): 542–43.

Gwaltney, John Langston. *Drylongso: A Self Portrait of Black America*. 1980. Reprint. New York: Vintage Books, 1981.

Hall, Gwendolyn Midlo. *Africans in Colonial Louisiana: The Development of Afro-Creole Culture in the Eighteenth Century*. Baton Rouge: Louisiana State University Press, 1992.

Hall, Perry A. *In the Vineyard: Working in African American Studies*. Knoxville: University of Tennessee Press, 1999.

Hall, Stuart. "Cultural Identity and Diaspora." In *Identity, Community, Culture, Difference*, edited by Jonathan Rutherford, 222–37. London: Lawrence and Wishart, 1990.

Hamilton, Edith. *Mythology*. New York: Mentor Books, 1969.

Hare, Nathan, and Julia Hare. *The Endangered Black Family: Coping with the Unisexualization and Coming Extinction of the Black Race*. San Francisco: Black Think Tank, 1984.

Harper, Michael. "Gayl Jones: An Interview." *Massachusetts Review* 18 (Winter 1977): 692–715.

———. "Interview: Gayl Jones and Michael S. Harper." In *Chant of Saints: A Gathering of Afro-American Literature, Art, and Scholarship*, edited by Michael S. Harper and Robert B. Stepto, 352–75. Urbana: University of Illinois Press, 1979.

Harper, Phillip Brian. *Are We Not Men? Masculine Anxiety and the Problem of African American Identity*. New York: Oxford University Press, 1998.

Harris, E. Lynn. "For All I Know." *The Advocate*, November 24, 1998: 67.

Harris, Joel Chandler. *Gabriel Tolliver*. 1902. Reprint. Ridgewood, N.J.: Gregg Press, 1967.

———. *Uncle Remus: His Songs and Sayings*. 1880. Reprint. New York: Appleton–Century, 1938.

Harris, Trudier. *Exorcising Blackness: Historical and Literary Lynching and Burning Rituals*. Bloomington: Indiana University Press, 1984.

———. "On *The Color Purple*, Stereotypes, and Silence." *Black American Literature Forum* 18 (Winter 1984): 155–61.

Harris, William J. "Al Young." *Afro-American Fiction Writers After 1955*. In *Dictionary of Literary Biography*, Vol. 33, edited by Thadious M. Davis and Trudier Harris, 300–306. Detroit: Gale, 1984.

———. " 'I Write the Blues:' An Interview With Al Young." *Greenfield Review* 10 (Summer/Fall 1982): 1–19.

Hastings, James. *A Dictionary of the Bible*, Vol 1. New York: Charles Scribner's Sons, 1908.

Hayden, Robert. "Preface." In *The New Negro*, edited by Alain Locke, i–xxiv. 1925. Reprint. New York: Atheneum, 1968.

Heath, Stephen, trans. and ed. *Image, Music, Text: Roland Barthes*. New York: Hill and Wang, 1977.

Heermance, Noel. *William Wells Brown and Clotelle: A Portrait of the Artist in the First Negro Novel*. Hamden: Archon Books, 1969.

Hemenway, Robert. "Are You a Flying Lark or a Setting Dove?" In *African American Literature: The Reconstruction of Instruction*, edited by Dexter Fisher and Robert B. Stepto, 122–52. New York: Modern Language Association of America, 1979.

Hemphill, Essex, ed. *Brother to Brother: New Writings by Black Gay Men.* Boston: Alyson Books, 1991.

Henderson, Richard. *The King in Every Man: Evolutionary Trends in Onitsha Ibo Society and Culture.* New Haven: Yale University Press, 1972.

Henson, Josiah. *The Life of Josiah Henson, Formerly a Slave, Now an Inhabitant of Canada.* Boston: A. D. Phelps, 1849.

Hernton, Calvin. "The Sexual Mountain and Black Women Writers." *Black American Literature Forum* 18 (Winter 1984): 139–45.

Herskovits, Melville J., and Frances S. Herskovits. *Dahomean Narrative.* Evanston: Northwestern University Press, 1958.

———. *Life in a Haitian Valley.* New York: Alfred A. Knopf, 1937.

———. *The Myth of the Negro Past.* Boston: Beacon Press, 1941.

Hill, Herbert. "Reflections on Richard Wright: A Symposium on an Exiled Native Son." In *Anger, and Beyond: The Negro Writer in the United States,* edited by Herbert Hill, 196–212. 1966. Reprint. New York: Perennial Library, 1968.

Himes, Chester. *My Life of Absurdity.* New York: Paragon, 1990.

———. *The Quality of Hurt.* New York: Paragon, 1990.

Hogness, Peter. "How Walter Mosley Discovered His Audience—And the Voice of His Fiction." *Writer's Digest* 76 (March 1996): 8–9.

Holloway, Joseph E. "The Origins of African-American Culture." In *Africanisms in American Culture,* edited by Joseph E. Holloway, 1–18. Bloomington: Indiana University Press/Midland Books, 1991.

Holman, C. Hugh, and William Harmon. *A Handbook to Literature.* 5th ed. New York: Macmillan, 1986.

Holt, Patricia. "PW Interviews: David Bradley." *Publishers Weekly,* April 10, 1981: 12–14.

hooks, bell. *Ain't I a Woman: Black Women and Feminism.* Boston: South End Press, 1981.

———. *Feminist Theory: From Margin to Center.* Boston: South End Press, 1984.

———. "Representing Whiteness in the Black Imagination." In *Cultural Studies,* edited by Lawrence Grossberg et al., 338–346. New York: Routledge, 1992.

———. *Yearning: Race, Gender, and Cultural Politics.* Boston: South End Press, 1990.

Huggins, Nathan I. *Harlem Renaissance.* New York: Oxford University Press, 1971.

———, Martin Kilson, and Daniel Fox, eds. *Key Issues in the Afro-American Experience.* 2 vols. New York: Harcourt Brace Jovanovich, 1971.

Hughes, Carl Milton. *The Negro Novelist: A Discussion of Writing of American Negro Novelists, 1940–1950.* 1953. Reprint. New York: Citadel Press, 1979.

Hughes, Langston. *The Big Sea.* 1940. Reprint. New York: Hill and Wang, 1968.

———. "The Negro Artist and the Racial Mountain." *Nation,* June 23, 1926: 692–94.

———. "The Negro Speaks of Rivers." 1926. Reprint. In *Modern and Contemporary Afro-American Poetry,* edited by Bernard W. Bell, 38. Boston: Allyn and Bacon, 1972.

———, and Arna Bontemps, eds. *The Book of Negro Folklore.* New York: Dodd, Mead, 1958.

Huizinga, Johan. *Homo Ludens: A Study of the Play Element in Culture.* London: Routledge and Kegan Paul, 1949.

Hutchinson, George. *The Harlem Renaissance in Black and White.* Cambridge: Belknap Press, 1995.

Hutcheon, Linda. *A Poetics of Postmodernism: History, Theory, Fiction.* New York: Routledge, 1988.

———. *The Politics of Postmodernism*. New York: Routledge, 1989.

Hyman, Stanley E., and Ralph Ellison. "The Negro Writer in America: An Exchange." *Partisan Review* 25 (Spring 1958): 197–222.

Hymes, Dell, ed. *Pidginization and Creolization of Languages: Proceedings of a Conference Held at the University of West Indies Mona, Jamaica, April 1968*. London: Cambridge University Press, 1974.

Ingarden, Roman. *The Cognition of the Literary Work of Art*. Translated by Ruth Ann Crowley and Kenneth Olson. Evanston: Northwestern University Press, 1973.

"An Interview with Percival Everett." *University Press of New England*. 16 Oct. 2002. 22 Nov. 2002, http://www.upne.com/features/EverettQ&A.html

Iser, Wolfgang. *The Act of Reading: A Theory of Aesthetic Response*. Baltimore: Johns Hopkins University Press, 1978.

Jackson, John G. *Introduction to African Civilizations*. New York: University Books, 1970.

Jacobs, Harriet A. *Incidents in the Life of a Slave Girl, Written by Herself*, edited by Jean Fagan Yellin. Cambridge: Harvard University Press, 1987.

Jacques-Garvey, Amy. *Garvey and Garveyism*. New York: Collier Books, 1970.

———, ed. *Philosophy and Opinions of Marcus Garvey*. New York: Atheneum, 1970.

Jahn, Janheinz. *Muntu: An Outline of the New African Culture*. Translated by Marjorie Green. New York: Grove Press, 1961.

———. *Neo–African Literature: History of Black Writing*. Translated by Oliver Coburn and Ursula Lehrburger. New York: Evergreen, 1969.

Jay, Gregory S. *American Literature and the Culture Wars*. Ithaca: Cornell University Press, 1997.

Jehlen, Myra. "Introduction: Beyond Transcendence." In *Ideology and Classic American Literature*, edited by Sacvan Bercovitch and Myra Jehlen, 1–18. Cambridge: Cambridge University Press, 1986.

Johnson, Barbara E. "Response [to Henry Louis Gates Jr.]." In *Afro-American Literary Study in the 1990s*, edited by Houston A. Baker and Patricia Redmond, 39–44. Chicago: University of Chicago Press, 1989.

Johnson, Brett. "Omar Tyree: Raw and Uncut." *Black Issues Book Review* (July–Aug. 2002): 40–43.

Johnson, Charles. *Being and Race*. Bloomington: Indiana University Press, 1988.

———. "Interview with Samuel Delany." *Callaloo* (Fall 1984): 27–35.

———. *Black Humor*. Chicago: Johnson Publishing Co., 1970.

Johnson, James Weldon. "Dilemma of the Negro Author." *American Mercury* 15 (December 1928): 477–88.

———. *God's Trombones*. New York: Viking Press, 1927.

———. *In the Shadow of the Plantation*. 1934. Reprint. Chicago: University of Chicago Press, 1966.

———, ed. *The Book of American Negro Poetry*. Rev. ed. New York: Harcourt, Brace and World, 1931.

Jones, LeRoi. *Home: Social Essays*. New York: William Morrow, 1966.

Jordan, Winthrop D. *White over Black: American Attitudes toward the Negro, 1550–1812*. Chapel Hill: University of North Carolina Press, 1968.

Josephy, Alvin M., Jr. *The Indian Heritage of America*. New York: Alfred A. Knopf, 1968.

Joyce, James. *Finnegans Wake*. New York: Penguin Books 1999.

July, Robert W.*A History of the African People*. New York: Scribner and Sons, 1970.

Kammen, Michael. *People of Paradox: An Inquiry Concerning the Origins of American Civilization*. New York: Alfred A. Knopf, 1972.

Kaplan, Amy. "'Left Alone with America': The Absence of Empire in the Study of American Culture." In *Cultures of United States Imperialism*, edited by Amy Kaplan and Donald E. Pease, 3–21. Durham: Duke University Press, 1993.

Kaplan, Carla, ed., *Zora Neale Hurston: A Life in Letters*. New York: Doubleday, 2002.

Karenga, Maulana. "Black and Latino Relations: Context, Challenge, and Possibilities." In *Multi–America: Essays on Cultural Wars and Cultural Peace*, edited by Ishmael Reed, 196–200. New York: Penguin Books, 1998.

———. "Black Art: A Rhythmic Reality of Revolution." *Negro Digest* 17, no. 3 (January 1968): 5–9.

———. *Introduction to Black Studies*. Los Angeles: University of Sankore Press, 1993.

———. *Kwanzaa: A Celebration of Family, Community and Culture*. Los Angeles: University of Sankore Press, 1998.

Katz, Jonathan Ned. *Gay American History: Lesbians and Gay Men in the U.S.A.* New York: Meridian, 1972. Rev. ed. 1992.

———. *Gay/Lesbian Almanac: A New Documentary*. 1983. Reprint. New York: Carroll and Graf, 1994.

Katz, William Loren, ed. *Five Slave Narratives*. New York: Arno Press and *The New York Times*, 1969.

Keil, Charles. *Urban Blues*. Chicago: University of Chicago Press, 1966.

Kelley, Norman. "Rhythm Nation: The Political Economy of Black Music."*Black Renaissance/Renaissance Noire* 2, no. 2 (Summer 1999): 8–21.

Kelley, Robin D. G. *Race Rebels*. New York: Free Press, 1994.

Kelley, William Melvin. *Dancers on the Shore*. 1964. Reprint. Chatham, N.J.: Chatham Bookseller, 1973.

Kent, George E. "Ethnic Impact in American Literature: Reflections on a Course." *College Language Association Journal* 11 (September 1967): 24–37.

Kermode, Frank. *The Sense of an Ending: Studies in the Theory of Fiction*. New York: Oxford University Press, 1967.

Killens, John O. "The Black Writer vis-à-vis His Country." In his *Black Man's Burden*, 23–54. New York: Trident Press, 1965.

Klinkowitz, Jerome. *Literary Disruptions: The Making of a Post-Contemporary American Fiction*. 2nd ed. Urbana: University of Illinois Press, 1980.

Knotts, Kristina. "Walter Mosley." In *Contemporary African American Novelists: A Bio–Bibliographical Critical Sourcebook*, edited by Emmanuel S. Nelson, 350–54. Westport, Conn.: Greenwood Press, 1999.

Kochman, Thomas, ed. *Rappin' and Stylin' Out: Communication in Urban Black America*. Urbana: University of Illinois Press, 1972.

Kress, David C. "Middle Voice Moves in Nathaniel Mackey's *Djbot Baghostus's Run*." *Callaloo* 23, no. 3 (Spring 2000): 765–83.

Lacan, Jacques. "The Mirror Stage as Formative of the Function of the I." In his *Ecrits*, translated by Alan Sheridan, 1–7. New York: W. W. Norton, 1977.

Ladner, Joyce A. *Tomorrow's Tomorrow: The Black Woman*. Garden City, N.Y.: Anchor Books, 1972.

Lambert, Gregg. "On the Uses and Abuses of Literature for Life." In *Deleuze and Literature*, edited by Ian Buchanan and John Marks, 135–66, Edinburgh: Edinburgh University Press, 2000.

Lane, Ann J., ed. *The Debate over Slavery: Stanley Elkins and His Critics*. Urbana: University of Illinois Press, 1971.

Laney, Ruth. "A Conversation with Ernest Gaines." *Southern Review* 10 (January 1974): 1–14.

Larimer, Kevin. "Industrial Strength in the Information Age: A Profile of Colson Whitehead." *Poets & Writers Magazine* (July–Aug. 2001): 21–25.

Leakey, L.S.B. *The Progress and Evolution of Man in Africa*. New York: Oxford University Press, 1961.

Lefkowitz, Mary. *Not out of Africa: How Afrocentrism Became an Excuse to Teach Myth as History*. New York: Basic Books, 1996.

"The Lemba Jews." *60 Minutes*. CBS. April 23, 2000.

Lerner, Gerda, ed. *Black Women in White America: A Documentary History*. New York: Vintage Books, 1973.

Levine, George. *The Realistic Imagination: English Fiction from Frankenstein to Lady Chatterley*. Chicago: University of Chicago Press, 1980.

Levine, Lawrence W. *Black Culture and Black Consciousness: African American Folk Thought from Slavery to Freedom*. New York: Oxford University Press, 1977.

———. "The Concept of the New Negro and the Realities of Black Culture." In *Key Issues In the Afro-American Experience*. Vols. 1 and 2, edited by Nathan I. Huggins, Martin Kilson, and Daniel Fox, 2: 125–47. New York: Harcourt Brace Jovanovich, 1971.

Lewis, David Levering. *W. E. B. Du Bois: Biography of a Race, 1868–1919*. New York: Owl Books, 1994.

Lewis, Vashti Crutcher. "Gloria Naylor." *American Novelists since World War II*. 5th series. In *Dictionary of Literary Biography*, Vol. 173, edited by James R. Giles and Wanda H. Giles, 170–76. Detroit: Gale, 1996.

Lindfors, Bernth. "Amos Tutuola: Debts and Assets." *Cahiers d'Etudes Africaines* 10 (1970): 306–34.

———. "Critical Approaches to Folklore in African Literature." In *African Folklore*, edited by Richard Dorson, 223–34. Bloomington: Indiana University Press, 1972.

Lindsay, Vachel. "Congo: A Study of the Negro Race." In his *The Congo and Other Poems*, 3–11. New York: Macmillan, 1914.

Locke, Alain, ed. *The New Negro*. 1925. Reprint. New York: Atheneum, 1968.

Long, Richard. "Alain Locke: Cultural and Social Mentor." *Black World* (November 1970): 87–90.

Longstreet, Augustus. *Georgia Scenes: Characters, Incidents, & Etc. in the First Half Century of the Republic*. 1835. New York: Harper and Brothers, 1874.

Loomba, Ania. *Colonialism/Postcolonialism*. New York: Routledge, 1998.

Lovell, John, Jr. *Black Song: The Forge and the Flame; The Story of How the African American Spiritual Was Hammered Out*. New York: Macmillan, 1972.

Lukács, Georg. *Realism in Our Time: Literature and the Class Struggle*. Translated by John and Necke Mander. 1963. Reprint. New York: Harper, 1964.

Lyotard, Jean-François. *The Postmodern Condition: A Report on Knowledge*. 1979. Reprint.

Translated by Geoff Bennington and Brian Massumi. Minneapolis: University of Minnesota Press, 1993.

Mack, S. Thomas. "Percival L. Everett." In *Cyclopedia of World Authors*. Vol. 2. 3rd rev. ed., edited by Frank N. Magill, 654–65. Pasadena, Calif.: Salem Press, 1997.

Major, Clarence. *The Dark and Feeling: Black American Writers and Their Work*. New York: Third Press, 1974.

———. *Swallow the Lake*. Middletown, Conn.: Wesleyan University Press, 1970.

Majors, Richard G., and Jacob U. Gordon, eds. *The American Black Male: His Present Status and His Future*. Chicago: Nelson-Hall, 1994.

Marable, Manning. *How Capitalism Underdeveloped Black America: Problems in Race, Political Economy, and Society*. Boston: South End Press, 1983.

———. "We Need New and Critical Study of Race and Ethnicity." *Chronicle of Higher Education* February 25, 2000: B4–B7.

Marshall, Paule. "Shadow and Act." *Mademoiselle* 79, no. 2 (June 1974): 82–83.

———. *Reena and Other Stories*. Old Westbury, N.Y.: Feminist Press, 1983.

Martin, Reginald. "Ishmael Reed." In *Black Writers*, Vol. 2, edited by Linda Metzger, 478–84. Detroit: Gale Research Inc., 1989.

Marx, Leo. *The Machine in the Garden: Technology and the Pastoral Idea in America*. 1964. Reprint. New York: Galaxy, 1967.

Massiah, Louis. "How She Came by Her Name." In *Deep Sightings and Rescue Missions: Fiction, Essays, and Conversations*, edited by Toni Cade Bambara, 201–45. New York: Pantheon Books, 1996.

Mather, Cotton. *Rules for the Societies of Negroes*. 1693. Reprint. Boston: Bartholomew Green, 1714.

Matthiessen, F. O. *American Renaissance: Art and Expression in the Age of Emerson and Whitman*. 1941. Reprint. New York: Oxford University Press, 1979.

Mays, Benjamin. *The Negro's God as Reflected in His Literature*. 1938. Reprint. New York: Atheneum, 1968.

McCaffery, Larry, and Linda Gregory. "Major's *Reflex and Bone Structure* and the Anti-Detective Tradition." *Black American Literature Forum* 13 (Summer 1979): 39–45.

McCullough, Bob. "Walter Mosley." *Publishers Weekly*, May 23, 1994: 67–68.

———, and Jerzy Kutnik. " 'I Follow My Eyes': An Interview with Clarence Major." *African American Review* 28 (Spring 1994): 121–38.

McDowell, Deborah E. "New Directions for Black Feminist Criticism." In *The New Feminist Criticism: Essays on Women, Literature, and Theory*, edited by Elaine Showalter, 186–99. New York: Pantheon Books, 1985.

McFeely, William. "Unfinished Business: The Freedman's Bureau and Federal Action in Race Relations." In *Key Issues in the Afro-American Experience*, edited by Nathan I. Huggins, Martin Kilson, and Daniel Fox, 2: 5–25. New York: Harcourt Brace Jovanovich, 1971.

McHenry, Susan. "Octavia Butler's Mind Trip into the Near Future." *Black Issues Book Review* (Jan–Feb 1999): 14–18.

McKay, Claude. *Harlem: Negro Metropolis*. 1940. Reprint. New York: Harvest Books, 1968.

McKay, Nellie. "An Interview with Toni Morrison." In *Conversations with Toni Morrison*, edited by Danielle Taylor-Guthrie, 138–55. Jackson: University Press of Mississippi, 1994.

McLuhan, Marshall. *The Gutenberg Galaxy: The Making of Typographic Man*. 1962. Reprint. New York: Signet Books, 1969.

McWhorter, John. *The Word on the Street: Fact and Fable about American English*. New York: Plenum Trade, 1998.

Merriam-Webster's Collegiate Dictionary. 10th ed. Springfield, Mass.: Merriam-Webster, 1999.

Mibiti, John S. *African Religions and Philosophy*. Garden City, N.Y.: Anchor Books, 1970.

Michaels, Walter Benn "Political Science Fictions," *New Literary History* 31, no. 4 (2001): 649–64.

Mintz, Sidney. "Foreword." In *Afro-American Anthropology: Contemporary Perspect.ives*, edited by Norman E. Whitten and John F. Szwed, 1–16. New York: The Free Press, 1970.

———., and Richard Price. *An Anthropological Approach to the African American Past: A Caribbean Perspective*. Philadelphia: Institute for the Study of Human Issues, 1977.

Mitchell, Henry H. *Black Preaching*. New York: J. B. Lippincott, 1970.

Mitchell, Margaret. *Gone with the Wind*. New York: Scribner and Sons, 1996.

Montejo, Esteban. *The Autobiography of a Runaway Slave*. Translated by Jocasta Innes, edited by Miguel Barnet. New York: Vintage Books, 1973.

Moore, Richard. "Du Bois and Pan Africa." *Freedomways* (First Quarter 1965): 166–87.

Morrison, Toni. "Rootedness: The Ancestor as Foundation." In *Black Women Writers (1950–1980): A Critical Evaluation*, edited by Mari Evans, 339–45. Garden City, N.Y.: Anchor Books, 1984.

Moses, Wilson Jeremiah. *Afrotopia: The Roots of African American Popular History*. New York: Cambridge University Press, 1998.

Moynihan, D. Patrick. *The Negro Family: The Case for National Action*. Washington, D.C.: United States Department of Labor, Office of Policy Planning and Research, 1965.

Mudimbe, V. Y. *The Idea of Africa*. Bloomington: Indiana University Press, 1994.

Mufwene, Salikoko S., et al., eds. *African American English: Structure, History, and Use*. New York: Routledge, 1998.

Murray, Albert. *The Omni-Americans: Some Alternatives to the Folklore of White Supremacy*. 1970. Reprint. New York: Vintage Books, 1983.

Musher, Sharon Ann. "Contesting 'The Way the Almighty Wants It': Crafting Memories of Ex-Slaves in the Slave Narrative Collection." *American Quarterly* 53, no. 1 (2001): 1–31.

Myrdal, Gunnar. *An American Dilemma: The Negro Problem and Modern Democracy*. 1944. Reprint. New York: Harper and Row, 1962.

Nathan, Hans. *Dan Emmett and the Rise of Early Negro Minstrelsy*. Norman: University of Oklahoma Press, 1962.

Navasky, Victor. "Counter Espionage." *New York Times*, February 27, 1966, sec. 8: p. 5.

Naylor, Gloria, and Toni Morrison. "A Conversation." *Southern Review* 21 (1985): 567–93.

Naylor, Paul, ed. *Nathaniel Mackey: A Special Issue. Calliloo* 23, no. 3 (Spring 2000).

Neal, Larry. "The Black Arts Movement." In *The Black Aesthetic*, edited by Addison Gayle Jr., 272–90. 1971. Reprint. Garden City, N.Y.: Anchor Books, 1972.

———. "And Shine Swam On." In *Black Fire: An Anthology of Afro-American Writing*, edited by LeRoi Jones and Larry Neal, 643–48. New York: William Morrow, 1968.

"The Negro in Art: How Shall He Be Portrayed, A Symposium." *The Crisis* 31, no. 4 (February 1926): 163–166.

Nero, Charles I. "Toward a Black Gay Aesthetic: Signifying in Contemporary Black Gay Literature." In *In Cornerstones: An Anthology of African American Literature*, edited by Melvin Donalson, 971–89. New York: St. Martin's Press, 1996.

Nichols, Charles. *Many Thousands Gone: The Ex–Slaves' Account of Their Bondage and Freedom*. 1963. Reprint. Bloomington: Indiana University Press, 1969.

Norris, Frank. *McTeague*. 1899. Reprint. New York: Library of America, 1986.

———. *The Octopus*. 1901. Reprint. Boston: Houghton Mifflin, 1958.

Nunez, Elizabeth, and Brenda M. Green, eds. *Defining Ourselves: Black Writers in the 1990s*. New York: Peter Lang, 1999.

Obiechina, Emmanuel. *Culture, Tradition, and Society in the West African Novel*. London: Cambridge University Press, 1975.

O'Brien, John, ed. *Interviews with Black Writers*. New York: Liveright, 1973.

———. "Seeking a Humanist Level: Interview with John A. Williams." *The Humanist Alternative* (Spring–Summer 1973): 94–99.

O'Connor, Margaret Anne. "Octavia Butler." In *Dictionary of Literary Biography*, Vol. 33: 35–41. Detroit: Gale Research Co., 1984.

Okpewho, Isidore. *African Oral Literature: Backgrounds, Character, and Continuity*. Bloomington: Indiana University Press, 1992.

O'Leary, Peter. "An Interview with Nathaniel Mackey." *Chicago Review* 43, no. 1 (Winter 1997): 30–46.

Olsen, Marvin E. "Power as a Social Process." In his *Power in Societies*, 2–10. New York: Macmillan, 1970.

Omi, Michael, and Howard Winant. *Racial Formation in the United States from the 1960's to the 1990's*. 2nd ed. New York: Routledge, 1994.

Ong, Walter J. *The Presence of the Word: Some Prolegomena for Cultural and Religious History*. New Haven: Yale University Press, 1967.

Osborne, Gwendolyn. "The Legacy of Ghetto Pulp Fiction." *Black Issues Book Review* (September–October 2001): 53.

———. "Old School Masters of Blaxploitation Lit." *Black Issues Book Review* (September–October 2001): 54–56.

Osofsky, Gilbert, ed. *Puttin' on Ole Massa: The Slave Narratives of Henry Bibb, William Wells Brown, and Solomon Northup*. New York: Harper Torchbooks, 1969.

Ostendorf, Bernhardt. *Black Literature in White America*. Totowa, N.J.: Barnes and Noble Books, 1982.

———. "Black Poetry, Blues, and Folklore: Double Consciousness in African American Oral Culture." Unpublished Manuscript, 1975.

Ottley, Roi, and William J. Weatherby. *The Negro in New York: An Informal Social History, 1626–1940*. New York: Praeger, 1969.

Ozick, Cynthia. "Literary Blacks and Jews." In her *Art and Ardor*, 90–113. New York: Alfred A. Knopf, 1983.

Page, Thomas Nelson. *In Old Virginia; Or, Marse Chan, and Other Stories*. 1887. Reprint. Ridgewood, N.J.: Gregg Press, 1968.

———. *Red Rock: A Chronicle of Reconstruction*. 1898. Reprint. Ridgewood, N.J.: Gregg Press, 1968.

Park, Robert E. "Community Organization and Juvenile Delinquency." In *The City,* edited by Robert E. Park, Ernest W. Burgess, and Roderick D. McKenzie, 99–112. Chicago: University of Chicago Press, 1925.

———. "Mentality of Racial Hybrids." *Journal of Sociology* 36 (January 1931): 535–51.

———, and Ernest W. Burgess. *Introduction to the Science of Sociology*. Chicago: University of Chicago Press, 1921.

Parks, Gordon. *The Learning Tree.* 1963. Reprint. New York: Crest Books, 1964.

Parrington, Vernon L. *Main Currents in American Thought:* Vol. 3, *The Beginnings of Critical Realism in America, 1860–1920.* New York: Harbinger Books, 1930.

Patell, Cyrus R. K. *Negative Liberties: Morrison, Pynchon, and the Problem of Liberal Ideology.* Durham: Duke University Press, 2001.

Patterson, Orlando. "Race by the Numbers." *New York Times,* May 8, 2001: A31.

Paulsen, Ronald. *Satire and the Novel in Eighteenth-Century England.* New Haven: Yale University Press, 1967.

Pearson, John H. "Larry Duplechan." In *Contemporary Gay American Novelists: A Bio-Bibliographical Critical Sourcebook,* edited by Emmanuel S. Nelson. Westport, Conn.: Greenwood Press, 1993.

Peplow, Michael W., and Robert S. Bravard. *Samuel R. Delany: A Primary and Secondary Bibliography, 1962–1979.* Boston: G. K. Hall, 1980.

"Percival Everett." *Contemporary Authors.* 25 Feb. 2002. Gale. 20 Nov. 2002, http://www.galenet.com.

Perry, Theresa, and Lisa Delpit, eds. *The Real Ebonics Debate: Power, Language, and the Education of African American Children.* Boston: Beacon Press, 1998.

Pettigrew, Thomas. *A Profile of the Negro American.* Princeton: Van Nostrand, 1964.

Pettis, Joyce. "A MELUS Interview: Paule Marshall." *MELUS* 17, no. 4 (Winter 1991–92): 117–29.

Phillips, Ulrich B. *American Negro Slavery: A Survey of the Supply, Employment, and Control of Negro Labor as Determined by the Plantation Regime.* 1918. Reprint. Baton Rouge: Louisiana Paperbacks, 1969.

———. *Life and Labor in the Old South.* New York: Grosset and Dunlap, 1929.

Pickens, William. *The New Negro: His Political, Civil, and Mental Status and Related Essays.* 1916. Reprint. New York: Negro Universities Press, 1969.

Piers, Gerhart, and Milton B. Singer. *Shame and Guilt: A Psychoanalytic and a Cultural Study.* Springfield, Ill.: Charles C. Thomas, 1953.

Pinsker, Sanford. "John Updike and the Distractions of Henry Bech, Professional Writer and American Jew." *Modern Fiction Studies* 37, no. 1 (1991): 97–111.

Pizer, Donald. *Twentieth–Century American Literary Naturalism: An Interpretation.* Carbondale: Southern Illinois University Press, 1982.

Pleck, J. H. *The Myth of Masculinity.* Cambridge: M.I.T. Press, 1981.

Poe, Edgar Allan. "The Murders in the Rue Morgue." 1841. Reprint. In *The Annotated Tales of Edgar Allan Poe,* edited by Stephen Peithman, 195–223. New York: Avenel Press, 1986.

———. "The Mystery of Marie Roget." 1842. Reprint. In *The Annotated Tales of Edgar Allan Poe,* edited by Stephen Peithman, 224–61. New York: Avenel Press, 1986.

———. "The Purloined Letter" 1845. Reprint. In *The Annotated Tales of Edgar Allan Poe,* edited by Stephen Peithman, 299–313. New York: Avenel Press, 1986.

Poe, Richard. "Negro: by Definition." *Negro History Bulletin* 40 (1977): 668–70.

The Poetic Edda. 2nd rev. ed. Translated by Lee H. Hollander. Austin: University of Texas Press, 1962.

Prince, Gerald. *Dictionary of Narratology: Human Agency and Language*. Lincoln: University of Nebraska Press, 1987.

The Prose Edda of Snorri Sturluson: Tales from Norse Mythology. Translated by Jean I. Young. Berkeley: University of California Press, 1973.

Quarles, Benjamin. *The Negro in the American Revolution*. Chapel Hill: University of North Carolina Press, 1961.

Raboteau, Albert J. *Slave Religion: The "Invisible Institution" in the Antebellum South*. New York: Oxford University Press, 1980.

Rainwater, Lee, and William L. Yancey. *The Moynihan Report and the Politics of Controversy*. Cambridge.: M.I.T. Press, 1967.

Rawick, George P. *The American Slave: A Composite Autobiography*. 19 vols. Amherst: University of Massachusetts Press, 1974.

———. *From Sundown to Sunup*. Westport, Conn.: Greenwood Press, 1972.

Record, Wilson. *The Negro and the Communist Party*. 1951. Reprint. New York: Atheneum, 1971.

Redding, Saunders. *Strangers and Alone*. 1950. Reprint. New York: J and J Harper, 1969.

Redfield, Robert. *Tepoztlan*. Chicago: University of Chicago Press, 1930.

Reed, Ishmael. *Conjure: Selected Poems, 1963–1970*. Amherst: University of Massachusetts Press, 1972.

———. "Hoodoo Manifesto #2: The Baker-Gayle Fallacy." *Umnum Newsletter* 4, no. 3–4 (1975): 8–11.

———. *Multi-America: Essays on Cultural Wars and Cultural Peace*. New York: Penguin Books, 1998.

———. *19 Necromancers from Now*. Garden City, N.Y.: Anchor Books, 1970.

———. "The Writer as Seer: Ishmael Reed on Ishmael Reed." *Black World* 23, no. 8 (June 1974): 20–34.

Retamar, Roberto Fernandez. *Caliban and Other Essays*. Translated by Edward Baker. Minneapolis: University of Minnesota Press, 1989.

Rickford, John Russell, and Russell John Rickford. *Spoken Soul: The Story of Black English*. New York: John Wiley and Sons, 2000.

Ringer, Benjamin B., and Elinor R. Lawless. *Race-Ethnicity and Society*. New York: Routledge, 1989.

Roberts, John W. *From Trickster to Badman: The Black Folk Hero in Slavery and Freedom*. Philadelphia: University of Pennsylvania Press, 1989.

Rogers, Katharine M. *The Troublesome Helpmate: A History of Misogyny in Literature*. Seattle: University of Washington Press, 1966.

Rosenberg, Bruce. *The Art of the American Folk Preacher*. New York: Oxford University Press, 1970.

Rourke, Constance. *American Humor: A Study of the National Character*. New York: Harcourt, Brace, 1931.

Rowell, Charles. "Poetry, History and Humanism: An Interview with Margaret Walker." *Black World* 25, no. 2 (1975): 4–17.

Rushing, Andrea Benton. "Family Resemblances: A Comparative Study of Women Protagonists in Contemporary African-American and Anglophone-African Novels." Diss. University of Massachusetts, Amherst, 1983.

———. "Images of Black Women in Afro-American Poetry." In *The Afro-American Woman: Struggles and Images*, edited by Sharon Harley and Rosalyn Terborg–Penn, 74–84. Port Washington, N.Y.: Kennikat Press, 1978.

———. "Images of Black Women in Modern African Poetry: An Overview." In *Sturdy Black Bridges: Visions of Black Women in Literature*, edited by Roseanne P. Bell, Bettye J. Parker, and Beverly Guy-Sheftall, 18–24. Garden City, N.Y.: Anchor Books, 1979.

Sagan, Dorian. "Gender Specifics: Why Women Aren't Men." *New York Times*, June 21, 1998, sec. 15: 1+.

Said, Edward. *Culture and Imperialism*. New York: Alfred A. Knopf, 1993.

San Juan, E., Jr. *Beyond Postcolonial Theory*. New York: St. Martin's Press, 1998.

Saussure, Ferdinand de. *Course in General Linguistics*. 1915. Reprint. Translated by Wade Baskin. New York: McGraw–Hill, 1966.

Schlesinger, Arthur M. The Disuniting of America: Reflections on a Multicultural Society. New York: W. W. Norton, 1991.

Scholes, Robert. *The Fabulators*. New York: Oxford University Press, 1967.

Schultz, Elizabeth. "Albert L. Murray." *Afro-American Writers after 1955: Dramatists and Prose Writers*. In *Dictionary of Literary Biography*, Vol. 38, edited by Thadious M. Davis and Trudier Harris, 214–224. Detroit: Gale, 1985.

Schulz, Max F. *Black Humor Fiction of the Sixties: A Pluralistic Definition of Man and His World*. Athens: Ohio University Press, 1973.

Scroggins, Mark. "Nathaniel Mackey." In *American Poets since World War II: Fifth Series*, edited by Joseph Conte, 179–91. Detroit: Gale, 1996.

Sedgwick, Eve Kosofsky. *Epistemology of the Closet*. Berkeley: University of California Press, 1990.

See, Carolyn. "*Suder*." *Los Angeles Times Book Review*, July 31, 1983.

Senghor, Léopold, ed. *New Anthology of the New Black and Malagasy Poetry*. Paris: Presses Universitaires de France, 1948.

Shakespeare, William. *The Tempest*. New York: Cambridge University Press, 2000.

Shockley, Ann Allen. "The Black Lesbian in American Literature: An Overview." In *Home Girls: A Black Feminist Anthology*, edited by Barbara Smith, 83–93. New York: Kitchen Table: Women of Color Press, 1983.

Showalter, Elaine, ed. *The New Feminist Criticism: Essays on Women, Literature, and Theory*. New York: Pantheon Books, 1985.

Silberman, Charles. *Crisis in Black and White*. New York: Vintage Books, 1964.

Simmons, Ron. "Some Thoughts on the Challenges Facing Black Gay Intellectuals." In *In Cornerstones: An Anthology of African American Literature*, edited by Melvin Donalson, 805–20. New York: St. Martin's Press, 1996.

Smith, Barbara. "Toward a Black Feminist Criticism." In *The New Feminist Criticism: Essays on Women, Literature, and Theory*, edited by Elaine Showalter, 168–85. New York: Pantheon Books, 1985.

Smith, David Lionel. "The Black Arts Movement and Its Critics." *American Literary History* (Spring 1991): 93–110.

Smith, Valerie. "David Bradley." *Afro-American Fiction Writers after 1955*. In *Dictionary of*

Literary Biography, Vol. 33, edited by Thadious M. Davis and Trudier Harris, 28–32. Detroit: Gale, 1984.

Smitherman, Geneva. *Talkin and Testifyin: The Language of Black America*. Boston: Houghton Mifflin, 1977.

———. "'What Is Africa to Me?': Language, Ideology, and AFRICAN AMERICAN," *American Speech* 66, no. 2 (1991): 115–32.

Soitos, Stephen F. *The Blues Detective: A Study of African American Detective Fiction*. Amherst: University of Massachusetts Press, 1996.

Sollors, Werner. *Beyond Ethnicity: Consent and Descent in American Culture*. New York: Oxford University Press, 1986.

———, and Maria Diedrich, eds. *The Black Columbiad: Defining Moments In African American Literature and Culture*. Cambridge: Harvard University Press, 1994.

Sowell, Thomas. *Black Education: Myths and Tragedies*. New York: David McKay, 1972.

Spillers, Hortense. "Mama's Baby, Papa's Maybe: An American Grammar Book." *Diacritics* 17, no. 2 (Summer 1987): 64–81.

Spivak, Gayatri Chakravorty. "Can the Subaltern Speak?" In *Marxism and the Interpretation of Culture*, edited by Cary Nelson and Lawrence Grossberg, 271–313. Urbana: University of Illinois Press, 1988.

———. *Outside in the Teaching Machine*. New York: Routledge, 1993.

———. "Poststructuralism, Marginality, Postcoloniality and Value." In *Literary Theory Today*, edited by Peter Collier and Helga Geyer-Ryan, 219–44. Cambridge: Polity Press, 1990.

———. "Subaltern Studies: Deconstructing Historiography." In her *In Other Worlds: Essays in Cultural Politics*, 197–221. New York: Methuen, 1987.

Stampp, Kenneth M. *The Peculiar Institution: Slavery in the Ante-Bellum South*. New York: Vintage Books, 1956.

Staples, Brent. "Unearthing a Riot." *New York Times Magazine*, December 19, 1999: 64.

Stepto, Robert B. *From behind the Veil: A Study of Afro-American Narrative*. Urbana: University of Illinois Press, 1979.

Stevenson, Rosemary. "Octavia Butler." In *Black Women in America: A Historical Encyclopedia*, Vol. 1, edited by Darlene Clark Hine, Elsa Barkley Brown, and Rosalyn Terborg-Penn, 208–10. Bloomington: Indiana University, 1993.

———. "Octavia Butler's Mind Trip into the Near Future." *Black Issues Book Review* (Jan.–Feb. 1999): 14–18.

Stewart, James. "Reaching for Higher Ground: Toward an Understanding of Black/Africana Studies." *The Afrocentric Scholar* 1, no. 1 (May 1992): 1–63.

Stewart, William A. "Sociolinguistic Factors in the History of American Negro Dialects." *Florida Foreign Language Reporter* 5, no. 2 (1967): 11–29.

Stonequist, Everett V. *The Marginal Man: A Study in Personality and Culture Conflict*. New York: Charles Scribner's Sons, 1937.

Styron, William. *The Confessions of Nat Turner*. New York: Random House, 1967.

Sundquist, Eric. *The Hammers of Creation*. Athens: University of Georgia Press, 1992.

Suvin, Darko. *Metamorphoses of Science Fiction: On the Poetics and History of a Literary Genre*. New Haven: Yale University Press, 1979.

Summer, Bob. "Ernest J. Gaines." *Publishers Weekly* May 24, 1993, 62 and 64.

Swados, Harvey, ed. *The American Writer and the Great Depression.* New York: Bobbs-Merrill, 1966.

Takaki, Ronald, ed. T. *Violence in the Black Imagination: Essays and Documents.* New York: Putnam, 1972.

Tansill, Charles, ed. *Documents Illustrative of the Formation of the Union of the American States.* Washington, D.C.: U.S. Government Printing Office, 1927.

Tate, Claudia, ed. *Black Women Writers at Work.* New York: Continuum, 1983.

Tate, Greg. "Funking Intellect." *Vibe* (June/July 1997): 70.

Taylor, Charles. *The Ethics of Authenticity.* Cambridge: Harvard University Press, 1991.

———. *Human Agency and Language.* Cambridge: Cambridge University Press, 1985.

Thiong'o, Ngugi wa. *Weep Not, Child.* 1964. Reprint. London: Heinemann, 1987.

Thompson, Robert Farris. *Flash of the Spirit: African and African American Art and Philosophy.* 1983. Reprint. New York: Vintage Books, 1984.

Todorov, Tzvetan. "Race, Writing, and Culture." Translated by Loulou Mack. In *"Race," Writing, and Difference,* edited by Henry Louis Gates Jr., 370–80. Chicago: University of Chicago Press, 1986.

Toll, Robert C. *Blacking Up: The Minstrel Show in Nineteenth–Century America.* New York: Oxford University Press, 1974.

Trilling, Lionel. *Sincerity and Authenticity.* Cambridge: Harvard University Press, 1971.

Trudgill, Peter. *Sociolinguistics: An Introduction to Language and Society.* New York: Penguin Books, 1987.

"Tulsa Burning." *60 Minutes II.* News segment summary. 10 July 2001. 12 July 2001, http://cbsnews.com/now/story/0,1597,69603-412,00.shtml.

Turner, Victor W. *The Ritual Process: Structure and Anti-Structure.* Middlesex, England: Penguin Books, 1974.

Turville-Petrie, Edward. *Myth and Religion of the North: The Religion of Ancient Scandinavia.* New York: Holt, Rinehart and Winston, 1964.

Tuttleton, James. "Tracking the American Novel into the Void." *The World & I* (May 1989): 451–67.

U.S. Department of Commerce. *The Social and Economic Status of the Black Population in the United States: A Historical View, 1790–1978.* Washington, D.C.: U.S. Government Printing Office, 1979.

Valentine, Charles A. *Culture and Poverty: A Critique and Counter–Proposals.* Chicago: University of Chicago Press, 1968.

van Gennep, Arnold. *The Rites of Passage.* Translated by Monika B. Vizedom and Gabrielle L. Caffee. Chicago: University of Chicago Press, 1960.

Van Vechten, Carl. *For My People.* New York: Arno Press and *The New York Times,* 1968.

———. *Nigger Heaven.* 1926. Reprint. New York: Harper Colophon, 1971.

Wade, Nicholas. "DNA Backs a Tribe's Tradition of Early Descent from the Jews." *New York Times,* May 9, 1999, late ed., sec. 1: 1+.

———. "Taking New Measurements for Jefferson's Pedestal." *New York Times,* March 7, 1999, late ed., sec. 1: 32+.

Walcott, Ronald. "The Novels of Hal Bennett: Part 1." *Black World* 23, no. 8 (June 1974): 36–48; 89–97.

———. "The Novels of Hal Bennett: Part 2." *Black World* 23, no. 9 (July 1974): 78–96.

Walcutt, Charles C. *American Literary Naturalism: A Divided Stream*. Minneapolis: University of Minnesota Press, 1956.

Walker, Alice. *In Search of Our Mothers' Gardens: Womanist Prose*. New York: Harvest/Harcourt Brace Jovanovich, 1984.

———. *Once*. 1968. Reprint. New York: Harcourt Brace Jovanovich, 1976.

Walker, David. "Appeal to the Coloured Citizens of the World." 1829. Reprint. In *A Documentary History of the Negro People in the United States*, edited by Herbert Aptheker, 1: 93–97. 3rd ed. New York: Citadel Press, 1965.

Walker, Jeanne Murray. "Reciprocity and Exchange in Samuel Delany's *Nova*." *Extrapolation* 23, no. 3 (Fall 1982): 221–34.

Walker, Margaret. *How I Wrote "Jubilee."* Chicago: Third World Press, 1972.

Wallace, Michele. *Black Macho and the Myth of the Superwoman*. 1979. Reprint. New York: Verso, 1990.

Wardhaugh, Ronald. *An Introduction to Sociolinguistics*, 3rd ed. Malden, Mass.: Blackwell, 1998.

Washington, Mary Helen. "Black History: His Story or Hers." *Washington Post Book World*, April 12, 1981: 3, 13.

———. "Introduction: In Pursuit of Our Own History." In *Midnight Birds: Stories of Contemporary Black Women Writers*, edited by Mary Helen Washington, xiii–xxv. Garden City, N.Y.: Anchor Books, 1980.

———, ed. *Black Eyed Susans: Classic Stories by and about Black Women*. Garden City, N.Y.: Anchor Books, 1975.

Watkins, Mel. "Thirteen Runaway Slaves and David Bradley." *New York Times Book Review*, April 19, 1981: 20–21.

Watkins, Patricia D. "Sutton Griggs: The Evolution of a Propagandist." Master's thesis, Howard University, 1970.

Weber, Max. *The Theory of Social and Economic Organization*. Translated by. A. M. Henderson and Talcott Parsons, edited by Talcott Parsons. New York: The Free Press, 1964.

Weedman, Jane Branham. *Samuel R. Delany*. Mercer Island, Wash.: Starmont House, 1982.

Welch, Dave. "Post Office to Unveil Colson Whitehead Stamp." *Powells.com*. 14 June 2001. 22 Nov. 2002, http://www.powells.com/authors/whitehead.html.

White, Deborah Gray. *Ar'n't I a Woman?: Female Slaves in the Plantation South*. New York: W. W. Norton, 1985.

White, Walter. *Rope and Faggot: A Biography of Judge Lynch*. 1929. Reprint. New York: Arno Press and *The New York Times*, 1969.

Whitten, Norman E., and John F. Szwed, eds. *Afro-American Anthropology: Contemporary Perspectives*. New York: The Free Press, 1970.

Whorf, Benjamin Lee. *Language, Thought, and Reality: Selected Writings*, edited by John B. Carroll. Cambridge: M.I.T. Press, 1956.

Wideman, John Edgar. "Frame and Dialect: The Evolution of the Black Voice in Fiction." *American Poetry Review* 5 (1976): 33–37.

Wiggins, William H., Jr. "Black Folktales in the Novels of John O. Killens." *Black Scholar: Journal of Black Studies and Research* 3 (November 197l): 50–58.

Williams, John A. *The Angry Ones*. New York: Pocket Books, 1969.

———. "Career by Accident." In his *Flashbacks: A Twenty-Year Diary of Article Writing*, 393–406. Garden City, N.Y.: Doubleday, 1973.

———. "John A. Williams." In *Contemporary Authors Autobiography Series*, Vol. 3, edited by Adele Sarkissian, 413–33. Detroit: Gale Research Company, 1986.

Williams, Raymond. *The Country and the City*. New York: Oxford University Press, 1973.

———. *Culture and Society, 1780–1950*. 1958. Reprint. New York: Harper and Row, 1966.

———. *Marxism and Literature*. London: Oxford University Press, 1977.

Williams, Robert L., ed. *Ebonics: The True Language of Black Folks*. St. Louis: Robert L. Williams and Associates, 1975.

Wirth, Louis. *The Ghetto*. Chicago: University of Chicago Press, 1928.

Wittgenstein, Ludwig. *On Certainty*. Oxford: Blackwell, 1969.

Wittke, Carl. *Tambo and Bones: A History of the American Minstrel Stage*. 1930. Reprint. Westport, Conn.: Greenwood Press, 1968.

Wolters, Raymond. *Negroes and the Great Depression: The Problem of Economic Recovery*. Westport, Conn.: Greenwood Press, 1970.

Wood, Peter. *Black Majority: Negroes in Colonial South Carolina from 1670 through the Stono Rebellion*. New York: Alfred A. Knopf, 1974.

Woods, Paula, ed. *Spooks, Spies, and Private Eyes: Black Mystery, Crime, and Suspense Fiction*. New York: Doubleday, 1995.

Woodson, Carter G. *The Negro in Our History*. Washington D.C.: Associated Publishers, 1922. *The World Almanac and Book of Facts*. Mahwah, N.J.: Almanac Books, 2001.

Wright, Richard. "Blueprint for Negro Writing." *New Challenge* 2 (Fall 1937): 53–65.

———. "Introduction." In *Black Metropolis: A Study of Negro Life in a Northern City*, edited by Clair Drake and Horace Cayton, i–xxxiv. New York: Harcourt, Brace and World, 1945.

———. *Savage Holliday*. 1954. Reprint. New York: Award Books, 1965.

———. *Twelve Million Black Voices: A Folk History of the Negro in the United States*. New York: Viking Press, 1941.

Yellin, Jean Fagan. *The Intricate Knot: Black Figures in American Literature, 1776–1863*. New York: New York University Press, 1972.

Yetman, Norman, ed. *Life under the "Peculiar Institution": Selections from the Slave Narrative Collection*. New York: Holt, Rinehart and Winston, 1970.

Yohe, Kristine A. "Gloria Naylor." In *The Oxford Companion to African American Literature*, edited by William L. Andrews, Frances Smith Foster and Trudier Harris, 527–29. New York: Oxford University Press, 1997.

Young, Al. *Drowning in the Sea of Love: Musical Memoirs*. Hopewell, N.J.: The Ecco Press, 1995.

———. *Kinds of Blue: Musical Memoirs*. San Francisco: D. S. Ellis, 1984.

———, and Janet Coleman. *Mingus Mingus: Two Memoirs*. Berkeley: Creative Arts Books, 1989.

———, and Ishmael Reed, eds. *Yardbird Lives!* New York: Grove Press, 1972.

Zangwill, Israel. *Melting Pot: A Drama in Four Acts*. New York: Macmillan, 1911.

Index

Index

Index

Index

Index

Index